# Lecture Notes in Artificial Intelligence    10284

Subseries of Lecture Notes in Computer Science

More information about this series at http://www.springer.com/series/1244

Dylan D. Schmorrow · Cali M. Fidopiastis (Eds.)

# Augmented Cognition

## Neurocognition and Machine Learning

11th International Conference, AC 2017
Held as Part of HCI International 2017
Vancouver, BC, Canada, July 9–14, 2017
Proceedings, Part I

Springer

*Editors*
Dylan D. Schmorrow
SoarTech
Orlando, FL
USA

Cali M. Fidopiastis
Design Interactive, Inc.
Orlando, FL
USA

ISSN 0302-9743          ISSN 1611-3349   (electronic)
Lecture Notes in Artificial Intelligence
ISBN 978-3-319-58627-4          ISBN 978-3-319-58628-1   (eBook)
DOI 10.1007/978-3-319-58628-1

Library of Congress Control Number: 2017940838

LNCS Sublibrary: SL7 – Artificial Intelligence

Printed on acid-free paper

This Springer imprint is published by Springer Nature
The registered company is Springer International Publishing AG
The registered company address is: Gewerbestrasse 11, 6330 Cham, Switzerland

# Foreword

The 19th International Conference on Human–Computer Interaction, HCI International 2017, was held in Vancouver, Canada, during July 9–14, 2017. The event incorporated the 15 conferences/thematic areas listed on the following page.

A total of 4,340 individuals from academia, research institutes, industry, and governmental agencies from 70 countries submitted contributions, and 1,228 papers have been included in the proceedings. These papers address the latest research and development efforts and highlight the human aspects of design and use of computing systems. The papers thoroughly cover the entire field of human–computer interaction, addressing major advances in knowledge and effective use of computers in a variety of application areas. The volumes constituting the full set of the conference proceedings are listed on the following pages.

I would like to thank the program board chairs and the members of the program boards of all thematic areas and affiliated conferences for their contribution to the highest scientific quality and the overall success of the HCI International 2017 conference.

This conference would not have been possible without the continuous and unwavering support and advice of the founder, Conference General Chair Emeritus and Conference Scientific Advisor Prof. Gavriel Salvendy. For his outstanding efforts, I would like to express my appreciation to the communications chair and editor of *HCI International News*, Dr. Abbas Moallem.

April 2017                                                    Constantine Stephanidis

# HCI International 2017 Thematic Areas
# and Affiliated Conferences

Thematic areas:

- Human–Computer Interaction (HCI 2017)
- Human Interface and the Management of Information (HIMI 2017)

Affiliated conferences:

- 17th International Conference on Engineering Psychology and Cognitive Ergonomics (EPCE 2017)
- 11th International Conference on Universal Access in Human–Computer Interaction (UAHCI 2017)
- 9th International Conference on Virtual, Augmented and Mixed Reality (VAMR 2017)
- 9th International Conference on Cross-Cultural Design (CCD 2017)
- 9th International Conference on Social Computing and Social Media (SCSM 2017)
- 11th International Conference on Augmented Cognition (AC 2017)
- 8th International Conference on Digital Human Modeling and Applications in Health, Safety, Ergonomics and Risk Management (DHM 2017)
- 6th International Conference on Design, User Experience and Usability (DUXU 2017)
- 5th International Conference on Distributed, Ambient and Pervasive Interactions (DAPI 2017)
- 5th International Conference on Human Aspects of Information Security, Privacy and Trust (HAS 2017)
- 4th International Conference on HCI in Business, Government and Organizations (HCIBGO 2017)
- 4th International Conference on Learning and Collaboration Technologies (LCT 2017)
- Third International Conference on Human Aspects of IT for the Aged Population (ITAP 2017)

# Conference Proceedings Volumes Full List

# Augmented Cognition

Program Board Chair(s): **Dylan D. Schmorrow and Cali M. Fidopiastis, USA**

- Débora N.F. Barbosa, Brazil
- Murat Perit Çakir, Turkey
- Martha E. Crosby, USA
- Rodolphe Gentili, USA
- Michael W. Hail, USA
- Monte Hancock, USA
- Øyvind Jøsok, Norway
- Ion Juvina, USA
- Benjamin J. Knox, Norway
- Chloe Chun-Wing Lo, Hong Kong, SAR China
- David Martinez, USA
- Santosh Mathan, USA
- Chang S. Nam, USA
- Banu Onaral, USA
- Robinson Pino, USA
- Mannes Poel, The Netherlands
- Stefan Sütterlin, Norway
- Anna Skinner, USA
- Robert A. Sottilare, USA
- Midori Sugaya, Japan
- Ayoung Suh, Hong Kong, SAR China
- Christian Wagner, Hong Kong, SAR China
- Peter Walker, USA
- Martin Westhoven, Germany
- John K. Zao, Taiwan

The full list with the Program Board Chairs and the members of the Program Boards of all thematic areas and affiliated conferences is available online at:

**http://www.hci.international/board-members-2017.php**

# HCI International 2018

The 20th International Conference on Human–Computer Interaction, HCI International 2018, will be held jointly with the affiliated conferences in Las Vegas, NV, USA, at Caesars Palace, July 15–20, 2018. It will cover a broad spectrum of themes related to human–computer interaction, including theoretical issues, methods, tools, processes, and case studies in HCI design, as well as novel interaction techniques, interfaces, and applications. The proceedings will be published by Springer. More information is available on the conference website: http://2018.hci.international/.

General Chair
Prof. Constantine Stephanidis
University of Crete and ICS-FORTH
Heraklion, Crete, Greece
E-mail: general_chair@hcii2018.org

**http://2018.hci.international/**

# Contents – Part I

**Eye Tracking in Augmented Cognition**

**Physiological Measuring and Bio-sensing**

**Machine Learning in Augmented Cognition**

# Contents – Part II

**Brain-Computer Interfaces**

## Human Cognition and Behavior in Complex Tasks and Environments

# Electroencephalography and Brain Activity Measurement

# My Brain Is Out of the Loop:
# A Neuroergonomic Approach of OOTL
# Phenomenon

Bruno Berberian[1]([⊠]), Jonas Gouraud[1], Bertille Somon[1], Aisha Sahai[1],
and Kevin Le Goff[2]

[1] French Aerospace Lab (ONERA), Salon, France
bruno.berberian@onera.fr
[2] Airbus Group, Toulouse, France

**Abstract.** The world surrounding us has become increasingly technological. Nowadays, the influence of automation is perceived in each aspect of everyday life and not only in the world of industry. Automation certainly makes some aspects of life easier, faster and safer. Nonetheless, empirical data suggests that traditional automation has many negative performance and safety consequences. Particularly, in cases of automatic equipment failure, human supervisors seemed effectively helpless to diagnose the situation, determine the appropriate solution and retake control, a set of difficulties called the "out-of-the-loop" (OOL) performance problem. Because automation is not powerful enough to handle all abnormalities, this difficulty in "takeover" is a central problem in automation design.

The OOL performance problem represents a key challenge for both systems designers and human factor society. After decades of research, this phenomenon remains difficult to grasp and treat and recent tragic accidents remind us the difficulty for human operator to interact with highly automated system. The general objective of our research project is to improve our comprehension of the OOL performance problem. To address this issue, we aim (1) to identify the neuro-functional correlates of the OOL performance problem, (2) to propose design recommendations to optimize human-automation interaction and decrease OOL performance problem occurrence. Behavioral data and brain imaging studies will be used to provide a better understanding of this phenomenon at both physiological and psychological levels.

## 1 Introduction

Over the past 50 years, automation technology has profoundly changed our everyday life. There is perhaps no facet of modern society in which the influence of automation technology has not been felt. Whether at work or at home, while travelling or while engaged in leisurely pursuits, human beings are becoming increasingly accustomed to using and interacting with sophisticated computer systems designed to assist them in their activities. Even more radical changes are anticipated in the future, as computers increase in power, speed and "intelligence".

D.D. Schmorrow and C.M. Fidopiastis (Eds.): AC 2017, Part I, LNAI 10284, pp. 3–18, 2017.
DOI: 10.1007/978-3-319-58628-1_1

We have usually focused on the perceived benefits of new automated or computerized devices. This is perhaps not surprising, given the sophistication and ingenuity of design of many such systems (e.g., the automatic landing of a jumbo jet, or the docking of two spacecraft). Automation certainly makes some aspects of life easier: by allowing people with disabilities to be able to move and communicate; faster: with the generalization of computerized devices and the increase of productivity; and safer: the accident rate in aviation or high-risk industry has dropped thanks to the implementation of automated systems [1]. In same time, the economic benefits that automation can provide, or is perceived to offer, also tend to focus public attention on the technical capabilities of automation. However, this fascination often obscures the fact that automation does not simply supplant human activity but rather changes it, often in ways unintended and unanticipated by the designers of automation [2]. Understanding the impact of this evolution for the human operator is crucial for successful design of new automated systems.

## 1.1 Automation and Human Operator Performance

For a long time, developers have assumed that adding "automation" was a simple substitution of a machine activity for human activity (substitution myth, see [3]). Unfortunately, empirical data on the relationship of people and technology suggest that this is not the case. Particularly, it is now well accepted that traditional automation has many negative consequences for performance and safety, including human vigilance decrements (e.g., lack of operator sensitivity to signals), complacency (e.g., over trust in highly reliable computer control) and loss of operator situation awareness [2]. This phenomenon has been called the out-of-the-loop (OOL) performance problem [4]. As a major consequence, the OOL performance problem causes a set of difficulties encountered by the operator in case of failure. Amongst other, we can cite a longer latency to determine what has failed, to decide if an intervention is necessary and to find the adequate course of action. Such difficulties are illustrated in several tragic accidents. Three examples suffice: the crash of flight 447 of Air France between Rio de Janeiro and Paris in 2009, the Three Mile Island nuclear incident of 1979, and the case of Knight Capital which lost about 400M$ due to a computer bug in 2012. Although these previous cases are from different domains, they highlight that when the automatic equipment fails, supervisors seemed dramatically helpless for diagnosing the situation and determining the appropriate solution because they were not aware of the system state prior to the failure. Numerous experimental results confirm these difficulties.

For example, Endsley and Kiris [4] provided evidence that performance during failure mode following a fully automated period were significantly degraded, as compared to a failure mode following a fully manual control. Merat and Jamson [5] reported similar conclusion. In a driving simulation task, they demonstrated that drivers' responses to critical events were slower in the automatic driving condition than in the manual condition. Because automation is not powerful enough to handle all abnormalities, this difficulty in takeover is a central problem in automation design.

## 1.2    Automation and the Place of the Human Operator

Together with this security issue, replacing the human by automated tools in the control loop gives rise to several critical issues. A first concern relates to the system acceptability. Improving acceptance of new technology and system by human operators is an important area of concern to equipment suppliers [6]. To be acceptable, new technology must be reliable, efficient and useful. However, such qualities do not guarantee acceptability from human operator. As pointed by Shneiderman and Plaisant [7], users "strongly desire the sense that they are in charge of the system and that the system responds to their actions". Increase in automation has the potential to seriously threat this sense of control, as confirmed by Baron when he claimed:

*"Perhaps the major human factors concern of pilots in regard to introduction of automation is that, in some circumstances, operations with such aids may leave the critical question, who is in control now, the human or the machine?"* [8].

This is not a simple question, and it is certainly not merely a matter of pilots' self-esteem being threatened by the advance of the machine age. "The question goes to the very heart of the nature of piloting, the seemingly divided authority between human and machine, and mainly, what is the role of the pilot as minder of equipment that is not only increasingly sophisticated but increasingly autonomous" [9].

A second concern relates to the penal responsibility of human operator in case of incident. It is well accepted that we have to control our action, intentionally, to be judged as responsible. With the interaction with highly automated system, the notion of responsibility becomes less clear. If automation technology decreases human operator performance, what about the responsibility of this operator in case of mistake? This is particularly important in safety critical systems and in semi-automated systems where a human supervising the task is held responsible for task failures. With the next generation of full-automated cars (i.e., google car project), this penal issue should become a major concern.

A third concern relates to ethical problems. The interposition of more and more automation between the pilot and the vehicle tends to distance human operators from many details of the operation. They are isolated from most of the physical structures of the system. In the same time, the automation tends to isolate the crew from the operations of the system. The automatic equipment monitors and controls it, providing little or no trace of its operations to the crew, isolating them from the moment-to-moment activities of the system and of the controls. This combination of relative physical and mental isolation tends to distance the human operator from the results of their action. At the extreme, some pilots argue that automation reduces the status of the human to a "button pusher" [10]. This form of disengagement regarding the result of the action has the potential to disturb the mechanism classically used to regulate human behaviour. Indeed, different works have proved that involvement in the consequence of your action is a necessary condition to act with ethics, to act with moral judgement [11–13]. Military robots are a perfect illustration of this ethical issue. Autonomy of this robot increases in same time than the technology progress. If the last decision remains to the operator at the moment, the distance (physically and cognitively) between human operator and its action clearly ask question, for the society in one part, but also for the operators themselves.

### 1.3    Understanding the OOL Performance Problem: A Key Challenge

The OOL performance problem represents a key challenge for both systems designers and human factor society. After decades of research (from [14] to [15]), this phenomenon remains difficult to grasp and treat and recent tragic accidents remind us the difficulty for human operator to interact with highly automated system. Moreover, with the development of autonomous cars, which should come onto our roads in a few years, everyone (not only expert operators) could be concerned by such difficulties, and the issue becomes universal. In this project, we aim to improve our comprehension of the OOL performance problem and to develop a new methodology for specification and evaluation of "agentive" HMI (i.e., HMI which have the property to keep the operator in the loop of control).

## 2    Characterizing the OOL Performance Problem at the Physiological Level

As previously explained, the OOL performance appears as a first concern in the human factors literature. Cognitive engineering literature has discussed at length the origins of vigilance decrements (e.g., low signal rates, lack of operator sensitivity to signals), complacency (e.g., over trust in highly reliable computer control) and the decrease in situation awareness (use of more passive rather than active processing and the differences in the type of feedback provided) in automated system supervision and has established associations between these human information processing shortcomings and performance problems. However, this OOL performance problem remains difficult to characterize and quantify, excepted by difficulties in takeover situation. Detecting the occurrence of this phenomenon, or even better detecting the dynamics toward this degraded state, is an important issue in order to develop tools for evaluation and monitoring.

In this project, we assume that the recent progress made by neuroscientists about the characterization of the processes of vigilance, attention and performance monitoring could help in this job. In this sense, the first goal of this project is to characterize the OOL performance problem at the physiological level. Particularly, we aim to identify the neuro-functional correlates of the OOL performance problem. We assume that such characterization will help to both understand and quantify the transformation induced by the OOL performance problem.

### 2.1    Physiological Markers

One important behavioral aspect of the OOL performance problem is reflected in an insufficient monitoring and checking of automated functions, i.e., information on the status of the automated functions is sampled less often than necessary [16]. Automated systems typically are highly reliable—with the exception of some automated alerting systems, which can have high false alarm rates. This, together with their opacity and complexity, can lead operators to rely unquestioningly on automation [17, 18]. This overreliance on automation represents an important aspect of misuse that can result from several form of human error, including decision biases and failure of monitoring [19–21]. The lack of operator involvement in process or automated systems control in supervisory modes and passive information processing will contribute to critical human cognitive errors, specifically the loss of operator situation awareness, to which some of the safety incidents discussed above have been attributed.

Beginning of these premises, our project aims to quantify the degradation of the monitoring process during OOL performance problem. In this sense, we propose to use recent insight about the anatomical substrate of action monitoring in humans (see for example [22, 23]) to characterize the degradation involved in OOL phenomenon. Particularly, evidence from neuroimaging, EEG, and invasive recordings in humans and nonhuman primates converges on the currently widely accepted view that this performance monitoring function is implemented by a cortico-subcortical network connected to the posterior medial frontal cortex (pMFC). Since the discovery of the error-related negativity (ERN) and the error positivity (Pe) [24], several further temporally and topographically defined event-related potentials (ERPs) have been linked to performance monitoring at different stages of goal-directed behavior (i.e., the error-related negativity or ERN, the error positivity or Pe, the feedback-related negativity or FRN, the prediction error or PE, and so on). Each of these signals could be considered as a physiological marker of response-monitoring processes in case of self-action. In this project, we assume that similar mechanisms of performance monitoring could be involved in case of the supervision of others' action, based on the pMFC activity.

Using EEG recordings in supervisory task, we propose to study (1) the brain activity related to the performance monitoring function in case of artificial agent supervision, (2) the impact of OOL performance problem on such activity, first in a simplified laboratory environment, and then in a cockpit simulation. Particularly, we make the hypothesis (1) that same kind of event-related potential could appears when you supervise automated system and detect system error than in case of self-action monitoring, (2) that the OOL performance problem is linked to the degradation of this performance monitoring function characterized by a decrease of the pMFC activity (decrease of the amplitude and/or increase in the latency of the evoked potential related to the performance monitoring activity). This degradation of the performance monitoring could serve as a physiological marker of the OOL phenomenon.

A two steps approach is proposed:

*Step 1: The identification of the neural substrates of performance monitoring in case of supervisory task.* As previously explained, several further temporally and topographically defined event-related potentials (ERPs) have been linked to performance monitoring at different stages of goal-directed behavior (i.e., the error-related negativity or ERN, the error positivity or Pe, the feedback-related negativity or FRN, the prediction error or PE, and so on) in case of self-action. We assume that similar mechanisms of performance monitoring should be involved in case of the supervision of others' action. To make evidence of this performance monitoring activity, we propose to realize a set of experiment where the participants have to supervise an automated system and detect system errors, first in a simplified laboratory environment (artificial agent doing a Simon task for example) then in a cockpit simulation using ONERA simulation facilities (supervision of Flight Managing System or Air Traffic Management system, see for example [25]). Using EEG recordings, we propose to systematically study the relation between the apparition of event-related potential in the pMFC (but also in other brain regions) and the capacity to the operator to detect and correct system errors. By this way, we aim to identify physiological markers of response-monitoring processes in case of supervisory task.

*Step 2: The characterization of the degradation of this process in case of OOL episodes.* It is well accepted that the OOL performance problem is reflected in an insufficient monitoring and checking of automated functions. Interestingly, the pMFC activity is known to be sensitive to performance. Particularly, the properties (amplitude, reaction time) of certain evoked potential (NE, Nelike, ERN) appears directly link to the efficiency of response monitoring [26]. If so, we should observe some signs of the deficiency of response-monitoring processes in case of OOL episodes. To make evidence of the degradation of this performance monitoring process when OOL episodes occur, we propose to replicate the experiment realized in Step 1 in condition stimulating the apparition of OOL episodes. Amongst other, system opacity, system reliability, automation level or time on task are different factors supporting the apparition of this OOL performance problem. We propose to manipulate these different factors to place the human operator in OOL performance episodes and to study the impact of this phenomenon on the pMFC activity, particularly on the amplitude and the reaction time of the evoked potential link to performance monitoring.

## 2.2  Physiological Precursors

The closed loop with the system requires human attention and several studies show that sustained attention over hours cannot be achieved [27–29]. Moreover, there is some consensus for the existence of a decrease of human operator vigilance in case of interaction with highly automated system [30, 31]. Both change in vigilance level and deterioration of the attentional mechanisms could cause degradation of the monitoring process involved in supervisory task.

In this project, we propose to document the relation between vigilance, attention and the degradation of the monitoring activities. Particularly, we propose to study the dynamics of vigilance and attentional mechanisms during the emergence of OOL performance problem. Using EEG recordings and oculometric measures, we will explore the impact of both change in vigilance and attentional on the monitoring activities. Because vigilance and attention refer to two different mechanisms - vigilance or arousal refer to the state of physiological reactivity of the subject [32, 33] whereas attention is perceived as the appropriate allocation of processing resources to relevant stimuli [34] – our project will take in consideration the respective part of these two processes in the apparition of the OOL performance problem, but also their mutual interaction. Moreover, regarding the factors impacting the vigilance and attentional processes (motivation, stress, fatigue, habituation, see [35]), we propose to study how the context could modify these relations.

Our project also proposed to specifically question the relation between the emergence of mind wandering episodes and the OOL performance problem. Mind wandering episodes correspond to the emergence of task unrelated thoughts and affects that are attracting the attention away from the task at hand [36, 37]. Not surprisingly, mind wandering episodes occur in our everyday life quite often. Interestingly, mind wandering has been associated with lower level of alertness and vigilance, a mental state with limited external information processing where attention is decoupled from the environment. Supporting this hypothesis, human subjects exhibited decreased performance in rate-target oddball detection tasks during mind wandering [38]. In addition, the amplitude of the P300 event-related potential component was reduced during mind wandering, suggesting a decrease in attentional resources directed towards stimulus processing [39]. We assume that mind wandering episodes occur more frequently in case of OOL performance problem. In a recent work, Braboszcz and Delorme [40] have studied the brain dynamics associated with mind wandering. They have shown that mind wandering episodes are associated with an increase in theta (4–7 Hz) and delta (2–3.5 Hz) EEG activity and a decrease in alpha (9–11 Hz) and beta (15–30 Hz) EEG activity. We propose to study the potential to use such pattern of activity as marker of OOL phenomenon. Using EEG recordings in supervisory task, we will study the relation between automation and mind wandering. An interesting and opening question is the relation between mind wandering and operator performance. We will tackle this question by systematically exploring the relation between the performance and the mind wandering episodes regarding the frequency of these episodes and their moment of emergence.

Taking together, these results will help us to characterize the state of the brain leading to the degradation of the monitoring activities. We assume that such physiological characterization could be used as physiological precursor of the OOL phenomenon. In this sense, our project could help (1) to characterize the OOL phenomenon and develop new methodology to evaluate current/future HMIs that would keep the crew "in the loop", but also (2) to monitor the operator state and identify operator loop output times. Both (1) and (2) have important implications. (1) could enforce safety and diminish fatigue of humans when interacting with highly automated system. (2) could pave the future to new brain computer interfaces to facilitate the exchange between human and machines.

To progress on this question, two experiments are proposed. The goal of the first experiment is to study the attentional and vigilance dynamics during OOL emergence and to determine the relation between change in vigilance and attention and the emergence of OOL episodes. The general methodology will be as follow. Using an adaptation of the supervisory task proposed by Berberian and collaborators [25], we will explore how vigilance and attention evolved with the time spent on the task. Both EEG recordings and oculometric measures will be performed to quantify these cognitive states. Alpha and theta activities in the waking electroencephalography (EEG) [41–44] and pupil dilatation [45] will be used to track the evolution of vigilance level. Pupillary response and eye fixations will also be used to track the dynamics of attention [46, 47]. Additionally, we will systematically explore the relation between these physiological markers of vigilance and attention and the amplitude/the reaction time of the evoked potential and eye field related potential related to the performance monitoring process. This paradigm should enable to explore how vigilance and attention mutually impact the performance monitoring process.

The second experiment will explore the relation between mind wandering and performance monitoring function. As previously noted, Braboszcz and Delorme [40] have studied the brain dynamics associated with mind wandering. They have shown that mind wandering episodes are associated with an increase in theta (4–7 Hz) and delta (2–3.5 Hz) EEG activity and a decrease in alpha (9–11 Hz) and beta (15–30 Hz) EEG activity. We propose to study the potential to use such activity patterns as marker of OOL phenomenon. Using EEG recordings in supervisory task, we will study the relation between automation and mind wandering. An interesting and opening question is the relation between mind wandering and operator performance. We will tackle this question by systematically exploring the relation between performance monitoring functions and the mind wandering episodes regarding the frequency of these episodes and their moment of emergence. In this sense, we propose to detect on line mind wandering episodes and to introduce system failure during or just after one of these episodes. Brain activity related to performance monitoring function, but also operators' failure detection and pertinence of the takeover maneuver will inform of the impact of mind wandering on operator performance.

## 3 Characterizing the OOL Performance Problem at the Psychological Level

In the current context of a continued increase in automation, understanding the sources of difficulties in the interaction with automation and finding solutions to compensate such difficulties are crucial issues for both system designer and human factor society. In this sense, the second objective of this project is to provide a new methodology for the design of the next generation of technological systems regarding their capacity to keep the human operator in the loop of control.

### 3.1 The Classical Approach

To explain the difficulties observed during human-automation interaction, the classical approach has consisted in considering how human characteristics and limitations influence the use (or misuse) of this automation. Regarding the difficulties for human operator to interact with highly automated system, designers have concluded that monitoring is a role for which humans are generally ill-suited [20, 48] and different solutions to compensate this weakness has been proposed. Some of them consist to train human operator to produce efficient behavior in case of system failure. For example, Bahner and colleagues [49] show that exposing operators to automation failures during training significantly decreased complacency and thus represents a suitable means to reduce this risk, even though it might (see also [50]). A more popular solution consists to manipulate the level of system automation (originally introduced by [51]), sharing the authority between the automation and the human operator (for example MABA-MABA methods, adaptive function allocation). In an attempt to prevent operators from being reduced to automated control system supervisors, monitors and passive information processors, the level of system automation allocates system functions to human and computer controllers based on consideration of the capabilities and capacities of each under normal operating conditions and failure modes. It has been hypothesized that by keeping the human involved in system operations, some intermediate level of system automation may provide better human/ system performance and situation awareness than that found with highly automated systems [4, 52]. From this time, empirical data has confirmed such hypothesis [1, 53, 54].

If these techniques have the virtue to partially decrease the negative consequences of automation technology, we assume that such explanation remains incomplete. Indeed, such approach rests on the hypothesis that new technology can be introduced as a simple substitution of machines for people - preserving the basic system while improving it on some output measures. Unfortunately, such assumption corresponds to a vague and bleak reflection of the real impact of automation: automation technology transforms human practice and forces people to adapt their skills and routines [55]. Whatever the merits of any particular automation technology, adding or expanding the machine's role changes the cooperative architecture, changing the human's role, often in profound ways [56]. Creating partially autonomous machine agents is, in part, like adding a new team member. One result is the introduction of new coordination demands and the emergence of new classes of problems which are due to failures in the human-machine relationship.

## 3.2    How to Make Automation a Collaborative Agent?

The key for designers is to depart from this quantitative, substitutional practice of function allocation [57, 58] because substitution assumes a fundamentally uncooperative system architecture in which the interface between human and machine has been reduced to a trivial "you do this, I do that" barter. As stated by Deker and Woods [55], the question for successful automation is not "who has control over what or how much" but "how do we get along together". Where designers really need guidance today is how to support the coordination between people and automation, not only in foreseeable standard situations, but also during novel, unexpected circumstances. In this sense, the main problem with automation is not the presence of automation, but rather its inappropriate design. It was recently proposed that the key for designers is to "socialize our interactions with technology" [57]. How to design collaborative agent has known a particular interest during the last years [59–64]. Our project aims to contribute to this effort by introducing recent insight about how humans understand and control joint action. Indeed, we can assume that operators interpret the intentions and the outcomes' actions of a system with their own "cognitive toolkit". Thus, understanding how this "cognitive toolkit" works could be relevant to propose design principles for potentially controllable/collaborative systems.

### A New Theoretical Framework: The Sense of Agency
The mechanisms underlying the experience of intentional causation and the sense of control of our own actions are the first concern of the science of agency [65]. Gallagher [66] defined agency as "the sense that I am the one who is causing or generating an

action". Put differently, agency corresponds to our capacity to make things happens, to change the world thorough our action. Although, the mental processes contributing to the sense of agency are not fully understood at this time, the different approaches propose that we derive a sense of being the agent for our own actions by a cognitive mechanism that computes the discrepancies between the predicted consequences of our own actions' actual consequences of these actions, similarly to action control models [67–69].

What makes our understanding of agency especially pertinent is the fact that an increasing number of our everyday agentive interactions involve technology. During interactions with technology, the simple process of producing an action to cause an intended outcome is endowed with a whole host of possible variables that can alter the agentive experience dramatically (for a review see [70]). Automation is one of them. With the progress of technology, current man-made complex systems tend to develop cascades and runaway chains of automatic reactions that decrease, or even eliminate predictability and cause outsized and unpredicted events [71]. This is what we will call system opacity: the difficulty for human operator to see the arrow from system intention to actual state and to predict the sequence of events that will occur.

Regarding the central place of predictability in the concept of agency, we could imagine that such opacity could dramatically change our experience of agency. Such degradation has been recently confirmed by empirical data [25]. Manipulating the level of automation in an aircraft supervision task, we have demonstrated a decrease in agency (both for explicit and implicit measures) concomitant to the increase in automation.

Regarding our initial question – make automation a collaborative agent – Pacherie [72] have recently argued that the different mechanisms underlying sense of agency for individual actions are the same kind of those underlying sense of agency one experiences when engaged in joint action. That is, the sense of agency in joint action is based on the same principle of congruence between predicted and actual outcomes. In this sense, we assume that a way to design a more collaborative interface is to consider the supervision as a joint action between a human operator and an artificial co-agent following the same principles as a biological coagent.

We can imagine that in the same manner as two people working together, the supervisors must be able to predict automated systems' actions and their outcomes in order to facilitate the cooperation between them and built a "we-agency" (or joint agency). This proposition echoes that of Norman [57] when he assumed that continual feedback about the state of the system is needed, in a normal natural way, much in the manner that human participants in a joint problem-solving activity will discuss the issues among themselves. The use of the theoretical background of agency will make it easier to achieve this objective. Therefore, we argue, in this project, for a mediated agency: an approach to HMI interactions that takes into account how the information provided by an automated system influences how an operator feels in mutual control.

Beginning from this premise, we aim to apply the concept of sense of agency to the human machine interaction domain and take into account the role of the information provided by an automated system in facilitating the operator's understanding and control of the system. Recent developments in the science of agency provide new conceptual tools and measures to analyse agent-system interactions. As proposed by Wegner [73], the experience we have of causing our own actions arises whenever we draw a causal inference linking our thought to our action. This inference occurs in accordance with principles - priority, consistency and exclusivity - that follow from research on cause perception and attribution. In an initial study (Le Goff, Haggard, Rey, & Berberian, submitted), we have shown that manipulating the characteristic of the interaction between the human operator and the automated system (automation intention feedback) in accordance to these principles could increase human operator performance in case of takeover situations. Particularly, using ONERA simulator, we have tested the performance of human operators in a supervision task where they have to supervise a highly automated aeronautical systems (FMS, automated detect and avoid functions) and detect potential errors. We have observed an increase in performance (system error detection) in presence of priming information in advance of the action indicating the intention of the system.

We assume that using the tools proposed by the framework of agency, ergonomists could design automation interfaces that are more predictable, and therefore more acceptable and more controllable. In this sense, we propose to translate existing results from laboratory studies of sense of agency towards situations of human system interaction. This project aims to study how these principles could help to develop more collaborative automation technology. In this sense, we will try to understand (1) how to design predictable system, (2) the link between system predictability and OOL episodes occurrence, and (3) how recover human control when these OOL episodes occur.

Again, a two steps approach is proposed:

*Step 1: Study the relation between system predictability and OOL episodes occurrence.* The goal is to highlight the degradation of the performance monitoring function when human operator interacts with opaque system. The general methodology will be as follow. Using an adaptation of the supervisory task proposed by Le Goff and collaborators (Le Goff, Haggard, Rey,& Berberian, submitted), we will explore how the performance monitoring function degrades with the time on task in different condition of system opacity. Participant will supervise an "air traffic management". This system will detect the presence of obstacle in environment and implement automatically change in the course of the aircraft. We have recently proved that using feedback to alert the operator to the current intention of the system will significantly improve human operator performance in the case of unexpected situations. In this sense, we will test two conditions. In a first condition, the supervised system will offer no information regarding the new course implemented (opaque system). In a second condition, the supervised system will alert the human operator of its intention before each avoidance maneuver (predictable system). Using EEG recordings, we will explore how the performance monitoring function will evolve with time regarding the predictability of the system. We assume that the brain activity relating to PM function will decrease in the case of opaque system.

*Step 2: Propose design for predictable system.* We will perform a set of experiment to understand how to use the Wegner principle to design predictable system. As proposed by Wegner [73], the experience we have of causing our own actions arises whenever we draw a causal inference linking our thought to our action. We propose to manipulate the characteristic of the interaction between the human operator and the automated system (automation intention feedback) in accordance to these principles and observe the impact of this manipulation on both performance in take over and performance monitoring function. Regarding these design recommendations, a crucial question refers to the amount of information transferred to the pilot. In this sense, we will test the minimum of information necessary to keep the human operator in the loop of control. For example, we will compare situation in which intention of the system is proposed all the time with situation in which intention of the system is sent occasionally. In the same vein, we will explore the pertinence to keep the operator in the loop all the time in comparison to situation in which we use system predictability only in critical situation.

# 4    Conclusion

As previously suggested, automation technology have the potential to dramatically change the way we interact with our environment. This transformation clearly asks the place of the human operator in the future technological systems. Dealing with these different issues is a necessary step to make future systems safer, more acceptable, more usable.

The general objective of this research project is to improve our comprehension of the OOL performance problem and to develop a new methodology for specification and evaluation of "agentive" HMI (i.e., HMI which have the property to keep the operator in the loop of control). To address this issue, our project will meet the following goals: (1) to identify physiological correlates of the OOL performance problem, (2) to propose design recommendations to optimize human-automation interaction and decrease OOL episodes occurrence.

To address this issue, we propose a new theoretical approach of the change induced by automation technology based on recent data from neurosciences. We assume that such approach will lead to the creation of new tools for Human Machine Interface (HMI) specification and evaluation and lead to the creation of knowledge that inspires new ways of working for system designers.

**Acknowledgement.** This project is supported by an ANR grant (Young researcher program).

# References

1. Kaber, D.B., Onal, E., Endsley, M.R.: Design of automation for telerobots and the effect on performance, operator situation awareness, and subjective workload. Hum. Factors Ergon. Manuf. **10**(4), 409–430 (2000)
2. Parasuraman, R., Sheridan, T.B., Wickens, C.D.: A model for types and levels of human interaction with automation. IEEE Trans. Syst. Man Cybern. Part A Syst. Hum. **30**(3), 286–297 (2000)

3. Woods, D.D., Tinapple, D.: W3: watching human factors watch people at work. In: Presidential Address, presented at the 43rd Annual Meeting of the Human Factors and Ergonomics Society, Houston, TX, September 1999
4. Endsley, M.R., Kiris, E.O.: The out-of-the-loop performance problem and level of control in automation. Hum. Factors: J. Hum. Factors Ergon. Soc. 37(2), 381–394 (1995)
5. Merat, N., Jamson, A.H.: The effect of stimulus modality on signal detection: implications for assessing the safety of in-vehicle technology. Hum. Factors: J. Hum. Factors Ergon. Soc. 50(1), 145–158 (2008)
6. Horberry, T., Stevens, A., Regan, M.A. (eds.): Driver Acceptance of New Technology: Theory, Measurement and Optimisation. Ashgate Publishing Ltd., Farnham (2014)
7. Shneiderman, B., Plaisant, C.: Designing the User Interface: Strategies for Effective Human-Computer Interaction, 4th edn. Pearson Education, London (2004)
8. Baron, S.: Pilot control. In: Wiener, E.L., Nagel, D.C. (eds.) Human Factors in Aviation, pp. 347–386. Academic Press, San Diego, CA (1988)
9. Wiener, E.L.: Cockpit automation. In: Wiener, E.L., Nagel, D.C. (eds.) Human Factors in Aviation, pp. 433–459. Academic Press, San Diego, CA (1988)
10. Wiley, D.: The Coming Collision Between the Automated Instruction and Learning Communities Camps of Online Learning Research. Working Draft. Accessed 22 June 2003
11. Bandura, A., Barbaranelli, C., Caprara, G.V., Pastorelli, C.: Mechanisms of moral disengagement in the exercise of moral agency. J. Pers. Soc. Psychol. 71(2), 364 (1996)
12. Bratman, M.: Structures of Agency: Essays. Oxford University Press, Oxford (2007)
13. Borg, J.S., Hynes, C., Van Horn, J., Grafton, S., Sinnott-Armstrong, W.: Consequences, action, and intention as factors in moral judgments: an fMRI investigation. J. Cogn. Neurosci. 18(5), 803–817 (2006)
14. Bainbridge, L.: Ironies of automation. Automatica 19(6), 775–779 (1983)
15. Baxter, G., Rooksby, J., Wang, Y., Khajeh-Hosseini, A.: The ironies of automation: still going strong at 30? In: Proceedings of the 30th European Conference on Cognitive Ergonomics, New York, USA, pp. 65–71. ACM (2012)
16. Kaber, D.B., Endsley, M.R.: Out-of-the-loop performance problems and the use of intermediate levels of automation for improved control system functioning and safety. Process Saf. Prog. 16(3), 126–131 (1997)
17. Moray, N., Inagaki, T.: Attention and complacency. Theoret. Issues Ergon. Sci. 1(4), 354–365 (2000)
18. Sheridan, T.B., Parasuraman, R.: Human–automation interaction. In: Nickerson, R.S. (ed.) Reviews of Human Factors and Ergonomics, vol. 1, pp. 89–129. Human Factors and Ergonomics Society, Santa Monica (2006)
19. Parasuraman, R., Molloy, R., Singh, I.L.: Performance consequences of automation induced 'complacency'. Int. J. Aviat. Psychol. 3(1), 1–23 (1993)
20. Parasuraman, R., Riley, V.: Humans and automation: use, misuse, disuse, abuse. Hum. Factors: J. Hum. Factors Ergon. Soc. 39(2), 230–253 (1997)
21. Singh, I.L., Molloy, R., Parasuraman, R.: Automation-induced "complacency": development of the complacency-potential rating scale. Int. J. Aviat. Psychol. 3(2), 111–122 (1993)
22. Bonini, F., Burle, B., Liégeois-Chauvel, C., Régis, J., Chauvel, P., Vidal, F.: Action monitoring and medial frontal cortex: leading role of supplementary motor area. Science 343(6173), 888–891 (2014)
23. Ullsperger, M., Fischer, A.G., Nigbur, R., Endrass, T.: Neural mechanisms and temporal dynamics of performance monitoring. Trends Cogn. Sci. 18(5), 259–267 (2014)
24. Falkenstein, M., Hohnsbein, J., Hoormann, J., Blanke, L.: Effects of cross-modal divided attention on late ERP components. II. Error processing in choice reaction tasks. Electroencephalogr. Clin. Neurophysiol. 78(6), 447–455 (1991)

25. Berberian, B., Sarrazin, J.C., Le Blaye, P., Haggard, P.: Automation technology and sense of control: a window on human agency. PLoS ONE **7**(3), e34075 (2012)

26. Allain, S., Carbonnell, L., Falkenstein, M., Burle, B., Vidal, F.: The modulation of the Ne-like wave on correct responses foreshadows errors. Neurosci. Lett. **372**(1), 161–166 (2004)

27. Davies, D.R., Parasuraman, R.: The psychology of vigilance. Academic Press, Cambridge (1982)

28. Matthews, G., Davies, D.R.: Individual differences in energetic arousal and sustained attention: a dual-task study. Pers. Individ. Differ. **31**(4), 575–589 (2001)

29. Methot, L.L., Huitema, B.E.: Effects of signal probability on individual differences in vigilance. Hum. Factors: J. Hum. Factors Ergon. Soc. **40**(1), 102–110 (1998)

30. O'Hanlon, J.F.: Boredom: practical consequences and a theory. Acta Psychol. **49**(1), 53–82 (1981)

31. Strauch, B.: Investigating Human Error: Incidents, Accidents, and Complex Systems. Ashgate, Burlington (2002)

32. Broadbent, D.E.: Decision and Stress. Academic Press, New York (1971)

33. Kahneman, D.: Attention and Effort, p. 246. Prentice-Hall, Englewood Cliffs (1973)

34. Coull, J.T.: Neural correlates of attention and arousal: insights from electrophysiology, functional neuroimaging and psychopharmacology. Progress Neurobiol. **55**(4), 343–361 (1998)

35. Oken, B.S., Salinsky, M.C., Elsas, S.M.: Vigilance, alertness, or sustained attention: physiological basis and measurement. Clin. Neurophysiol. **117**(9), 1885–1901 (2006)

36. Mason, M.F., Norton, M.I., Van Horn, J.D., Wegner, D.M., Grafton, S.T., Macrae, C.N.: Wandering minds: the default network and stimulus-independent thought. Science **315** (5810), 393–395 (2007)

37. Smallwood, J., Schooler, J.W.: The restless mind. Psychol. Bull. **132**(6), 946 (2006)

38. Giambra, L.M.: A laboratory method for investigating influences on switching attention to task-unrelated imagery and thought. Conscious. Cogn. **4**(1), 1–21 (1995)

39. Smallwood, J., Beach, E., Schooler, J.W., Handy, T.C.: Going AWOL in the brain: mind wandering reduces cortical analysis of external events. J. Cogn. Neurosci. **20**(3), 458–469 (2008)

40. Braboszcz, C., Delorme, A.: Lost in thoughts: neural markers of low alertness during mind wandering. Neuroimage **54**(4), 3040–3047 (2011)

41. Daniel, R.S.: Alpha and Theta EEC in vigilance. Percept. Mot. Skills **25**(3), 697–703 (1967)

42. Duffy, F.H., Albert, M.S., McAnulty, G., Garvey, A.J.: Age-related differences in brain electrical activity of healthy subjects. Ann. Neurol. **16**(4), 430–438 (1984)

43. Berka, C., Levendowski, D.J., Lumicao, M.N., Yau, A., Davis, G., Zivkovic, V.T., Olmstead, R.E., Tremoulet, P.D., Craven, P.L.: EEG correlates of task engagement and mental workload in vigilance, learning, and memory tasks. Aviat. Space Environ. Med. **78** (1), B231–B244 (2007)

44. Jung, T.P., Makeig, S., Stensmo, M., Sejnowski, T.J.: Estimating alertness from the EEG power spectrum. IEEE Trans. Biomed. Eng. **44**(1), 60–69 (1997)

45. Goldinger, S.D., Papesh, M.H.: Pupil dilation reflects the creation and retrieval of memories. Curr. Dir. Psychol. Sci. **21**(2), 90–95 (2012)

46. Verney, S.P., Granholm, E., Marshall, S.P.: Pupillary responses on the visual backward masking task reflect general cognitive ability. Int. J. Psychophysiol. **52**(1), 23–36 (2004)

47. Wierda, S.M., van Rijn, H., Taatgen, N.A., Martens, S.: Pupil dilation deconvolution reveals the dynamics of attention at high temporal resolution. Proc. Nat. Acad. Sci. **109**(22), 8456–8460 (2012)

48. Endsley, M.R.: Automation and situation awareness. In: Parasuraman, R., Mouloua, M. (eds.) Automation and Human Performance: Theory and Applications, pp. 163–181. Lawrence Erlbaum, Mahwah (1996)

49. Bahner, J.E., Hüper, A.D., Manzey, D.: Misuse of automated decision aids: complacency, automation bias and the impact of training experience. Int. J. Hum.-Comput. Stud. **66**(9), 688–699 (2008)

50. Plat, M., Amalberti, R.: Experimental crew training to deal with automation surprises. In: Cognitive Engineering in the Aviation Domain, pp. 287–308. Lawrence Erlbaun Associates, Hillsdale (NJ) (2000)

51. Sheridan, T.B., Verplank, W.L.: Human and Computer Control of Undersea Teleoperators (1978)

52. Endsley, M.R.: The application of human factors to the development of expert systems for advanced cockpits. In: Proceedings of the Human Factors and Ergonomics Society Annual Meeting, Vol. 31, no. 12, pp. 1388–1392. SAGE Publications (1987)

53. Endsley, M.R.: Level of automation effects on performance, situation awareness and workload in a dynamic control task. Ergonomics **42**(3), 462–492 (1999)

54. Kaber, D.B., Endsley, M.R.: The effects of level of automation and adaptive automation on human performance, situation awareness and workload in a dynamic control task. Theoret. Issues Ergon. Sci. **5**(2), 113–153 (2004)

55. Dekker, S.W., Woods, D.D.: MABA-MABA or abracadabra? Progress on human–automation coordination. Cogn. Technol. Work **4**(4), 240–244 (2002)

56. Sarter, N.B., Woods, D.D., Billings, C.E.: Automation surprises. In: Handbook of Human Factors and Ergonomics, vol. 2, pp. 1926-1943 (1997)

57. Norman, D.A.: The 'problem' with automation: inappropriate feedback and interaction, not 'over automation'. Philos. Trans. R. Soc. B: Biol. Sci. **327**(1241), 585–593 (1990)

58. Hollnagel, E.: From function allocation to function congruence. In: Dekker, S.W.A., Hollnagel, E. (eds.) Coping with computers in the cockpit, pp. 29– 53 (1999)

59. Christoffersen, K., Woods, D.D.: How to make automated systems team players. Adv. Hum. Perform. Cogn. Eng. Res. **2**, 1–12 (2002)

60. Klein, G., Woods, D.D., Bradshaw, J.M., Hoffman, R.R., Feltovich, P.J.: Ten challenges for making automation a "team player" in joint human-agent activity. IEEE Intell. Syst. **19**(6), 91–95 (2004)

61. Hoc, J.M.: Human and automation: a matter of cooperation. In: HUMAN 2007, pp. 277–285. Université de Metz (2007)

62. Hoc, J.M., Carlier, X.: Role of a common frame of reference in cognitive cooperation: sharing tasks between agents in air traffic control. Cogn. Technol. Work **4**(1), 37–47 (2002)

63. Dragan, A.D., Lee, K.C., Srinivasa, S.S.: Legibility and predictability of robot motion. In: 2013 8th ACM/IEEE International Conference on Human-Robot Interaction (HRI), pp. 301–308. IEEE, March 2013

64. Zimmermann, M., Bauer, S., Lutteken, N., Rothkirch, I.M., Bengler, K.J.: Acting together by mutual control: evaluation of a multimodal interaction concept for cooperative driving. In: 2014 International Conference on Collaboration Technologies and Systems (CTS), pp. 227–235. IEEE, May 2014

65. Pacherie, E.: The sense of control and the sense of agency. Psyche **13**(1), 1–30 (2007)

66. Gallagher, S.: Philosophical conceptions of the self: implications for cognitive science. Trends Cogn. Sci. **4**(1), 14–21 (2000)

67. Blakemore, S.J., Wolpert, D.M., Frith, C.D.: Abnormalities in the awareness of action. Trends Cogn. Sci. **6**(6), 237–242 (2002)

68. Frith, C.D., Blakemore, S.J., Wolpert, D.M.: Explaining the symptoms of schizophrenia: abnormalities in the awareness of action. Brain Res. Rev. **31**(2), 357–363 (2000)

69. Wegner, D.M.: The Illusion of Conscious Will. MIT press, Cambridge (2002)
70. Moore, J.W., Obhi, S.S.: Intentional binding and the sense of agency: a review. Conscious. Cogn. **21**(1), 546–561 (2012)
71. Taleb, N.N.: Antifragile: Things that Gain from Disorder. Random House Incorporated, New York (2012)
72. Pacherie, E.: Action (2012)
73. Wegner, D.M., Wheatley, T.: Apparent mental causation: sources of the experience of will. Am. Psychol. **54**(7), 480 (1999)

# Testing the Specificity of EEG Neurofeedback Training on First- and Second-Order Measures of Attention

Eddy J. Davelaar[✉]

Department of Psychological Sciences, Birkbeck College, University of London,
Malet Street, London WC1E 7HX, UK
e.davelaar@bbk.ac.uk

**Abstract.** During electroencephalography (EEG) neurofeedback training, individuals learn to willfully modulate their brain oscillations. Successful modulation has been shown to be related to cognitive benefits and wellbeing. The current paper addresses the specificity of three neurofeedback protocols in influencing first- (basic Stroop effect) and second-order (Gratton effect) measures of attentional control. The data come from two previously presented studies that included the Stroop task to assess attentional control. The three neurofeedback protocols were upregulation of frontal alpha, sensorimotor (SMR), and mid-frontal theta oscillations. The results show specific effects of different EEG neurofeedback protocols on attentional control and are modulated by the cognitive effort needed in the Stroop task. To summarize, in less-demanding versions of the Stroop task, alpha training improves first- and second-order attentional control, whereas SMR and theta training had no effect. In the demanding version of the Stroop task, theta training improves first-order, but not second-order control and SMR training has no effect on either. Using a drift diffusion model-based analysis, it is shown that only alpha and theta training modulate the underlying cognitive processing, with theta upregulation enhancing evidence accumulation. Although the current results need to be interpreted with caution, they support the use of different neurofeedback protocols to augment specific aspects of the attentional system. Recommendations for future work are made.

**Keywords:** EEG neurofeedback · Stroop effect · Gratton effect · Attention training

## 1 Introduction

Biofeedback is a paradigm in which individuals are trained to modulate their biological processes by providing them corrective feedback about the target biological variable. Commonly known target variables are the heart rate and heart rate variability. However, biofeedback of neuroelectrical signals as measured with electroencephalography (EEG) has also been shown in the clinical practice and in the research laboratories. Several clinical disorders have been purported to be ameliorated by specifically designed EEG neurofeedback training protocols (see for reviews, [1–4]). In the field of

© Springer International Publishing AG 2017
D.D. Schmorrow and C.M. Fidopiastis (Eds.): AC 2017, Part I, LNAI 10284, pp. 19–27, 2017.
DOI: 10.1007/978-3-319-58628-1_2

cognitive neurofeedback, the research focuses on cognitive enhancement and peak performance [5, 6]. For example, training the alpha band frequency has been associated with improved attentional control and working memory [7, 8]. Investigating attentional control is typically done with tasks such as the Stroop task, in which a color word is printed in a font color that is either the same (congruent) or different (incongruent) than what the word represents and the participant is required to name the font color. The slowed response time to naming incongruent compared to congruent stimuli is the Stroop effect and is the prototypical measure of attentional control. In addition to the simple difference of response times, recent theories of attentional control postulate that the amount of incongruency experienced on a preceding trial influences the amount of control exerted on the current trial [9, 10]. That is, the cognitive system reacts to the increase in cognitive conflict by increasing the attention paid to the task. This leads to an interaction effect whereby the Stroop effect is larger after congruent trials than after incongruent trials. This pattern, called the Gratton effect, is a marker of cross-trial fluctuations of attention and thus a more sensitive measure of how attention is distributed over time.

In a recent study, we showed that second-order measures of attentional control, i.e., the Gratton effect, was influenced by upregulation of frontal alpha oscillations [11]. In particular, the alpha training lead to a decrease in the Gratton effect, which was interpreted as a decreased need to exert reactive control. It was postulated that the increase in frontal alpha made the attentional control system more efficient, leading to less cognitive conflict and thereby to smaller Gratton effects.

An important consideration in neurofeedback research is the specificity of the results (see e.g., [12]). For example, it is yet unclear whether the effect observed with alpha neurofeedback is specific for that protocol or whether any other neurofeedback protocol produces the same result. To test this, we compare three neurofeedback protocols. The first is the frontal alpha protocol described above. The second and third are a mid-frontal theta and a sensorimotor (SMR) protocol, respectively. The latter two protocols were used in a large-scale study investigating their effects on a range of cognitive tests and phenomenological experiences. The study used two variants of the Stroop task that will be reanalyzed in this paper.

In the next section, the two studies are described to provide the context within which each study was conducted. Although the methods vary, they do use the same cognitive task. This is followed by two sets of analyses. The first set addresses first- and second-order measures of attention across the three protocols. The second set follows after an intermezzo about decomposition of response times in underlying latent cognitive processes and looks at cross-protocol differences in drift rate, boundary separation, and non-decision time. The paper closes with a speculative integration of the findings based on the conflict/control-loop theory.

## 2  Description of Studies

In the first study [11], participants were trained over 5 consecutive days to enhance the alpha oscillation over the prefrontal cortex (Fp2) using a virtual reality system. The task within the virtual world was to levitate a vase that rested on a table in a room. This study consisted of two groups: a 3D group and a 2D group. The aim of the study was to assess the effect of immersive feedback on the learning rate. It used the Stroop task to measure the attentional focus. The task required participants to respond to the strings RED, BLUE, and &&&& by pressing one of two keys denoting the font color of the string (red versus blue). This created three trial types: congruent, incongruent, and neutral. In each group, data from 10 participants were used in the analyses. The main results were that the immersion due to the virtual environment (3D vs 2D) lead to a higher rate of neural learning. The rate of enhancement of alpha over 5 training sessions was associated with the amount of decrease in the Stroop and Gratton effect.

The second study [13] had a different aim and experimental design. Participants were trained over 10 sessions to either enhance mid-frontal theta (Fz) oscillations or central sensorimotor rhythm (SMR). The choice of mid-frontal theta was based on the findings that the anterior cingulate cortex (ACC) is a critical neural component in the attentional control system [9, 10] and is the cortical source for theta oscillations. The SMR protocol was used as an active control condition, although in clinical practice, the SMR protocol is used to address symptoms associated with attention-deficit/hyperactivity disorder. Complete datasets were available from 10 and 16 participants in the SMR and theta group, respectively. Participants were given a standard feedback interface (not immersive) that provided visual and auditory (beeps) feedback every time the power in the target frequency was above threshold. A battery of cognitive tests was administered before and after the training period. Among these were two variants of the Stroop test. The first was the same version as used in the alpha study. The second, and more demanding, variant included an auditory beep that was present on 25% of the trials and signaled to the participant to withhold the response. Thus, in this variant, the participant had to keep two task goals in mind.

In sum, both studies included the Stroop task as the cognitive task to assess attentional control and the second study also varied the demand characteristics. We now turn to the results which are analyzed both across studies and for each training protocol separately.

**Results: Stroop Effects**

Although earlier reports presented the mean response times of all trials [11, 13], here the mean response times of congruent and incongruent trials that followed a neutral trial are presented. The rationale is that these trials are uncontaminated by the influence of reactive control. This also prevents confounding the first- and second-order measures, as data points will only contribute to one set of analyses.

Figure 1 presents the mean correct response times for all congruent and incongruent trials in the Stroop tasks for all training groups. Data from the two alpha groups were combined in the analysis to increase statistical power, but are shown separately for information. A $2 \times 2 \times 3$ mixed factorial ANOVA crossing the factors trial type (congruent/incongruent), session (before/after), and neurofeedback group (alpha/SMR/theta) revealed a Stroop effect [$F(1,43) = 8.78$, MSe = 1059.95, $p < .01$, partial $\eta^2 = .17$], an overall speed up from pre- to post-training [$F(1,43) = 12.47$, MSe = 4665.69, $p = .001$, partial $\eta^2 = .23$], an interaction between session and trial-type [$F(1,43) = 8.90$, MSe = 1431.11, $p < .01$, partial $\eta^2 = .17$], which was part of the

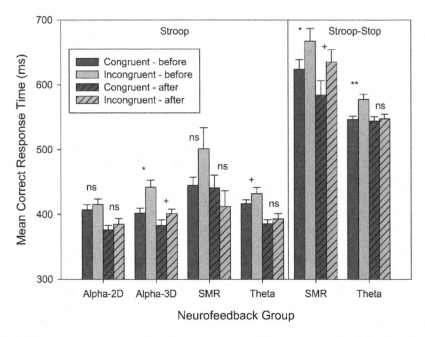

**Fig. 1.** Mean correct response times for congruent and incongruent trials (following neutral trials) before and after neurofeedback training. Error bars represent standard error of the within-subject mean. Simple effects comparing pre- and post-training scores are indicated: ** $p < .01$, * $p < .05$, + $p < .10$, ns = nonsignificant.

three-way interaction [$F(2,43) = 3.96$, MSe = 1431.11, $p < .05$, partial $\eta^2 = .16$]. The interaction was due to the SMR group not showing any Stroop effects.

For the Stroop-Stop task, a $2 \times 2 \times 2$ factorial ANOVA revealed a marginal speed up across sessions [$F(1,24) = 3.74$, MSe = 4450.61, p .065, partial $\eta^2 = .14$] and a significant Stroop effect [$F(1,24) = 17.55$, MSe = 1480.10, $p < .001$, partial $\eta^2 = .42$].

### Results: Gratton Effects

Figure 2 presents the mean correct response times for all congruent and incongruent trials in the Stroop tasks for all training groups as a function of the previous Stroop trial type.

The overall Gratton effect was present [previous x current trial type interaction F (1,43) = 9.38, MSe = 2225.25, $p < .01$, partial $\eta^2 = .18$], as was the across-session speed up [$F(1,43) = 12.24$, MSe = 9236.23, p = .001, partial $\eta^2 = .22$] and Stroop effect [$F(1,43) = 9.08$, MSe = 2071.59, $p < .01$, partial $\eta^2 = .17$]. However, the Gratton effect differed across groups [$F(2,43) = 4.73$, MSe = 2225.25, $p < .05$, partial $\eta^2 = .18$] and across sessions [$F(1,43) = 5.06$, MSe = 1085.20, $p < .05$, partial $\eta^2 = .11$], due to absence of the effect in the theta group.

For the Stroop-Stop task, the Stroop effect was significant [$F(1,23) = 8.79$, MSe = 2271.61, $p < .01$, partial $\eta^2 = .28$], but the Gratton effect was marginally significant [$F(1,23) = 3.69$, MSe = 3350.13, p = .067, partial $\eta^2 = .14$] and failed to reach statistical significance in the interaction with session and group (p = .21).

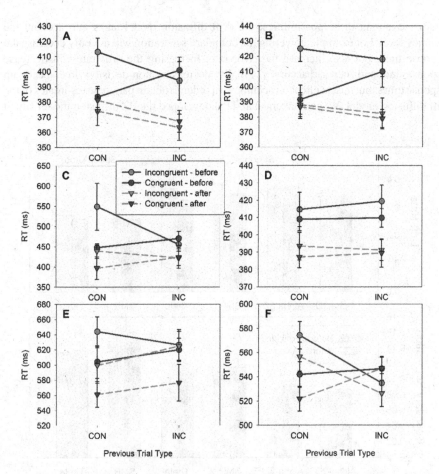

**Fig. 2.** Mean correct response times for congruent and incongruent trials before and after neurofeedback training broken down by previous trial type. Error bars represent standard error of the within-subject mean. A = alpha 2D (Stroop), B = alpha 3D (Stroop), C = SMR (Stroop), D = theta (Stroop), E = SMR (Stroop-Stop), F = theta (Stroop-Stop).

## 3   Decomposition of Response Times

The results in the previous section focused on response times, which are the main data of interest for most, if not all, of the Stroop literature. However, a particular response time is the result of a series of cognitive events that can be roughly broken down into a decision and a non-decision component. An influential theoretical explanation of response times is the drift diffusion model (for a recent review see, [14]). According to this theory, response times are a linear combination of the two components, with the decision component being governed by two further parameters: drift diffusion and boundary separation. The latter dictates the threshold at which a particular decision is made, whereas the former reflect the speed at which the system approaches this threshold. Fast responses can therefore be due to short non-decision times, fast drift rates, or lower boundary separations. In order to adjudicate among these possibilities, the drift diffusion model takes into account the accuracy level. For example, lowering the boundary separation will not only decrease the response time, but also increase the error rate. Increasing the drift rate will decrease response time and increase accuracy. Finally, decreasing non-decision time speeds up response times, but has no effect on accuracy. In order to obtain parameter estimates of the drift diffusion model, Wagenmakers et al. [15] developed the EZ diffusion model which

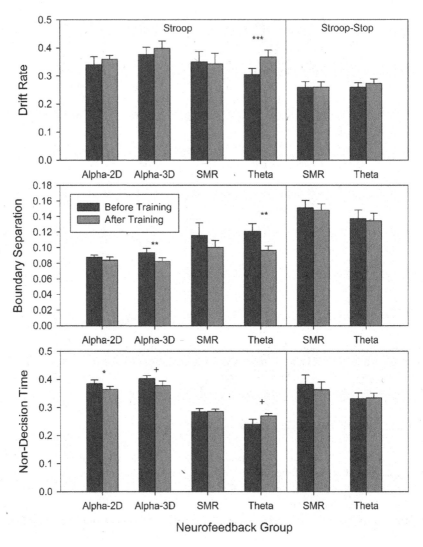

**Fig. 3.** EZ diffusion parameter estimates for each neurofeedback training group. *** p < .001, ** p < .01, * p < .05, + p < .10

simplifies the original diffusion model[1] to a closed-form expression. In order to obtain estimates of the drift rate, boundary separation, and non-decision time, all that is needed are the mean correct response time (in seconds), the variance (in seconds$^2$), and the proportion of correct trials.

### EZ Diffusion Model Decomposition

In order to obtain the parameter estimates, only the neutral trials in the tasks were used. The rationale for this selection was that the congruent and incongruent stimuli are invoking additional processes that warrant the diffusion model inappropriate as a reasonable model for extracting cognitive parameter estimates.

### Results: Diffusion Model Parameter Estimates

Figure 3 shows the parameter estimates for each group in each task. For the Stroop-Stop task none of the parameter estimates changed due to neurofeedback training. For the Stroop task, only alpha and theta training modified parameter estimates. Alpha training decreased non-decision time [session x group interaction $F(1,43) = 6.45$, MSe $= 0.001$, $p < .01$, partial $\eta^2 = .23$] and boundary separation [session x group interaction $F(1,43) = 2.70$, MSe $< 0.001$, $p = .079$, partial $\eta^2 = .11$], whereas theta upregulation lead to an increase in non-decision time, a decrease in boundary separation, and a strong increase in drift rate [session x group interaction $F(2,43) = 2.76$, MSe $= 0.003$, $p = .074$, partial $\eta^2 = .11$]. No effects were observed for the SMR group.

## 4   Discussion

The current analyses addressed the specificity of EEG neurofeedback protocols on measures of attentional control obtained in the Stroop task. The numerical results (and simple effects analyses) showed that training theta leads to decrease in the Stroop effect, while not affecting the Gratton effect. This pattern was only observed in a version of the Stroop task that was made more cognitively demanding by including a stop-signal on 25% of the trials. In the less-demanding version, Stroop and Gratton effects did not reach statistical significance.

In the SMR group, the Gratton effect in the less-demanding version was marginal before training and non-significant after training with no influence on the Stroop effect. In the more demanding Stroop version, Stroop effects were present before and after SMR-training and a Gratton effect was absent. Finally, Stroop and Gratton effects decreased with alpha neurofeedback.

The results on alpha oscillations supports theories claiming that alpha is associated with the inhibition of distracting information. Enhancing the power of alpha oscillations would thus lead to' decrease in Stroop effects and of the Gratton effect. The

---

[1] The diffusion model contains many more parameters, most of which are variance parameters, in order to account for complete response time distributions. In order to fit the full model to empirical data, many data observations are needed and a complex fitting procedure be employed. The EZ diffusion model has been shown to be reasonably accurate in estimating the underlying model parameter values. Its simplicity lends itself to application to cognitive data obtained from the neurofeedback studies.

mid-frontal region, the cortical source of theta oscillations, has been associated with monitoring cognitive effort and triggering top-down control. Enhancing theta power specifically affects the incongruent stimuli, leading to a decrease in Stroop effect. However, the Gratton effect, an interaction effect, is not affected. The absence of a training effect with SMR underscores its use as an active control condition.

**Strength and Limitations**

Although the current analyses provide insights into the specificity of neurofeedback protocols, there are some limitations that should inspire further empirical work. First, Stroop effects were not always observed in the pre-training session, making it difficult to infer any improvement in attentional deployment. This was inevitably due to the small sample size from which data was available. It is recommended that the pre-training test session be used to select for neurofeedback training those participants who show initial cognitive effects. Although this would require a larger sample size from the outset, it would prevent a situation where the number of completers is insufficient to observe cognitive effects at the group level, as is the case here for the SMR group. Second, the analyses compared data from two studies that varied in methodology. It is not impossible that some of the observed differences can be attributed to these. Future work could therefore aim to use the same methodology and vary only the neurofeedback protocol in a large multi-protocol study. This would also allow the opportunity for replication to assess whether any of the reported findings were statistical anomalies. The nature of EEG neurofeedback requires multiple training sessions to observe learning and as individuals vary in their rate of learning this will inevitably lead to datasets that include this uncontrolled variance.

Despite these methodological issues, the current paper demonstrates two data-analytic directions for neurofeedback research that can lead to understanding the cognitive mechanisms underlying neurofeedback success. First, the second-order measure, the Gratton effect, is a theoretically articulated pattern coming from an understanding of the cognitive processes involved in the Stroop task. The use of theory-driven analyses can ground neurofeedback results in an existing theoretical framework, from which new testable predictions can emerge. Second, the use of the EZ diffusion model presents an example in which a computational model is used to extract latent cognitive parameters to allow evaluation of the impact of neurofeedback on these parameters. Model-based data analyses like this provides insights beyond the dependent measures observed and speak directly to the question of which cognitive processes are influenced by neurofeedback training. It should be noted that both types of data-analytics can be applied to any cognitive and brain training program to evaluate its efficacy. In doing so, the analyses bridge the theoretical literature with the literature on cognitive enhancement.

## 5   Conclusion

EEG neurofeedback training has been shown to influence first- and second-order measure of attentional deployment. Three training protocols demonstrate different impact profiles on the Stroop task, evidencing that the protocols influence specific components in the cognitive system supporting attentional control. Whereas frontal alpha enhances efficient deployment of top-down attention, mid-frontal theta leads to faster conflict resolution.

**Acknowledgements.** I thank my co-authors on the two studies (in alphabetical order), Soma Almasi, Joe Barnby, Anna Berger, Virginia Eatough, Emily Hickson, Natasha Kevat, and Sonny Ramtale. Parts of this research was supported by a Faculty of Science Research grant and an ISSF grant to E.J. Davelaar and V. Eatough.

# References

1. Arns, M., de Ridder, S., Strehl, U., Breteler, M., Coenen, A.: Efficacy of neurofeedback treatment in ADHD: the effects on inattention, impulsivity and hyperactivity: a meta-analysis. Clin. EEG Neurosci. **40**, 180–189 (2009)
2. Schabus, M., Heib, D.P.J., Lechinger, J., Griessenberger, H., Klimesch, W., Pawlizki, A., Kunz, A.B., Sterman, B.M., Hoedlmoser, K.: Enhancing sleep quality and memory in insomnia using instrumental sensorimotor rhythm conditioning. Biol. Psychol. **95**, 126–134 (2014)
3. Scott, W.C., Kaiser, D., Othmer, S., Sideroff, S.I.: Effects of an EEG biofeedback protocol on a mixed substance abusing population. Am. J. Drug Alcohol Abuse **31**, 455–469 (2005)
4. Tan, G., Thornby, J., Hammond, D.C., Strehl, U., Canady, B., Arnemann, K., Kaiser, D.A.: Meta-analysis of EEG biofeedback in treating epilepsy. Clin. EEG Neurosci. **40**, 173–179 (2009)
5. Gruzelier, J.H.: EEG-neurofeedback for optimising performance. I: a review of cognitive and affective outcome in healthy participants. Neurosci. Biobehav. Rev. **44**, 124–141 (2014)
6. Gruzelier, J.H.: EEG-neurofeedback for optimising performance. II: creativity, the performing arts and ecological validity. Neurosci. Biobehav. Rev. **44**, 142–158 (2014)
7. Klimesch, W.: EEG Alpha and Theta oscillations reflect cognitive and memory performance: a review and analysis. Brain Res. Rev. **29**, 169–195 (1999)
8. Nan, W., Rodrigues, J.P., Ma, J., Qu, X., Wan, F., Mak, P.-I., Mak, P.U., Vai, M.I., Rosa, A.: Individual Alpha neurofeedback training effect on short term memory. Int. J. Psychophysiol. **86**, 83–87 (2012)
9. Botvinick, M.M., Braver, T.S., Barch, D.M., Carter, C.S., Cohen, J.D.: Conflict monitoring and cognitive control. Psychol. Rev. **108**(3), 624–652 (2001)
10. Botvinick, M.M., Cohen, J.D., Carter, C.S.: Conflict monitoring and anterior cingulate cortex: an update. Trends Cogn. Sci. **8**, 539–546 (2004)
11. Davelaar, E.J., Berger, A.: Enhanced reactive cognitive control through virtual reality EEG neurofeedback. Front. Hum. Neurosci. (2016). doi:10.3389/conf.fnhum.2016.220.00045. Conference Abstract: SAN2016 Meeting
12. Gruzelier, J.H.: EEG-neurofeedback for optimising performance. III: a review of methodological and theoretical considerations. Neurosci. Biobehav. Rev. **44**, 159–182 (2014)
13. Davelaar, E.J., Eatough, V., Almasi, S., Barnby, J.M., Hickson, E., Kevat, N., Ramtale, C.: Neurofeedback training and cognitive performance: a pilot study using an integrated cognitive and phenomenological approach. Front. Hum. Neurosci. (2016). doi:10.3389/conf. fnhum.2016.220.00033. Conference Abstract: SAN2016 Meeting
14. Ratcliff, R., McKoon, G.: The diffusion decision model: theory and data for two-choice decision tasks. Neural Comput. **20**, 873–922 (2008)
15. Wagenmakers, E.-J., van der Maas, H.L.J., Grasman, R.P.P.P.: An EZ-diffusion model for response time and accuracy. Psychon. Bull. Rev. **14**, 3–22 (2007)

# Neural Dynamics of Spontaneous Thought: An Electroencephalographic Study

Manesh Girn[1(✉)], Caitlin Mills[1], Eric Laycock[1], Melissa Ellamil[2], Lawrence Ward[1], and Kalina Christoff[1]

[1] University of British Columbia, Vancouver, Canada
maneshg@alumni.ubc.ca
[2] Max Planck Institute for Human Cognitive and Brain Sciences, Leipzig, Germany

**Abstract.** Spontaneous thinking is a ubiquitous aspect of our mental life and has increasingly become a hot topic of research in cognitive neuroscience. To date, functional neuroimaging studies of spontaneous thought have revealed general brain recruitment centered on a combination of default mode network and executive regions. Despite recent findings about general brain recruitment, very little is known about how these regions are recruited dynamically over time. The current research addresses this gap in the literature by using EEG to investigate the fine-grained temporal dynamics of brain activity underlying spontaneous thoughts. We employed the first-person reports of experienced meditators to index the onset of spontaneous thoughts, and examined brain electrical activity preceding indications of spontaneous thought onset. An independent component analysis-based source localization procedure recovered sources very similar to those previously found with fMRI (Ellamil et al. in NeuroImage 136:186–196, 2016). In addition, phase synchrony analyses revealed a temporal trajectory that begins with default network midline and salience network connectivity, followed by the incorporation of language and executive regions during the period from thought generation to appraisal.

**Keywords:** Spontaneous thought · Neural dynamics · Electroencephalography · Default mode network · Frontoparietal control network · Independent-component analysis

## 1 Introduction

The human brain has a remarkable propensity to spontaneously generate mental content that captures our attention. Memories and projections into the future arise in our awareness unbidden, a previously contemplated problem may suddenly return to cognizance, and so on. Such mental phenomena fall under the rubric of 'spontaneous thought,' which can be understood as unintended mental phenomena that occur without conscious generation, and which are relatively free-flowing with a lack of strong deliberate control [1]. Types of spontaneous thought include mental states such as dreaming, mind wandering, and creativity [1]. Psychological research has linked spontaneous thought to various both beneficial (creativity, prospective planning, etc.

© Springer International Publishing AG 2017
D.D. Schmorrow and C.M. Fidopiastis (Eds.): AC 2017, Part I, LNAI 10284, pp. 28–44, 2017.
DOI: 10.1007/978-3-319-58628-1_3

[2]) and detrimental (disruptions and reductions in memory encoding [3, 4]) processes and outcomes [5, 6]. However, much less is understood about the neural markers of spontaneous thought, particularly with respect to its initial generation and onset – a focus of the current research.

To date, functional neuroimaging studies of spontaneous thought have revealed general brain recruitment centered on a combination of default mode network (DMN) and frontoparietal control network (FPCN) regions [1, 7]. The DMN, which encompasses medial temporal memory regions, is thought to supply the general content of thought [8], while the FPCN likely pertains to processes such as attentional appraisal, thought evaluation and elaboration, as well as maintenance in working memory [9, 10]. This general network recruitment has been further fractionated into distinct sub-components and specific brain regions, each of which putatively has a distinct functional contribution to spontaneous thought [8, 11].

Moreover, in line with the highly dynamic and interactive nature of the brain, these various sub-components are very unlikely to be uniformly recruited; rather, they are likely to be differentially integrated into varying dynamic patterns contingent on both the content of the thought, as well as the current temporal stage of the thought process [11–13]. Thus, it is reasonable to expect that different stages of neural activity may map onto different stages in the subjective experience of spontaneous thought: thought generation, attentional appraisal, evaluation, and elaboration.

We currently know very little about the neural dynamics underlying the temporal components of spontaneous thought. A particular challenge has been to isolate the neural activity corresponding to the initial generation of a spontaneous thought and its subsequent attentional appraisal. The reason for this is evident in the methodological difficulty of experimentally isolating the onset of an elusive mental phenomenon such as a spontaneous thought. By definition, a spontaneous thought cannot be induced by external means; it must rise of its own accord – thus differentiating it from the stimulus-based paradigms that constitute the bulk of cognitive neuroscience research. Moreover, there is currently no known objective neural or behavioral index for the moment of spontaneous thought onset. Studies that hope to investigate this phenomenon, therefore, must employ first-person measures. Yet, first-person measures are also imperfect given individuals' typically poor ability to indicate the onset of mental content, often only realizing their engagement in a mind-wandering episode some time after the fact [5, 14].

One study by Ellamil and colleagues found a way to address these challenges: using trained meditators to investigate the temporal dynamics of spontaneous thought [11]. Indeed, experienced meditators are suggested to have a refined introspective capacity, and may as such constitute a uniquely suitable population to investigate subtler aspects of first-person experience. This contention is encapsulated by the 'neurophenomenology' research program [15], which promotes understanding the neural basis of first-person experience by relating rigorous first-person reports from individuals with introspective training to neural measures [16].

Meditation is generally conceived as a form of attentional training [17], and mindfulness meditation in particular has an explicit goal of increasing one's ability to maintain awareness of the rise and fall of spontaneous mental phenomena [18]. Meditators/mindfulness practitioners have been shown to display greater awareness of subtle emotional and interoceptive feelings [19, 20] and have shown increased meta-cognitive accuracy on memory judgments [21]. In addition, meditators have shown improved ability on a number of perceptual tasks, presumably as a result of increased attentional stability and efficiency [22, 23]. Performance improvements also include, for example, increased perceptual sensitivity and vigilance on a visual threshold line-length discrimination task [24] and improved detection of the second target during attentional blink tasks [25]. As such, experienced meditators appear to be an ideal population to investigate subtler aspects of spontaneous thought, as their attentional capacities may enable them to recognize the onset of thoughts with greater accuracy.

Ellamil and colleagues took advantage of the heightened metacognitive abilities of meditators and employed a procedure that had long-term meditators self-report the onset of spontaneous thoughts while they were maintaining a meditative focus. They characterized brain region recruitment in blocks of 2 s prior to and after indications of spontaneous thought onset [11]. This study found activations spanning both the DMN and FPCN, with a distinct temporal trajectory that originated in the medial temporal lobes as well as lateral and posteromedial parietal cortex (2 s preceding onset), spread to a number of regions including medial prefrontal cortex (onset), and later spread to executive regions such as dorsolateral prefrontal cortex and anterior cingulate cortex (2 s following onset) [11]. Notably, however, this study was greatly limited by the relatively poor temporal resolution of fMRI. Neural activity contains significant variability at the sub-second level, and as such a large amount of information is lost in the use of 2-second blocks. Here we aim to extend the findings of the Ellamil study by using EEG to address the temporal limitations of fMRI.

## 1.1 Current Study and Research Questions

The present study employed high-density electroencephalography (EEG) to overcome the temporal limitations inherent in fMRI. High-density EEG is useful in this context as it allows the measurement of brain electrical activity at the millisecond time scale while also offering reasonably accurate source localization. Notably, at least one previous study has successfully used EEG source localization to recover putative spontaneous thought-related regions [26]. We adopted a similar experimental paradigm to Ellamil et al. [11], capitalizing on the improved first-person reports afforded by using experienced meditators as participants.

Our primary goals were (1) to determine whether brain regions activated during spontaneous thought converge across our EEG analyses and the previous fMRI findings [11], and (2) to investigate the temporal progression of interregional functional connectivity (information sharing) between these regions. In line with our first goal, we hypothesized that we would recover sources of neural electrical activity that correspond to regions previously implicated in spontaneous thought, including DMN regions such as the posterior cingulate cortex, medial prefrontal cortex, and medial temporal lobes, and executive regions such as dorsolateral prefrontal cortex and dorsal anterior cingulate [1, 7]. Moreover, we expected a particular temporal trajectory of activations spanning these regions. In line with the results of Ellamil and colleagues' study [11], we hypothesized that spontaneous-thought related activity will first begin in the medial temporal lobe (MTL), and then spread to medial and lateral parietal regions, followed by other default-mode network regions such as the medial prefrontal cortex (MPFC). Additionally, executive regions, such as the dorsolateral prefrontal cortex (DLPFC), are expected to only show activity immediately prior to responses, and not during the early onset stage. This expectation is consistent with the DLPFC's role in the volitional top-down deployment of cognitive control [27], implying that executive regions may not play a role early on in the spontaneous thought generation process.

In line with our second goal, we made a number predictions afforded by the greater degree of temporal specificity in comparison to the previous fMRI results [11]. Importantly, we analyze brain activity at much smaller time intervals, up to four times smaller than the previous fMRI study. For example, Ellamil and colleagues found a peak in both medial temporal lobe (MTL) and posterior cingulate cortex (PCC) activity at −2 s relative to thought onset indication, followed by medial prefrontal cortex activation at 0 s (thought onset) [11]. Using EEG, we were able increase the temporal specificity from 2 s temporal windows to 500 ms. We expect connectivity to begin between the MTL and PCC, immediately followed by PCC-MPFC and PCC-lateral parietal connectivity. This is consistent with a recent intracranial EEG study that found that MTL-retrosplenial cortex (a region ventrally adjacent to the PCC) phase locking peaked at around ∼200 ms following cued autobiographical memory retrieval, with retrosplenial cortex activity peaking ∼300 ms later [28]. We expect this to then be followed by connectivity with the MPFC in virtue of dense MPFC-PCC interconnectivity and frequent coactivation [29], and connectivity with lateral parietal regions in virtue of previous electrophysiological work indicating PCC and lateral parietal coactivation during episodic memory retrieval [30].

## 2 Methods

### 2.1 Participants and Design

A total of 23 participants took part in the study (13 females; mean age = 31.4 years old, SD = 5.3). 3 participants had to be excluded either because of too few thought reports (>20), or because of technical issues with the data acquisition software. Participants were experienced meditators recruited from the Greater Vancouver area. Minimum meditation experience cut-off was 500 total hours within the past 2 years (mean meditation experience = 726.6 h, SD = 374.4 h). Participants received $10 an hour as compensation.

We employed a within-subjects yoked-control design (Fig. 1), similar to the one used in Ellamil et al. [11]. Participants engaged in two 10-minute conditions while sitting in front of a computer monitor: a thought condition (monitoring and reporting spontaneous thoughts) and a word condition (monitoring and reporting words that appeared onscreen, yoked to the timing of the thought condition). The two conditions were completed back-to-back twice, totaling 20 min each (40 min total).

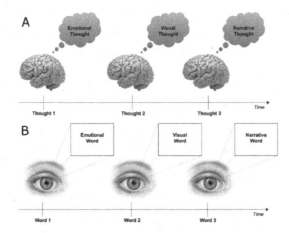

**Fig. 1.** A visual representation of the two experimental conditions. Adapted from Ellamil et al. [11] with permission.

## 2.2 Materials

The task and stimuli were implemented and presented using E-Prime 2.0 (Psychology Software Tools, Sharpsburg, PA, USA). The words and fixation cross appeared as gray font on a black background.

**Word Task Stimuli.** Words in the 'verbal' list consisted of 30 nouns (e.g., work, money, family, goals, health) selected from the Edinburgh Associative Thesaurus (EAT) [31]. The specific words were chosen based on their association with the typical concerns that constitute the bulk of spontaneous thought content [32]. These included home and household matters; employment and finance; partner, family, and relatives; friends and acquaintances; love, intimacy, and sexual matters; self-changes; education and training; health and medical matters; spiritual matters; and hobbies, pastimes, and recreation. The 'visual' list consisted of 30 nouns (e.g., mountain, beach, rain, sun, pet) selected from the Medical Research Council (MRC) Psycholinguistics Database [33] which had imageability, concreteness, and familiarity ratings of 500–700 (on scales of 100 = very low to 700 = very high). The 'somatic' list consisted of 30 nouns and adjectives selected from the EAT that were associated with various body sensations (e.g., warmth, tickle, vibration, pressure, pain), whereas the the 'affective' list consisted of 30 adjectives associated with various emotions (e.g., happiness, sadness, anger, disgust, fear, surprise) [31]. Across all types, each word contained 3–10 letters and 1–3 syllables.

## 2.3 Procedure

**Thought Condition.** Participants were instructed to focus their attention on an aspect of their breathing (sensations on the nostrils or the rise and fall of the abdomen) throughout both conditions. They were told to rest their eyes on a black computer screen with a white fixation cross in the center. Participants reported when they detected the onset of a spontaneous thought by pressing 'I' on the keyboard, then immediately indicated the type of thought it was with an' additional button press (I = verbal, J = visual, K = somatic, L = affective). Verbal thoughts were defined as thoughts that represent an internal narrative and/or that were embedded in terms of language/inner speech. Visual thoughts were defined as any form of mental imagery or symbols. Somatic thoughts were defined as thoughts directly related to bodily sensa-tions. Affective thoughts were defined as thoughts directly related to emotions. These thought types were chosen to correspond the categories of thought frequently identified during mindfulness training [34].

**Word Condition.** For the word condition, participants were also instructed to attend to their breathing and rest their eyes on a black computer screen with a white fixation cross in the center. Rather than reporting on thoughts, however, participants were instructed to press a button when a word was presented on the computer screen. Word presentation was yoked to the thought condition, matched precisely for timing and type of thought reported in the preceding thought condition via a real-time algorithm. Participants were explicitly instructed to read and interpret the word prior to responding with a button press, and each word stayed onscreen until the first button press. The first button press was always followed by an asterisk (*) and the second by two asterisks (**), in order to indicate that the responses were received. Participants were explicitly told not to report thoughts during the word condition.

# 3   EEG Acquisition and Analysis

## 3.1   EEG Recording and Data Pre-processing

EEG was recorded using 60 electrodes on a standard electrode cap (International 10–10 System). The reference electrode was over the right mastoid and electrode AFz served as the ground. Eye movements were recorded by 4 peri-ocular electrodes. Electrode impedances were below 10 k$\Omega$ (input impedance of the amplifier was 2 g$\Omega$).

Prior to analysis, all signals were re-referenced to an average reference and down-sampled to 250 Hz. Signals were also digitally filtered using the EEGLAB toolkit in MATLAB [35], to only contain activity within the 1–50 Hz range. The continuous data were then separated into 10-second time-bins (epochs) time locked to the thought/word onset button presses (5.5 s prior and 4.5 s after). Distinct sets of epochs were delineated for each type of thought (verbal, visual, somatic, affective) and for the word category in general – for a total of 5 conditions, which were used for comparisons. Epoching was performed in order to remove task-irrelevant inter-trial activity.

## 3.2   EEG Source Localization

In order to recover the sources of neural activity responsible for the EEG signals, we ran independent component analysis (ICA) on the EEG data. ICA is a method of blind

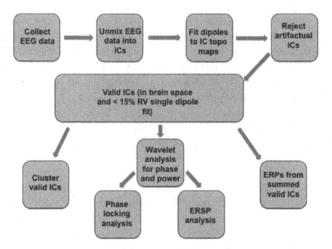

**Fig. 2.** EEG data analysis pipeline. Event-related spectral perturbations (ERSPs) and event-related potentials (ERPs) were excluded from discussion in the present paper.

source separation, which separates the EEG data into apparent neural sources without a priori constraints. Essentially, ICA takes into account the activity across all 60 channels of the raw EEG data, and organizes it into a new set of 60 new channels (independent components; ICs) that are free of the volume conduction that characterizes the raw scalp EEG [36]. ICs represent non-Gaussian neural sources that are maximally independent of each other, as defined by sharing minimal mutual information. Specifically, the procedure involves iteratively solving a neural network for an IC x channel 'unmixing' matrix, U, according to $I = UX$, where X is the electrode channel x time data matrix and I is the IC x time matrix of independent component activations. We computed ICA by using the *runica* function in EEGLAB, which implements extended infomax ICA [36].

Once IC's were derived from the data of all 23 participants (a total of 1380 ICs), we began the process of pruning and rejecting artifactual and unreliable sources. First, we localized the neural sources of the ICs using the *dipfit* algorithm in EEGLab. Electrode locations were co-registered to the Montreal Neurological Institute (MNI) average brain, which enabled the production of Talairach brain space coordinates for the IC dipoles. All ICs with dipoles localized outside of the brain were rejected as artifacts. We then examined the spectral distributions for all of the included ICs, and rejected the ICs that significantly deviated from a 1/f distribution; which would be indicative of non-neural sources of activity such as eye movements or muscle twitches [37].

Clusters were then created using EEGLAB's k-means clustering algorithm, which minimizes intra-cluster distances while maximizing the inter-cluster distances, based on each IC's location in Talairach brain space. Large values of k relative to the number of ICs yield many small, highly localized, clusters with only a few ICs per cluster, whereas small values of k yield a few large, diffuse, non-localized, clusters with many ICs per cluster. We investigated a range of k-values from 10 to 20, and ultimately settled on a k-value of 13: thirteen clusters composed from a total of 289 valid ICs (ranging from 11 to 17 ICs contributed by each participant). Importantly, other k-values within this range produced highly similar results.

In addition, we compared these results to the clusters generated by a seed-based cluster analysis. This analysis generated clusters based on their Euclidean distance from apriori ROIs (distance <3 cm), as defined based on the Talaraich coordinates of the peak activations from Ellamil et al. [11]. We compared the clusters across these two analyses in order to better determine sources of convergence and divergence between our results and those of the original fMRI study.

We then selected the six IC clusters that best overlapped between the two cluster analyses, based on their putative relationship with spontaneous thought-relevant processing. Although several of the unselected clusters are also of some interest, their ICs were not analyzed further in the interest of our focus on spontaneous thought and of minimizing statistical error. We pruned these six clusters to contain only the most representative IC from each participant, which consisted in choosing the IC in closest proximity to the centroid and with the best fit to a single dipole. In a few ambiguous cases, we also examined scalp maps and event-related spectral perturbations to determine the inclusion of a particular IC over another.

It is important to emphasize here that dipole localization and clustering is for interpretational purposes only, and has no bearing on the subsequent spectral and connectivity analyses. These subsequent analyses are computed solely on the basis of the statistically derived IC activations themselves.

In order to decompose the broadband signals into their component frequencies, we applied wavelet analyses on all of the included ICs. Specifically, a Morlet wavelet analysis on each IC time series yielded wavelet coefficients of the sinusoidal oscillations between 1 and 50 Hz, from which phase at each time-frequency point was calculated to be used in computing phase synchrony analyses.

### 3.3   Phase Synchrony Analysis

In order to assess functional connectivity (an index of information sharing) between regions, we conducted phase synchrony analyses. To do this, we computed phase-locking values (PLVs) between IC pairs of interest, each of which were localized to a specific brain region. PLVs were computed via the following formula [35]:

$$PLV_{1,2}(f,t) = \frac{1}{N} \sum_{k=1}^{N} \frac{W_{1,k(f,t)} W_{2,k}^{*}(f,t)}{|W_{1,k(f,t)} W_{2,k}(f,t)|}$$

where $W_{i,k}(f,t)$ are the wavelet coefficients for each time point, t, and frequency, f, for each IC, i, and k = 1 to N is the index of epochs. The PLVs as computed by this equation represent the degree to which the phase differences between signals at a specific oscillatory frequency are constant across trials. PLVs can range from 0 to 1, where 0 indicates a total absence of phase locking, and 1 indicates that the phase difference between two ICs at any given time point remains constant across all trials. Due to neural noise, only $0 < PLV < 1$ is expected from any time series of brain activity.

We first identified the ICs from participants that were common to both clusters and then computed PLVs across all cluster pairs, across all conditions (verbal thought, somatic thought, affective thought, visual thought, word condition), and all frequency bands. We then ran t-tests comparing the PLVs between each thought condition and the word condition. This gave us a PLV/time two-dimensional matrix for each comparison (a total of four), for each region pair. We then looked at each frequency band separately (theta, alpha, beta, gamma). Ultimately, for the scope of this paper we decided to focus on the alpha frequency band for subsequent analyses. The reasoning for this was two-fold. First, previous work has indicated that alpha processing plays a critical role in attentional processes [38–40], and also in internally-oriented processing [38, 41]. Second, and in line with the abovementioned findings, activity in the alpha band displayed the greatest amount of significant activity around the events of interest.

Looking at the alpha frequency band, we calculated the maximum t value at each time point (i.e., across its component frequencies; 8–12 Hz). This was to determine the most significant point in this frequency band at a given point in time; allowing us to collapse across the band to one t value per time point. We then determined whether each of these maximum t values was statistically significant at $p < 0.01$. This gave us a binary output: 0 if not statistically significant, 1 if statistically significant.

Next, we did a chi-squared analysis as a means to measure synchrony over time in 500 ms time-bins. This analysis technique and time-bin length was chosen in order to overcome limitations associated with the number of trials we received. We looked at time bins of 500 ms, from 4 s pre-button press to the button press. Chi Squared tests were used to determine whether the proportion of significant time points (the number of 1 s from the t value analysis) within a given time bin was significantly greater at $p < 0.01$ in one condition relative to a comparison. We compared each individual thought condition relative to the word condition, and the word condition relative to the thought condition as a whole. As an additional check, the condition in question also required at least one instance of a full cycle (133 ms for alpha) of consecutive significant time points within the time bin to be considered significant. This was to control for spurious inconsistent time points of significance within a time bin. Ultimately, these tests indicate whether one condition is exhibiting higher connectivity between a given region pair, during a given time bin.

## 4   Results

### 4.1   Behavioral Results

Before addressing our main research questions, we first assessed the frequency and types of thoughts reported by the meditators. Participants reported a mean of 46 thoughts (2.3 thoughts per minute). Verbal thoughts were the most common (40%), followed by somatic (37%), visual (16%), and affective thoughts (7%). As mentioned in the methods, the words were yoked to the reported thoughts in the preceding thought condition and thus had the same frequency and distribution. The trials for each individual thought type were collapsed (into four groups), and all of the words types were collapsed into one group. In subsequent analyses, we focused on the verbal thought type due to their high frequency (most common) and comparability with the word condition, where participants were asked to interpret the meaning of a word.

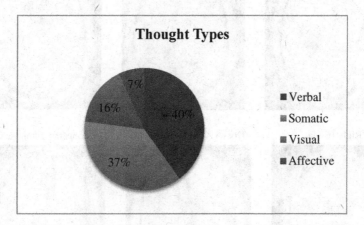

**Fig. 3.** Thought type frequencies.

## 4.2   EEG Sources Converge with Neuroimaging Data

Next, we determined whether the sources of neural activity recovered from the EEG data spatially aligned with the regions implicated by previous fMRI investigations of spontaneous thought. Specifically, we assessed whether prominent clusters localized using EEG converged with regions from Ellamil et al. [11]. In line with our hypotheses, a number of the clusters that were recovered through the ICA, dipole fitting, and cluster analysis exhibited high spatial correspondence to regions previously identified with fMRI using the same paradigm (see Table 1 and Fig. 2) [11]. The scalp maps of the ICs indicated single dipole sources (Fig. 3), which further suggests that these locations represent compact cortical generators [42]. Convergence between our EEG analyses and previously reported hemodynamic results strongly suggests that we have indeed identified reliable regions of spontaneous thought-related activity.

**Table 1.**  Talaraich coordinates for the centroid of recovered neural source clusters.

| Region | Talaraich coordinates (centroid) | | | | |
|---|---|---|---|---|---|
| | L/R/M | BA | x | y | z |
| Medial frontal gyrus (MPFC) | M | 10 | −3 | 47 | 25 |
| Dorsal anterior cingulate | M | 32 | −8 | 2 | 36 |
| Middle frontal gyrus (DLPFC) | L | 9 | −30 | 37 | 31 |
| Insula | R | 13 | 43 | −12 | 16 |
| Posterior cingulate cortex | M | 31 | −19 | 45 | 21 |
| Superior temporal gyrus | L | 22 | −62 | −12 | 1 |

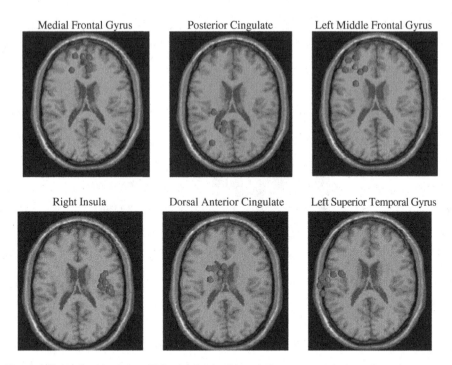

**Fig. 4.** Cluster locations on a Talaraich brain. Blue circles represent independent components, and the red circle is the centroid. (Color figure online)

However, one notable absence was evident: our analyses did not localize a medial temporal lobe (MTL) cluster. On the one hand, this is surprising given that MTL activity prior to thought onset was a primary finding in the previous fMRI study of the same paradigm [11]. MTL regions are consistently recruited by spontaneous thoughts, and are associated with a number of relevant mnemonic processes [1, 8, 43, 44]. On the other hand, the absence of MTL activity makes sense given the relatively poor ability of EEG to detect signals from deeper brain regions. EEG detects the scalp distribution of the aggregate electrical charge of sets of neurons (dipoles). Due to the conductivity of neural tissue, a charge generated by a deeper structure will spatially spread on the way to the surface, and will therefore have weaker detectability (and localizability) at the scalp [45]. As such, due to the location of MTL regions deep below the cortical surface, it would require a very strong and consistent activation for them to be detected by EEG. This kind of activity may not have been feasible with the current paradigm and/or with the number of trials we observed. Future studies should further explore whether EEG can detect MTL structures in relation to spontaneous thought.

### 4.3    Functional Connectivity over Time

Our second research question was addressed using phase synchrony analyses, which allowed us to observe changes in interregional functional connectivity (i.e., information sharing) over time. We were specifically interested in contrasting the significant activity that occurred in small windows prior thought to onset. This was done using two key comparisons: (1) all words vs. all thoughts, and (2) verbal thoughts vs. all words.

We focused on connectivity between the IC clusters that exhibited high spatial overlap with regions previously detected with fMRI. As mentioned in Sect. 3.4, we investigated four time-bins of 500 ms leading up to thought onset to give us finer-grained temporal resolution compared to the previous fMRI investigation. Our chi-squared analysis (see Sect. 2) gave us connectivity matrices, which were then projected onto three-dimensional brains (see Figs. 5 and 6 for results projected on an MNI brain). In Figs. 5 and 6, lines are drawn between two regions when the comparison condition (i.e. Fig. 5: all words, Fig. 6: verbal thoughts) significantly differs from the control condition (i.e. Fig. 5: all thoughts, Fig. 6: all words). More specifically, lines indicate there was (1) a significantly greater proportion of time points of significant alpha-band synchrony between those two regions and (2) at least one instance of a full alpha cycle's worth of consecutive significant time-points.

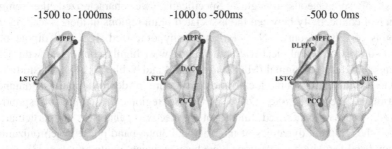

**Fig. 5.** Greater alpha synchrony for all words relative to all thoughts.

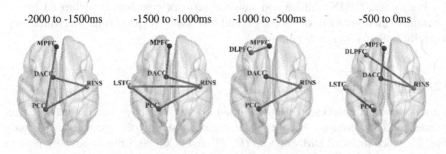

**Fig. 6.** Greater alpha synchrony for verbal thoughts relative to all words.

Comparing all words vs. all thoughts ultimately served as a check of methodological validity. Based on previous studies of word reading and evaluation [10, 46], we should see consistent LSTG connectivity with DMN midline and executive region involvement. For this comparison (Fig. 5), we used a time window of −1.5 s to the button press. This window was chosen due to the fact that individuals indicated word onset at a mean of 1128 ms following word presentation. Indeed, LSTG connectivity was consistent with our predictions, providing evidence for our methodological approach.

The verbal thoughts vs. all words comparison is the key analysis interest. A time window of −2 s relative to the button press was used for the verbal thoughts vs. all words comparison. We chose this window because there was very sparse significant connectivity prior to this window of time; consistent with participants focusing on their breath during this time. In line with our general hypotheses, we observed a progression of DMN connectivity followed by greater executive region recruitment closer to thought onset. Also, we interestingly found consistent significant connectivity between putative 'salience network' [47] network regions.

## 5    Discussion

### 5.1    Overview

Following up on an fMRI study that employed the same behavioral paradigm [11], we used EEG to investigate the neural dynamics underlying the generation and attentional appraisal of spontaneous thoughts. Specifically, we characterized the temporal dynamics of connectivity between the associated brain regions in the 2 s leading up to indications of thought onset. Notably, and as hypothesized, ICA and dipole fitting revealed sources of neural electrical activity that were highly convergent with activation peaks found in the original fMRI study (Fig. 4 and Table 1) [11]. This study is the second to use this EEG source localization procedure to identify putative spontaneous thought-related neural activity [26]. With these regions of spatial correspondence recovered, we then conducted functional connectivity analyses. In particular, we examined the temporal dynamics of interregional alpha-band phase synchronization, a frequency band for which oscillations have been associated with attention [38–40] and internally-directed processing [38, 41]. These analyses revealed a general trajectory that begins with DMN midline and salience network connectivity, followed by the subsequent incorporation of language and executive regions (Fig. 5), which was generally in line with our hypotheses.

### 5.2    Major Findings

We recovered six sources of electrical brain activity that have general spatial correspondence to spontaneous-thought related regions found by the previous fMRI study (Fig. 2), which included DMN regions (MPFC and PCC) [8], salience network regions (DACC and RINS) [47], a language processing region (LSTG) [48], and an executive region (DLPFC) [27]. As mentioned, we analyzed changes in significant connectivity between these regions (in pairs) in 500 ms time-bins, from −2 s to indications of thought onset.

Although we did not recover any MTL activity as hypothesized, we observed connectivity between the MPFC and PCC early in the thought generation process (−2000 to −1500 ms). As mentioned, the PCC is highly structurally and functionally connected with the MTL [29], and was coactivated with the MTL in the original fMRI study [11]. It has also been found to activate in response to a variety of episodic memory-based tasks [44]. This offers the interpretation that the PCC may serve as a (likely temporally delayed) proxy of MTL activity. Further support for this comes from the recent intracranial EEG finding that MTL-retrosplenial cortex phase locking occurred early during autobiographical memory retrieval [28].

The MPFC-PCC connectivity may represent the initial evaluative processing and affective valuation of the spontaneously arising mental content [8]. The concurrent connectivity between the RINS and DACC may indicate initial bottom-up salience processing of this mental content [49]. Interestingly, the RINS also indicated significant connectivity with the PCC. Although causal directionality cannot be inferred based on the current analyses, it is intriguing to consider whether the RINS could be engaging its putative network switching role in this instance by recruiting the PCC to switch from external to internal processing in response to emerging mental content [49].

The second following time-bin, −1500 to −1000 ms, features LSTG connectivity with the RINS and PCC. We interpret the LSTG-PCC coupling as possibly representing a form of linguistic encoding of thought content, consistent with the LSTG's role in language processing [48]. Underscoring this interpretation, comparisons with other thought types (not presently discussed) revealed that LSTG-PCC coupling only occurred in relation to verbal thoughts. The LSTG-RINS connectivity during this time-bin may be indicative of the RINS signaling the need for LSTG thought encoding, as a result of salience tagging [49].

The time-bin from −1000 to −500 ms uniquely includes DLPFC-MPFC connectivity, which may represent evaluative processes occurring on the emergent mental content; consistent with past work implicating these regions in thought evaluation [10].

The final 500 ms immediately preceding the thought onset-button presses, may pertain to the conscious attentional/emotional appraisal of the thought culminating in the decision to report via button press. The RINS-DLPFC connectivity found here very likely indicates salience network recruitment of the executive network in the initiation of the required behavioral response [27, 49].

## 5.3    Limitations and Methodological Considerations

There are a number of notable limitations to the present study. Firstly, although the recovered sources had high spatial correspondence to the results of an fMRI studying using the same paradigm, it is impossible to be certain that they represent the same activity. Moreover, since each measure has its basis in a different indicator of brain activity (i.e., electrical vs. hemodynamic), it is unclear whether exact spatial overlap is to be expected or required for the validation of the EEG results. Our use of EEG source localization combined with a measure of the temporal progression of interregional synchrony is, to our knowledge, the first of its kind as applied to spontaneous thought. As such, this study was as much a proof-of-principle methodological evaluation as it was a study of spontaneous thought. The correspondence and interpretability of the results in relation to previous research is suggestive, but further research employing a similar set of analyses is required to validate the approach.

Another limitation corresponds to the use of meditator's self-reports to index the onset of spontaneous thought. Although we specifically only recruited individuals with a moderate to high amount of meditation experience (range: ~ 500–2000 h), it was not possible to evaluate the accuracy with which they were able to report the emergence of a spontaneous thought. Additionally, it was also not possible to objectively evaluate their meditation expertise and validate the hours of experience that they claimed to possess. We were also limited in our analyses due to the relatively low amount of trials. This precluded our ability to characterize differential patterns of activity for each individual thought type, may have also contributed to our inability to detect MTL regions, and limited us to 500 ms time-bins.

## 6  Concluding Remarks

Our results are generally consistent with those of Ellamil et al. [11] and additionally move beyond them to provide a more fine-grained temporal analysis of the neural dynamics underlying spontaneous thought. The electrophysiological dynamics revealed by EEG appear to share similar sources to the regions found in the original study, but the sequence of connectivity revealed at the millisecond level indicate that there may be important specificities that are overlooked by fMRI. These results underscore the neural heterogeneity of different temporal stages of spontaneous thought, and the need for additional studies in characterizing their dynamics. Our results also suggest that EEG spatial localization combined with phase synchrony analysis may constitute a useful approach to study the neural dynamics of spontaneous thought. Overall, the present study, in addition to Ellamil et al. [11], suggests that the neural correlates pertaining to the temporally distinct processes of thought generation, crystallization, and appraisal can be differentiated, and future research is needed to further fractionate the complex dynamic process of spontaneous thought.

## References

1. Christoff, K., Irving, Z.C., Fox, K.C., Spreng, R.N., Andrews-Hanna, J.R.: Mind-wandering as spontaneous thought: a dynamic framework. Nat. Rev. Neurosci. **17**, 718–731 (2016)
2. Baird, B., Smallwood, J., Schooler, J.W.: Back to the future: autobiographical planning and the functionality of mind-wandering. Conscious. Cogn. **20**, 1604–1611 (2011)
3. Unsworth, N., McMillan, B.D.: Mind wandering and reading comprehension: examining the roles of working memory capacity, interest, motivation, and topic experience. J. Exp. Psychol. Learn. Mem. Cogn. **39**, 832 (2013)
4. Mrazek, M.D., Smallwood, J., Franklin, M.S., Chin, J.M., Baird, B., Schooler, J.W.: The role of mind-wandering in measurements of general aptitude. J. Exp. Psychol. Gen. **141**, 788 (2012)
5. Smallwood, J., Schooler, J.W.: The science of mind wandering: empirically navigating the stream of consciousness. Annu. Rev. Psychol. **66**, 487–518 (2015)
6. Mooneyham, B.W., Schooler, J.W.: The costs and benefits of mind-wandering: a review. Can. J. Exp. Psychol. **67**, 11–18 (2013)
7. Fox, K.C.R., Spreng, R.N., Ellamil, M., Andrews-Hanna, J.R., Christoff, K.: The wandering brain: meta-analysis of functional neuroimaging studies of mind-wandering and related spontaneous thought processes. NeuroImage **111**, 611–621 (2015)

8. Andrews-Hanna, J.R., Smallwood, J., Spreng, R.N.: The default network and self-generated thought: component processes and dynamic control. Ann. New York Acad. Sci. **1316**, 29–52 (2014)
9. Vincent, J.L., Kahn, I., Snyder, A.Z., Raichle, M.E., Buckner, R.L.: Evidence for a frontoparietal control system revealed by intrinsic functional connectivity. J. Neurophysiol. **100**, 3328–3342 (2008)
10. Ellamil, M., Dobson, C., Beeman, M., Christoff, K.: Evaluative and generative modes of thought during the creative process. NeuroImage **59**, 1783–1794 (2012)
11. Ellamil, M., Fox, K.C., Dixon, M.L., Pritchard, S., Todd, R.M., Thompson, E., Christoff, K.: Dynamics of neural recruitment surrounding the spontaneous arising of thoughts in experienced mindfulness practitioners. NeuroImage **136**, 186–196 (2016)
12. Zabelina, D.L., Andrews-Hanna, J.R.: Dynamic network interactions supporting internally-oriented cognition. Curr. Opin. Neurobiol. **40**, 86–93 (2016)
13. Dixon, M.L., Andrews-Hanna, J.R., Spreng, R.N., Irving, Z.C., Mills, C., Girn, M., Christoff, K.: Interactions between the default network and dorsal attention network vary across default subsystems, time, and cognitive states. NeuroImage **147**, 632–649 (2016)
14. Nisbett, R.E., Wilson, T.D.: Telling more than we can know: verbal reports on mental processes. Psychol. Rev. **84**, 231 (1977)
15. Varela, F.J.: Neurophenomenology: a methodological remedy for the hard problem. J. Conscious. Stud. **3**, 330–349 (1996)
16. Lutz, A., Thompson, E.: Neurophenomenology: integrating subjective experience and brain dynamics in the neuroscience of consciousness. J. Conscious. Stud. **10**, 31–52 (2003)
17. Lutz, A., Slagter, H.A., Dunne, J.D., Davidson, R.J.: Attention regulation and monitoring in meditation. Trends Cogn. Sci. **12**, 163–169 (2008)
18. Tang, Y.-Y., Hölzel, B.K., Posner, M.I.: The neuroscience of mindfulness meditation. Nat. Rev. Neurosci. **16**, 213–225 (2015)
19. Nielsen, L., Kaszniak, A.W.: Awareness of subtle emotional feelings: a comparison of long-term meditators and nonmeditators. Emotion **6**, 392 (2006)
20. Fox, K.C.R., Zakarauskas, P., Dixon, M.L., Ellamil, M., Thompson, E., Christoff, K.: Meditation experience predicts introspective accuracy. PLoS ONE **7**, e45370 (2012)
21. Baird, B., Mrazek, M.D., Phillips, D.T., Schooler, J.W.: Domain-specific enhancement of metacognitive ability following meditation training. J. Exp. Psychol. Gen. **143**, 1972 (2014)
22. Kozasa, E.H., Sato, J.R., Lacerda, S.S., Barreiros, M.A., Radvany, J., Russell, T.A., Sanches, L.G., Mello, L.E., Amaro Jr., E.: Meditation training increases brain efficiency in an attention task. NeuroImage **59**, 745–749 (2012)
23. Lutz, A., Slagter, H.A., Rawlings, N.B., Francis, A.D., Greischar, L.L., Davidson, R.J.: Mental training enhances attentional stability: neural and behavioral evidence. J. Neurosci. **29**, 13418–13427 (2009)
24. MacLean, K.A., Ferrer, E., Aichele, S.R., Bridwell, D.A., Zanesco, A.P., Jacobs, T.L., King, B.G., Rosenberg, E.L., Sahdra, B.K., Shaver, P.R.: Intensive meditation training improves perceptual discrimination and sustained attention. Psychol. Sci. **21**, 829–839 (2010)
25. Slagter, H.A., Lutz, A., Greischar, L.L., Francis, A.D., Nieuwenhuis, S., Davis, J.M., Davidson, R.J.: Mental training affects distribution of limited brain resources. PLoS Biol. **5**, e138 (2007)
26. Kirschner, A., Kam, J.W.Y., Handy, T.C., Ward, L.M.: Differential synchronization in default and task-specific networks of the human brain. Front. Hum. Neurosci. **6**, 139 (2012)
27. Niendam, T.A., Laird, A.R., Ray, K.L., Dean, Y.M., Glahn, D.C., Carter, C.S.: Meta-analytic evidence for a superordinate cognitive control network subserving diverse executive functions. Cogn. Affect. Behav. Neurosci. **12**, 241–268 (2012)

28. Foster, B.L., Kaveh, A., Dastjerdi, M., Miller, K.J., Parvizi, J.: Human retrosplenial cortex displays transient theta phase locking with medial temporal cortex prior to activation during autobiographical memory retrieval. J. Neurosci. **33**, 10439–10446 (2013)

29. Greicius, M.D., Supekar, K., Menon, V., Dougherty, R.F.: Resting-state functional connectivity reflects structural connectivity in the default mode network. Cereb. Cortex **19**, 72–78 (2008)

30. Foster, B.L., Rangarajan, V., Shirer, W.R., Parvizi, J.: Intrinsic and task-dependent coupling of neuronal population activity in human parietal cortex. Neuron **86**, 578–590 (2015)

31. Kiss, G.R., Armstrong, C., Milroy, R., Piper, J.: An associative thesaurus of English and its computer analysis. Comput. Literary Stud. 153–165 (1973)

32. Klinger, E., Cox, W.M.: Dimensions of thought flow in everyday life. Imagination Cogn. Pers. **7**, 105–128 (1987)

33. Wilson, M., Psycholinguistic, M.R.C.: Database: machine-usable dictionary, version 2.00. Behav. Res. Methods, Instrum. Comput. **20**, 6–10 (1988)

34. Sayadaw, M., Maung, T.N.: Fundamentals of Vipassana Meditation (2002)

35. Delorme, A., Makeig, S.: EEGLAB: an open source toolbox for analysis of single-trial EEG dynamics including independent component analysis. J. Neurosci. Methods **134**, 9–21 (2004)

36. Bell, A.J., Sejnowski, T.J.: An information-maximization approach to blind separation and blind deconvolution. Neural Comput. **7**, 1129–1159 (1995)

37. Viola, F.C., Thorne, J., Edmonds, B., Schneider, T., Eichele, T., Debener, S.: Semi-automatic identification of independent components representing EEG artifact. Clin. Neurophysiol. **120**, 868–877 (2009)

38. Palva, S., Palva, J.M.: Functional roles of alpha-band phase synchronization in local and large-scale cortical networks. Front. Psychol. **2**, 204 (2011)

39. Green, J.J., McDonald, J.J.: Electrical neuroimaging reveals timing of attentional control activity in human brain. PLoS Biol. **6**, e81 (2008)

40. Doesburg, S.M., Bedo, N., Ward, L.M.: Top-down alpha oscillatory network interactions during visuospatial attention orienting. NeuroImage **132**, 512–519 (2016)

41. Cooper, N.R., Burgess, A.P., Croft, R.J., Gruzelier, J.H.: Investigating evoked and induced electroencephalogram activity in task-related alpha power increases during an internally directed attention task. NeuroReport **17**, 205–208 (2006)

42. Delorme, A., Palmer, J., Onton, J., Oostenveld, R., Makeig, S.: Independent EEG sources are dipolar. PLoS ONE **7**, e30135 (2012)

43. Squire, L.R., Stark, C.E., Clark, R.E.: The medial temporal lobe. Annu. Rev. Neurosci. **27**, 279–306 (2004)

44. Spreng, R.N., Mar, R.A., Kim, A.S.: The common neural basis of autobiographical memory, prospection, navigation, theory of mind, and the default mode: a quantitative meta-analysis. J. Cogn. Neurosci. **21**, 489–510 (2009)

45. Luck, S.J.: An Introduction to the Event-Related Potential Technique. MIT Press, Cambridge (2014)

46. Bedo, N., Ribary, U., Ward, L.M.: Fast dynamics of cortical functional and effective connectivity during word reading. PLoS ONE **9**, e88940 (2014)

47. Seeley, W.W., Menon, V., Schatzberg, A.F., Keller, J., Glover, G.H., Kenna, H., Reiss, A. L., Greicius, M.D.: Dissociable intrinsic connectivity networks for salience processing and executive control. J. Neurosci. **27**, 2349–2356 (2007)

48. Jobard, G., Crivello, F., Tzourio-Mazoyer, N.: Evaluation of the dual route theory of reading: a metanalysis of 35 neuroimaging studies. NeuroImage **20**, 693–712 (2003)

49. Menon, V., Uddin, L.Q.: Saliency, switching, attention and control: a network model of insula function. Brain Struct. Funct. **214**, 655–667 (2010)

# Deep Transfer Learning for Cross-subject and Cross-experiment Prediction of Image Rapid Serial Visual Presentation Events from EEG Data

Mehdi Hajinoroozi[1(✉)], Zijing Mao[1], Yuan-Pin Lin[2], and Yufei Huang[1]

[1] University of Texas at San Antonio, San Antonio, USA
Mehdi.hajinoroozi@my.utsa.edu, mzjl68@hotmail.com,
Yufei.huang@utsa.edu
[2] Institute of Medical Science and Technology, National Sun Yat-sen University,
Kaohsiung, Taiwan
yplin@mail.nsysu.edu.tw

**Abstract.** Transfer learning (TL) has gained significant interests recently in brain computer interface (BCI) as a key approach to design robust predictors for cross-subject and cross-experiment prediction of the brain activities in response to cognitive events. We carried out in this.aper the first comprehensive investigation of the transferability of deep convolutional neural network (CNN) for cross-subject and cross-experiment prediction of image Rapid Serial Visual Presentation (RSVP) events. We show that for both cross-subject and cross-experiment predictions, all convolutional layers and fully connected layers contain both general and subject/experiment-specific features and transfer learning with weights fine-tuning can improve the prediction performance over that without transfer. However, for cross-subject prediction, the convolutional layers capture more subject-specific features, whereas for cross-experiment prediction, the convolutional layers capture more general features across experiment. Our study provides important information that will guide the design of more sophisticated deep transfer learning algorithms for EEG based classifications in BCI applications.

**Keywords:** Transfer learning · Deep convolutional neural networks · EEG signals

## 1 Introduction

Rapid Serial Visual Presentation (RSVP) is a widely used EEG-based brain computer interface (BCI) paradigm designed to study human brain response to time-lock rare target stimuli [1]. RSVP has also found many applications including BCI keyboard, smart learning, etc. Like in most BCI systems, designing robust classifier for accurate prediction of RSVP target event from EEG measurements is a crucial component and it has benefited from the advancement in machine learning and signal processing. While the XDAWN filter [2] and Bayesian linear discriminant algorithm (BLDA) [3]

© Springer International Publishing AG 2017
D.D. Schmorrow and C.M. Fidopiastis (Eds.): AC 2017, Part I, LNAI 10284, pp. 45–55, 2017.
DOI: 10.1007/978-3-319-58628-1_4

represent two state-of-the-art shallow algorithms for RSVP target event classification, deep learning has also gained much interest for this classification recently. To this end, we have conducted comprehensive investigations of convolutional neural network (CNN) models and showed that the spatial-temporal CNN (STCNN) model can achieve considerable performance improvement over both XDAWN and BLDA in predicting RSVP events, [4] demonstrating the ability of deep learning to learn robust and complex EEG discriminate features.

To achieve this improved performance, deep learning requires a large amount of training data. However, collecting large training data for a single user is expensive and laborious. Prolonged BCI training time can also induce fatigue, thus deteriorating user performance. It is therefore desirable to integrate data from other subjects performing the same or similar BCI experiments. However, it is well known that there is a large variation in individual brain responses to the same stimuli and brute-force combing data from different subjects might degrade rather than improve the performance. Instead, transfer learning [5–7] provides a principle paradigm for identifying and adapting discriminate information in data across different subjects or experiments to help improve subject-specific classification performance. However, developing deep learning based transfer learning algorithms for RSVP event prediction and general EEG-based classification is still an open topic, yet to be investigated.

Because of the nature of deep learning algorithm and architecture, transfer deep learning models can be easily implemented through its fine tune process. However, fine-tuning does not always lead to improved performance and an important investigation of feature transferability of CNN models for image recognition [11] has showed that the transferability decreases with layers, where the lower convolution layers tend to learn general features more transferable and higher fully connected layers are more likely to learn less transferable, task-specific features. This result has inspired new deep transfer learning algorithms such as deep adaptive network that optimize the transferable features in CNN.

However, the extent to which the STCNN (as a deep convolutional neural network) layers can be transferred and if the transferability result for image recognition still holds for RSVP event prediction and general EEG-based classification are unclear. To answer this very important question, in this work, we investigate how transferable the layers of STCNN are. Specifically, we determine if the features learned in each layer of the STCNN are general to different subjects or experiments or subject-/experiment specific in the case of RSVP event prediction. We investigated both cross-subject and cross-experiment predictions and interestingly, we showed that the fully connected layer features are specific features and cannot be transferred. On the other hand, the convolution layer features are extracting some general features but are not completely general. In addition, transferring the features from source domain to target domain and performing fine-tuning result in the best classification in target domain.

The rest of this paper is organized as follows. In Sect. 2, we introduce the datasets used for this investigation. In Sect. 3, we explain the STCNN architecture for RSVP event classification. In Sect. 4, we discuss the procedures of our investigation of feature transferability in different layers of the STCNN and demonstrate the results for both cross-subject and cross-experiment predictions. Concluding remarks are provided in Sect. 5.

## 2 Description of Data

In this work, we used EEG data from three RSVP experiments to study STCNN feature transferability for both cross-subject and cross-experiment event prediction. In an RSVP experiment, subjects are asked to identify a target image from a continuous burst of image clips presented at a high rate. The target image can be predefined or decided by certain rules. Subjects EEG signals are recorded during this process. The patterns in EEG signals are different when the subject is presented with target or non-target images. Three different RSVP data sets used in this work are CT2WS [19], Static Motion [20] and Expertise RSVP [24]. In the CT2WS RSVP experiment, short grayscale video clips as target and non-target stimuli (targets are moving people or vehicles, and non-targets are plants or buildings) are presented at 2 Hz (every 500 ms). The experiment included 15 subjects, where each subject participated in a 15-min. session, where EEG data were recorded by Biosemi device with 64 channels, at sampling rate of 512 Hz. In the Static motion RSVP experiment, target and non-target images static images presented at speed of 2 Hz. 16 subjects have taken part, where each subject participated in a 15-min. session, and EEG data were collected with a Biosemi headset with 64 electrodes at a sampling rate 512 Hz. The Expertise RSVP experiment consists of a 5-Hz presentation of color images of indoor and outdoor scenes, where the target images come from one of following five categories: stair, container, poster, chair, and door [25]. The experiment consists of 10 subjects, where each subject participated in 5 sessions of 60-min. presentation. EEG data were collected with Biosemi EEG headsets with 256 electrodes at a sampling rate of 512 Hz. The data from all three datasets were first band-pass filtered with a bandwidth of 0.1–55 Hz to remove DC and electrical noise and then down-sampled to 128 Hz to reduce feature dimension and cover the whole frequency band after filtering. For Expertise RSVP, only 64 channels (based on the 10–20 system) were selected. Following the procedure described in [17], one-second epochs of the EEG samples time-locked to each target/non-target onset were extracted for all subjects, where the size of each EEG epoch is $64 \times 128$. For cross-subject prediction, we used Expertise RSVP. Specifically, we called samples from subject 1 to 5 including 65831 epochs as dataset A and those from subject 6 to 10 including 62553 epochs as dataset B. For cross-experiment prediction, we combined the EEG epochs from CT2WS and Static Motion data sets which contain 21680 EEG epochs and we call this C data set.

## 3 Spatial-Temporal CNN for RSVP Event Prediction

In this section we provide the explanation for STCNN architecture and also how the transfer learning can be performed by STCNN.

### 3.1 Architecture of Spatial-Temporal CNN

We discuss next the architecture of spatial-temporal convolutional neural network (STCNN), a deep learning model for classification of the RSVP EEG data sets [7–13].

STCNN is a CNN model, specially designed in order to extract spatial correlations and local temporal correlations of the EEG signals. STCNN similar to regular CNNs structure includes convolutional layers as feature extractors and fully connected layers (FC) on top of the neural network as classifier. Let $\mathbf{v} \in \mathcal{R}^{M \times 1}$ denote an input vector with $M = C \times T$, where both C (channel size) and T (time samples) are 64 in this case. Also, let $W_{ct}^{pq}$ represent the cth and tth weight of the pth feature map for hidden layer k and qth feature map for hidden layer $k - 1$, where $c = 1, \ldots, c'$, $t = 1, \ldots, t'$ with $c' \times t'$ as the kernel size and p = 1,...,P, q = 1,...,Q, where P, Q are feature map sizes (FMS) as hyper-parameters to be learned. Then, the $p^{\text{th}}$ FM at the output of the convolutional layer is:

$$\text{convolution}(\mathbf{v})_{ct}^{p} = \text{ReLU}\left(\sum_{q=1}^{Q} W_{ct}^{pq} * \mathbf{v}_{ct} + b_p\right) \qquad (1)$$

where $\mathbf{v}_{ct}$ is input element corresponding to the EEG measurement from channel $c$ at time $t$, ReLU represents the rectified linear function [19, 20] $f(x) = max(0, x)$. Asterisk sign is convolution operation as $W_{ct}^{pq} * \mathbf{v}_{ct} = \Sigma_{u=-c'}^{c'}\Sigma_{v=-t'}^{t'} W_{ct}^{pq}\mathbf{v}_{c-u,t-v}$ and $b_p$ is the bias parameter for $p^{\text{th}}$ feature map. We can see from (1) that the kernel filters for all channels at time $t$ form a spatial filter. After the convolutional layer, an MLP is added to combine all FMs for prediction of target/non-target events. In current design which is specific for EEG signals STCNN contains two convolution layers to capture both spatial and temporal correlations in EEG signals. In the first convolutional layer, kernels of size $64 \times$ Conv1W ($c' = 64, t' =$ Conv1W) is applied to sub-epochs, where each kernel slides in the whole epoch from the start to the end to generate a $1 \times (128\text{-Conv1W} + 1)$ feature map [21–23]. Figure 1 shows the structure of the STCNN.

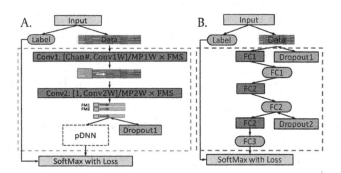

**Fig. 1.** STCNN architecture. **A.** The designed CNN architecture. There are $N$ convolution layers and blue boxes are convolution operations, where the texts inside represent [kernel shape]/MP width $\times$ feature map size. "FM" denotes feature map. **B.** The detailed architecture of the DNN Module in A. The gray ovals are hidden units. (Color figure online)

## 3.2  Transfer Learning with Spatial-Temporal CNN

Suppose that we have two datasets, generated from the same experiment but for different subjects or from two similar experiments (e.g. two RSVP experiments). Particularly, we call them as source and target domain datasets separately. We further assume that a STCNN has been trained by using the source domain dataset. The goal of transfer learning is to train another STCNN by using the target domain dataset and by transferring the architecture and common features from source domain STCNN. Common features between source and target domain refers to the features learned by STCNNs that are general across these two domains. To perform transfer learning with STCNN, we consider in the paper simple weight transfer and fine-tuning, i.e., we copy the weights of the source domain STCNN to the target domain STCNN and then perform fine tuning. The weight transfer can be carried out by layers. The investigation of transferability of a layer is to study if the source domain weights in this layer contain general or task-specific features. We investigate two approaches. In the first approach, we transfer the weights of a certain layer and fix them in target domain model, which means that the transferred weights will not change and no fine-tuning will be performed on them when the target domain STCNN is trained. We call the first approach "Frozen (fixed) transferred layer approach". For the second approach, we can transfer the weights of a layer from source domain STCNN to target domain model and then that transferred layer gets fine-tuned while the target domain STCNN is being trained. We called the second approach the "fine-tuned transferred layer approach".

# 4  Results

In this section, we show the results on the transferability of STCNN for both cross-subject and cross-experiment predictions. We used area under the curve (AUC) as a measurement of the prediction performance. To obtain an AUC for an algorithm, a 10-fold cross validation (CV) was performed, where for each CV, the data were randomly separated into 10 equal sized parts with one part used for validation and the remaining 9 parts used for the trained the model. This is done 10 times and the average performance is considered as classification performance of the model. In following sections, we first show the baseline performance of STCNN and other state-of-the-art shallow algorithms and then present the results on the transferability of STCNN for both cross-subject and cross-experiment predictions.

## 4.1  Baseline Performance of STCNN

We first evaluated the baseline performances of STCNN in dataset A, B and C, respectively, and compared with the state-of-the-art shallow learning algorithms including Bagging, XDAWN-LDA (XLDA) and LDA. Figures 2, 3 and 4 show the classification AUC performances for dataset A, B and C, respectively. They show that STCNN outperforms all three tested shallow machine learning algorithms in all three datasets. STCNN has the highest gain in dataset B, where it achieved $\sim 8\%$ improvement.

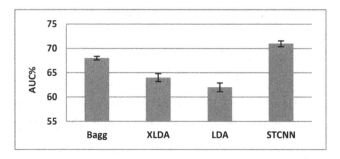

**Fig. 2.** AUC classification performances for dataset A.

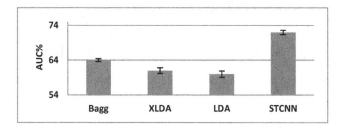

**Fig. 3.** AUC classification performances for dataset B.

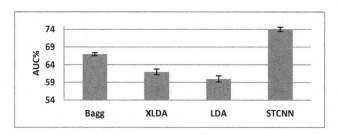

**Fig. 4.** AUC classification performances for dataset C.

## 4.2   Investigation of STCNN Transferability for Cross-subject Prediction

In this section, we investigate how transferable are the weights learned in different layers of the STCNN for cross-subject prediction. In this case, we first train a STCNN model using a source domain dataset and our goal is to transfer this model to a target data set. Apparently in cross-subject prediction the source domain contains the EEG epochs of the subjects, which are not seen in target domain and source domain and target domain contain completely different subjects. In order to study the transfer learning for cross subject prediction, we alternate dataset A and B as source and target datasets.

In the following, we used AnB(+) and BnA(+) to represent how the transfer learning is being performed, where AnB means that A is the source domain, B is the target domain, there are n transferred layers and If "+" is also included, then the transferred layers are also fined-tuned. Figure 5 depicts the results for transferring from A to B. The green dot (Base B) is the baseline classification performance of the STCNN trained only using dataset B. The blue dots which are named AnB show the performance of the frozen transferred layer approach and the red dots AnB+ show the performances of the fine-tuned transferred layer approach. We can see that AnB performance drops continuously from the convolutional layers to the fully connected layer, comparing with the baseline performance, where the drops in convolutional layers are higher than in fully connected layers. This suggests that all the layers contain subject-specific features, where convolutional layers seem to capture most of these subject-specific features as performances of frozen fully connected layers does not induce too much drop anymore. The fact that the largest performance drop is about 5% also suggests that all layers also contain a significant amount of general information. This is confirmed by the results of the fine-tuned transferred layer approach (AnB+), where fine-tuning after weights transfer significantly improves the performance and the improvement is pronounced particularly for the convolutional layers. Moreover, when all the layers are transferred and fine-tuned, the highest classification performance 73.28% is achieved, which is 2.69% higher than the baseline performance.

Figure 6 shows the results of transferring from B to A. Very similar results can be seen in this case. In addition, fine-tuning of all transferred layers results in the highest classification performance 72.42%. Taken together, the results show that for cross-subject predictions, both convolutional and fully connected layers in STCNN contain both general features that can be transferred and subject specific information that cannot be transferred. It is notable that fine-tuning of all the transferred layers using the target domain data achieves the best performance and improves the baseline performance.

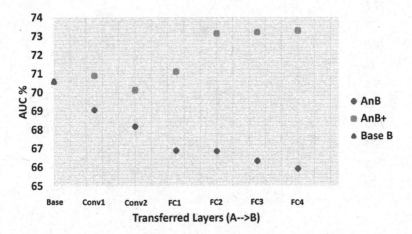

**Fig. 5.** AUC classification performance of the target domain **B** when the features transferred from source domain **A**. (Color figure online)

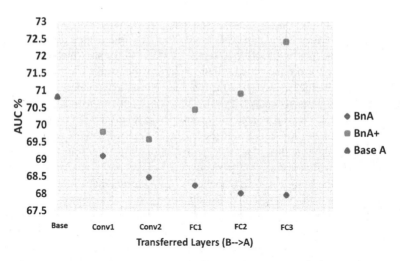

**Fig. 6.** AUC classification performance of the target domain **A** when the features transferred from source domain **B**.

### 4.3 Experimental Results for Cross-experiment Transferability Study

In this section, we study the cross-experiment transferability with STCNN. In this case, we consider dataset C as the source domain and A and B are considered two individual target domain datasets. Figures 7 and 8 depict the transferability from C to A and B, respectively. Once again, the green dot is baseline performance trained with only the target domain data. The blue dots named CnA and CnB show the results for the frozen transferred layer approach and the red dots in CnA+ and CnB+ show the results for the fine-tuned transferred layer approach. From CnA and CnB we observe again that the

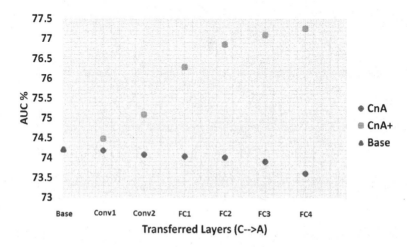

**Fig. 7.** AUC classification performance of the target domain A when the features transferred from source domain C. (Color figure online)

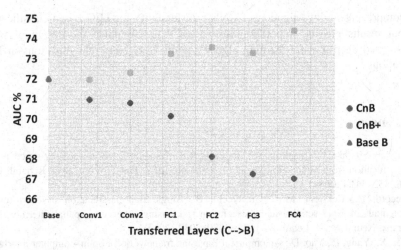

**Fig. 8.** AUC classification performance of the target domain B when the features transferred from source domain C. (Color figure online)

performance drops with layers, suggesting that all layers learn experimental-specific feature. However, this time there is a lot less amount of drop in convolutional layer; there is almost no significant drop in convolutional layers for C to A. This suggests that the convolutional layers capture a significant portion of features that are general across two different RSVP experiments. In contrast, the fully connected layers contain more experiment-specific features. Since both convolutional and fully connected layers contain experimental specific features, as expected fine-tuning improves the performance and once again fine-tuning of all layers obtains the highest performance 77.24% and 74.38% for transferring from C to A and B respectively.

## 5 Conclusion

In this work, we studied the transferability of STCNN layers in performing for cross-subject and cross-experiment classification of RSVP target and non-target events using EEG data. We showed that for both cases, all convolutional layers and fully connected layers contain both general and subject/experiment-specific features. For cross-subject prediction, the convolutional layers capture more subject-specific features, whereas for cross-experiment prediction, the convolutional layers capture more general features across experiment. This suggests that the convolutional layers are more likely transferable for cross-experiment predictions. Previously, it has been shown for image recognition that convolutional layers contain general features that can be transferred. Apparently, for EEG based BCI classification, the characteristics of transferability is more complicated. Nevertheless, we show that fine-tuning can improve the baseline performance, which suggests that transfer learning with STCNN has the ability to transfer general features from source domain to improve the performance in the target domain for EEG based classification. This study represents the first comprehensive investigation of CNN transferability for EEG based classification and our results provide important information that will guide the design of more sophisticated deep transfer learning algorithms for EEG based classifications in BCI applications.

# References

1. Bigdely-Shamlo, N., Vankov, A., Ramirez, R.R., Makeig, S.: Brain activity-based image classification from rapid serial visual presentation. IEEE Trans. Neural Syst. Rehabil. Eng. **16**, 432–441 (2008)
2. Cecotti, H., Eckstein, M.P., Giesbrecht, B.: Single-trial classification of event-related potentials in rapid serial visual presentation tasks using supervised spatial filtering. IEEE Trans. Neural Netw. Learn. Syst. **25**, 2030–2042 (2014)
3. Lei, X., Yang, P., Yao, D.: An empirical Bayesian framework for brain–computer interfaces. IEEE Trans. Neural Syst. Rehabil. Eng. **17**, 521–529 (2009)
4. Rivet, B., Souloumiac, A., Attina, V., Gibert, G.: xDAWN algorithm to enhance evoked potentials: application to brain–computer interface. IEEE Trans. Biomed. Eng. **56**, 2035–2043 (2009)
5. Pan, S.J., Yang, Q.: A survey on transfer learning. IEEE Trans. Knowl. Data Eng. **22**(10), 1345–1359 (2010)
6. Cook, D., Feuz, K.D., Krishnan, N.C.: Transfer learning for activity recognition: a survey. Knowl. Inf. Syst. **36**(3), 537–556 (2013)
7. Hinton, G., Deng, L., Yu, D., Dahl, G.E., Mohamed, A.-R., Jaitly, N., et al.: Deep neural networks for acoustic modeling in speech recognition: the shared views of four research groups. IEEE Signal Process. Mag. **29**, 82–97 (2012)
8. Shao, L., Zhu, F., Li, X.: Transfer learning for visual categorization: a survey (2014)
9. Razavian, A.S., et al.: CNN features off-the-shelf: an astounding baseline for recognition. In: 2014 IEEE Conference on Computer Vision and Pattern Recognition Workshops (CVPRW). IEEE (2014)
10. Donahue, J., et al.: Decaf: a deep convolutional activation feature for generic visual recognition. arXiv preprint arXiv:1310.1531 (2013)
11. Yosinski, J., et al.: How transferable are features in deep neural networks? In: Advances in Neural Information Processing Systems (2014)
12. Krizhevsky, A., Sutskever, I., Hinton, G.E.: Imagenet classification with deep convolutional neural networks. In: Advances in Neural Information Processing Systems (2012)
13. Patel, A.B., Nguyen, T., Baraniuk, R.G.: A probabilistic theory of deep learning. arXiv preprint arXiv:1504.00641 (2015)
14. Hinton, G.E., Osindero, S., Teh, Y.-W.: A fast learning algorithm for deep belief nets. Neural Comput. **18**(7), 1527–1554 (2006)
15. Mirowski, P.W., et al.: Comparing SVM and convolutional networks for epileptic seizure prediction from intracranial EEG. In: IEEE Workshop on Machine Learning for Signal Processing, MLSP 2008. IEEE (2008)
16. Aytar, Y., Zisserman, A.: Tabula rasa: model transfer for object category detection. In: 2011 IEEE International Conference on Computer Vision (ICCV). IEEE (2011)
17. Li, X.: Regularized adaptation: theory, algorithms and applications. Ph.D. thesis, University of Washington, USA (2007)

18. Yang, J., Yan, R., Hauptmann, A.: Adapting SVM classifiers to data with shifted distributions. In: ICDM Workshops 2007 (2007)
19. U.S Department of Defense Office of the Secretary of Defense: Code of federal regulations, protection of human subjects. 32 CFR 219 (1999)
20. U.S. Department of the Army. Use of volunteers as subjects of research. AR 70-25. Government Printing Office, Washington, DC (1990)
21. Hajinoroozi, M., et al.: Feature extraction with deep belief networks for driver's cognitive states prediction from EEG data. In: 2015 IEEE China Summit and International Conference on Signal and Information Processing (ChinaSIP). IEEE (2015)
22. Hajinoroozi, M., Mao, Z., Huang, Y.: Prediction of driver's drowsy and alert states from EEG signals with deep learning. In: IEEE 6th International Workshop on Computational Advances in Multi-sensor Adaptive Processing (CAMSAP). IEEE (2015)
23. Hajinoroozi, M., Mao, Z., Jung, T.P., Lin, C.T., Huang, Y.: EEG-based prediction of driver's cognitive performance by deep convolutional neural network. Signal Process. Image Commun. (2016)
24. Touryan, J., Apker, G., Kerick, S., Lance, B., Ries, A.J., McDowell, K.: Translation of EEG-based performance prediction models to rapid serial visual presentation tasks. In: Schmorrow, D.D., Fidopiastis, C.M. (eds.) AC 2013. LNCS (LNAI), vol. 8027, pp. 521–530. Springer, Heidelberg (2013). doi:10.1007/978-3-642-39454-6_56
25. Touryan, J., Apker, G., Lance, B.J., Kerick, S. E., Ries, A. J. McDowell, K.: Estimating endogenous changes in task performance from EEG. In: Using Neurophysiological Signals That Reflect Cognitive or Affective State, p. 268 (2015)

# Using Portable EEG to Assess Human Visual Attention

Olave E. Krigolson$^{(\boxtimes)}$, Chad C. Williams, and Francisco L. Colino

Neuroeconomics Laboratory, University of Victoria, Victoria, BC, Canada
{krigolson, ccwillia, fcolino}@uvic.ca

**Abstract.** Over the past ten years there has been a rapid increase in the number of portable electroencephalographic (EEG) systems available to researchers. However, to date, there has been little work validating these systems for event-related potential (ERP) research. Here we demonstrate that the MUSE portable EEG system can be used to quickly assess and quantify the ERP responses associated with visuospatial attention. Specifically, in the present experiment we had participants complete a standard "oddball" task wherein they saw a series of infrequently (targets) and frequently (control) appearing circles while EEG data was recorded from a MUSE headband. For task performance, participants were instructed to count the number of target circles that they saw. After the experiment, an analysis of the EEG data evoked by the target circles when contrasted with the EEG data evoked by the control circles revealed two ERP components – the N200 and the P300. The N200 is typically associated with stimulus/perceptual processing whereas the P300 is typically associated with a variety of cognitive processes including the allocation of visuospatial attention [1]. It is important to note that the physical manifestation of the N200 and P300 ERP components differed from reports using standard EEG systems; however, we have validated that this is due to the quantification of these ERP components at non-standard electrode locations. Importantly, our results demonstrate that a portable EEG system such as the MUSE can be used to examine the ERP responses associated with the allocation of visuospatial attention.

**Keywords:** EEG · ERP · Attention · Visuospatial attention · Portable technology

## 1 Introduction

The collection of electroencephalographic (EEG) data used to be associated with expensive (>$25,000 USD), large electrode array systems. However, in the past ten years there has been a rapid increase in the availability and number of "low-cost" EEG systems available to researchers. However, what remains problematic is the extent to which these low-cost systems record data of sufficient quality for research purposes. Indeed, in a seminal paper Picton and colleagues [2] outlined standards that a "research grade" EEG system needed to have to be able to record a level of data quality necessary to allow collection of event-related brain potential (ERP) data. In particular, the Picton

© Springer International Publishing AG 2017
D.D. Schmorrow and C.M. Fidopiastis (Eds.): AC 2017, Part I, LNAI 10284, pp. 56–65, 2017.
DOI: 10.1007/978-3-319-58628-1_5

group [2] noted that electrode type, electrode quality [3, 4], number of electrodes [5], and amplifier specifications [6] all had minimum values that were necessary to meet a sufficient research standard. Initially, the low-cost systems that were available to researchers did not meet these standards and as such there was a paucity of published research using these systems. However, in recent years the quality of low-cost EEG systems has improved sufficiently that there is now a small, but rapidly increasing number of studies that have successfully used low-cost EEG systems to conduct ERP research [7–14].

Electroencephalography provides an excellent methodology for examining human visuospatial attention. Indeed, given the excellent temporal resolution of the technique, EEG and more specifically, ERPs provide a means to directly examine neural responses and their sensitivity to the allocation of attentional resources. While there are a myriad of ERP components that have been shown to be sensitive to attentional processing, here we will focus on two specific components – the N200 and the P300.

## 1.1   The N200

The N200 ERP component is a negative going deflection in the ERP waveform that occurs between 180 and 300 ms post stimulus onset [15] with the scalp topography depending on the how the N200 is elicited. Specific to the present study, the N200b ([16]: simply referred to in this paper as the N200) has a topography that ranges from central to posterior and is evoked by the occurrence of infrequent stimuli during performance of the visual oddball paradigm. Indeed, the amplitude of the N200 is sensitive to target frequency – thus it is evoked by any stimulus but is increasingly more negative with increasing target rarity. Changes in the amplitude of the N200 have been yoked to visual attention [17]. Specifically, the amplitude of the N200 evoked during oddball paradigms is typically reduced when the target is stimulus is not being attended.

## 1.2   The P300

The P300 ERP component reflects a positive, posterior deflection in the ERP waveform that can be as early as 300 ms post-stimulus onset but that can be observed as late as 800 ms post-stimulus onset [1]. Seminal work on the P300 associated it with context-updating [18]. The context-updating hypothesis posits that the P300 is sensitive to an updating of an internal model of the world, and as a result, it is sensitive to changes in stimulus frequency. The P300 is also a marker for visuospatial attention. Specifically, previous research [19, 20] has shown that the amplitude of the P300 is reduced for non-attended stimuli. In this manner, the P300 is reflective of underlying attentional processes, even if it is not a direct measure of visuospatial attention itself. Indeed, the amplitude of the P300 has been shown to be proportional to the amount of attentional resources that are available for stimulus processing [21, 22].

## 1.3   Hypotheses

In the present study we wanted to determine whether or not the MUSE EEG system (www.choosemuse.com) was capable of quantifying two ERP components associated with visual processing and the allocation of visuospatial attention, the N200 and the P300. As noted above, both the N200 and the P300 have been shown to be sensitive to the allocation of attentional resources. Here, participants completed a standard visual oddball task while EEG data was recorded via a MUSE EEG system. Importantly, our experimental setup was such that task presentation and data collection were completed on a single Macbook Air laptop. Our hypothesis was simple, we predicted that the MUSE EEG system would be able to record data of sufficient quality that the N200 and the P300 ERP components would be visible in the grand average ERP waveforms. Further, we predicted that a standard mean peak detection analysis would be able to statistically verify N200 and P300 ERP component existence.

## 2   Methods

### 2.1   Participants

Sixty undergraduate students (n = 60; 34 female, mean age: 21) from the University of Victoria participated in the experiment. All participants had normal or corrected-to-normal vision, no known neurological impairments, volunteered for extra course credit in a psychology course and provided informed consent approved by the Human Research Ethics Board at the University of Victoria. The study followed ethical standards as prescribed in the 1964 Declaration of Helsinki. We note here that the data used here is subset of a larger study that specifically validated the MUSE EEG system against a more conventional large array EEG system (Brain Products ActiChamp).

### 2.2   Apparatus and Procedure

Participants were seated in a sound dampened room in front of a Macbook Air computer and completed a visual oddball task while EEG data were recorded via a MUSE EEG system. The oddball task was coded in the MATLAB programming environment (Version 8.6, Mathworks, Natick, U.S.A.) using the Psychophysics Toolbox extension [23].

During the oddball task participants saw a series of blue (MATLAB RGB value = [0 0 255]) and green (MATLAB RGB value = [0 255 0]) coloured circles that appeared for 800 to 1200 ms in the center of a dark gray screen (MATLAB RGB value = [108 108 108]). Prior to the onset of the first circle and in between the presentation of subsequent circles a black fixation cross was presented for 300 to 500 ms (MATLAB RGB value = [0 0 0]). Participants were not told that the frequency of the blue and green circles differed: the blue circles appeared less frequently (oddball: 25%) than the green circles (control: 75%) with the sequence order of presented circles being completely random. Participants were instructed to mentally count the number of blue circles (oddballs) within each block of trials. Participants completed 3 blocks of 40 trials during performance of the oddball task. For a full time line of the task see Fig. 1.

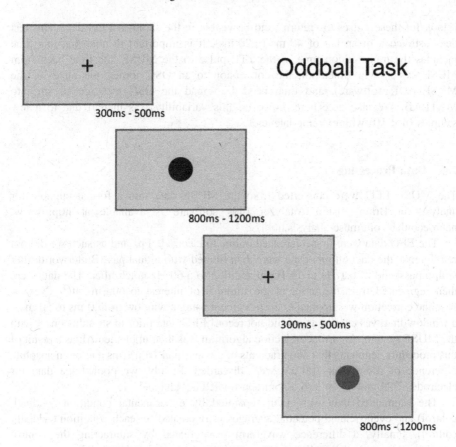

**Fig. 1.** Experimental timeline of the oddball task

## 2.3 Data Acquisition

EEG data in the MUSE group were recorded from a MUSE EEG headband with research preset AD (500 Hz sampling rate, no onboard data processing: InteraXon, Ontario, Canada) (see http://developer.choosemuse.com/hardware-firmware/hardware-specifications for full technical specifications). The MUSE EEG system has electrodes located analogous to Fpz, AF7, AF8, TP9, and TP10 with electrode Fpz utilized as the reference electrode. Using the muse-io SDK we streamed data from the MUSE EEG system directly to MATLAB via the open sound control (OSC) protocol (see http://www.neuroeconlab.com/muse.html for all configuration, setup, and acquisition methods and software). In essence, following the presentation of each experimental stimulus of interest we directly sampled 1000 ms of streaming data into MATLAB – subject to a small, varying inherent timing lag due to the Bluetooth connection (see http://developer.choosemuse.com/protocols/data-streaming-protocol). We tested the latency and variability of the latency of the Bluetooth EEG data stream by sending a series of 5000 TTL pulses into the MUSE auxiliary port from MATLAB and measuring the time it took for these pulses to "return" and be visible in the sampled EEG data. This test demonstrated a mean lag of 40 ms ($\pm$20 ms). It is important to note that this time includes the transmission time of the TTL pulse to the MUSE, the time back from MUSE system via Bluetooth, the conversion to an OSC format via muse-io (the MUSE SDK software), and time needed to read the OSC message stream into MATLAB. We also note here, however, this variability was in part due to a few samples (n < 10) with extreme latencies.

## 2.4  Data Processing

The MUSE EEG were converted from the MUSE data into a format suitable for analysis in Brain Vision Analyzer (this software is available at http://www.neuroeconlab.com/muse-analysis.html).

The EEG data were first referenced online to electrode Fpz and as such we did not re-reference the data offline. Data were then filtered with a dual pass Butterworth filter with a passband of 0.1 Hz to 15 Hz in addition to a 60 Hz notch filter. The data were then segmented from the onset of the stimulus of interest to 600 ms after. Next, a baseline correction was applied to each segment using a window from 0 ms to 50 ms – a window that was chosen as we did not record EEG data prior to stimulus onset with the MUSE system. An artifact rejection algorithm was then implemented; as a result of this procedure segments that had gradients of greater than 10 $\mu$V/ms and/or an absolute difference of more than 100 $\mu$V were discarded. Finally, we pooled the data for electrodes TP9 and TP10 into a common pooled TP channel.

The segmented data were then separated by experimental condition (oddball, control) and event-related potential averages were created for each condition (oddball, control). Finally, a difference waveform was created by subtracting the control waveforms from the oddball waveforms. For each conditional and difference waveform, a grand average waveform was created by averaging corresponding ERPs across all participants. ERP components of interest were quantified by first identifying the time point of maximal deflection from zero $\mu$V on the grand average difference waveform in the time range of the component where this deflection was maximal (N200: 240 ms; P300: 335 ms). All peaks were then quantified on an individual basis by taking the mean voltage $\pm$ 25 ms of the respective time points for each participant.

## 2.5  Data Analysis

For all analyses the same statistical procedures were used. For each component (N200, P300) analyses were conducted on the mean peak amplitudes extracted from the difference waves. To confirm the differences between conditions of each component, we compared the mean peak difference data to zero using three statistical methods: 95% confidence intervals, t-tests ($\alpha$ = 0.05), and 95% highest density Bayesian credible intervals.

# 3   Results

Our analyses of the grand average difference waveforms revealed components with a timing consistent with the N200 and P300 (see Fig. 2). Furthermore, all statistical tests determined that there was indeed a difference in the N200 and P300 component peaks as a function of experimental condition for all analyses (see Fig. 3).

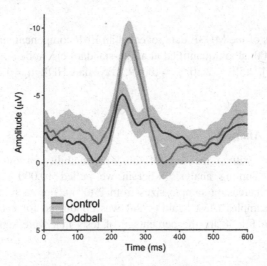

**Fig. 2.** Grand average conditional waveforms locked to the onset of the target and non-target stimuli at the averaged TP electrode. To allow meaningful interpretation of differences, the waveforms are shown with 95% confidence intervals.

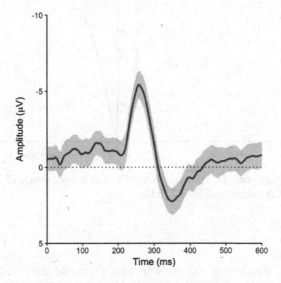

**Fig. 3.** The grand average difference waveform locked to the onset of the target and non-target stimuli at the averaged TP electrode. To allow meaningful interpretation of differences, the waveform is shown with its 95% confidence interval.

### 3.1 The N200

Our analysis of the MUSE data revealed a component was similar to the standard N200 ERP component ($M_d = -4.85$ µV [$-5.95$ µV $-3.76$ µV], $t(59) = -8.89$, $p < .0001$, Bayesian HDI: $\mu = -4.80$ µV [$-5.91$ µV $-3.69$ µV]).

### 3.2 The P300

Again, our analysis of the MUSE data revealed an ERP component similar to previous accounts of the P300, albeit quantified at a non-standard electrode site ($M_d = 1.37$ µV [$0.39$ µV $2.35$ µV], $t(59) = 2.80$, $p = .0069$, Bayesian HDI: $\mu = 1.36$ µV [$0.36$ µV $2.36$ µV]).

### 3.3 Resampling Analysis

To provide readers with a measure of the reproducibility of our result, we also implemented a resampling analysis wherein we pulled 10,000 samples from the existing data with increasing sample sizes from 2 to 60. For each sample size (e.g., n = 10), a single samples t-test against zero was conducted for each of the 10,000 samples. Plotted in Fig. 4 are the percentage of tests that were significant for each sample size.

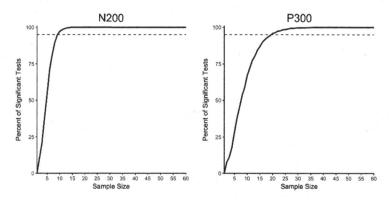

**Fig. 4.** The resampling analysis. The curve reflects a fit of the percentage of significant single sample t-tests for each sample size from 2 to 60.

## 4 Discussion

Our results clearly demonstrate that we were able to see and statistically quantify two ERP components associated with the processing and allocation of visuospatial attention, the N200 and the P300. Specifically, both the N200 and P300 ERP components were clearly visible in the grand average conditional and difference waveforms. Further, a peak detection analysis statistically verified the existence of these two ERP components. We also implemented a resampling analysis that demonstrated that the N200 ERP component was reliably visible with a sample size of 10 participants. In terms of the P300, the resampling analysis demonstrated that a larger sample size of 20 participants is needed to reliably quantify this ERP component. The larger sample size needed to quantify the P300 is possibly related to the fact that we had to use non-standard ERP electrode locations with the MUSE EEG system (i.e., TP9 and TP10 as opposed to more standard posterior midline electrodes used to examine this component).

Importantly, our results show that we can measure some of the electroencephalographic correlates of visuospatial attention with in a simple and efficient manner. Attention has been studied quite extensively with electroencephalography. Indeed, in a prominent review paper in 2000, Luck and colleagues [24] reviewed 30 years' worth of research on the major findings of electroencephalographic studies of attention. Typically, ERP studies of attention focus on the P100 and the N100 components. However, with our technique and from pilot data in our lab to date we have not been able to detect these components. Most likely, this is due to the relatively small effect size seen in differences with these components and given the noise inherent in markerless approach we used with the MUSE system the "temporal jitter" in our data washes these components out. Conversely, the N200 and the P300 are quite large in terms of voltage effect size and thus we are able to observe them with our approach. As outlined above, the N200 and P300 have been shown to be sensitive to the allocation of visuospatial attention [15–21]. Thus, the MUSE EEG system and the approach used here can be quantify some of the processes that underlie, or at least sensitive to, the allocation of visuospatial attention.

Our data provide further support for the use of low-cost, portable EEG systems such as the MUSE for field research [9]. More specifically, our results increase the research capability of researchers to collect EEG data in clinical settings and out in the "real world" by demonstrating a simple to use, portable, low-cost methodology for collecting ERP data. Given these factors (ease of use, cost, etc.), researchers using this technology will now have the ability to collect large numbers of participants with relative ease. Supporting this, the data collected in the present study was done on average in less than 6 min per participant – a time that includes EEG system setup, task performance, and post experiment cleanup. Further, we remind the reader that our setup was done with a single MacBook Air laptop computer and a single MUSE EEG system – there were no wired connections thus further increasing the portability of the system. Indeed, the portability of data collection with MUSE is being demonstrated by a variety of projects in our laboratory – we have collected data from doctors working in hospitals, in a monastery in Nepal, and even from rock climbers during ascent of a climbing wall. We note here that to some extent our approach replicates previous work [25, 26] but our technique greatly improves the portability and ease of use of mobile ERP data collection.

## 5  Conclusions

In the present study, we have demonstrated that it is possible to quantify two of the electroencephalographic correlated of visuospatial attention – the N200 and the P300 – in a quick and efficient manner using the MUSE EEG system. Further, we demonstrate that this can be done with a single laptop computer. Combined with the low invasiveness of the system (it is a headband) and the Bluetooth connection our methodology opens the doors to the study of visuospatial attention in a variety of novel contexts.

## References

1. Patel, S.H., Azzam, P.N.: Characterization of N200 and P300: selected studies of the event-related potential. Int. J. Med. Sci. **2**(4), 147–154 (2005)
2. Picton, T.W., Bentin, S., Berg, P., Donchin, E., Hillyard, S.A., Johnson, R., et al.: Guidelines for using human event-related potentials to study cognition: recording standards and publication criteria. Psychophysiology **37**(02), 127–152 (2000)
3. Coles, M.G.H., Gratton, G., Kramer, A.F., Miller, G.A.: Principles of signal acquisition and analysis. In: Psychophysiology: Systems, Processes and Applications, pp. 183–221 (1986)
4. Kutas, M.: Views on how the electrical activity that the brain generates reflects the functions of different language structures. Psychophysiology **34**(4), 383–398 (1997)
5. Srinivasan, R., Tucker, D.M., Murias, M.: Estimating the spatial Nyquist of the human EEG. Behav. Res. Methods Instrum. Comput. **30**(1), 8–19 (1998)
6. Cadwell, J.A., Villarreal, R.A.: Electrophysiologic equipment and electrical safety. In: Aminoff, M.J. (ed.) Electrodiagnosis in clinical neurology 4, pp. 15–33. Churchill Livingstone, New York (1999)
7. Badcock, N.A., Mousikou, P., Mahajan, Y., de Lissa, P., Thie, J., McArthur, G.: Validation of the Emotiv EPOC® EEG gaming system for measuring research quality auditory ERPs. PeerJ **1**, e38 (2013)
8. Badcock, N.A., Preece, K.A., de Wit, B., Glenn, K., Fieder, N., Thie, J., McArthur, G.: Validation of the Emotiv EPOC EEG system for research quality auditory event-related potentials in children. PeerJ **3**, e907 (2015)
9. Debener, S., Minow, F., Emkes, R., Gandras, K., de Vos, M.: How about taking a low-cost, small, and wireless EEG for a walk? Psychophysiology **49**, 1617–1621 (2012)
10. Duvinage, M., Castermans, T., Petieau, M., Hoellinger, T., Cheron, G., Dutoit, T.: Performance of the Emotiv Epoc headset for P300-based applications. Biomed. Eng. online **12**(1), 56 (2013)
11. Gramann, K., Ferris, D.P., Gwin, J., Makeig, S.: Imaging natural cognition in action. Int. J. Psychophysiol. **91**, 22–29 (2014)
12. Kuziek, J.W., Shienh, A., Mathewson, K.E.: Transitioning EEG experiments away from the laboratory using a Raspberry Pi 2. J. Neurosci. Methods **277**, 75–82 (2017)
13. Maskeliunas, R., Damasevicius, R., Martisius, I., Vasiljevas, M.: Consumer-grade EEG devices: are they usable for control tasks? PeerJ **4**, e1746 (2016)
14. Wascher, E., Heppner, H., Hoffmann, S.: Towards the measurement of event-related EEG activity in real-life working environments. Int. J. Psychophysiol. **91**(1), 3–9 (2014)
15. Hoffman, J.E.: Event-related potentials and automatic and controlled processes. In: Rohrbaugh, J.W., Parasuraman, R., Johnsón Jr., R. (eds.) Event Related Brain Potentials, pp. 145–157. Oxford University Press, New York (1990)

16. Sams, M., Alho, K., Näätänen, R.: Sequential effects on the ERP in discriminating two stimuli. Biol. Psychol. **17**, 41–58 (1983)
17. Folstein, J.R., Van Petten, C.: Influence of cognitive control and mismatch on the N2 component of the ERP: a review. Psychophysiology **45**, 152–170 (2008)
18. Donchin, E., Coles, M.G.H.: Is the P300 component a manifestation of context updating? Behav. Brain Sci. **11**(3), 357–427 (1988)
19. Duncan-Johnson, C.C., Donchin, E.: On quantifying surprise: the variation in event-related potentials with subjective probability. Psychophysiology **14**, 456–467 (1977)
20. Duncan-Johnson, C.C., Donchin, E.: The P300 component of the event-related brain potential as an index of information processing. Biol. Psychol. **14**, 1–52 (1983)
21. Gray, H.M., Ambady, N., Lowenthal, W.T., Deldin, P.: P300 as an index of attention to self-relevant stimuli. J. Exp. Soc. Psychol. **40**, 216–224 (2004)
22. Johnson Jr., R.: The amplitude of the P300 component of the event-related potential: review and synthesis. Adv. Psychophysiol. **3**, 69–137 (1988)
23. Brainard, D.H.: The psychophysics toolbox. Spat. Vis. **10**, 433–436 (1997)
24. Luck, S.J., Woodman, G.F., Vogel, E.K.: Event related potential studies of attention. Trends Cogn. Sci. **4**(11), 432–440 (2000)
25. Vos, M.D., Gandras, K., Debener, S.: Towards a truly mobile brain computer interface: exploring the P300 to take away. Int. J. Psychophysiol. **91**, 46–53 (2014)
26. Wong, S.W.H., Chan, R.H.M., Mak, J.N.: Spectral modulation of frontal EEG during motor skill acquisition: a mobile EEG study. Int. J. Psychophysiol. **91**, 16–21 (2014)

# Investigating Brain Dynamics in Industrial Environment – Integrating Mobile EEG and Kinect for Cognitive State Detection of a Worker

Pavle Mijović[1], Miloš Milovanović[2], Ivan Gligorijević[1],
VanjaKović[3], Ivana Živanović-Mačužić[4], and Bogdan Mijović[1(✉)]

[1] mBrainTrain LCC, Belgrade, Serbia
{pavle.mijovic,ivan,bogdan}@mbraintrain.com
[2] IT Department, Faculty of Organizational Sciences, University of Belgrade,
Belgrade, Serbia
milos.milovanovic@mmklab.org
[3] Department for Psychology, Faculty of Philosophy, University of Belgrade,
Belgrade, Serbia
vanja.kovic@f.bg.ac.rs
[4] Department of Anatomy and Forensic Medicine Faculty of Medical Sciences,
University of Kragujevac, Kragujevac, Serbia
ivanaanatom@yahoo.com

**Abstract.** In the present work we used wearable EEG sensor for recording brain activity during simulated assembly work, in replicated industrial environment. We investigated attention related modalities of P300 ERP component and engagement index (EI), which is extracted from signal power ratios of $\alpha$, $\beta$ and $\theta$ frequency bands. Simultaneously, we quantified the task unrelated movements, which are previously reported to be related to attention level, in an automated way employing kinect[TM] sensor. Reaction times were also recorded and investigated. We found that during the monotonous task, both the P300 amplitude and EI decreased as the time of the task progressed. On the other hand, the increase of the task unrelated movement quantity was observed, together with the increase in RTs. These findings lead to conclusion that the monotonous assembly work induces the decrease of attention and engagement of the workers as the task progresses, which is observable in both neural (EEG) and behavioral (RT and unrelated movements) signal modalities. Apart from observing how the attention-related modalities are changing over time, we investigated the functional relationship between the neural and behavioral modalities by using Pearson's correlation. Since the Person's correlation coefficients showed the functional relationship between the attention-related modalities, we proposed the creation of the multimodal implicit Human-Computer Interaction (HCI) system, which could acquire and process neural and behavioral data in real-time, with the aim of creating the system that could be aware of the operator's mental states during the industrial work, consequently improving the operator's well-being.

**Keywords:** Wireless EEG · Kinect · ERP · P300 · Attention · Neuroergonomics

© Springer International Publishing AG 2017
D.D. Schmorrow and C.M. Fidopiastis (Eds.): AC 2017, Part I, LNAI 10284, pp. 66–78, 2017.
DOI: 10.1007/978-3-319-58628-1_6

# 1   Introduction

Roughly 50 years from the introduction of IBM 360, the way we interact with computers has changed immensely. Communicating with a computer required humans to learn a specific, limited set of commands that, when issued to a computer, produced a certain effect. Today, we witness a fast movement of computer technology towards more natural model of interaction with humans. This is attributed to rapid development of sensing technology and improvement of algorithms that can interpret the acquired signals. Sensing technology does not only serves for explicit interaction between the computers and our environment (such as in smart cities, houses, vehicles etc.), but it also opens a novel way of understanding humans as the technology is deployed to monitoring our behaviors and mental states. Ultimately, computers now act as a link between humans and their environment.

Vinton Cerf states that in a world of humanoid and functional robots, smart cities, smart dwellings, and smart vehicles we cannot disregard the notion of instrumented and augmented bodies [1]. By enabling computers to sense human neural states and behavior, we can also enable them to create dynamic user-state representations and respond dynamically and context-specifically to changes in actual human mental states (the user states). One way of achieving this is by expanding the conventional modelling in HCI, which is explicit in nature, by introduction of implicit interaction [2]. Implicit HCI assumes that actions performed by the user are not primarily aimed to interact with a computerized system, but the system may still understand the actions as an input [2].

A fertile ground for the introduction of implicit interaction can be found in an industrial workplace. Although It is generally known that industry tries to reach the "lights-out" manufacturing [3] (i.e. fully automated factories) for decades, there are still many industrial processes relying on human operators [4], which are often characterized as the most fallible element in the production line [5, 6]. The main cause of this are limited mental and physical endurance that can sometimes cause behavior and reactions to be unpredictable [6]. Our motivation is to develop an automated system capable of detecting a drop in mental and physical performance so that appropriate action (e.g. a break or a change in task) can be taken to prevent errors and improve the productivity and quality of manual tasks. In this study, we analyzed worker's neural (electroencephalography- EEG) and behavioral (reaction times - RT and the quantity of the task unrelated movements) signals in order to interpret the implicit multimodal interaction [7] between the worker and the workplace in manual assembly tasks. The ultimate goal is to achieve a system that will be able to perform online detection of mental strain and monitor attention fluctuation thereby preventing the occurrence of operating errors [8] and improving the worker experience.

# 2   State-of-the-Art

We approach the problem of worker's online attention monitoring by analyzing the relationship between brain dynamics and the active behavior during execution of work activities [9]. This is done by recording brain activity, using unobtrusive wearable EEG in parallel with motion capture sensors in naturalistic industrial environment. Although industry conceived the use of wearables for over a decade now [10], the majority of their applications are still oriented towards explicit interaction and providing workers with the information about their task [11], or for augmenting the reality [12], rather than for collecting and exploiting data about the task being performed or the worker performing the task.

The only available and reliable tool for direct brain activity monitoring in a naturalistic workplace environment is wearable EEG [13]. Nowadays, the EEG research is mainly oriented towards Brain Computer Interface (BCI), which uses brain activity to allow humans to interact with computers without any physical contact or verbal exchange of commands [14]. BCI research already had some success in medical applications, mainly in helping people reacquire the lost ability of moving a certain body part. Moving away from its primary usage, however, a novel direction in BCI (passive BCI) is orienting towards continuous analysis of the recorded brain signals in human-machine interaction, with the aim to objectively assess the user states [15].

A clear momentum of passive BCI technology [15] recently opened new doors to application in industry, empowering the research area of neuroergonomics [16]. This emerging scientific field is focused on merging classical ergonomics methods with neuroscience, while exploiting the benefits of both [16]. Mainly, it provides precise analytical parameters of the work efficiency of individuals, by investigating the relationship between neural and behavioral activity [17]. The advantage of this approach is avoidance of unreliable results about the cognitive state of the workers based only on theoretical constructs [17]. As EEG sensors became wearable, it is finally possible to reach the ultimate goal of neuroergonomics and examine how the brain carries out complex tasks in real working environments [16]. Specific EEG features that can be used for estimating human attention level and cognitive engagement are event-related potentials (ERPs) and Engagement index (EI), respectively.

ERPs represent the voltage fluctuations of the EEG signal that are related to the specific event (stimuli) [18], and its components are defined by the polarity and latency from the event occurrence. As such, the P300 ERP component represents the positive deflection that occurs approximately 300 ms upon the stimulus presentation. The P300 component is the most prominent over the central and parieto-central scalp locations (Fz, Cz, CPz and Pz, the central portion of Fig. 2; [18]). It has been largely accepted that the magnitude of the P300 component's peak directly correlate to the attention level of the person - higher amplitude values of the P300 correspond to the higher attentive state [18].

The cognitive engagement of a person can be measured from the EEG signal through EI. The brain rhythms are usually investigated through four distinct frequency bands: gamma ($\gamma$ = 0–4 Hz), theta ($\theta$ = 4–8 Hz), alpha ($\alpha$ = 8–12 Hz) and beta ($\beta$ = 12–30). The low frequency waves are usually high in amplitude and are dominant in the state of rest, relaxation, sleepiness, low alertness etc. Conversely, the high frequency and low amplitude waves reflect the alert state, state of wakefulness, state of task engagement, etc. EI represents the ratio between the high frequency waves ($\beta$), and the summation of the low frequency waves ($\alpha + \theta$), i.e. EI = $\beta/(\alpha + \theta)$. Therefore, a higher EI indicates the higher engagement of the person in the task, whereas the low values of EI indicate that person is not actively engaged with some aspect of the environment during the task [19].

Apart from direct observation of brain functions with the neuroimaging techniques, the user state assessment can be conducted with behavioral measurements. For instance, in early stages of experimental psychology, the researchers relied mostly on behavioral measurement (e.g. reaction times – RTs) to estimate the cognitive state. RTs reflect various cognitive processes and are recorded simply by measuring the time elapsed from stimulus presentation to initiation of the required action. Although RTs reflect cognitive processes to an extent, they lack the temporal precision and fail to provide deeper insights to the underlying brain activity [20].

Another measureable aspect of human behavior is body movements [9]. Research has indicated that variability in movement that is not directly related to the task could be an important indicator of the user's state assessment [21]. Behavioral activity analyses of movements are usually carried out off-line, since researchers typically record the participants with the RGB camera and then perform manual analysis, which mostly comes down to counting the number of different types of movements [21]. Advances in HCI and computer vision technology allowed an on-line and automated processing of these movements. The structured light technology in unison with additional sensors, as can be found in Microsoft Kinect$^{TM}$, opens the possibility of automatic acquisition of the information on behavioral activities. The Kinect$^{TM}$ interprets human body with the stick figure, where the joints (e.g. elbow, shoulder, etc.) are represented in terms of key-points and they can be retrieved in real-time. This enables installment of simple behavioral models based on movement energy (ME) that we propose and which will be described further in text.

The combination of neural and behavioral modalities can open a deeper understanding of human mental states during complex work activities [9]. Until very recently, research that investigated the relationship between brain dynamics and human behavior was confined to strictly controlled laboratory conditions, where the obtrusiveness and immobility of EEG and motion sensors was the main culprit for this. However, as the technology matures, EEG eventually became wearable, thus enabling experiments in the realistic workplace conditions. In order to investigate the possibility of implicit interaction between worker and workplace, we developed the replicated workplace that was equipped with the computing entities capable of sensing workers' neural states and interpreting behavioral activities. We named such a workplace "sensitive workplace".

# 3 Methods

## 3.1 Participants

Six participants were engaged in the study. All participants had normal or corrected-to-normal vision. They have agreed to participation and signed informed consent after reading the experiment summary. The study was approved by the Ethical committee of the University of Kragujevac.

Participants started with a 15-minute training session, after which they confirmed their readiness to participate in the study. The experiment consisted of two tasks, where each task's duration was around 90 min, and between the tasks they had a 15-minute break (the total duration of the experiment was 4 h). The tasks were counterbalanced across the participants.

## 3.2  Replicated Workplace

We replicated the physical workplace of an automotive sub-component manufacturing company where we simulated the assembly of the hoses used in the hydraulic brake systems of the vehicles (see Fig. 1).

**Fig. 1.** Real life workplace (on the left) compared to the replicated laboratory workplace (on the right)

The operation was divided into six sub-steps as follows: (1) – Picking the rubber hose (blue box, on the right hand of participant in the study); (2) – picking the metal extension, that should be crimped to the hose (yellow box, on the left hand side of the participant); (3) – placing metal extension on the rubber hose; (4) – Placing unassembled part in the improvised machine (white box in front of participant); (5) – pressing the pedal foot switch, with the right foot, in order to initiate the simulated crimping process; (6) – removing the assembled part from the machine and placing it inside the box with the assembled parts (grey box in front of participant).

## 3.3  Sensitive Workplace Architecture

A combination of sensing technologies was installed to the replicated workplace in order to acquire neural and behavioral data. Figure 2 depicts the system architecture of the resulting sensitive workplace environment.

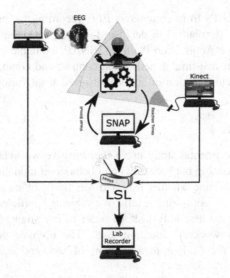

**Fig. 2.** Sensitive workplace system architecture

For neural data, we opted for wireless EEG signal acquisition, using SMARTING system (mBrainTrain, Serbia). SMARTING is a small and lightweight EEG amplifier, tightly connected to the EEG recording cap (EasyCap, Germany), thus minimizing movement related artefacts making it usable in real-life environments (Fig. 2 – upper left corner).

The movement data were acquired with the Microsoft Kinect$^{TM}$ that was mounted above and in front of a person. The human body is tracked based on structured light technology and is interpreted in a form of a stick figure. Since the device comes with an software development kit (SDK), we were able to develop standalone motion-acquisition module capable of simultaneously recording and streaming the data (Fig. 2).

When acquiring the neural and behavioral signal modalities in a real-world environments, a precise synchronization between multiple sensor modalities represents a major challenge. This is even more challenging when requiring synchronization of the sensors that are different in both the type of data and the sampling rate, e.g. EEG, RTs and movement data. For example, during acquisition of EEG signals, and particularly for extraction of ERPs, a millisecond precision in the data synchronization is mandatory. This problem becomes prominent with wireless technologies, where grouping sensors or making a common reference signal is not feasible.

To deal with this issue, we used the open source platform "Lab Streaming Layer" (LSL, https://github.com/sccn/labstreaminglayer). LSL is a real-time data collection and distribution system, capable of synchronously streaming multiple streams of multi-channel data which are heterogeneous in both type and sampling rate [9, 22], to the recording program "Lab Recorder" (bottom central panel, Fig. 2). LSL has a built-in synchronized time facility for all recorded data and it is capable of achieving sub-millisecond accuracy on computers connected in a local area network (LAN) [22].

In order to elicit ERPs from continuous EEG recording we provided visual stimulation to the subjects (Explained in detail in the Sect. 3.4). For this we used Simulation and Neuroscience Application Platform (SNAP, available at https://github.com/sccn/SNAP) capable of real-time experimental control, and compatible with the LSL. SNAP also supports interpretation of actions retrieved from various input devices.

### 3.4    Experimental Task

We conducted an experimental study using the sensitive workplace, with the aim of investigating the relationship between EEG and behavioral modalities. One goal of the experiment was to determine whether RTs and ME (in combination with EEG) could provide reliable attention monitoring results. We subjected participants to the change in task during the simulated assembly task, in order to investigate how the changes in mental workload alter workers' attention level. The ultimate goal is to propose a real-time system for the on-line measurement of workers' attention in industrial environments.

Participants in this study sat in a chair in front of the improvised machine (shown in the right panel of Fig. 1), while performing the simulated assembly task. In order to investigate the time-locked features of neural signals (ERPs), two verified psychological tests for estimating cognitive ability were presented to participants on the 24" screen from a distance of approximately 100 cm (the task specifications were programmed in SNAP). The tests we used were the modified Sustained Attention to Response Task (SART) and the Arrow task.

The SART paradigm represents the 'go/no-go' task. The numbers ranging from '1' to '9' are presented to participants in random order, where they are required to initiate the action, with the exception if the number '3' appears on the screen. Therefore, numbers other than '3' are target stimuli and the probability of the appearance of the target stimuli was set to 90%. The Arrow task is also a 'go/no-go' task, where participants are required to initiate the action once the white arrow appears on the screen (also a target stimulus, with 90% probability of appearance), whereas they should withhold the action if the red arrow appears.

The main difference between the SART and Arrow task was in the level of mental workload to which participants were subjected. SART is monotonous psychological test, being suitable for investigating the neural correlates of the attention decline. In this task, participants could freely choose which hand they will initiate the action with. On the other hand, in the Arrow task we imposed a slightly higher workload to participants, as in this task they were instructed to initiate the action alternating the hand according to the direction of the white arrow presented on the screen. Thus, the direction of white arrow determined the order of action execution.

### 3.5    Sensing the Operators' State

In order to estimate the user state through EEG signals, we extracted and analyzed specific features of ERPs and Engagement index (EI). The behavioral modalities of

RTs and ME of the participants were analyzed together, during the periods when they were not physically engaged with the task. Finally, we investigated the relationship between attention- and cognitive engagement -related behavioral and neural modalities. Methodology outline is presented on Fig. 3 and explained further in text.

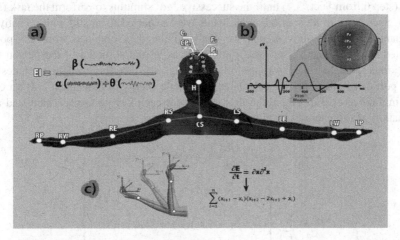

**Fig. 3.** Methodology outline: (a) Engagement Index equation; (b) Visualisation of P300 window; (c) Motion Energy equation. Central Segment presents joint positions (also called key-points) for motion analysis (Left, Right, Central/Palm, Wrist, Elbow, Shoulder, Head) and position of used EEG electrodes (Fz, Cz, CPz and Pz)

### P300 and EI - Attention Related EEG Modalities

In order to calculate the P300 component's amplitude, the EEG signal was first bandpass filtered from 1–35 Hz, then re-referenced to the channels on mastoid locations, followed by the eye movement and muscle artifacts removal using Independent Component Analysis (ICA; [22]). Finally, the signal was segmented to the period of - 200 to 800 ms, according to the timestamps of stimulus presentation. We used the mean peak amplitude measure, meaning that we calculated the P300 peak amplitude as the mean value of the window in the range between 230–450 ms following stimulus onset (shaded section in the upper right corner on Fig. 3).

We further analyzed the Engagement Index (EI; [19]). In order to quantify the power contained in different signal bands, bandpass filtering was applied in three frequency bands ($\theta$, $\alpha$ and $\beta$), followed by re-referencing the signal, and artifact removal with ICA [23]. The EEG signal was then segmented according to the timestamps of the stimuli appearance and the signal segments of 1 s preceding the stimulus appearance was used for the further analysis. Finally, the signal Power Spectral Densities (PSDs) were calculated for each frequency band and then EI is calculated according to the equation ($EI = \beta/(\alpha + \theta)$), that is graphically represented in the upper left corner of the Fig. 3.

### Reaction Times and Motion Energy – Attention Related Behavioral Modalities

Reaction Times are recognized as a tool for estimating the level of attention, where the shorter RTs are often considered as an indicator of higher attentive state, with the exception in case of speed-accuracy trade-off. We calculated RTs as an elapsed time between the stimulus presentation and the beginning of the machine crimping action (i.e. between steps 1 and step 5 that were explained in Sect. 3.2).

The quantity of task unrelated movements is another behavioral modality analyzed. We measured the amount of movement, from the period where participants assembled a part (step 6 from Sect. 3.2) until the successive 'go' stimulus to perform the task (step 1 from Sect. 3.2). In this period, participants were expected to sit still with no activity. To quantifying these movements, we analyzed the data obtained from key-points provided by the Kinect$^{TM}$ sensor. In this analysis, a seated model of the person was used (joints indicated in central portion of the Fig. 3), since the machine occludes the lower portion of the body. We calculated the kinetic energy of movement [24] for each point in three axes (Eq. 1) and the final energy for each key point was calculated as a summation of the energies produced for each axis (Eq. 2).

$$\frac{\partial Ex}{\partial t} = \partial x \partial^2 x; \frac{\partial Ey}{\partial t} = \partial y \partial^2 y; \frac{\partial Ez}{\partial t} = \partial z \partial^2 z \tag{1}$$

$$\text{ME} = \sum_{i=1}^{n} \left\{ \begin{array}{c} [(x_{i+1} - x_i)(x_{i+2} - 2x_{i+1} + x_i)] \\ + \\ [(y_{i+1} - y_i)(y_{i+2} - 2y_{i+1} + y_i)] \\ + \\ [(z_{i+1} - z_i)(z_{i+2} - 2z_{i+1} + z_i)] \end{array} \right\} \tag{2}$$

### 3.6   Statistical Analysis

We conducted an off-line data analysis in order to investigate the relationship between neural and behavioral attention related modalities. First, we conducted Spearman's correlation, mainly to investigate whether any of the four attention-related modalities can reveal a decline in attention and cognitive engagement as the task progresses, i.e. with the Spearman correlation we investigated the general trend of each modality over the time course of the task. Further, we performed Pearson's correlation between all the modalities recorded in the study with the aim of comparing RTs and ME to the EEG data.

## 4   Results and Discussion

The results of the Spearman correlation are shown in the upper panel of Fig. 4 (note that the "+"/"−" sign represents positive/negative correlation (trend), "−" with the $p < .05$, while the empty field represent statistically insignificant values). The results revealed that in the monotonous (SART) task the behavioral activity of ME is increasing, while the P300 amplitude and EI are decreasing over the experiment progression, regardless of the order of task presentation. The Spearman correlation further revealed that in the more demanding (Arrows) task, the results depended on the order of the Arrows task presentation, that is, the results were identical to the SART task, if the Arrows were presented as a first task. However, when the arrows task was presented as second task, the P300 amplitude increased as the task progressed, while the ME and EI decreased during the task. It is noteworthy that RTs were independent from both task type and task order and it was decreasing with the time-on-task, probably caused by the effect of rehearsing as the task progresses.

From Spearman correlation results (presented in lower panel of Fig. 4), it can be inferred that the monotonous task (SART) induces the attention decline, regardless of the task order. Spearman correlation revealed that the P300 amplitude and EI declined as the time of the task increased, while ME increases as the task progresses. On the other hand, results in the more mentally demanding task (Arrows) depended on the presentation order. This is especially notable through evaluation of the P300 amplitude, as it increases during the task if the Arrow task follows SART. Although EI was still decreasing, proving that mental engagement of the participants was decreasing during the task, the evaluation of the P300 amplitude revealed that the participants were able to maintain higher attention state during the task. This is also notable through evaluation of ME, as only in case where Arrows were a second task, the ME was decreasing with time elapsed, i.e. the participants were making less task unrelated movements.

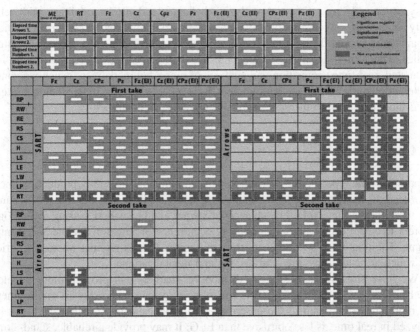

**Fig. 4.** Results retrieved from experimental study. Upper left table – Spearman's correlations of elapsed task time with neural and behavioral factors; Bottom table – Pearson's correlations between behavioral and neural factors; The fields with "+"/"–" sign represent positive/negative correlation results (p < .05), while the empty fields are representing the statistically non-significant results (p > .05). Fz, Cz, CPz and Pz represent the electrode sites from which we calculated P300 amplitudes and EI. The rows in the lower table represents the key point locations derived from Kinect, explained on Fig. 3. The last rows represent the reaction times (RTs).

Bottom part of Fig. 4 depicts Pearson's correlation results. It is notable that expected negative correlation between P300 amplitudes and ME is more distinguished in case of low demanding, monotonous (SART), than it can be seen in more mentally demanding (Arrow) task. This finding is not surprising, as in the existing literature the quantity of movements, which are not related to the task, are reported to be linked to the attention decline in monotonous tasks [21]. Further, when the more monotonous task is presented first, the EI was negatively correlated for each key-point, while in the more demanding task almost no correlations were found between neural and behavioral attention-related modalities. Finally, if the Arrows were presented as the first task, the only negative correlation with the P300 amplitude was at the LP, LW, RP and RW key-points, while the EI was positively correlated with the ME on almost all key-points. This could be explained through the notion of re-activation, as participants in more mentally demanding task use the task unrelated movements in order to re-activate the attention related resources in the brain [18], thus staying more focused on the task. This was not obvious if the SART was following the Arrow task. In fact, again in the more monotonous task the P300 amplitude was negatively correlated to the ME on majority of key-points. From all these results, we can infer that during low demanding and monotonous tasks, the ME that is unrelated to the task is negatively correlated with the attention level.

Presented results support our intention on monitoring the operators' attention level by synchronously recording and analyzing behavior and EEG modalities, with relatively simple and low-cost unobtrusive sensor network. However, an obvious limitation is that we did not use the on-line attention analysis, which is expected to occur in future studies. The future steps will include the development of advanced algorithms for automated, real-time acquisition and analysis of presented modalities, which we could further implement in factory environment for sensing the user state. Such a system could ultimately lead to increase of overall workers' wellbeing.

## 5   Conclusion

Monotonous and repetitive tasks, commonly seen in manual assembly production lines, often lead to mental strain, due to limited mental and physical endurance of humans. Our work focused on exploiting advances in neural and behavioral sensing technology in order to detect users' states that indicate occurrence of attention decline and mental fatigue. The final goal is to prevent errors that might lead to product waste or injuries and which are caused by attention decline and mental fatigue.

We have shown that neural and behavioral markers can provide more detailed insight in human attention level. This was done in a realistic workplace environment and represents a first step of the described HCI model paradigm. ME, which can be analyzed in real time, is less obtrusive than EEG. It may provide a reliable, stand-alone tool for attention monitoring, especially in industrial scenario. An obvious follow-up is to provide real-time processing of these features and put them in a feedback loop with some sort of indication communicated to workers. That way, a person is informed about the attention drops in a close-to real-time manner, which could serve to prevent errors and dangerous consequences. This could then become basis of a true future implicit human-computer interaction.

**Acknowledgments.** This research is financed under EU - FP7 Marie Curie Actions FP7-PEOPLE-2011-ITN.

# References

1. Cerf, V.G.: Cognitive implants. Commun. ACM **57**(2), 7 (2014)
2. Schmidt, A.: Implicit human computer interaction through context. Pers. Technol. **4**(2–3), 191–199 (2000)
3. Tompkins, J.A., et al.: Manufacturing systems (chap. 8). In: Facilities Planning. Wiley (2010)
4. Shappel, S.A., Wiegmann, D.A.: The human factors analysis and classification system–HFACS (No. DOT/FAA/AM-00/7). US Federal Aviation Administration, Office of Aviation Medicine (2000)
5. Bainbridge, L.: Ironies of automation. Automatica **19**(6), 775–779 (1983)
6. Hamrol, A., Kowalik, D., Kujawińsk, A.: Impact of selected work condition factors on quality of manual assembly process. Hum. Factors Ergon. Manuf. Serv. Ind. **21**(2), 156–163 (2011)
7. Obrenovic, Z., Starcevic, D.: Modeling multimodal human-computer interaction. IEEE Comput. **37**(9), 65–72 (2004)
8. Mijović, P., et al.: Towards creation of implicit HCI model for prediction and prevention of operators' error. In: Proceedings of the 17th International Conference on Human-Computer Interaction, Los Angeles, CA, August 2015
9. Gramann, K., et al.: Cognition in action: imaging brain/body dynamics in mobile humans. Rev. Neurosci. De Gryter **22**(6), 593–608 (2011)
10. Stanford, V.: Wearable computing goes live in industry. IEEE Pervasive Comput. **1**(4), 14–19 (2002)
11. Lukowicz, F., et al.: Wearit@ work: toward real-world industrial wearable computing. IEEE Pervasive Comput. **6**(4), 8–13 (2007)
12. Thomas, B.H., Sandor, C.: What wearable augmented reality can do for you. IEEE Pervasive Comput. **8**(2), 8–11 (2009)
13. Wascher, E., Heppner, H., Hoffmann, S.: Towards the measurement of event-related EEG activity in real-life working environments. Int. J. Psychophysiol. **91**(1), 3–9 (2014)
14. Wolpaw, J.P., et al.: Brain-computer interface technology: a review of the first international meeting. IEEE Trans. Rehabil. Eng. **8**(2), 164–173 (2000)
15. Zander, T.O., Kothe, C.: Towards passive brain–computer interfaces: applying brain–computer interface technology to human–machine systems in general. J. Neural Eng. **8**(2), 1–5 (2011)
16. Parasuraman, R.: Neuroergonomics: research and practice. Theor. Issues Ergon. Sci. **4**(1–2), 5–20 (2003)
17. Fafrowicz, M., Marek, T.: Quo vadis, neuroergonoics? Ergonomics **50**(11), 1941–1949 (2007)
18. Picton, T.W., et al.: Guidelines for using human event-related potentials to study cognition: recording standards and publication criteria. Psychophysiology **37**(02), 127–152 (2000)
19. Prinzel, L.J., et al.: A closed-loop system for examining psychophysiological measures for adaptive task allocation. Int. J Aviat. psychol. **10**(4), 393–410 (2000)
20. Luck, S.J., Woodman, G.F., Vogel, E.K.: Event-related potential studies of attention. Trends Cogn. sci. **4**(11), 432–440 (2000)
21. Rogé, J., Pebayle, T., Muzet, A.: Variations of the level of vigilance and of behavioral activities during simulated automobile driving. Accid. Anal. Prev. **33**(2), 181–186 (2001)

22. Bigdely-Shamlo, N., Kreutz-Delgado, K., Robbins, K., Miyakoshi, M., Westerfield, M., Bel-Bahar, T., Kothe, C., Hsi, J., Makeig, S.: Hierarchical event descriptor (HED) tags for analysis of event-related EEG studies. In: Global Conference on Signal and Information Processing (GlobalSIP), 2013 IEEE, pp. 1–4. IEEE (2013)
23. Viola, F.C., et al.: Semi-automatic identification of independent components representing EEG artifact. Clin. Neurophysiol. **120**(5), 868–877 (2009)
24. Arnold, V.I.: Mathematical Methods of Classical Mechanics, vol. 60, 2nd edn. Springer Science & Business Media, New York (1989)

# Characteristic Alpha Reflects Predictive Anticipatory Activity (PAA) in an Auditory-Visual Task

Julia A. Mossbridge[1,2(✉)]

[1] Institute of Noetic Sciences, Petaluma, USA
jmossbridge@gmail.com
[2] Department of Psychology, Northwestern University, Evanston, USA

**Abstract.** Several lines of evidence suggest that humans can predict events that seem to be unpredictable through ordinary sensory means. After reviewing the literature in this controversial field, I present an exploratory EEG study that addresses this hypothesis. I used a pattern classification algorithm drawing on EEG data prior to stimulus presentation to successfully predict upcoming motor responses that were constrained by the upcoming stimulus. Both the phase of peak alpha activity and overall amplitude at $\sim 550$ ms prior to the presentation of the stimulus were useful in predicting the upcoming motor response. Although these results support the idea that brain activity may reflect precognitive processes in certain situations, due to the exploratory nature of this study, additional pre-registered confirmatory experiments are required before the results can be considered solid. Implications for creating a closed-loop predictive system based on human physiology are discussed.

**Keywords:** Predictive anticipatory activity · Presentiment · Precognition · Prospection · EEG · Alpha · Auditory-visual

## 1 Introduction

Many organisms can use associations from past experiences to help predict future ones. For instance, planarian worms that have been trained to expect electrical shock following a light burst will demonstrate a conditioned response to the light alone [1]. Here we discuss some neurophysiological correlates of a different kind of prediction – one that does not seem to be based on inferences from past experiences. This kind of prediction is known as *precognition* – the beyond-chance prediction of future events

---

The original analysis and some of the results described in this paper was registered with the Koestler Parapsychology Registry at http://www.koestler-parapsychology.psy.ed.ac.uk/Doc-uments/Study_Results_1004.pdf. Further, that document briefly describes how the initial prediction from the first 20 participants was assessed in the second 20 participants, and was not upheld (unless the alpha level for significance was relaxed). The results shown in more detail here are from a combined analysis of data from all 40 participants. Thus, any meta-analysis including this manuscript should not include the data registered there, to avoid data duplication.

© Springer International Publishing AG 2017
D.D. Schmorrow and C.M. Fidopiastis (Eds.): AC 2017, Part I, LNAI 10284, pp. 79–89, 2017.
DOI: 10.1007/978-3-319-58628-1_7

that are not predictable through ordinary means. In humans, the physiological analogue to precognition has been called *presentiment* [2], or more recently, *predictive antici-patory activity* (PAA; [3]). After a brief review of the behavioral precognition and PAA literature, I will describe an EEG experiment in which I used characteristic alpha measures to examine PAA in an auditory-visual task. While we do not currently understand the mechanisms underlying PAA, the results of this experiment add to converging evidence that it may be possible to engineer a closed-loop system drawing on PAA or related phenomena to predict seemingly unpredictable future events.

## 2  Background

Given that we normally experience a linear order of events in time, it seems reasonable that our minds or bodies could accurately predict future events only if those future events can be inferred from the past. On the other hand, given that we know about the order of events in time is largely based on our conscious perceptual experiences, one also might consider that nonconscious processes (of which we are not normally aware) may have access to what we call the "future" (e.g., [4, 5]).

Regardless, it is safe to say that if an organism can predict a future event with any level of accuracy beyond chance, using whatever means, this ability is likely to be adaptive. Whether that event is predictable based on our present-day understanding of time may not eventually turn out to be of practical importance. Instead, what I suggest is important for our survival is the ability to harness any sort of predictive ability, regardless of its source, and use it to predict events such as strokes, terrorist attacks, explosions, and violent riots [6]. Via the process of this harnessing project, we may better understand the unfolding of events in time.

The evidence that both human behavior and physiology are influenced by seemingly unpredictable events in the future has recently been highlighted in two meta-analyses. Behavioral evidence for precognition in humans was recently examined in a meta-analysis including 90 implicit precognition experiments examining the hypothesis that even when participants aren't asked directly about future events, behaviour in the present is related at a level beyond chance to randomly selected future events that are not known in the present by experimenters or participants in the experiments [7]. While the overall effect was highly statistically significant, it was also small. Interestingly, an admittedly post-hoc but nonetheless revealing analysis of the data showed that the overall effect was carried by the subset of the experiments in which participants were asked to use less deliberation ("fast-thinking" behavioural systems [8]). This subset of the experiments had a bigger, significant overall effect, whereas the other subset (using "slow-thinking" systems) was smaller and not statistically significant. This analysis suggests that conscious, deliberative control may obscure information about future events. In support of this idea, I took a precognition experiment that originally required extended deliberation, and after consulting with the experimenter's designer (Daryl Bem), I created a low-deliberation version of the experiment, which revealed a significant precognitive effect for events that would occur minutes in the future [9]. I am currently conducting an attempted replication of this effect. Further supporting the idea that behavior precognition represents a real, albeit unexplained effect, experiments in birds [10] and planarian worms [11] have revealed statistically significant differences in predictive behavioral changes in these animals prior to two classes of randomly selected behavioral stimuli.

Physiological precognition, otherwise known as predictive anticipatory activity or PAA, was examined in a meta-analysis including 26 PAA experiments in humans [3]. The meta-analysis examined the hypothesis that physiology in the present is related at a level beyond chance to randomly selected future events that are not known in the present by experimenters or participants in the experiments. The meta-analysis found a statistically significant small-to-medium overall effect, and spurred some reasonably friendly debate [12, 13].

## 3 Motivation and Study Overview

In the abstract and conclusion of the PAA meta-analysis, we included the following sentence: "The cause of this anticipatory activity, which undoubtedly lies within the realm of natural physical processes (as opposed to supernatural or paranormal ones), remains to be determined." The dual aims of understanding the natural physical processes underlying PAA and, in order to do so, enhancing the signal-to-noise ratio of the effect, are what drove me to undertake the PAA experiment using EEG that I describe here.

To understand the context of this experiment, it is important to know that Libet [14] and later others [15, 16] found neurophysiological signals called readiness potentials, which are generally considered to be neurophysiological reflection of unconscious decision-making processes tied to upcoming choices. Further, Matthewson et al. [17] showed that EEG activity in the alpha range (7.5–12 Hz), especially alpha phase, predicts whether an upcoming near-threshold visual stimulus will be detected or not, which was reported via a motor response. It seemed possible that perhaps both phenomena could be interpreted as PAA signals that predict upcoming motor responses, especially given that there is tentative evidence that precognition may be associated with alpha activity (for review, see [18]). To examine this idea, I designed a task in which the motor response is not a free choice, as it is in a traditional readiness potential experiment, but instead is constrained according to task directions about which of two buttons to press in response to randomly selected auditory and visual stimuli. Then I analysed current-source density transformed ERPs and EEG alpha activity that occurred prior to the software's decision about which stimulus to present to the participant, within the time frame of readiness potentials termed "type I" as originally found by Libet [14], to determine whether this activity could predict the upcoming button press.

## 4 Brief Methods

### 4.1 Hypothesis

The hypothesis of this study was that future motor responses to randomly selected auditory and visual stimuli could be predicted from brain activity that occurred prior to the selection of the stimuli.

## 4.2   Participants

Forty participants, ages 18–26, completed the study in two groups of 20. All participants were right-handed native speakers of English, and none had been diagnosed with neurological deficits. Some participants received course credit in exchange for their participation, while others received payment ($10/h for 2 h). All participants signed a consent form, describing procedures approved by the Northwestern University Institutional Review Board.

## 4.3   Task and Stimuli

The task was a speeded response task coded in Presentation software, in which I asked participants to press the left key of a computer mouse after seeing a white number "1" on a dark computer monitor or hearing a low-pitched tone (250 Hz) over headphones, and to press the right key of a computer mouse after seeing a white number "2" on the dark computer monitor or hearing a high-pitched tone (1 kHz) over the headphones (Fig. 1). All button presses were to be made with the right hand. I wanted participants to monitor attention in more than one sensory system because I suspected that this could ensure that they did not fall asleep as they did the task (a problem I had had with other EEG studies). Further, the auditory-visual nature of the task allowed me to test a different hypothesis that I do not explore here.

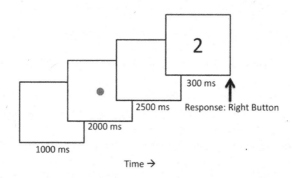

**Fig. 1.** Schematic showing timing and example of the correct response on a sample visual trial of the auditory-visual task, as it would appear to a participant.

All stimuli were randomized according to a pseudorandom number generator, which selected from the four possible stimulus types with equiprobability. The selection of the stimulus type was made just prior to the beginning of the pre-stimulus delay.

The order of events in the task and their durations were:

(1)  black screen with no visual or auditory input (1000 ms),
(2)  presentation of a red fixation dot in the center of the screen (2000 ms),
(3)  random selection of stimulus type (with no display or indication of type),
(4)  pre-stimulus delay with no visual or auditory input (2500 ms),

(5) presentation of the selected visual stimulus alone or auditory stimulus alone (300 ms),
(6) [user responds according to task requirements; all records with response times > 700 ms removed from analysis],
(7) return to 1.

## 4.4   Procedure

After the participant read and signed the consent form, I fitted 64 active EEG electrodes (BioSemi cap) to the participant's scalp. I explained that I was interested in understanding how neural activity as recorded by EEG electrodes could be related to expectation of future events. I did not discuss precognition. I told participants that while I knew this was an easy task, they should try to be as accurate and as fast in their responses as possible. The goals of this instruction were: first, to help participants attend to the task and not fall asleep, and second, to push response times into the domain in which fast-thinking processes could dominate. I also asked participants to blink during the presentation of the red fixation dot and to withhold blinking after that until they responded, because this would produce fewer eye movement artifacts during the 2.5 s leading up to the stimulus presentation.

The first 20 participants performed 120 trials of the task and the second 20 participants performed 100 trials of the same task. The reason for the change in the number of trials in the second group of participants was that I wanted to shorten the duration of the experiment because several of the first 20 participants had complained about boredom, and the analysis data from the initial 20 participants suggested that 100 trials was enough to obtain the effect. All analyses shown here were derived from the first 100 trials of all 40 participants.

## 4.5   EEG Analysis

I recorded EEG with a 64 + 8 active-electrode (Biosemi) system, using a 1024-Hz sampling rate and bandpass filtering between 0.1 and 100 Hz. Using Matlab (EEGlab Toolbox), I re-referenced data offline to a nose electrode. I baselined each value in the 2500-ms pre-response trace preceding a correct response to the average of the first 500 ms of that 2500-ms pre-response trace, and removed blinks and movement artifacts using standard methods. I used current-source density transformation in Matlab to improve resolution (CSD Toolbox Version 1), and performed all remaining analyses on the CSD-transformed traces. After examining the data, I focused on two different dependent variables that seemed to predict upcoming motor movements: mean (within-participant, across-trial) CSD trace magnitude, and phase of the mean CSD trace (within-participant, across-trial) at each individual's peak alpha frequency in the CSD traces. Each were calculated twice for each participant; one time each for the trials preceding right- and left-button presses. To calculate the mean CSD trace magnitudes for each person at each electrode and for each of the two response types, I averaged the values of CSD traces in 25 ms intervals between ∼1850 to ∼1975 ms (∼650 to ∼525 ms prior to stimulus presentation; times approximate because analysis was done on the points sampled at 1024 Hz). Thus for each of the response types, each person had 320 CSD trace magnitudes (64 electrodes × 5 epochs). I calculated peak alpha activity by first using a Fast Fourier Transform on each trace to find the frequency with greatest energy in the alpha range (7.5–12 Hz), then using a Butterworth filter to create a trace containing just that isolated frequency. Then for each electrode for each participant and each response type, I calculated the mean CSD trace within each participant, finally calculating absolute phases of this mean trace at the same 25 ms intervals (calculated every 25 ms between ∼1850 and ∼1975). Thus for each of the response types, each person had 320 CSD peak alpha phase values.

### 4.6 Pattern Classification

I used a random forest pattern ensemble pattern classification algorithm to objectively determine which of the dependent variables were best able to classify the future motor response (left or right button press). More details about this algorithm are available in my previous work [19], but briefly, the algorithm performs a series of analyses using decision trees to separate the data, and it includes a generalization test in which it uses a subset of the data as a training dataset and then tests on the remaining portion of the data (i.e., out-of-bag error estimation). Thus, only the error rate based on attempts at classifying the upcoming response using the instances that are not used during the training phase are reported as the final, or "generalization" error rate. It also allows for post-test querying to determine which features are most important in each classification attempt. The classifier was run with 640 sets of dependent variables for each of the response types, for each of the 40 participants (see Sect. 4.5 *EEG analysis*). The classifier was executed using the actual data versus a scrambled version of the same data to create a fair comparison, given that there were many dependent variables. This scrambled version was created on each run of the classifier by randomly selecting 50% of the left-button trials and renaming them as right-button trials, and vice versa. I ran the classifier 1000 times each, for the original data and the scrambled version of the same data, and recorded the generalization error rates for both datasets and the most important features for the original data.

## 5 Results

Here I report only the EEG results of this study; the behavioral results were not remarkable in relation to the present hypothesis. Grand means of CSD-transformed traces for correct trials showed a differential time course depending on the appropriate response to the upcoming stimulus (Fig. 2). The differential activity (black lines) deviates from zero primarily in the left-frontal region, suggesting that in the time domain, scalp electrodes in this region are best at separating future right- from left-button presses during time prior to stimulus presentation.

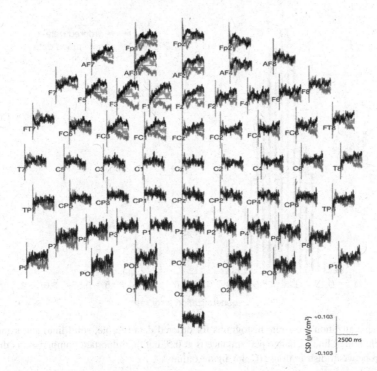

**Fig. 2.** Grand mean CSD traces for the 2500-ms pre-stimulus period (including the 500 ms baseline period) for correct trials on the auditory-visual task (N = 40 participants). Left upcoming response is indicated by green (middle trace); right upcoming response is indicated by pink (bottom trace); the difference is indicated by black (top trace). Correct responses were tied to the stimulus presented at 2500 ms, according to task instructions. (Color figure online)

Our statistical method allowed us to compare two distributions of generalization errors rate across 1000 attempts at classification of the across-participant data (Fig. 3). A distribution tail-test comparing classification error rates based on data presented in the original order versus data presented in scrambled orders gave a statistically significant result ($p < 2.5 \times 10^{-6}$). The classification method allowed us to determine the relative criticality for the 10 most critical electrodes and time points for each of the two dependent variables with the data in the original order; these were the three electrodes that were calculated by the classifier as the most necessary to produce robust classification (i.e., without these electrodes, classification all but failed). Averaging the relative criticality weighting of these electrodes over the 1000 classification attempts indicated that, on average, the most critical electrodes for the CSD-trace magnitude data were in the midline-to-left-frontal region (Fig. 4, left), and the most critical electrodes for the peak alpha-phase data were in the midline-to-right-parietal region, with some left-frontal involvement (Fig. 4, right). Further, the activity at the most critical electrode for both the CSD-trace magnitude data and the peak alpha phase data occurred at ∼550 ms prior to stimulus presentation (∼1950 ms), suggesting that this time point contains more information about the future response than any other tested timepoint.

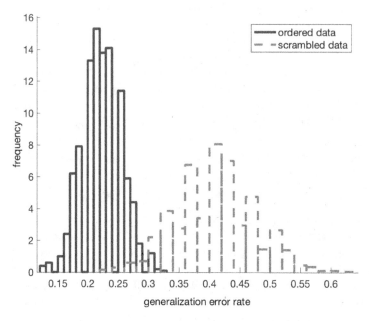

**Fig. 3.** Generalization error rate histograms for ordered data (purple; solid line) and scrambled data (green; dotted line). Chance performance is at 0.5, but the important comparison is the lack of overlap between distributions. (Color figure online)

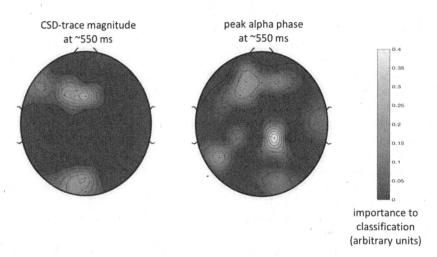

**Fig. 4.** The most critical features among the two types of dependent variables for predicting future left versus right responses. Hotter colors indicate higher importance. (Color figure online)

# 6  Conclusions

It appears that it is possible to use CSD magnitude and the phase of peak alpha activity prior to a seemingly unpredictable upcoming motor response to predict the type of that motor response, at least when possible responses are binary. Further, this predictive ability was best for data obtained 550 ms prior to the stimulus presentation that induced a pre-planned response linked to the stimulus, which is in the time frame associated with type I readiness potentials, the type that occur with some preplanning of future motor movements (i.e., starting at about 1050 ms prior to initiation of the motor movement; [14]). The left frontal (contralateral to the motor response) and midline-to-right-parietal involvement indicated in the critical electrode plots (Fig. 4) is within the boundaries of what might be expected based on previous examinations of type I readiness potentials [14–16], In addition, it may be a coincidence, but the average response time across participants was about 550 ms following the stimulus, suggesting a compelling form of time symmetry. To test this idea, a fruitful future approach may be to reanalyze the data using a trial-by-trial analysis, in which the dependent variables for each trial are the CSD-trace magnitude and the peak alpha phase exactly X ms prior to the stimulus presentation, where X = response time for that trial.

Three important flaws with this study must be highlighted. First, the random selection of the upcoming trial type should be performed following the pre-stimulus period. Although the software did not act on this selection in any way except to store the trial type in the computer's memory, if there is some way in which the participant could sense the presence of this selection remotely then it is difficult to interpret the results as reflecting a precognitive process. Second, these results were obtained with an exploratory step in which the dependent variables were selected, so it is crucial that they are replicated independently prior to drawing firm conclusions. Third, the results were obtained with a pseudorandom number generator, which does not mimic real-life uncertainty, so if a closed-loop system used to predict future events were to be created, it should be based off of data obtained with a truly random (quantum) number generator.

If these results are replicated independently using a random selection using a truly random number generator following the pre-stimulus period, two compelling conclusions can be explored. These are: (1) brain activity may predict motor responses that are, by ordinary means, unpredictable, and (2) type I readiness potentials (and potentially the alpha phase effects observed by Matthewson and others [17]) may be redundant with predictive anticipatory activity, or PAA.

In terms of the implications for creating a closed-loop system based on human physiology, I have several recommendations that arise from the results of this experiment as well as others; some of these recommendations were previously mentioned in an earlier review of PAA [6].

(1) Interindividual differences make the search for a single stereotyped signal difficult; one solution is to use machine learning to better isolate the predictive signal for a given event for each individual.
(2) The complexity of the nervous system may allow for better isolation of signals tied to an array of different future events as compared to a simple binary comparison.

(3) On the other hand, the quick-responding nature of the nervous system, assuming this quick response applies also to the "reverse" temporal direction, is likely to be poorly suited to predict events for purposes that would require seconds to minutes of preparations. In contrast, implicit behavioral effects, like those investigated in the precognition meta-analysis already discussed [7], are among the slowest effects. Thus, if temporal symmetry around an event is a general rule, it is likely that these implicit behavioral measures will also reveal the upcoming event earlier in time than other measures, because they respond later than other measures.

In sum, the results, if replicated independently, support converging evidence that there is some mechanism by which events in time are mirrored by behavioral and physiological systems. Whether these events in time are motor responses (as in this study) or sensory stimuli (as in many others, as machine learning techniques improve, it may be possible to create a closed-loop system able to predict events that previously were thought to be unpredictable. Note that one common concern that impedes the development of such a device is that it would cause a temporal paradox – for instance, the so-called "grandfather paradox" in which an anti-hero can go back in time and kill her own grandfather at a stage in life prior to when her own mother was conceived, thereby making our anti-hero cease to exist. One way to avoid this paradox is to assume that events in time are conditioned according to both information from the past and the future – in other words, what is happening in the present is only possible because past and future events agree with it. An interpretation of quantum mechanics sympathetic with this view has been advanced recently [20], and a formulation of closed timelike curves has been tested to show that it solves for the grandfather paradox using a similar idea [21]. If we can successfully build a closed-loop system that allows people to avoid future dangers, then we will also be better positioned to understand why the system worked. The mechanisms underlying precognition, while still unknown, may well become better understood as we attempt to create such a system.

**Acknowledgements.** Bial Foundation Bursary 141/10 supported this work. Also, thank you to Kyle Matthewson for creating and modifying the Matlab script to calculate alpha phase, and Satoru Suzuki, Marcia Grabowecky, and Ken Paller for office space, lab space, and financial support related to the completion of this project.

# References

1. Thompson, R., McConnell, J.: Classical conditioning in the planarian, Dugesia dorotocephala. J. Comp. Phys. Psychol. **48**, 65 (1955)
2. Radin, D.: Unconscious perception of future emotions: an experiment in presentiment. J. Sci. Explor. **11**, 163–180 (1997)
3. Mossbridge, J., Tressoldi, P.E., Utts, J.: Predictive physiological anticipation preceding seemingly unpredictable stimuli: a meta-analysis. Front. Psychol. **3**, 390 (2012)
4. Mossbridge, J.A.: Time and the unconscious mind. arXiv:1503.01368v1 [q-bio.NC] (2015)
5. Baruš, I., Mossbridge, J.: Transcendent Mind: Rethinking the Science of Consciousness. American Psychological Association Books, Washington DC (2016)

6. Mossbridge, J.A., Tressoldi, P., Utts, J., Ives, J.A., Radin, D., Jonas, W.B.: Predicting the unpredictable: critical analysis and practical implications of predictive anticipatory activity. Front. Hum. Neurosci. **8**, 146 (2014)
7. Bem, D., Tressoldi, P.E., Rabeyron, T., Duggan, M.: Feeling the future: a meta-analysis of 90 experiments on the anomalous anticipation of random future events (2016). SSRN: http://f1000research.com/articles/4-1188/v2
8. Kahneman, D.: Thinking, Fast and Slow. Farrar, Straus and Giroux, New York (2011)
9. Mossbridge, J.: Examining the nature of retrocausal effects in biology and psychology. Amer. Inst. Phys.: Conf. Proc. (in press)
10. Alvarez, F.: Anticipatory alarm behavior in Bengalese finches. J. Sci. Explor. **24**, 599–610 (2010)
11. Alvarez, F.: An experiment on precognition with planarian worms. J. Sci. Explor. **30**, 217–226 (2016)
12. Schwarzkopf, D.S.: We should have seen this coming. Front. Hum. Neurosci. **8**, 332 (2014)
13. Mossbridge, J.A., Tressoldi, P., Utts, J., Ives, J.A., Radin, D., Jonas, W.B.: We did see this coming: response to, we should have seen this coming, by D.S. Schwarzkopf. arXiv:1501.03179v2 [q-bio.NC] (2015)
14. Libet, B.: Do we have free will? J. Conscious. Stud. **6**, 47–57 (1999)
15. Bode, S., He, A.H., Soon, C.S., Trampel, R., Turner, R., Haynes, J.D.: Tracking the unconscious generation of free decisions using uitra-high field fMRI. PLoS ONE **6**, e21612 (2011)
16. Soon, C.S., Allefeld, C., Bogler, C., Heinzle, J., Haynes, J.D.: Predictive brain signals best predict upcoming and not previous choices. Front. Psychol. **5**, 406 (2014)
17. Mathewson, K.E., Gratton, G., Fabiani, M., Beck, D.M., Ro, T.: To see or not to see: prestimulus α phase predicts visual awareness. J. Neurosci. **29**, 2725–2732 (2009)
18. Morris, R.L.: The Psychobiology of Psi. Cosimo, Inc., New York (2016)
19. Mossbridge, J.A., Grabowecky, M., Paller, K.A., Suzuki, S.: Neural activity tied to reading predicts individual differences in extended-text comprehension. Front. Hum. Neurosci. **7**, 655 (2013). doi:10.3389/fnhum.2013.00655
20. Kastner, R.E.: Cramer's transactional interpretation and causal loop problems. Synthese **150**, 1–14 (2006)
21. Lloyd, S., Maccone, L., Garcia-Patron, R., Giovannetti, V., Shikano, Y., Pirandola, S., Steinberg, A.M.: Closed timelike curves via postselection: theory and experimental test of consistency. Phys. Rev. Lett. **106**, 040403 (2011)

# Influence of Spontaneous Rhythm on Movement-Related Cortical Potential - A Preliminary Neurofeedback Study

Lin Yao[1], Mei Lin Chen[1], Xinjun Sheng[2],
Natalie Mrachacz-Kersting[3], Xiangyang Zhu[2], Dario Farina[4],
and Ning Jiang[1(✉)]

[1] Engineering Bionics Lab, Department of Systems Design Engineering,
University of Waterloo, Waterloo, Canada
ning.jiang@uwaterloo.ca
[2] State Key Lab of Mechanical System and Vibration,
Shanghai Jiao Tong University, Shanghai, China
[3] Center for Sensory-Motor Interaction, The Faculty of Medicine,
Aalborg University, Aalborg, Denmark
[4] Department of Bioengineering, Imperial College London, London, UK

**Abstract.** In this work, the variation of the waveform of the movement related cortical potential (MRCP) was investigated in a real-time neurofeedback study, in which the spontaneous slow cortical potential (SCP) within the same frequency band as MRCP ([0.05 3] Hz) was provided as feedback to the subjects. Experiments have shown that the background SCP activity has a strong influence on the waveform of the self-paced MRCP. Negative potential SCP has been shown to increase the negative peak of the MRCP waveform, while positive potential SCP has been shown to reduce the negative peak. The variation of the single-trial MRCP waveform was correlated with the background SCP activity. This study provided a new approach to evaluate and modulate MRCP waveform, which directly determines the brain switch detection BCI performance.

**Keywords:** Brain-computer interface (BCI) · Movement related cortical potential (MRCP) · Slow cortical potential (SCP) · Neurofeedback

## 1 Introduction

Brain-computer Interface (BCI) provides an alternative communication and control channel for healthy or disabled users to interact with the external environment through brain activity alone [1]. Scalp-recorded EEG is comprised of a wide variety of oscillatory activities, such as delta ([2 4] Hz), theta ([4 8] Hz) alpha ([8 13] Hz), beta ([13 26] Hz), gamma ([30 70] Hz), even near to direct current (DC) component (< 1 Hz), which we call slow cortical potential (SCP) [2]. Among those oscillatory activities, sensorimotor rhythm frequency band ([8 to 30] Hz) has been shown to be correlated with movement or imagined movement intention [3], and also somatosensory attention [4]. By detection of the changes of band power, subjects' motor or sensation intention can be reliably recognized by the BCI system and transferred to control external

© Springer International Publishing AG 2017
D.D. Schmorrow and C.M. Fidopiastis (Eds.): AC 2017, Part I, LNAI 10284, pp. 90–98, 2017.
DOI: 10.1007/978-3-319-58628-1_8

devices [5, 6]. However, there is a latency, usually in the order of seconds, between the motor imagery (MI) task and the generation of SMR patterns [7–9], making it difficult to develop a highly interactive BCI. This is especially the case in stroke neuroreha-bilitation [10, 11], when the delay between motor intention and the corresponding detection is required to render the Hebbian principle effective [12, 13].

Another signal modality, called movement-related cortical potential (MRCP) has been shown able to reflect the subject's motor intentions within a few hundreds of milliseconds, thus it is critical for the afferent feedback to be timed to arrive in syn-chrony with the movement intention [14–16]. The MRCP based closed-loop BCI would provide a novel neuromodulation system to enhance the neuroplasticity more effectively. The performance of the MRCP based BCI system is a key factor influencing stroke recovery, as it is necessary to accurate single-trial detection of the MRCP waveform in real-time. However, the waveform of MRCP can vary substan-tially and therefore affect the performance of the brain switch. Factors influencing the waveform of MRCP need to be quantified, in part, by quantitatively analyze its trial by trial variability. Understanding the MRCP variability in a single-trial basis would provide a new way to enhance the corresponding BCI detection performance.

The MRCP consists of a Bereitschafts potential (BP) [17], followed by a motor potential (MP) [18] and a movement monitoring potential (MMP) [19, 20]. The BP consists of a slow decrease in EEG amplitude starting approximately 1500 ms prior to the onset of the movement, and is considered as a cortical representation of motor preparation. MRCP is one kind of a slow cortical potentials, within the frequency range of 0.05 to 3 Hz, but the waveform is related to movement – either real movement or imagined movement. The SCP can be self-regulated through neurofeedback training [21], i.e. the voluntary production of negative and positive potential shifts. There is an apparent overlap in frequency band between MRCP and SCP, both near the DC fre-quency range, hence the spontaneous SCP would be one of the factors influencing the MRCP waveform. The variability of single-trial waveform would be explained by the background SCP activity.

In this study, the spontaneous SCP will be topographically presented to subjects in real-time, and subjects will be instructed to perform self-paced real movement in the following three conditions: (1) without neurofeedback; (2) with negative SCP potential feedback; and (3) with positive SCP potential feedback. The variability of the MRCP waveform will be systematically investigated and compared between conditions.

## 2  Methods

**Subjects**
Four healthy subjects participated in the experiments (two female, all right handed, average age 22 ± 3.5 years), all were BCI naïve subjects. All participants have normal or corrected to normal vision, and none reported to be diagnosed with any neurological disorder. This study was approved by the Ethics Committee of the University of Waterloo, Waterloo, Canada. All participants signed an informed consent form before participation.

## EEG Recording and EMG Recording

EEG signals were recorded using a 44-channel g.USBamp EEG system (g.tec, Austria). The electrodes were placed according to the extended 10/20 system, as shown in Fig. 1. The reference electrode was located on the right earlobe, and the ground electrode on the forehead. A hardware notch filter at 60 Hz was applied to the raw signals. The signals were digitally sampled at 1200 Hz.

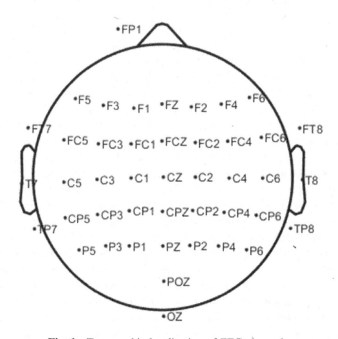

**Fig. 1.** Topographic localization of EEG electrodes.

One channel surface electromyography (EMG) was also recorded with the g. USBamp amplifier. EMG was acquired in monopolar montage from the tibialis anterior (TA) muscle with disposable electrodes. The electrode was placed on the mid-belly of the right TA muscle, while the reference and ground electrodes were placed on the bony surface of the right knee and right ankle, respectively.

## Real-Time Spontaneous SCP Neurofeedback Interface

The EEG signals were continually filtered between 0.05 to 3 Hz using a second order Butterworth filter. The filtered SCP signals was then averaged within 100 ms windows. The potential across electrodes was presented to subjects on a color scalp topographic map, which was updated every 100 ms, as shown in Fig. 2.

## Experimental Procedure

The experiment paradigm was shown in Fig. 2. Subjects were required to perform movement tasks according to different conditions: (1) No neurofeedback, (2) Neurofeedback with Negative Potential, (3) Neurofeedback with Positive Potential.

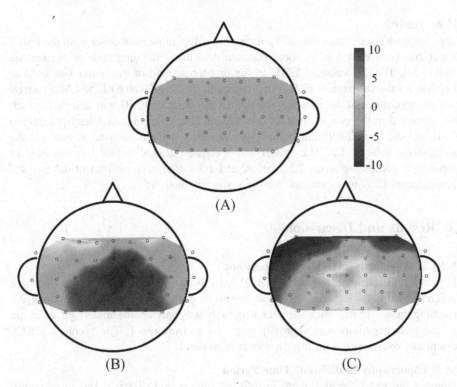

**Fig. 2.** Graphic Demonstration of Experiment Paradigm. (A) No neurofeedback was pre-sented to subjects. (B) Neurofeedback was presented to subjects, when negative potential was presented around Cz vertex subjects performed a real movement. (C) Neurofeedback was pre-sented to subjects, when positive potential was presented around Cz vertex subjects performed a real movement. Color bar indicates the voltage value. (Color figure online)

The subject was seated on a comfortable armchair, with both forearms and hands resting on the armrests. The subjects were instructed to limit their eye, facial and arm movements. Every subject performed three runs of foot dorsiflexion task, with 20 trials per run. Before the start of every run, subjects were required to stay still and not make any foot movement in the first 10 s, which was used as baseline for the subsequent online EMG detection. During the first run, subjects performed self-paced foot dorsiflexion, with 5–8 s between each task. No neurofeedback was provided to the participants in this run, as shown in Fig. 2(A). During the second run, subjects received the real-time slow cortical potential maps (the whole scalp), and subjects were instructed to perform foot dorsiflexion when the center of the scalp (Cz) turns into blue color, which corresponded to negative potential as shown in Fig. 2(B), and rest for 5–8 s before next task. During the third run, the participants received the same neurofeedback as in the second run, but were instructed to perform the foot dorsiflexion task when the center of the scalp turns to red color, as shown in Fig. 2(C), which corresponded to positive potential. Subjects rested 4 to 10 min between runs.

## Data Analysis

The Teager–Kaiser energy operator was used to detect movement onset from the EMG, which has been shown to be more accurate than using the amplitude of the surface EMG [22]. The TK value of EMG in the first ten second of every run was used as baseline for the subsequent EMG onset detection. If the TK value of the EMG surpass that of three times of the baseline value, then the onset of EMG was detected, which corresponded to the start of the foot dorsiflexion task. A band-pass filter from 0.05 to 3 Hz and the large Laplacian spatial filter centered at Cz were used to enhance the signal-noise ratio of Cz. The spatial and spectrally filtered virtual Cz was used in subsequent processing steps. 2.5 s before and 1.5 s after each movement onset of the preprocessed EEG was extracted for the waveform analysis.

## 3   Results and Discussion

### MRCP Waveform in Different Conditions

Figure 3 illustrates the averaged MRCP waveforms ([0.05 3] Hz) under the three different conditions. Evidently, the peak negativity peak in run 2 was more pronounced, reaching up to −15 uv, while the peak negativity was only approximately −5 uv in run 3. The peak negativity was approximately −10 uv from run 1. The averaged MRCP essentially overlapped with the waveform from run 1.

### SCP Topography in different Time Period

Figure 4 illustrates the SCP maps in different time period ([0.05 3] Hz) in no neuro-feedback condition (run 1), 0 corresponds to the onset on movement as detected by EMG. The potential with the corresponding time window was averaged, including time window of [−2.0 −1.8] s, [−1.5 −1.3] s, [−1.0 −0.8] s, [−0.5 −0.3] s, [−0.2 0] s, [0 0.2] s, [0.4 0.6] s, and [0.8 1] s.

Figure 5 illustrates the SCP maps in different time period in neurofeedback with negative potentials (run 2). Figure 6 illustrates the SCP maps in different time period in neurofeedback with positive potentials (run 3).

From the time period between −2.0 s to −1.8 s, the potential distribution around the scalp were similar among the three conditions. While in the time period between −0.5 s to −0.3 s, there was a clear difference between the three conditions; there was a more negative potential around the Cz channel in the negative potential neurofeedback condition, and a more positive potential around the Cz channel in the positive potential neurofeedback condition. These differences were explicitly induced by our experiment protocol, and it is clear that they are influencing factors for the subsequent MRCP amplitude changes. At around 0 s, the resulting negative potential was more pronounced in run 2 than that in both run 1 and run 3.

In this preliminary neurofeedback study, the background SCP changes were found to be correlated to the variation of the MRCP waveform. To the best of our knowledge, this was the first study to address the waveform variation due to the background SCP changes. Through the proposed neurofeedback strategy, the MRCP amplitude can be enhanced or reduced. This confirmed our hypothesis that there would be an additive effect between the background SCP and self-induced MRCP signal in the resulting waveform.

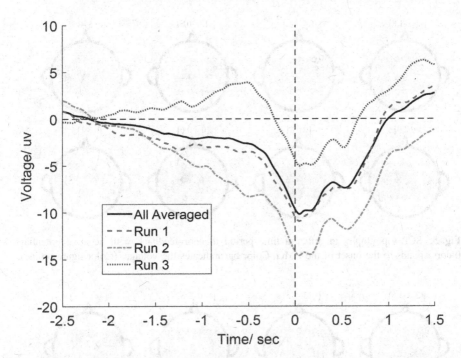

**Fig. 3.** MRCP waveform in different neurofeedback conditions. Black line indicates the averaged waveform across all trials (20 × 3 = 60 trial); red dashed line indicates the waveform in Run 1; green dash-dotted line indicates the waveform in Run 2; blue dotted line indicates the waveform in Run 3. 0 s indicates the start of the task. (Color figure online)

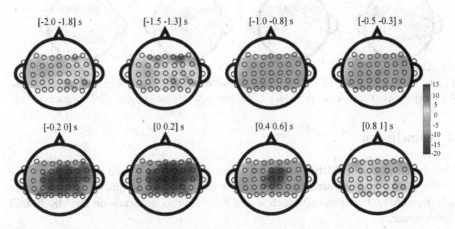

**Fig. 4.** SCP topography in different time period in no neurofeedback condition. 0 corresponds to the onset of the EMG. Color bar indicates the voltage. (Color figure online)

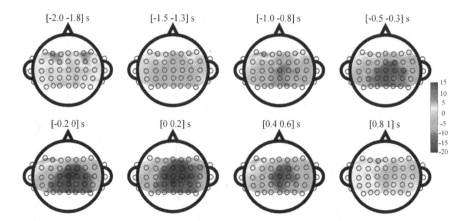

**Fig. 5.** SCP topography in different time period in neurofeedback with negative potentials. 0 corresponds to the onset of the EMG. Color bar indicates the voltage. (Color figure online)

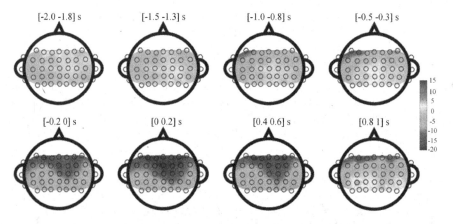

**Fig. 6.** SCP topography in different time period in neurofeedback with positive potentials. 0 corresponds to the onset of the EMG. Color bar indicates the voltage. (Color figure online)

## 4   Conclusion

The variation of the MRCP was influenced by the background spontaneous SCP activity. Real-time neurofeedback provided a new approach to quantify and affect the self-paced MRCP waveform, which would have a direct influence on the MRCP BCI performance.

**Acknowledgement.** We thank all volunteers for their participation in the study. This work is supported by the University Starter Grant of the University of Waterloo (No. 203859), the National Natural Science Foundation of China (Grant No. 51620105002, 51375296, 51421092), the Research Project of State Key Laboratory of Mechanical System and Vibration MSV201607.

# References

1. Wolpaw, J.R., Birbaumer, N., McFarland, D.J., Pfurtscheller, G., Vaughan, T.M., et al.: Brain-computer interfaces for communication and control. Clin. Neurophysiol. **113**(6), 767–791 (2002)
2. Birbaumer, N., Cohen, L.G.: Brain-computer interfaces: communication and restoration of movement in paralysis. J. Physiol. **579**(Pt 3), 621–636 (2007)
3. Pfurtscheller, G., Neuper, C.: Motor imagery and direct brain-computer communication. Proc. IEEE **89**(7), 1123–1134 (2001)
4. Yao, L., Sheng, X., Zhang, D., Jiang, N., Farina, D., Zhu, X.: A BCI system based on somatosensory attentional orientation. IEEE Trans. Neural Syst. Rehabil. Eng. **4320**(c), 1 (2016)
5. Meng, J., Zhang, S., Bekyo, A., Olsoe, J., Baxter, B., He, B.: Noninvasive electroencephalogram based control of a robotic arm for reach and grasp tasks. Sci. Rep. **6**(November), 38565 (2016)
6. Pfurtscheller, G., Müller, G.R., Pfurtscheller, J., Gerner, H.J., Rupp, R.: 'Thought'–control of functional electrical stimulation to restore hand grasp in a patient with tetraplegia. Neurosci. Lett. **351**(1), 33–36 (2003)
7. Doud, A.J., Lucas, J.P., Pisansky, M.T., He, B.: Continuous three-dimensional control of a virtual helicopter using a motor imagery based brain-computer interface. PLoS ONE **6**(10), e26322 (2011)
8. Kaiser, V., Bauernfeind, G., Kreilinger, A., Kaufmann, T., Kübler, A., Neuper, C., Müller-Putz, G.R.: Cortical effects of user training in a motor imagery based brain-computer interface measured by fNIRS and EEG. Neuroimage **85**(Pt 1), 432–444 (2014)
9. Pichiorri, F., De Vico Fallani, F., Cincotti, F., Babiloni, F., Molinari, M., Kleih, S.C., Neuper, C., Kübler, A., Mattia, D.: Sensorimotor rhythm-based brain-computer interface training: the impact on motor cortical responsiveness. J. Neural Eng. **8**(2), 25020 (2011)
10. Pichiorri, F., Fallani, F.D.V., Cincotti, F., Babiloni, F., Molinari, M., Kleih, S.C., Neuper, C., Kübler, A., Mattia, D.: Sensorimotor rhythm-based brain–computer interface training: the impact on motor cortical responsiveness. J. Neural Eng. **8**(2), 25020 (2011)
11. Ramos-Murguialday, A., Broetz, D., Rea, M., Läer, L., Yilmaz, Ö., Brasil, F.L., Liberati, G., Curado, M.R., Garcia-Cossio, E., Vyziotis, A., Cho, W., Agostini, M., Soares, E., Soekadar, S., Caria, A., Cohen, L.G., Birbaumer, N.: Brain-machine interface in chronic stroke rehabilitation: a controlled study. Ann. Neurol. **74**(1), 100–108 (2013)
12. Mrachacz-Kersting, N., Kristensen, S.R., Niazi, I.K., Farina, D.: Precise temporal association between cortical potentials evoked by motor imagination and afference induces cortical plasticity. J. Physiol. **590**(7), 1669–1682 (2012)
13. Mrachacz-Kersting, N., Jiang, N., Stevenson, A.J.T., Niazi, I.K., Kostic, V., Pavlovic, A., Radovanovic, S., Djuric-Jovicic, M., Agosta, F., Dremstrup, K., Farina, D.: Efficient neuroplasticity induction in chronic stroke patients by an associative brain-computer interface. J. Neurophysiol. (2015). doi:10.1152/jn.00918.2015
14. Niazi, I.K., Jiang, N., Jochumsen, M., Nielsen, J.F., Dremstrup, K., Farina, D.: Detection of movement-related cortical potentials based on subject-independent training. Med. Biol. Eng. Comput. **51**(5), 507–512 (2013)
15. Xu, R., Jiang, N., Lin, C., Mrachacz-Kersting, N., Dremstrup, K., Farina, D.: Enhanced low-latency detection of motor intention from EEG for closed-loop brain-computer interface applications. IEEE Trans. Biomed. Eng. **61**(2), 288–296 (2014)

16. Xu, R., Jiang, N., Mrachacz-Kersting, N., Lin, C.: A closed-loop brain-computer interface triggering an active ankle-foot orthosis for inducing cortical neural plasticity. Trans. Biomed. Eng. **61**(7), 2092–2101 (2014)
17. Jahanshahi, M., Hallett, M.: The Bereitschaftspotential: Movement-Related Cortical Potentials. Springer Science & Business Media, Heidelberg (2003)
18. Deecke, L., Grözinger, B., Kornhuber, H.H.: Voluntary finger movement in man: cerebral potentials and theory. Biol. Cybern. **23**(2), 99–119 (1976)
19. Kristeva, R., Keller, E., Deecke, L., Kornhuber, H.H.: Cerebral potentials preceding unilateral and simultaneous bilateral finger movements. Electroencephalogr. Clin. Neurophysiol. **47**(2), 229–238 (1979)
20. Libet, B., Gleason, C.A., Wright, E.W., Pearl, D.K.: Time of conscious intention to act in relation to onset of cerebral activity (readiness-potential). Brain **106**(3), 623–642 (1983)
21. Hinterberger, T., Schmidt, S., Neumann, N., Mellinger, J., Blankertz, B., Curio, G., Birbaumer, N.: Brain-computer communication and slow cortical potentials. IEEE Trans. Biomed. Eng. **51**(6), 1011–1018 (2004)
22. Solnik, S., Rider, P., Steinweg, K., Devita, P., Hortobágyi, T.: Teager-Kaiser energy operator signal conditioning improves EMG onset detection. Eur. J. Appl. Physiol. **110**(3), 489–498 (2010)

# Multiple Human EEG Synchronous Analysis in Group Interaction-Prediction Model for Group Involvement and Individual Leadership

Jiacai Zhang[✉] and Zixiong Zhou

College of Information Science and Technology, Beijing Normal University,
No. 19, Xinjiekouwai Street, Haidian, Beijing, People's Republic of China
Jiacai.zhang@bnu.edu.cn

**Abstract.** Successful communication relies on the ability to express and obtain information and fast adaptability to the communication that others think has high quality [1]. The one with high exchange quality in group-based communication is generally supposed to have leadership. The leader's neural mechanism during the communication is not deeply studied in the previous researches. In this paper, a new method is proposed to evaluate the leadership in group activity by utilizing the characteristic of EEG. We collect the brain electrical activity of the group members with non-intrusive high precision wireless EEG acquisition device to reduce the barrier in exchange activity. Through classification of interactive and noninteractive multivariate analysis with multi-person EEG electrode, it's found that the left temporal lobe cerebral region of leader elected by voting features obvious activation of electrode after receiving messages from others. Further, his α EEG is significantly inhibited and β EEG is obviously activated. This cerebral region is considered to be the one disposing and predicting errors, which indicates that the leader is good at analyzing each person's information and disposing errors and used the resources for predicting and planning after accepting the problem. Besides, the frontal lobe α wave of the leader during the stage of communication and discussion is inhibited obviously and it is the same as the voting result.

**Keywords:** EEG · Leadership · Synchronization and multi-person interaction

## 1 Introduction

When many people participate in team interaction, they exchange messages through a series of behaviors. Different individuals are adapted to their communication means through in-depth tightly coupled alignment. Multi-person team interaction process can be considered to be the frequent two-person communication with different objects. However, it is different from the two-person communication. Due to the randomness of multi-person communication object, the individual is required to fast synchronize with different objects. If the effect of tightly coupled alignment is not desirable, the communication quality will be reduced.

© Springer International Publishing AG 2017
D.D. Schmorrow and C.M. Fidopiastis (Eds.): AC 2017, Part I, LNAI 10284, pp. 99–108, 2017.
DOI: 10.1007/978-3-319-58628-1_9

To be different from team, social group is defined as two or more interacting and mutually influencing each other [2]. Some social psychologists think that the member of "group" as regards those in his group as "us" instead of "them". The difference between social group and team is that the team consists of members who are highly differentiated and mutually dependent while social group consists of members who are homogeneous and substitutive. It can be understood that team is a group with special form. Human society consists of human group. However, people are consciously divided into different teams to improve efficiency in modern society. The leader, as the core of the team, should possesses strong communication ability, for which the leader should rapidly synchronize with the followers and get to know the thought and intention of the followers so as to divide the homogeneous group into the teams with special trait.

It's poorly understood how the brain supports the social function in current researches, most of which are centrally carried out under experimental environment. However, there tends to be blank researches carried out under natural environment. In this paper, one leader marker is defined to evaluate the leadership of individual in group. Meanwhile, the similar but different experimental contents made with same members can be used as the result reference for the task completion result with or without leader. Then, the task is expanded to the practical problem (built with building blocks) from the topic discussion. According to the result, it shows that task completion and evaluation of the predicted group under the leadership of the leader is superior to the control group without leader.

To be specific, according to the previous research on synchronic dual-EEG, it's found that the power spectrum of the parietal lobe $\alpha$ wave (about 10 Hz) has the tendency of synchronization when focusing on common thing namely when synchronization occurs. That is to say, when focusing on the same thing, there is synchronic tendency for the beginning and ending time of the activating and inhibiting strength of $\alpha$ wave. When not focusing on same thing, the power spectrum strength of $\alpha$ wave is not obviously associated. In a bid to eliminate the error between external disturbance and wireless device, a small interactive-blink test is designed before the experiment is officially implemented. That is, the eyes are opened according to the order of experimenter and all group members are completely stochastic. Opening and closing eyes alternatively at regular of 10 s shall be regarded as the basis for static data (base-data) and evaluating wireless connection quality.

## 2  Materials and Methods

### 2.1  Participants

25 subjects (12 males, averagely aged: $23.52 \pm 3.02$) have no cerebral diseases and bad habits. All participants receive the experimental notes and don't repeatedly participate in experiment.

## 2.2  Task and Procedure

The subjects can see each other and observe the expressions of others during the dialogue. The subjects have 5 min' rest before the experiment starts and then begin discussing the topics. Two conditions are discussed in the experiment. Firstly, the whole-follower's state of the group leader is not designated. Secondly, the leader-follower of the group leader is designated.

**(1) Whole-Follower.** At this time, all group members can make statements freely at their will and the experimenter read the topic for all subjects once and then discuss it. There is no fixed answer for the question. The subjects can involve any fields that they are adept in during the discussion. The subjects shall keep gentle and should not be excited and nervous during the explanation. The discussion lasts 20 min all group members shall select a group leader after times run out, and the group leader will report the final result. During the discussion, two DV cameras will record video from different directions for recording such information as the demeanor of the group members, beginning & ending time of communication and mood and serve as one of reference basis for evaluating the communication quality.

Each subject will have to fill in one questionnaire for inquiring about the voting result of the group leader selected by each subject and evaluating their attentions to the question, communication quality and level of their interest in the topic. Each question is divided into 1-10 grades. The answer of questionnaire will be used as the basis for future classification.

**(2) Designated Leader-Follower.** There are 10 min for rest after the last stage, then the group leader selected by the last group is designated as the leader, taking the lead in topic discussion. After the experimenter explains the question, the subjects can begin the discussion. The discussion process requirement, video recording detail and questionnaire shall be the same as those for the last stage.

Besides, two extra stages are designed to explore difference in activation of cerebral region of the leader and follower.

**(3) Whole-Follower (Task).** At this time, all group members can make statements at their will and complete building of electronic bricks (environment is minecraft creative model) on computer. All group members connect the network through LAN. There has existed a building in the task. All materials have been given out. The group members are required to repeatedly build a same building. The construction process can be discussed. The subjects shall keep gentle and should not be excited and nervous. The time is 20 min according to the discussion and building process, it is required to reduce head and body movements as far as possible, mutually communicate with each other over the earphone and record video with PC camera and serve as one of reference basis for evaluating the communication quality and attention in the late stage. The subjects should fill in questionnaire after completion of construction. The content shall be referred to that at the first stage.

**(4) Designated Leader-Follower (Task).** One leader (voted through investigation questionnaire at the third stage) shall be designated at the very beginning, then the leader give commands in completing the building of the target. To prevent the repeated work from bringing influences to the result, the difficulty in building at the second stage is the same as that at the third stage but the structure is different from that at the third stage. All subjects participated in teaching and are all skilled at operation before. The requirements and specific details are the same as those at the third stage (Fig. 1).

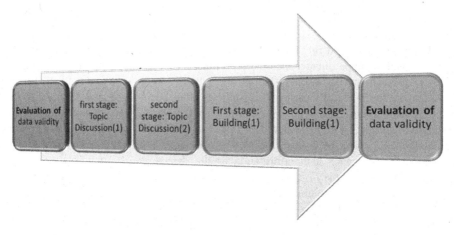

**Fig. 1.** Specific flow chart

## 2.3    EEG Recordings

All members of each group collect EEG data synchronically. 5 32-channel electrode caps are used, for which international standard electrode location (standard-10–10) is adopted. 5 groups of independent wireless receiving devices are connected in parallel with synchronic annunciator, which sends out beginning and ending signals to ensure the synchronization among 5 groups of devices. The recorded bandwidth is 0.1 Hz–60 Hz and the sampling frequency is 250 Hz.

## 2.4    EEG Data Preprocessing

EEGLab (version No.: 13_6_5b) is used for data processing and analysis and MATLAB software toolbox for data processing. All periods shall be expected to be manually classified. It's necessary to differentiate each subject is at the state of listening or expressing according to the video recording and record area. If the expressing time is long, it's necessary to select −1–1.5 s before start, 1 s during the expression and −1.5–1 s before the ending time. All expressing time length shall be standardized within 6 s. The data before normal form is used shall be adopted as the baseline correction standard to remove DC offset.

## 2.5    Artifact Removal

The data is further processed with ICA. Because the normal form of experiment is mainly constituted by the dialogue, head movement and blink, the influence on EEG cannot be avoided. The electrode cap is equipped with gyroscope, which can collect acceleration data of axis X, Y and Z, judge the component of blink, eye and head movement by combining accelerometer and PCA, and then remove it. Then, the main component is extracted through PCA to reduce the data dimension and non-main leading component. Besides, PCA is also helpful for reducing distortion of frequency domain. Main 6 components are calculated through PCA as the classification basis in the late stage.

## 2.6  Spectral Analysis

To standardize the state of cerebral activity of different participants, the time for communication is standardized. The expression time is intercepted. Every intercepted section only involves expression that man is the expression state with the remaining participants considered to be at listening state. WT (wavelet transform) is adopted. Hamming window length is 2 s. It's supposed that the intercepted standard length is a trail. To reduce the data error, the corresponding power spectrum is calculated after average of data overlay of each trail is taken. The range that we are interested in is centralized at two frequency bands $\alpha$ (8–12 Hz) and $\beta$ (13–30 Hz). The selection of channel is calculated according to correlation test of whole-brain channel to select EEG channel with high correlativity. In the meantime, the previous research shows that there is obvious difference in activation of temporal lobe of the bran when the leader communicates with non-leader [3].

Figure 2 shows the change in whole brain power strength of the leader at different frequency bands during expression and listening. It could be known from the figure that the activation degree of parietal & temporal lobes in the left side and temporal lobe in

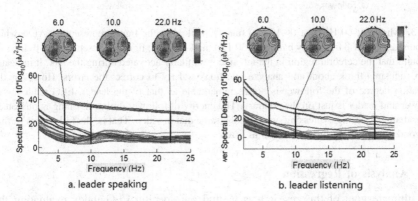

a. leader speaking          b. leader listenning

**Fig. 2.** Midpoint of frequency band $\alpha$ (8–12 Hz) mainly marked in a and b 10 Hz represents wave $\alpha$ and midpoint 22 Hz of $\beta$ frequency band (13–30 Hz) marked in the figure represents wave $\beta$. It could be found that the electrode in parietal lobe in the left side and temporal lobe in the right side of the brain is activated obviously during the communication. B wave power during the talk is obviously larger than that during listening while $\alpha$ wave power during listening is obviously larger than that during the talk. The energy during listening is mainly centralized in low-frequency band (0 < 15 Hz); the energy distribution during listening is more average than that during listening. The proportion of high frequency band (15 > 30 Hz) is larger.

the right side during the expression is obviously higher than that during the listening. According to psychological and related research results, it's supposed that the errors that have already made or might be made during the expression are judged and corrected in advance. Figure 2a and b shows that the leader is more relaxed during listening and more concentrated during the expression.

Figure 3 shows the change in whole brain power strength of follower during representation and listening at different frequency bands. Similarly, the cerebral region in the left side is activated obviously during communication. However, to be different from the leader, the difference in energy of activated and other electrodes of follower is small. Besides, energy of wave $\alpha$ and $\beta$ is obviously smaller than that of leader. It indicates that the follower is more relaxed during the talk for the error-tolerant rate of follower during expression is higher and the responsibility is small. Therefore, the follower is in relaxing state during expressing.

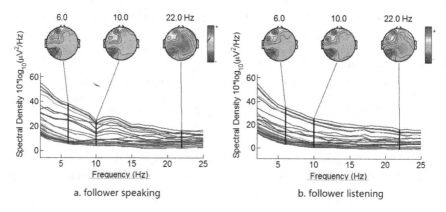

a. follower speaking                    b. follower listening

**Fig. 3.** Midpoint 10 Hz of a (8–12 Hz) mainly marked in the figure represents wave $\alpha$ while midpoint 22 Hz of $\beta$ frequency band (13–30 Hz) marked in the figure represents wave $\beta$. It could be found that the cerebral region in the left side is similarly activated during the talk. It indicates the participants think about and analyze questions and try to correct the errors. However, the activation degree of the follower is not as remarkable as that of the leader. EEG tendency of follower and leader is just on the contrary. The energy of follower during listening is obviously larger than that during expressing, which is the same that in video. That is, the follower is further not good at expressing but is inclined to listen.

## 2.7  Analysis of Regression

The ultimate goal of this research is to find out specific EEG index evaluating the individual leadership and build a prediction model through this index to predict the efficiency of the group, and give out the recommended leader. Therefore, it's ultimately necessary to build a regression model. There are 5 members in each group. Each participant collects 32 channels of EEG data and has discussion or numerous groups of dialogues will be had in the experiment. The data dimensionality for EEG analysis is large. The specific characteristic is selected for the data. SVM is finally selected as the classifier and RBF kernel is selected for kernel function.

Due to data nonlinearity, the data is not completely stochastic. The classification effect of linear kernel function and Gaussian kernel is not good. When the regression function is made, the data is divided into two parts: 80% for training set and 20% for the test set. The training data is put into SVM to monitor learning. To improve the performance of classifier, the parameter c and g of SVM is optimized through grid search to search for the optimal parameter. Searching range: parameter $c:2^{\wedge}(-8)-2^{\wedge}8$; parameter $g:2^{\wedge}(-8)-2^{\wedge}8$. The stepping is 1. Because the experimental content is fixed and the noise reduction & filtering and standardization of data is implemented before it is finally put in SVM. To simplify calculation step, once the optimal parameter is determined through grid search it will be no longer modified. Though it may not be optimal parameter for different data sets, it can be considered to approach the optimal parameter.

## 2.8   Effectiveness Evaluation of Data

For EEG is collected with wireless device. There is high requirement for environment. Channel disturbance and mutual interference among devices might have great influence on experimental result. Therefore, the data validity is evaluated before beginning and ending of experiment. The specific step is: order group members to sit when facing the wall for 5 min, and then open and close eyes alternatively according to the order of the experimenter. The eye opening or closing state lasts 10 s. 3–5 groups shall be made cyclically. Then, the subjects shall sit when facing the wall according to the order of experimenter. If the data validity proves that the environmental interference belongs to the acceptable range, it's necessary to start the experiment after resting for 5 min.

After the experiment is finished, it's necessary to repeat the same evaluation step. If the assessment result is data validity, then it's considered that the data is reliable. Once the assessment result is data invalidity, the data for the experiment will be abandoned and the subjects also cannot join in experiment again.

Up to now, there have been research on influences of eye opening & closing on EEG carried out. There are unified opinions in the circle. Therefore, it's necessary to verify the data validity through alternative eye opening and closing. If the data analysis result is the same as the opinions in the circle, the data will be considered to be valid, vice versa.

# 3   Result

## 3.1   Individual Leadership

It's mentioned in the above text that the activation of left hemisphere of leader or follower during communication is obvious, in which the electrode activation of temporal and parietal lobes is obvious. The cerebral region activation of the leader is obviously higher than that of the follower. Simultaneously, the leader is more relaxed during listening and communication than the follower. In this way, the leader has clear thought and improves the efficiency in solving the problem. However, there is no especially obvious trend for the follower. Even if some followers are more concentrated during listening, the activation level of their cerebral region is far lower than that of the leader's.

Because there are many featured electrodes and activated electrodes of different subjects and role are also not the same, the features might be lost if few featured electrodes are selected for the classification. Therefore, 8 motors in left parietal and temporal lobes, etc. are selected for classification. To facilitate Fig. 4, feature of P3 electrode (international standard motor location is channel 24) is only displayed. By combining the time frequency map and investigation questionnaire of follower's P3 electrode, it's found that the electrode activation of left temporal lobe of followers with high executive force during listening is obvious, which indicates that the followers summarize and extract the orders or tasks of the leader consciously or subconsciously. Meanwhile, it also indicates that the leader has good expressing ability.

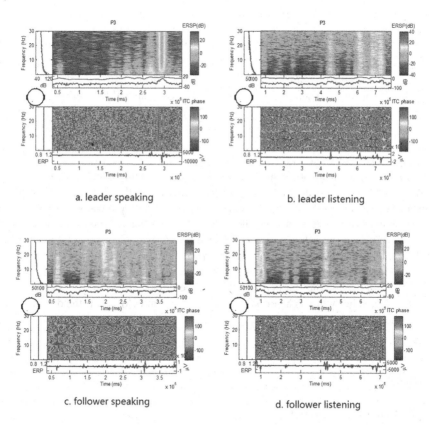

**Fig. 4.** Middle-stage (about 3 s of data after standardization, representing the middle part of communication stage) P3 electrode activation of leader during the talk is obvious. (a) P3 electrode activation of leader during the middle and back periods (about 4.5 s and 6–7.5 s of data after standardization, representing the middle and ending parts of listening stage) during listening is obvious, in which α wave plays a dominating role. (b) P3 electrode of follower during the whole stage of communication is activated but the activation level is obviously lower than that of leader. (c) P3 electrode activation of follower at beginning and ending stage during communication and listening is obvious, which indicates that beginning and ending of communication excites the follower greatly.

It's also found that the cerebral region of follower doesn't have obvious features at all stages, which is identical to the research conclusion reached previously. For high precision EEG acquisition device is used in this paper, the inconspicuous activation features still can be found. It proves that the followers participate in discussing and thinking about the topic but the strength is not the same. This conclusion fills the blank in analysis of thinking mode in previous researches. In addition, the hypothesis is verified with experimental data.

Further, data is classified through the searched out. The average classification accuracy reaches above 90%, which proves that the features searched out can indeed be regarded as the classification basis and can differentiate from the follower and leader. By building regression model through classifier to predict the individual leadership and comparing the predicting result into the voting result of questionnaire, it's found that the predicting accuracy is about 70% and even higher. If the prediction accuracy is found out for the optimal parameter of classification parameter during construction of prediction model, there is still the trend for promoting.

## 3.2    Behavioral Results

Through analysis of the communication video of experimental paradigm, it's found that the individual leader is not directly associated with communication frequency, but the person with high communication frequency is indeed easily selected by voting. The individual with high leadership can fast understand others' thought and give satisfying answers to others. When the individual with high leadership makes speech, short-term collaboration comes up with others' $\alpha$ EEG. That is, when the individual makes speech, the difference in change trend of power spectrum intensity of others' $\alpha$ EEG is small. This feature only will emerge when the communication quality of individual with high leadership is high. Besides, once the expressing stage ends, EEG of others will fast lose synch state.

**Acknowledgments.** This work is supported by the NSFC Key Program (91520202), and General Program (61375116). This work is also supported by Beijing Advanced Innovation Center for Future Education with grant No. BJAICFE2016IR-003.

# References

1. Konvalinka, I., Bauer, M., Stahlhut, C., et al.: Frontal alpha oscillations distinguish leaders from followers: multivariate decoding of mutually interacting brains. NeuroImage **94**, 79–88 (2014)
2. Spiegelhalder, K., Ohlendorf, S., Regen, W., et al.: Interindividual synchronization of brain activity during live verbal communication. Behav. Brain Res. **258**, 75–79 (2014)
3. Jiang, J., Chen, C., Dai, B., et al.: Leader emergence through interpersonal neural synchronization. Proc. Natl. Acad. Sci. **112**(14), 4274–4279 (2015)
4. Caetano, G., Jousmäki, V., Hari, R.: Actor's and observer's primary motor cortices stabilize similarly after seen or heard motor actions. Proc. Natl. Acad. Sci. **104**(21), 9058–9062 (2007)

5. Hari, R.: Action–perception connection and the cortical mu rhythm. Prog. Brain Res. **159**, 253–260 (2006)
6. Hari, R., Forss, N., Avikainen, S., et al.: Activation of human primary motor cortex during action observation: a neuromagnetic study. Proc. Natl. Acad. Sci. **95**(25), 15061–15065 (1998)
7. Amodio, D.M., Frith, C.D.: Meeting of minds: the medial frontal cortex and social cognition. Nat. Rev. Neurosci. **7**(4), 268–277 (2006)
8. Fliessbach, K., Weber, B., Trautner, P., et al.: Social comparison affects reward-related brain activity in the human ventral striatum. Science **318**(5854), 1305–1308 (2007)
9. Babiloni, F., Astolfi, L.: Social neuroscience and hyperscanning techniques: past, present and future. Neurosci. Biobehav. Rev. **44**, 76–93 (2014)
10. Hari, R., Himberg, T., Nummenmaa, L., et al.: Synchrony of brains and bodies during implicit interpersonal interaction. Trends Cogn. Sci. **17**(3), 105–106 (2013)
11. Duan, L., Dai, R.N., Xiao, X., et al.: Cluster imaging of multi-brain networks (CIMBN): a general framework for hyperscanning and modeling a group of interacting brains. Front. Neurosci. **9** (2015)
12. Hasson, U., Nir, Y., Levy, I., et al.: Intersubject synchronization of cortical activity during natural vision. Science **303**(5664), 1634–1640 (2004)
13. Wen, X., Mo, J., Ding, M.: Exploring resting-state functional connectivity with total interdependence. Neuroimage **60**(2), 1587–1595 (2012)
14. King-Casas, B., Tomlin, D., Anen, C., et al.: Getting to know you: reputation and trust in a two-person economic exchange. Science **308**(5718), 78–83 (2005)
15. Jensen, O., Mazaheri, A.: Shaping functional architecture by oscillatory alpha activity: gating by inhibition. Front. Hum. Neurosci. **4**, 186 (2010)
16. Kourtis, D., Sebanz, N., Knoblich, G.: Predictive representation of other people's actions in joint action planning: an EEG study. Soc. Neurosci. **8**(1), 31–42 (2013)
17. Kuhlman, W.N.: Functional topography of the human mu rhythm. Electroencephalogr. Clin. Neurophysiol. **44**(1), 83–93 (1978)
18. Davis, M.H.: Measuring individual differences in empathy: evidence for a multidimensional approach. J. Pers. Soc. Psychol. **44**(1), 113–126 (1983)
19. Konvalinka, I., Roepstorff, A.: The two-brain approach: how can mutually interacting brains teach us something about social interaction? Front. Hum. Neurosci. **6**, 215 (2012)
20. Maris, E., Oostenveld, R.: Nonparametric statistical testing of EEG-and MEG-data. J. Neurosci. Methods **164**(1), 177–190 (2007)
21. Fiebelkorn, I.C., Saalmann, Y.B., Kastner, S.: Rhythmic sampling within and between objects despite sustained attention at a cued location. Curr. Biol. **23**(24), 2553–2558 (2013)
22. Haegens, S., Händel, B.F., Jensen, O.: Top-down controlled alpha band activity in somatosensory areas determines behavioral performance in a discrimination task. J. Neurosci. **31**(14), 5197–5204 (2011)
23. Delorme, A., Makeig, S.: EEGLAB: an open source toolbox for analysis of single-trial EEG dynamics including independent component analysis. J. Neurosci. Methods **134**(1), 9–21 (2004)
24. Sharot, T., Riccardi, A.M., Raio, C.M., et al.: Neural mechanisms mediating optimism bias. Nature **450**(7166), 102–105 (2007)

# Interactive Image Segmentation Method of Eye Movement Data and EEG Data

Jiacai Zhang[✉], Song Liu, and Jialiang Li

Beijing Normal University, No. 19, Xinjiekouwai Street, Haidian, Beijing,
People's Republic of China
Jiacai.zhang@bnu.edu.cn, {201521210012, 201421210018}
@mail.bnu.edu.cn

**Abstract.** Interactive image segmentation method plays a vital role in various applications, such as image processing, computer vision and other fields. Traditional interactive image segmentation methods focus on using the way of manually adding interactive information, such as sketching the edges, distinguishing foreground backgrounds with dotted frames, and so on. The information acquisition and decoding technology has become more mature, such as in eye movement and electroencephalogram, and based on which, this paper presents an interactive image segmentation method that uses eye movement trajectory and EEG as interactive information. While observing the image, it collects the data from EEG and eye movement, based on these physiological signals to establish a more natural interactive image object segmentation method. The results show that the method of brain-computer interaction based image segmentation has advantages in the following aspects: first, it is hand-free, and can be applied to special occasions; second, there will be higher efficiency and better results in multi-target image segmentation. This research provides a new way to establish a new method of image segmentation based on human-computer cooperation.

**Keywords:** Interactive image segmentation method · Human-computer cooperation

## 1 Introduction

Image segmentation is one of the important branches of image processing. Fast and reliable image segmentation is not only the cornerstone of image editing and image analysis, but also an indispensable catalyst for pattern recognition, computer vision and artificial intelligence. Image segmentation plays an irreplaceable role as an initial step in target detection and tracking, image retrieval, shape from silhouette and other applications (Vezhnevets and Konouchine 2005).

Although the automatic image segmentation is developing continuously, the segmentation effect has been greatly improved. However, any kind of fully automatic image segmentation method can only have a good segmentation result and cannot be generalized for a specific case (Hernández-Vela et al. 2011). In the process of image segmentation intervention, it can get better results (Veksler et al. 2010) by making

D.D. Schmorrow and C.M. Fidopiastis (Eds.): AC 2017, Part I, LNAI 10284, pp. 109–120, 2017.
DOI: 10.1007/978-3-319-58628-1_10

interruption moderately, so more researchers are increasingly turning to the interactive image segmentation.

The interactive methods of early interactive image segmentation methods are mostly tedious and the method of image segmentation is not very effective. For example, Intelligent paint (Harley and Reese 1999) uses a region-based hierarchical segmentation method to link similar image regions together automatically (Mortensen and Barrett 1998; Mortensen and Barrett 1999) and it takes each pixel as a section of the picture, and then it makes image segmentation through graph theory finding the shortest distance. While in the aspect of interaction, the algorithm needs to sketch the approximate edge contour artificially, and uses artificial sketch edge to generate the shortest path. However, when the background texture is complex, multiple shortest paths may be generated to influence the final segmentation effect. In this case, additional relay points are needed to fit the shortest path to the contour of the target object. Therefore, it obtains a better segmentation effect, which virtually enhances the complexity of human-computer interaction process.

In order to improve the image segmentation results and interactive methods, many image segmentation methods turn to differentiate the foreground and background, such as GraphCut (Boykov and Jolly 2001; Greig et al. 1989) which is also an image segmentation method based on graph theory. Each pixel as a graph node, the algorithm maintains a global label, and the label is divided into two categories: the foreground and background; it uses maximum flow, shortest path method to maintain all the pixels of the label, the global optimization of the foreground label It can be used as the basis of image segmentation to complete the whole process of image segmentation. The purpose of interaction is to define the foreground and background as the initial parameters of maximum flow and shortest path. When the foreground and background texture are similar, GrabCut (Rother et al. 2004) is an extension of the GraphCut method that adds an iterative process to the GraphCut. GrabCut first determines the approximate range of the foreground and background by the human frame, initializing the foreground and background of the label, then each iteration is to re-calculate the weight of each edge of the graph. It uses new weights for the image segmentation algorithm, re-segmentation of the image, after several iterations, the image segmentation algorithm will gradually converge to a better result; GrabCut can also improve the segmentation results of irregular shapes of transitional edge objects by adding detail edge shapes.

There are some limitations in foreground background segmentation using maximum flow and shortest path algorithm of graph theory, including only one foreground object can be segmented, and interactive mode is inevitable to divide foreground background. In view of these problems, a variety of image segmentation algorithms are introduced into the interactive image segmentation method to improve the image segmentation effect and simplify the interactive mode. GrowCut (Vezhnevets and Konouchine 2005) is still focused on the division of the foreground and background, and it uses prospects, background tags as the basis for image segmentation; GrowCut uses cellular automata idea, before it starts the image segmentation by the user through the interaction of the target object position, outline and location of the background, as a foreground seed and background seed, through the growth of cellular automata, the user does not specify the pixels into the foreground or background. During the whole growth process, the foreground label and background tags are all completed, and the use of dual-tag can complete the target object segmentation. TouchCut (Wang et al. 2014) is a simple image segmentation method based on level set and interaction. TouchCut first requires the user to input the position of a target object. Through the edge information of the image and the GMM color model, scholars (Qiu et al. 2014) use the energy function of edges, textures and geometries to obtain the contours of the level set and then use the evolution of the level set to obtain the final target object segmentation. The super-pixel segmentation and merging approach are to achieve image segmentation; in the image preprocessing, it aims to complete the super-pixel segmentation and the initial merger, to add the object to determine the location and approximate shape of the line, the super-pixel is merged to complete the image segmentation process (Table 1).

**Table 1.**  Comparison of several methods

| Methods | Image segmentation method | Interactive mode |
|---|---|---|
| Intelligent paint | Based on areas | Draws the target contour |
| Intelligent scissors | Based on graph theory | Draws the target contour |
| GraphCut | Based on graph theory | Painting the background and simple outline |
| GrabCut | Based on graph theory | Frame and detail shapes |
| GrowCut | Cellular automata | Draw the target position and the contour line |
| TouchCut | Based on level sets | Draw the target location |
| LinedCut | Super-pixel segmentation | Draw the target location and shape |

As can be seen from the above description, interactive image segmentation methods are moving in the direction of more diverse image segmentation methods and simpler and more natural way of interaction. Amid which a class of methods such as the intelligent paint and intelligent scissors, in the present view, whether it is from the result of image segmentation or interactive mode of simplicity, both are unsatisfactory. In the graph-based interactive image segmentation method, GraphCut further applies the maximum flow and shortest path algorithm of graph theory in the image segmentation domain, and GrabCut obtains better results by iterative method. The interactive way is from drawing foreground background to drawing. It is more convenient to distinguish the foreground background from the earlier interactive segmentation methods. However, the image segmentation methods based on graph theory are not flexible enough. The only parameter is the weights between the graph nodes. The interaction can only provide foreground and background seed information. It is not suitable for image segmentation, and this method is more suitable for the classification problem of binary objects, that is, the classification of single object and background is not suitable for multi-target image segmentation (Vezhnevets and Konouchine 2005). GrowCut, and TouchCut use the cellular automata and level set methods to get the labels from the seed point growth iterations. LinedCut uses the method of super-pixel segmentation and merging for image segmentation. These methods are more suitable than the graph theory method for obtaining target object segmentation, but the interaction of multi-target segmentation will become more complex.

While except for that it does not apply to multi-objective image segmentation, the above methods, whether using the mouse or touch-based, are not able to get rid of the step that add interactive information manually. So, for the special cannot use the hand to add interactive information occasions, such as handicapped people, these methods are not able to adapt.

Thoughts to put forward this method:

In view of the above problems, this paper presents an interactive idea: when the viewer watches the images, they only need to watch the images naturally, without the need to add interactive information. When the viewer watches, the eye movement trajectory of the viewer is collected, The EEG signal is collected and processed to measure the attention of each point of interest. The attention is monitored by the attention, and the segmentation process of the image is monitored by the attention point.

The entire interactive image segmentation method uses the SLIC super-pixel segmentation (Achanta et al. 2012a) as the initial step; the eye tracker used to acquire the eye trajectory has an accuracy of 0.4° (Larivière et al. 2015), and the eye-tracking trajectory can be well used in the image compression field (Nguyen 2006). We use EEG signal as the supervisory information of eye movement trajectory, and we introduce the EEG signal as the monitoring information of eye movement trajectory, in which the alpha rhythmic wave is used to monitor the eye movement track. The alpha rhythmic wave (8–12 Hz) can be a good measure of the viewer's attention when viewing the image as the viewer focuses on the picture (Thut et al. 2006; Worden et al. 2000; Sauseng et al. 2005); by filtering the attention points and monitoring the merging process of ultra-pixels using the filtered points of interest, an interactive image segmentation method combining eye movement trajectories and EEG signals can be realized.

## 2  Methods

### 2.1  Data Acquisition and Data Set

The eye tracking device is the Tobii TX120 Eye Tracker, which can operate at 60 Hz or 120 Hz sampling rate; the EEG acquisition device uses NeuroSky's MindWave single-electrode device; the display is a 23-inch display with a resolution of 1920 * 1080; The NeuroSky SDK is developed under Windows environment. The device connection, device calibration, synchronous data acquisition and human - computer interaction is realized in C# language, and the image processing part such as super - pixel segmentation and merge is realized by C++ language.

## 2.2    Process

Combined EEG and eye movement data of the image segmentation system is mainly composed by two parallel processes. First, the target image is displayed to the user, and the eye movement tracker and the EEG synchronizer are used to collect the eye movement trajectory and the EEG signal of the user during the user viewing process. And then, it obtains the focus by processing the eye movement data and gets the attention by processing the EEG. The use of focus and attention is to obtain the interests points of users in the process of viewing images; While the user views the image, the other part of the system simultaneously makes super-pixel segmentation to the image, and then splits the good super-pixel block to optimize the merger to reduce the number of super-pixel block to facilitate the next super-pixel combination of computing time. After the completion of the super-pixel optimization, the part will wait for the end of the user's viewing process and the eye movement trajectory, and EEG signal pro-cessing. When the focus and attention calculation have been completed, it will merge users' super-pixel blocks interests by using optimized hyper-pixel block and attention information and the super-pixel blocks which are not interested by the user are removed, and the output image is the image object segmentation obtained by the user's eye movement trajectory and EEG signal (Fig. 1).

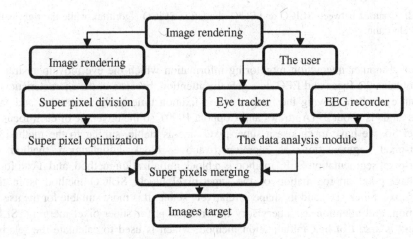

**Fig. 1.** Flow chart of image segmentation system combined with eye movement and EEG method

## 2.3    Core Algorithm

The core algorithm of the system is divided into three parts: super-pixel segmentation and optimization, simultaneous acquisition and joint analysis of EEG signals and eye movement signals, and super-pixel merging using interactive information monitoring to obtain the image segmentation of target objects (Fig. 2).

Super pixel segmentation as a starting point for the entire segmentation algorithm, it can obtain a basic similar block of pixels, that is the super-pixel. Because we use

**Fig. 2.** Contrast between SLICO and SLIC, the left is SLICO algorithm, while the right is the SLIC algorithm.

human-computer interaction monitoring information which the eye movement trajectory obtains the focus and EEG data gets the attention, because of the characteristics of human eye when viewing the image, whose fixation time is about 600 ms, and saccades angle is about 3° (Andrews and Coppola 1999), so the coverage of each focus is stable. So, we have to choose a super-pixel size as stable, similar to the method of super-pixel segmentation, as mentioned above, block initialization method of super-pixel segmentation SLIC method is a block initialization method, and it can form a square pixel approximation of the super-pixel block. SLICO method is in the super-pixel block size, and its shape is relatively stable. It is more suitable for the use of attention, and attention as supervisory information is for super-pixel merging. SLIC method is a sort of box initialization method, which is used to calculate the relative parameters automatically. The generated super-pixel blocks are more similar to regular polygons and are more regular. After contrast experiment, we find that the SLICO method is more regular, but it is not precise enough for small edge detection. SLIC method is to generate the shape of the super-pixel and sometimes it is not so neat but it has more accurate detection of small edges, so when we make super-pixel segmentation according to different images, it needs us to choose a different method.

The average size of each super-pixel block is calculated as the initial parameter of the super-pixel segmentation according to the characteristics of the human eye, the human-to-screen distance, the screen size, and the image size. The formula is as follows:

$$L = 2x^*\tan3°2x^*\tan3 \quad S1 = W^*H \quad n = S1/S$$

SLIC/SLICO is a Kmeans-based super-pixel segmentation method, so this method will eventually form an approximation to the initial set K value of the number of ultra-pixel block, but for large areas of similar color areas, such as the background, it is a solid color or close to a solid color texture, this method will be divided into many initialization box size of the background of the super-pixel size, similar objects in the color close to the object will be divided into an indefinite number of super pixels. These meaningless super-pixels block only merges with the complexity and time-consuming of subsequent super-pixel, so we need to optimize the merger of these meaningless super-pixel blocks. The general super-pixel merging mainly uses the greedy algorithm, but for the color texture complex image, it is difficult to determine a similarity threshold or a number of pixels' threshold. While for inappropriate threshold, belong to different objects or belong to the foreground background of the super pixel block maybe merged together to influence the effect of the final target object segmentation. Unlike the traditional greedy merge method, we use a clustering method that takes the BOC of each super-pixel block as a feature, since the color distribution of each super-pixel block is sparse, so it is easy to use clustering methods to super-pixel blocks merged into a small number of clusters, thus greatly reducing the number of super-pixel blocks.

We first obtain the BOC feature of the whole image according to the method of (Wengert et al. 2011), and then use Kmeans' clustering method to get the color dictionary, that is, several color feature vectors of the whole picture. The clusters are clustered by clustering centers. The color vector is also calculated for each super-pixel block, i.e. the BOC characteristics of each super-pixel block. Then we use each of the above-obtained super-pixel block vectors to do Kmeans clustering to several color vector centers of the whole image. Since the SLIC/SLICO method is a super-pixel segmentation in the CIE-Lab space, two points are in the Lab color space. The distance between them is the same as the distance between the two points in the European space. Therefore, the clustering process automatically classifies the adjacent hyper-pixel blocks into the same cluster, so after clustering, the super-pixel blocks with close vector distance are merged, so that the super-pixel blocks of different objects are not merged together, and the error merging caused by the greedy algorithm can be greatly reduced when the image color texture is complicated (Fig. 3).

The EEG signal is used as reference information of the eye movement trajectory to eliminate the inattention of the user during the process of viewing the image. That is to say, the EEG signal is processed to form the attention information synchronously with the eye movement trajectory.

EEG signal processing first uses short-time Fourier transform, and the short-time Fourier transform the main idea is to window the time-domain signal, and then windowed signal after Fourier transform to the frequency domain, time domain Window can be a very short period of time-domain signal extraction, the time window in the entire time domain sliding, you can get any location of the local spectrum, that is, the localization of the spectrum. Using the energy distribution of the local spectrum, we can obtain the energy amplitudes of $\alpha$ wave, $\theta$ wave and $\beta$ wave. A waves are thought to reflect the local excitability of the brain-related cortical areas (Kanwisher et al. 1997).

**Fig. 3.** Super-pixel contrast before and after the merger, the left side is the SLICO algorithm based on the size of the super-pixel block calculated by the super-pixel segmentation, the right is with the combination of color dictionary for the super-pixel block clustering optimization results, showing a significant number of super pixels cut back. (Color figure online)

Studies of $\theta$-waves and $\beta$-waves have shown that $\theta$ and $\beta$ waves can also produce amplitude changes under vision, (Raymond et al. 2005; Egner and Gruzelier 2004), which reflects the degree of excitement and attention of the brain under visual stimulation. The three-rhythm wave normalized to 0–100 between the uses of three rhythmic wave energies. Expressed concern about the level of the formula is as follows:

$$Att = \beta - \theta - 10 * \alpha$$

Where Att represents the attention of the viewer when viewing the image, i.e., the degree of attention is the particular point of interest in the image.

In the short-time Fourier transform, it needs to determine the width of the time window. In order to synchronize the points of interest and attention as closely as possible, it is necessary to make the frequency of the attention information as close as possible to the frequency of the attention information. In the above environment, the sampling rate of the TX120 eye tracker is 120 Hz or 60 Hz, and the sampling rate of MindWave is 1000 Hz. Set the global sampling rate in the system, eye tracker set the sampling rate in accordance with the global sampling rate, window width is set to w = 1000/rate, allows the rhythm wave frequency similar to the eye movement sampling rate, eye movement data Synchronization with EEG data.

While eye movement data is being collected, since the frequency has been adjusted to the same level as the eye movement data while the EEG data is being processed, the time between the eye movement data and the EEG data is removed with the time stamp while the eye movement data is acquired The eye movement data is synchronized with the EEG data, and the synchronized eye movement data is filtered according to the attention degree acquired by EEG data processing to remove eye movement data with insufficient attention.

Then, the eye movement data are divided into two categories, one is the fixation point and the other is the glance point. We consider that the eye movement point within $3°$ in 600 ms which is the same fixation point (Andrews and Coppola 1999). The eye movement point between the fixation points is a scanning trajectory. For the present system, the scanning of the target image does not help, so we only use the gaze as the target image of the monitoring data. The gaze center, the gaze time, and the number of eye movement points included in one gaze point can be calculated at the same time as the gaze point is divided,

$$R = (time/1000) * (L/2)$$

Obtaining the radius of interest, superimposing each circle of interest with the super-pixel block information, can obtain the attention by each super-pixel block, and if the pixel block is covered by only one fixation point, the pixel will be covered by the pixel. If the pixel block is covered by multiple fixation points, the fixation result will be the attention of the pixel block. The focus on below a certain threshold of ultra-pixel block removal is to retain the user to watch the process of attention and focus on the part of the focus, that is, the user is to watch the target object.

## 3   Results and Discussion

In this paper, we use the part of the BSDS300 image library to test our image segmentation method, and compared with the classic and better interactive image segmentation algorithm of Grubcut (Fig. 4).

It can be seen from the previous section that the interactive image segmentation method using eye movement trajectory combined with EEG signal processing as interactive is better than Grubcut in average. Single object segmentation has more advantages in multi-object segmentation, and the image segmentation method using the eye movement trajectory as the main interactive mode is satisfactory in the result (Fig. 5).

The interactive way of the traditional interactive image segmentation methods, whether it is crossed, frame or draw points, are inevitably added manually after viewing the interactive information, both in terms of speed or ease of interaction are not enough human. While eye movement trajectory as interactive information, only the user to view the image at the same time to collect the user's eye movement information and EEG information in the process of viewing the user to automatically get the interactive information, after viewing the image will be completed after the entire interactive image Segmentation process, from the interaction speed to the convenience of inter-action are far superior to the traditional interactive way. It can be said that this new interactive image segmentation method is more natural and more efficient.

**Fig. 4.** Compared effect with Grubcut

Traditional interactive methods cannot interact with each other in many special cases. In many situations where hand cannot be used, such as disabled persons or patients whose hands cannot work normally on the battlefield, traditional interactive image segmentation is degraded into a non-interactive method, and the use of eye movement can meet most of these needs, then the use of eye movement trajectory image segmentation method can also be applied naturally in many areas, such as the battlefield computer equipment, computer vision, paralysis, disabled after a simple training. By which, those people can achieve the use of computers, the network of new interactive means, real-world enhance (AR) realm more real content, faster and virtual content integration.

Confidence level of the traditional interaction cannot meet the needs in specific situations, such as the trial suspects want to know that the pictures are more concerned about the target object to provide ideas for the detection of cases, the use of traditional interaction is clearly not easy to obtain real attention to the target object. But with the eye track as the main interactive way, combined with EEG signal as the auxiliary monitoring information, you can effectively get the image in the view of the real concern to the target object.

**Fig. 5.** Results

## 4  Conclusion

In this paper, an interactive image segmentation method that does not require additional hands-on interaction by the viewer is realized. The eye movement trajectory and the EEG signal acquired by the observer at the same time are all interactive information in the image segmentation. It is difficult for the observer to add fake supervisory information in the tracking of eye movements and EEG signals. In the case of suspect interrogation, it is necessary to divide the image into real images. This method can segment the object with one or several viewers at the same time in one viewing process, which can effectively solve the problem of traditional interactive image segmentation system in multi-object segmentation, or in the costs to pay time or the complexity of the problem of interaction.

**Acknowledgments.** This work is supported by the NSFC Key Program (91520202), and General Program (61375116). This work is also supported by Beijing Advanced Innovation Center For Future Education with grant No. BJAICFE2016IR-003.

# References

Vezhnevets, V., Konouchine, V.: GrowCut: interactive multi-label ND image segmentation by cellular automata. In: Proceedings of Graphicon, vol. 1, pp. 150–156 (2005)

Hernández-Vela, A., Hernández-Vela, A., Primo, C., et al.: Automatic user interaction correction via multi-label graph cuts. In: 2011 IEEE International Conference on Computer Vision Workshops (ICCV Workshops), pp. 1276–1281. IEEE (2011)

Veksler, O., Boykov, Y., Mehrani, P.: Superpixels and supervoxels in an energy optimization framework. In: Daniilidis, K., Maragos, P., Paragios, N. (eds.) ECCV 2010. LNCS, vol. 6315, pp. 211–224. Springer, Heidelberg (2010). doi:10.1007/978-3-642-15555-0_16

Harley, K., Reese, E.: Origins of autobiographical memory. Dev. Psychol. **35**(5), 1338 (1999)

Mortensen, E.N., Barrett, W.A.: Toboggan-based intelligent scissors with a four-parameter edge model. In: IEEE Computer Society Conference on Computer Vision and Pattern Recognition, vol. 2, pp. 452–458. IEEE (1999)

Boykov, Y.Y., Jolly, M.P.: Interactive graph cuts for optimal boundary & region segmentation of objects in ND images. In: Proceedings of Eighth IEEE International Conference on Computer Vision, ICCV 2001, vol. 1, pp. 105–112. IEEE (2001)

Rother, C., Kolmogorov, V., Blake, A.: Grabcut: interactive foreground extraction using iterated graph cuts. In: ACM Transactions on Graphics (TOG), vol. 23, no. 3, pp. 309–314. ACM (2004)

Wang, T., Han, B., Collomosse, J.: Touchcut: fast image and video segmentation using single-touch interaction. Comput. Vis. Image Underst. **120**, 14–30 (2014)

Ablikim, M., Achasov, M.N., Albayrak, O., et al.: Observation of a charged charmoniumlike structure in e + e − →(D* D⁻*) ± π∓ at s = 4.26 GeV. Phys. Rev. Lett. **112**(13), 132001 (2014)

Achanta, R., Shaji, A., Smith, K., et al.: SLIC superpixels compared to state-of-the-art superpixel methods. IEEE Trans. Pattern Anal. Mach. Intell. **34**(11), 2274–2282 (2012)

Thut, G., Nietzel, A., Brandt, S.A., et al.: α-Band electroencephalographic activity over occipital cortex indexes visuospatial attention bias and predicts visual target detection. J. Neurosci. **26**(37), 9494–9502 (2006)

Worden, M.S., Foxe, J.J., Wang, N., et al.: Anticipatory biasing of visuospatial attention indexed by retinotopically specific-band electroencephalography increases over occipital cortex. J. Neurosci. **20**(RC63), 1–6 (2000)

Sauseng, P., Klimesch, W., Stadler, W., et al.: A shift of visual spatial attention is selectively associated with human EEG alpha activity. Eur. J. Neurosci. **22**(11), 2917–2926 (2005)

Larivière, V., Haustein, S., Mongeon, P.: The oligopoly of academic publishers in the digital era. PLoS ONE **10**(6), e0127502 (2015)

Stankovich, S., Dikin, D.A., Dommett, G.H.B., et al.: Graphene-based composite materials. Nature **442**(7100), 282–286 (2006)

Andrews, T.J., Coppola, D.M.: Idiosyncratic characteristics of saccadic eye movements when viewing different visual environments. Vis. Res. **39**(17), 2947–2953 (1999)

Wengert, C., Douze, M., Jégou, H.: Bag-of-colors for improved image search. In: Proceedings of the 19th ACM International Conference on Multimedia, pp. 1437–1440. ACM (2011)

Kanwisher, N., McDermott, J., Chun, M.M.: The fusiform face area: a module in human extrastriate cortex specialized for face perception. J. Neurosci. **17**(11), 4302–4311 (1997)

Raymond, J., Varney, C., Parkinson, L.A., et al.: The effects of alpha/theta neurofeedback on personality and mood. Cogn. Brain. Res. **23**(2), 287–292 (2005)

Egner, T., Gruzelier, J.H.: EEG biofeedback of low beta band components: frequency-specific effects on variables of attention and event-related brain potentials. Clin. Neurophysiol. **115**(1), 131–139 (2004)

# Eye Tracking in Augmented Cognition

# Geometry and Gesture-Based Features from Saccadic Eye-Movement as a Biometric in Radiology

Folami T. Alamudun[1,2(✉)], Tracy Hammond[1,2], Hong-Jun Yoon[1],
and Georgia D. Tourassi[1]

[1] Biomedical Sciences, Engineering, and Computing Group,
Oak Ridge National Laboratory, Oak Ridge, TN 37831, USA
{yoonh,tourassig,alamudunft}@ornl.gov, hammond@cs.tamu.edu
[2] Sketch Recognition Lab, Department of Computer Science and Engineering,
Texas A&M University, College Station, TX 77843, USA
http://www.ornl.gov/bsec, http://srl.tamu.edu

**Abstract.** In this study, we present a novel application of sketch gesture recognition on eye-movement for biometric identification and estimating task expertise. The study was performed for the task of mammographic screening with simultaneous viewing of four coordinated breast views as typically done in clinical practice. Eye-tracking data and diagnostic decisions collected for 100 mammographic cases (25 normal, 25 benign, 50 malignant) and 10 readers (three board certified radiologists and seven radiology residents), formed the corpus for this study. Sketch gesture recognition techniques were employed to extract geometric and gesture-based features from saccadic eye-movements. Our results show that saccadic eye-movement, characterized using sketch-based features, result in more accurate models for predicting individual identity and level of expertise than more traditional eye-tracking features.

**Keywords:** Eye-tracking · Biometrics · Sketch recognition · Mammography

## 1 Introduction

Survival of *breast cancer* disease is largely dependent on early detection through the annually recommended mammographic screening process. Studies show that

F.T. Alamudun—This manuscript has been authored by UT-Battelle, LLC under Contract No. DE-AC05-00OR22725 with the U.S. Department of Energy. The United States Government retains and the publisher, by accepting the article for publication, acknowledges that the United States Government retains a non-exclusive, paid-up, irrevocable, world-wide license to publish or reproduce the published form of this manuscript, or allow others to do so, for United States Government purposes. The Department of Energy will provide public access to these results of federally sponsored research in accordance with the DOE Public Access Plan (http://energy.gov/downloads/doe-public-access-plan).

D.D. Schmorrow and C.M. Fidopiastis (Eds.): AC 2017, Part I, LNAI 10284, pp. 123–138, 2017.
DOI: 10.1007/978-3-319-58628-1_11

through early detection, while the disease is localized, patients have a 98.5% relative survival rate in comparison to a 25% survival rate when the cancer is metastasized; a point at which the disease becomes incurable [42].

The timely detection of breast cancer is made possible through a process known as mammographic cancer screening. Mammographic screening is a specialized examination of X-ray images of interior breast tissues by a trained radiologist. Achieving expertise in radiology requires specialized training, which consists of 5–7 years of Radiology residency and fellowship, and years of experience during which the practitioner develops an *intuition* for the task. Expert radiologists exhibit notably outstanding characteristics, such as increased speed and higher overall accuracy with which he/she makes decisions on the pathology of an image, which differentiate them from non-experts. However, the length of training, and the specific nature and duration experience necessary to achieve expertise has been the subject of much research in medical imaging [5, 23, 30].

Although the exact relationship between experience and expertise remains unclear, one approach to establishing a quantitative relationship between the two, within the context of mammography, is through identifying differences in visual search behavior between experts and non-expert image readers [23, 30]. In a study of six image readers (board certified radiologists and Radiology residents), Krupinski [22] compared cumulative cluster dwell times on 20 mammographic cases between experience groups. A comparison of the median values for experienced and inexperienced image readers revealed that experienced readers tend to have shorter dwell times. Their findings suggest that temporal measures of visual search behavior may be important factors in differentiating experience level of image readers.

Kundel et al. [25] evaluated the eye-movements of 24 subjects, which included laymen, medical students, and experienced radiologists while viewing normal and abnormal chest radiographs. They reported an evolution of observers' scanpaths from the localized central patterns of first-year medical students to the circumferential patterns of the experienced radiologist. They noted that, in addition to the distinct nature of experienced radiologists' scanning patterns, experienced radiologists also moved their eyes to the target faster and were more accurate at interpreting what they saw. Kundel and LaFolette's findings suggest that *geometric properties* of scanning patterns formed during visual search may be important factors in differentiating between experienced and inexperienced image readers.

To investigate human factors associated with proficiency of diagnostic pathology, Krupinski et al. [24] conducted a study examining the eye-movement of nine image readers of varied experience level (medical students, Pathology residents, and pathologists). They reported that, when compared with Radiology residents and medical students, experienced pathologists exhibited longer saccades on average (measured in seconds). A similar trend was noted when comparing medical students Radiology residents.

In addition, they reported that the average saccade velocity for experienced pathologists was lower in comparison with Radiology residents, who's average velocity was higher than those recorded for medical students. They noted that the decreasing trend in saccade velocity with years of experience was consistent within the experienced pathology group (board certified pathologists), with the more experienced pathologists exhibiting a significantly lower average saccade velocity than the less experienced pathologists. Krupinski et al.'s findings suggest that distance and velocity measures of eye-movement during visual search in diagnostic pathology may also be important factors in differentiating between experienced and inexperienced readers.

In this paper, we describe a novel application of sketch gesture recognition to extract discriminative information from eye-tracking data for the purpose of user identification and for determination of task proficiency in Radiology. The remainder of this paper is organized as follows. Section 2 provides a general introduction to the domain of sketch recognition along with related. Section 2 also covers related work in eye movement-based biometric identification. Section 3 describes our experimental procedure and data processing methods. Section 4 presents the results from our experiments. Section 5 gives a brief discussion of results followed by conclusions (Sect. 6) and acknowledgements respectively.

## 2 Related Work

### 2.1 Sketch Gesture Recognition

Sketch is considered a natural form of communication involving free form shapes, letters, and numbers, which encode contextual meaning. Sketches can be considered as a special class of gestures. The fundament in sketch recognition involves encoding patterns contained within a sketch gesture in a manner, which permits accurate interpretation and inference based on the intent of the author of the sketch gesture [16]. The domain of sketch recognition utilizes machine intelligence to capture and interpret intent of the author making the sketch gestures. The correct interpretation of gesture intent enables the integration of sketch gestures in user interface systems, which in turn enables intelligent manipulation and computation on the recognized input.

There are numerous algorithmic contributions to general artificial intelligence from the domain of sketch recognition. The majority of sketch recognition algorithms fall into one of three broad categories: geometry-based algorithms [34], vision-based (appearance-based) recognition algorithms [20,32], and gesture-based (motion-based) algorithms [27,40], or hybrid combinations of these [7].

Geometry-based algorithms apply geometric relationships and constraints to describe primitive (basic) shapes, which combine to form recognizable high-level shapes [34]. Appearance-based recognition algorithms rely on the appearance of a sketched shape; ignoring timing and ordering constraints of data points [38]. These algorithms rely on recognition techniques, such as template-matching, on the snapshot of a sketched shape to distinguish between shapes [20,32]. Gesture-based (motion-based) recognition algorithms rely primarily on the path of motion of a strokes that make up a sketch shape. Gesture-based algorithms characterize shapes based on how individual strokes are drawn (the path of each stroke) in contrast with the shape of the stroke, even though the latter can be correlated. These types of algorithms were initially conceptualized for identification of a small set of application-specific gesture commands [27,40]. Rubine [40] developed a pen input gesture-based recognition system (GRANDMA), which enabled recognition of single stroke gestures through simple trainable linear classifiers. In this work, Rubine proposed and evaluated 13 features for classifying ten different gesture datasets, each containing 15 classes, and reported an average accuracy of 98%. In a followup work, Long et al. [27] proposed 11 additional features to those developed by Rubine.

Sketch recognition algorithms were previously applied to solve challenging pattern recognition problems in other domains [14,26,43]. Dixon and Hammond in 2010 [9,15] and Pramanik and Bhattacharjee in 2012 [36] applied sketch recognition algorithms to identify faces in images from sketched drawings. They reported an average of 86% similarity with the top five matches using their method, which was significantly higher than averages from the two alternatives presented (eigenface: 43%, and sketch transform method: 80%).

Cig and Sezgin [6] developed a eye-movement interaction system, which interprets eye-movement patterns as auxiliary commands to augment pen-based gestures as a mode selection mechanism (drag, minimize, scroll etc.) during sketch interaction. Their results demonstrated that manipulation commands can be recognized with 88% accuracy using natural gaze behavior during pen interactions. In [32], Ouyang and Davis presented a robust, multiple domain sketch recognition system, which uses vision based decomposition methods to classify hand-drawn symbols. Their system represented symbols as a set of feature images, in contrast to geometric or temporally ordered data points. These image features capture properties of the constituent strokes in a sketch symbol, such as orientation and the location of end points.

More advanced systems [13,45] are able to identify high-level shapes by using geometry-based algorithms to characterize its constituent low-level shapes. Valentine et al. developed *Mechanix*, an intelligent, interactive, on-line tutoring system, which allows engineering students to enter planar truss and free-body diagram solutions to homework problems [45]. The work reported in this paper does not represent the first time sketch-based features have been applied to human motions other than pen [2,29,33], but it is the first time they have been applied to characterize eye-movement.

### 2.2   Eye-Movement as a Biometric

Biometrics refer to authentication techniques, which rely on easily verifiable physical characteristics of an individual. Biometric *identifiers* are categorized as measurable physiological and behavioral properties of the individual. Physiological characteristics are measures related to some property of the physical body, which include fingerprint, footprint, palmprint, palm veins, face, DNA, iris, and retina. Behavioral characteristics are measures specific the behavior of a person (behaviometrics), which include typing cadence, gait, hand-writing, and voice. Eye-movements do not easily lend themselves to forgery, since they are largely dependent on brain activity and extra-ocular muscle characteristics, which are *unique* to the individual not unlike the biomechanics of walking (gait). This property makes eye-movement an attractive option for biometric identification.

In a previous work, Noton and Stark [31] observed that individuals tend to repeat certain scanpath trajectories during repeated viewings of a given pattern. In their experiments, they tested this theory, coined *scanpath theory*, and found that the general scanpath for a subject during a first viewing of a pattern was repeated in initial eye-movements of approximately two-thirds (65%) of subsequent viewings. In addition, Noton and Stark observed that the scanpath produced by an individual for a given stimulus pattern was unique and varied for each subject [31]. These findings were also supported by subsequent research in reading related information processing [39,41].

Eye-movements were first explored as a potential biometric identifier in [21]. In this work, Kasprowski and Ober used a combination of eye reaction time (the period of time between introduction of stimulus and eye reaction), and stabilization time (the time taken for the eye to fixate on a new location after stimulus), as features for a predictive model. Using data from nine subjects, they reported a best average false acceptance rate of 1.48% achieved with a k-nearest neighbor classifier (k = 3).

Subsequently, researchers explored various eye-movement measures including: gaze trajectory [8,11], gaze velocity [46], and pupil size [3] with reasonable success. Galdi et al. developed a gaze analysis (GAS) soft-biometric based on user behavior during observation of particular objects such as facial images [11]. The GAS system constructs a user profile using a fixed area of interest-based feature vector, which is computed using the order-independent cumulative duration of fixations on the respective area of interest. The system was tested on 88 subjects and gave encouraging results on user identification by computing the profile with the lowest Euclidean distance from the test sample.

Yoon et al. explored gaze as a biometric by examining the scanpath of 12 subjects viewing 50 images of patterns with varied spatial characteristics. They modeled gaze velocity using Hidden Markov Models to create unique profiles for each subject. Using a leave-one-out cross-validation scheme, they reported an average performance accuracy in user identification ranging between 53% and 76% [46].

Holland and Oleg evaluated eye movement-based metrics as a feature for biometric identification. They recorded eye-movements while subjects performed a challenging reading task. From the recorded data, they extracted eye-tracking features and scanpath measures including: fixation count, fixation duration, saccade amplitude and velocity. Applying an information fusion method, they combined these features and reported a 27% error rate in a subject identification task [18].

## 3    Materials and Methods

### 3.1    Image Dataset

For the proposed study, we selected 100 screen-film mammograms from a corpus of mammographic images, digitized using a high resolution LUMISYS scanner (50 m per pixel, 12 bit), sourced from the University of South Floridas Digital

Database for Screening Mammography (DDSM) [17]. Each case provided by the DDSM database is accompanied by associated patient information, the cranio-caudal (CC) and the mediolateral oblique (MLO) view mammographic images of both the left and the right breasts. Abnormal cases are accompanied by dupli-cate images containing pixel level ground truth markings of abnormalities, and ground truth subtlety values using the BI-RADS$^{TM}$ lexicon [37] established via biopsy, additional imaging, or two-year follow-up. The selected set included clin-ically actionable cases covering a broad range of mass margin and shape char-acteristics. Of the 100 selected cases, 50 cases included biopsy-proven malignant masses, 25 cases included biopsy-proven benign masses, and the remaining 25 cases were normal as determined during a 2-year cancer-free follow-up patient evaluation. A description of the images used in our experiments are provided in greater detail in a previous publication [1].

### 3.2   Experimental Procedure

Ten readers with varied levels of expertise (Radiology residents and board cer-tified radiologists) were recruited from an academic institution to conduct a blind review of the selected mammograms for this study. Each reader was out-fitted with an H6 headmounted eye-tracking device developed by Applied Sci-ence Laboratories (ASL, Bedford, MA, USA). Readers were then presented with the selected mammographic images on medical grade monitors (dual-head 5MP mammo-grade Totoku LCD monitors calibrated to the DICOM display stan-dard), and asked to report on location and provide a corresponding BI-RADS$^{TM}$ rating of any suspicious mass through a graphical user interface (GUI) custom designed for this experiment. A more detailed overview of the study participants, software and hardware, and the experimental protocol is provided in greater detail in a previous publication [1].

### 3.3   Eye-Movement Detection

Eye-movements refer to voluntary and involuntary change in the configuration of the eyes, which help the subject to acquire, fixate or track visual stimuli. The movement of the human eye is controlled by pairs of muscles, who's combined and coordinated effect (depicted in Fig. 1) is responsible for horizontal (yaw), vertical (pitch), and torsional (roll) eye-movements, respectively; enabling them to control the three-dimensional orientation of the eye.

Three antagonistic pairs of muscles: the lateral and medial rectus muscles, the superior and inferior rectus muscles, and the superior and inferior oblique mus-cles, are responsible for the characteristic eye-movements (illustrated in Fig. 1) along different axes: horizontal adduction toward the nose or abduction away from it, vertical elevation or depression, and intorsion or extorsion movements that bring the top of the eye toward or away from the nose respectively.

According to Donders law [44], orientation uniquely determines the direction of gaze independent of how the eye was previously orientated. Large sections of the brain control the eye muscles to direct gaze to the desired location in space. Humans primarily engage in seven types of voluntary and involuntary

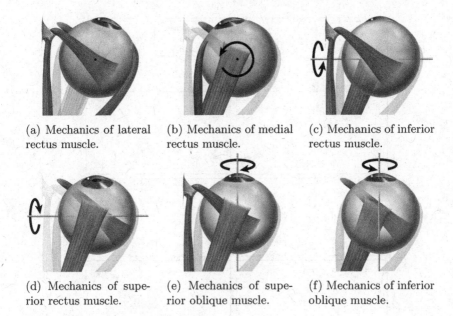

(a) Mechanics of lateral rectus muscle.

(b) Mechanics of medial rectus muscle.

(c) Mechanics of inferior rectus muscle.

(d) Mechanics of superior rectus muscle.

(e) Mechanics of superior oblique muscle.

(f) Mechanics of inferior oblique muscle.

**Fig. 1.** Superior view of muscles responsible for horizontal (yaw), vertical (pitch), and torsional (roll) eye-movements (From Lynch [28]).

eye-movement: fixation, saccade, glissade, smooth pursuit, microsaccade, tremor, and drift [19]. From eye-tracking data recorded from each reader while reviewing the four mammographic images across two monitors, we extracted fixations and saccades.

A fixation refers to a state in which the eyes remain relatively still (or within a minute spatial radius) over a period of time, such as when the eyes pause on a given word while reading text. The rapid motion of the eye from one fixation to another (such as from one word to another while reading text) is known as a *saccade*. Saccades are considered the fastest movement the body can produce; typically taking 30–80 ms to complete. An important peculiarity of saccades is that they rarely take the shortest path between two points, but instead undergo one of several (often suboptimal) paths resulting in *shapes* and *curvatures* Fig. 2.

Although there is no universally excepted method for computing fixations, there are parameters based on eye physiology, which permit a reasonable criteria for approximating fixations from gaze data. To identify fixations, we computed the average $x$ and $y$ coordinates for gaze points measured over a period of time during which the point-of-gaze continuously remains within an area (approximately 1° visual angle) for a minimum amount of time (approximately 100 ms for our algorithm). Since saccades are described in terms of the gaze data between fixations, we computed saccadic events as gaze points connecting the completion of one fixation to the beginning of the next fixation. Saccadic movements between

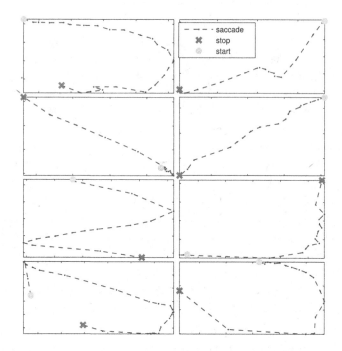

**Fig. 2.** Sample saccade recorded during a mammographic reading.

displays (jumping from one screen to the other), thus between mammographic image views, were excluded from our analysis.

### 3.4 Gesture-Based and Geometry-Based Features

Once fixation and saccadic events were computed, we applied feature extraction algorithms developed for sketch recognition to characterize the *shape* and *curvature* of individual saccadic movements. Since gaze scanpath is an aggregate shape consisting of individual saccadic movements, aggregating features extracted from saccadic movements will, in principle, provide an accurate characterization of the scanpath (Fig. 3).

Gesture-based features are dependent on how individual strokes are drawn (i.e. the path of each stroke) in contrast to the final geometric shape of the stroke, although the latter can be correlated. For this reason, gesture-based features contain subtle user-dependent variations, which are useful in differentiating between users [10]. Based on work by Rubine [40], Long et al. [27], and Paulson et al. [35], we extracted 29 gesture-based and vision-based features, which were previously demonstrated as being efficiently computable in real-time given a large input size, robust to noise, and capable of encoding semantically meaningful and discriminative information about shapes.

Drawing inspiration from work by Ouyang and Davis [32], we computed an orientation based feature, which captures the direction of the scanpath. The

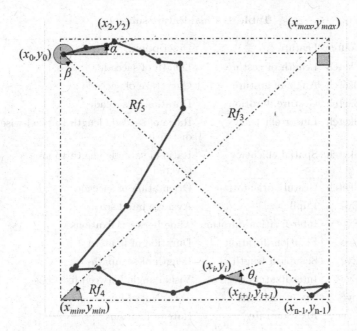

**Fig. 3.** Rubine's features capture properties associated with the shape a sample saccade from mammographic reading.

intuition behind this feature is the tendency of the readers' gaze scanpath to follow a specific direction indicating individual behavioral adaptations resulting in a preferred direction for scanning an image. This value is computed as an aggregate of point to point directionality of constituent gaze points in a saccade mapped to one of 12 angles indicating the cardinal direction.

## 4    Analysis and Results

In this section, we present performance results of sketch-based eye-movement features on two tasks: predicting reader identity, and predicting reader expertise. For comparison purposes, we examined the performance results of traditional eye-tracking features on the same set of tasks. For both sets of features, we first performed feature subset selection to reduce dimensionality of feature representation.

First, since the dependent variable (reader identity) is nominal, features were ranked using a combination of model-based, information gain ratio-based, and correlation-based ranking. To compute the model-based ranking, a k-nearest neighbor classifier was trained (one per feature) on a randomly selected training and test subset to predict the identity of each reader.

Information gain ($IG$) measures the expected reduction in entropy resulting from a partitioning of a dataset based on the values of a given feature. However, $IG$ is not normalized and can therefore be biased in favor of large-valued features.

**Table 1.** Final feature subsets.

| No. | Source | Feature | Description |
|-----|--------|---------|-------------|
| s8 | Sketch | Length of gesture | Length of saccade |
| s10 | Sketch | Angle of gesture | Curvature of saccade |
| s12 | Sketch | Gesture duration | Duration of saccade |
| s17 | Sketch | Linear efficiency | Ratio of saccade length to pixel-wise distance |
| s18 | Sketch | Spatial efficiency | Ratio of saccade length to area covered |
| s30 | Sketch | Gesture orientation | Orientation of saccade |
| f1 | Eye | Pupil size | Average pupil size |
| f2 | Eye | Inter-fixation duration | Time between fixations |
| f3 | Eye | Fixation duration | Duration of fixation |
| f4 | Eye | Scanpath length | Length of scanpath |
| f5 | Eye | Inter-fixation degree | Visual angle between fixations |
| f6 | Eye | No. of fixations | Total No. of fixations |
| f7 | Eye | Fixation rate | Rate of fixations |

For this reason, we employ the information gain ratio to obtain a gain ratio-based rank for each feature. The information gain ratio ($IGR$) resolves the limitations of $IG$ by taking the number and size of partitions into account when choosing an attribute, thereby reducing bias towards large-valued attributes.

Next, the ten highest ranked features were selected by combining the gain ratio-based and model-based ranking methods. The final feature set was further reduced by eliminating highly correlated features. Table 1 provides the final subset of features from both the sketch-based features and the traditional eye-tracking features.

We then evaluated the efficacy of both feature subsets by training a Random Forest classifier [4] using a k-fold cross-validation scheme ($k = 10$). For each fold, a 90% of the cases were set aside for training the model, and the remainder 10% was utilized for model evaluation. Note that for each fold, identical cases (identified by case id) were selected from each reader for model training and evaluation. The aggregated (mean) predictive value over all $k$ folds served as the final performance evaluation for the predictive model. All training and testing evaluations were performed using $WEKA$ software package [12]; an open source machine learning software for building and testing predictive models.

## 4.1  Predicting Reader Identity

To test the effectiveness of sketch-based features on a biometric identification, we developed a between-subject predictive model using a Random Forest classifier evaluated using a k-fold cross-validation partitioning scheme ($k = 10$)

**Table 2.** Performance metrics (*F-score*) for sketch-based and traditional eye-tracking features for biometric identification task.

| Reader | Sketch | Eye-tracking | ZeroR |
|--------|--------|--------------|-------|
| N1 | 0.94 | 0.75 | 0.1 |
| N2 | 0.88 | 0.74 | 0.1 |
| N3 | 0.9 | 0.66 | 0.1 |
| A1 | 0.87 | 0.59 | 0.1 |
| A2 | 0.87 | 0.65 | 0.1 |
| A3 | 0.92 | 0.64 | 0.1 |
| A4 | 0.95 | 0.86 | 0.1 |
| E1 | 0.87 | 0.8 | 0.1 |
| E2 | 0.88 | 0.7 | 0.1 |
| E3 | 0.84 | 0.62 | 0.1 |
| Avg. | 0.89 | 0.7 | 0.1 |

**Table 3.** Confusion matrix for sketch-based features for biometric identification task.

| ACTUAL | PREDICTED | | | | | | | | | |
|--------|-----|-----|-----|-----|-----|-----|-----|----|----|----|
| | NR1 | NR2 | NR3 | AR1 | AR2 | AR3 | AR4 | E1 | E2 | E3 |
| NR1 | 93 | 1 | 0 | 2 | 0 | 1 | 0 | 0 | 0 | 3 |
| NR2 | 0 | 90 | 1 | 1 | 1 | 0 | 3 | 4 | 0 | 0 |
| NR3 | 2 | 0 | 91 | 3 | 0 | 0 | 3 | 0 | 0 | 1 |
| AR1 | 1 | 2 | 0 | 94 | 0 | 0 | 0 | 0 | 1 | 2 |
| AR2 | 2 | 0 | 1 | 2 | 83 | 3 | 0 | 2 | 2 | 5 |
| AR3 | 4 | 3 | 0 | 1 | 3 | 89 | 0 | 0 | 0 | 0 |
| AR4 | 0 | 1 | 0 | 2 | 0 | 0 | 96 | 1 | 0 | 0 |
| E1 | 1 | 2 | 2 | 0 | 0 | 0 | 0 | 85 | 7 | 3 |
| E2 | 0 | 1 | 1 | 3 | 2 | 0 | 0 | 8 | 85 | 0 |
| E3 | 3 | 1 | 3 | 4 | 1 | 0 | 0 | 2 | 3 | 83 |

as previously described. Multiple ($k$) rounds of cross-validation were performed using different partitions, and the validation results were averaged over all rounds in to reduce variability. As a baseline, we include the results of a majority classifier (ZeroR). A ZeroR classifier is a simple majority rule classifier, which classifies all input test samples as the majority or modal class independent of feature values of the input sample. In Table 2, we report *F-score* (the harmonic mean of precision and recall) performance metrics for the biometric identification task using sketch-based features. For comparison purposes, Table 2 also includes performance metrics using eye-tracking features for the same task. The confusion matrix provided in Table 3 illustrates the instances of error when predicting the actual class label for the sketch-based models.

## 4.2   Predicting Reader Expertise

We grouped each of the 10 participating readers into one of three experience levels: new trainee resident (NR), advanced trainee resident (AR), and expert radiologist (E). Next, utilizing a similar cross-validation partitioning scheme, we evaluated the efficacy of sketch-based features in predicting the experience level (expertise) of each reader. In Table 4, we report *F-score* performance metrics for the reader expertise prediction task using sketch-based features and include the performance of eye-tracking features for the same task for comparison. The confusion matrix provided in Table 5 illustrates the instances of error when predicting the actual class label for the sketch-based models.

**Table 4.** Performance metrics (*F-score*) for sketch-based and eye-tracking features for reader expertise prediction task.

| Class | Sketch | Eye-tracking | ZeroR |
|-------|--------|--------------|-------|
| NR    | 0.9    | 0.77         | 0.4   |
| AR    | 0.93   | 0.8          | 0.4   |
| E     | 0.91   | 0.83         | 0.4   |
| Avg.  | 0.91   | 0.8          | 0.4   |

**Table 5.** Confusion matrix of predictive model for reader expertise using sketch-based features from eye-movement.

| ACTUAL | | PREDICTED | | |
|--------|----|-----|-----|-----|
|        |    | NR  | AR  | E   |
|        | NR | 270 | 17  | 13  |
|        | AR | 15  | 370 | 15  |
|        | E  | 15  | 13  | 272 |

## 5   Discussion

The final set of features (see Table 1) include four measures related to motion: the orientation, duration, length, and rotational change of the shape formed by the saccade, and two measures of visual appearance: ratio of saccade length to overall size (*s16*), and the ratio of saccade length to the actual inter-fixation distance (*s17*). The highest ranked feature, saccade orientation, explains the tendency of the image readers' saccadic scanpath to follow a specific direction. We speculate that this feature captures coordinated muscle movements resulting from adaptations of repetitive behavior over time, which are specific to the individual. This observation is not unlike the uniqueness of the biomechanics of walking (gait). However, more detailed studies and experimental data is required to validate this speculative statement.

Previous studies in mammography have identified some measures of direction, duration, and lengths of saccadic movements as containing discriminative information about the experience in radiology [24,25,30]. Intuitively, both density metrics ($s16$ and $s17$) capture the spatial efficiency of the saccadic movements. While $s16$ measures the linear efficiency of the scanpath, $s17$ measures the two-dimensional spatial efficiency of the scanpath. Both features give a piecewise decomposition of the geometric properties of the scanpath formed by the image reader during the screening process. Previous studies have suggested that measures of overall scanpath formed during the viewing of a mammographic case are related to the individual and experience [25,31]. The scanpath has also been studied as a biometric for individual identification under varied image viewing conditions unrelated to mammography [18,46]. To the best of our knowledge, these features were never applied in predictive models as biometric identifiers or for predicting experience level. Additionally, the characterization using gesture recognition methods have never been explored until now.

# 6 Conclusions

In this study, we proposed and evaluated two methods for extracting features, which contain discriminative information about the identity and the level of expertise of a radiologist in screening mammography. These features characterize changes in positional and non-positional measures of eye-movement. First, we applied sketch recognition algorithms to extract gesture and geometry-based features from eye-tracking data. These features give a fine-grained characterization of the scanpath by aggregating the spatial (shape), directional, and kinetic properties of individual saccadic movements. We compared the effectiveness of these sketch-based features with more traditional metrics from eye-tracking.

Using a corpus of eye-movement and pupillary data from 100 mammographic cases reviewed by ten readers of varied experience level, recorded under clinically equivalent experimental conditions, the findings presented in this study establishes the following generalizable trends:

1. During the mammographic screening task, positional and non-positional measures of changes in the eye can provide sufficient discriminative information about the identity of an image reader.
2. Positional and non-positional measures of changes in the eye provide sufficient discriminative characterization of the readers' level of expertise for a given task (mammographic screening).
3. Both positional and non-positional measures perform significantly better than random chance at predicting the readers' identity and level of expertise.
4. Sketch-based features of eye-movement result in more accurate predictive models when compared with more traditional eye-tracking features.

**Acknowledgement.** This material is based upon work supported by the U.S. Department of Energy and the Office of Science under contract number DE-AC05-00OR22725. The authors also thank Kathleen B. Hudson, MD, and Garnetta Morin-Ducote, MD for contributions during data collection.

# References

1. Alamudun, F., Yoon, H.J., Hudson, K.B., Morin-Ducote, G., Hammond, T., Tourassi, G.D.: Fractal analysis of visual search activity for mass detection during mammographic screening. Med. Phys. (2017). http://dx.doi.org/10.1002/mp. 12100

2. Bartley, J., Forsyth, J., Pendse, P., Xin, D., Brown, G., Hagseth, P., Agrawal, A., Goldberg, D.W., Hammond, T.: World of workout: a contextual mobile RPG to encourage long term fitness. In: Proceedings of the 2nd ACM SIGSPATIAL International Workshop on the Use of GIS in Public Health, pp. 60–67. ACM (2013)

3. Bednarik, R., Kinnunen, T., Mihaila, A., Fränti, P.: Eye-movements as a biometric. In: Kalviainen, H., Parkkinen, J., Kaarna, A. (eds.) SCIA 2005. LNCS, vol. 3540, pp. 780–789. Springer, Heidelberg (2005). doi:10.1007/11499145_79

4. Breiman, L.: Random forests. Mach. Learn. **45**(1), 5–32 (2001)

5. Chi, M.T., Glaser, R., Farr, M.J.: The Nature of Expertise. Psychology Press, Park Drive (2014)

6. Çığ, Ç., Sezgin, T.M.: Gaze-based prediction of pen-based virtual interaction tasks. Int. J. Hum.-Comput. Stud. **73**, 91–106 (2015). http://www.sciencedirect.com/ science/article/pii/S1071581914001244

7. Corey, P., Hammond, T.: Gladder: combining gesture and geometric sketch recognition. In: Proceedings of the 23rd National Conference on Artificial Intelligence, vol. 3, pp. 1788–1789. AAAI Press (2008)

8. Deravi, F., Guness, S.P.: Gaze trajectory as a biometric modality. In: BIOSIGNALS, pp. 335–341 (2011)

9. Dixon, D., Prasad, M., Hammond, T.: iCanDraw: using sketch recognition and corrective feedback to assist a user in drawing human faces. In: Proceedings of the SIGCHI Conference on Human Factors in Computing Systems, pp. 897–906. ACM (2010)

10. Eoff, B.D., Hammond, T.: Who dotted that'i'?: context free user differentiation through pressure and tilt pen data. In: Proceedings of Graphics Interface 2009, pp. 149–156. Canadian Information Processing Society (2009)

11. Galdi, C., Nappi, M., Riccio, D., Cantoni, V., Porta, M.: A new gaze analysis based soft-biometric. In: Carrasco-Ochoa, J.A., Martínez-Trinidad, J.F., Rodríguez, J.S., Baja, G.S. (eds.) MCPR 2013. LNCS, vol. 7914, pp. 136–144. Springer, Heidelberg (2013). doi:10.1007/978-3-642-38989-4_14

12. Hall, M., Frank, E., Holmes, G., Pfahringer, B., Reutemann, P., Witten, I.H.: The weka data mining software: an update. ACM SIGKDD Explor. Newsl. **11**(1), 10–18 (2009)

13. Hammond, T., Gajos, K., Davis, R., Shrobe, H.E.: An agent-based system for capturing and indexing software design meetings. In: Proceedings of the International Workshop on Agents in Design (WAID 2002). Citeseer (2002)

14. Hammond, T., O'Sullivan, B.: Recognizing freeform hand-sketched constraint network diagrams by combining geometry and context. In: Proceedings of the Eurographics Ireland (2007)

15. Hammond, T., Prasad, M., Dixon, D.: Art 101: learning to draw through sketch recognition. In: Taylor, R., Boulanger, P., Krüger, A., Olivier, P. (eds.) SG 2010. LNCS, vol. 6133, pp. 277–280. Springer, Heidelberg (2010). doi:10.1007/ 978-3-642-13544-6_30

16. Hammond, T.A.: Ladder: A perceptually-based language to simplify sketch recognition user interface development. Ph.D. thesis, Massachusetts Institute of Technology (2007)

17. Heath, M., Bowyer, K., Kopans, D., Kegelmeyer Jr., P., Moore, R., Chang, K., Munishkumaran, S.: Current status of the digital database for screening mammography. In: Karssemeijer, N., Thijssen, M., Hendriks, J., van Erning, L. (eds.) Digital Mammography, vol. 13, pp. 457–460. Springer, Heidelberg (1998)

18. Holland, C., Komogortsev, O.: Biometric identification via eye movement scanpaths in reading. In: 2011 International Joint Conference on Biometrics (IJCB), pp. 1–8, October 2011

19. Holmqvist, K., Nyström, M., Andersson, R., Dewhurst, R., Jarodzka, H., Van de Weijer, J.: Eye Tracking: A Comprehensive Guide to Methods and Measures. Oxford University Press, Oxford (2011)

20. Kara, L.B., Stahovich, T.F.: An image-based, trainable symbol recognizer for hand-drawn sketches. Comput. Graph. **29**(4), 501–517 (2005). http://www.sciencedirect.com/science/article/pii/S0097849305000853

21. Kasprowski, P., Ober, J.: Eye movements in biometrics. In: Maltoni, D., Jain, A.K. (eds.) BioAW 2004. LNCS, vol. 3087, pp. 248–258. Springer, Heidelberg (2004). doi:10.1007/978-3-540-25976-3_23

22. Krupinski, E.A.: Influence of experience on scanning strategies in mammography. Proc. SPIE Med. Imaging **2712**, 95–101 (1996). International Society for Optics and Photonics

23. Krupinski, E.A., Graham, A.R., Weinstein, R.S.: Characterizing the development of visual search expertise in pathology residents viewing whole slide images. Hum. Pathol. **44**(3), 357–364 (2013)

24. Krupinski, E.A., Tillack, A.A., Richter, L., Henderson, J.T., Bhattacharyya, A.K., Scott, K.M., Graham, A.R., Descour, M.R., Davis, J.R., Weinstein, R.S.: Eye-movement study and human performance using telepathology virtual slides. Implications for medical education and differences with experience. Hum. Pathol. **37**(12), 1543–1556 (2006). http://www.sciencedirect.com/science/article/pii/S0046817706005302

25. Kundel, H.L., Paul, S., La Follette, J.: Visual search patterns and experience with radiological images. Radiology **103**(3), 523–528 (1972). pMID: 5022947. http://dx.doi.org/10.1148/103.3.523

26. Li, W., Hammond, T.: Recognizing text through sound alone. In: Proceedings of the Twenty-Fifth AAAI Conference on Artificial Intelligence, AAAI 2011, pp. 1481–1486. AAAI Press (2011). http://dl.acm.org/citation.cfm?id=2900423.2900657

27. Long Jr., A.C., Landay, J.A., Rowe, L.A., Michiels, J.: Visual similarity of pen gestures. In: Proceedings of the SIGCHI Conference on Human Factors in Computing Systems, CHI 2000, pp. 360–367. ACM, New York (2000). http://doi.acm.org/10.1145/332040.332458

28. Lynch, P.J.: Eye movements abductors, December 2006. https://en.wikipedia.org/wiki/File:Eye_movements_abductors.jpg

29. Miller, J., Hammond, T.: Wiiolin: a virtual instrument using the wii remote. In: Proceedings of the 2010 Conference on New Interfaces for Musical Expression (NIME), pp. 497–500 (2010)

30. Nodine, C.F., Kundel, H.L., Mello-Thoms, C., Weinstein, S.P., Orel, S.G., Sullivan, D.C., Conant, E.F.: How experience and training influence mammography expertise. Acad. Radiol. **6**(10), 575–585 (1999). http://www.sciencedirect.com/science/article/pii/S1076633299802529

31. Noton, D., Stark, L.: Scanpaths in eye movements during pattern perception. Science **171**(3968), 308–311 (1971). http://science.sciencemag.org/content/171/3968/308

32. Ouyang, T.Y., Davis, R.: A visual approach to sketched symbol recognition. In: Proceedings of the 21st International Joint Conference on Artificial Intelligence, IJCAI 2009, pp. 1463–1468. Morgan Kaufmann Publishers Inc., San Francisco (2009). http://dl.acm.org/citation.cfm?id=1661445.1661680

33. Paulson, B., Cummings, D., Hammond, T.: Object interaction detection using hand posture cues in an office setting. Int. J. Hum.-Comput. Stud. **69**(1), 19–29 (2011)

34. Paulson, B., Hammond, T.: Paleosketch: accurate primitive sketch recognition and beautification. In: Proceedings of the 13th International Conference on Intelligent User Interfaces, IUI 2008, pp. 1–10. ACM, New York (2008). http://doi.acm.org/10.1145/1378773.1378775

35. Paulson, B., Rajan, P., Davalos, P., Gutierrez-Osuna, R., Hammond, T.: What!?! no rubine features?: using geometric-based features to produce normalized confidence values for sketch recognition. In: HCC Workshop: Sketch Tools for Diagramming (VL/HCC), pp. 57–63 (2008)

36. Pramanik, S., Bhattacharjee, D.: Geometric feature based face-sketch recognition. In: 2012 International Conference on Pattern Recognition, Informatics and Medical Engineering (PRIME), pp. 409–415, March 2012

37. American College of Radiology: BI-RADS Committee. Breast imaging reporting and data system. American College of Radiology (1998)

38. Rajan, P., Hammond, T.: From paper to machine: extracting strokes from images for use in sketch recognition. In: Proceedings of the 5th Eurographics Conference on Sketch-Based Interfaces and Modeling, pp. 41–48. Eurographics Association (2008)

39. Rayner, K.: Eye movements in reading and information processing: 20 years of research. Psychol. Bull. **124**(3), 372 (1998)

40. Rubine, D.: Specifying gestures by example. SIGGRAPH Comput. Graph. **25**(4), 329–337 (1991). http://doi.acm.org/10.1145/127719.122753

41. Schnitzer, B.S., Kowler, E.: Eye movements during multiple readings of the same text. Vis. Res. **46**(10), 1611–1632 (2006). http://www.sciencedirect.com/science/article/pii/S0042698905004864

42. Smith, R.A., Cokkinides, V., von Eschenbach, A.C., Levin, B., Cohen, C., Runowicz, C.D., Sener, S., Saslow, D., Eyre, H.J.: American cancer society guidelines for the early detection of cancer. CA Cancer J. Clin. **52**(1), 8–22 (2002)

43. Taele, P., Peschel, J., Hammond, T.: A sketch interactive approach to computer-assisted biology instruction. In: Proceedings of IUI 2009 Workshop on Sketch Recognition (2009)

44. Tweed, D., Vilis, T.: Geometric relations of eye position and velocity vectors during saccades. Vis. Res. **30**(1), 111–127 (1990). http://www.sciencedirect.com/science/article/pii/0042698990901314

45. Valentine, S., Vides, F., Lucchese, G., Turner, D., Kim, H.H., Li, W., Linsey, J., Hammond, T.: Mechanix: a sketch-based tutoring system for statics courses. In: Proceedings of the 24th Innovative Applications of Artificial Intelligence Conference on Artificial Intelligence (IAAI), pp. 2253–2260. AAAI (2012)

46. Yoon, H.J., Carmichael, T.R., Tourassi, G.: Gaze as a biometric. In: Proceedings of SPIE, pp. 903707–903707 (2014)

# Assessing Workload with Low Cost Eye Tracking During a Supervisory Control Task

Joseph T. Coyne[1]([⊠]), Ciara Sibley[1], Sarah Sherwood[2],
Cyrus K. Foroughi[1], Tatana Olson[3], and Eric Vorm[4]

[1] Naval Research Laboratory, Washington, DC, USA
{joseph.coyne, ciara.sibley, cyrus.foroughi.ctr}
@nrl.navy.mil
[2] Embry Riddle University, Daytona Beach, FL, USA
sherwoo9@my.erau.edu
[3] Naval Aerospace Medical Institute, Pensacola, FL, USA
tatana.m.olson.mil@mail.mil
[4] Indiana University, Bloomington, IN, USA
esvorm@umail.iu.edu

**Abstract.** Automation is fundamentally shifting the tasks that many humans perform. Unmanned aerial vehicles, which originally had stick and rudder control, now rely on waypoint based navigation. The future operators of these systems are increasingly becoming supervisors of automated systems and their primary role is shifting to simply monitoring those systems. This represents a challenge for assessing human performance since there is limited interaction with the systems. Low cost eye tracking, specifically measures of pupil diameter and gaze dispersion, may serve as a means of assessing operator engagement and workload while using these automated systems. The present study investigated the use of a low cost eye tracking system to differentiate low and high workload during an unmanned vehicle supervisory control task. The results indicated that pupil diameter significantly increased during periods of high workload; however, there was no change in the distribution of eye gazes. These results suggest that low cost eye tracking may be an effective means of determining an operator's workload in an automated environment, however more research is needed on the relationship between gaze distribution, workload and performance within a supervisory control environment.

**Keywords:** Supervisory control · Workload · Eye tracking · Automation · Pupil diameter

## 1 Introduction

Advances in automation have shifted many tasks previously controlled by unmanned aerial vehicle (UAV) operators to automated systems. These technological advances, coupled with a proliferation of unmanned systems, have pushed the military to explore a supervisory control paradigm for future UAV operations. However, one of the problems experienced by current UAV operators, dramatic fluctuations in workload based on mission context, is also expected to impact future UAV supervisory control

© Springer International Publishing AG 2017
D.D. Schmorrow and C.M. Fidopiastis (Eds.): AC 2017, Part I, LNAI 10284, pp. 139–147, 2017.
DOI: 10.1007/978-3-319-58628-1_12

operators. For example, the waypoint-based navigation of current UAVs only requires the operator to set the route; once the platform is enroute, it controls the flight systems and the operator's role is reduced to monitoring the automated system. Assessing human performance in highly automated systems is challenging because the operator's direct interaction with the system can be limited. How can one assess whether an operator is engaged and monitoring a system when the operator doesn't need to interact with the system for extended periods of time?

Eye tracking may be an effective means of continuously assessing both operator attention and engagement when interacting with complex automated systems. Eye tracking data is typically broken down to periods where the eye is relatively still (fixating) on a given region and periods where it is moving [1]. Individuals can only process new visual information during the periods where the eye is relatively still or fixating. This makes gaze position, particularly fixations, an important measure of an individual's overt attention [2]. However, analysis of fixations usually emphasizes areas of interest, comparing where and how long fixations occur in different regions. The results of these types of analyses are very task and even situation specific since the visual field needs to be broken up into task dependent regions.

One newer approach to analyzing gaze data, which does not require the visual field to be divided into areas of interest, is the Nearest Neighbor Index (NNI) [3, 4]. The NNI is the ratio of the average distance of each object to its nearest neighbor, compared to distance one would expect if the distribution were random. This technique was originally developed as a means of characterizing spatially distributed populations [5] and only recently applied to eye tracking data [3]. When NNI has been applied to eye tracking data, it has been shown to be sensitive to changes in task load. Specifically, NNI increases as workload increases. These changes in NNI were characterized as the distribution of gazes becoming more random. The results have been found in both a video game task [3] as well as during a simulated flight [4]. The researchers have suggested that under periods of high workload that an individual might have a more dispersed pattern of gazes so that they are more ready to process incoming information. NNI has only been applied to a limited number of tasks and has not been used in environments where participant's primary role is to monitor automated systems.

Eye trackers not only measure where an individual directs their visual attention, but also measures the size of an individual's pupils. The link between increases in pupil diameter and increases in working memory demand has been well documented since the 1960's [6, 7]. Although much of the early research linking pupil size to mental workload focused on basic tasks such as a digit span task [8], more recent research has shown pupil diameter increases within more complex visual environments such as driving, [9] and unmanned vehicle control [10]. Although low cost eye trackers have been shown to be capable of measuring pupil diameter changes in response to workload in basic tasks with consistent luminance levels [11], they have not been investigated within more complex visual tasks.

The present research seeks to determine if a low cost system can assess changes in workload within a supervisory control task. The goal for this study is to demonstrate that low cost eye tracking can be used to measure changes in workload via increased pupil diameter as well as a more random gaze pattern as accessed by the NNI.

# 2 Method

## 2.1 Participants

Nineteen (18 men and 1 woman) Navy and Marine Corps student pilots and flight officers aged 22–29 were recruited from Naval Air Station Pensacola, Florida. Participants were run in two groups. Eye tracking data for one of the participants was not recorded.

## 2.2 Equipment and Setup

Each of the 10 workstations in the lab were equipped with the Gazepoint GP3 eye tracker, which is capable of collecting both left and right gaze position as well as left and right pupil diameter size at 60 Hz. The task was displayed on a 25 in. Acer monitor at 2560 × 1440 resolution. Participants were all seated approximately 65 cm from the display.

## 2.3 Supervisory Control Task

Participants in the study used a single-screen version of the Supervisory Control Operations User Testbed (SCOUT) [12]. SCOUT (see Fig. 1) was developed to be a game-like environment where participants are awarded points for simultaneously completing a number of tasks associated with supervising three highly autonomous UAVs. There are three primary tasks within SCOUT including route management, sensor monitoring, and responding to communications. Within the route management

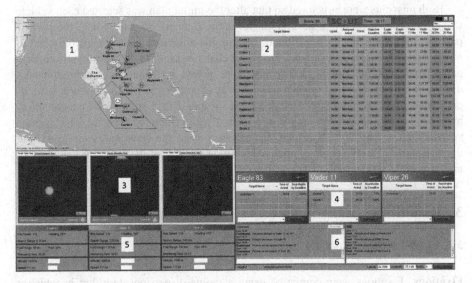

**Fig. 1.** Screen shot from the Supervisory Control Operations User Testbed (SCOUT). SCOUT consists of six main screen areas including the (1) moving map, (2) target information table, (3) sensor task, (4) route builder, (5) vehicle status, and (6) communications.

task, the participant develops a plan by assigning their vehicles to pursue objectives with varying priority levels, search area sizes, and deadlines. The initial plan may be modified as new objectives become available or changes to the parameters of an existing objective occur during the mission.

SCOUT's sensor monitoring task begins when the vehicle arrives within an objective's specified search area. The participant has to monitor the vehicle's sensor for the target shape specified for the objective and then clicking on it when it appears in the feed. The final task is responding to communication queries and command. For a communication query, the participant is asked to provide information on a specific vehicle or objective. For a communication command, the participant is asked to update a parameter of a vehicle (e.g. altitude) or objective (e.g., longitude). The version of SCOUT used in this study was modified so that all of the information could be displayed on a single display.

### 2.4  Procedure

Participants first completed an informed consent and then performed Gazepoint's calibration process (looking at a circle as it moved to 9 different positions on the display). Participants next completed a self-paced SCOUT training session that lasted approximately 35 min, followed by a 10-min practice mission. Once familiarized with the SCOUT environment, they completed two 30-min experimental mission scenarios: Prototype and Legacy. In the Prototype scenario, participants could choose to use automation during the payload task. They were told the automation would always find the target but was subject to false alarms; false alarms resulted in point loss. In the Legacy scenario, participants did not have sensor automation available.

Both missions were structured so that after the initial plan was selected each vehicle would proceed to its initial destination for approximately 15 min, where the participants would experience low workload. During this downtime, participants only had to monitor progress and answer one incoming chat message. In the Prototype mission, participants had the option of earning more points by requesting additional chat messages. The second half of each mission was characterized by a heavy task load, as participants had to monitor the payload task, respond to a stream of frequent information requests, and update target information and vehicle commands. The average and maximum subjective workload was assessed using the crew status survey [13] at the beginning of each scenario, after planning, at the end of the low task load period, and at the end of the high task load period.

## 3  Results

### 3.1  Eye Tracking Analysis

**Fixations.** Fixations were computed using a radius dispersion algorithm in which a packet was either considered to be part of a fixation or not. The dispersion based algorithm identified a fixation when a series of consecutive packets that met the minimum time duration (100 ms) were all within 50 pixels of their computed centroid. The 50 pixels equates to approximately 1° of visual angle. The fixation criteria were selected because they are comparable with those used for complex visual tasks [1]. For the fixation to be extended beyond the minimum duration a new centroid was computed and then compared to each packet to ensure they were all less than the maximum distance from the centroid. This definition of fixation was used to compare average fixation duration as well as to assess NNI. Fixations were compared during the planning phase during six five minute blocks of time (three low task load and three high task load) throughout the mission (excluding times when the scenario was paused for a workload probe or SA probe). For the data to be included in the analysis at least 50 fixations, the suggested minimum for NNI, were needed for each time segment. Sixteen percent of the total blocks did not meet this minimum.

*Fixation Duration.* The fixation duration analysis looked at the mean during the planning phase (variable length) and the six five minute time segments. A 2 way repeated measures ANOVA (Automation scenario × Time segment) was performed on average fixation duration. There was a significant effect of time segment $F(6,98) =$ 3.312, $P < .005$ on the mean fixation duration. There was a trend for fixation duration to decrease over each 5 min block, however Post Hoc analysis revealed that only the difference between the first five minutes after planning and the last five minutes of the experiment were significantly different. Figure 2 shows the average fixation duration

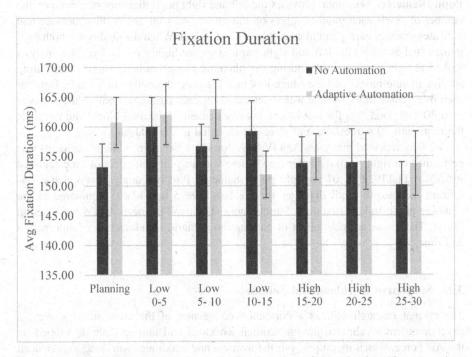

**Fig. 2.** Average fixation duration for both the no automation and adaptable automation scenarios for the planning phase and six 5-min time blocks. Error bars represent standard error of the mean

for each of the time segments. There was no main effect of Automation scenario or interaction of automation and time.

Nearest Neighbor Index. The NNI was computed using fixations from each of the six time blocks and planning period for each scenario using the convex hull method of computing area. A 2 way repeated measures ANOVA (Automation scenario × Time segment) did not find any significant main effects or interactions for NNI. The NNI's for each time segment are shown in Table 1.

**Table 1.** Nearest neighbor index for each time segment

| Time segment | NNI |
|---|---|
| Planning | 0.642452 |
| Low 0–5 | 0.663226 |
| Low 5–10 | 0.625114 |
| Low 10–15 | 0.629899 |
| High 15–20 | 0.62045 |
| High 20–25 | 0.652253 |
| High 25–30 | 0.638474 |

**Pupil Diameter.** Gazepoint provides the left and right pupil diameter measured by the number of pixels each pupil occupies on the camera, as well as a quality measure that indicates whether each particular sample is good or bad. When the quality for both eyes is indicated as valid, the left and right pupil sizes are highly correlated. The analysis looked at right pupil diameter during the planning phase (variable length) and during six five minute blocks of time (three low task load and three high task load). Data for each five minute block of time were considered for each participant only if there was at least 30 s of good data for that block. Twenty percent of the total blocks did not meet the minimum 30 s threshold and were not included in the analysis.

A 2 way repeated measures ANOVA (Automation Scenario × Time segment) was performed on right pupil diameter data. There was a significant effect of time segment $F(6,96) = 11.119$, $P < .01$ on right pupil diameter. Post hoc analysis revealed a significant increase in pupil diameter for the last three 5 min blocks compared to the planning phase and the first three 5-min blocks. The pupil diameter data is presented in Fig. 3. There was no main effect of automation scenario or interaction of automation and time.

## 3.2 Subjective Workload and Fatigue

The current research utilized a computerized version of the crew status survey, a psychometrically validated unidimensional workload and fatigue scale developed by the Air Force, which measures both the average and maximum workload experienced

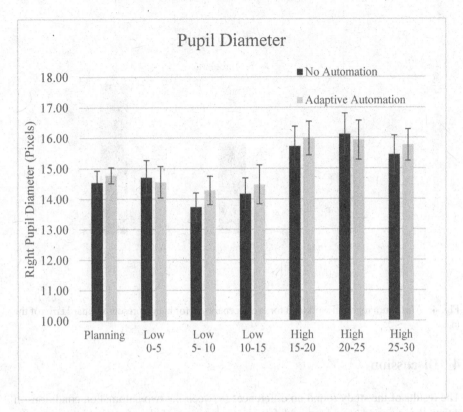

**Fig. 3.** Right pupil diameter over time for each scenario. Error bars represent standard error of the mean.

on a 7 point anchored scale [13]. A 2 way repeated measures ANOVA (Automation Scenario × Task load) performed on both the average and maximum workload yielded the same pattern of results. There was a significant effect of scenario task load $F_{(2,38)} = 14.714$, $P < .01$ (Average workload) and $F_{(2,38)} = 13.563$, $P < .01$ (Maximum workload). Post hoc analyses for both revealed a significant increase in reported workload during the high task load compared to the low task load and planning. Results for the maximum reported workload are shown in Fig. 4. There was no main effect of automation scenario or interaction of task load and automation scenario for the subjective workload probe.

There were no main effects or interactions for the fatigue portion of the crew status survey.

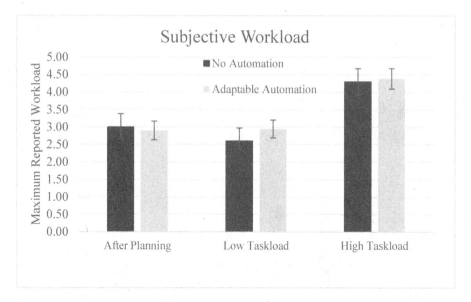

**Fig. 4.** Maximum reported workload for each scenario. Error bars represent standard error of the mean

## 4  Discussion

The results of the study found no differences between the two automation conditions in either the reported workload and fatigue, or for any of the eye tracking measures. However, both the eye tracking measures, particularly pupil diameter and the subjective workload scale, were able to detect changes in workload across the periods of high and low task load within each scenario.

The pupil diameter results are consistent with those found in a number of other studies in that pupil diameter is shown to increase as mental effort increases [6, 8, 9, 11]. The results are meaningful since they were found in a task with varying levels of luminance across the different regions of the screen. Despite the lack of control for screen luminance, the low cost system was still able to detect a pupillary response to increased task load. This suggests that pupillary response may be a robust measure of mental workload even in visually complex environments.

The authors expected to see significant increases in the Nearest Neighbor Index as workload increased, however this was not the case. The nearest neighbor index did not show any significant differences or even non-significant trends in the data. It is not clear if this is due to problems with data quality, problems with accuracy of the eye trackers, or a lack of sensitivity of the NNI. Although not reported in the paper, the authors adjusted the fixation criteria to allow for both shorter fixation durations and larger dispersion; however using different fixation criteria did not meaningfully alter the outcome of the NNI analysis. To date NNI has only been applied to a limited number of task domains and additional research on NNI needs to be done to see if it is a robust measure of workload.

One of the main limitations of the present study was that there was a large amount of data marked as poor quality by the eye trackers. The authors took a liberal criteria in accepting eye tracking data. The high data loss is most likely due to the participants moving outside of the Gazepoint GP3's limited head box. This problem was exacerbated by the fact that participants were seated at rolling chairs which could recline.

Overall, despite problems with data quality, the low cost eye trackers, specifically the measures of pupil diameter, demonstrated that they could differentiate between high and low task load in a complex visual task.

# References

1. Holmqvist, K., Nyström, M., Andersson, R., Dewhurst, R., Jarodzka, H., Van de Weijer, J.: Eye Tracking: A Comprehensive Guide to Methods and Measures. Oxford University Press, New York (2011)
2. Rayner, K.: Eye movements and attention in reading, scene perception, and visual search. Q. J. Exp. Psychol. **62**, 1457–1506 (2009)
3. Di Nocera, F., Terenzi, M., Camilli, M.: Another look at scanpath: distance to nearest neighbour as a measure of mental workload. In: de Waard, D., Brookhuis, K.A., Toffetti, A. (eds.) Developments in Human Factors in Transportation, Design, and Evaluation, pp. 295–303. Shaker Publishing, Maastricht (2006)
4. Di Nocera, F., Camilli, M., Terenzi, M.: A random glance at the flight deck: pilots' scanning strategies and the real-time assessment of mental workload. J. Cogn. Eng. Decis. Mak. **1**, 271–285 (2007)
5. Clark, P.J., Evans, F.C.: Distance to nearest neighbor as a measure of spatial relationships in populations. Ecology **35**, 445–453 (1954)
6. Hess, E.H., Polt, J.M.: Pupil size in relation to mental activity during simple problem-solving. Science **143**, 1190–1192 (1964)
7. Beatty, J., Lucero-Wagoner, B.: The pupillary system. In: Cacioppo, J.T., Tassinary, L.G., Berntson, G.G. (eds.) Handbook of Psychophysiology, pp. 142–162. Cambridge University Press, Cambridge (2000)
8. Beatty, J.: Pupillometric measurement of cognitive workload. In: Proceedings of 12th Annual Conference on Manual Control (1976)
9. Palinko, O., Kun, A.L., Shyrokov, A., Heeman, P.: Estimating cognitive load using remote eye tracking in a driving simulator. In: Proceedings of the 2010 Symposium on Eye-Tracking Research and Applications, pp. 141–144. ACM (2010)
10. Sibley, C., Coyne, J.T., Doddi, A., Jasper, P.: Pupillary response as an indicator of processing demands within a supervisory control simulation environment. In: The 18th International Symposium on Aviation Psychology, pp. 506–511. Wright State University (2015)
11. Coyne, J., Sibley, C.: Investigating the use of two low cost eye tracking systems for detecting pupillary response to changes in mental workload. In: Proceedings of the Human Factors and Ergonomics Society Annual Meeting, pp. 37–41. SAGE Publications (2016)
12. Sibley, C., Coyne, J., Thomas, J.: Demonstrating the Supervisory Control Operations User Testbed (SCOUT). In: Proceedings of the Human Factors and Ergonomics Society Annual Meeting, pp. 1324–1328. SAGE Publications (2016)
13. Ames, L.L., George, E.J.: Revision and verification of a seven-point workload estimate scale. Air Force Flight Test Center (1993)

# The Analysis and Prediction of Eye Gaze When Viewing Statistical Graphs

Andre Harrison[1(✉)], Mark A. Livingston[2], Derek Brock[2],
Jonathan Decker[2], Dennis Perzanowski[2], Christopher Van Dolson[2],
Joseph Mathews[2], Alexander Lulushi[2], and Adrienne Raglin[1]

[1] Army Research Laboratory, Adelphi, MD, USA
{andre.v.harrison2.civ,
adrienne.j.raglin.civ}@mail.mil
[2] Naval Research Laboratory, Washington, DC, USA
{mark.livingston,derek.brock,jonathan.decker,
dennis.perzanowski,christopher.vandolson,
joseph.matthews,alexander.lulushi}@nrl.navy.mil

**Abstract.** Statistical graphs are images that display quantitative information in a visual format that allows for the easy and consistent interpretation of the information. Often, statistical graphs are in the form of line graphs or bar graphs. In fields, such as cybersecurity, sets of statistical graphs are used to present complex information; however, the interpretation of these more complex graphs is often not obvious. Unless the viewer has been trained to understand each graph used, the interpretation of the data may be limited or incomplete [1]. In order to study the perception of statistical graphs, we tracked users' eyes while studying simple statistical graphs. Participants studied a graph, and later viewed a graph purporting to be a subset of the data. They were asked to look for a substantive change in the meaning of the second graph compared to the first.
To model where the participants would direct their attention, we ran several visual saliency models over the graphs [2–4]. Visual saliency models try to predict where people will look in an image; however, visual saliency models are typically designed and evaluated to predict where people look in natural images (images of natural or real world scenes), which have lots of potential information, subjective interpretations, and are not typically very quantitative. The ideal observer model [2], unlike most saliency models, tries to predict where people look based on the amount of information contained within each location in an image. The underlying theory of the ideal observer model is that when a person sees a new image, they want to understand that image as quickly as possible. To do this, the observer directs their attention first to the locations in the image that will provide the most information (i.e. give the best understanding of the information).
Within this paper, we have analyzed the eye gaze from a study on statistical graphs to evaluate the consistency between participants in the way they gazed at graphs and how well a saliency model can predict where those people are likely to look in the graph. During the study, as a form of mental diversion to the primary task, participants also looked at natural images, between each set of graphs. When the participants looked at the images, they did so without guidance, i.e. they weren't told to look at the images for any particular reason or

D.D. Schmorrow and C.M. Fidopiastis (Eds.): AC 2017, Part I, LNAI 10284, pp. 148–165, 2017.
DOI: 10.1007/978-3-319-58628-1_13

objective. This allowed the viewing pattern for graphs to be compared to eye gaze data for the natural images, while also showing the differences, in the processing of simple graphs versus complex natural images.

An interesting result shows that viewers processed the graphs differently than natural images. The center of the graph was not a strong predictor of attention. In natural images, a Gaussian kernel at the center of an image can achieve a receiver operating characteristic (ROC) score of over 80% due to inherent center bias in both the selection of natural images and the gaze patterns of participants [5]. This viewing pattern was present when participants looked at the natural images during the diversion task, but it was not present when they studied the graphs. Results from the study also found fairly consistent, but unusually low inter-subject consistency ROC scores. Inter-subject consistency is the ability to predict one participant's gaze locations using the gaze positions of the other $(n - 1)$ participants [3]. The saliency model itself was an inconsistent predictor of participants' eye gaze by default. Like the participants, the saliency model identified titles and axis labels as salient. The saliency model also found the bars and lines on the graphs to be salient; however, the eye gaze of most participants rarely fell or focused on the line or bar graphs. This may be due to the simplicity of the graphs, implying that very little time or attention needed to be directed to the actual bar or line graph in order to remember it.

**Keywords:** Cognitive modeling · Perception · Emotion and interaction · Understanding human cognition and behavior in complex tasks and environments · Visual salience · Information theory · Statistical graphics

# 1  Introduction

Statistical graphs (SG) are visual representations used to represent high-order relations into different facets of data sets of a variety of types through the use of symbolic systems [6]. SGs present data as different types of images to take advantage of the advanced pattern detection capabilities of the human visual system and to allow an easy and consistent interpretation of information. SGs have numerous uses, including data exploration, structure investigation, outlier and anomaly detection, model verification, network flow, dimensional analysis, and more. Basic SGs include line graphs, bar graphs, and scatter plots. Line graphs and bar graphs are two of the most commonly used types of SG's and the type of SG used to present data can constrain or infer how that data is to be interpreted. In many fields, sets of SG's are used to detect and monitor complex types of information (widely known as "information dashboards"). Typically, the more specialized the use of the SG's is the harder it is for a novice to understand the information and the more time it takes to train a novice to be able to use these systems.

There has been substantial work in the design of SG according to human factors guidelines [7–10], which could help make these graphs more intuitive and reduce the learning curve of new trainees, but these guidelines are rarely used to create SG's in practice [7]. At the same time, some human factors guidelines can interfere with the intended application of the SG. It has been shown that features that make a graph more memorable can actually interfere with the comprehension of that graph [11, 12].

In this paper, we describe the results from a study aimed at studying the perception and comprehension of graph content, by seeing if participants could detect when the content in an SG changed. Participants studied a graph, and later viewed a graph purporting to be a subset of the data. They were asked to look for a substantive change in the meaning of the second graph compared to the first. In this paper, we analyzed the recorded eye gaze locations when the participants were examining the SG and the natural image in order to model the participants' perception of the SG by applying a visual saliency model to those same SG and comparing the results. Visual saliency refers to how likely items in an image are to attract a person's attention.

In Subsect. 1.1, we describe some of relevant work in the design of SGs, similar studies in the perception of SGs, as well as a brief background in modeling of visual salience. In Sect. 2, we briefly discuss the study that was conducted and the types of analyses done on the eye tracking data collected during the study. In Sect. 3, we discuss the results of the analysis on the patterns of eye gaze and the prediction of eye gaze using different saliency models. In the last section, we provide a short conclusion of the analysis and modeling done in this work.

## 1.1  Relevant Work

**The Design of Graphs.** There have been several papers on the design of SG [7–10]. The goal of these papers has been focused on how best to design graphs to convey an easily understood message to the reader, when a graph should be used to present information, and what type of graph should be used for different types of information [13, 14]. Research in the design of SGs has looked at how to make graphs more easily understood [8, 9], more memorable [11, 12], or how to control the aesthetic quality [15, 16].

There are many choices to be made when creating a graph, from the type of graph to use, the style of the text, the placement of text in the graph, as well as the types of graphical cues to use. Each of these choices can have an impact on the memorability of the graph and how easy it is to understand the primary and secondary meanings (if any) contained within the graph [7–10, 17–19]. In general, a graph with the simplest layout and the fewest number of variables and extraneous clutter is the easiest to understand, while a graph that is visually striking or has natural objects is more memorable.

Research into the memorability of graphs, by Borkin et al., has shown that the most memorable items in a graph are identified and encoded within the first 10 s of viewing [11, 12]. At the same time, they found that human recognizable objects in a graph improved a person's ability to recognize or recall the graphs. For graphs with less easily memorable features or objects standard text elements of a graph were used to recall and recognize those graphs, with title being the most popular point of recognition and recall [11, 12].

Understanding or interpreting the meaning of a graph starts with the type of graph used to represent the information. Certain types of graphs are selected based on the common interpretation of data when it is shown in a graph of that type [17]. Graph understanding is further colored by the salience of different graphical elements, the use of graphical cues, and the types of graphical cues used [17]. In general, graphical cues have a strong impact on the interpretation and perception of an SG dominating attention over salient effects [17]. Work on the comprehension or understanding of graphs has shown that comprehending the trends or the effects that depend on inter-actions across graphs is difficult without training [18]. Untrained individuals don't see all of the information present in graphs, but what they do see they remember [18].

Work on the perception of SGs has focused on higher level descriptions of how the information in SGs could be encoded and represented within the brain [20, 21]. These descriptions are organizational; much like feature integration theory (FIT) by Treisman and Gelade [22], models of the perception of graphs like saliency models break up graph comprehension in terms of bottom-up and top-down processes. Most models, however, are not computational. Given a sample SG, these models can be used to tell a person how to evaluate how easily a graph can be understood or what level of knowledge a person needs to understand a particular graph [20].

**Predicting Where People Look.** Computational models of visual salience are a popular way to model visual perception. Visual salience is the aspect of visual per-ception that attracts a person's attention to a particular location in an image over others. Visual saliency models thereby predict where people look by identifying the most salient locations in an image and then assume that these locations are likely to be where a person will look. There are two main factors that influence the salience of an object or location in salience models, top-down factors and bottom-up factors. Top-down factors are learned or goal directed factors that affect visual attention. In short, they are external factors that influence where a person may look. In the realm of SGs, a common situation with a strong top-down factor is when a person is looking at an SG to answer a specific question. Top-down factors are also related to higher level processing tasks like object recognition, classification, and some aspects of segmentation [23–26]. Bottom-up influences are more sensory based; eye gaze is affected in this case by changes in contrast, texture, intensity, or color. Accounting for top-down influences in a model generally requires some sort of learning or training step that must employ a large database of positive and negative examples of objects or patterns. As a result, almost all current saliency models with top-down influences have only been trained on natural images. In the rest of this paper we focus only on bottom-up approaches to saliency. A benefit of bottom-up approaches is that while they have been developed and tested primarily on natural images their underlying assumptions and approaches are tied primarily to low level models of vision and so they can be generalized to most domains of vision.

Most bottom-up models of where people look take the natural approach to modeling attention by basing some or all of the components of their models on the neural circuitry involved in eye gaze [4, 27–31]. The theory of how attention works, on which these models are based, is from FIT by Treisman and Gelade [22] and Koch and Ullman [32]. Treisman and Gelade proposed that the extraction of features from a scene or image occurs in a parallel fashion extracting all the features from the image in one pass, while attention is a serial process and must jump from one region of the scene to another. Koch and Ullman expanded upon this theory by proposing the idea that the movement of attention from one part of a scene to another occurs in a winner-take-all (WTA) process and they first coined the term of "saliency map." There were several features initially thought to be extracted by Treisman and Gelade [22]; however, most biologically inspired bottom-up saliency models extract only three types of features intensity, color, and orientation at multiple spatial scales [4, 27, 28, 33].

Another approach that has been used to develop saliency models is to look at fixation from an information theoretic perspective. The underlying idea of these models is that when a person looks at a new image or scene they want to learn as much about the scene as quickly as possible. The locations that are gazed or attended to first are the ones that have the most information. In these models information is typically measured as entropy [2, 34–36] or self-information [5, 37, 38]. Other saliency models have been based in different areas of mathematics than information theory, like graph theory [3], and Bayesian estimation [39].

## 2    Materials and Methods

The objective of the study on SGs was to explore the manipulation of the information content in SGs. The approach taken in the study was to manipulate SGs (line graphs and bar graphs) in two ways. The first way the graphs were manipulated was by reducing the amount of information presented in each graph, thus graphs with 3–6 elements were modified into graphs with 1–3 elements. The other change was to sometimes change the message of the original graph, such that it no longer presented the same information. Each participant's task was to detect if the information stated in the simplified graph was stated in the original graph (where "not stated" could imply a conflict or simply new information).

### 2.1    Procedure

The procedure followed within this study was to show each participant a very simple SG, then present the participant a series of distractors, afterwards the participant viewed a modified version of that same graph. The distractors were a series of natural images and a brief paragraph. For the images of SGs participants were given at least 30 s to study each image. For the natural images participants were told to free view the natural images for 3 s each. For the paragraph, participants were asked to read it, as they would have to answer questions about the paragraph, which they did after they were shown the simplified graph. For each trial, participants had their eye gaze tracked and recorded; however, while the eye gaze of the participants was tracked during the paragraph reading and answer sections they were not analyzed in this paper and so that aspect of the eye gaze data won't be discussed further nor did we analyze the pattern of eye gaze when the participants viewed the modified graph. Each modified graph was only viewed by 4–5 of the participants.

### 2.2    Stimuli

The participants were shown 12 different SGs, 6 line graphs and 6 bar graphs. The graphs were chosen to be relatively simple and straight forward in meaning, such that if the information was changed in the simplified graph the change would be clear. The natural images were selected primarily to serve as distractors to the main task, but they were selected from the MIT1003 dataset [40], which would allow the eye tracks to be compared to another natural image eye gaze dataset.

## 2.3 Participants

Twenty-four participants completed the study (20 men, 4 women) between the ages of 19–58 with a mean and median age of 38. Most participants were heavy computer users (at least 20 h per week). All but five participants said that they read or created graphs regularly (at least weekly).

## 2.4 Equipment

The participants' eye gaze was tracked using a Gazepoint GP3 eye tracker. The system, after calibration, tracked the participants' eye gaze for the rest of the study.

## 2.5 Analysis

**Fraction of Valid Eye Tracks.** The Gazepoint GP3 eye tracker is a desktop mounted eye tracker that tracks the left and right eye gaze of the person sitting in front of the device. It also maps the location each eye is looking into the pixel based coordinates of the display by using a 9-point calibration method where the viewer is prompted by the Gazepoint software to look at nine specific locations on the display. The nine different points of gaze allows the system to triangulate not just the user's eye gaze, but also the relative position of the user to the display and eye tracker in three dimensions. However, two main things can and did interfere with the eye tracker's ability to determine where on the screen the viewer was looking. (1) The viewer would sometimes look away from the screen, or at least outside the region where the SGs or images were presented. (2) The presence of eye glasses or any form of corrective lenses in front the participant's eyes. Glare from the computer screen or overhead lights could create specular reflections or highlights confusing the system's ability to locate the eye. Also the unknown prescription can refract the light in ways that can't be compensated for using the default calibration [41].

**Observed Differences in Eye Gaze.** It has become a typical finding that when analyzing the locations of gaze from a group of individuals who have been looking at a natural image without any stated objective there is a distinct central bias regardless of the content of the image [5, 29, 42]. This is present in every unguided eye tracking dataset using natural images. There have been several potential reasons given to explain this behavior. Commonly in eye tracking studies, participants are asked to focus on the center of the screen before the image is shown, therefore many eye fixations are found in the center. A similar justification is that when studying an image going back to the center is optimal from the perspective of minimizing the travel time to any location in the image. Another explanation often given is that natural images used in studies are often taken by people and typically people take pictures so that the most salient object is located in the center of the image [43, 44]. We will compare the aggregated eye gaze locations for all users over all natural image against the aggregated eye gaze locations from the SGs to view any differences in viewing bias between the two classes of images.

**Saliency Analysis.** Saliency models are typically designed with the assumption that the image that will be analyzed is a natural one; with "natural" meaning an image that could be found in the real world. Thus, it could be argued that saliency models have no applicability to SGs. But the human visual system has evolved looking only at natural scenes, hence any image viewed by the human visual system may be initially processed as if it were a natural image. This is especially likely for bottom-up models of vision. So bottom-up saliency models may not be too far off in predictive accuracy when applied to SGs, in terms of identifying what might be salient. To evaluate how well saliency algorithms predict where people look in SGs when participants aren't trying to answer a specific question, we analyzed the SGs and natural images in this study using several visual saliency algorithms.

The best predictor of where people will look in an image is where other people look when they see that same image, under the same circumstances. This is more formally known as the inter-subject consistency and if there are N participants in a study it is calculated by blurring the aggregated eye gaze locations of $N - 1$ of the participants into a 2D eye gaze map, treating it like a saliency map, and then using that map to predict the eye gaze locations of the Nth participant. This is done for all N participants and then the average similarity value is calculated for all participants. Typically, the average inter-subject consistency represents the highest achievable accuracy possible by a saliency model. But the specific value has also been interpreted as a measure of the consistency of interpretation due to the consistency between the gaze locations [45]. We calculated the inter-subject consistency using two different saliency measures for the natural images and SGs used in this study. We also calculated the inter-subject consistency of the natural images using the eye fixation from the MIT1003 dataset [40], which is the original dataset the natural images came from.

There are several different similarity measures to compare a saliency map against a map of eye gaze [46]. In this paper, we selected two popular similarity measures, the receiver operator characteristic (ROC) and the Kullback-Leibler divergence (KL divergence). The receiver operating characteristic is a widely-used measure of the performance of a binary classifier. For succinctness, we have used the single-value version of the ROC and calculate the area under the ROC curve (AUC). The ROC curve compares the true positive rate vs. the false positive rate for each saliency map. By doing this it assesses the rank ordering of the values in the saliency map for each saliency model. The Kullback-Leibler divergence is a standard statistical measure for comparing the difference between two distributions; thereby comparing the overall pattern of fixation versus salience.

## 2.6   Results

**Fraction of Valid Eye Tracks.** A substantial portion of the eye gaze samples from the participant data was found to be invalid. This was partially due to the fact that three of the participants had no valid eye gaze information recorded at all. Discarding the users who had less than 10% valid eye gaze samples we found that 19.97% of the remaining eye gaze samples were invalid due to the eye tracker marking the recorded gaze as inaccurate, while, 37.52% of the gaze locations were not considered as the user's eye gaze didn't fall anywhere on the graph or image that was being shown. Overall only 13 participants had a sufficient number of eye gaze samples to be analyzed. From the remaining participants, the ratio of valid eye gaze samples had a mean and standard deviation of ($\mu = 0.4196$; $\sigma = 0.1563$). If the eye gaze samples are partitioned between whether the participant was looking at an SG vs. a natural image we find that 60.57% of the eye gaze samples are valid for the natural images and 38.86% of the eye tracks are valid for the SGs. If we further restrict the eye tracks of the SGs to the first 3 s 21.53% of the eye tracks are valid. Overall this means that there are 59,679, 11,656, and 188,986, valid samples of eye gaze when participants were looking at the natural images, at the SGs for three seconds, and at the SGs for the full study period, respectively.

It is of note that 13 of the 24 participants reported wearing some sort of prescription corrective lenses and 3 additional participants reported that they use non-prescription reading glasses. However, whether the participants were wearing some form of corrective lenses during the study was not recorded and not every participant who was eliminated from the analysis wore some form of corrective lenses. To determine the correlation between invalid eye gaze samples and corrective lenses we computed three binary dummy variables for eyewear:

1. Any form of eye correction = 0 or "Poor" and No correction = 1 or "Good"; this variable is called "No Correction"
2. Prescription eyeglasses = 0 or "Poor" and anything else = 1 or "Good"; this variable is called "No Script Glasses"
3. Prescription or Non-prescription eyeglasses = 0 or "Poor" and anything else = 1 or "Good"; this variable is called "No Glasses".

Any form of correction includes contact lenses, prescription eyeglasses, and non-prescription reading glasses. We suspected based on the literature and conversations with experts that prescription eyeglasses would create challenges for the eye tracker, because the frames and (often) thick lenses create unexpected reflections in the images that the eye tracker uses to locate the pupils. By similar logic, we suspected reading glasses to create challenges as well, since they have frames (and despite the lenses generally being thinner than prescription glasses). We did not expect contact lenses to create challenges for the eye tracker, since the lens is so close to the cornea. Our three dummy variables include (respectively) all three corrections (hypothesis: too restrictive), just prescription eyeglasses (hypothesis: too permissive), prescription or non-prescription glasses (hypothesis: best predictor). All these hypotheses are supported by the following analysis.

We computed analysis of variance (ANOVA) for the dummy variables. This also showed that the three dummy variables encapsulating the use of eyewear were a significant factor in the percentage of valid eye gaze data (Table 1). Note that the generalized effect size (GES) for each variable is considered large.

**Table 1.** Analysis of variance (ANOVA) for dummy variables regarding eyewear and the percentage of valid eye gaze data. Each (binary) dummy variable shows a significant main effect on the percentage of valid data, indicating that, in particular, eyeglasses – whether prescription or not – seemed to create challenges for the eye tracker to acquire valid eye gaze data. GES is generalized effect size; it is considered large for each variable, implying that each variable could explain a significant amount of the variance in percentage of valid data. It appears that the best hypothesis is that any form of eyeglasses created challenges for the eye tracker, whereas including contact lenses wear as a predictor of poor performance explained less of the variance.

| | F (1,22) | P | GES | Mean ratios | |
| --- | --- | --- | --- | --- | --- |
| | | | | Good (SEs) | Poor (SEs) |
| No correction | 4.4040 | 0.0481 | 0.1734 | 0.38 (0.08) | 0.19 (0.05) |
| No script glasses | 9.3274 | 0.0060 | 0.3076 | 0.36 (0.06) | 0.11 (0.05) |
| No glasses | 9.6320 | 0.0054 | 0.3144 | 0.40 (0.07) | 0.14 (0.05) |

**Observed Differences in Eye Gaze.** Aggregating the eye gaze locations from all of the valid participants across all of the images shown creates a picture of the viewing patterns and biases people employ when viewing imagery. In Fig. 1a, a blurred version of the aggregated eye gaze locations from all of the valid participants over all of the natural images used in this study shows the aforementioned central bias typically found in unguided eye gaze studies of natural images. Repeating that procedure for the SGs creates a very different pattern of eye gaze, Fig. 1b. The pattern of eye gaze on SGs shows that in this study there was consistently more than one location that drew a participant's attention. The fixation pattern for the SGs shows clusters of fixations near the edges of the image, falling where text for the graph is usually found: the title, the y-axis label, the x-axis label, and the legend. Strangely however, the actual content (the line in the line graph or bars in the bar graph) does not seem to attract as much attention as does the text on the x and y-axis, the title, or the legend. Part of this is likely due to the simplicity of the graphs. There are few data points in the line or bar graphs and there are no secondary factors or interactions to interpret. If the participants are viewing the graphs for upwards of 30 s, simple bars and lines are unlikely to require much attention. There is slightly more information in the text and the numbers for each axis, especially since the task was to study the graph in order to identify differences later. Patterns of eye gaze are typically different in free viewing tasks compared to memorization tasks. In memorization tasks there is a stronger top-down influence, there tend to be more eye fixation locations, and the average distance between fixation locations is larger [47]. The increased length of time the participants viewed the SGs meant that both bottom-up and top-down factors were guiding the participants viewing behavior. In the first 3 s of viewing the SG bottom-up effects are likely to dominate the eye gaze pattern. Samples from the first 3 s of viewing the SGs seem to primarily be drawn to the x-axis label for both bar and line graphs, Fig. 1c. Two of the implications of this behavior are that eye gaze is largely controlled by information content and initial fixation or optimal search strategies are not the main cause of central bias in natural images [43, 44].

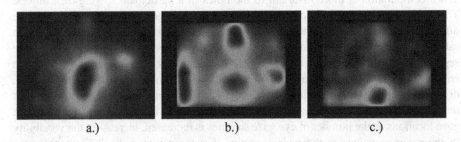

a.)    b.)    c.)

**Fig. 1.** Aggregated eye fixation for all of the participants. (a) Shows the aggregated eye fixations for all of the participants when they were looking at a natural image. (b) Shows the aggregated eye fixations of all of the participants over all the SGs for the entire time they were looking at each graph. (c) Shows the aggregated eye fixations of all of the participants over all of the SGs for the first three seconds that they were looking at the graph. The SGs were smaller than the natural images and so there is an empty border around the aggregated eye fixations for the SGs.

**Saliency Analysis.** The calculated inter-subject consistency for the SG and natural images used in the study on SG has fairly low AUC values, Table 2. As a point of reference the calculated inter-subject consistency of the participants' eye gaze patterns when looking at natural images from the SG study compared to the MIT1003 study shows a substantial drop in consistency using the AUC measure. The differences in the inter-subject consistency of the natural images shows that, assuming the different pools of participants are interchangeable, the substantially lower scores from this study are likely a result of the dropped eye gaze samples. The substantially lower inter-subject consistency scores from this study are likely due to participants with a smaller percentage of valid eye gaze samples or participants whose valid eye gaze locations are close together. If locations where most of the other participants directed their gaze didn't coincide with the eye gaze location of the reaming participant due to dropped samples, then that location is marked as a false positive lowering the overall consistency score and changes the rank ordering of the salient and non-salient locations.

**Table 2.** Comparison of the inter-subject consistency of the eye gaze patterns analyzed by this paper broken out by image type (natural image and SGs) and the per image trial length (the entire trial vs 3 s). Also on the table is the inter-subject consistency using the eye gaze patterns from the MIT1003 dataset.

|  | AUC | KL divergence |
|---|---|---|
| Statistical graph (all) | 0.6460 ($\sigma$ = 0.0789) | 1.2864 ($\sigma$ = 0.6524) |
| Statistical graph (3 s) | 0.6216 ($\sigma$ = 0.0397)* | 5.0776 ($\sigma$ = 1.3348)* |
| Natural images | 0.6606 ($\sigma$ = 0.0888) | 3.2033 ($\sigma$ = 1.7713) |
| Natural images (MIT) | 0.8674 ($\sigma$ = 0.0363) | 2.7507 ($\sigma$ = 0.7234) |

158    A. Harrison et al.

Conversely, the inter-subject consistency values for the KL divergence seems to show no real difference when comparing the eye gaze patterns over the natural images. This suggests that the KL divergence values for the SGs represent a true upper bound of the best a saliency model could be expected to do in terms of predicting where a person would look when memorizing an SG. This also suggests, that the KL divergence computation is more invariant to the holes in a participant's eye gaze samples. This seems like a reasonable conclusion as the KL divergence basically compares the difference in distribution of the saliency values where a participant looked against the saliency values where they didn't look. So even if there is missing data so long as the separation in saliency values between gaze locations and non-gaze locations is wide enough the KL divergence values won't be affected. This also explains why the KL divergence value is so much lower when the KL divergence is calculated using all of the eye gaze samples from the SG trial vs. the first 3 s of the trial. There are more eye gaze locations as the number of eye gaze samples is increased, increasing the variability in the saliency values at the gaze locations thereby reducing the differences in the distributions.

We applied several different saliency models to the images of the SGs (the Itti model) [4], the graph based visual saliency model (GBVS) [3], and the ideal observer model (ioM) [2]. In the evaluation of the saliency models we also include a saliency map that is simply a Gaussian kernel centered in the middle of the image. The accuracy

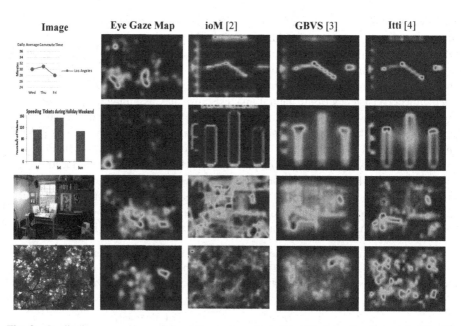

**Fig. 2.** Qualitative comparison of the saliency maps from the different saliency models. The 1st column, the leftmost column, shows the original images used within the study. The 2nd column shows the aggregated eye fixations for each image. The 3rd, 4th and 5th columns shows the saliency maps generated by the ideal observer model (ioM) [2], the graph based visual saliency (GBVS) model [3], and the Itti et al. model [4].

of the Gaussian kernel sets a minimum level of required predictive accuracy since the predictions are solely based on central bias and don't change with image content. Each saliency model generated a saliency map for each image, showing a 2D probability of the likelihood that each location would attract someone's attention, Fig. 2. These maps were compared against the aggregated maps of eye gaze for each SG, Fig. 1. Consistently across all of the saliency models the saliency maps of SGs find not just the text areas salient, but they also identify the graph and bars as salient. However, it is unclear what impact this has on each measure of accuracy.

In the first evaluation, we compared the ability of the saliency models to predict eye gaze when people looked at natural images, at the SGs for 3 s, or the SG for the entire memorization time (>30 s) Fig. 3. We specifically compared the output of the saliency models against the gaze patterns from the first 3 s of the SG trial for two reasons: (1) The participants could only look at the natural images for three seconds, so using only the first three seconds of the eye gaze patterns for the SGs makes for a more appropriate comparison. (2) In the first three seconds, bottom-up influences are still a strong predictor of eye gaze.

Across all of the models the predictive strength of the saliency models for the AUC measure follows an expected progression, Fig. 4. Every model has a higher accuracy when applied to a natural image, a slightly lower accuracy predicting eye gaze in the first 3 s of viewing an SG and even less accuracy predicting eye gaze for the entire time participants were viewing the SG. The results of the KL divergence however, shows a more unusual pattern. Each saliency model still has the highest accuracy predicting eye

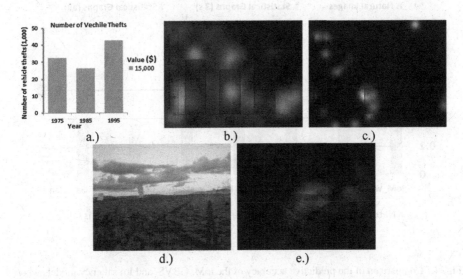

**Fig. 3.** (a) Sample SG used in the study. (b) Aggregated eye fixations of all the participants overlaid over the original graph. (c) Shows the aggregated eye fixations of all the participants during the first three seconds of viewing the graph. (d) Sample natural image used in the study. (e) Aggregated eye fixations of all the participants overlaid over the original image. Each eye fixation location is blurred to ∼1° of visual angle. This visualizes the approximate accuracy of the Gazepoint eye tracker and the coverage area of the fovea of the average participant.

gaze on for natural images, but the accuracy in predicting eye gaze from the entire SG trial is higher than for the first three seconds. A possible reason is that with the longer viewing time the pattern of eye gaze is more spread out over the entire image. When the KL divergence calculates the distribution differences between saliency map values at eye gaze locations vs non-eye gaze locations the longer eye gaze time reduces the number of non-eye gaze locations that fall on a high saliency map value.

Finally, a more anomalous pattern shown in Fig. 4a and b is that that even though the saliency models have a higher predictive accuracy when applied to natural images they have the same or a lower similarity score than the Gaussian kernel using the AUC similarity measure. However, all of the saliency models have a higher similarity measure than the Gaussian kernel when predicting eye gaze locations during the first

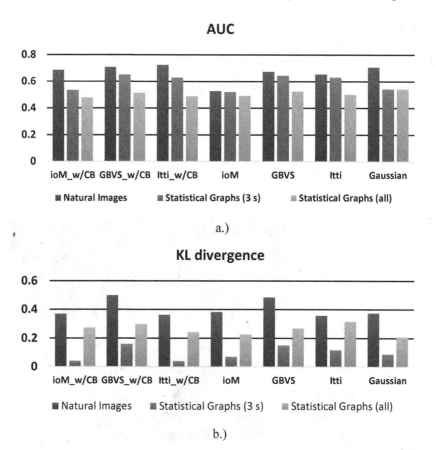

a.)

b.)

**Fig. 4.** Comparison of the predictive accuracy of the ioM, GBVS, and Itti saliency models when applied to natural images, and SGs using different similarity measures. (a) Uses the area under the curve of the receiver operating characteristic similarity measure. (b) Uses the Kullback-Leibler divergence similarity measure. Results are shown for the saliency models with center bias (left three groups of bars) and without center bias (right three groups of bars). The results of the Gaussian kernel are typically considered minimum necessary performance for minimum accuracy.

3 s of the SG trial, but only for the KL divergence similarity measure. When predicting the eye gaze for the entire SG trial most of the saliency models have a higher AUC score compared to the Gaussian Kernel, but in this case, all of the tested saliency models had a higher KL divergence similarity measure than the Gaussian kernel.

We also compared how the predictive accuracy of the saliency models used in this paper changed when eye gaze locations from the MIT1003 dataset were used, Fig. 5. For both similarity measures, an improvement in the predictive accuracy occurred in all of the saliency models we tested. Another improvement that occurred is that the Gaussian kernel no longer matches or outperforms the predictive accuracy of the saliency models using the eye gaze information from the MIT1003 dataset. Hopefully, this means that by using a more precise eye tracker, the predictive accuracy of the tested saliency models will also improve, using the AUC similarity measure when applied to SGs. What all of this most likely means is that bottom-up saliency models can with some accuracy, predict where people first look at simple SGs, but a more precise eye tracking system is necessary to definitively show this.

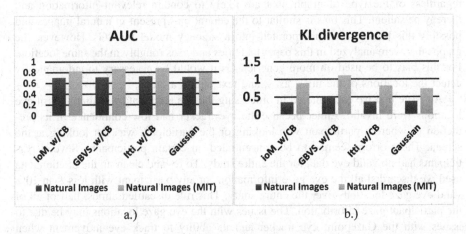

**Fig. 5.** Comparison of the predictive accuracy of the ioM, GBVS, and Itti saliency models with center bias when applied to the natural images in this study, but evaluated using the eye gaze locations from this study vs. the eye gaze locations from the MIT1003 dataset using different similarity measures. (a) This graph uses the area under the curve of the receiver operating characteristic similarity measure. (b) This graph uses the Kullback-Leibler divergence similarity measure.

## 3 Conclusion

Within this paper, we have analyzed the eye gaze of participants while they memorized SGs and natural images. We have shown that a person's viewing pattern when looking at simple SGs is different from their viewing pattern when looking at natural images. When a person looks at a natural image there is a strong unimodal bias near the center of the image. This strong central bias allows a person's gaze to be predicted, at higher than chance levels, using just a Gaussian mask centered in the middle of the image. The viewing pattern for the SGs analyzed is far more multimodal. For the graphs used in the study that we analyzed there were distinct attractors of the participants' gaze that was consistent across graph type and graph content. These attractors of attention are focused on the graph axes, title, and to a lesser degree the graph legend. These results are consistent with the results of other studies that have looked at the eye gaze patterns of individuals when they looked at natural images or SGs [11, 48].

Many visual saliency models try to predict where people will look in an image by trying to model some component of the human visual system. These models are typically only applied to natural images, but using bottom up principles of vision SGs can be processed like any other image. Based on the performance of the different saliency models in the results section it does seem like saliency models can predict where people will look in a graph, for the first few seconds at least, with accuracies better than chance and better than just assuming the center of the image is important. One hindrance to improving the predictive accuracy of saliency models is likely due to the fact that SGs are generally more structured than natural images. There are certain locations, regardless of the type of graph, that are likely to contain relevant information and thereby be salient. This bias is similar to the central bias present in natural images and possibly this bias can be incorporated into a saliency model for SGs. However, the graphs that were analyzed in this paper had titles and axes roughly in the same location. For this bias to be used on more generic SGs it would be necessary to automatically detect the locations of the titles, axes, and text within a graph.

. An issue that we encountered in processing the eye track data was that a lot of eye locations were invalid. Either because the eye tracker had low confidence in its prediction of where a participant was looking or the participant was not looking at the screen. These errors seemed to be concentrated on certain participants. Several participants had no valid eye data for the entire study. To try and clean up the fixation data used we discarded all the eye gaze information for any participant with less than 10% valid eye gaze locations over the entire study. This rule discarded almost half of all of the participant gaze information. The issues with the eye gaze locations may be due to issues with the Gazepoint eye tracker and its ability to track eye movement when participants wore corrective lenses. This is a common issue with eye trackers due to the way certain eye trackers calculate the pose of the eye [41]. Even after removing the eye tracks of users whose eye gaze couldn't be tracked effectively the wide variation in the inter-subject consistency and low average inter-subject consistency prevented the establishment of a true upper bound in predictive accuracy of the saliency models using the AUC similarity measure though the KL divergence similarity measure was more insensitive to issues with lost eye gaze samples.

, The issues with the missing eye gaze locations from the participants we did use also affected the results of the saliency model evaluation for both similarity measures, since the performance of the saliency models was much higher when the eye gaze information from the MIT1003 dataset was used for the natural images. Even though the KL divergence measure was more insensitive there was a distinct increase in the similarity measure score for the MIT1003 dataset. This suggests that with higher confidence eye gaze information the measured predictive quality of saliency models on SGs would also increase. Looking forward it would be ideal to evaluate the predicting accuracy of saliency models using the SGs and eye gaze information from the MASSVIS dataset to see if the SG based biasing improves the performance of a standard visual saliency model [11].

# References

1. Kosslyn, S.M.: Understanding charts and graphs. Appl. Cogn. Psychol. **3**, 185–225 (1989)
2. Harrison, A., Etienne-Cummings, R.: An entropy based ideal observer model for visual saliency. In: 2012 46th Annual Conference on Information Sciences and Systems (CISS), pp. 1–6. IEEE (2012)
3. Harel, J., Koch, C., Perona, P.: Graph-based visual saliency. In: Advances in Neural Information Processing Systems, pp. 545–552 (2007)
4. Itti, L., Koch, C., Niebur, E.: A model of saliency-based visual attention for rapid scene analysis. IEEE Trans. Pattern Anal. Mach. Intell. **20**, 1254–1259 (1998)
5. Zhang, L., Tong, M.H., Marks, T.K., Shan, H., Cottrell, G.W.: SUN: a Bayesian framework for saliency using natural statistics. J. Vis. **8**, 32.1–32.20 (2008)
6. Gattis, M., Holyoak, K.J.: How graphs mediate analog and symbolic representation. In: Proceedings of the 16th Annual Conference of the Cognitive Science Society (1994)
7. Aumer-Ryan, P.: Visual rating system for HFES graphics: design and analysis. In: Proceedings of the Human Factors and Ergonomics Society Annual Meeting, pp. 2124–2128 (2006)
8. Fausset, C.B., Rogers, W.A., Fisk, A.D.: Visual graph display guidelines, Atlanta, GA (2008)
9. Gillan, D.J., Wickens, C.D., Hollands, J.G., Carswell, C.M.: Guidelines for presenting quantitative data in HFES publications. Hum. Factors: J. Hum. Factors Ergon. Soc. **40**, 28–41 (1998)
10. Petkosek, M.A., Moroney, W.F.: Guidelines for constructing graphs. In: Human Factors and Ergonomics Society Annual Meeting, pp. 1006–1010 (2004)
11. Borkin, M.A., Bylinskii, Z., Kim, N.W., Bainbridge, C.M., Yeh, C.S., Borkin, D., Pfister, H., Member, S., Oliva, A.: Beyond memorability: visualization recognition and recall. IEEE Trans. Vis. Comput. Graph. **22**, 519–528 (2016)
12. Borkin, M.A., Vo, A.A., Bylinskii, Z., Isola, P., Sunkavalli, S., Oliva, A., Pfister, H.: What makes a visualization memorable? IEEE Trans. Vis. Comput. Graph. **19**, 2306–2315 (2013)
13. Vessey, I., Galletta, D.: Cognitive fit: an empirical study of information acquisition. Inf. Syst. Res. **2**, 63–84 (1991)
14. Vessey, I.: Cognitive fit: a theory-based analysis of the graphs versus tables literature. Decis. Sci. **22**, 219–240 (1991)
15. Ngo, D.C.L., Samsudin, A., Abdullah, R.: Aesthetic measures for assessing graphic screens. J. Inf. Sci. Eng. **16**, 97–116 (2000)
16. Zen, M., Vanderdonckt, J.: Towards an evaluation of graphical user interfaces aesthetics based on metrics (2014)
17. Acartürk, C.: Towards a systematic understanding of graphical cues in communication through statistical graphs. J. Vis. Lang. Comput. **25**, 76–88 (2014)
18. Greenberg, R.A.: Graph comprehension: difficulties, individual differences, and instruction (2014)
19. Halford, G.S., Baker, R., McCredden, J.E., Bain, J.D.: How many variables can humans process? Psychol. Sci. **16**, 70–76 (2005)
20. Pinker, S.: Theory of graph comprehension (1959)

21. Trickett, S.B., Trafton, J.G.: Toward a comprehensive model of graph comprehension: making the case for spatial cognition. In: Barker-Plummer, D., Cox, R., Swoboda, N. (eds.) Diagrams 2006. LNCS (LNAI), vol. 4045, pp. 286–300. Springer, Heidelberg (2006). doi:10.1007/11783183_38

22. Treisman, A.M., Gelade, G.: A feature-integration theory of attention. Cogn. Psychol. **12**, 97–136 (1980)

23. Oliva, A., Torralba, A., Castelhano, M.S., Henderson, J.M.: Top-down control of visual attention in object detection. In: Proceedings 2003 International Conference on Image Processing (Cat. No. 03CH37429), p. I-253-6. IEEE (2003)

24. Gao, D., Vasconcelos, N.: Integrated learning of saliency, complex features, and object detectors from cluttered scenes. In: 2005 IEEE Computer Society Conference on Computer Vision and Pattern Recognition (CVPR 2005), pp. 282–287. IEEE (2005)

25. Gao, D., Vasconcelos, N.: Discriminant saliency for visual recognition from cluttered scenes. Adv. Neural. Inf. Process. Syst. **17**, 1 (2004)

26. Torralba, A., Oliva, A., Castelhano, M.S., Henderson, J.M.: Contextual guidance of eye movements and attention in real-world scenes: the role of global features in object search. Psychol. Rev. **113**, 766–786 (2006)

27. Parkhurst, D.J., Law, K., Niebur, E.: Modeling the role of salience in the allocation of overt visual attention. Vis. Res. **42**, 107–123 (2002)

28. Itti, L., Koch, C.: A saliency-based search mechanism for overt and covert shifts of visual attention. Vis. Res. **40**, 1489–1506 (2000)

29. Zhao, Q., Koch, C.: Learning a saliency map using fixated locations in natural scenes. J. Vis. **11**, 1–15 (2011)

30. Chauvin, A., Herault, J., Marendaz, C., Peyrin, C.: Natural scene perception: visual attractors and images processing. In: Connectionist Models of Cognition and Perception - Proceedings of the Seventh Neural Computation and Psychology Workshop, pp. 236–248. World Scientific Publishing Co. Pte. Ltd., Singapore (2002)

31. Lin, Y., Fang, B., Tang, Y.: A computational model for saliency maps by using local entropy. In: AAAI Conference on Artificial Intelligence (2010)

32. Koch, C., Ullman, S.: Shifts in selective visual attention: towards the underlying neural circuitry. Hum. Neurobiol. **4**, 219–227 (1985)

33. Peters, R.J., Iyer, A., Itti, L., Koch, C.: Components of bottom-up gaze allocation in natural images. Vis. Res. **45**, 2397–2416 (2005)

34. Kadir, T., Brady, M.: Saliency, scale and image description. Int. J. Comput. Vis. **45**, 83–105 (2001)

35. Tamayo, N., Traver, V.J.J.: Entropy-based saliency computation in log-polar images. In: Proceedings of the International Conference on Computer Vision Theory and Applications, pp. 501–506 (2008)

36. Wang, W., Wang, Y., Huang, Q., Gao, W.: Measuring visual saliency by site entropy rate. In: 2010 IEEE Computer Society Conference on Computer Vision and Pattern Recognition, pp. 2368–2375. IEEE (2010)

37. Bruce, N.D.B., Tsotsos, J.K.: Saliency based on information maximization. Adv. Neural. Inf. Process. Syst. **18**, 155–162 (2006)

38. Bruce, N.D.B., Tsotsos, J.K.: Saliency, attention, and visual search: an information theoretic approach. J. Vis. **9**, 5.1–5.24 (2009)

39. Itti, L., Baldi, P.: Bayesian surprise attracts human attention. Adv. Neural Inf. Process. Syst. **18**, 547 (2006)

40. Judd, T., Ehinger, K., Durand, F., Torralba, A.: Learning to predict where humans look. In: 2009 IEEE 12th International Conference on Computer Vision, pp. 2106–2113. IEEE (2009)

41. Dahlberg, J.: Eye tracking with eye glasses (2010)

42. Tatler, B.W.: The central fixation bias in scene viewing: selecting an optimal viewing position independently of motor biases and image feature distributions. J. Vis. **7**, 4 (2007)
43. Hart, B.M., Vockeroth, J., Schumann, F., Bartl, K., Schneider, E., Konig, P., Einhäuser, W., Marius, B., Vockeroth, J., Bartl, K., Schneider, E., Einhäuser, W.: Gaze allocation in natural stimuli: comparing free exploration to head-fixed viewing conditions. Vis. Cogn. **17**, 1132–1158 (2009)
44. Schumann, F., Einhäuser-Treyer, W., Vockeroth, J., Bartl, K., Schneider, E., König, P.: Salient features in gaze-aligned recordings of human visual input during free exploration of natural environments. J. Vis. **8**, 12.1–12.17 (2008)
45. Bylinskii, Z., Borkin, M.A.: Eye fixation metrics for large scale analysis of information visualizations. In: ETVIS Workshop on Eye Tracking and Visualization (2015)
46. Borji, A., Itti, L.: State-of-the-art in visual attention modeling. IEEE Trans. Pattern Anal. Mach. Intell. **35**, 185–207 (2013)
47. Cooper, R.A., Plaisted-Grant, K.C., Baron-Cohen, S., Simons, J.S.: Eye movements reveal a dissociation between memory encoding and retrieval in adults with autism. Cognition **159**, 127–138 (2017)
48. Tilke, J., Ehinger, K., Durand, F., Torralba, A.: Learning to predict where humans look. In: Proceedings of IEEE International Conference on Computer Vision, pp. 2106–2113 (2009)

# Performance Evaluation of the Gazepoint GP3 Eye Tracking Device Based on Pupil Dilation

Pujitha Mannaru[1(✉)], Balakumar Balasingam[1], Krishna Pattipati[1], Ciara Sibley[2], and Joseph T. Coyne[2]

[1] Department of Electrical and Computer Engineering,
University of Connecticut, Storrs, CT, USA
{pujitha.mannaru,balakumar.balasingam,krishna.pattipati}@uconn.edu
[2] Warfighter Human Systems Integration Lab, Naval Research Laboratory,
Washington DC, USA
{ciara.sibley,joseph.coyne}@nrl.navy.mil

**Abstract.** Eye tracking is considered one of the most salient methods to study the cognitive demands of humans in human computer interactive systems, due to the unobtrusiveness, flexibility and the development of inexpensive eye trackers. In this work, we evaluate the applicability of these low cost eyetrackers to study pupillary response to varying memory loads and luminance conditions. Specifically, we examine a low-cost eye tracker, the Gazepoint GP3, and objectively evaluate its ability to differentiate pupil dilation metrics under different cognitive loads and luminance conditions. The classification performance is computed in the form of a receiver operating characteristic (ROC) curve and the results indicate that Gazepoint provides a reliable eye tracker to human computer interaction applications requiring pupil dilation studies.

**Keywords:** Low-cost eye trackers · Eye tracker performance · Gazepoint · Pupil dilation · Memory load · TEPR · Power spectral density

## 1 Introduction

Eye tracking metrics are found to be useful indicators of visual attention and cognitive workload in numerous application areas, including reading and language comprehension [1], driving [2], individual differences [3], gaming devices [4], and medical applications [5]. Eye tracking devices (eye trackers) are used to collect measurements, such as pupil dilation, gaze locations and eye-closing patterns. Recent technical advances in video sensors and miniaturized computing power have resulted in cost-effective mass produced eye tracking devices; thus, several low-cost eye tracking devices have become available for researchers. However, the effectiveness of these low-cost devices to study human behavior remains an ongoing investigation [6–13] and is the objective of this paper. Specifically, we examine a low-cost eye tracker, the Gazepoint GP3 (cost ≈ $500), and objectively evaluate its ability to differentiate pupil dilation metrics under different

© Springer International Publishing AG 2017
D.D. Schmorrow and C.M. Fidopiastis (Eds.): AC 2017, Part I, LNAI 10284, pp. 166–175, 2017.
DOI: 10.1007/978-3-319-58628-1_14

cognitive loads and luminance conditions. To our knowledge, this is one of the first studies reporting the effectiveness of Gazepoint GP3 in capturing pupillary data.

Several pupillary metrics have been proposed in the past as useful indices of cognitive context [14–16]. Out of those, we employ two widely accepted metrics in this paper: one computed in the time domain and the other in the frequency domain. Using data collected by the Gazepoint GP3 eye tracking device, a time domain measure, task evoked pupillary response (TEPR) [17], as well as a recently published frequency domain measure, pupillary power spectral density (PSD) [18], are computed and evaluated as indicators of mental workload under different luminance conditions. It has been well established that pupil diameter is impacted by both mental workload and luminance conditions [19–24]. Therefore, the objective of our experiment is to verify the potential use of Gazepoint system to study the impact of these two factors on pupil diameter in studies involving cognitive context analysis.

Towards this end, we employed the digit span task [19] experiment under different luminance conditions, which is explained in Sect. 2. The rest of the paper is organized as follows: data collection and analysis methods are described in Sects. 2 and 3, respectively, the results of classification analysis are presented and discussed in Sect. 4, and the paper is concluded in Sect. 5.

## 2 Experiment

### 2.1 Subjects

Twenty participants ranging in age from 22 to 29 years ($M = 23.9, SD = 2.41$) voluntarily participated in the experiment conducted by researchers from the Naval Research laboratory (NRL) at the Naval Aerospace Medical Institute (NAMI).

### 2.2 Apparatus

All the eye tracking data were collected using the Gazepoint GP3 system. The system was calibrated for each user according to the Gazepoint Application Program Interface (API) manual [25]. GP3 collects the pupillary data, specifically, pupil size in pixels for each eye and their corresponding binary quality factor (valid/invalid) at 60 samples/s.

### 2.3 Task

A visual *digit span task* (also known as memory span task), which is a common technique used for assessing working memory capacity, was employed to assess the pupillary response of the participants to mental workload. In this task, participants are presented with a series of numbers and are then asked to recall the digits in the order they saw them. Longer series of numbers present more of a challenge for working memory, while shorter series are expected to be easier.

A *luminance change task* was employed to assess the pupillary response of the participants to the screen luminance. While completing the digit span task, participants were fixating on a monitor which varied in the background luminance (black, gray, and white).

## 2.4   Procedure

As mentioned in the previous section, participants engaged in a digit span task. Each participant was given four sets of digits of sizes 3, 5, 7 and 9 under three different screen luminance conditions (black, gray and white). The experiment utilized a within subject design (i.e., repeated measures) in which each participant completed all digit span set sizes (3, 5, 7 and 9, randomly ordered and exhaustive) three times for each of the 3 different background colors (white, gray, and black). Thus, a total of 36(= 4 set sizes × 3 colors × 3 times) trials were conducted. Participants were told to focus on a central fixation cross (a "+" sign ~50 pixels tall and wide) that was offset from the background color (80 brighter for the black and gray backgrounds, and 80 darker for the white background). The string of numbers was then sequentially presented ~1 s per number. Following each number set (e.g., "2, 6, 1, 8, 4"), a numeric keypad appeared on the screen and participants used the mouse to input the string of numbers ("2, 6, 1, 8, 4") by clicking on the corresponding numbers in order. The keypad was used to ensure that participants continued to fixate on the screen, while they were making a response. When satisfied, the participants clicked the submit button. Participants were not given performance feedback on their response accuracy. Following each set of digits, there was a pause of ≈3 s before presenting the participant with a numeric keypad on the monitor to enter his/her response. The pupillary measures from this time segment, known as the *encoding phase* of the memory, are analyzed here. The total time to complete the digit span task varied from 10–15 min, depending on the participant's response times.

# 3   Data Analysis

The Gazepoint GP3 collects the following pupillary data: pupil size in pixels for each eye and their corresponding binary quality factors (valid/invalid) at 60 samples/s, the scale factor of each eye pupil (unitless), whose value equals 1 at calibration depth, is less than 1 when the user is closer to the eye tracker and greater than 1 when the user is further away. Only data from the encoding time segment are analyzed in this work, as it has been established by the human factors researchers that the maximum pupil dilation occurs during the encoding of the stimulus materials for short term memory recall tasks [26,27].

## 3.1   Data Preprocessing

For *time-domain analysis* (TEPR), the poor quality samples (quality factor = 0) of the pupil size signals were marked as missing values (or NaN in

MATLAB® [28]). Pupil size data of the eye with fewer missing observations [29] were utilized for analysis. A "clean-up" function was employed to remove all the data below 4th percentile and above 98th percentile, in order to remove any sudden dips/peaks in the pupil size signal. Then, a hampel filter (of order 6) [30] was applied to remove outliers and a linear interpolator was used to recover missing values. Figure 1a shows an example of raw data and filtered data signals.

For *frequency-domain analysis* (PSD), the linear trend in the above pre-processed signals was removed using the *detrend* function in MATLAB® and the resulting signals were passed through a zero-phase lowpass butterworth filter with a cutoff frequency $f_c = 4$ Hz using the *filtfilt* function, since most of the pupillary activity falls in the frequency range of 0–4 Hz [31]. Figure 1b shows an example of detrended data and filtered data signals.

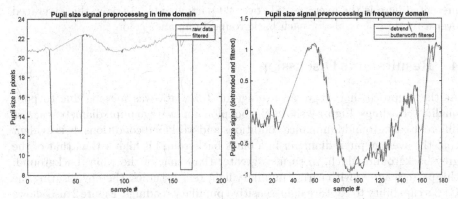

(a) Preprocessing for Time domain analysis  (b)  Preprocessing  for  frequency-domain analysis

**Fig. 1.** Pupil size signal preprocessing

## 3.2  Data Analysis

**Task Evoked Pupillary Response (TEPR):** To evaluate the ability of the eye tracker in capturing the changes in pupil diameter caused by mental workload changes, we analyzed the data of set sizes 3 (labeled as EASY), 5 (labeled as MEDIUM) and 7 (labeled as HARD) only. The set size 9 was excluded from the analysis since recall performance dropped to 65% (i.e., only remembering 65% of the 9 numbers) and there was increased variability between participants, suggesting it was either too difficult for some participants or that some participants gave up. For classification purposes, the median values of the pupil size in the encoding phase (TEPR), for each person, for each set size, each background color, and for each trial, (e.g., pupil size of person 13, set size 3 in a black background for the first trial) were computed over a sliding window of size

30 samples with an overlap of 25 samples ($\approx$80% overlap). A simple cut-point grouping into binary classes was implemented for pairs of set sizes 3 (EASY) vs. 7 (HARD), 3 (EASY) vs 5 (MEDIUM) and 5 (MEDIUM) vs. 7 (HARD) for the corresponding pairs of the moving-median filtered signals. The Receiver Operating Characteristic (ROC) curves [32] were drawn by varying the cut-points from the minimum of the two signals, in steps of 0.01 pixels, to the maximum value of the two signals.

**Power Spectral Density (PSD):** PSD of the pupil diameter signals was computed for each person using the Welch's method with segments of 50 samples with 50% overlap [18]. Each segment was windowed with a Hamming window. Only the 'encoding' phase was considered when computing PSD under the memory tasks of set size 3 (EASY) vs set size 5 (MEDIUM) vs. set size 7 (HARD). PSD presented here is the average PSD over 20 participants * 3 trials; thus averaged over a total of 60 trials for each background luminance color.

## 4    Results and Discussion

At the preprocessing stage, an average of 37% data was missing due to poor quality recordings. Figure 2 shows the boxplots for average pupil diameters across different background luminance conditions and workload conditions. It is evident that the average pupil diameter in a black background is higher than that of the grey background which, in turn, is greater than that of the white background; this pattern agrees with earlier pupillary light reflex studies, thereby assuring the GP3's capability to capture light-sensitive pupillary readings. Figure 2 also shows the differences in average pupil diameter for different workload tasks within the same background conditions and it can be seen that the average pupil diameter for set size 3 is lower than that of set size 7 under all 3 luminance conditions. However, the pupil diameters of set size 5 is not clearly greater than (or lesser than) for set size 3 (or for set size 7) under black and grey background luminance conditions.

To further analyze the differences in TEPRs corresponding to the different set sizes, we plotted the ROC curves from classification as described in Sect. 3. An example set of ROC curves for one person are shown in Figs. 3, 4 and 5. For this particular example, Fig. 3 shows a 100% accuracy in classifying pupil size signals of set size 3 vs. 7 for all three background conditions, whereas a 68% accuracy in classifying pupil size signals of set size 3 vs. 5 in grey background conditions and a 78% accuracy in classifying pupil size signals of set size 5 vs. 7 in white background conditions. Table 1 gives the average classification accuracy values over all participants and over all 3 repeated trials. Therefore, the minimum average classification accuracy is approximately 80%, which is considered a significant value by psychologists in detecting human cognitive context.

Figure 6 shows the results of PSD analysis, where Figs. 6(a–c) correspond to black, grey and white background conditions, respectively. The results agree with earlier studies only in the average power spectral densities of set size 3 vs.

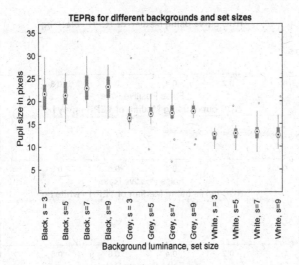

**Fig. 2.** Boxplot of average pupil diameters under different backgrounds and mental workloads

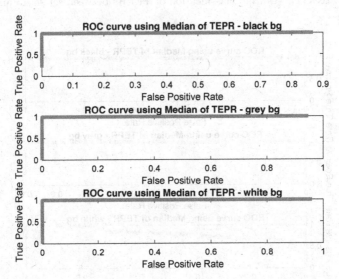

**Fig. 3.** ROC curves from classification of TEPRs between set size 3 and 7

set size 5 or 7. However, the results we obtained do not conform to the finding that average PSD increases in the frequency range of 0.1–0.5 Hz and 1.6–3.5 Hz with increase in cognitive workload as the average PSD in set size 5 is seen to be greater than that of set size 7. This could be due to the recovery of lost data points by using a linear interpolator or due to similar spectral behavior of pupils during set sizes 5 and 7. Also, to our knowledge, there is no detailed mechanism

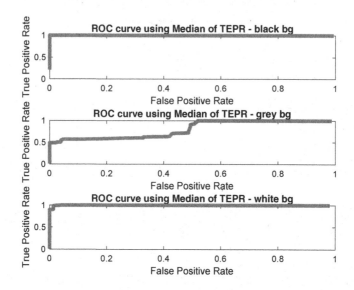

**Fig. 4.** ROC curves from classification of TEPRs between set size 3 and 5

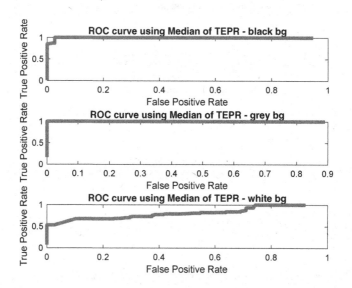

**Fig. 5.** ROC curves from classification of TEPRs between set size 5 and 7

for this phenomena of pupil control and PSD, yet. Future research will integrate the PSD metrics in classification studies to attempt to validate the findings of Peysakhovich et al. [18] and Nakayama and Shimizu [31].

**Table 1.** Average accuracies in TEPR classification

| Average accuracies in % | | | |
| --- | --- | --- | --- |
| Background luminance conditions | Set size 3 vs. 7 | Set size 3 vs. 5 | Set size 5 vs. 7 |
| Black | 90.73 | 79.83 | 83.28 |
| Grey | 87.53 | 80.92 | 81.77 |
| White | 86.89 | 81.45 | 79.68 |

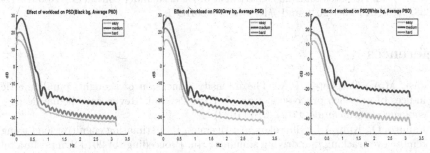

(a) PSD in black luminance conditions (b) PSD in grey luminance conditions (c) PSD in white luminance conditions

**Fig. 6.** Power spectral density under different workload conditions

## 5   Summary and Conclusion

In this paper, we evaluated the performance of Gazepoint GP3, a low-cost eye tracker, by using pupillary metrics that are already tested and used by human factors researchers: TEPRs and PSD. We collected pupil size data from 20 volunteers engaged in a visual digit span task. First, a preprocessing routine was employed to filter out outliers from the data for time domain analysis, and low pass filtering was performed prior to frequency domain analysis. Then, TEPRs and PSDs were computed and studied for different digit set sizes. The classification performance is computed in the form of a receiver operating characteristic (ROC) curve and the results show the applicability and limitations of low-cost eye tracking devices by cognitive workload researchers.

The results indicate that the Gazepoint GP3 is an easy and inexpensive tool that can be utilized in psychological studies involving pupil diameter data. The classification results indicate that the eye tracker does a good job in classifying mental workloads under different background luminance conditions; however, it is not a robust tool for frequency domain analysis which could be attributable to linear interpolation of poor quality readings. Researchers, with budget constraints, who are interested in incorporating pupillary measures of cognitive workload now have access to a reliable inexpensive eye tracker. However, they should keep in mind the GP3 is limited to collecting pupil diameter data for tasks which use a single screen and is vulnerable to loss of chunks of data. Finally, we believe that the low cost eyetrackers are of great value to researchers from all disciplines trying to incorporate human factors aspects in their systems.

**Acknowledgements.** The authors would like to thank Dr. Jeffrey Morrison and the Command Decision Making (CDM) program at the U.S. Office of Naval Research and Department of Defense High Performance Computing Modernization Program for supporting this work. In addition, the authors would like to thank the symposium organizers for their encouragement of this work. This research was funded by the U.S. Office of Naval Research and the Department of Defense under contracts #N00014-12-1-0238, #N00014-16-1-2036 and #HPCM034125HQU.

# References

1. Just, M.A., Carpenter, P.A.: The intensity dimension of thought: pupillometric indices of sentence processing. Can. J. Exp. Psychol./Revue canadienne de psychologie expérimentale **47**(2), 310 (1993)
2. Palinko, O., Kun, A.L., Shyrokov, A., Heeman, P.: Estimating cognitive load using remote eye tracking in a driving simulator. In: Proceedings of 2010 Symposium on Eye-Tracking Research and Applications, pp. 141–144. ACM (2010)
3. Odenheimer, G., Funkenstein, H., Beckett, L., Chown, M., Pilgrim, D., Evans, D., Albert, M.: Comparison of neurologic changes in'successfully aging'persons vs the total aging population. Arch. Neurol. **51**(6), 573–580 (1994)
4. Ekman, I.M., Poikola, A.W., Mäkäräinen, M.K.: Invisible eni: using gaze and pupil size to control a game. In: CHI 2008 Extended Abstracts on Human Factors in Computing Systems, pp. 3135–3140. ACM (2008)
5. Ren, P., Barreto, A., Gao, Y., Adjouadi, M.: Affective assessment of computer users based on processing the pupil diameter signal. In: Engineering in Medicine and Biology Society, EMBC, 2011 Annual International Conference of the IEEE, pp. 2594–2597. IEEE (2011)
6. Zugal, S., Pinggera, J.: Low–cost eye–trackers: useful for information systems research? In: Iliadis, L., Papazoglou, M., Pohl, K. (eds.) CAiSE 2014. LNBIP, vol. 178, pp. 159–170. Springer, Cham (2014). doi:10.1007/978-3-319-07869-4_14
7. Dalmaijer, E.: Is the low-cost eyetribe eye tracker any good for research? Technical report, PeerJ PrePrints (2014)
8. Ooms, K., Dupont, L., Lapon, L., Popelka, S.: Accuracy and precision of fixation locations recorded with the low-cost eye tribe tracker in different experimental setups. J. Eye Mov. Res. **8**(1) (2015)
9. Ferhat, O., Vilariño, F.: Low cost eye tracking. Comput. Intell. Neurosci. **2016**, 17 (2016)
10. Coyne, J., Sibley, C.: Investigating the use of two low cost eye tracking systems for detecting pupillary response to changes in mental workload. In: Proceedings of Human Factors and Ergonomics Society Annual Meeting, vol. 60, pp. 37–41. SAGE Publications (2016)
11. Funke, G., Greenlee, E., Carter, M., Dukes, A., Brown, R., Menke, L.: Which eye tracker is right for your research? Performance evaluation of several cost variant eye trackers. In: Proceedings of Human Factors and Ergonomics Society Annual Meeting, vol. 60, pp. 1240–1244. SAGE Publications (2016)

12. Gibaldi, A., Vanegas, M., Bex, P.J., Maiello, G.: Evaluation of the Tobii EyeX eye tracking controller and Matlab toolkit for research. Behav. Res. Methods 1–24 (2016)
13. Janthanasub, V., Meesad, P.: Evaluation of a low-cost eye tracking system for computer input. King Mongkuts Univ. Technol. North Bangk. Int. J. Appl. Sci. Technol. **8**(3), 185–196 (2015)
14. Causse, M., Sénard, J.-M., Démonet, J.F., Pastor, J.: Monitoring cognitive and emotional processes through pupil and cardiac response during dynamic versus logical task. Appl. Psychophysiol. Biofeedback **35**(2), 115–123 (2010)
15. Mannaru, P., Balasingam, B., Pattipati, K., Sibley, C., Coyne, J.: Cognitive context detection in UAS operators using pupillary measurements. In: SPIE Defense+Security, p. 98510Q. International Society for Optics and Photonics (2016)
16. Mandrick, K., Peysakhovich, V., Rémy, F., Lepron, E., Causse, M.: Neural and psychophysiological correlates of human performance under stress and high mental workload. Biol. Psychol. **121**, 62–73 (2016)
17. Beatty, J.: Task-evoked pupillary responses, processing load, and the structure of processing resources. Psychol. Bull. **91**(2), 276 (1982)
18. Peysakhovich, V., Causse, M., Scannella, S., Dehais, F.: Frequency analysis of a task-evoked pupillary response: luminance-independent measure of mental effort. Int. J. Psychophysiol. **97**(1), 30–37 (2015)
19. Kahneman, D., Beatty, J.: Pupil diameter and load on memory. Science **154**(3756), 1583–1585 (1966)
20. Tryon, W.W.: Pupillometry: a survey of sources of variation. Psychophysiology **12**(1), 90–93 (1975)
21. Taptagaporn, S., Saito, S.: How display polarity and lighting conditions affect the pupil size of VDT operators. Ergonomics **33**(2), 201–208 (1990)
22. Goldinger, S.D., Papesh, M.H.: Pupil dilation reflects the creation and retrieval of memories. Curr. Dir. Psychol. Sci. **21**(2), 90–95 (2012)
23. Winn, B., Whitaker, D., Elliott, D.B., Phillips, N.J.: Factors affecting light-adapted pupil size in normal human subjects. Investig. Ophthalmol. Vis. Sci. **35**(3), 1132–1137 (1994)
24. Peysakhovich, V., Vachon, F., Dehais, F.: The impact of luminance on tonic and phasic pupillary responses to sustained cognitive load. Int. J. Psychophysiol. **112**, 40–45 (2017)
25. Gazepoint API. http://www.gazept.com/dl/Gazepoint_API_v2.0.pdf
26. Beatty, J., Lucero-Wagoner, B.: The pupillary system. Handb. Psychophysiol. **2**, 142–162 (2000)
27. Gardner, R.M., Beltramo, J.S., Krinsky, R.: Pupillary changes during encoding, storage, and retrieval of information. Percept. Mot. Skills **41**(3), 951–955 (1975)
28. MATLAB: R2016a. The MathWorks Inc., Natick (2016)
29. Papesh, M.H., Goldinger, S.D., Hout, M.C.: Memory strength and specificity revealed by pupillometry. Int. J. Psychophysiol. **83**(1), 56–64 (2012)
30. Pearson, R.K.: Outliers in process modeling and identification. IEEE Trans. Control Syst. Technol. **10**(1), 55–63 (2002)
31. Nakayama, M., Shimizu, Y.: Frequency analysis of task evoked pupillary response and eye-movement. In: Proceedings of 2004 Symposium on Eye Tracking Research Applications, pp. 71–76. ACM (2004)
32. Fawcett, T.: An introduction to ROC analysis. Pattern Recogn. Lett. **27**(8), 861–874 (2006)

# Patterns of Attention: How Data Visualizations Are Read

Laura E. Matzen$^{(\boxtimes)}$, Michael J. Haass, Kristin M. Divis,
and Mallory C. Stites

Sandia National Laboratories, Albuquerque, USA
{lematze,mjhaass,kmdivis,mcstite}@sandia.gov

**Abstract.** Data visualizations are used to communicate information to people in a wide variety of contexts, but few tools are available to help visualization designers evaluate the effectiveness of their designs. Visual saliency maps that predict which regions of an image are likely to draw the viewer's attention could be a useful evaluation tool, but existing models of visual saliency often make poor predictions for abstract data visualizations. These models do not take into account the importance of features like text in visualizations, which may lead to inaccurate saliency maps. In this paper we use data from two eye tracking experiments to investigate attention to text in data visualizations. The data sets were collected under two different task conditions: a memory task and a free viewing task. Across both tasks, the text elements in the visualizations consistently drew attention, especially during early stages of viewing. These findings highlight the need to incorporate additional features into saliency models that will be applied to visualizations.

**Keywords:** Data visualizations · Text · Eye tracking

## 1 Introduction

Data visualizations are widely used to convey information, yet it is difficult to evaluate whether or not they are effective. Previous work on graph comprehension has suggested that the effectiveness of a graph depends on the relationships between the visual properties of the graph, the experience and expectations of the user, and the type of information to be extracted from the graph (reviewed in [26]). As such, the recommendations for the "best" way to present as dataset may differ for every new visualization created.

Eye tracking can provide insight into how people comprehend data visualizations. It is a useful measure of where visual attention is being directed, as attention is typically closely linked with gaze location (see [24] for review). Eye tracking measures are divided into fixations (periods of relative stability) and saccades (ballistic movements, during which effectively no new visual information is processed). In general, people tend to spend more time looking at, and make more fixations on, areas of a display that are difficult to process or important to their current task goals [24]. Graph comprehension researchers have devised various metrics to evaluate ease of processing information from graphs. For example, the time to the first fixation in a region is taken

© Springer International Publishing AG 2017
D.D. Schmorrow and C.M. Fidopiastis (Eds.): AC 2017, Part I, LNAI 10284, pp. 176–191, 2017.
DOI: 10.1007/978-3-319-58628-1_15

as an indicator of how easy the region was to find. The time from landing in a region to making a decision about a graph is taken as an indicator of how easy the information was to process after it was found (see [5, 12] for discussions of other useful metrics). In this way, eye movement patterns can provide a window into the ongoing cognitive processes taking place as people comprehend data visualizations.

Although eye tracking metrics have the potential to be useful in evaluating the effectiveness of a data visualization in conveying information to a viewer, they must be evaluated within the context of many different factors that affect viewers' eye movement patterns. One factor is the viewer's task, which has a large impact on his or her eye movements. For example, Goldberg and Helfman [12] found more fixations to a graph when viewers subtracted or added data than when they were tasked with simply extracting values. Similarly, Strobel et al. [27] found more fixations to line graphs than bar graphs when users were performing trend analyses. The type of visualization technique used also impacts how users take in the same information, with, for example, more fixations for unfamiliar or difficult visualizations [10, 11]. Characteristics of the viewer also influence eye movement behaviors. More experienced users can extract information in less time and may pay attention to different aspects of a visualization than less experienced viewers [20].

To address the diversity of factors that can influence what aspects of a data visualization draw the viewer's attention, it is useful to distinguish between top-down and bottom-up visual attention. Top-down, or goal-oriented, visual attention is driven by the viewer's goals and expectations. Meanwhile, bottom-up visual attention is driven by the physical characteristics of the image, such as color and contrast [9, 22]. There are existing models of bottom-up visual attention that use the visual properties of an image to predict which parts of the image will draw a viewer's attention (cf. [16]). These models take an input image and generate a map of visual saliency, where the salient regions are those that are more likely to attract bottom-up visual attention. To assess the ability of the models to predict where people will look, the saliency maps are compared to eye tracking data collected under free viewing conditions (i.e. the participants view the images for a fixed amount of time with no specific task to complete [2]).

In prior work, we developed evaluation approaches for data visualizations that incorporate eye tracking data, saliency maps, and sensor phenomenology [20]. We demonstrated that comparing saliency maps to eye tracking data collected from experienced and inexperienced viewers can highlight the differences between features that are highly salient and features that are highly task-relevant. Using saliency maps and eye tracking data in combination was informative for teasing apart which aspects of the data drew viewers' attention from both the bottom-up and top-down perspectives. This information can then be applied to improving the visual representation of the data and to assessing feature detection algorithms.

In subsequent work, we have attempted to extend this general approach from the realm of sensor data into the domain of abstract data visualizations. Predicting what parts of a visualization will draw the user's attention would be a useful first pass at evaluation [25]. However, our work has found that existing saliency maps do not work well for predicting where viewers will look in abstract data visualizations. In Haass et al. [13], we evaluated the ability of multiple models of visual saliency to explain viewing behaviors in natural scenes as well as data visualizations. The models performed well for natural scenes, but they were poor predictors of viewing patterns for abstract data visualizations. Based on comparisons of the saliency maps and fixations, a large part of the discrepancy seems to be due to people attending to text in the data visualizations. The text elements received a high proportion of the viewers' fixations, but were generally not identified as salient in the saliency maps. The visual properties of text are quite different from those of features in natural scenes, so models designed to predict eye movement in scene viewing do not account for the text's influence on the viewer's patterns of attention.

The findings of Haass et al. [13] highlight the point that abstract data visualizations are very different from natural scenes – each element was chosen by a designer and is there for a reason. In this way, data visualizations share some commonalities with print ads, which are also comprised of a combination of images and text to convey a message. Eye-tracking techniques have been applied to the print ad literature (see review in [14]), and their findings have largely echoed the graph comprehension literature in showing that the viewer's goals have a huge influence over eye movement guidance. One robust finding is that when viewers are asked to learn about a product or decide on a product to purchase, they tend to look at the text of an ad earlier and for more time—roughly 70% of viewing time—than when they are evaluating an ad for its likeability or effectiveness (in which case viewers show a preference for fixating the images). Readers are also more likely to fixate, and spend more time viewing, ads with large text relative to small text, although the same is not true for photo size. Importantly, the characteristics of eye movements also change when people look at different elements of ads: readers make longer fixation durations and saccades on graphical elements compared to text.

It is worth noting that the graphical elements in ads and data visualizations serve different purposes (display a product versus convey numeric information, respectively), and so different mechanisms might influence viewing patterns for these two visualization types. However, gaining an understanding of the features that drive eye movements in a range of visualizations is an important first step in understanding how viewers allocate their attention between text and graphics during successful comprehension. Uncovering these basic features will help inform models of visual saliency. Our previous work has already shown that simple saliency maps are not sufficient to explain viewing patterns in visualizations [13]. Updating these models to incorporate insights regarding how users allocate their attention between text and graphics might help visualization designers to assess their designs more accurately than models that treat text similarly to graphics.

In the present study, we take a closer look at viewers' attention to text in data visualizations. First, we analyzed eye tracking data collected by Borkin et al. [3] in the context of a memory study. While their study included a wide range of visualizations, we selected and analyzed a subset of the data that included frequently-used graph types, such as bar charts and line graphs. We then assessed how much attention participants devoted to different regions of the visualizations, paying particular attention to how attention was allocated to regions that contained text compared to those that did not. The data collected by Borkin et al. [3], henceforth referred to as the MASSVIS data, was collected during a memory study. The parameters of this task are somewhat different from those used in the eye tracking datasets that are commonly used to evaluate visual saliency models. To address this, we collected eye tracking data from a new group of participants who completed a free viewing task for the same subset of the MASSVIS images and an additional set of newly created data visualizations.

## 2 Viewing Data Visualizations in a Memory Task

To study how viewers divide their attention between text and graphics in data visualizations, we began with an analysis of a subset of the MASSVIS dataset (http://massvis.mit.edu/). These data were collected during a memory study in which participants viewed images for 10 s and were later tested on their memory for the visualizations via recognition and recall tests [3].

For the present analysis, we selected a subset of 35 images from the MASSVIS study. These images represented a variety of commonly used types of data visualizations, all of which contained some combination of text and graphical representations of data. The subset included four area plots, four bar charts, one bubble plot, four column charts (including two double Y-axis plots in which a line graph was overlaid on the column charts), three correlation plots, three line graphs, two map-based visualizations, three network diagrams, three pie charts, and five scatter plots. In addition to these 32 images, we included the three visualizations that had the best match between the eye tracking data and the saliency maps in our prior evaluation of saliency models [13]. These included two infographics and one line graph.

Regions of interest (ROIs) were defined for the stimulus set, dividing the visualizations into the following regions: Title, Data, Data Area, X-Axis, X-Axis Label, Y-Axis, Y-Axis Label, Legend, Data Labels, and Text. For each visualization, the ROIs were marked using GIMP software (www.gimp.org). The ROIs were tightly drawn to the edges of each region.

Scan paths, representing the sequence of fixations across the ROIs for each participant and each visualization where constructed using MATLAB [19]. Fixations were counted as falling within an ROI if their center, defined as the geometric median of all points in the fixation, fell within a 1° viewing angle of the ROI, approximating the participants' useful field of view. If the same fixation could be assigned to multiple ROIs, multiple variants of the scan path were generated. However, for the purpose of this analysis, only the first variant was used. A total of 562 scan paths were analyzed, with an average of 16 scan paths from different participants for each visualization. There were an average of 36 fixations per scan path (range 6–51).

### 2.1 Analyses

For each visualization, the number of participants who fixated within each ROI in the visualization at least once was calculated. The average proportion of participants who fixated on an ROI (when present) across all of the visualizations is shown in Table 1. Unsurprisingly, participants nearly always fixated on the data in the visualizations. They were also highly likely to fixate on the title, legend, and data labels, when those ROIs were present.

To determine where the participants allocated their attention in the visualizations, we calculated the proportion of each participant's fixations that fell within each ROI for each visualization. The average proportion of fixations in each ROI is also shown in Table 1. The Data ROI received the highest average proportion of fixations, but this proportion was relatively low. On average, only 27% of the participants' fixations were in the Data ROI, while the Title and Data Labels ROIs received similar proportions of fixations (25% and 26%, respectively).

**Table 1.** Attention to each ROI in the analysis of the MASSVIS data, including average proportions and (standard deviations).

| ROI name | Number of visualizations containing ROI | Average proportion of participants viewing ROI | Average proportion of fixations to ROI |
|---|---|---|---|
| Title | 26 | 0.94 (0.10) | 0.25 (0.10) |
| Data | 35 | 0.98 (0.05) | 0.27 (0.17) |
| Data area | 21 | 0.55 (0.26) | 0.04 (0.03) |
| X-axis | 24 | 0.64 (0.20) | 0.05 (0.03) |
| X-axis label | 11 | 0.67 (0.14) | 0.06 (0.05) |
| Y-axis | 24 | 0.70 (0.22) | 0.12 (0.17) |
| Y-axis label | 15 | 0.73 (0.25) | 0.10 (0.08) |
| Legend | 23 | 0.89 (0.15) | 0.20 (0.11) |
| Data label | 15 | 0.88 (0.22) | 0.26 (0.16) |
| Text | 24 | 0.56 (0.28) | 0.07 (0.10) |

To test our hypothesis that participants disproportionately pay attention to text in data visualizations, the ROIs were categorized based on whether or not they contained text for each stimulus. For example, the X-Axis ROIs contained text in some visualizations but not in others. For each visualization, we then calculated the proportion of fixations that fell in ROIs containing text, the proportion of fixations to the data and data area, and the proportion of fixations that fell in other ROIs that did not contain text (including graphics, symbols, numbers, etc.). On average across all of the visualizations, 59.9% (SD = 16.1%) of the participants' fixations fell into ROIs containing text relative to 30.0% (SD = 15.6%) of fixations in the data ROIs and 10.1% (SD = 6.6%) of fixations in the other non-text ROIs.

As another measure of how participants weighted the relative importance of each ROI, we assessed how often each ROI was one of the first three ROIs visited by a participant. This was calculated as the proportion of scan paths in which the ROI was one of the first three fixated (for visualizations where that ROI was present). Note that this does not necessarily mean that one of the first three *fixations* in the trial fell in that ROI. For example, if a participant began a trial by fixating four times on the title, then fixating three times on the data, and then fixating once on the legend, then the title, data, and legend would be counted as the first three ROIs visited on that trial. In other words, we assessed the order in which the ROIs were viewed irrespective of the number of fixations in the sequence.

The Title ROI was the most likely to be one of the first three ROIs visited. When the Title ROI was present in a visualization, it was one of the first three visited in 87.8% of the scan paths. The Data ROI was a close second at 83.5%. The proportions were much lower for the other ROIs (51.1% for Data Labels; 39.8% for Legend; 34.7% for the combination of Y-Axis and Y-Axis Labels; 17.0% for the combination of X-Axis and X-Axis Labels; 14.8% for Text). Some of the X- and Y-Axis ROIs contained words (e.g. the names of countries or months) while others were numerical (e.g. years or values). The axis ROIs were subdivided into those that contained text (other than the axis labels) and those that did not. When the X-Axis ROI contained text, it was one of the first three ROIs visited in 48.5% of the scan paths.[1] When the X-Axis ROI did not contain text, it was one of the first three ROIs visited in 12.4% of the scan paths. The difference was even more dramatic for the Y-Axis ROI, which was in the first three ROIs visited in 80.9% of the scan paths when the ROI included text, but only 13.0% of the scan paths when it did not.

To explore the data further, we looked at correlations between the number of words in an ROI and the proportion of fixations in the ROI. If a participant is spending time reading the text in a particular ROI, we would expect to see a high correlation between the number of words and the proportion of fixations. The correlations were significant for the Title ($R^2 = 0.73$, $p < 0.001$), Text ($R^2 = 0.82$, $p < 0.001$), X-Axis Label ($R^2 = 0.69$, $p < 0.02$), and Y-Axis Label ($R^2 = 0.83$, $p < 0.001$) ROIs. For the Legend and Data Label ROIs, which received relatively high proportions of fixations on average, there was not a significant correlation between the number of words and the proportion of fixations (Legend: $R^2 = 0.39$, $p = 0.07$; Data Labels: $R^2 = 0.41$, $p = 0.15$).

The axes themselves provide an interesting opportunity for investigating the effect of text on where viewers spend their time when studying a visualization. As mentioned above, some of the X- and Y-Axis ROIs contained words and others contained only numbers. When the axes contained words, there was a significant correlation between the number of words and the proportion of fixations to the axis (X-Axis: $R^2 = 0.48$, $p < 0.02$; Y-Axis: $R^2 = 0.90$, $p < 0.001$). In contrast, when the X-Axis contained only numerical values, there was no correlation between the number of numerical values and the proportion of fixations ($R^2 = 0.09$, $p = 0.68$). When the Y-Axis contained only numerical values, there was a significant *negative* correlation ($R^2 = -0.46$, $p < 0.03$).

## 2.2  Discussion

The results of our analyses indicate that participants disproportionately viewed regions of the visualizations that contained text in the MASSVIS study. Although the

---

[1] However, there were only two visualizations in this category, with a total of 33 scan paths. The other groupings contained much higher numbers of visualizations and scan paths.

participants did spend time looking at the visualized data, the majority of their fixations were devoted to regions containing text. For some of those regions, including the Title, Text and Axis Label ROIs, significant correlations between the number of fixations and the number of words in the ROIs indicate that participants were spending time reading the text. For other regions, namely the Legend and Data Label ROIs, there was not a significant correlation between the number of fixations and the number of words. These ROIs received relatively high proportions of fixations overall, so the absence of a correlation between the number of words and the proportion of fixations in these regions likely indicates that the participants read the text in those regions but also referred back to them more than once as they studied the visualizations.

Interestingly, the axes of graphs seemed to attract participants' attention when they contained text but not when they contained numbers. Axes containing text were much more likely to be one of the first three ROIs viewed than axes containing only numbers, and for the Y-Axis ROI there was a significant negative correlation between the number of fixations and the number of numerical values along the axis. There are several possible explanations for this pattern, but it seems plausible that numerical axes can be comprehended at a glance, making repeated fixations and revisits unnecessary.

An important point to note is that the MASSVIS eye tracking dataset was collected in the context of a memory study, which may have had a substantial influence on how participants allocated their attention. For example, they may have devoted a lot of attention to the titles of the graphs, thinking that the titles would be easier to remember than the details of the visualized data. To explore the impact of the task on patterns of attention to the visualizations, we conducted a study in which participants viewed data visualizations in a free viewing task.

## 3   Viewing Data Visualizations in a Free Viewing Task

When eye tracking datasets are used to assess saliency maps, the participants in the eye tracking studies are typically given a free viewing task. For example, in the widely used MIT Saliency Benchmark eye tracking datasets (http://saliency.mit.edu), participants completed a free viewing task in which they viewed each image for 5 s [2, 6, 17]. In this study, we used the same task and presentation duration to examine eye movement patterns on a larger set of data visualizations and a larger group of participants. Participants viewed the same subset of MASSVIS stimuli that were used in the analysis described above and an additional 27 data visualizations in the context of a larger free viewing experiment.

### 3.1   Method

**Participants**
Thirty participants were recruited from students, faculty, and staff in the University of Illinois community (10 males; mean age = 30.53 years, SD = 13.06) and compensated $20 for their time. All participants were tested for color vision deficiencies (24 plate

Ishihara Test [15]) and near vision acuity prior to completing the study. Data from an additional five participants was discarded because: they failed the colorblindness and/or acuity tests prior to beginning the experiment (2 participants); the eye tracker failed to successfully capture their eye movements for a significant portion of the experiment (1 participant); they fell asleep for any portion of the experiment (1 participant); or there was a problem with the experimental apparatus (1 participant).

**Materials**
Four blocks of images were used in this study, consisting of a total of 108 images. Each image was centered and gray padded to fill the dimensions of the screen.

Two of the blocks consisted of line drawings (30 images) and fractals (16 images) drawn from the MIT Saliency Benchmark CAT2000 dataset [2]. Those blocks are not analyzed in the present study. One block contained thirty-five data visualizations pulled from the MASSVIS dataset [3, 4]. These were the same visualizations as those analyzed in Sect. 2. The final block contained twenty-seven data visualizations that were created specifically for this experiment (3 bar charts, 3 boxplots, 3 bubble graphs, 3 column charts, 3 line plots, 3 parallel coordinates plots, 3 pie charts, 3 scatterplots, and 3 violin plots[2]). These stimuli were selected to represent a variety of common types of data visualizations. To mirror the visualizations in the MASSVIS set, not all of the visualizations contained all of the possible ROIs and the placement of specific ROIs (such as the Legend) varied across visualizations. The newly generated visualizations also differed from the MASSVIS set because they did not contain infographics or additional text, such as text indicating the source of the data.

The order in which the four blocks of images were presented was counterbalanced across participants. Within each block, the stimuli were shown in a random order.

**Procedure**
The experiment was completed in a dark room at a nominal viewing distance of 0.8 m. Stimuli were presented on a large monitor ($0.932 \times 0.523$ m; $1920 \times 1080$ pixels) while eye movements were recorded with two Smart Eye Pro cameras. Participants first underwent the standard Smart Eye camera setup procedure and 9-point calibration.

Participants were instructed to view each image as it was presented. Each trial began with a 2-s fixation cross in the center of the screen. The fixation cross was followed by the presentation of an individual image, which was displayed on the screen for 5 s.

**Analysis**
In the resulting dataset, fixations were defined as samples for which the velocity over the preceding 200 milliseconds (ms) was less than 15 degrees per second. The first fixation in each trial and any fixations with a duration less than 100 ms were dropped from the analysis. For all of the analyses described below, the visualizations pulled from the MASSVIS set and the visualizations created specifically for this experiment

---

[2] Due to a programming error, 11 of these images were dropped (leaving a total of 97 images in this experiment). Because they were still of interest, the dropped images were included in a subsequent data collection. The participants in that data collection were recruited in the same manner as the initial group of participants. The group consisted of thirty participants (7 males; mean age = 29.57, stdev = 13.79). Two participants completed both data collection sessions.

are pooled together. A total of 1834 scan paths were included in the analysis. There were an average of 11 fixations per scan path (range 1–19).

As in our earlier analysis, the number of participants who fixated within each ROI at least once was calculated for each visualization. The average proportion of participants who fixated on an ROI (when present) across all of the visualizations is shown in Table 2. In addition, we calculated the proportion of each participant's total fixations that fell within each ROI for each visualization. The average proportion of fixations in each ROI is also shown in Table 2. As before, the three ROIs receiving the highest proportion of fixations were the Data (37%), Title (22%) and Data Label (19%) ROIs.

**Table 2.** Attention to each ROI for the visualizations in the second analysis, including average proportions and (standard deviations).

| ROI name | Number of visualizations containing ROI | Average proportion of participants viewing ROI | Average proportion of fixations to ROI |
|---|---|---|---|
| Title | 43 | 0.71 (0.21) | 0.22 (0.14) |
| Data | 62 | 0.91 (0.12) | 0.37 (0.18) |
| Data area | 43 | 0.53 (0.23) | 0.10 (0.06) |
| X-axis | 46 | 0.43 (0.18) | 0.07 (0.04) |
| X-axis label | 23 | 0.17 (0.11) | 0.02 (0.02) |
| Y-axis | 47 | 0.52 (0.22) | 0.10 (0.10) |
| Y-axis label | 33 | 0.39 (0.23) | 0.07 (0.07) |
| Legend | 42 | 0.68 (0.21) | 0.14 (0.08) |
| Data label | 17 | 0.70 (0.30) | 0.19 (0.13) |
| Text | 24 | 0.24 (0.29) | 0.05 (0.08) |

The ROIs were categorized based on whether or not they contained text for each stimulus. For each visualization, we then calculated the proportion of fixations that fell in ROIs containing text, the proportion of fixations to the data and data area, and the proportion of fixations that fell in other ROIs that did not contain text (including graphics, symbols, numbers, etc.). On average across all of the visualizations, 40.8% (SD = 19.5%) of the participants' fixations fell into ROIs containing text relative to 44.4% (SD = 18.3%) of fixations in the data ROIs and 14.8% (SD = 0.07%) of fixations in the other non-text ROIs.

We assessed how often each ROI was one of the first three ROIs fixated by a participant using the same procedure defined above. In this experiment, the Data ROI was most often one of the first three ROIs fixated. It was one of the first three ROIs fixated for 80.5% of the scan paths. The Title ROI was second at 67.5%. Once again, the proportions were lower for the other ROIs (50.8% for Data Labels; 40.5% for

Legend; 40.3% for the combination of Y-Axis and Y-Axis Labels; 18.7% for the combination of X-Axis and X-Axis Labels; 13.8% for Text). The axis ROIs were subdivided into those that contained text (other than the axis labels) and those that did not. When the X-Axis ROI contained text, it was one of the first three ROIs viewed in 22.2% of the scan paths. When the X-Axis ROI did not contain text, it was one of the first three ROIs viewed in 14.4% of the scan paths. The Y-Axis ROI was one of the first three ROIs viewed in 56.4% of the scan paths when the ROI included text and 22.0% of the scan paths when it did not.

As before, we also assessed the correlations between the number of words in an ROI and the proportion of fixations in the ROI. The correlations were significant for the Title ($R^2 = 0.90$, $p < 0.001$), Text ($R^2 = 0.81$, $p < 0.001$), X-Axis Label ($R^2 = 0.57$, $p < 0.01$), Y-Axis Label ($R^2 = 0.64$, $p < 0.001$), Legend ($R^2 = 0.39$, $p < 0.02$) and Data Label ($R^2 = 0.60$, $p < 0.02$) ROIs.

As in the first analysis, some of the X- and Y-Axis ROIs contained words and others contained only numbers. For the X-Axis, there was not a significant correlation between the number of items and the proportion of fixations for axes consisting of words ($R^2 = 0.27$, $p = 0.07$) or numbers ($R^2 = 0.03$, $p = 0.86$). For the Y-Axis, there was a significant correlation between the proportion of fixations and the number of words ($R^2 = 0.89$, $p < 0.001$), and, as in the first analysis, a significant negative correlation for numbers ($R^2 = -0.41$, $p < 0.01$).

For a more detailed assessment of how participants allocated their attention to the ROIs, plots were created to show the time course of attention to various parts of the visualizations. Every trial was divided into 313 consecutive 16 ms time windows, from trial onset until the five second trial cutoff time. For each time window, we calculated whether a fixation was made, and if so, which ROI the fixation fell into. An ROI was given a value of 1 for the time window if it received a fixation, and a 0 if it did not. Time windows of 16 ms were chosen to coincide with the sampling rate of the eye-tracker. Fixations were counted as occurring within a time bin if any part of the fixation fell in the window (i.e., even if the fixation ended or started during the time window). Only one fixation was allowed to occur in a single 16 ms time window; if multiple fixations occurred during a time window, only the first ROI visited was counted, and the fixation to the second ROI was assigned as starting in the next time window. However, given that it takes roughly 30–50 ms to make a saccade, it is highly unlikely that two separate fixations would have been possible in the small time window. The first fixation of the trial was excluded, as it began with the disappearance of the fixation cross and did not represent a volitional look to any ROI.

The data plotted in Fig. 1 shows the viewing patterns collapsing across all visualizations. The x-axis represents time from trial start, the y-axis represents the probability of fixating an ROI, and each line represents a different ROI. Note that the probabilities do not necessarily sum to 1 at every time point, because not every participant made a fixation during every time point (e.g., due to saccades or track loss). Overall, participants tended to look at the Title ROI early in the trial, with Title fixations peaking between 750–1000 ms after trial onset and then quickly declining. Fixations to the Data ROI surpassed looks to the Title beginning ~1500 ms after trial onset, and continued to increase throughout the duration of the trial until peaking at ~4500 ms. The next most-fixated ROI was the Legend region, which had a numerically higher probability of fixation than the rest of the ROIs from ∼750 ms after trial onset until the end of the trial. However, the low probability of fixating the other ROIs could be due the fact that not all ROIs were present in all visualizations, meaning that many ROIs had zeros for several visualizations. This plot highlights that although users made more fixations to the data ROI *overall*, this pattern was only true in the later part of the viewing period. Upon first viewing a new visualization, users tended to look at the Title first, after which they shifted their attention to other areas of the visualization.

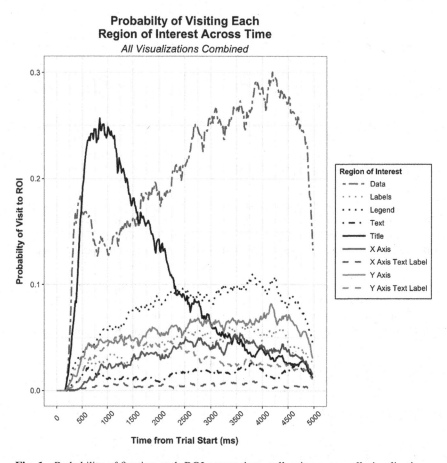

**Fig. 1.** Probability of fixating each ROI across time, collapsing across all visualizations.

The data plotted in Fig. 2 shows viewing patterns to visualizations without text in the y-axis (top panel) versus with text in the y-axis (bottom panel). In both cases, Title fixations peaked early in the trial (∼500 ms in vis without y-axis text and ∼1000 ms in vis with y-axis text).

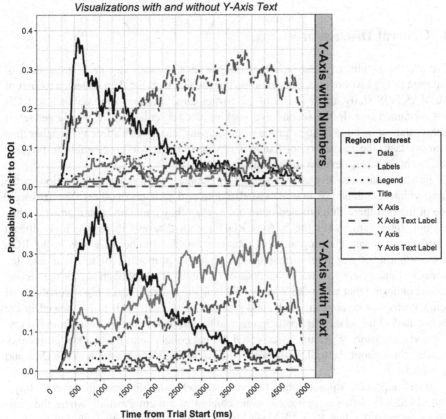

**Fig. 2.** Probability of fixating each ROI across time, plotted separately for visualizations without y-axis text (top panel) and with y-axis text (bottom panel).

However, striking differences are apparent in the pattern of looks to the y-axis. In visualizations *with* y-axis text, users showed clear preference for fixating the y-axis over the data area after ~500 ms into the trial, and fixations to the y-axis exceeded Title fixations after ~2250 ms. Conversely, in visualizations without y-axis text, participants made very few looks to the y-axis, and instead focused most of their fixations on the Title early in the trial, and to the Data ROI later in the trial (after ~1500 ms). There was a small preference for fixating the Labels ROI, relative to the non-Data ROIs, from ~3000–4500 ms, suggesting the need to seek out text to understand the plots when it was not present in the y-axis. This pattern clearly shows that users' viewing patterns to the y-axis were strongly influenced by the presence of text. Users made many more y-axis fixations when text was present compared to when it was not, and even made more fixations to the y-axis than to the Data when text was present, highlighting the emphasis that users place on text during visualization comprehension.

## 4 General Discussion

Overall, the results of these analyses suggest that viewers devote a great deal of attention to the text in data visualizations. For the eye tracking data collected as part of the MASSVIS study, the majority of the participants' fixations were devoted to ROIs that contained text. In the second eye tracking dataset, collected using a larger set of data visualizations and a larger group of participants along with a free view rather than memory task, the proportion of fixations devoted to text was comparable to the proportion of fixations devoted to the data.

For both datasets, it was instructive to examine the participants' attention to the axes, which contained text in some visualizations and numbers in others. The axes were one of the first three ROIs fixated more often when they contained text than when they did not. Interestingly, for the Y-Axis ROI in both datasets, there was a significant correlation between the proportion of fixations and the number of words in the ROI, and a significant negative correlation between the proportion of fixations and the number of numerical values. An analysis of the time course of fixations for the second dataset indicated that when the Y-Axis ROI contained text, it had a high probability of being visited throughout the trials, and was the most likely ROI to be viewed in the second half of the trials, after participants had turned their attention away from the title of the visualization. When the Y-Axis ROI did not contain text, it had a low probability of visits throughout the trial, with participants devoting more attention to the Data and Legend ROIs.

It is important to note that the two datasets are different in several ways. The MASSVIS data was collected in the context of a memory study where the visualizations were displayed for 10 s each. It consisted of visualizations that were found "in the wild." Although we selected a subset of the visualizations that represented common types of data visualizations, these images often contained descriptive titles, annotations, and text noting the source of the data. In other words, the data itself was contextualized by the text in the visualizations. In the second study, we added an additional set of visualizations that were generated in the lab rather than being found in the wild. These visualizations tended to be simpler and had less contextual information. In addition, to mirror the experimental parameters that have been used for assessing visual saliency maps, participants were given a free viewing task[3] with only 5 s for examining the visualizations. The simpler text and shorter viewing times in the second dataset may have driven the difference in the overall proportions of fixations to the text versus the data. However, even in the second dataset, the ROIs containing text were viewed almost as often as the data ROIs, indicating that the text still draws viewers'

---

[3] It is worth noting that a free viewing task may be more representative of how people interact with visualizations in the wild than a memory task. When a person encounters a data visualization in *The Economist*, for example, they are essentially doing a free viewing task.

attention even when they have little time and the text provides relatively little information.

Our finding that viewers focused on the text elements in data visualizations is consistent with prior research. Some studies have found that users spend as much as 60–70% of viewing time reading the title, data labels and axes of simple graphs [1, 8, 18]. Users are also more likely to re-fixate text-based areas, such as the legend [3, 21, 28]. In our current analysis, we investigated a wider variety of visualization types and complexities, but the overall tendency to devote a large amount of viewing time to text-based regions remained the same.

The analyses presented here have several limitations. First, the relatively small size of the text in visualizations may necessitate more direct fixations due to the limits of visual acuity [23]. This may have an impact on overall viewing time. Second, the participants in these studies had no particular expertise with interpreting data visualizations, and their tasks did not require them to find specific information in the visualizations, or even to understand the gist of the data presented. While this approach may be realistic for understanding how people process visualizations that they encounter in daily life, such as an infographic presented in a magazine, patterns of attention are likely to be quite different in cases where a viewer is using a visualization to obtain specific information in the context of a larger task. Domain experience also plays an important role in how people attend to data visualizations. Our own prior work found large differences between professional imagery analysts and novice viewers looking at radar imagery [20], and other researchers have found that even brief instructions on how to interpret a plot can change how people allocate their attention [7]. Individual differences in information processing also play an important role. For example, dyslexic individuals spend disproportionately more time on text than typical readers [18]. None of these factors operate in isolation, and taking their combination into account can result in complex interactions between such factors as chart type, task difficulty, and the user's perceptual speed [28].

Despite these limitations, the general finding that text in data visualizations draws the viewer's attention has important implications for the development of visual saliency models that apply to visualizations. As discussed above, the ability to make predictions about where viewers will look in data visualizations could be a useful evaluation tool. To make accurate predictions, these models must take attention to text into account. In our future work, we plan to develop a new saliency model that incorporates text as a visual feature. We will test how to weight this feature relative to the other visual features that are commonly used in saliency models (color, contrast, and orientation). If successful, this approach will provide an improved tool that will allow visualization designers to evaluate their designs from the perspective of human visual processing.

**Acknowledgements.** This work was funded by the Laboratory Directed Research and Development (LDRD) Program at Sandia National Laboratories. Sandia is a multiprogram laboratory operated by Sandia Corporation, a Lockheed Martin Company, for the Department of Energy's National Nuclear Security Administration under Contract DE-AC04-94AL85000.

The authors would like to thank Deborah Cronin and Jim Crowell for collecting the eye tracking data at the University of Illinois at Urbana-Champaign, as well as Hank Kaczmarski and Camille Goudeseune for their support.

# References

1. Acarturk, C., Habel, C., Cagiltay, K., Alacam, O.: Multi-media comprehension of language and graphics. J. Eye Mov. Res. **1**(3), 2, 1–15 (2008). doi:10.16910/jemr.1.3.2
2. Borji, A., Itti, L.: CAT2000: a large scale fixation dataset for boosting saliency research. In: CVPR 2015 Workshop on "Future of Datasets" (2015). arXiv preprint: arXiv:1505.03581
3. Borkin, M., Bylinskii, Z., Kim, N., Bainbridge, C.M., Yeh, C., Borkin, D., Pfister, H., Oliva, A.: Beyond memorability: visualization recognition and recall. IEEE Trans. Vis. Comput. Graph. (Proc. InfoVis) (2015). doi:10.1109/TVCG.2015.2467732
4. Borkin, M., Vo, A., Bylinskii, Z., Isola, P., Sunkavalli, S., Oliva, A., Pfister, H.: What makes a visualization memorable? IEEE Trans. Vis. Comput. Graph. (Proc. InfoVis) (2013). doi:10.1109/TVCG.2013.234
5. Bylinskii, Z., Borkin, M.A.: Eye fixation metrics for large scale analysis of information visualizations. In: Proceedings of ETVIS 2015, First Workshop on Eyetracking and Visualizations (2015)
6. Bylinskii, Z., Judd, T., Borji, A., Itti, L., Durand, F., Oliva, A., Torralba, A.: MIT saliency benchmark. http://saliency.mit.edu/
7. Canham, M., Hegarty, M.: Effects of knowledge and display design on comprehension of complex graphics. Learn. Instr. **20**, 155–166 (2010). doi:10.1016/j.learninstruc.2009.02.014
8. Carpenter, P.A., Shah, P.: A model of the perceptual and conceptual processes in graph comprehension. J. Exp. Psychol. Appl. **4**(2), 75–100 (1998). doi:10.1037//1076-898x.4.2.75
9. Connor, C.E., Egeth, H.E., Yantis, S.: Visual attention: bottom-up versus top-down. Curr. Biol. **14**(19), R850–R852 (2004). doi:10.1016/j.cub.2004.09.041
10. Fu, B., Noy, N.F., Storey, M.A.: Eye tracking the user experience – an evaluation of ontology visualization techniques. Semant. Web **8**(1), 23–41 (2017). doi:10.3233/SW-140163
11. Goldberg, J.H., Helfman, J.I.: Comparing information graphics: a critical look at eye tracking. In: Proceedings of the 3rd BELIV 2010 Workshop: BEyond Time and Errors: Novel EvaLuation Methods for Information Visualization, pp. 71–78 (2010). doi:10.1145/2110192.2110203
12. Goldberg, J.H., Helfman, J.I.: Eye tracking for visualization evaluation: reading values on linear versus radial graphs. Inf. Vis. **10**(3), 182–195 (2011). doi:10.1177/1473871611406623
13. Haass, M.J., Wilson, A.T., Matzen, L.E., Divis, K.M.: Modeling human comprehension of data visualizations. In: Lackey, S., Shumaker, R. (eds.) VAMR 2016. LNCS, vol. 9740, pp. 125–134. Springer, Cham (2016). doi:10.1007/978-3-319-39907-2_12
14. Higgins, E., Leigenger, M., Rayner, K.: Eye movements when viewing advertisements. Front. Psychol. **5**, 210 (2014). doi:10.3389/fpsyg.2014.00210
15. Ishihara, S.: Tests for Colour-Blindness: 24 Plates Edition. Kanehara Shuppan Co., Ltd., Tokyo (1972)
16. Itti, L., Koch, C.: Computational modelling of visual attention. Nat. Rev. Neurosci. **2**, 194–203 (2001). doi:10.1038/35058500
17. Judd, T., Durand, F., Torralba, A.: A benchmark of computational models of saliency to predict human fixations (2012). https://dspace.mit.edu/handle/1721.1/68590
18. Kim, S., Lombardino, L.J.: Comparing graphs and text: effects of complexity and task. J. Eye Mov. Res. **8**(3), 2, 1–17 (2015). doi:10.16910/jemr.8.3.2
19. MATLAB Release 2015b: The MathWorks, Inc., Natick

20. Matzen, L.E., Haass, M.J., Tran, J., McNamara, L.A.: Using eye tracking metrics and visual saliency maps to assess image utility. Electron. Imaging **16**, 1–8 (2016). doi:10.2352/ISSN. 2470-1173.2016.16.HVEI-127

21. Peebles, D., Cheng, P.C.-H.: Modeling the effect of task and graphical representation on response latency in a graph reading task. Hum. Factors **45**(1), 28–46 (2003). doi:10.1518/ hfes.45.1.28.27225

22. Pinto, Y., van der Leij, A., Sligte, I.G., Lamme, V.A.F., Scholte, H.S.: Bottom-up and top-down attention are independent. J. Vis. **13**, 1–14 (2013). doi:10.1167/13.3.16

23. Rayner, K.: Eye movements in reading and information processing: 20 years of research. Psychol. Bull. **124**(3), 372–422 (1998). doi:10.1037/0033-2909.124.3.372

24. Rayner, K.: Eye movements and attention in reading, scene perception, and visual search. Q. J. Exp. Psychol. **62**(8), 1457–1506 (2009). doi:10.1080/17470210902816461

25. Rosenholtz, R., Dorai, A., Freeman, R.: Do predictions of visual perception aid design? ACM Trans. Appl. Percept. (TAP) **8**(2), 12 (2011). doi:10.1145/1870076.1870080

26. Shah, P., Hoeffner, J.: Review of graph comprehension research: implications for instruction. Educ. Psychol. Rev. **14**(1), 47–69 (2002). doi:10.1023/A:1013180410169

27. Strobel, B., Sass, S., Lindner, M.A., Köller, O.: Do graph readers prefer the graph type most suited to a given task? Insights from eye tracking. J. Eye Mov. Res. **9**(4), 4, 1–15 (2016). doi:10.16910/jemr.9.4.4

28. Toker, D., Conati, C., Steichen, B., Carenini, G.: Individual user characteristics and information visualization: connecting the dots through eye tracking. In: Proceedings of the SIGCHI Conference on Human Factors in Computing Systems, pp. 295–304 (2013). doi:10. 1145/2470654.2470696

# Eye Tracking for Dynamic, User-Driven Workflows

Laura A. McNamara[✉], Kristin M. Divis, J. Daniel Morrow,
and David Perkins

Sandia National Laboratories, Albuquerque, NM 87185, USA
{lamcnam,kmdivis,jdmorr,dnperki}@sandia.gov

**Abstract.** Researchers at Sandia National Laboratories in Albuquerque, New Mexico, are engaged in the empirical study of human-information interaction in high-consequence national security environments. This focus emerged from our longstanding interactions with military and civilian intelligence analysts working across a broad array of domains, from signals intelligence to cybersecurity to geospatial imagery analysis. In this paper, we discuss how several years' of work with Synthetic Aperture Radar (SAR) imagery analysts revealed the limitations of eye tracking systems for capturing gaze events in the dynamic, user-driven problem-solving strategies characteristic of geospatial analytic workflows. We also explain the need for eye tracking systems capable of supporting inductive study of dynamic, user-driven problem-solving strategies characteristic of geospatial analytic workflows. We then discuss an ongoing project in which we are leveraging some of the unique properties of SAR image products to develop a prototype eyetracking data collection and analysis system that will support inductive studies of visual workflows in SAR image analysis environments.

**Keywords:** Visual search · Synthetic Aperture Radar · Information foraging · Eye tracking · Imagery analysis

## 1 Introduction

In this paper, we are interested in how computational hardware and software have changed geospatial imagery analysis in the United States Intelligence Community, and consider the implications of that shift for characterizing, modeling, and supporting humans in the visual interpretation of imagery. In particular, we have become acutely aware of the technological limitations of eye tracking systems for studying visual attention in natural settings.

Computational technologies have profoundly changed how humans generate, store, share, and interact with data and information. As a result, office work today relies on quite a different set of technologies than it did even twenty years ago, when the electric typewriter was an unremarkable desktop artifact. These days, typewriters are a rarity: instead, we rely on desktop computers, network cables, routers, servers, and mice, icons and electronic displays to work more creatively and flexibly with ever greater amounts of data and information. As many commentators have noted, the same systems

© Springer International Publishing AG 2017
D.D. Schmorrow and C.M. Fidopiastis (Eds.): AC 2017, Part I, LNAI 10284, pp. 192–205, 2017.
DOI: 10.1007/978-3-319-58628-1_16

that are enabling us to work with all that information are also *generating* new types of data and information at an astounding rate. The resulting information glut presents capability and capacity challenges for even the most technologically sophisticated sectors of Western economies.

This data glut is problematic even among the institutions comprising the United States' military and civilian intelligence community (or IC). Although these are among the most sophisticated developers and consumers of new technology, even they are struggling to adapt to the rapid evolution of their local information ecologies [1].

Of particular importance is the remote sensing revolution that has swept the intelligence community since 2001. Conflict in Afghanistan and Iraq spurred the United States government to invest heavily in developing, deploying, and integrating a dizzying array of sensor systems into the country's suite of collection technologies. Sensor investments blossomed quickly, producing a data harvest that has strained the capacity of national information transmission, storage and processing systems. Over the past few years, leaders in both military and civilian intelligence functions have expressed concern that their analytic experts are "swimming in sensors and drowning in data," as Air Force Lieutenant General David Deptula famously put it [2, 3].

To help military and intelligence agencies realize the information return on their country's sensor investment, technology developers have increasingly turned their attention to enhancing the analytic performance of *human* operators. They are doing so by developing systems aimed at helping human analysts discover, assess, and make decisions about the signatures and patterns captured in national datasets. Such systems include methods, algorithms, software, data products, and visualizations that are rapidly making their way to the ground stations, cubicles and open workspaces of the intelligence community.

In the best of worlds, analysts would be able to adopt these new technologies into their workflows, leveraging their wealth of data to make better sense of complicated events, trends and shifts in the world around us. Yet the extent to which new analytics and interaction models are actually enabling people to identify important patterns in the flood of sensor data remains an open question – one that will challenge human-computer interaction researchers to expand their evaluative frameworks to increasingly complex forms of perceptual and cognitive work.

## 1.1   Previous Work

The authors of this paper include an anthropologist, a cognitive neuroscientist, a computer scientist and a software-engineer-turned-data-scientist. We have spent much of the past decade studying human-information interaction among imagery analysts in the intelligence community, most recently with Synthetic Aperture Radar (SAR) analysts affiliated with Sandia National Laboratories. Sandia is a multi-program, federally funded research and development center (FFRDC) owned by the United States Department of Energy and headquartered in Albuquerque, New Mexico and Livermore, California. Sandia's national security mission includes a wide array of basic and applied research and development activities, including the design and engineering of remote sensing systems used in operational, tactical and strategic mission areas.

Sandia is internationally recognized for its expertise in developing SAR systems. These radars rely on the movement of a platform, such as an air vehicle, to synthesize a photographic aperture. As the platform travels over an area to be imaged, the radar emits pulses of radio energy to "illuminate" terrain features. Reflected energy is captured and processed by image formation algorithms that create two-and-three dimensional renderings of terrain features [4].

As researchers working at the intersection of human, SAR technologies, and national security, our proximity to sensor engineers and their operational users has given us a unique opportunity for studying real-world intelligence workflows. In previous papers, we have leveraged this experience to describe some of the challenges that accompany designing, fielding, and then evaluating the usability and utility of remote sensing systems in the operational workplace. We have discussed the use of ethnographic field study methods with cognitive work analysis and cognitive task analysis frameworks, an approach that has informed the development of experimental visual search studies we have conducted with imagery analysts [5–7]; offered guidance to radar engineers for designing usable operational interfaces for deployed systems [8]; and examined how eyetracking data can be leveraged with measures of visual saliency and radar image quality metrics to assess the utility of an image product for a particular class of signature detection tasks [9].

## 1.2    Purpose of This Paper

This paper is different from our previous reports: it is a position paper asserting the need to re-think task models that describe visual inspection of image products; and data collection systems and analysis frameworks that enable researchers to perform inductive studies of dynamic, user-driven visual workflows.

In the following pages, we explain how new technologies have changed imagery analysis in ways that challenge the task-based models frequently described in the visual inspection literature [10–13]. We suggest that many imagery analysis activities involve *visual information foraging* workflows, in which analysts pull selectively across a heterogeneous assortment of data and information types to inform decisions about whether or not an indicator meets accepted criteria for "something that matters" [14–17]. This is somewhat of a departure from traditional visual inspection models, which do not explicitly account for the presence of easily accessible electronic data and information in today's workplaces.

Characterizing the complex, dynamic workflows of imagery analysis will require us to develop systems that accurately and precisely capture the behaviors indicative of resource foraging decisions in interactive workflows. Of particular importance are eyetracking data collection systems and analysis methods that enable researchers to identify what features seem to be cueing analysts to seek additional information in the electronic resources available to them. To this end, we briefly discuss a recent initiative to develop a prototype system that associates gaze events with geospatial point data, which we hope will enable us to capture and model the trajectory of a user's movement through large, heterogeneous information spaces.

## 2  Imagery Analysis as Visual Inspection and Profession

In the academic literature, imagery analysis has traditionally been studied using models of visual inspection derived from well-established research in human factors and industrial engineering. However, as we discuss below, desktop computing and enterprise information systems have changed analytic practice in the intelligence community, in ways that challenge older models of visual inspection.

### 2.1  Imagery Analysis as Visual Inspection

From a human-information interaction perspective, imagery analysts are using their visual systems seek, detect and characterize features of interest in geospatial information products; i.e., they are performing *visual inspection*, which involves the deployment of our evolved capacity for *visual search* in purposeful work.

Visual inspection and visual search are related but not synonymous scientific research areas. As Wang et al. have pointed out, in the academic literature the term "visual search" has historically denoted the study of physical and neuropsychological processes associated with perception, cognition and attention in the context of scanning a stimulus in the visual field [18–21]. In contrast, inspection is the purposeful activity of examining and artifact to identify anomalies, signatures of signals associated with an event or trend of significance [11–13].

Researchers in human factors, industrial and engineering psychology have been developing empirical and theoretical models of visual inspection processes for decades. This research is the empirical foundation for qualitative and quantitative models that have, in turn, provided structure for examination of the factors that influence human inspection performance [22, 23]. Models of inspection processes typically decompose these workflows into distinct goal states which can be described in terms of specific behaviors, perceptual activity, cognitive activity, and decisions that mark a transition from one task state to another.

1. *Selection* of the item to be examined;
2. *Manipulation* of the item or one's workspace to facilitate visual examination;
3. *Visual scanning* of the item for anomalous features;
4. *Detection* of an anomaly/feature of interest;
5. *Evaluation* of the anomaly to determine its meaning, cause and significance; and
6. A *decision* about whether the anomaly merits action (see discussions in [12, 13, 22, 23].

Task models such as the one delineated above are very useful for researchers studying visual work in organizational settings. They enable close study of specific stages of a workflow, including the experimental identification of factors that promote successful outcomes, such as the identification of a fault indicative of an impending mechanical failure. They have enabled practitioners to develop and evaluate training protocols used to prepare inspectors for evaluating high-consequence sociotechnical systems, such as power grid components or commercial aircraft [10, 11, 18, 23]. Finally, they have supported the design and execution of controlled laboratory studies to document eye movement events and patterns associated with different stages in an inspection workflow, with studies of gaze behavior dating back to the 1970s (for example, [24]).

Interestingly, over the past decade, scientists traditionally associated with laboratory studies of visual search have shifted attention to studying visual inspection. Of particular importance are observational and experimental studies of feature detection behaviors and performance among airport baggage screeners [26–28]. Eye tracking studies that capture patterns of gaze behavior have enabled researchers to explore how vocational experience influences search strategies and performance; i.e., by comparing the strategies and detection performance of non-professional searchers with trained airport security officers; and by developing skill acquisition models to explain the performance of professional inspectors [26, 28].

These studies have has generated some lively, entertaining debates about basic understandings of visual attention, perception and cognition, but have also highlighted the difficulties that attend the application of laboratory methods and approaches in actual work environments [27, 29]. One particular challenge is the adaptation of eye tracking data collection and analysis to sample gaze behaviors as people perform tasks in real-world work environments, where it is difficult – sometimes impossible – to put a full suite of experimental controls on stimuli, the environment, and the behaviors of the human operators. As we discuss below, this is a significant barrier to understanding how people interact with data and information to develop intelligence assessments with remote sensing data products.

## 2.2 Imagery Analysis as a Profession

Imagery interpretation and analysis are common tasks in many domains, from medical diagnostics to drought monitoring. However, in the intelligence community, "imagery analysis" is a recognized professional domain. Both civilian and military intelligence agencies hire geospatial imagery analysts, commonly referred to as "IAs," to review and assess geospatial datasets derived from the nation's array of remote sensing systems (e.g., electro-optical, infrared, radiometric). Geospatial imagery analysts use a range of software tools, data and information resources, and assessment methods to detect and evaluate evidence of important trends and events. They are responsible for communicating intelligence findings to military and civilian stakeholders to support tactical, operational and strategic decision- and policy-making.

As is true in most Western office environments, technology has dramatically changed how these professionals work with data and information. In 2010, one of the authors (McNamara) spent a year performing a multi-site field study of imagery analyst workflows. Interviews and observational research with imagery analysts brought McNamara in contact with imagery analysts across a range of experience levels, from recently-hired novices to senior intelligence personnel with decades of experience in the agency. It was from this latter category of seasoned domain experts that she was made aware of how much the world of imagery analysis had changed over the previous decade – a change described as the shift from "hardcopy" to "softcopy" imagery analysis.

## 2.3   The Softcopy Revolution in Imagery Analysis

As the term implies, "hardcopy" describes images printed on paper or rendered in transparent/semitransparent films. In contrast, "softcopy" images are stored electronically and accessed via computer on a display terminal. In the intelligence community, both have been around for decades [30], but only recently have softcopy image products and analysis methods overtaken hardcopy imagery as the primary work focus of geospatial intelligence analysis.

When asked to compare hardcopy and softcopy workflows, senior imagery analysts invariably pointed to differences in the artifacts used in their intelligence activities. In the days of hardcopy analysis, filing cabinets, films and light tables were the key tools of the imagery analyst. One analyst had fond memories of walking down rows of filing cabinets to locate a particular cabinet, then a particular drawer, and then thumbing through files to identify the relevant films. Once she had returned to her desk, she removed the films from their protective envelopes to be displayed against the glowing surface of her light table. She examined her selected images for indicators of strategically-important activities, using her hands to move optical tools (such as magnifying lenses) and measurement instruments to examine fine detail and evaluate features in the scenes. This focused, manual-visual workflow enabled her to assess trends in a region of interest, for inclusion in reporting products that were disseminated to military decision-makers across the Department of Defense.

Of all the resources that imagery analysts used, the light table may have been the hallmark artifact of the profession. One of McNamara's interviewees spent his career examining electro-optical imagery for evidence of change in Soviet military posture. At one point in the interview, he observed that he had likely spent more of his adult life with his light table than with his wife or children.

However, in today's intelligence workplace, light tables are about as common as electronic typewriters. As enterprise computing systems took hold in government workplaces in the 2000s, filing cabinets, films and light tables were gradually supplanted by desktop computers, servers, routers, mice and keyboards, and so-called "electronic light tables" – i.e., hardware and software setups that analysts use to retrieve, manipulate, enhance, compare, measure, and mark imagery that is rendered on digital displays and/or CRT monitors (the latter still prized by analysts for the stability and clarity they afford).

Imagery analysts who developed their skills in the days of hardcopy inspection often express dissatisfaction with electronic light tables. They point out that even the highest resolution digital displays can perceptibly pixelate fine details in an object or scene. However, this is only one way in which softcopy analysis has changed human-information interaction in this domain.

## 2.4   The Complexity of Softcopy

The digitization of geospatial information has opened the door to more dynamic and interactive models of analyst-imagery interaction. First, not only are remote sensing systems generating more data; they are generating greater array of image products, and in seemingly ever-increasing quantities. The data flooding the intelligence community's networks and servers has given image scientists exciting new research challenges. They have responded by developing new mathematical models and algorithms that exploit everything from the statistical properties of image pixels to the physics of radiometric datasets. Their creativity has provided the intelligence community with new image products and new ways to analyze geospatial data; for example, by integrating temporal and geospatial information to examine patterns of activity at local and regional levels.

Second, the metaphor of the "electronic light table" underestimates what softcopy analysis entails. Today's commercial imagery analysis platforms do far more than simply reproduce the physical manipulation of hardcopy artifacts on a light table. Softcopy systems enable a remarkable array of interactions with geospatial datasets. For example, an analyst might apply different spectral filters to electro-optical imagery to assess changes in the moisture content of agricultural topsoil; or import records of other types of intelligence reporting, such as captured radio communications, to help her determine if recent vehicular activity indicates expanding military presence in a region of interest. Softcopy systems also facilitate the creation and rapid dissemination of new intelligence products; for example, an analyst could create a KML (Keyhole Markup Language) to represent all known military vehicle and tank positions in the past month, and provide the file as part of a geospatial analysis package for her customers.

## 2.5  Softcopy Imagery Analysis Is Visual Information Foraging

As technology has evolved in the intelligence workplace, so have the strategies people use to work with data and information. The hardcopy-and-light-table inspection model is inadequate to account for the range of behaviors comprising softcopy analytic workflows. Certainly, softcopy image analysis can be described in terms of source selection, manipulation, examination, detection, evaluation and decision-making. However, desktop computing enables people to perform a wider range of operations at each stage of an inspection task. In particular, when an analyst detects a feature of interest, he often sets aside the primary stimulus (e.g., an electro-optical satellite image) to seek complementary data to characterize and resolve ambiguous features.

For this reason, we have come to think of visual imagery analysis as visual-inspection-plus-information foraging. Information foraging theory was first articulated by Peter Pirolli and Stuart Card in the late 1990s [14]. Derived from ecological models of resource foraging "in the wild," information foraging theory posits that human information seeking can be modeled as a tradeoff between the amount of time spent seeking sources of relevant information (working "between patches" of information); and the amount of time one spends ingesting relevant information (realizing the information value "within patch"). An efficient foraging strategy is one that minimizes the former while maximizing the latter.

Information foraging theory is one of the most powerful descriptive models of human-information behaviors with electronic data, influencing the design of information retrieval systems for large, heterogeneous spaces, such commercial search engines used with the World Wide Web (Chi et al.). Although it has not been widely used in the design and evaluation of systems for geospatial intelligence analysis, information theory's principles can usefully expand visual inspection models to account for the expanded range of behaviors that we have observed with imagery analysts working with softcopy systems. Indeed, a recent paper by Paik and Pirolli extended information theory to develop a computational cognitive of information selection in map-based geospatial intelligence retrieval and integration tasks [15].

Among imagery analysts, the availability of so many information sources means that foraging activities have become part and parcel of the image inspection workflow. For example, detecting a feature of interest in an electronic image frequently shifts an analyst's attention away from inspecting that image into a foraging mode. She may open other image products for comparison with the scene at hand; or begin searching complementary datasets to determine if there are other indicators of the suspected activity. If a signature seems meaningful, the analyst will often engage in "patch enrichment" behavior: pulling complementary information from the selected databases and compiling a reference set she can use to contextualize the anomaly for her stakeholders.

## 3 SAR Imagery Analysis: A Dynamic Workflow

Since 2011, most of our work has focused on understanding how imagery analysts working with the US military use products from SAR systems to identify and evaluate indicators of operationally important events, such as the movement of illicit cargo through remotely populated areas in a military theater. As previously described, SAR systems are radiometric sensors that actively illuminate a scene, generating rich datasets whose physical properties can be exploited to generate a range of image types. Sophisticated geo-registration algorithms enables accurate spatial alignment of images generated at different points in time. This makes SAR systems particularly useful for detecting and revealing changes in a scene, such as the appearance of a car near the side of a building.

Because SAR datasets are so information dense, SAR researchers have been able to develop a variety of algorithms for highlighting different types of objects in a scene, as well as changes in the state or position of scene features. Many of these products are intended to help SAR analysts detect and make sense of signatures indicative of behaviors of interest. However, as image scientists expand the range, quantity and quality of SAR image products, it is worth assessing whether or not image products are helping analysts as intended. After all, introducing new information into an established workflow may benefit performance *or* lead to decrements, depending on whether people are able to integrate it into their decision-making framework. This requires us to understand how analysts use their perceptual and attentional resources to identify significant indicators, so that we can ensure our products support human requirements.

### 3.1 Characterizing Analyst-Imagery Interactions in SAR Operations

Between 2011 and 2014, we performed a series of observational and experimental data collection activities with SAR imagery analysts generating near-real time intelligence for tactical decision-making in military theaters of operation [5–7, 9]. The SAR systems in question were regularly used to image key terrain areas, so that the analysts could detect and characterize signatures associated with known illicit activities. Because it was used so regularly, this system was generating a tremendous amount of radiometric data, and Sandia's image scientists were continuously working to improve and/or provide more useful image products to help analysts detect and assess key signatures. At the time we became involved with the program, the system was generating more than a half-dozen types of distinct image products on a regular basis, across many linear miles of terrain.

To facilitate analytic inspection and decision-making, Sandia had provided the SAR analyst teams with custom-designed, SAR-specific softcopy display and analysis software, which the analytic teams used to select, display, manipulate, and mark image products containing indicators of potentially important events. We were asked to support a comparative evaluation of two different image products using two slightly different analysis algorithms, to determine if analysts would find one more useful than the other.

As described in [5], we performed ethnographic interviews using frameworks from Cognitive Work Analysis and cognitive task analysis to develop descriptive models of the SAR operational system. We also observed training sessions with pilots, radar operators, and imagery analysts comprising the deployed teams. Although we identified a number of distinct work processes and activities that contributed to system success, we focused on the analysis of newly-generated SAR imagery as the keystone task that integrated team members and technologies in the execution of the intelligence mission. The importance of this workflow highlighted the need to understand how imagery analysts were using the Sandia softcopy system to interact with different SAR image products to detect and characterize the signatures of interest.

SAR analysts work quickly. In fact, it is not unusual for an experienced analyst to exhaustively scan several hundred square meters of terrain in a few seconds, and do so using a number of complementary image products. This made observational documentation impossible.

Instead, we instrumented a copy of the Sandia softcopy display system so that we could log analyst interactions as they executed an operationally realistic inspection task. For our stimulus set, we selected four sets of SAR images, each consisting of a few dozen frames of imaged terrain, from operationally deployed systems. For every frame in these sets, we provided the full suite of SAR image products, as well as thirty days' worth of historical imagery for each frame, providing the participants with a total of several hundred image products available for review. Each of the four sets contained one frame displaying a verified signature of illicit activity, as well as multiple distractors; i.e., visually similar but operationally irrelevant markings scattered throughout the scenes. We marked each of the four target frames and several of the distractor frame with the word "STOP."

Twelve SAR analysts volunteered to perform our simulated search task. Each participant was assigned two of the four image sets we had curated. They were instructed to search the entire set of image products, as though they were performing an operational assessment; but to stop at each of the marked frames and report whether or not the frame contained any operationally meaningful features. Once the analyst had completed evaluating both sets of imagery, we played back a screen video recording of their session and asked them to narratively describe their search strategy and actions as they were examining the images.

## 3.2 Dynamic Foraging in Analytic Workflows

As discussed in [5], we discovered that analysts were actually using the image products differently than the system engineers had expected. However, what really caught our attention were the interaction patterns we extracted from the log files. Our customized logging system captured detailed information about the operations each analyst performed on the datasets we had assigned them. The logs allowed us to see the order in which each frame was examined; which image products each analyst accessed when evaluating the content of each frame; the amount of time spent on the frame; selection and manipulation of the image products associated with each of the frames (such as panning, zooming, and flickering across the half-dozen image products the SAR system generated for each scene); mouse clicks on a feature to mark anomalies; and opening additional image windows to access and display any of the previous months' image products.

By comparing the log files with the video recordings and voiceover narratives we collected from the analysts, we identified interaction behaviors that seemed to be associated with different stages in an inspection workflow: moving rapidly from one frame to another, with minimal zooming or flickering, indicated the analyst was quickly scanning frames for anomalies of interest without detecting anything meaningful. Stopping on an image product, then manipulating the frame by panning around its content or zooming in and out of features in the frame, indicated a deeper investment of attention. Rapid, repeated flickering among different image products within the frame indicated a level of expectation that an anomaly might be present, since analysts rely on the animation effects of rapid flickering to facilitate the detection of new objects. When such a feature was detected, the analyst would position the feature of interest in the center of her display, then zoom to a useful level of resolution before moving into an extended flicker pattern among multiple image products, examining the area for additional evidence of an important event. If the feature seemed like it might meet the criteria for a signature of intelligence significance, the analyst would engage in seeking-and-enrichment behavior: opening a new display window and populating it with previously collected SAR imagery for the same frame, comparing and contrasting changes over time to put the anomaly into an activity context.

As we examined the log file captures and identified consistent interaction behaviors associated with different stages in the SAR analysis workflows, we realized that the analysts were engaged in complex, dynamic type of search and inspection, interwoven with behaviors characteristic of information foraging in electronic datasets. By "feature contingent," we mean that detection of a potential feature in a frame seemed to occasion a shift in the analyst's interaction strategy, as indicated by a change in the pattern of interaction with particular image products (from panning across frames to flickering within a frame, for example). This opened up the possibility of using information foraging theory to develop models of efficiency gains as imagery analysts developed proficiency in the work environment. However, we realized that we were also missing key component of information: What features, in what areas of which of the images, were capturing the participants' attention, precipitating the detected shift in their behavioral patterns?

Empirical studies of information foraging behaviors have capitalized on mouse-element interactions, or "clicks," in an interface [17]. However, when an imagery analyst is using a softcopy system to select, display and manipulate image sources, she may not be leaving a path of click events to inform an empirical description of her workflow. Studies of visual attention require the use of eye tracking systems, which became an important data collection resource in our studies of SAR analysts. Although we were able to develop and implement experimental protocols that revealed important sources of search efficiency between novice and experienced analysts (e.g., [9]), we quickly realized that eye tracking systems are simply not built for studying the unpredictable dynamics of foraging behaviors.

## 4    Needed: Eye Tracking in Dynamic, User-Driven Workflows

This experience is leading us to developing a prototype system for collecting gaze data in dynamic, user-driven workflows, so that we can develop what we think of as "gaze-informed information foraging models."

As Clark et al. have pointed out [27], it can be extremely difficult to translate laboratory-based theory and methods into operational field settings, if only because of the degrees of freedom one must account for in naturalistic environments. This is particularly the case with eye tracking systems, which evolved in a research paradigm that privileges highly constrained tasks with static stimuli to test hypotheses about perception and attention. In principle, eyetracking data could reveal how imagery analysts perceive and respond to visual cues in geospatial datasets. In practice, it is *extremely* difficult to study gaze-contingent analytic decision-making in realistic, user-driven workflows. Underlying the design of most eyetracking systems is a deductive model of inquiry that assumes the researcher can formulate hypotheses about how participants will interact with a stimulus, or some feature within a stimulus. Another important assumption is the degree of control exercised over the presentation of the stimulus; and, to a lesser extent, the degree to which one can predict the range of actions the participant can take with the stimulus.

These assumptions are not valid in the context of dynamic, user-directed workflows, like the ones we studied with our instrumented SAR analysis package. Log files can reveal quite a bit about which image products an analyst selects, and in what order, and how he manipulates those to facilitate the detection and characterization of items that have attracted his attention. Unfortunately, they tell us next to nothing about which scene features our analyst is attending, nor how his visual system examines different elements of information across different image products to build an integrated narrative about the meaning of an anomaly and whether it merits the investment of additional resources.

What is needed are eye tracking data collection systems and analysis protocols that support *inductive* studies of analytic interactions with softcopy imagery inspection. Such a system would enable researchers to sample gaze activity as people are solving an imagery analysis problem, then calculate key events (fixations and clusters of fixations) and associate those with the content rendered on the display screen.

This is the kind of system we are beginning to build for our own work with SAR imagery analysts. SAR imagery has a number of properties that make it ideal for the kind of eye tracking data collections and analysis platform we envision: for one thing, every pixel is associated with a stable set of geo-coordinates. Because these systems are equipped with highly accurate geo-registration algorithms, pixels locations are stable across image products – useful for determining if people are shifting their attention from one area of a scene to another as they move among image products depicting features in that scene. Secondly, the SAR research community has developed and implemented efficient algorithms for accurate and reliable segmentation of SAR images into regions of like pixels. This clustering reduces dynamic range in the data and facilitates the association of calculated gaze events, such as a fixation, with a mathematically calculated feature in the content. Over the next eighteen months, we will be working to iteratively develop, test, and then expand a prototype system that integrates gaze data collected using a COTS eyetracker with features in SAR imagery.

## 4.1   Conclusion

Two decades ago, Spencer described the work of aircraft inspectors as a multisensory process, involving "...such behaviors as looking, listening, feeling, smelling, shaking, and twisting" [22]. Similarly, the work of imagery analysts has become more complex as technology affords a wider range of data and information sources, as well as an expanded repertoire of operations with those information sources.

In the United States, leaders in the military and civilian intelligence community remain concerned about how to manage the flow of data and information that their analysts must evaluate. The community needs analysis software systems that that genuinely support the perceptual and cognitive work of intelligence analysts, whose work increasingly requires they become efficient foragers in the wild world of big data. Without the ability to robustly characterize and identify interaction.

Developing inductively-oriented algorithms and software for gaze tracking studies could expand the applicability of eye tracking systems for the complex perceptual cognitive workflows associated with information foraging. In particular, we suggest that gaze data and the associated user behaviors and stimuli can be treated as a high-dimensional point dataset amenable to a number of decomposition and pattern analysis techniques, including matrix decomposition and graph algorithms. Expanding the repertoire of mathematical models, algorithms and software used with eye tracking systems could provide an entirely novel source of data for documenting the search behaviors that characterize information foraging in large, complex data environments.

**Acknowledgments.** This research was funded by the Sandia National Laboratories' Laboratory Research and Development Program. Sandia National Laboratories is a multiprogram laboratory managed and operated by the Sandia Corporation, a wholly owned subsidiary of the Lockheed Martin Corporation, for the U.S. Department of Energy's National Nuclear Security Administration under contract DE-AC04-94AL85000.

# References

1. Nardi, B.A., O'Day, V.: Information Ecologies: Using Technology with Heart. MIT Press, Cambridge (1999)
2. Magnuson, S.: Military swimming in sensors and drowning in data. In: National Defense, p. 1, January 2010
3. Ackerman, S.: Air force chief: it'll be 'years' before we catch up on drone data. In: Wired Magazine (2012). http://www.wired.com/dangerroomn/2012/05/air-force/drone-data/
4. Doerry, A.W., Dieckey, F.M.: Synthetic aperture radar. Opt. Photonics News 15(11), 28–33 (2004)
5. McNamara, L.A., Cole, K., Haass, M.J., Matzen, L.E., Daniel Morrow, J., Stevens-Adams, S.M., McMichael, S.: Ethnographic methods for experimental design: case studies in visual search. In: Schmorrow, D.D., Fidopiastis, C.M. (eds.) AC 2015. LNCS (LNAI), vol. 9183, pp. 492–503. Springer, Cham (2015). doi:10.1007/978-3-319-20816-9_47
6. Cole, K., Stevens-Adams, S., McNamara, L., Ganter, J.: Applying cognitive work analysis to a synthetic aperture radar system. In: Harris, D. (ed.) EPCE 2014. LNCS (LNAI), vol. 8532, pp. 313–324. Springer, Cham (2014). doi:10.1007/978-3-319-07515-0_32
7. Stevens-Adams, S., Cole, K., McNamara, L.: Hierarchical task analysis of a synthetic aperture radar analysis process. In: Harris, D. (ed.) EPCE 2014. LNCS (LNAI), vol. 8532, pp. 545–554. Springer, Cham (2014). doi:10.1007/978-3-319-07515-0_54
8. McNamara, L.A., Klein, L.M.: Context sensitive design and human interaction principles for usable, useful and adoptable radars. In: Proceedings of SPIE Decision Support Systems, Baltimore, MD. SPIE (2016)
9. Matzen, L.E., Haass, M., Tran, J., McNamara, L.: Using eye tracking metrics and visual salience maps to assess image utility. In: Proceedings of Conference on Human Vision and Electronic Imaging, Baltimore, MD, pp. 1–8. SPIE (2016)
10. Drury, C.G.: Inspection performance. In: Handbook of Industrial Engineering, pp. 2283–2314. Wiley, New York (1992)
11. Drury, C.G., Watson, J.: Good Practices in Visual Inspection. US Department of Transportation, Federal Aviation Administration, Washington, DC (2002)
12. Sarac, A., Batta, R., Drury, C.G.: Extension of the visual search models of inspection. Theor. Issues Ergon. Sci. 21(3), 531–556 (2007)
13. See, J.E.: Visual Inspection: A Review of the Literature (SAND 2012-8590). Sandia National Laboratories, Albuquerque (2012)
14. Chi, E.H., Pirolli, P., Chen, K., Pitkow, J.: Using information scent to model user information needs on the web. In: Proceedings of the SIGCHI Conference on Human Factors in Computing Systems, pp. 490–497. ACM (2001)
15. Paik, J., Pirolli, P.: ACT-R models of information foraging in geospatial intelligence tasks. Comput. Math. Organ. Theory 21(3), 274–295 (2015)
16. Pirolli, P., Card, S.: Information foraging. Psychol. Rev. 106(21), 643–675 (1999)
17. Chi, E.H., Gumbrecht, M., Hong, L.: Visual foraging of highlighted text: an eye-tracking study. In: Jacko, J.A. (ed.) HCI 2007. LNCS, vol. 4552, pp. 589–598. Springer, Heidelberg (2007). doi:10.1007/978-3-540-73110-8_64
18. Wang, M.K., Lin, S.C., Drury, C.G.: Training for strategy in visual search. Int. J. Ind. Econ. 20, 101–108 (1997)
19. Triesman, A., Gelade, G.: A feature integration theory of attention. Cogn. Psychol. 12, 97–136 (1980)
20. Wolfe, J.: Visual search. In: Pashler, H. (ed.) Attention, pp. 13–73. Psychology Press, Taylor and Francis, New York (1998)

21. Wolfe, J.: Guided search 4.0: current progress with a model of visual search. In: Gray, W.D. (ed.) Integrative Models of Cognitive Systems, pp. 99–119. Oxford University Press, New York (2007)
22. Spencer, F.W.: Visual inspection research report on benchmark inspections, Department of Transportation, Federal Aviation Administration (1996)
23. Gramopadhye, A.K., Drury, C.G., Prabhu, P.V.: Training strategies for visual inspection. Hum. Factors Ergon. Manuf. 7(3), 171–196 (1997)
24. Megaw, E.D.: Factors affecting visual inspection accuracy. Appl. Ergon. 10, 27–32 (1979)
25. Megaw, E.D., Richardson, J.: Eye movements and industrial inspection. Appl. Ergon. 10(3), 145–154 (1979)
26. Biggs, A.T., Cain, M.S., Clark, K., Darling, E.F., Mitroff, S.R.: Assessing visual search performance differences between Transportation Security Administration Officers and nonprofessional visual searchers. Vis. Cogn. 21(3), 330–352 (2013)
27. Clark, K., Cain, M.S., Adamo, S.H., Mitroff, S.: Overcoming hurdles in translating visual search research between the lab and the field. In: Dodd, M.D., Flowers, J.H. (eds.) The Influence of Attention, Learning, and Motivation on Visual Search. Nebraska Symposium on Motivation, pp. 147–181. Springer, New York (2012)
28. McCarley, J.S., et al.: Visual skills in airport-security screening. Psychol. Sci. 15(5), 302–306 (2004)
29. Duchowski, A.T.: A breadth-first survey of eye-tracking applications. Behav. Res. Methods Instrum. Comput. 34(4), 455–470 (2002)
30. Latshaw, G.L., Zuzelo, P.L., Briggs, S.J.: Tactical photointerpreter evaluations of hardcopy and softcopy imagery. In: 1978 Technical Symposium East. International Society for Optics and Photonics (1978)

# Investigating Eye Movements in Natural Language and C++ Source Code - A Replication Experiment

Patrick Peachock, Nicholas Iovino, and Bonita Sharif$^{(\boxtimes)}$

Youngstown State University, Youngstown, OH 44555, USA
{prpeachock,nriovino}@student.ysu.edu, bsharif@ysu.edu

**Abstract.** Natural language text and source code are very different in their structure and semantics. Source code uses words from natural language such as English mainly in comments and identifier names. Is there an inherent difference in the way programmers read natural language text compared to source code? Does expertise play a role in the reading behavior of programmers? In order to start answering these questions, we conduct a controlled experiment with novice and non-novice programmers while they read small short snippets of natural language text and C++ source code. This study is a replication of an earlier study by Busjahn et al. [1] but uses C++ instead of Java source code. The study was conducted with 33 students, who were each given ten tasks: a set of seven programs, and three natural language texts. They were asked one of three random comprehension questions after each task. Using several linearity metrics presented in an earlier study [1], we analyze the eye movements on source code and natural language. The results indicate that novices and non-novices both read source code less linearly than natural language text. We did not find any differences between novices and non-novices between natural language text and source code. We compare our results to the Busjahn study and provide directions for future work.

**Keywords:** Eye tracking study · C++ · Program comprehension · Natural language

## 1 Introduction

Programmers are required to not just write source code, but read and comprehend it as well. The better a programmer comprehends code, the better they will be at debugging and finding faults. Programming is not as straightforward as it may seem to the beginner programmer. While it may look linear in its structure, source code is very different from natural text. It is not commonly read and executed left to right, top to bottom. Rather, it skips up and down, only using what part of the program is needed at the time that it is called i.e. the control flow. Natural text such as English prose, on the other hand is read from top to down and left to right.

© Springer International Publishing AG 2017
D.D. Schmorrow and C.M. Fidopiastis (Eds.): AC 2017, Part I, LNAI 10284, pp. 206–218, 2017.
DOI: 10.1007/978-3-319-58628-1_17

We derive our inspiration from a study conducted by Busjahn et al. [1]. They compared eye movements of novice and expert programmers who were asked to read and comprehend natural language text and Java programs. They found that novices read source code less linearly than the natural language texts. In addition, the experts were found to read code even less linearly than the novices. In this paper, we replicate the Busjahn et al. study because we wanted to determine if their results still hold for C++ on a different sample. We do not label our participants as experts and we did not have any participants from industry. Rather, we split our participants as novices and non-novices as detailed in Sect. 3.

The motivation behind this replication is to add to the growing research that is focused in the area of natural language and source code comparison. Current research shows little to no proof that being a novice or expert programmer affects the readability of source code. Since it is very likely that programmers start with reading code written by others, code comprehension plays an important role in programming. In this paper, we propose two different research questions.

- RQ1: Is there an inherent difference in the way novice and non-novice programmers read natural language text compared to source code?
- RQ2: Does expertise play a role in the reading behavior of programmers, in particular, with respect to linear reading?

If we can begin to analyze these patterns and behaviors, it can help to better our methods and practices of teaching and programming overall.

The paper is organized as follows. We discuss some related work in the area in the next section. In Sect. 3, we introduce the study and discuss the results in Sect. 4. Finally we present our conclusions and future work.

## 2 Related Work

Eye trackers are devices that are able to detect where on a screen a user is looking. An eye tracker will typically record two different types of data, saccades and fixations. A fixation is where an eye has come to rest on part of the screen for a given amount of time. A saccade is the movement from that fixation, to the next fixation. The time for these can vary but is frequently between 200 and 300 ms. Analysis programs will often mark fixations with a dot that grows the longer a user focuses on a spot on the screen. These dots are connected by a line called a scan path [2].

The area of investigation of our study falls under the general area of program comprehension. A program is defined as a set of instructions that are written to perform a specified task. Program comprehension can be defined as the understanding of these lines of code typically written in some language such as Java or C++. There have been several different studies done in the field of program comprehension, many focusing around fragments of code or beacons. While these beacons still play a major part in program comprehension, it has been shown that they are not often the same between all users. That is to say that different programmers see code in different ways [3].

A more recent study took a look into the way that students can retain information by reading in a less linear pattern. Raina et al. ran a study to see if information presented in a segmented pattern as opposed to a linear pattern would help students to better understand what was presented to them [4]. Using an eye tracker they were able to look at reading scores and reading depth to gather data. The study conducted used a group of 30 students (cut down to 19 due to inaccurate calibrations). Using a control group and a treatment group, they were given the same module in C++. The control group had the module in a linear format. The treatment group used a segmented format. Results showed that when reading in segments, students had higher reading and depth scores. They were able to not only focus on the information presented but understood it better than those reading in a linear fashion.

To expand and study the way that users read programming code, a study was done on the way that programmers read code with syntax highlighting [5]. The study looked to find if it was beneficial to the student to have syntax highlighting (colorization of specific keywords and constructs) from different software development environments. The study included 31 participants using the C# programming language and separated them into two groups: black and white code and code with syntax highlighting. The program having no errors, and the omitting of a time limit gave the programmers adequate time to go through the program to determine its output. The data was recorded with several metrics including fixations, regressions, and scan percentage. In conclusion, the study showed that there was minimal difference between all three metrics. This suggests that syntax highlighting, while possibly more pleasing to the eye, does not make a significant difference in the reading patterns of a programmer. However, in a different study, Sarkar found that highlighting did help with task completion but the effect decreased as programming experience increases [6].

One of the first studies done on natural language versus computer language led to a belief that natural language may be simpler than programming code. Having only been studied on novice programmers, this left room to expand research to include both novice, non-novice, and expert programmers [7]. Following on Crosby's research into beacons [7], Fan's study focused on beacons and comments within programming code and the benefits they have on program comprehension. The study showed the same findings as Crosby in that beacons are noticed differently by each programmer. It also did find that comments within code helped improve code comprehension [8].

Focusing on a different area than natural language and code comprehension, Sharif et al. turned to the comparison of programming languages. The study used students that were studying programming, broken into groups based on their knowledge of both Python and C++ programming languages. The C++ group did have more participants, this was directly related to the amount of programming courses offered to the students. The students had three different tasks that involved finding bugs as well as the overview of two different tasks. Using accuracy, time, fixation counts, and fixation duration, the study showed that accuracy higher in C++, also that novices took longer overall in C++. This group also had higher fixation counts than the Python group. The students doing Python tasks took longer than those using C++. While these metrics showed different, the final data analysis showed that there was no significant statistical difference when comparing the two programming languages [9].

Sharif and Maletic took a look into using an eye tracker to gather data on the different identifier styles i.e., underscores versus camel case [10]. The eye tracker was an improvement on a previous study [11] that used response time to get data between the two styles. Using the eye tracker, it was found that the different naming styles had a different effect on time as well as effort to detect identifiers within source code. It was shown that camel-casing affected speed of novice programmers. The final data analysis revealed that there was a large improvement when it came to speed and effort when underscores were used.

Focusing on a different aspect of code reading than styles or languages, a group of programmers took a look directly at the reading of code reviewers. Code reviewing has been used and proven to help improve already written code. A study done in 2002 on code reviewing sought to find out if a different code reading technique prevailed over others. They took a look at different metrics such as duration, gazes, glances, line identification and line reading. A lot of the software was developed in house so that the data the eye tracker recorded suited their needs for analysis. The five programmers chosen were to review six programs. Among the programmers it was commonly found that the reviewers would read code in a linear fashion the first time (referred to as a scan) reading and then go back and piece apart the code. Results showed that different code reviewers used different reading patterns involving recursive styles and focus on variables [12].

Using eye-tracking to aid in computer science education is an ever growing field of interest. In 2010 a study was done that looked at program comprehension for educators in the computer science field [13]. It broke down a programmer's thought process into different sections to help better identify learning concepts. External representation is any part of a program outside of the programmers current known knowledge. Cognitive structure is what is already known to the programmer, and assimilation process is how a programmer tackles the current programming problem. They broke down program comprehension into several different models. In the end, the study concluded that there is no single way to learn reading and comprehension of programs. Also that being open to how a program operates by reading code, is like different patches of knowledge coming together to better understand a program as a whole.

In 2013 when Busjahn and Schulte studied code reading, they found with a small group of 6 participants that there was a direct link to comprehension of algorithms and code constructs used [14]. Following this study a workshop was conducted that determined that even after a single programming course it's possible for the reading techniques of a programmer to change. Even from the beginning of a programming class, to the end, a novice programmer can read code different.

Eye-tracking and code comprehension studies are very detail oriented and can often be time consuming. A study done by Marter et al. [15] took a look at reducing study time by doing a study on the readabilty of source code using natural text. Marter's study had a unique setup in that it did not use programmers or programming code. The program was focused on using identifiers and the readability of those identifiers. They primarily did this study due to the claims that programming experiments can be quite costly and time consuming. The study set out to with one primary focus, finding if the similarity and the number of identifiers has a part in the readability of source code. They set out to do this study by having users read short snippets of natural language text with identifiers in it. After having read the text each user was asked two questions. One of these questions would relate to an identifier that was associated to the text, the other fulfilling criteria within the text. Each one of these readings was timed until a correct answer was given. The results of the study showed that while it is easy to produce a quick experiment and get data from multiple subjects, there are strong risks that come in to play. Whether a study of this type can relate directly to source code and the understanding of source code being one of them. The study itself does show a way to create quick lightweight studies, used for specific experiment types. They should not replace a controlled study confirming a hypothesis [7].

## 3   The Study

This study seeks to analyze and compare the reading and comprehension of natural language text and C++ source code. The main purpose of this study is to determine if natural text is read differently from source code and determine if novice programmers read differently than non-novices.

### 3.1   Data Collection and Tools

We used a Tobii X60 eye tracker which recorded at 60 Hz and was able to generate 60 samples of eye movements per second. The device is a non-intrusive eye tracker, meaning that a user does not need to wear it. The eye tracker is stationary on a desk between the user and monitor. The eye tracker is capable of compensating for head movements. We used a High Definition 24" monitor at $1920 \times 1080$ resolution for the study and an identical monitor for the moderator. Audio and video was recorded via a webcam. We used several different metrics via the Tobii Studio software that included fixations, durations, validity, areas of interest, gaze positions, timestamps, pupil size, validity codes, as well as start and end times for each trial.

### 3.2   Study Variables

The independent variables are the type of stimulus: source code or natural language text and the expertise (non-novice or novice) of the test participant. The dependent variables being the linearity metrics shown below taken from Busjahn et al. [1].

- Vertical Next Text: The percentage of forward saccades that either stay on the same line or move one line down.
- Vertical Later Text: The percentage of forward saccades that either stay on the same line or move down any number of lines.
- Horizontal Later Text: The percentage of forward saccades within a line.
- Regression Rate: The percentage of backward saccades of any length.
- Line Regression Rate: The percentage of backward saccades within a line.

In addition to the linearity metrics, we also measure *Saccade Length*, which is the average Euclidean distance between every successive pair of fixations and *Element Coverage*, measured by the fraction of words that the participant looked at. Element Coverage and Saccade Length were used to measure the differences between non-novices and novices while the first five measures were used to analyze reading styles and were mostly used to compare source code to natural language text.

## 3.3 Participants

For the study we used 33 students from Youngstown State University ranging from 0 to 5 years or more of programming experience. We grouped the students into two groups. We consider a non-novice to be a student who was exposed to programming in a prior course. They are typically students enrolled in a higher level course. Novices on the other hand had little or no programming background. The novices were recruited from the Introduction to Programming course and were all given extra credit. They were familiar with various concepts such as variables, looping structures, and data types all done in C++. All participants filled out a questionnaire before the study, we had a total of 18 male and 15 female participants between the ages of 18 and 27. All students were able to speak, read, and write in English, the native language of a majority of participants.

## 3.4 Tasks

Tasks given to the students were three different natural text paragraphs and seven small C++ programs. The different natural language text programs were all non related topics and were the same ones used by Busjahn et al. [1]. They discussed government and economy, the history of black powder, and the effects of dung beetles into a new environment. The C++ programs were all formulated with the understanding that novice programmers were part of the study. Given that information, we made the programs easy enough for a student going through the Introduction to Programming course to figure out. We included different concepts in each program including loops and nested loops, as well as input statements. While there was a range in difficulty of the programs, they were not overly difficult.

The natural text tasks were presented first (in a random order) followed by the seven source code tasks (in a random order). Subjects announced out loud when they were ready to begin the test and used the mouse to continue on to the next slide. Subjects selected one of three numbers (in a random order) after each task and answered the question that followed using the mouse or keyboard. After each task, subjects were presented with a short questionnaire about the difficulty of the task and their confidence in their answer. After all tasks were answered, test subjects were presented with a post questionnaire that asked about difficulty, time needed, and if any problems occurred during the test.

There was no time limit given to the participants of the study. They were allowed as much time as needed to finish each Natural language and source code task. Participants were also given as much time as needed to answer the comprehension questions. Each comprehension question was one of three types; a summary of the task, a multiple choice question about the task, or a fact about the text/the output of the source code. The comprehension questions, chosen at random, helped to better understand a participants ability to read a program. The random options helped deter participants from discussing answers with each other. A replication package with all tasks and study material is available at http://sereslweb.csis.ysu.edu/HCII2017.

## 4    Study Results

We present the results in terms of our two research questions. We first describe how the data was processed followed by comprehension task and timing results. Threats to validity and a discussion is also presented.

Before we ran statistical tests on the data, we needed to map the fixations on source code elements, which was done using eyeCode [16]. eyeCode is able to automatically determine lines and words given an image stimulus. These lines and words form the areas of interest (AOI). In our case the image stimulus is the natural language and source code tasks. eyeCode also maps the fixations on corresponding words so we are able to determine which fixation falls on which word in natural text or source code. We use the abbreviation NT for natural language texts and SC for source code.

### 4.1    Comprehension Scores

We observe that overall non-novices scored higher than novices. We also observer the gap between novices and non-novices per task. The gaps are larger for difficult programs like SignChecker and PrintPattern. The other programs that fell into the medium and easy difficulty category had less of a gap between novices and non-novices. This indicates that novices had a hard time giving a correct answer for difficult problems. See Fig. 1 for the average comprehension score for novices vs. non-novices within each task.

### 4.2    Response Time

We recorded the time that it took each user to go through each task. The time differences showed similar results to the comprehension scores. Both novices and

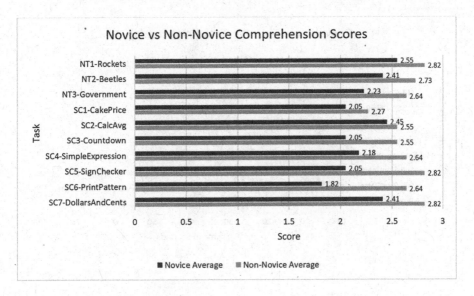

**Fig. 1.** Average comprehension scores for all participants.

non-novices spent the least amount of time in SC4 which was a small and simple program. Similar to comprehension scores, the gaps between novices and non-novices are much more apparent in difficult programs. Non-novices also tend to take the study more seriously compared to novices and so they spend more time on the tasks. A Mann-Whitney test reveals no significant differences in time between novices and non-novices ($p = 0.866$, $U = 126$). See Fig. 2 for completion time per task for novices vs. non-novices.

## 4.3 Element Coverage and Saccade Length

*Novices:* For element coverage, we found that 31.7% of NT in novices were looked at and 34% of elements were looked at for SC. Both saccade length ($p < 0.001$) and element coverage ($p = 0.03$) are significantly different between NT and SC indicating that these two types of stimuli are quite different in terms of their cognitive load for novices.

*Non-novices:* For element coverage, we found that 28.37% of NT in non-novices were looked at and 33.43% of elements were looked at for SC among non-novices. Both the saccade length ($p = 0.001$) and coverage ($p = 0.01$) were significantly different for NT and SC in the non-novices group as well.

We also notice that the saccade length is higher for NT than SC for novices. This means that in NT they jumped a few lines more than in the SC. The same can be seen in the non-novices group. However, we find that the saccade length in the non-novices SC category is lower (by 9 points) than the novices SC category. For NT, the non-novices have higher (15 points more) saccade length compared to the novices NT category.

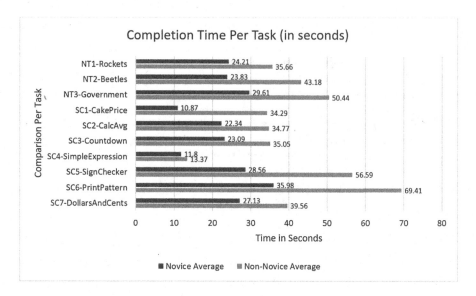

**Fig. 2.** Average time measurements for all participants

### 4.4    Research Questions Revisited

In order to answer RQ1, we report on the linearity metrics we introduced in the previous Section. We notice that the measures Vertical Next Text, Vertical Later Text, and Horizontal Later Text are all higher for NT compared to SC. These are all linearity measures indicating that NT is read more linearly than SC. The regression measures deal with non-linear reading. The line regression rates were higher in NT than SC i.e., participants went back to read a line more often in NT than SC. We ran the Wilcoxon paired test within novices and within non-novices to see if the above measures were significantly different in these groups. Table 1 shows the results of the Wilcoxon test. We see that the measures Vertical Next Text, Vertical Later Text, and Horizontal Later Text and Line Regression Rate are all significantly different between NT and SC for

**Table 1.** Wilcoxon signed ranked test for NT vs. SC for non-novices and novices

| Linearity measure | Sum of positive signed ranks | Non-novices | Novices |
|---|---|---|---|
| | | $p$ | $p$ |
| Vertical next text | 253 | 0.001* | <0.001* |
| Vertical later text | 253 | 0.001* | <0.001* |
| Horizontal later text | 253 | 0.001* | <0.001* |
| Regression rate | 136 | 0.01* | 0.775 |
| Line regression rate | 246 | 0.002* | <0.001* |

non-novices. The Regression Rate which involves regressions of any length is not significant in the novices groups but is significant in the non-novices group. This means that there are significant more line regressions in SC vs. NT reading in the non-novices group.

In order to answer RQ2, we ran the Mann-Whitney test on all participants. We did not find any major differences between the novice group and the non-novice group. These results are shown in Table 2. This could be due to the fact that our non-novices were still students and not what could be considered an expert in the programming industry. This leaves room to expand on this research with expert programmers compared to novices and non-novices. In contrast, Busjahn et al. found significant differences in these linearity measures (except line regression rate) for novices vs. experts in their study.

Table 2. Mann Whitney results for novices vs non-novices over all tasks

| Linearity measure | U | $p$ |
| --- | --- | --- |
| Vertical next text | 546 | 0.406 |
| Vertical later text | 539 | 0.461 |
| Horizontal later text | 536 | 0.487 |
| Regression rate | 540 | 0.453 |
| Line regression rate | 487 | 0.973 |

## 4.5   Story Order Among Novices

We now discuss the alignment of NT and SC to Story Order among novices and show the results of the Needleman-Wunch (N-W algorithm) in Table 3. Story order is basically reading the stimulus one line at a time from top to bottom (typically the way we read natural language text). The N-W algorithm is used as a string matching algorithm to determine story order. It has also been used by Cristino et al. [17] in earlier work on eye movement research. We also use it in order to compare our work with Busjahn et al. [1]. The algorithm gives a similarity score where a high score indicates that two sequences are close to each other. The difference between naïve and dynamic scores is whether repetitions through the code are counted. So if we care about how many times the person

Table 3. Needleman-Wunch results comparing the story order for NT and SC for novices

| Story order | NT | SC | $p$ |
| --- | --- | --- | --- |
| Naïve N-W score | −8.27 | −21.16 | <0.001 |
| Dynamic N-W score | 18.71 | −4.06 | <0.001 |
| Repetitions | 3.42 | 2.6 | <0.001 |

read through the code, we keep repeating the string matching with the story order and the eye gaze movements to get a dynamic score, exactly the same as done in [1].

These scores are not close to one another. This means that even novices do not start with an approach that is very top down and left to right (contrary to what Busjahn [1] found for novices). The results indicate that both natural language text and source code were both read multiple times. The NT was read 3.42 times compared to SC which was read 2.6 times. The more read-throughs the higher the N-W alignment score. We found a significant difference between NT and SCs story order for novices. In comparison to the Busjahn study, the NT was read 6.35 times compared to the SC which was read 3.89 times. Busjahn did not find a significant difference between NT and SC which indicates that their novices start out with a primarily linear approach to code reading. We found a clear differences in our novice group as shown by the numbers in Table 3. We leave the same comparison of story order and eventually execution order (how the program is actually executed) for the novices and non-novices group as part of our future work.

### 4.6   Post Questionnaire Results

After all tasks were complete, each participant was asked if they felt that the given time that it took to go through the tasks was enough. All agreed that they had enough time. Within the group of participants, the difficulty ranking varied. 10% found it to be very easy, 34% easy, 41% average, and 16% found it difficult. The main difficulty that seven participants reported was trying to remember the given stimuli when presented with the comprehension question after the fact.

### 4.7   Threats to Validity

To account for different control structures in source code as well as different word lengths in natural language text, we used three NT passages and seven source code passages. The fact that we did not find any differences between novices and non-novices indicates that they are possibly at the same level in reading skills. In order to find differences in linearity, it might be necessary to study expert programmers in industry who program on a daily basis and have been working in industry for more than 10 years. One major threat to validity is the skewness that occurs in eye tracking data. The linearity metrics are directly dependent on how accurately the fixations are mapped to words or source code elements. We did not manually correct skewness for this study. We did however make sure our calibrations were done well and since our study didn't last more than 20 min, the drift was minimal. We also discarded all trials with less than 60% mapping on source code elements and found the same significant results. This indicates that we might find even more strength and effect in our findings if all the data was manually corrected. Also, on examining the scan paths, we found that most of them were close to the word that they were looking at. We strongly believe that after correction, we should see even stronger significance. We have left this as an immediate future exercise.

## 5 Conclusions and Future Work

The paper presents a study that characterized linearity in eye movements between natural language text and source code in C++. This study replicates an earlier study by Busjahn et al. [1] that looked at Java code. Similar to Busjahn, our results show that both non-novices and novices read source code significantly different than natural language text, while most natural text is read left to right, top to bottom with few regressions, source code is read in a less linear manner with more regressions. Unlike Busjahn our study did not find any significant differences between novices and non-novices. As these findings are different, it calls for more studies to be conducted. It is very likely that this difference was not visible in our study since our non-novices was not comparable to experts from industry used in the Busjahn study.

As part of future work, we are currently conducting a second phase of this study with the same group of students. The purpose is to determine if the eye movements differ at the end of the semester indicating if any learning occurred. The second phase of the study is being conducted during the last week of the semester. We are also taking a look at fixations and durations on specific areas (beacons) in the code provided and want to determine if the difficulty of a task makes a difference on how both novices and experts read the code. Beacons are places in the code that non-novices tend to focus on as one chunk of data. More studies and replications need to be done to add to the body of knowledge and thereby advance the state of the art of eye movement research in programming.

## References

1. Busjahn, T., Bednarik, R., Begel, A., Crosby, M., Paterson, J.H., Schulte, C., Sharif, B., Tamm, S.: Eye movements in code reading: relaxing the linear order. In: Proceedings of the 2015 IEEE 23rd International Conference on Program Comprehension, ICPC 2015, Piscataway, NJ, USA, pp. 255–265. IEEE Press (2015). http://dl.acm.org/citation.cfm?id=2820282.2820320
2. Rayner, K., Chace, K.H., Slattery, T.J., Ashby, J.: Eye movements as reflections of comprehension processes in reading. Sci. Stud. Read. 10, 241–255 (2006)
3. Brooks, R.: Towards a theory of the comprehension of computer programs. Int. J. Man-Mach. Stud. 18(6), 543–554 (1983). http://www.sciencedirect.com/science/article/pii/S0020737383800315
4. Raina, S., Bernard, L., Taylor, B., Kaza, S.: Using eye-tracking to investigate content skipping: a study on learning modules in cybersecurity. In: 2016 IEEE Conference on Intelligence and Security Informatics (ISI), pp. 261–266, September 2016
5. Beelders, T., du Plessis, J.-P.: The influence of syntax highlighting on scanning and reading behaviour for source code. In: Proceedings of the Annual Conference of the South African Institute of Computer Scientists and Information Technologists, SAICSIT 2016, pp. 5:1–5:10. ACM, New York (2016). http://doi.acm.org/10.1145/2987491.2987536

6. Sarkar, A.: The impact of syntax colouring on program comprehension. In: PPIG, July 2015

7. Crosby, M.E.: Natural versus computer languages: a reading comparison. Ph.D. dissertation, University of Hawaii at Manoa (1986)

8. Fan, Q.: The effects of beacons, comments, and tasks on program comprehension process in software maintenance. Ph.D. dissertation, Catonsville, MD, USA (2010)

9. Turner, R., Falcone, M., Sharif, B., Lazar, A.: An eye-tracking study assessing the comprehension of C++ and Python source code. In: Proceedings of the Symposium on Eye Tracking Research and Applications, ETRA 2014, pp. 231–234. ACM, New York (2014). http://doi.acm.org/10.1145/2578153.2578218

10. Sharif, B., Maletic, J.I.: An eye tracking study on camelcase and under_score identifier styles. In: Proceedings of the 2010 IEEE 18th International Conference on Program Comprehension, ICPC 2010, Washington, DC, USA, pp. 196–205. IEEE Computer Society (2010). http://dx.doi.org/10.1109/ICPC.2010.41

11. Binkley, D., Davis, M., Lawrie, D., Maletic, J., Morrell, C., Sharif, B.: The impact of identifier style on effort and comprehension. Empir. Softw. Eng. J. (Invit. Submiss.) **18**(2), 219–276.(2013)

12. Uwano, H., Nakamura, M., Monden, A., Matsumoto, K.-I.: Analyzing individual performance of source code review using reviewers' eye movement. In: Proceedings of the 2006 Symposium on Eye Tracking Research Applications, ETRA 2006, pp. 133–140. ACM, New York (2006). http://doi.acm.org/10.1145/1117309.1117357

13. Schulte, C., Clear, T., Taherkhani, A., Busjahn, T., Paterson, J.H.: An introduction to program comprehension for computer science educators. In: Proceedings of the 2010 ITiCSE Working Group Reports, ITiCSE-WGR 2010, pp. 65–86. ACM, New York (2010). http://doi.acm.org/10.1145/1971681.1971687

14. Busjahn, T., Schulte, C.: The use of code reading in teaching programming. In: Proceedings of the 13th Koli Calling International Conference on Computing Education Research, Koli Calling 2013, pp. 3–11. ACM, New York (2013). http://doi.acm.org/10.1145/2526968.2526969

15. Marter, T., Babucke, P., Lembken, P., Hanenberg, S.: Lightweight programming experiments without programmers and programs: an example study on the effect of similarity and number of object identifiers on the readability of source code using natural texts. In: Proceedings of the 2016 ACM International Symposium on New Ideas, New Paradigms, and Reflections on Programming and Software, Onward! 2016, pp. 1–14. ACM, New York (2016). http://doi.acm.org/10.1145/2986012.2986020

16. Hansen, M.: GitHub - synesthesiam/eyecode-tools: a collection of tools for analyzing data from my eyeCode experiment. https://github.com/synesthesiam/eyecode-tools

17. Cristino, F., Mathôt, S., Theeuwes, J., Gilchrist, I.D.: ScanMatch: a novel method for comparing fixation sequences. Behav. Res. Methods **42**(3), 692–700 (2010). http://www.springerlink.com/index/10.3758/BRM.42.3.692

# Adapting Human-Computer-Interaction of Attentive Smart Glasses to the Trade-Off Conflict in Purchase Decisions: An Experiment in a Virtual Supermarket

Jella Pfeiffer[1]([✉]), Thies Pfeiffer[2], Anke Greif-Winzrieth[1], Martin Meißner[3,4], Patrick Renner[2], and Christof Weinhardt[1]

[1] Karlsruhe Institute of Technology, Karlsruhe, Germany
jella.pfeiffer@kit.edu
[2] CITEC, Bielefeld University, Bielefeld, Germany
[3] University of Southern Denmark, Esbjerg, Denmark
[4] Monash University, Melbourne, Australia

**Abstract.** In many everyday purchase decisions, consumers have to trade-off their decisions between alternatives. For example, consumers often have to decide whether to buy the more expensive high quality product or the less expensive product of lower quality. Marketing researchers are especially interested in finding out how consumers make decisions when facing such trade-off conflicts and eye-tracking has been used as a tool to investigate the allocation of attention in such situations. Conflicting decision situations are also particularly interesting for human-computer interaction research because designers may use knowledge about the information acquisition behavior to build assistance systems which can help the user to solve the trade-off conflict. In this paper, we build and test such an assistance system that monitors the user's information acquisition processes using mobile eye-tracking in the virtual reality. In particular, we test whether and how strongly the trade-off conflict influences how consumers direct their attention to products and features. We find that trade-off conflict, task experience and task involvement significantly influence how much attention products receive. We discuss how this knowledge might be used in the future to build assistance systems in the form of attentive smart glasses.

## 1 Introduction

When we make decisions, we usually have to trade-off favorable against unfavorable attributes of several alternatives. For example, going to a decent restaurant during a lunch break instead of grasping a burger at the next fast food store has the advantage of eating healthier food and relaxing more during the break, but most likely this alternative will also be more expensive and take more time. Detecting situations in which decision makers experience such trade-off conflicts

© Springer International Publishing AG 2017
D.D. Schmorrow and C.M. Fidopiastis (Eds.): AC 2017, Part I, LNAI 10284, pp. 219–235, 2017.
DOI: 10.1007/978-3-319-58628-1_18

and gathering knowledge about how they cope with conflicting decision situations is of large interest for human-computer interaction designers of assistance systems.

Users of assistance systems, for example, will most likely refer to help when they experience difficulties in making a cognitively demanding decision because of conflicting attributes. The system should provide exactly the right information that is required to come to a decision. Consequently, there is a need to understand how trade-off conflicts influence human information acquisition behavior.

This work is part of a larger research line on assistance systems in form of attentive smart glasses that monitor the user's attention to follow her decision making progress (see Fig. 1). The intelligent glasses include eye-tracking facilities to record and analyze eye movements in real time. In addition to that, the glasses monitor the environment with a scene camera and use computer vision to detect objects relevant in supported application domains. Based on these two information sources, environmental context and interaction progress, the smart glasses augment reality with appropriate information with little to none explicit interaction efforts by the user.

**Fig. 1.** Example of the eye-tracking enabled smart glasses with augmented reality capabilities based on the Epson Moverio BT-200.

The basic research question to which we contribute in this article is how trade-off conflicts influence attentional processes. From a practical viewpoint, this knowledge will help us to build attentive smart glasses that enable the user to focus on decision-relevant information in order to make better decisions. Based on our findings, we formulate guidelines for the design of human-computer interaction with the attentive smart glasses. We study the information acquisition behavior using mobile eye tracking in the context of consumer decision making in front of a supermarket shelf. This domain is particularly suited because consumers face many trade-off decisions when making day-to-day purchases.

In the development of interactive systems, an iterative, user-centered design process is crucial. Studies on mobile decision making in complex interaction scenarios such as a supermarket, however, are resource intense endeavor.

The annotation of the recorded eye movements (i.e. assigning the fixations to specific areas of interest) in particular is an error-prone and time consuming task. To make the gathering of data on larger user groups more feasible and to allow us to reproduce exactly the same decision situations in many design iterations, we created a life-sized virtual supermarket shelf for studies in immersive virtual reality. This also increases our level of experimental control and data quality. In particular, in the virtual shelf, we can easily randomize the products and their positions and detect the user's gaze in real time.

Our empirical study involved 33 participants who made four purchase decisions. After each of the decisions between 20 products on the shelf, participants saw additional information for two attributes (nutrition facts and customer rating) for the chosen product in the simulated augmented reality (see Fig. 2). Participants then received recommendations for six products that all were in trade-off conflict with the previously chosen product. Our results show that the overall product attention as well as the time participants spend on looking at conflicting information is strongly influenced by the degree of trade-off conflict. Thus, trade-off conflict exhibits a strong influence on participants' attentional processes.

**Fig. 2.** Two examples from users interacting with the virtual shelf. The scene on the left is taken from the condition with additional information displays in AR-style. The scene on the right shows that participants could pick-up products from the shelf for further inspections. (Color figure online)

Assuming that longer attention to objects is related to a higher complexity for the user to process the information, these results have several implications for designers of smart glasses. First, by analyzing the users' eye movements, we can infer the cognitive complexity of the decision situation for the consumer. The next logical step is to detect which attributes are in conflict and provide targeted recommendations when assistance is needed. Second, in future work, we need to develop an interface that can help users to reduce the difficulty that is caused by trade-off conflicts. Thus, the interface might lead to faster decision-making processes. Third, the empirical results of our study show that the user characteristics, such as product involvement and task experience, also influence the allocation of attention. As a consequence, an attentive system should take such information into account when interpreting the attentional processes.

## 2    Attentive Smart Glasses

Augmented reality has become famous through smartphone apps that provide information about the environment once the user points the smartphone at the object of interest. In our project, we push augmented reality one step further by proposing attentive smart glasses that include mobile eye-tracking and provide information not only depending on the environmental context, but also based on cognitive processing. The hardware system is thus a combination of wearable mobile eye tracking [27] and augmented reality classes, similar to Toyama et al. [24]. These intelligent glasses learn about the user's attention through processing the user's eye movements. At the same time, they project back information about the user's environment on a display. In contrast to the above described existing smartphone apps, the attentive smart glasses can thus detect the context and augment the reality with little user effort. The user neither has to manually scan nor observe the environment with the smartphone. Furthermore, in contrast to the already existing smart glasses, the attentive smart glasses can gather information about the user's attentional and behavioral processes in greater detail by using eye-tracking technology.

The proposed system provides the technical basis for augmented cognition in an open-loop interactive system [23]. In combining eye tracking as a basis for cognitive state analysis and computer vision on the scene camera for context analysis, it can automatically assign eye fixations to objects of interest [10,20,21]. Once the semantic link between eye fixation and object of interest is established, patterns of eye movements can be analyzed. Detecting and interpreting these eye movement patterns is the basis for the cognitive state and situation analysis of the proposed augmented cognition system, which should then be enabled to present adequate assistance to the user, e.g. by displaying relevant information. First of all, however, eye movement patterns for different relevant situations have to be identified. Work on this is in the primary focus of this paper.

We thus present a study about the usage of attentive smart glasses at the point-of-purchase. Imagine the potential use case: A customer wants to buy a muesli. She has a standard one that she usually buys. However, she would be really interested in getting the information on how other consumers rate the mueslis available in the supermarket and on how healthy the mueslis are based on nutritional facts. The intelligent glasses that she is wearing are able to detect the muesli she is currently looking at and displays customer rating and nutrition information to her in the augmented reality, once she fixates a muesli for a certain amount of time, indicating her interest in this product. Displaying this additional information, however, might evoke an additional conflict. The other mueslis might be better to the muesli she usually buys with respect to the customer rating and worse with respect to the nutrition information, or vice versa. When we design attentive smart glasses, we first of all need to understand how the trade-off conflict influences how much attention the decision maker directs to products being in conflict.

## 3   Trade-Off Conflict and Decision Making

Most decision situations which consumers in supermarkets face involve a large number of different products (which we will also call alternatives in the following). These decisions will result in trade-off conflicts if the products differ with respect to many of their characteristics (also called product attributes). More precisely, trade-off conflicts occur when the available alternatives have advantages and disadvantages, i.e. when there is no dominant alternative which is better than all other alternatives in terms of all its product attributes. The investigation of trade-off conflicts is of central research interest in the field of decision-making because it is a key question how decision makers make use of conflicting information [22].

A trade-off conflict which we observe frequently in the market is the one between price and quality. Products with a higher product quality most often will also have higher prices which is a source of conflict for consumers as they will have to decide whether to trade in quality for lower prices [8]. In line with previous research from the area of decision-making and marketing [6], we therefore define trade-off conflict as the "degree to which alternatives under consideration have different advantages and disadvantages" [6, p. 217]. According to this definition, one way to quantify the trade-off conflict is to compare the alternatives with respect to how similar they are. This definition of conflict goes back to Festinger [9] who suggested that the degree of conflict should decrease if decision alternatives are largely similar. Vice versa, if two alternatives are dissimilar with respect to many of their attributes, the degree of conflict between the two options will be higher.

The marketing literature has been particularly interested in how trade-off conflicts between attributes influence the difficulty of making a decision [4,12]. One of the important findings is that attributes may substantially vary with respect to how difficult it is to make trade-offs between them [15]. It is, for example, easier for decision-makers to make trade-offs for attributes that can be directly compared and exchanged along a common dimension [16,26]. If the information for both attributes is presented on the same type of rating scale, it will be easier for decision makers to make trade-offs between the two attributes compared to a situation in which the information is visualized in different ways.

The literature has largely focused on how trade-off conflict influences decision-making behavior in choice situations including multiple decision alternatives. Dhar [6], for example, has shown that decision-makers will more likely defer making a decision if the conflict between the decision alternatives is larger. Moreover, researchers have shown that decision makers will spend more time in choice situations that involve more conflict [11]. With increasing trade-off conflict decision makers will also consider more product attributes [13], show more consistent choice patterns [2] and use simplifying decision heuristics to a larger extend [17]. Furthermore, [17] showed that the influence of trade-off conflict on the decision heuristic used is stronger than the influence of the number of attributes or alternatives characterizing the decision situation.

To the best of our knowledge, research so far has not investigated how the trade-off conflict between two alternatives influences information processing in an augmented reality setting. Our goal therefore is to validate whether an increasing trade-off conflict between additionally provided information in the augmented reality will increase participants' overall attention to products as well as attention to the particular information that evokes the conflict. The level of conflict will be manipulated in the experiment in order to test how the degree of conflict influences the overall product attention. In addition, we will test whether the allocation of attention changes when participants make a sequence of repeated decisions. In line with previous research investigating decision making in repeated choices [14], we expect to find a significant decrease in the overall amount of attention to products in later tasks as participants will learn how to more efficiently direct their attention. We will also test whether a higher personal product involvement significantly increases overall product attention. A higher product involvement will mean that the product category is more relevant for the participant. The participant will therefore care more about which product she will choose in the respective decision situation.

## 4   Study Design

In this section, we present an experiment on the effect of trade-off conflict on consumers' attentional processes. The experiment took place in front of a virtual shelf in a Cave Automatic Virtual Environment (CAVE) [5]. Altogether, 33 students (mean age = 23.8, min. 19, max 31 years) from various fields completed the study. One session took about 30 min and participants were endowed with €8.00 for their purchase in the virtual supermarket in the beginning of the experiment. We incentive-aligned the participants using the following mechanism: Participants received one of the four products they chose plus the money remaining after subtracting the price of this product from the €8.00. Due to technical problems the data was not recorded or stored correctly for seven sessions, so the analyses are based on only 26 participants.

### 4.1   Technical Setup

We collected the data in a virtual supermarket realized in a CAVE at the virtual reality lab at CITEC. The CAVE has two screens (front and floor forming an L-shape) measuring 3 m times 2.25 m each. The projectors project a pixel size of 1.41 mm. Passive stereo projection based on INFITEC is implemented. For tracking participants' movements the Advanced RealTime Tracking (ART) TrackPack 4 (60 Hz) is used. For eye-tracking the SMI eye-tracking glasses which record gaze data with 60 Hz on both eyes (binocular) were integrated into the system [19]. The interaction device used is the ART FlyStick.

## 4.2   Procedure

Participants had to make four product decisions in total. For each of the four decisions, participants faced a product shelf containing 20 products from one product category (muesli or baking mixture)[1]. After each of the decisions, participants saw additional information for two attributes (nutrition facts and customer rating) for the chosen product. This information was shown in a simulated augmented reality style by displaying a red box next to the product. It popped up as soon as the participants gazed at the particular product. Participants then received recommendations for six products that all were in trade-off conflict with the previously chosen product. These recommendations were highlighted using a blue frame. Each of the purchase decisions a participant made consisted of three scenes and the final purchase decision was made in the last scene (see Fig. 3).

In the first scene, participants chose their favorite product from the product shelf and confirmed their choice by putting the product into a virtual shopping cart.

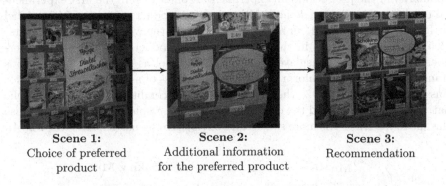

| **Scene 1:** | **Scene 2:** | **Scene 3:** |
| Choice of preferred product | Additional information for the preferred product | Recommendation |

**Fig. 3.** Scenes in the study. (Color figure online)

In the second scene, they faced the same shelf again, but the product they had chosen before was highlighted with a red frame and additional product information was displayed in a bubble next to the product when the participant looked at it. For every product, participants saw additional information about nutrition facts and a customer rating. Participants could take as much time as they wanted to look at the provided information for their favorite product and then switched to the third scene.

In this last scene, we asked participants to make their final decision. Taking into account the participant's preferences in terms of taste (chocolate vs. fruit vs. other in the muesli category) and type of the product (muffin vs. ordinary cake in the baking mix category) as revealed by the choice of the preferred product

---

[1] In sum, we modeled 49 different mueslis and 44 different baking mixtures from different brands and chose the 20 products shown in each shelf randomly from this set of products of the respective product category.

in the first scene, we recommended six products by highlighting them with blue frames and provided additional information when the participant looked at one of these highlighted products. This third scene is the most relevant for this work because each recommended product either has a higher nutrition rating and a lower customer rating or a lower nutrition rating and a higher customer rating than the initially chosen, preferred product. As a result, every decision consumers face in the third scene includes trade-offs.

The nutrition ratings were calculated using a scoring system based on the colors in the traffic light label and the customer ratings were assigned such that the attributes of each recommended product were in conflict with those of the initially preferred one[2]. The participant then had to decide whether she wants to keep the product chosen in the first scene in her shopping cart or would like to switch to one of the other six recommended products.

The experiment varied the format of the scales used for these two product attributes. The customer rating ranged from 2 (lowest possible rating indicating a low popularity of the product) to 5 (highest possible rating indicating a high popularity of the product) in all experimental conditions. In the first experimental condition, we displayed the healthiness of a product using a nutrition label with stars ranging from 1 (unhealthiest product in the whole range of products) to 5 (healthiest product in the whole range of products). In the other experimental condition, we displayed a traffic light label as proposed by the foods standards agency [3] to inform about the healthiness of a product[3]. However, for this work, we only analyze the first experimental condition, in which both the nutrition information and the customer rating were displayed with stars because this made the trade-offs more salient and obvious to the participants (see Fig. 4).

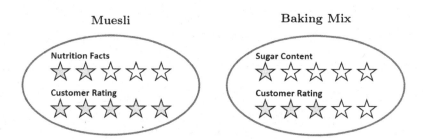

**Fig. 4.** Additional product information for nutrition information and customer ratings. (Color figure online)

---

[2] After the experiment subjects were informed that the customer ratings were fictitious.

[3] In the muesli category this traffic light label contains information about the amounts of sugar, fat, sag fats, and salt in 100 grams of the product. In the baking mixture category it only contains information about the amount of sugar. Depending on the amounts the corresponding part of the label is colored in green (low amount), amber (medium amount), or red (high amount).

**Preferred Product:**

NR: 1 (1)
CR: 5 (7)
T: c

NR: nutriton rating [# stars] (rank)
CR: customer rating [# stars] (rank)
TOC: trade-off conflict with preferred product
T: type [chocolate, fruit, other]

**Recommended Products:**

low ———————— trade-off conflict ———————— high ▷

| NR: 1.5 (2) | NR: 1.5 (3) | NR: 1.5 (4) | NR: 2 (5) | NR: 2.5 (6) | NR: 3 (7) |
| CR: 4.5 (6) | CR: 4 (5) | CR: 3.5 (4) | CR: 3 (3) | CR: 2.5 (2) | CR: 2 (1) |
| TOC: 1 | TOC: 1.5 | TOC: 2 | TOC: 3 | TOC: 4 | TOC: 5 |
| T: f | T: o | T: c | T: c | T: c | T: c |

**Fig. 5.** Exemplary choice set and assigned ratings. (Color figure online)

In this second experimental group, the trade-off conflict was manipulated. Figure 5 shows an example of a choice set given in the third scene and illustrates the algorithm we used to assign the customer ratings: After the participant had chosen the preferred product, we randomly draw six products out of the remaining ones. Please note that in the muesli category we always recommended four products of the same type as the preferred product and two of another type. The types were "chocolate", "fruits" and "other" in the muesli category and "cake" and "muffins/cupcakes" in the baking mix category. Thus, the recommendations were in fact six randomly chosen products. We sorted them in ascending order according to their real nutrition ratings and assigned fictitious customer ratings from 2 to 5 stars in steps of 0.5 in descending order. Consequently, the product with the highest nutrition rating got the lowest customer rating, the product with the second highest nutrition rating got the second lowest customer rating and so on. If two or more products in the choice set had the same nutrition ratings, they were ordered alphabetically in the ascending sequence and received different customer ratings according to their position in this sequence. On rare occasions the preferred product was weakly dominated by a recommended product with a similar nutrition rating but a higher customer rating or the preferred product was weakly dominated by a recommended product with a similar nutrition rating but a lower customer rating[4]. Cases in which one product of the set was weakly dominated were excluded from further analyses. As a result of applying this algorithm (i) each recommended product was in conflict with the preferred product, (ii) trade-off conflict differed considerably between choice sets and (iii) at the same time we could realize the visualization of the real nutrition information. Showing fictitious nutrition information, which would have helped to increase the variance over trade-offs and to exclude weakly dominating products, was not an option because for some products nutrition information is provided on the package of the three-dimensional model. Thus, participants were able to see the real nutrition information.

### 4.3   Dependent Variables - Attentional Measures

To trace decision processes we recorded the participants' eye movements during the experiment. We defined separate areas of interest for the product package, the price tag, as well as the star-rating scales for every product. When assigning fixations to the areas of interest, our integration of eye tracking into virtual reality takes care of the fact that the position of the objects (products) in the three-dimensional space will change because participants move and interact with the shelf. If, for example, participants grab a product package from the shelf and turn it around, fixations on the package will automatically be correctly assigned based on the continuously changing position of the package. We focus our analysis on two attentional measures: First, we count the number of fixations to all areas of interest which belong to a product, which also includes the price tags and the rating-scale information (Number of fixations on product). This measure will quantify how much attention is directed to a each product. Second, we calculate the number of fixations on star-rating information (Number of fixations to star-ratings) because we are particularly interested in how much attention is directed to the rating-scale information provided in the augmented reality.

### 4.4   Independent Variables

**Trade-Off Conflict.** The experimental design guarantees that all recommended products are always in trade-off conflict with the initially chosen product, which means that each recommended product will have a higher rating on one of the scales, but a lower rating on the other scale compared to the initially chosen product. Given that we have a decision which involves trade-off conflict, we are interested in how strongly the degree of trade-off conflict influences how much attention participants direct to the products and corresponding

---

[4] The preferred product was weakly dominated in 15 choice sets and it dominated at least one recommended product in 44 choice sets.

star-ratings. In line with the above definition, we operationalize the trade-off conflict as the dissimilarity between a recommended product $i$ ($i \in \{1, \ldots, 6\}$) and the preferred product $P$. The degree of trade-off conflict is calculated as the sum of the absolute differences between the nutrition ratings $NR$ and the customer ratings $CR$ of both products:

$$\text{Trade-off conflict}_i = |NR_P - NR_i| + |CR_P - CR_i| \tag{1}$$

Six products were highlighted in the third scene of the experiment. We therefore get six observations for every participant-task combination.

**Task Experience.** In our experiment, every participant makes decisions in four tasks. We are therefore able to test whether the number of fixations changes with task experience. In line with previous findings in other choice contexts (see, for example, [14]) we expect that participants learn how to allocate their attention and therefore will be faster making their decisions in later tasks.

**Task Involvement.** In order to measure the participants' product involvement, we used the frequency of product consumption of a product. At the end of the experiment, we asked participants how often they purchase the respective product. We expect that a higher product involvement will prolong the search process because participants will care more about finding the right, i.e. preferred muesli or baking mixture.

**Product Category.** Previous studies have shown that the product category can influence which information is taken into account when making purchase decisions [1,7]. In order to control for potential differences between product categories, we also included the product category as an independent variable.

## 5 Results

Each recommended product was on average fixated 31 times (std dev. $= 34$). As expected, the number of fixations on average decreases from 34 (std dev. $= 30$) fixations in the first task to 29 fixations (std dev. $= 37$) in the last task. When we look at the amount of attention that was directed to the star-ratings we see that it does not change with task experience. In the first task, participants on average fixated the star-ratings 15 times (std dev. $= 16$) which is as often as in the last task (std dev. $= 31$). The relatively large increase in the standard deviation which we observe in the last task suggests that participants differed with respect to how much they use the star-rating information in later tasks. The result suggests that some participants will use that information to a larger extend.

In order to test the effect of all independent variables and their potential interactions on the two attentional measures, we build a general model of product attention. We count the number of fixations on each product (or correspondingly the star-ratings) in each task for every participant. A Poisson count model with a log-link function is used (similar to the model used by [14]). In this model, the expected frequency of looking at a product depends on the trade-off conflict, the task experience, the task involvement, and the product category. Because the observations are not independent, we include a random coefficient for participants. Trade-off conflict, task experience, and task involvement are continuous variables and are therefore standardized to facilitate the interpretation of the results. The product category is treated as a categorical variable. We used the GENLINMIXED procedure in SPSS to run the multi-level models.

## 5.1   Overall Attention to Products

Table 1 provides the multi-level model results for the overall attention to products. The Poisson model allows us to interpret the percentage changes in fixations to products. The percentage changes are derived by exponentiation of the raw Poisson coefficients. In the following, we will focus on the percentage changes because they allow us to appraise how strongly the independent variables impact the dependent variable.

**Table 1.** Multilevel analysis of factors influencing overall attention to products

| Model term | Number of fixations to product | | |
|---|---|---|---|
| | % Change | Coefficient (Standard error) | Significance |
| Trade-off conflict | +16% | .15 (.01) | $t = 12.45$, $p < .01$ |
| Trade-off conflict × Task experience | +20% | .19 (.01) | $t = 14.98$, $p < .01$ |
| Trade-off conflict × Task involvement | +3% | .03 (.01) | $t = 2.49$, $p = .01$ |
| Task experience | −12% | −.12 (.01) | $t = -10.15$, $p < .01$ |
| Task involvement | +28% | .25 (.02) | $t = 12.02$, $p < .01$ |
| Product category (Muesli) | −12% | −.13 (.03) | $t = -3.70$, $p < .01$ |
| Product category (Baking Mixtures) | . | . | . |

The result in the first row of Table 1 shows how the trade-off conflict (with respect to the star-ratings) influences the overall product attention. An increase of one unit in the trade-off conflict generates a 16% increase in the number of fixations given that all other independent numerous variables are at their mean levels. The result shows that, in line with our expectations, an increase in conflict has a strong positive effect on the overall amount of attention that participants direct to the products. We also find a significant interaction effect between trade-off conflict and task experience. The estimate is a $1.162 \times e^{-.186/2} - 1 = 5.9\%$ increase in fixations for the first task, but a $1.162 \times e^{+.186/2} - 1 = 27.5\%$ increase for the last task. This result can be interpreted as a learning effect. If products are in conflict with respect to the star-ratings, participants will more strongly use that information in later tasks to direct their attention to relevant products.

We also find a significant, but small, interaction effect for trade-off conflict and task involvement. Trade-off conflict has a slightly stronger effect on overall product attention for participants who have a higher product involvement.

In line with previous findings on repeated choices [14], we also find a main effect for task experience. The number of fixations drops by 12% from earlier to later tasks, indicating that participants make their decisions faster in later tasks. We also find that participants overall looked less frequently at mueslis than at baking mixtures. This general difference between the two product categories shows that it is important to control for the differences resulting from investigating different products. In line with our expectations, we also find a significant main effect for task involvement. Participants with a higher task involvement fixated the products more frequently. The number of fixations changes by 28% with a unit change in task involvement.

## 5.2 Attention to Star-Rating Information

Table 2 summarizes the results of the multi-level model for the attention to star-rating information. The results for trade-off conflict and the respective interactions are similar to the results for the overall attention to products. We find evidence that participants indeed more frequently look at star-rating information if the recommended and the initially chosen product are more in conflict regarding the star-ratings.

**Table 2.** Multilevel analysis of factors influencing attention to star-rating information

| Model Term | Number of fixations to star-ratings | | |
|---|---|---|---|
| | % Change | Coefficient (Standard error) | Significance |
| Trade-off conflict | +18% | .17 (.02) | $t = 9.51$, $p < .01$ |
| Trade-off conflict x Task experience | +21% | .19 (.02) | $t = 10.54$, $p < .01$ |
| Trade-off conflict x Task involvement | +3% | .03 (.02) | $t = 1.70$, $p = .09$ |
| Task experience | −7% | −.07 (.02) | $t = -4.05$, $p < .01$ |
| Task involvement | +49% | .40 (.03) | $t = 13.17$, $p < .01$ |
| Product category (Muesli) | −34% | −.42 (.05) | $t = -8.54$, $p < .01$ |
| Product category (Baking Mixtures) | . | . | . |

We also find that task experience has a smaller, but still significant effect on the number of fixations to the star-ratings. Across tasks, the amount of attention that is directed to the star-rating decreases by about 7%.

A new insight from this analysis is that task involvement influences the number of fixations to star-rating information even stronger than the overall attention to products. A unit change in task involvement leads to a 49% increase in the number of fixations to star-ratings. This result means that participants with higher task involvement focus much more on the star-rating information.

We conclude that the star-rating information is more important for participants with higher task involvement because they care more about the opinions of other consumers and the nutritional information provided by the simulated augmented reality.

## 6   Design Implications for Attentive Smart Glasses

Our results show that trade-off conflict strongly influences how much attention user direct to a decision situation. Thus, the degree of the trade-off conflict experienced by the user can be predicted by assistance systems that have integrated eye trackers, like our attentive smart glasses. Detecting the degree of trade-off conflict is important because users might defer their choice if they cannot resolve the conflict [6,25]. An assistance system could furthermore help users to resolve trade-off conflicts, for example, by displaying the conflicting information in an easy-to-understand way or by providing additional explanations regarding the attributes that are in conflict.

We also find that trade-off conflict has an even stronger effect on attention if users are more experienced. Yet, overall, more experience in task execution leads to less attention. Therefore, experience makes users being more selective in their attentional processes. Designers of attentive smart glasses must therefore pay attention to how much and which information to display to experienced shoppers as they might not be willed to spend too much time and effort on the additional information provided. For example, information that is not in conflict might not be processed in more detail by the user.

Furthermore, we find that the influence of the trade-off conflict is stronger for users with high product involvement. In particular, we find that users focus directly on the conflicting product information provided in the augmented reality. Thus, it seems that users with high product involvement might be particularly interested in receiving assistance to process and understand conflicting information.

In sum, our results imply that the users' characteristics, such as task experience and product involvement, influence their allocation of attention in these purchase situations. With regard to this point, we refer to our prior work [18] in which we detect further information about the decision context early on in the decision process based on eye movements.

## 7   Contributions and Limitations

In this paper, we analyzed the influence of trade-off conflict between products on users' attentional processes. We show that with increasing trade-off conflict, participants look more frequently at the products being in conflict. This increase in product attention comes along with an increase of attention on the conflicting additional product information. The effects are stronger for participants with larger product involvement. We furthermore find a learning effect as participants direct their attention to conflicting additional product information to a larger extend, when they have more task experience.

These findings not only add to the common understanding of human's attention in situations of conflicting information but also have important implications for the design of attentive smart classes.

Our study is limited by the fact that other product attributes, for example, the price, size of the package, or favorite ingredients could further increase the experienced trade-off conflict for the respondents. When measuring trade-off conflict these attributes were neglected. We solely focused on those two attributes that were prominently displayed in augmented reality. Furthermore, the attentive smart glasses are designed to work in the reality. Our results are derived from a study in the virtual reality that simulates the smart glasses because of several advantages, such as high experimental control, repeatability and simplified data analysis. Therefore, it remains an open question to what degree the results can be directly transferred to a real-world setting with consumers.

In future work, we plan to study how to best display conflicting information in order to avoid negative consequences of conflict like choice deferral and frustration. We would also like to test whether the experienced trade-off conflict can be reduced by highlighting important attributes in the augmented reality which are personally relevant for the individual consumer. Our vision is that assistance systems will help consumers to better cope with trade-off conflicts in order to allow them to make better decisions which are in line with their personal goals.

# References

1. Balasubramanian, S.K., Cole, C.: Consumers' search and use of nutrition information: the challenge and promise of the nutrition labeling and education act. J. Mark. **66**(3), 112–127 (2002)
2. Bettman, J.R., Johnson, E.J., Luce, M.F., Payne, J.W.: Correlation, conflict, and choice. J. Exp. Psychol. Learn. Mem. Cogn. **19**(4), 931 (1993)
3. British Department of Health: Guide to creating a front of pack (fop) nutrition label for pre-packed products sold through retail outlets (2013). https://www.gov.uk/government/publications/front-of-pack-nutrition-labelling-guidance
4. Carmon, Z., Wertenbroch, K., Zeelenberg, M.: Option attachment: when deliberating makes choosing feel like losing. J. Consum. Res. **30**(1), 15–29 (2003)
5. Cruz-Neira, C., Sandin, D.J., DeFanti, T.A.: Surround-screen projection-based virtual reality: the design and implementation of the cave. In: Proceedings of the 20th Annual Conference on Computer Graphics and Interactive Techniques, pp. 135–142 (1993)
6. Dhar, R.: Consumer preference for a no-choice option. J. Consum. Res. **24**(2), 215–231 (1997)
7. Ehrich, K.R., Irwin, J.R.: Willful ignorance in the request for product attribute information. J. Mark. Res. **42**(3), 266–277 (2005)
8. Fasolo, B., McClelland, G.H., Lange, K.A.: The effect of site design and interattribute correlations on interactive web-based decisions. In: Haugtvedt, C.P., Machleit, K.A., Yalch, R. (eds.) Online Consumer Psychology. Advertising and Consumer Psychology, pp. 325–344. Lawrence Erlbaum Associates, Mahwah (2005)

9. Festinger, L.: A Theory of Cognitive Dissonance. Stanford University Press, Stanford (1957)
10. Harmening, K., Pfeiffer, T.: Location-based online identification of objects in the centre of visual attention using eye tracking. In: Pfeiffer, T., Essig, K. (eds.) Proceedings of the First International Workshop on Solutions for Automatic Gaze-Data Analysis 2013 (SAGA 2013), pp. 38–40. Center of Excellence Cognitive Interaction Technology (2013)
11. Iglesias-Parro, S., De La Fuente, E.I., Ortega, A.R.: The effect of context variables on cognitive effort in multiattribute binary choice. Theor. Decis. **52**(2), 101–125 (2002)
12. Kivetz, R.: The effects of effort and intrinsic motivation on risky choice. Mark. Sci. **22**(4), 477–502 (2003)
13. Luce, M.F., Bettman, J.R., Payne, J.W.: Choice processing in emotionally difficult decisions. J. Exp. Psychol. Learn. Mem. Cogn. **23**(2), 384–405 (1997)
14. Meißner, M., Musalem, A., Huber, J.: Eye tracking reveals processes that enable conjoint choices to become increasingly efficient with practice. J. Mark. Res. **53**(1), 1–17 (2016)
15. Nowlis, S.M., Dhar, R., Simonson, I.: The effect of decision order on purchase quantity decisions. J. Mark. Res. **47**(4), 725–737 (2010)
16. Nowlis, S.M., Simonson, I.: Attribute-task compatibility as a determinant of consumer preference reversals. J. Mark. Res. **34**(2), 205–218 (1997)
17. Pfeiffer, J., Duzevik, D., Rothlauf, F., Bonabeau, E., Yamamoto, K.: An optimized design of choice experiments: a new approach for studying decision behavior in choice task experiments. J. Behav. Decis. Mak. **28**(3), 262–280 (2015)
18. Pfeiffer, J., Meißner, M., Prosiegel, J., Pfeiffer, T.: Classification of goal-directed search and exploratory search using mobile eye-tracking. In: Proceedings of the International Conference on Information Systems (ICIS 2014) (2014)
19. Pfeiffer, T.: Towards gaze interaction in immersive virtual reality: evaluation of a monocular eye tracking set-up. In: Schumann, M., Kuhlen, T. (eds.) Virtuelle und Erweiterte Realität - Fünfter Workshop der GI-Fachgruppe VR/AR, pp. 81–92. Shaker Verlag GmbH, Aachen (2008)
20. Pfeiffer, T., Memili, C.: Model-based real-time visualization of realistic three-dimensional heat maps for mobile eye tracking and eye tracking in virtual reality. In: Proceedings of the Ninth Biennial ACM Symposium on Eye Tracking Research and Applications, pp. 95–102. ACM Press (2016)
21. Pfeiffer, T., Renner, P., Pfeiffer-Leßmann, N.: EyeSee3D 2.0: model-based real-time analysis of mobile eye-tracking in static and dynamic three-dimensional scenes. In: Proceedings of the Ninth Biennial ACM Symposium on Eye Tracking Research and Applications, pp. 189–196. ACM Press (2016)
22. Slovic, P.: Comparison of Bayesian and regression approaches to the study of information processing in judgment. Organ. Behav. Hum. Perform. **6**(6), 649–744 (1971)
23. Stanney, K.M., Schmorrow, D.D., Johnston, M., Fuchs, S., Jones, D., Hale, K.S., Ahmad, A., Young, P.: Augmented cognition: an overview. Rev. Hum. Factors Ergon. **5**(1), 195–224 (2009)
24. Toyama, T., Dengel, A., Suzuki, W., Kise, K.: Wearable reading assist system: augmented reality document combining document retrieval and eye tracking. In: 2013 12th International Conference on Document Analysis and Recognition (ICDAR), pp. 30–34. IEEE (2013). http://ieeexplore.ieee.org/abstract/document/6628580/
25. Wang, J., Novemsky, N., Dhar, R., Baumeister, R.F.: Trade-offs and depletion in choice. J. Mark. Res. **47**(5), 910–919 (2010)

26. Yeung, C.W., Soman, D.: Attribute evaluability and the range effect. J. Consum. Res. **32**(3), 363–369 (2005)
27. Zhang, L., Li, X.Y., Huang, W., Liu, K., Zong, S., Jian, X., Feng, P., Jung, T., Liu, Y.: It starts with iGaze: visual attention driven networking with smart glasses. In: Proceedings of the 20th Annual International Conference on Mobile Computing and Networking, MobiCom 2014, pp. 91–102. ACM, New York (2014)

# Practical Considerations for Low-Cost Eye Tracking: An Analysis of Data Loss and Presentation of a Solution

Ciara Sibley[1(✉)], Cyrus K. Foroughi[1], Tatana Olson[2],
Cory Moclaire[2], and Joseph T. Coyne[1]

[1] Naval Research Laboratory, Washington, D.C., USA
{ciara.sibley,cyrus.foroughi.ctr,
joseph.coyne}@nrl.navy.mil
[2] Naval Aerospace Medical Institute, Pensacola, FL, USA
{tatana.m.olson.mil,cory.m.moclaire.ctr}@mail.mil

**Abstract.** This paper presents data loss figures from three experiments, varying in length and visual complexity, in which low-cost eye tracking data were collected. Analysis of data from the first two experiments revealed higher levels of data loss in the visually complex task environment and that task duration did not appear to impact data loss. Results from the third experiment demonstrate how data loss can be mitigated by including periodic eye tracking data quality assessments, which are described in detail. The paper concludes with a discussion of overall findings and provides suggestions for researchers interested in employing low-cost eye tracking in human subject experiments.

**Keywords:** Eye tracking · Data quality · Data loss · Supervisory control

## 1 Introduction

Several commercial off-the-shelf low-cost eye trackers have emerged on the market in the last few years, providing researchers the opportunity to inexpensively and unobtrusively collect eye tracking data across a variety of experimental protocols. Specifically, the Gazepoint GP3, Eye Tribe and Tobii EyeX have been available for under $500. Unfortunately, however, Eye Tribe is no longer selling their system due to its recent acquisition by Oculus [1] and the Tobii EyeX user agreement prohibits data from being recorded. Mobile or glasses-worn eye trackers are another low-cost option, but these are notoriously uncomfortable to wear for extended time periods. As such, at this point in time, the Gazepoint GP3 is the only off-the-head low-cost tracker truly available for research purposes.

Likely due to their nascence, only a limited number of studies have assessed the viability of low-cost eye trackers for research purposes. One team of researchers investigated the fixation accuracy and precision of the Eye Tribe system and generally found its performance acceptable for their research purposes [2, 3]. Another study concluded that Eye Tribe's pupillometry measurements were comparable to those of a high-quality tracker, when participants were exposed to black and white screen

D.D. Schmorrow and C.M. Fidopiastis (Eds.): AC 2017, Part I, LNAI 10284, pp. 236–250, 2017.
DOI: 10.1007/978-3-319-58628-1_19

backgrounds [4]. This ability to capture pupillary responses to changes in screen luminance was confirmed by the authors, who also included assessment of the Gazepoint GP3 system, and furthermore found both trackers capable of identifying pupillary responses to cognitive workload [5].

Researchers from the Air Force Research Laboratory conducted a more in depth performance comparison of two low-cost eye tracking systems (Eye Tribe and Tobii EyeX) to three more expensive alternatives [6]. They primarily assessed accuracy and precision of each system during a 9-min fixation task, but also provided data quality measures, as defined by the amount of data samples dropped by each system. Their analysis revealed that the low-cost trackers experienced more data loss than the higher cost-systems, with percentages of useable data at approximately 78% for both low-cost systems and between 90 to 100% useable data for the higher-cost systems.

The few evaluations that have been conducted to date have utilized short and visually simple tasks, involving either static images or fixation points. Data loss was typically reported in each study, but not discussed at length. This paper focuses exclusively on data quality, or data loss, since the authors believe this is an issue that is often overlooked but critical in determining whether low-cost eye tracking systems are appropriate for use in research and across a variety of experimental protocols, including longer tasks within visually complex environments.

Specifically, this paper presents data loss figures from the Gazepoint GP3 eye tracking system across three separate experiments. Tasks across each experiment varied in visual complexity and duration. The next section, Sect. 2, presents data from an experiment comprised of several short and visually simple tasks. Section 3 presents data from a longer, more visually complex experiment. Section 4 presents a technique used to mitigate data loss and shows improved results after its implementation. The final section discusses overall findings and provides suggestions for researchers interested in using low-cost eye tracking.

## 2 Experiment 1: Data Loss Across Visually Simple Tasks

### 2.1 Method

**Participants.** Eye tracking data was collected from 25 participants (24 male, 1 female) who were Naval and Marine Corps student pilots. They ranged in age from 22 to 29 ($M = 23.76$, $SD = 2.24$). An error occurred with one of the data files, so data from 24 participants are presented here.

**Equipment.** The Gazepoint GP3 eye tracking system was used to collect data from participants. This system is recommended for use with single displays up to 24″ and provides data at a 60 Hz sampling rate. Data recorded includes a user's left and right pupil diameter (in pixels, corresponding to a fraction of the camera image size) and left and right point-of-gaze (x and y-coordinates on the screen). The software also enables capture of the location of each eye in 3D space, with respect to the camera, as well as pupil size, all in meters. Fixation data (x and y-coordinates and duration) is also available. The system provides binary "validity" values for the following measurements:

left pupil size; right pupil size; left eye point-of-gaze (x and y screen coordinates); right eye point-of-gaze; average point-of-gaze; and fixation point-of-gaze. The validity parameter is coded as "1 if the data is valid, and 0 if it is not." [7]

Each eye tracking unit was centered immediately below a 17 inch monitor (1280 × 1024 resolution), using Gazepoint's tripod set up, as shown in Fig. 1. Eye trackers were placed at approximately arm's length distance from the participant, as instructed in Gazepoint's user manual. The appropriate distance is also verified using the native calibration software controller, discussed below.

**Fig. 1.** Laboratory set up showing Gazepoint GP3 beneath a 17 inch monitor

**Procedure.** This experiment took place in a group setting in which participants were seated at their own station, but beside other participants, as seen in Fig. 1. Data collection occurred over two sessions. Upon arrival, participants were provided informed consent documents. After giving consent, participants completed a brief demographic survey and then began Gazepoint's set up and calibration process. During set up, the user is shown a screen that verifies the camera is well positioned to track both eyes (see Fig. 2) and that the user is sitting at an appropriate distance. Distance is assessed by the dot shown above the image of the face; the dot moves horizontally across the top of the screen, shifting from red on the far left (user is positioned too far away from the camera) to green within the middle of the screen (user is positioned well) to red on the right (user is positioned too close to the monitor).

Each participant was verbally instructed to verify that their eyes were centered in the images and that the distance dot was green and positioned close to the center of the screen. If either was not true, they were told to move the camera and/or their body position. Experimenters then verified each participant's settings, after which participants were instructed to continue to the calibration. During calibration, participants tracked a white dot around the screen to nine different locations, which were presented in a 3 × 3 grid pattern. At the end, participants were able to see their eye gaze rendered on the screen in real time in order to qualitatively verify the accuracy of their

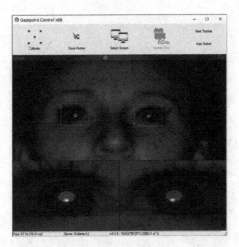

**Fig. 2.** Gazepoint GP3 setup screen showing a user correctly positioned in the camera's view and seated at an appropriate distance (Color figure online)

calibration. Participants were told to re-calibrate if their results were poor. Once calibration was successful participants were asked to be aware of body position relative to the tracker, however they were not reminded throughout experimentation.

**Tasks.** After calibration, participants were instructed to put headphones on and then engaged in three consecutive tasks in the following order: Operation Span (OSPAN), Direction Orientation Task (DOT), and Digit-Span Task. See: [5, 8, 9]; respectively, for comprehensive descriptions of these tasks. Most importantly, each of the three tasks required the participant to focus his/her attention in the center of the screen and all input was provided by mouse clicks on the screen, so participants did not have to divert visual attention away from the screen, to the keyboard. Each task took a variable length of time to complete, depending on how quickly participants input their responses: approximately 15 min for OSPAN; 6 min for DOT; and 14 min for Digit-Span. See Fig. 3 for screen grabs of the response screen for each task. All three tasks had a limited area in which relevant information was displayed and for purposes of this paper are considered to be low in visual complexity.

## 2.2 Results

As previously mentioned, the data presented here will only address data loss. Table 1 shows the proportion of point-of-gaze quality samples that Gazepoint marked as invalid. The correlation between pupil and point-of-gaze quality was very high, but point-of-gaze quality was used for analysis, since it is the slightly more conservative figure. Overall data loss represents the percentage of data where valid data from both eyes were not available. Note the high variance in the average data loss percentages, showing that some participants suffered much higher loss and others did much better.

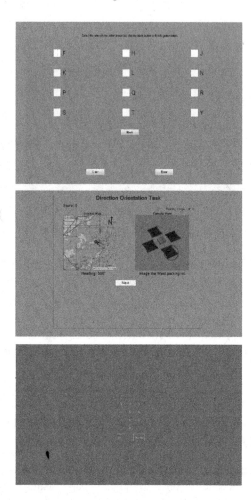

**Fig. 3.** Screen grabs from the OSPAN (top), DOT (middle) and Digit-span (bottom) tasks, demonstrating visual simplicity of each task

**Table 1.** Percentage of left, right, and overall data loss across tasks

| Task | Task duration | Monitor size | Left pupil % data loss | | Right pupil % data loss | | Overall % data loss | |
|---|---|---|---|---|---|---|---|---|
| | | | Average | St. Dev | Average | St. Dev | Average | St. Dev |
| OSPAN | ~15 min | 17″ | 20.59 | 20.79 | 22.07 | 21.50 | 23.20 | 20.40 |
| DOT | ~6 min | 17″ | 22.69 | 27.14 | 29.11 | 29.19 | 31.60 | 27.40 |
| Digit-Span | ~14 min | 17″ | 30.88 | 31.35 | 30.83 | 30.22 | 32.80 | 31.10 |

# 3  Experiment 2: Data Loss During Visually Complex Tasks

## 3.1  Method

**Participants.** Eye tracking data was collected from 19 participants (18 male, 1 female) who were Naval and Marine Corps student pilots, ranging in age from 22 to 29 ($M = 24.4$, $SD = 2.3$). Each experiment had a unique set of participants; no participant took part in multiple experiments.

**Equipment.** The Gazepoint GP3 eye tracking system was again used to collect data from participants with the same set up as Experiment 1, except a 25 inch monitor ($2560 \times 1440$ resolution) was used for this experiment.

**Procedure.** This experiment took place in a group setting over two sessions. Upon arrival, participants were provided informed consent documents. After giving consent, participants completed a brief demographic survey and then began Gazepoint's set up and calibration process. Participants were given the same instructions for set up and calibration as described in Experiment 1.

After calibration, participants were instructed to put headphones on and then began a self-paced training session, which took approximately 35 min, and instructed them how to interact with the Supervisory Control Operations User Testbed (SCOUT™). After completing training, participants completed one twelve minute practice mission followed by two thirty-minute missions. Half the participants received one mission scenario first, while the other half received the other first.

**Task.** The U.S. Naval Research Laboratory developed SCOUT to investigate future challenges operators will experience while managing missions involving multiple autonomous systems. SCOUT contains representative tasks that a future UAV supervisory controller will likely perform, assuming advancements in automation. The Gazepoint GP3 system is integrated with SCOUT in order to gather a more complete understanding of a user's state, including attention allocation, mental workload, and situation awareness, throughout a mission. SCOUT is available in a dual or single screen version, but the single screen version (see Fig. 4) was used in this data collection since the Gazepoint system does not yet reliably support use with multiple screens. See [10] for an overview of SCOUT functionality.

Throughout a mission the participant's primary responsibility was to determine how to dynamically assign unmanned assets to different objectives. Specifically, operators had to decide where to send each of their three UAVs to search for targets with different priority levels, uncertainty and deadlines. In addition, operators had to respond to requests for information and commands by typing in chat boxes. Finally, they had to monitor and click on sensor feeds when potential targets were present, and request access if they needed to fly through restricted airspace. Participants gained points for finding targets and providing timely and accurate information, and lost points for violating restricted airspace and missing potential targets on the sensor feeds. All tasking was driven by pre-scripted scenario files. See [11] for more information on research completed in SCOUT.

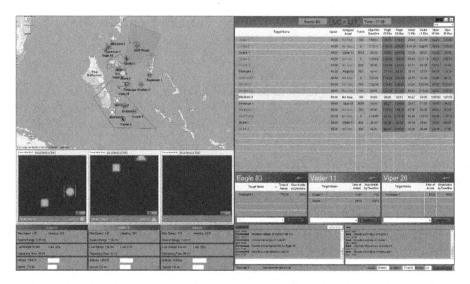

**Fig. 4.** Interface of single screen SCOUT on a 25 inch, 2560 × 1440 resolution monitor

### 3.2    Results

This analysis will focus on data from the two thirty minute mission scenarios, and not training or the practice scenario, since this is the data that would be of most interest for all other analyses. Table 2 presents the average proportion of data loss that occurred across all participants, broken out by the order in which they completed the SCOUT mission scenario and by eye. Again, overall data loss represents the percentage of data where valid data from both eyes were not available.

**Table 2.** Percentage of left, right, and overall data loss across tasks

| SCOUT mission order | Task duration | Monitor size | Left pupil % data loss | | Right pupil % data loss | | Overall % data loss | |
|---|---|---|---|---|---|---|---|---|
| | | | Average | St. Dev | Average | St. Dev | Average | St. Dev |
| #1 | 30 min | 25″ | 50.4 | 26.5 | 46.1 | 26.7 | 58.5 | 27.5 |
| #2 | 30 min | 25″ | 50.2 | 28.4 | 50.1 | 28.4 | 57.3 | 28.9 |

Figure 5 decomposes this data further into one minute increments, in order to consider the impact of data loss over time. Here, the percentage of good quality data (both eyes are being tracked), as opposed to data loss (in Table 2) is shown across the two 30-min SCOUT missions.

Figure 6 shows a representative sample of data from eight participants, binned into one minute increments, and across the two SCOUT mission scenarios. One can observe that there are many instances where the data drops out for long periods of time and sometimes reemerges for periods of time. There is also large variability across

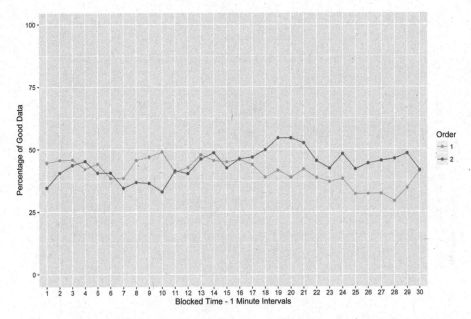

**Fig. 5.** Percentage of valid data each minute during the first and second SCOUT missions

individuals and does not appear to be an effect of time, where quality either improves or deteriorates. We hypothesized these large fluctuations were attributable to shifts in body position, outside of the head box of the eye tracker, which will be addressed in Experiment 3.

## 4   Experiment 3: Data Loss Mitigation Technique

### 4.1   Method

**Participants.** Eye tracking data was collected from 41 participants (40 male, 1 female) who were Naval and Marine Corps student pilots. They ranged in age from 22 to 29 ($M = 24.20$, $SD = 2.03$).

**Equipment.** All equipment was the same as described in Experiment 2.

**Procedure.** Data collection took place in a group setting, over four sessions. After giving consent, participants completed a brief demographic survey and then began Gazepoint's set up and calibration process, which was the same as in Experiment 1 and 2. Afterwards, participants put their headphones on and performed two brief baseline assessments, to assess accuracy and precision of the eye tracker and measure individual pupil size responses, both of which lasted only a few minutes. Next, participants completed an approximately five minute long digit-span task. This task was similar to the digit-span task run in Experiment 1, but included fewer trials. Following the digit-span task, participants completed the self-paced SCOUT training followed by the

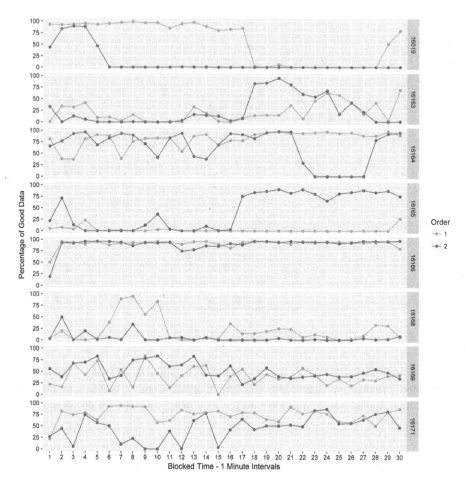

**Fig. 6.** Sample of eight participants' percentage of valid data, by minute, across the first and second SCOUT missions

twelve minute practice mission and one thirty-minute SCOUT mission. Afterwards they completed the baseline and digit-span tasks a second time.

**Data Quality Checks.** The SCOUT mission that participants experienced in Experiment 3 was different in one respect from Experiment 2: it included an additional eye tracking data quality check. These quality checks were appended to five pre-scripted workload freeze probes, which took place at approximately 6–7 min intervals throughout the SCOUT mission. Specifically, quality checks took place at the following mission clock times: 1:12, 7:25, 13:47, 20:28, 28:31. Quality checks comprised a position and accuracy assessment.

*Position Assessment.* Figure 7 shows the screen which participants encountered during the position assessment. Here, participants were instructed to position themselves in their chair so that the two green clusters of dots, which were being drawn on the screen in real time, fell within the bounds of the inner green rectangle. These dots

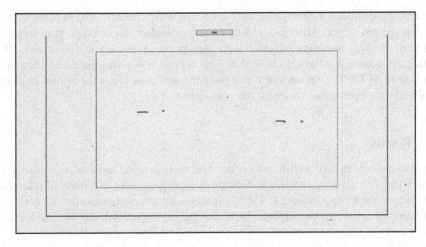

**Fig. 7.** Position assessment screen prior to recording, with a user's eyes positioned correctly within the green rectangle (Color figure online)

corresponded with the position of the eyes and essentially ensured that the user was positioned at an appropriate distance from the tracker, and that they were centered with respect to the tracker. Once participants' data fell within the green box, they were told to hit the start button, which would attempt to collect 300 samples, or 5 s, of continuous data, of which 75% or more had to be valid data for both eyes. The task continued until the eye tracker was able to collect the 5 s of good data.

*Accuracy Assessment.* After completing the position task, participants began the accuracy assessment task. Here, participants were instructed to look at the center of the target, shown in Fig. 8, and press start when they were ready for recording to begin.

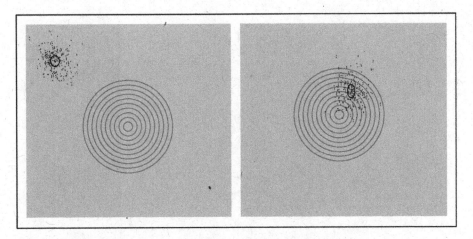

**Fig. 8.** Accuracy assessment screen showing two examples. Left image shows poor accuracy where the participant is told to consider recalibrating or redo the test. Right image shows acceptable accuracy and the user is told to continue. (Color figure online)

The recording collects 120 samples, or 2 s, of data which are rendered in black in real time on the red target. After data collection was complete, the average gaze location and one standard deviation of error were drawn as an ellipse on the screen. The participant was then informed either that their data accuracy was good and they may continue to SCOUT, or if accuracy was poor the user was given the option to either recalibrate the eye tracker or repeat the assessment.

## 4.2    Results

The data presented here will focus on the one thirty minute mission scenario, as in Experiment 2, but also includes data from both digit-span tasks as a point of reference and comparison to Experiment 1. Table 3 presents the average proportion of data loss that occurred across all participants. Note that the digit-span task did not include any

**Table 3.** Percentage of left, right, and overall data loss for experiment 1 and 2

| Task | Task duration | Monitor size | Left pupil % data loss | | Right pupil % data loss | | Overall % data loss | |
|---|---|---|---|---|---|---|---|---|
| | | | Average | St. Dev | Average | St. Dev | Average | St. Dev |
| Digit-Span | ~ 10 min | 25″ | 27.10 | 21.20 | 27.60 | 21.10 | 31.90 | 22.40 |
| SCOUT | 30 min | 25″ | 21.90 | 22.40 | 21.90 | 22.20 | 26.70 | 23.20 |

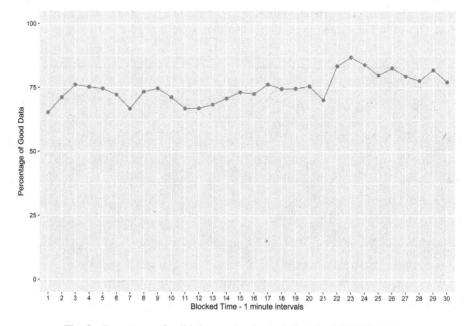

**Fig. 9.** Percentage of valid data each minute during the SCOUT mission

data quality checks and that the percentage of overall loss for this set of participants was within one percentage point of the group from Experiment 1. This suggests that there was nothing unique about this set of participants that could have resulted in better eye tracking data. Additionally, the increase in monitor size did not impact the data. Also note the large improvement in the percentage of data loss during the SCOUT scenario: down from approximately 58% in Experiment 2 to approximately 27% here.

Figure 9 presents the aggregate SCOUT data in one minute increments, again, to consider the impact of data loss over time. Here, the percentage of good quality data (both eyes are being tracked), is shown across the 30-min SCOUT mission.

Figure 10 shows a sample of data from eight participants, binned into one minute increments, and across the SCOUT mission scenario. One can observe a large improvement in the data quality for most participants, however, participant 170120 still experienced immense data loss. This general improvement in the data quality of participants can also be seen in the smaller standard deviation in data loss from

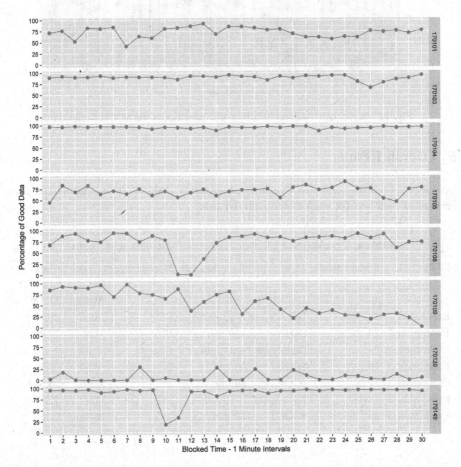

**Fig. 10.** Sample of data from eight participants, binned in one minute increments, across the SCOUT mission

Experiment 2 to Experiment 3 ($\sim$28.90 to 23.20). Figure 11 shows the variability in data quality across all participants for the entire SCOUT mission. Note two individuals who had close to zero percent good quality data.

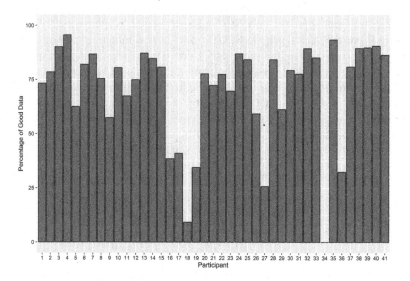

**Fig. 11.** Percentage of good data by participant across the SCOUT mission

## 5   Overall Results

For ease of comparison across the three experiments, Table 4 shows the overall percentage of data loss for each experiment, by task.

**Table 4.** Percentage of left, right, and overall data loss across tasks

| Study | # Participants | Task | Task duration | Monitor size | Overall % data loss | |
|---|---|---|---|---|---|---|
| | | | | | Average | St. Dev |
| Experiment 1 | 24 | OSPAN | $\sim$15 min | 17″ | 23.20 | 20.40 |
| Experiment 1 | 24 | DOT | $\sim$6 min | 17″ | 31.60 | 27.40 |
| Experiment 1 | 24 | Digit-Span | $\sim$14 min | 17″ | 32.80 | 31.10 |
| Experiment 2 | 19 | SCOUT #1 | 30 min | 25″ | 58.50 | 27.50 |
| Experiment 2 | 19 | SCOUT #2 | 30 min | 25″ | 57.30 | 28.90 |
| Experiment 3 | 41 | Digit-Span | $\sim$10 min | 25″ | 31.90 | 22.40 |
| Experiment 3 | 41 | SCOUT | 30 min | 25″ | 26.70 | 23.20 |

# 6  Discussion

Data collected from Experiments 1, 2 and 3 provided information on data loss from the Gazepoint GP3 system across a range of tasks. Tasking varied in both duration and visual complexity, requiring participants to focus primarily in the center of the screen or spread attention across the entire screen. Tasks in Experiment 1 were visually simple, while the SCOUT environment required participants to actively scan the entire display. Analysis from Experiments 1 and 2 revealed a significantly higher rate of data loss in the visually complex experiments. Furthermore, and contrary to initial assumptions, data quality did not systematically degrade over time. This finding suggests that visual complexity, rather than task duration, has a larger impact on data quality for tasks under an hour in length. The requirement to scan large areas of a screen likely perturbed participants' body positions with respect to the eye trackers, causing participants to fall outside the bounds eye tracker's head box. This finding motivated the inclusion of a data quality check in Experiment 3.

Utilizing an eye tracking data quality check at approximately 7 min intervals throughout the SCOUT scenario drastically improved the quality of data collected in Experiment 3, as compared to Experiment 2. Comparison of Figs. 5 and 9 show that the data at the beginning of the SCOUT mission in Experiment 3 was, on average, of higher quality than compared to Experiment 2. This is likely attributable to a quality check being presented during Experiment 3's practice scenario, which participants completed before the thirty minute SCOUT mission. The quality check successfully helped mitigate data loss, although it is not clear whether this was due to a greater awareness of maintaining appropriate body position, or whether it helped simply regain the appropriate position. Future studies will investigate use of a quality check which is triggered by a period of poor data quality, instead of utilizing pre-planned checks at specific time increments, even if data quality is high.

These results have widespread implications for researchers interested in utilizing eye tracking technologies for research. Although low-cost eye tracking systems are fast and easy to set up and use, the amount of data loss can be high if not carefully monitored and remediated (e.g., even simple solutions, such as using non-reclining chairs without wheels can have a large impact on data). Furthermore, the data loss was not uniformly distributed across time within participants; participants generally had lengthy periods of good data interspersed with lengthy periods of bad data. If, for example, half the data were present each minute, this might not be as problematic for some analyses, however, when several minutes of data is missing, it is highly questionable to employ techniques to deal with dropped data, such as linear interpolation. Therefore, the authors suggest researchers consider using a data quality check during experimentation. In addition, we suggest utilizing stringent cut-offs for determining inclusion of data, and consider each individual's data independently before determining whether it is appropriate to use for specific analysis purposes. Additionally, data loss figures should be presented for other researchers to assess.

In order for eye tracking to be an effective tool for research, it must be possible to employ in a truly unobtrusive manner and not inadvertently become a focal point of an experiment, which may add confounds. Future research will investigate how to further improve data quality in the least invasive manner possible. Overall, these results add to the corpus of literature showing that low-cost eye tracking has great promise for use in human subject experiments, but that data quality should also be carefully considered.

# References

1. Constine, J.: Oculus acquires eye-tracking startup The Eye Tribe. Tech Crunch, December 2016. https://techcrunch.com/2016/12/28/the-eye-tribe-oculus/
2. Ooms, K., et al.: Accuracy and precision of fixation locations recorded with the low-cost Eye Tribe tracker in different experimental set-ups. J. Eye Mov. Res. **8**, 1–24 (2015)
3. Popelka, S., et al.: EyeTribe tracker data accuracy evaluation and its interconnection with hypothesis software for cartographic purposes. Comput. Intell. Neurosci. **2016**, 9172506 (2016)
4. Dalmaijer, E.: Is the low-cost EyeTribe eye tracker any good for research? PeerJ PrePrints (2014)
5. Coyne, J., Sibley, C.: Investigating the use of two low cost eye tracking systems for detecting pupillary response to changes in mental workload. In: Proceedings of the Human Factors and Ergonomics Society Annual Meeting. SAGE Publications (2016)
6. Funke, G., et al.: Which eye tracker is right for your research? Performance evaluation of several cost variant eye trackers. In: Proceedings of the Human Factors and Ergonomics Society Annual Meeting. SAGE Publications (2016)
7. Gazepoint, Open Gaze API, in Version 2.0. http://www.gazept.com/dl/Gazepoint_API_v2.0.pdf
8. Turner, M.L., Engle, R.W.: Is working memory capacity task dependent? J. Mem. Lang. **28** (2), 127–154 (1989)
9. Ostoin, S.D.: An Assessment of the Performance-Based Measurement Battery (PBMB), the Navy's Psychomotor Supplement to the Aviation Selection Test Battery (ASTB). DTIC Document (2007)
10. Sibley, C., Coyne, J., Thomas, J.: Demonstrating the supervisory control operations user testbed (SCOUT). In: Proceedings of the Human Factors and Ergonomics Society Annual Meeting. SAGE Publications (2016)
11. Sibley, C., Coyne, J., Avvari, G.V., Mishra, M., Pattipati, K.R.: Supporting multi-objective decision making within a supervisory control environment. In: Schmorrow, D.D., Fidopiastis, C.M. (eds.) AC 2016. LNCS (LNAI), vol. 9744, pp. 210–221. Springer, Cham (2016). doi:10.1007/978-3-319-39952-2_21

# A Comparison of an Attention Acknowledgement Measure and Eye Tracking: Application of the as Low as Reasonable Assessment (ALARA) Discount Usability Principle for Control System Studies

Thomas A. Ulrich[1(✉)], Ronald L. Boring[2], Steffen Werner[1], and Roger Lew[1]

[1] University of Idaho, Moscow, ID, USA
{ulrich,werner}@uidaho.edu
[2] Idaho National Laboratory, Idaho Falls, ID, USA
ronald.boring@inl.gov

**Abstract.** The measurement of attention allocation is a valuable diagnostic tool for research. As Low As Reasonable Assessment (ALARA) is a research approach concerned with leveraging the simplest and most straightforward methods to capture usability data needed for the design process. Often complicated environments, such as nuclear process control, create an impetus to use accompanying complicated experimental designs and technical data collection methods; however, simple methods can in many circumstances capture equivalent data that can be used to answer the same theoretical and applied research questions. The attention acknowledgment method is an example of a simple measure capable of capturing attention allocation. The attention acknowledgment method assesses attention allocation via attention markers dispersed through the visual scene. As participants complete a scenario and interact with an associated interface, they perform a secondary acknowledgment task in which they respond to any attention markers they detect in their designated target state. The patterns of acknowledgment serve as a means to assess both location and temporal dimensions of attention allocation. The attention acknowledgment method was compared against a standard accepted measure of attention allocation consisting of infrared pupil and corneal reflection gaze tracking. The attention acknowledgment method is not able to measure attention at the same temporal and spatial resolution as the eye tracking method; however, the resolutions it is capable of achieving are sufficient to answer usability evaluation questions. Furthermore, the ease of administration and analysis of the attention acknowledgment measure are advantageous for rapid usability evaluation.

**Keywords:** Microworld · Simulation · Process control · Interface design

© Springer International Publishing AG 2017
D.D. Schmorrow and C.M. Fidopiastis (Eds.): AC 2017, Part I, LNAI 10284, pp. 251–260, 2017.
DOI: 10.1007/978-3-319-58628-1_20

# 1   Introduction

Nuclear power plant operators use a complex human-machine interface (HMI) in the form of a control room with control boards containing thousands of indicators and controls (Boring et al. 2013). Operators face the challenging task of monitoring and controlling the plant to ensure safe, efficient, and reliable electrical power production. The operators' process control task places considerable demands on the operators due to the complex relationships between the multitudes of systems involved with the nuclear power production process. Of the numerous approaches to evaluating HMI interactions, situation awareness is the most prominent method employed (Endsley and Kiris 1995). Acquiring situation awareness (SA) requires many perceptual and cognitive constructs, such as attention, visual perception, working memory, and decision making. All these underlying concepts play a role in building SA, but attention is particularly relevant, since it drives the selection of important information from the plethora of status and control information displayed across the control boards (Wickens 2008). Due to attention's prominent role in acquiring SA, a new measure of SA based on an attention acknowledgment measure is proposed to augment existing measures of attention allo-cation, such as eye tracking.

# 2   ALARA

Within human-computer interaction, ALARA is the acronym for "as low as reasonable assessment" which is a wordplay on an existing ALARA acronym within the nuclear industry for maintaining personnel exposure to radiation to levels "as low as reasonably achievable". Henceforth, ALARA is in reference to the as low as reasonable assessment, which is intended to convey the idea that simple measures can and should be used over more complicated measures. This is particularly important in complex human-computer interaction domains such as nuclear power plant control room usability studies, which are problematic for research. Operators have limited time due to their demanding work and training schedules and the simulator facilities typically used to support or directly conduct studies have limited availability due to their primary use for training operators. As such, making the most advantageous use of the time researchers have with operators to collect data is crucial. Discount usability and ALARA encompass this rationale and mandate using simple and easy to administer measures as opposed to more complicated measures. This new attention acknowledgment measure is intended to provide a simple and easy to administer method to human factors practitioners following the ALARA ideology. This simple measure is in direct contrast to an existing physiological measure of attention, eye tracking, which is traditionally used in usability studies on nuclear control rooms.

# 3   Eye Tracking Measure of Attention

Eye tracking is a popular technique to measure attention and its allocation through a visual scene based on the assumption that attention is typically yoked to the gaze position of the eyes (Duchowski 2011). Eye tracking entails measuring the gaze position using infrared camera systems. In the most common technique employed with commercially available eye trackers, the pupil and corneal reflection are captured to calculate where the eye is pointed (Holmqvist et al. 2011). Incorporating relative head position to a visual plane with the calculated direction of the eye provides gaze location within a visual plane.

Eye trackers are a useful research tool; however, they also suffer from several technical issues that make it challenging to use effectively in some environments. First, eye tracking suffers from numerous sources of errors that can lead to difficulty in accurately and reliably measuring each participants' gaze position. For example, a large portion of commercially available eye trackers rely on infrared cameras to detect the pupil and corneal reflection of each eye to determine the gaze position (Holmqvist et al. 2011). The process of capturing the pupil and corneal reflection suffers when the camera cannot accurately capture either of these two items. Some individual differences that can interfere with this process include drooping eyelids that occlude the pupil, contact lenses that diffuse the corneal reflection, and mascara or eye makeup that generate false corneal reflections (Holmqvist et al. 2011). Additionally, for stationary camera based systems, the head position must also be tracked along with the eye position which suffers from other sources of errors such as excessive participant movement and improper positioning away from the eye tracker (Holmqvist et al. 2011). Both the eye and head position tracking also suffer from interference based on lighting conditions (Holmqvist et al. 2011). Beyond accurately recording the gaze data, the analysis can prove cumbersome for eye tracking. The data generated by eye tracking must undergo extensive processing to manipulate it into a more human digestible format necessary to answer research questions (Holmqvist et al. 2011).

In addition to these general challenges associated with eye tracking, some environments pose specific challenges for eye tracking, such as the HSSL. The HSSL platform has been primarily used to perform applied research in collaboration with nuclear power utilities. As such, the timeline for running the experiments is tight and the cost of these experiments can be large (Ulrich et al. 2016). With the brief time course it is important to collect the needed data as quickly as possible. Often the simpler subjective response measures provided by the operator participants provide the most valuable insights to improve upon the usability of new interface designs undergoing evaluation within the simulator (Ulrich et al. 2016). The HSSL presents a challenge for eye tracking methodologies (Kovesdi et al. 2015), due to its complex three-dimensional environment containing many depth planes and spanning across 45 large displays with thousands of indicators and controls. Furthermore, several technical issues impede the use of eye tracking in this environment, including battery life constraints for the portable eye tracking glasses and their processing units worn by the operator participants and frequent recalibrations required between experimental trials to ensure the accuracy of the eye tracking. Furthermore, some eye tracking units use conflicting infrared camera systems and markers placed on the participant to determine head position. This type of infrared camera system for tracking head position is incompatible with the simulator touchscreen technology which also relies on an infrared camera system embedded within bezels mounted over the displays to detect touch positions. The touch capabilities were rendered functionless when this eye tracking system was operating due to the interference from the conflicting infrared camera systems. From a human perspective of managing participants, the operators do not enjoy wearing the bulky glasses-based systems that are compatible with the HSSL. These issues and others are encountered in other labs as well (Holmqvist et al. 2011), which provides the impetus to develop new measures that can answer the same questions in another fashion. The proposed attention acknowledgment measure would provide a way to simply identify where participants are attending to within an interface without relying on eye tracking techniques.

# 4   Attention Acknowledgment Measure

Ulrich et al. (2016) proposed a new attention acknowledgment measure consists of presenting visual attention markers that participants are instructed to acknowledge upon detection of the marker in its target state. The act of acknowledging the target via a response serves as an indication that the marker was attended to and underwent the necessary cognitive processing to elicit a response. This measure allows researchers to evaluate human-computer interactions by identifying what aspects of the interface were attended to while performing a task, see Fig. 1, for an example implementation of the attention acknowledgment measure embedded within an interface. The relative proportion of marker acknowledgments serves as an indication of the distribution of attention while the participant interacted with the interface. Within this example implementation, the markers are presented as part of or near interface elements to capture how often and when an individual attended to these interface elements. Using marker acknowledgments is a secondary task, which is inherently accompanied by some primary task intrusion, though this measure was developed to minimize any intrusion. The attention acknowledgment measure provides an easy to implement and assess method for measuring attention allocation. The setup involves overlaying the markers on the interface. The attention acknowledgment software system is configurable and allows the researcher to adjust the presentation and timing of the markers throughout the display. Furthermore, areas of interest can be defined and markers can be assigned to these areas of interest. The markers record correct acknowledgments via mouse clicks to yield total acknowledgment scores for each defined area of of interest. A primary advantage, in line with the concept of discount usability, is the simple to interpret results, which consist of acknowledgment counts for each area of interest.

## 4.1   Attention Acknowledgment Measure Development

This study is the latest in a series of studies conducted to develop an appropriate marker to be used for the attention acknowledgment measure, see Ulrich et al. (2016) for more details on these prior studies. These prior studies focused on establishing the viability of a rotating bar stimulus to serve as an attention marker for assessing where attention was allocated during a simple crosshair tracking task. In these experiments, participants were instructed to maintain the position of a crosshair in the center of its axis while detecting a single rotating marker among a matrix of stationary marker distractors. Participants demonstrated greater accuracy in correctly detecting rotating markers when the marker was located in close proximity to the crosshair task as opposed to located at further

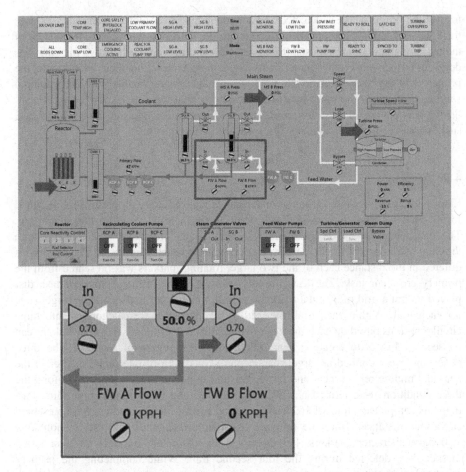

**Fig. 1.** Example implementation of attention acknowledgment markers embedded within an experimental interface used to assess situation awareness. Markers are positioned within areas of interested to identify distributions of attention while interacting with the interface.

distances away in the display. Furthermore, the time to identify rotating markers was shorter for close proximity markers as opposed to markers that were located more distantly away from the crosshair task. Since the primary task required participants to attend to that location within the display, the greater accuracy and shorter times to detect rotating markers near the primary crosshair task over more distant markers provides evidence that acknowledging nearby markers is a potentially viable method for localizing where attention was allocated during a simple primary task. In other words, the markers serve as an effective way to tag where attention is localized within a display.

This current study aimed to extend the prior research in two important ways to further establish the viability of the markers to serve as a measure of attention allocation. First, this study examined whether markers located nearest to the primary task were detected over more distant markers. In order to serve as a marker of the locus of attention for a primary task, it is important to establish that the marker positioned nearest the primary task is detected and acknowledged over more distant markers. Eye tracking was used to capture fixations prior to the detection and acknowledgement of the target marker. Using an established measure of attention, such as eye tracking was done to further verify that participants were in fact directing their attention to the primary crosshair task location and the acknowledged marker and ensure that attention was not directed to the more distant target marker that went unacknowledged. Establishing this pattern of attention corroborates the rationale for using a secondary task such as marker acknowledgment as a measure of attention.

## 4.2   Method

Eight participants required from an undergraduate psychology program were recruited for the study. The study consisted of a single factor three-level within subjects design. The distance of two target markers was manipulated, resulting in a total of three different conditions of target marker pairs presented to each participant. The conditions differed in the distance each of the two target rotating markers was presented from the primary crosshair task. The test stimuli consisted of the primary crosshair task displayed within a grid of 32 total markers, two of which were in the rotating target state for each trial. Within each trial, the grid of 32 markers were categorized into three circular regions based on each marker's distance from the primary crosshair task, as can be seen in Fig. 2 to create a near, middle, and far region of markers. The three conditions were defined as target marker pairs consisting of one target marker in the near and middle region, near and far region, and middle and far region. Therefore, the three condition were termed near-middle, near-far, and middle-far region pairs. Participants completed a total of 162 trials in which a pair of target markers were presented at various distances from the primary crosshair task against the grid of nontarget stationary distractor markers. Participants were instructed to select the first target marker they detected during the four second trail. While completing the primary crosshair and secondary target marker acknowledgment tasks during each trial, each participants' fixations were recorded using a Tobii X2-60 Eye Tracker, which consists of a desktop monitor mounted eye tracking camera.

*General Procedure.* Participants to were instructed to select the first marker they detected in the target rotating state, of two total markers in the rotating target state, as they performed the manual crosshair tracking task. During each trials participants responded with a mouse click to select the rotating marker upon detection.

*Crosshair Manual Tracking Task.* The manual tracking crosshair task required participants to maintain the vertical crosshair in the center of the horizontal crosshair while undergoing a pseudorandom disturbance. The horizontal disturbance was generated using a sum of sines method (Lew et al. 2014). Participants were instructed to use the left and the right arrow keys to counteract the disturbance and maintain the vertical crosshair at the center position of the horizontal crosshair. The instructions emphasized the importance of the crosshair task and explicitly stated the lower prioritization of identifying the marker objects in order to ensure participants directed their attention to the crosshair.

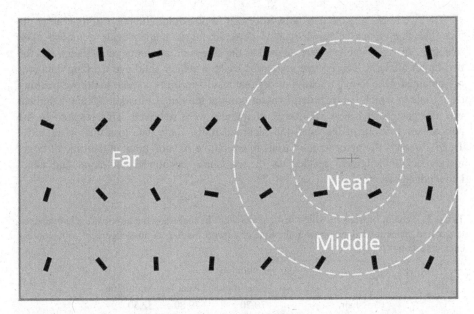

**Fig. 2.** Matrix of markers with the crosshair tracking task. Two markers were in the target state and presented at various distances from the crosshair task.

*Marker Detection Task.* The attention markers were organized into a 4 × 8 matrix spanning the entire display. The markers were categorized into near, mid, and far regions defined by the pixel distance away from the location of the crosshair task during each trial. The display consisted of a full matrix of 32 change detection objects as can be seen in Fig. 1. The marker detection task resembled a standard search task (Wolfe 1994) in which the participant had to find one of the two rotating markers, which provided both reaction times to detect the first rotating marker.

## 5 Results

To examine the effect of target distance pairings, i.e. near-middle, near-far, and middle-far region pairs of target markers on participant's acknowledgment rates of the closer target marker, a Chi-square test of independence was calculated. No significant interaction was found $X^2$ (3, N = 453) = 90.724, n.s.. Across all conditions the participants selected the closer target marker over the more distant target marker in more than 80% of the trials as can be seen in Table 1 below.

**Table 1.** Percentage of trials in which participants acknowledged the closer of two target markers presented within a matrix of nontarget stationary markers and a centrally located primary crosshair task.

| Condition | | |
|---|---|---|
| Near-middle | Near-far | Middle-far |
| 82.1 | 100 | 84.6 |

The eye tracking gaze data was processed to determine the point of fixation at the time the participant acknowledged a detected target marker with a mouse click selection. Areas of interest were defined as the crosshair, all nontarget markers, and the two target markers. There were numerous trials in which valid eye tracking data was not obtained. Due to eye tracking errors that results in trials without valid eye tracking data, trials in which the recorded fixation point at the time of marker acknowledgment was not categorized as a valid area of interest were removed. This resulted in the removal of 139 out of the total 453 recorded trails, for a data loss total of 30.68%. Table 2 depicts the percentage of trials in which the fixation point at the time of target marker acknowledgment resided on the crosshair, acknowledged target and unacknowledged target.

**Table 2.** Percent of trials in which participants were fixated upon the crosshair, acknowledged target, and unacknowledged target at the time of a target marker acknowledgement with a mouse click selection.

|  | Condition | | |
|---|---|---|---|
|  | Near-middle | Near-far | Middle-far |
| Crosshair | 70.70 | 79.80 | 52.50 |
| Acknowledged target | 24.24 | 20.20 | 45.00 |
| Unacknowledged target | 15.15 | 01.01 | 02.50 |

## 6 Discussion

The results of the current experiment further validated developed attention acknowledgment measure as a method to capture the locus of attention while performing a primary task. Participants reliably selected the closer target marker over the more distant target marker in the vast majority of trials. Indeed, in the near-far condition, participants selected the closer target marker in every trail. This provides strong supporting evidence that participants locus of attention centered around the primary task afforded them the ability to consistently detect and acknowledge the nearest most target marker. This result is quite promising for the attention acknowledgment measure for an important reason. The attention acknowledgment measure relies on a matrix of markers embedded within the interface to assess attention. In this configuration, multiple markers will be simultaneously in the target state to allow the individual to detect and acknowledge any of these target state markers. The location of attention within the interface drives which markers are detected and acknowledged. Therefore, a strong and reliable preference for selecting target marker nearest the locus of attention indicates that marker acknowledgments function as a means to tag where attention is allocated within the interface at a given point in time. The eye tracking results further corroborate these findings.

The eye tracking data illustrates the distinction between two visual strategies participants' used to detect and acknowledge target markers in close proximity to primary crosshair task in contrast to target makers in far proximity to the primary crosshair tasks. In both the near-middle and near-far conditions, which represent target markers in close proximity to the primary crosshair task, participants fixated upon the crosshair at the time of target marker acknowledgment in 70.70% and 79.80% of trials, respectively. The acknowledged target itself was fixated upon 24.24% and 20.20% of trials for these same two near-middle and near-far conditions. When taken together, this pattern of fixating primary upon the crosshair with a modest percentage of trials fixated upon the acknowledged target marker indicates that participants were actively engaged in the primary task and their locus of attention resided on the primary crosshair task at the time of the target marker acknowledgment. The close proximity of the closest of the two target markers in the near-middle and near-far conditions allowed the locus of attention to encompass the nearest target marker. Participants did not need to redirect attention away from the primary crosshair task to detect these close proximity target markers. The opposite visual strategy is apparent for the eye tracking data in the middle-far condition in which participants were forced to search for the closest target marker since it was outside of their locus of attention on the primary crosshair task. As a result the percentage of trials in which participants fixated upon the acknowledged target marker is much higher than in the near proximity target marker conditions with the 45% and the percentage of trails in which participants fixated upon the crosshair at the time of target marker acknowledgment is much lower at 52.50%.

With this latest study, the attention acknowledgment measure has been thoroughly vetted as a valid measure of attention and is now ready for use in a variety of applications. The next phase of research entails examining the scalability of the attention acknowledgment measure. This evaluation will determine if the attention acknowledgment measure can be scaled up from assessing attention in a simple primary crosshair tracking task to assessing attention in more complicated primary tasks. A microworld simulator consisting of a simplified nuclear process control task is the intended to serve as the next test application. The microworld requires participants to monitor and adjust various plant components to operate a simplified pressurized water reactor to generate steam, turn a turbine, and ultimately produce electrical power. This nuclear microworld application is a considerable increase in complexity from the simple crosshair task used to develop and test the attention acknowledgment measure thus far. The time course for assessing attention is considerably longer in the microworld with time spans on the order of minutes as opposed to seconds with the simple crosshair task. Secondly, the microworld entails a constantly shifting locus of attention as participants monitor the components and make any necessary adjustments while performing the primary electricity production task.

# References

Ulrich, T., Lew, R., Medema, H., Boring, R.: A Computerized Operator Support System Prototype. INL/EXT-13-29651. Idaho National Laboratory, Idaho Falls (2015a)

Quinn, T., Bockhorst, R., Peterson, C., Swindlehurst, G.: Design to Achieve Fault Tolerance and Resilience. INL/EXT-12-27205. Idaho National Laboratory, Idaho Falls (2012)

Endsley, M.R., Kiris, E.O.: The out-of-the-loop performance problem and level of control in automation. Hum. Factors: J. Hum. Factors Ergon. Soc. **37**(2), 381–394 (1995)

OHara, J., Higgins, J., Stubler, W., Goodman, C., Eckinrode, R., Bongarra, J., Galletti, G.: Human factors engineering review program model (NUREG-0711 rev. 3). US Nuclear Regulatory Commission, Washington, D.C. (2011)

Boring, R.L.: The use of simulators in human factors studies within the nuclear industry. In: Skjerve, A., Bye, A. (eds.) Simulator-based Human Factors Studies Across 25 Years, pp. 3–12. Springer, London (2010)

Boring, R., et al.: Digital Full-Scope Simulation of a Conventional Nuclear Power Plant Control Room, Phase 2: Installation of a Reconfigurable Simulator to Support Nuclear Plant Sustainability. Technical report INL/EXT-13-28432. Idaho National Laboratory, Idaho Falls (2013)

Hamstra, S.J., Brydges, R., Hatala, R., Zendejas, B., Cook, D.A.: Reconsidering fidelity in simulation-based training. Acad. Med. **89**(3), 387–392 (2014)

Rieber, L.P.: Seriously considering play: designing interactive learning environments based on the blending of microworlds, simulations, and games. Educ. Technol. Res. Dev. **44**(2), 43–58 (1996)

Romme, A.G.L.: Perceptions of the value of microworld simulation: research note. Simul. Gaming **35**(3), 427–436 (2004)

Vicente, K., Pawlak, W.: Cognitive work analysis for the DURESS II system. Cognitive Engineering Laboratory, Department of Industrial Engineering, University of Toronto, Toronto, Canada CEL, 94-03 (1994)

Boring, R., Kelly, D., Smidts, C., Mosleh, A., Dyre, B.: Microworlds, simulators, and simulation: framework for a benchmark of human reliability data sources. In: Joint Probabilistic Safety Assessment and Management and European Safety and Reliability Conference, 16B-Tu5-5, June 2012

Dyre, B.P., Adamic, E.J., Werner, S., Lew, R., Gertman, D.I., Boring, R.L.: A microworld simulator for process control research and training. In: Proceedings of the Human Factors and Ergonomics Society Annual Meeting, vol. 57, no. 1, pp. 1367–1371. SAGE Publications, September 2013

Lew, R., Boring, R.L., Ulrich, T.A.: A prototyping environment for research on human-machine interfaces in process control use of Microsoft WPF for microworld and distributed control system development. In: 2014 7th International Symposium on Resilient Control Systems (ISRCS), pp. 1–6. IEEE, August 2014

Ulrich, T.A., Werner, S., Boring, R.L.: Studying situation awareness on a shoestring budget an example of an inexpensive simulation environment for theoretical research. In: Proceedings of the Human Factors and Ergonomics Society Annual Meeting, vol. 59, no. 1, pp. 1520–1524. SAGE Publications (2015b)

Ulrich, T.A., Werner, S., Boring, R.L.: Change detection for measuring attention allocation: a new approach for capturing situation awareness. In: Proceedings of the Human Factors and Ergonomics Society Annual Meeting, vol. 60, no. 1. SAGE Publications (in press)

# Physiological Measuring and Bio-sensing

# Rim-to-Rim Wearables at the Canyon for Health (R2R WATCH): Experimental Design and Methodology

Glory Emmanuel Aviña[1(✉)], Robert Abbott[2],
Cliff Anderson-Bergman[1], Catherine Branda[1], Kristin M. Divis[2],
Lucie Jelinkova[3], Victoria Newton[2], Emily Pearce[3], and Jon Femling[3]

[1] Sandia National Laboratories, 7011 East Ave, Livermore, CA, USA
gremman@sandia.gov
[2] Sandia National Laboratories,
1515 Eubank Ave, Albuquerque, NM 87185, USA
[3] The University of New Mexico, Albuquerque, NM, USA
jfemling@salud.unm.edu

**Abstract.** The Rim-to-Rim Wearables At The Canyon for Health (R2R WATCH) study examines metrics recordable on commercial off the shelf (COTS) devices that are most relevant and reliable for the earliest possible indication of a health or performance decline. This is accomplished through collaboration between Sandia National Laboratories (SNL) and The University of New Mexico (UNM) where the two organizations team up to collect physiological, cognitive, and biological markers from volunteer hikers who attempt the Rim-to-Rim (R2R) hike at the Grand Canyon. Three forms of data are collected as hikers travel from rim to rim: physiological data through wearable devices, cognitive data through a cognitive task taken every 3 hours, and blood samples obtained before and after completing the hike. Data is collected from both civilian and warfighter hikers. Once the data is obtained, it is analyzed to understand the effectiveness of each COTS device and the validity of the data collected. We also aim to identify which physiological and cognitive phenomena collected by wearable devices are the most relatable to overall health and task performance in extreme environments, and of these ascertain which markers provide the earliest yet reliable indication of health decline. Finally, we analyze the data for significant differences between civilians' and warfighters' markers and the relationship to performance. This is a study funded by the Defense Threat Reduction Agency (DTRA, Project CB10359) and the University of New Mexico (The main portion of the R2R WATCH study is funded by DTRA. UNM is currently funding all activities related to bloodwork. DTRA, Project CB10359; SAND2017-1872 C). This paper describes the experimental design and methodology for the first year of the R2R WATCH project.

**Keywords:** Cognitive markers · Quantifying fatigue · Physiological markers · Bloodwork · Extreme environments · Early health indicators

© Springer International Publishing AG 2017
D.D. Schmorrow and C.M. Fidopiastis (Eds.): AC 2017, Part I, LNAI 10284, pp. 263–274, 2017.
DOI: 10.1007/978-3-319-58628-1_21

# 1 Introduction and Project Scope

When in extreme environments, such as the Grand Canyon, civilian hikers must remain healthy enough to complete the task. If their health deteriorates beyond recovery, they may require rescue out of the Grand Canyon or face extreme, even fatal, consequences. The situation is similar for warfighters, although in a different context. Warfighters must remain healthy to deliver peak performance and ensure mission success; if they do not, the consequences are also extreme and include mission incompletion, injuries of a fellow team member which slow down the unit, or death. The recent explosion in wearable and agile devices to collect data for various combinations of biomarkers and performance metrics presents the opportunity to use wearable devices to provide the earliest possible warning of deteriorating health. It is unclear currently which markers are most pertinent and reliable for early indication of emerging illness, determining likelihood of task success, or determining a cause for a detected health decline. Most research into biomarkers indicative of health deterioration use lab settings or mild tasks to gauge performance. Studying Rim-to-Rim (R2R) hikers provides an opportunity to quantify which health markers could provide the earliest indication of health and performance decrement.

In this study, we collect three different forms of health data: (1) physiological data through wearable devices, (2) cognitive data through a cognitive task taken every 3 hours, and (3) blood samples obtained before and after completing the hike. We collect this data to examine physiological measures such as heart rate and oxygenation, decision making abilities, and the deeper, changing composition of hikers' biological processes. Data is collected from two different populations, civilian and warfighter hikers, to apply findings to various activities performed in extreme environments. We will describe our approach for data analyses in this paper. Our goal is to:

- understand the effectiveness of each COTS device and the validity of the data
- identify which physiological and cognitive phenomena are the most associated with overall health and task performance in extreme environments
- ascertain which markers provide the earliest yet most reliable indication of health decline
- identify significant differences between civilians' and warfighters' markers and their relationship to performance.

# 2 Study Collaboration

Many of the same physiological and cognitive phenomena that serve as indicators of declining health due to infection or chemical exposure, such as changes in heart rate, respiration, body temperature, pupil dilation, alertness, response speeds, and fatigue (Harden et al. 2015), are also associated with the human body's response to extreme altitude and temperature changes during intense physical exertion (Chase et al. 2005; Wickens et al. 2015). Thus, determining measurable changes in physiology and cognitive aptitude over time for individuals subjected to extreme altitude and temperature changes during intense physical exertion will provide critical learnings for the further development of advanced wearables capable of relaying the earliest indications of warfighter infection or chemical exposure. Volunteers included in this study will be subjected to these conditions as they attempt to complete the Grand Canyon Rim-to-Rim (R2R) hike.

The Grand Canyon 24.2 mile R2R hike represents a rigorous performance task including extreme changes in altitude and external temperature; this 24.2-mile hike involves an elevation change of nearly 7000 feet from rim to canyon floor, with temperature differentials up to 50 °F. Completing the R2R hike in one day is discouraged by the park service, but nevertheless has become a goal for many thousands of hikers each season. Each year, over 300 hikers require rescue from the canyon, with 175 people being airlifted from the canyon by helicopter. Many hikers develop symptoms of heat illness and dehydration, while a handful also present with symptoms of exercise-associated hyponatremia, a dangerous condition of low blood sodium levels. These illnesses are a testament to the rigor of this hike, requiring the body to endure fatigue and stress, and to adapt to rapidly changing environmental conditions (Garigan and Ristedt 1999; Ghiglieri and Myers 2001).

The University of New Mexico (UNM) Emergency Medical Service Consortium, providing emergency medical services (EMS) medical direction to Grand Canyon National Park rangers, recognized the heightened expense and safety risks associated with these rescues, and became interested in identifying nutritional and biological characteristics of hikers that were most likely to develop these (hyponatremia, dehydration, heat illness) and other critical health conditions while hiking the Grand Canyon. For the last two years, UNM Emergency Response physician and professor, Dr. Jon Femling, and former NPS Preventive Search and Rescue Ranger, Emily Pearce, have collaborated to study the food and water intake of Grand Canyon visitors hiking from the North Rim to the South Rim, or vice-versa. UNM hopes to better prepare hikers for their physical endeavor by correlating food and water intake to successful hiking outcomes. This grew into a funded project through DTRA and a partnership with Sandia National Laboratories, specifically cognitive psychologist Dr. Glory Aviña and geneticist Dr. Catherine Branda. The study was expanded to collect and analyze cognitive and physiological data collected through wearable devices. The interdisciplinary team of physicians, psychologists, computer scientists, statisticians, and biologists, as represented by this paper's authorship, set this study up to collect and holistically analyze data across various fields.

## 3 Empirical Background and Literature Review

### 3.1 Physiological Markers

One study, in the *Journal of Human Performance in Extreme Environments*, collected physiological (blood pressure, pulse, skin resistance) and psychological (anxiety) data from eight mountaineers who climbed Mount Everest. The researchers concluded that the data was connected to inhibition of overload, hypersensibility, and exhaustion. This study encountered both opportunities and difficulties with wearable devices in extreme environments: telemedical assessment is possible and necessary in order to determine and predict deficits in behavior and health risks for individuals at high altitudes, but requires devices tailored to such conditions (Stück et al. 2005).

Sleep deprivation, which can be related to extreme fatigue, has also been studied in the context of extreme physical demands. In a sample of ultra-marathon runners, there was a positive correlation between sleep-time before the race and race completion time (Poussel et al. 2015). One can conclude that signs of fatigue are early indicators of performance decrement. Therefore, it is necessary to investigate the physiological and cognitive indicators of fatigue.

Sensitivity of physiological measures to evaluate workload has also been investigated. Heart rate, blood pressure (from beat to beat), respiration and eye blinks were recorded in 14 subjects while they performed a complex task in a flight simulator (Veltman and Gaillard 1998). It was found that heart rate and blood pressure were both affected by task difficulty.

Physiological relationships, such as the impact of nutrition on performance, have been recognized by military contexts. The Uniformed Services University hosted a conference in July 2008, entitled "Warfighter Nutrition: Advanced Technologies and Opportunities" with Health Affairs and the Defense Advanced Research Projects Agency to develop strategic and tactical plans that could enhance Force Health Protection (FHP) by optimizing warfighter nutrition within the Department of Defense (DoD). The conference concluded that nutritional optimization represents an integral and proactive approach to prevent illness, injury, and performance degradation throughout all phases of military service. The overarching consensus achieved was that warfighter nutrition, as a cornerstone of FHP, warrants the critical attention of both medical and line leadership to move quickly to support current initiatives and future advanced technologies (Deuster et al. 2009).

## 3.2  Cognitive Markers

Extreme fatigue and stress on the body, caused by the demands of the physical environment, has negative effects on cognitive functioning. Temperature and altitude are both characteristics of the physical environment that impact cognitive ability. Enander (1989) and Hancock and Vasmatzidis (1998) found that even mild levels of thermal stress can have a negative impact on human performance. In a study conducted by Hocking et al. (2001), the Digit Span task and the AX-continuous performance task were used to measure attention, memory, verbal learning, information processing, and concentration. These cognitive abilities were negatively impacted when participants were exposed to extreme temperatures. Time and vigilance have also been found to share a curvilinear relationship with temperature: performance increases up to 85 °F, at which point it reliably decreases (Grether 1973). Cold temperatures also have an impact. A series of studies have examined the effects of cold temperatures on physical and cognitive performance. Exposure to cold air resulted in decreased performance on serial choice-reaction time tasks (Ellis 1982; Ellis et al. 1985) and working memory deficits have been reported after core body temperatures dip beneath 36.7 °C. In a study of naval special operations forces during actual winter warfare training, Hyde et al. (1997) found that cold temperatures were associated with decrements in hand strength and fine motor skills. Additionally, performance was especially affected when temperature varied over time and had extremely high temperatures (Enander 1989).

Altitude is another environmental characteristic that affects cognition. Cognitive deficits, particularly in memory, have been associated with altitude change (Muza et al. 2004). A cognitive test battery known as WinsCAT, which stands for the Spaceflight Cognitive Assessment Tool for Windows, was designed to assess neurocognitive status of astronauts on missions of long duration at various altitudes (Lowe et al. 2007). Habituation to altitude change seems to occur: decreased performance in the running memory task of the WinsCAT was reported between 0.5 and 4 hours after ascent, however these were not present at the tests given at 12 and 24 hours. It could also be that cognitive performance is affected by variability in altitude over short periods of time. The cognitive deficits reported also largely occurred before physiologic symptoms of mountain sickness were reported, indicating the need for further research on the relationships between possible markers.

Fatigue and stress also negatively influence cognitive abilities such as attention, executive function, memory, and reaction time (Karatsoreos and McEwen 2010; Bourne and Yaroush 2003). Highly trained astronauts given a cognitive battery of tests after acute sleep deprivation showed reduced affect vigilant attention, cognitive throughput, and abstract reasoning (Basner et al. 2015). In studies of fatigue and performance, fatigue is consistently shown to negatively impact visual attention, vigilance, decision-making, and other complex cognitive functions (Bourne and Yaroush 2003). This reduction in cognitive ability could be particularly problematic in extreme environments such as the Grand Canyon R2R—even simple tasks such as drinking water can have extreme consequences if not executed properly (Wickens et al. 2015).

## 3.3   Biological Markers

Part of the endeavor to understand the relationships between psychophysiology and performance is to know how to mitigate and address health risks when they arise. For example, altitude illness refers to a group of environmentally mediated pathophysiologies. Many people will suffer acute mountain sickness shortly after rapidly ascending to a moderately hypoxic environment, and an unfortunate few will develop potentially fatal conditions such as high altitude pulmonary edema or high altitude cerebral edema. Some individuals seem to be predisposed to developing altitude illness, suggesting an innate contribution to susceptibility. The implication of altitude-sensitive and altitude-tolerant individuals has stimulated much research into the contribution of a genetic background to the efficacy of altitude acclimatization. To date, 58 genes have been investigated for a role in altitude illness and, of these, 17 have shown some association with the susceptibility to, or the severity of, these conditions. Additional research is needed to examine the genome and hypoxic environments that contribute to an individual's capacity to acclimatize rapidly and effectively to altitude (MacInnis et al. 2010).

Although we know that these three markers collectively are indicators of performance, little research has been to done to understand the relationships between them. There is also limited research on their collective relationship to performance.

## 4    Experimental Design

Data collection will occur twice a year over two weekends, once in May and then again in October. This project is anticipated to take place over three years from October 2016 to May 2019 and has already completed its first weekend of data collection. Note that UNM has already completed two years of nutritional and survey data prior to the R2R WATCH study, which had its first round of data collection in October 2016.

The R2R WATCH team sets up check-in stations at the three major trailheads at the Grand Canyon: South Kaibab (SK), North Kaibab (NK), and Bright Angel (BA). The check-in stations are equipped with the data collection materials and researchers to interact with study participants. Since the R2R hikers can complete the hike in multiple directions (SK to NK, BA to NK, NK to SK, NK to BA), the three trailheads are prepared to collect both start and finish survey data, to accommodate hikers starting or finishing the R2R. There is also a team of researchers at the bottom of the canyon at Phantom Ranch to collect mid-hike survey data.

When hikers first approach one of the trailheads to start their hike, they are asked if they will be attempting the Rim-to-Rim hike in a single day. If they respond yes, they are asked if they are 18 years or older and would like to participate in a voluntary research study. If they again respond positively, they are taken to the check-in station and a researcher walks them through a consent process, as approved by the human subjects boards of the researchers' institutions. Each hiker is told that their data will be anonymized and that personally identifiable information will not be collected at any point of the study. Each hiker is given a wrist band with a unique identification number and then completes the start-hike survey. Once they complete the survey, they are asked if they would be willing to participate in the wearable device and/or blood work parts of the study. If they respond yes to either or both, they are led to a team of researchers, who provide a package of wearable devices for the hiker to wear (more details below), and/or to an RV where medical professionals collect blood samples. The hiker may ask as many questions as needed and is informed that they may withdraw from the study at any time. The hiker then proceeds to start the R2R.

Data for the wearable devices and blood parts of the study are only collected going from South Kaibab (start) to North Kaibab (finish) to streamline data collection. The R2R WATCH team works in shifts and mans the check-in stations for about 48 hours, starting at 2:00 am one morning and completing at 11:55 pm the next day.

Once hikers complete the R2R at their own pace, there is a check-in station to collect post-hike data. As previously stated, the survey post-hike data can be completed at any of the three trailheads. For the bloodwork and device data, post-hike data is collected at the NK trailhead. After they are offered congratulations and a chair, hikers' wearable devices are turned off, the data is saved, and the devices are collected. Hikers who originally consented to be in the blood portion of the study are also led to a tent where a post-hike blood sample is collected by a team of trained phlebotomists. Hikers are reminded that their data is anonymous and thanked for their participation in the study.

## 4.1    Participants

Data is collected from two populations: day-of volunteer civilian hikers and warfighter hikers. Volunteer hikers show up to the Grand Canyon to hike the Rim-to-Rim hike and agree to participate in the study as they approach the trailheads and study check-in stations. Participants are not recruited to hike the Rim-to-Rim; only hikers who are already planning to hike the Rim-to-Rim are enrolled in this study. This is to avoid encouraging an unfit participant who may become ill or injured due to lack of preparedness. Warfighter hikers are from a specific group in the military and are asked prior to the study weekend if they will be interested in completing a hike at the Grand Canyon as a personal training exercise. They are provided with the details of the R2R WATCH study. Their time is on a volunteer basis and hikers are told that they are under no pressure to hike the Rim-to-Rim at the Grand Canyon. This method is taken to draw a warfighter population to the Grand Canyon but still prevent recruitment so as not to increase risk of unprepared hikers hiking the R2R. Warfighters show up to the check-in station the same as civilian hikers and blend in with the normal population for security and protection purposes. Their data is given a different form of identification number but is also anonymized.

In October 2016, 288 pre and post surveys were collected and 50 participants provided wearable device data. In combination between a very small pilot study in May 2016 and October 2016, 51 participants provided pre- and post-bloodwork samples. Surprisingly, hikers' willingness to participate in a research study such as the R2R WATCH, even moments before they are about to start their hike, is fairly high. Most people who decline to participate do so because there is already a crowd of participants at the check-in station and the hikers do not want to wait, especially when the weather is cold.

## 4.2    Survey

Potential participants are invited to participate in a simple, short survey which is administered at the start, middle, and finish of their R2R. The survey contains questions regarding nutritional intake, basic biometric data, previous experience, activity times, and self-reports of fatigue and preparedness.

## 4.3    Wearable Devices

Civilian hikers are given one of two wearable device packages. "Basic package 1" includes a fitness wristwatch device, an environment temperature recording device that hangs on their pack, and an iPod Touch which contains a cognitive battery. "Basic package 2" includes a different fitness wristwatch device, the same temperature recording device, an enhanced GPS recording device, and the iPod Touch with the same cognitive battery. For warfighter hikers, the "Advanced package 1" contains multiple types of wearable devices: a different fitness wristwatch device, two environment temperature recording devices, a chest strap, a smart hat, a core temperature device, and an option to wear sensor shorts. The "Advanced package 2" also contains the same two temperature devices, a different fitness wrist watch, a chest strap, and smart hat. Although the packages are slightly altered after each round of data collection, the goal is to have a low-maintenance package for hikers who do not have much time to spend checking in to the study and more in-depth packages for hikers who are willing to put more time and effort into the study. All wearable devices are non-invasive and commercial off-the-shelf products. The wearable devices are changed out each year of the study so as to validate data collected through two weekends of data collection with the same set of devices but also diversify data collected through various wearable devices.

Each hiker, whether they have a basic or advanced package, is given an iPod Touch that they can wear in an armband while hiking or put in their pack. Each iPod Touch has a cognitive battery, which is a 5–10 minutes task with three different cognitive "games." The cognitive battery is developed by Digital Artefacts, a company that has created an application entitled BrainBaseline (https://www.brainbaseline.com/). BrainBaseline is a series of validated cognitive tests that can be put into a customizable application. Our customized app, installed on each iPod, includes two to three cognitive tests plus a fatigue survey to ensure the tasks can be completed quickly. Every three hours, an alarm goes off to remind the hiker to take the cognitive battery. Each participant also completes the cognitive battery at the start and end of the hike.

## 4.4   Bloodwork

Participants are asked to participate in two blood draws (start and finish). Peripheral blood is acquired through venipuncture by individuals trained in phlebotomy. Approximately one 6 mL tube of blood for serum and an additional 6 mL tube of blood for plasma is drawn from each hiker both at the start and finish of the participants R2R.

## 4.5   Starting and Finishing the Rim-to-Rim Hike

Each trailhead (South Kaibab, North Kaibab, and Bright Angel) is equipped with check-in stations for the pre- and post-hike surveys. The Rim-to-Rim hikers who participate in the wearable devices and bloodwork parts of the study are checked in at the South Kaibab trailhead and travel to the North Kaibab trailhead where they are checked out of the study once they finish the Rim-to-Rim.

## 4.6   Data Extraction

Blood obtained from patients before and after crossing the Grand Canyon is processed on site to obtain plasma and serum. These samples are labelled with the subject's study ID only and frozen, stored and archived for future use in the PIs −80 °F freezer in his UNM HSC based laboratory (MRF 108). These stored samples will be used for measurement of blood chemistries, inflammatory markers, heat-shock protein analysis, and other analysis of immune function and human performance.

# 5 Data Analysis

Data collected will serve two purposes. First, to establish a correlation between cognitive performance and health indicators, we will use confirmatory analyses based on data collected from wearable devices for relationships between health indicators and performance. Second, once we have established the connection between health measurements and cognitive ability, we would like to build a model for accurately predicting change in cognitive abilities based on health measurements.

## 5.1 Confirmatory Analysis

The objective of the confirmatory analyses is to validate the connection between health measures and cognitive abilities. As such, the statistical methodology will emphasize robustness and interpretability. We propose using a derived variable analysis (Hedeker and Gibbons 2006) to build summary measures from the longitudinal data collected by the devices. These measures will be correlated with cognitive performance at each of the trial times. A mixed-effects model should be used to account for subject variability because repeated measures are taken from each subject.

## 5.2 Predictive Models

Ultimately, we would like to build models to predict decline in cognitive abilities from data collected by the wearable devices. While the models used for the confirmatory analysis will inherently have some predictive power, there will be some important distinctions between the predictive and confirmatory analysis. First, the predictive model's focus is on prediction rather than interpretability of effects and validity of hypothesis tests. This frees us to use standard machine learning strategies to build models with complex interactions between variables. Second, in the confirmatory analysis, we can use the controlled structure of the study to find reliable indicators of fatigue. In our predictive model, we intend to use features that can be reliably constructed outside the environment of the original study. We propose using a derived variable analysis to generate features from the device data, but will begin with traditional machine learning methods, such as support vector machine (SVM) or neural nets, to build the predictive model and validate the model using cross-validation.

# 6 Conclusion

The R2R WATCH study focuses on measuring physiological, cognitive, and biological data as participants hike the Rim-to-Rim to understand which markers are most related to human performance and fatigue in extreme, physically challenging environments. Data collection so far has occurred over one weekend in 2016 and is anticipated to continue for five more weekends over the next three years. Our goal is to contribute to gaps in the empirical research by:

- collecting larger sample sizes than traditionally reported in extreme environment settings;
- looking at differences between civilian and special military groups;
- analyzing individual and combined effects across physiological, cognitive, and biological markers;
- refining our experimental design to target validity and reliability across all data sources (e.g., optical heart rate, cadence)

Overall, we aim to further understand how to identify the earliest indicators of performance decrement and fuse cognitive process with physiological and biological processes.

## 7 Graphics

Pictures were taken during October 2016 Data Collection (Figs. 1, 2, 3, 4 and 5).

**Fig. 1.** Check in station at the trailhead. The tent in the back is specially used for bloodwork.

**Fig. 2.** Hikers are asked to complete the post-hike survey as well as take the cognitive battery one last time to get a post-hike score.

**Fig. 3.** The Grand Canyon Rim-to-Rim hike has an altitude change of 3000–5000 feet and a 30–50 degrees Fahrenheit temperature change.

**Fig. 4.** Hyponatremia is a water-salt imbalance that affects many hikers that cross the R2R.

**Fig. 5.** The research team collects data for 48 hours straight, starting at 2 am one morning and finishing at 11:55 pm the following day.

# References

Basner, M., Savitt, A., Moore, T.M., Port, A.M., McGuire, S., Ecker, A.J., Nasrini, J., Mollicone, D.J., Mott, C.M., McCann, T., Dinges, D.F., Gur, R.C.: Development and validation of the cognition test battery for spaceflight. Aerosp. Med. Hum. Perform. **86**(11), 942–952 (2015)

Bourne, L., Yaroush, R.A.: Stress and Cognition: A Cognitive Psychological Perspective (NAG2-1561). National Aeronautics and Space Administration (2003)

Chase, B., Karwowski, W., Benedict, M.E., Quesada, P.M., Irwin-Chase, H.M.: Effects of thermal stress on dual task performance and attention allocation. J. Hum. Perform. Extreme Environ. **8**(1–2), 27–39 (2005)

Deuster, P.A., Weinstein, A.A., Sobel, A., Young, A.J.: Warfighter nutrition: current opportunities and advanced technologies report from Department of Defense workshop. Mil. Med. **174**(7), 671 (2009)

Ellis, H.D.: The effects of cold on the performance of serial choice reaction time and various discrete tasks. Hum. Factors **24**, 589–598 (1982)

Ellis, H.D., Wilcock, S.E., Zaman, S.A.: Cold and performance: the effects of information load, analgesics, and the rate of cooling. Aviat. Space Environ. Med. **56**(3), 233–237 (1985)

Enander, A.E.: Effects of thermal stress on human performance. Scand. J. Work Environ. Health **15**, 27–33 (1989)

Garigan, T.P., Ristedt, D.E.: Death from hyponatremia as a result of acute water intoxication in an Army basic trainee. Mil. Med. **164**(3), 234 (1999)

Ghiglieri, M.P., Myers, T.M.: Over the Edge: Death in Grand Canyon (2001)

Grether, W.F.: Human performance at elevated environmental temperatures. Aerosp. Med. **44**(7), 747–755 (1973)

Hancock, P.A., Vasmatzidis, I.: Human occupational and performance limits under stress: the thermal environment as a prototypical example. Ergonomics **41**(8), 1169–1191 (1998). doi:10.1080/001401398186469

Harden, L.M., Kent, S., Pittman, Q.J., Roth, J.: Fever and sickness behavior: friend or foe? Brain Behav. Immun. **50**, 322–333 (2015)

Hedeker, D., Gibbons, R.D.: Longitudinal Data Analysis. Wiley, New York (2006)

Hocking, C., Silberstein, R.B., Lau, W.M., Stough, C., Roberts, W.: Evaluation of cognitive performance in the heat by functional brain imaging and psychometric testing. Comp. Biochem. Physiol.: Mol. Integr. Physiol. **128**, 719–734 (2001)

Hyde, D., Thomas, J.R., Schrot, J., Taylor, W.F.: Quantification of Special Operations Mission-Related Performance: Operational Evaluation of Physical Measures. Naval Medical Research Institute, Bethesda (1997)

Karatsoreos, I.N., McEwen, B.S.: Stress and allostasis. Handbook of Behavioral Medicine: Methods and Applications, pp. 649–658. Springer, New York (2010)

Lowe, M., Harris, W., Kane, R.L., Banderet, L, Levinson, D., Reeves, R.: Neuropsychological assessment in extreme environments. Arch. Clin. Neuropsychol. S88–S99 (2007)

MacInnis, M.J., Koehle, M.S., Rupert, J.L.: Evidence for a genetic basis for altitude illness: 2010 update. High Altitude Med. Biol. **11**(4), 349–368 (2010). doi:10.1089/ham.2010.1030

Muza, S.R., Kaminsky, D., Fulco, C.S., Banderet, L.E., Cymerman, A.: Cysteinyl leukotriene blockade does not prevent acute mountain sickness. Aviat. Space Environ. Med. **75**, 413–419 (2004)

Poussel, M., Laroppe, J., Hurdiel, R., Girard, J., Poletti, L., Thil, C., Didelot, A., Chenuel, B.: Sleep management strategy and performance in an extreme mountain ultra-marathon. Res. Sports Med. **23**(3), 330–336 (2015)

Stück, M., Balzer, H.-U., Hecht, K., Schröder, H.: Psychological and psychophysiological effects of a high-mountain expedition to Tibet. J. Hum. Perform. Extreme Environ. **8**(1), 4 (2005)

Veltman, J.A., Gaillard, A.W.K.: Physiological workload reactions to increasing levels of task difficulty. Ergonomics **41**(5), 656–669 (1998)

Wickens, C.D., Keller, J.W., Shaw, C.: Human factors in high-altitude mountaineering. J. Hum. Perform. Extreme Environ. **12**(1), 1 (2015). doi:10.7771/2327-2937.1065

# Investigation of Breath Counting, Abdominal Breathing and Physiological Responses in Relation to Cognitive Load

Hubert K. Brumback[✉]

Department of Educational Psychology and Hawai'i Interdisciplinary
Neurobehavioral and Technology Laboratory (HINT Lab), University of Hawai'i
at Mānoa, 1776 University Avenue, Honolulu, HI 96822, USA
brumback@hawaii.edu

**Abstract.** Computers and mobile devices can enhance learning processes but may also impose or exacerbate stress. This fact may be particularly applicable to some college and university students who already experience high stress levels. Breathing has long been used in meditative traditions for self-regulation and Western science has clearly shown the complex relationship between breathing, blood circulation and the autonomic nervous system. Since breathing is both automatic and volitional, this study seeks to examine if college students can manage physiological responses from a cognitive load imposed by a Stroop color word test by using either breath counting, abdominal breathing or the two combined. The findings of this study may provide evidence which promotes the idea of teaching breath-based self-regulation strategies in college and university settings. The findings may also be of interest to designers of affective computer systems by suggesting that device interfaces and software can be configured to monitor users' cognitive load indirectly through physiological signals and alert the user to irregularities or adapt to the user's needs.

**Keywords:** Breath counting · Abdominal breathing · Cognitive load · Stress · Stroop color word task · Students · Physiological response · Meditation

## 1 Introduction

Computers and mobile devices are ubiquitous in most university and college environments but for some, the advantages these devices bring to the learning process are offset by stress that continuous use of these devices can cause. One such risk is irregular breathing patterns [1, 2], which can instigate or compound stress. Breathing interruptions have been observed in other learning scenarios without electronic devices, when some individuals inadvertently hold their breath during periods of intense concentration (also called striving) [3] or unwittingly change their breathing in response to a demanding task [4].

It has long been known that breathing can be used for self-regulation, particularly for stress management [5]. A variety of studies have explored the use of breathing exercises in educational settings and suggest that these exercises are useful for in managing stress [6–9]. Particularly of note are two, basic exercises: breath counting

D.D. Schmorrow and C.M. Fidopiastis (Eds.): AC 2017, Part I, LNAI 10284, pp. 275–286, 2017.
DOI: 10.1007/978-3-319-58628-1_22

and abdominal breathing. If individuals are able to become mindful of their breathing in learning scenarios, it may be possible for individuals to better manage mental stress brought about by sustained cognitive load, especially when using computers or mobile devices.

## 2  Theoretical Background

### 2.1  Breathing and Self-regulation

For millennia adherents of religious traditions have used breathing to calm and focus the mind as part of individual meditative practices. Eastern traditions of Buddhism and Hinduism are commonly noted by Western scholars in this regard, but breath use for similar objectives can be found in a variety religions and in many indigenous spiritual practices.

Western medical science has also empirically established that breathing can both cause stress and help mitigate it. The complex relationship between the process of breathing, blood circulation and the autonomic nervous system is well documented [10–12]. Irregular breathing (regardless of cause) alters the body's homeostasis and depending on the breathing pathology, can alter blood pH, which activates the autonomic nervous system, and causes cascading physiological effects including but not limited to increased heart rate, increased blood pressure, and vasoconstriction. These physiological responses can then lead to or exacerbate physical and mental stress and further agitate breathing.

**Breath Counting.** Beyond being a means of establishing breath rate [13], breath counting can be used to focus one's attention on breathing, which can lead to breath awareness. Breath counting is a basic meditative technique [14–17] which has been suggested as a behavioral measure of mindfulness [18]. A limitation of some mindfulness studies of breath counting with students is that the studies employ other treatments in addition to breath counting, which can confound attribution of positive effects. While breath counting has been advocated for use in educational settings [19] and with children [17], the opportunity still remains to specifically examine breath counting with college students, especially for self-regulation.

**Abdominal Breathing.** Slow and deliberate breathing in which one purposefully and fully moves the diaphragm up and down while breathing is known as abdominal breathing [20]. This breathing pattern is further characterized by abdominal expansion and reduction corresponding to diaphragm movement [21]. It is also known as diaphragmatic [9, 20, 22, 23], diaphragmal [24], belly [20, 25], deep and slow [24] or slow-deep [7] breathing. Abdominal breathing appears in the literature as a means of eliminating or managing a variety of conditions such as asthma [26], pain [24, 27], anxiety [7, 28] and prehypertension [29].

Some studies have explored the use of abdominal breathing with children [7, 9], others with college students [6, 30]. For college students, abdominal breathing has been employed for anxiety management and as part of larger student health interventions. Similar to the aforementioned mindfulness studies, the studies involving college students did not exclusively employ abdominal breathing as a unique treatment, which makes it challenging to definitively attribute any positive effects to abdominal breathing.

## 2.2 Cognitive Load

**Cognitive Load Theory.** The notion that cognitive load can interfere with learning was first described by Sweller [31, 32] and is the basis of the Cognitive Load Theory. At the theory's core is the concept that instructional material can be designed to enable students to make effective use of limited cognitive resources [33, 34]. The cognitive load theory also applies to the use and design of computer systems and applications, where users' cognitive loads must be considered [35]. Closely related to system and software design is the fact that that users' cognitive load during computer-based tasks can be assessed through physiological measures [36–39].

While engaged in an activity, perceived stress due to cognitive load likely varies due to individual factors such differences in perception of and experience with the subject matter, one's ability to concentrate and one's motivation level [40, 41]. Individual differences may help explain why some perceive stress in response to cognitive load for a task and others do not [40]. For some, extended periods of cognitive load can lead to mental fatigue [42].

College and university students generally experience high degrees of stress for a variety of reasons including academic workload, social situations and environmental adaptation [6, 43–46]. Computer and mobile device use can also can cause or contribute to stress for members of these student populations [1, 47]. Given the relationships between learning, cognitive load, stress, and computer use, and the confluence of these factors in academic settings, it may be worthwhile to consider these factors together.

**Physiological Responses.** Both cognitive load and stress can elicit several measurable physiological responses including increases in breathing [4], skin conductance [48], and heart rate [41, 49]. Prolonged cognitive load can lead to mental fatigue and hyperactivity of the sympathetic nervous system [42]. Independent of the theoretical approaches to and categorizations of cognitive load and stress, the physiological responses of changes in breathing, skin conductance and heart rate can all be provoked by a computer-based activity.

**Stroop Task.** The Stroop effect refers to the interference caused by the presentation of two color stimuli simultaneously: the actual color (word font) and the word for the color [50]. For example, if the word BLUE is displayed in red font, one takes longer (in milliseconds) to name the color, and will make more erroneous responses than when the color when color word and the font color match. Stroop tasks are were initially applied to studies of human attention [51] and have also been used to investigate stress [52–57] and cognitive load [4, 58]. There is evidence that computer-based Stroop color word tasks are efficient laboratory stressors [59] and since interference caused by Stroop tasks cannot be individually controlled [60], it may explain why practice effects for Stroop tasks are only apparent after intensive exposure [61].

## 2.3    Hypotheses

From the material reviewed for this project related to breathing, cognitive load, stress, computer and mobile device use, and college students, there are three avenues for investigation. Two include exclusive examination of the specific breathing practices:

H1:    College students can learn a simple breath counting exercise to regulate physiological response to cognitive load.

H2:    College students can learn a simple abdominal breathing exercise to regulate physiological response to cognitive load.

The third is an examination of the two breathing exercises together:

H3:    When an individual applies simple abdominal breathing and breath counting exercises together, there will be greater effect on regulation of physiological responses to cognitive load.

For this study, cognitive load is indirectly assessed by measuring in the physiological responses evidenced by changes in breathing, heart rate and skin conductance.

## 3    Method

The purpose of this study is to investigate the efficacy of university student use of breath counting and abdominal breathing protocols to regulate physiological responses due to cognitive load from a computer-based task. Because individuals experience cognitive load differently, with some thriving on the challenge and others experiencing stress, it is it is important to employ a task that will be consistently challenging for all participants. In an endeavor to standardize individual cognitive load experience, this study applies a computer-based Stroop color word task to impose cognitive load.

### 3.1    Participants

Participants will be healthy state university undergraduate and graduate college students with normal color vision, whom will receive cash payment for their participation. This study seeks to record data from 150 participants (50 for each treatment) and employs a repeated measures design.

### 3.2    Task

Baseline physiological measures for each participant will first be recorded during a ten-minute period of sitting quietly. Participants will then complete a series of computer-based Stroop color word tasks [62] immediately followed by ten-minute periods of sitting quietly or ten minute breath task periods. The sequence of tasks is specified in Fig. 1.

| 1. | 2. | 3. | 4. | 5. | 6. | 7. | 8. | 9. |
|---|---|---|---|---|---|---|---|---|
| Sitting | Stroop | Sitting | Stroop | Sitting | Stroop | Breath | Stroop | Breath |
| Quietly | Task | Quietly | Task | Quietly | Task | Task | Task | Task |
| 10 min | 2 min | 10 min | 2 min | 10 min | 2 min | 10 min | 2 min | 10 min |

**Fig. 1.** Activity sequence

**Cognitive Load.** For the Stroop color word task, items are displayed to the participant in a random order with half of the items having matching color word and font color and half with the color word and font color that do not match. Regardless of the name of the color presented in the text, participants are instructed to respond by pressing the key on the computer keyboard that corresponds with the first letter of the color of the font. For example, if the word GREEN is displayed in blue font, the participant presses the b-key. Only four colors are used: red, green, yellow and blue. After each correct response, the message "Correct. Press SPACE to continue." appears. After each incorrect response, the message "INCORRECT. Don't rush." appears. Two minutes are allocated for each Stroop task but participants may finish early if they correctly complete 24 items (incorrect responses use time, but are not recorded).

Participants are instructed to complete the task as quickly and accurately as they are able. Task measures include the total amount of time used to complete the task and response time for each item. The primary purpose of the Stroop task is to elicit physiological responses from the participants but individual task measures are still recorded and analyzed.

### 3.3 Treatments

Participants will be randomly assigned to one of three conditions: (a) breath counting, (b) abdominal breathing and (c) combined breath counting and abdominal breathing. For each condition, after participants' baseline physiological measures are recorded for ten minutes, participants then complete two sets of the computer-based Stroop task paired with and followed by ten minutes of sitting quietly (Fig. 1, items 2–5). After the first two sets, the participants are given instructions for the respective breathing task for their group and then complete two sets of a Stroop task followed by ten minutes of a breathing task (Fig. 1, items 6–10).

**Sitting Quietly.** For baseline, physiological response measurements, participants are instructed to relax and sit quietly for ten minutes. Participants are also instructed to maintain a comfortable sitting position with their backs straight, to breathe normally, refrain from talking and to keep their minds as calm and clear as they are able.

**Breath Counting.** In the breath counting condition, participants are provided a breath counting worksheet and instructed to sequentially mark the rectangle on the worksheet that corresponds with each of four breath events as the events occur: the (a) beginning and (b) end of each (c) inhalation and (d) exhalation. Participants are also asked to keep their minds focused on marking the worksheet precisely at the exact occurrence of each breath event. After ten minutes, the participants are asked to tally the number of breaths they completed during the ten-minute period and calculate the average breaths per minute (BPM) by dividing by ten.

**Abdominal Breathing.** In the abdominal breathing condition, the participants are instructed to place their dominant hands on center of their chest and the other on the center of their abdomen. They are then asked to keep their abdomen completely relaxed and permit their abdomen to expand as they inhale to reduce as they exhale while keeping their chest as still as possible. Participants are also asked to keep their minds focused on the physical sensations of abdominal breathing.

**Combined.** In the combined condition, the participants are instructed to complete the breath counting and abdominal breathing tasks simultaneously with the following minor modifications. Instead of placing their dominant hand on the chest, participants use the dominant hand to mark the breath counting worksheet. Participants are also asked to keep their minds focused on marking the worksheet precisely at the exact time of each breath event while ensuring their abdomen remains relaxed and moving with each breath.

**Independent Variable.** The independent variable is the treatment task consisting of the three conditions described previously: breath counting, abdominal breathing and the combined breathing activity.

**Dependent Variables.** The dependent variables are breath rate, breath pauses (apnea), breath pattern (abdominal or thoracic), heart rate, heart rate variability, electrodermal activity (EDA) and global stress level. Breath rate is measured using two strain gauges: one around the participant's abdomen and one around the participant's thorax. Heart activity is recorded via two electrocardiogram (ECG) sensors placed on each of the participant's anterior forearms, inferior to the antecubital space. EDA is recorded via two skin conductance sensors placed next to each other on the medial longitudinal arch of the plantar surface of the participant's foot. Global stress is measured at the beginning of the session with a self-report questionnaire.

### 3.4    Procedures

The complete session will take approximately 90 min which includes one hour for the experimental procedure and thirty minutes for the questionnaire, sensor application/ removal, debriefing and general administration. The experimental procedure will be approved by the university Intuitional Review Board (IRB). Upon providing informed consent, participants begin by taking a single survey designed to capture handedness, demographics and global stress. Global stress is measured using questions from Feldt's 11-item college student stress scale (CSSS) [44, 63, 64]. They will then complete the experimental procedure seated in front of a computer workstation in a partitioned section of a lab room. The computer workspace is comparable to a standard 64-inch by 64-inch office cubicle. The lab room, which is air-conditioned, has a drop ceiling with acoustic tiles and fluorescent lighting.

**Experimental Procedure.** Participants will be seated in a common, static office chair to help minimize unnecessary movement. The computer workstation is equipped with a 15-inch monitor, keyboard and mouse. The experiment proctor will explain the process for attaching the physiological sensors and answer any questions the participant may have. Once all sensors have been applied and are functioning properly, the participant will be instructed to sit quietly for ten minutes. Next, the proctor will give the participant written instructions for the computer-based Stroop color word task and the participant will then complete task. After saving the Stroop test results, the proctor will give the participants instructions to sit quietly for ten more minutes. The participant will complete a total of two sets of one Stroop task followed by ten minutes of sitting quietly.

The proctor will then give the participant instructions that correspond with the breathing task for the treatment condition they have been randomly assigned to: (a) breath counting, (b) abdominal breathing or (c) breath counting and abdominal breathing combined. The participant will then complete two sets of one Stroop task followed by 10 min of the specified breathing activity. For the entire procedure, the proctor will mark the data from the physiological measurements to indicate the beginning and end of each event.

Once the participant has completed the experimental procedure, the proctor will remove the physiological sensors and debrief the participant. For the debriefing, the proctor will read a standard written statement describing the full scope and purpose of the experiment. The proctor will answer any questions the participant may have and ask the participant not to share the details of the experiment with anyone. The proctor will then thank and pay the participant.

**Instrumentation.** Data are collected using a BIOPAC MP150 system. The system is equipped with two strain gauge belt sensors to measure breath, electrocardiogram (ECG) sensors to measure heart rate and electrodermal activity (EDA) sensors to measure skin conductance. Data is recorded at 1000 Hz on four channels using the BIOPAC AcqKnowledge software.

## 3.5   Data Preparation

BIOPAC AcqKnowledge software is also used to remove artifacts from breath, ECG and electrodermal data and to aggregate the data to mean values per second. Change values for each channel are calculated by subtracting the physiological signal level at the beginning of each task period with the signal level at the end of the task period. Breath ratio is calculated by dividing the measures of abdominal breaths by the measures of thoracic breaths. Mean values for breath apnea periods are calculated for every task by dividing total apnea time by total task time. Each Stroop task is measured by total time used to complete the task and mean value for individual item response is calculated by adding all Stroop task times and dividing the total by 24. Global stress scores are calculated by adding the Likert scale values for each of the eleven instrument responses.

### 3.6   Data Analysis

Potential relationships between variables will first be examined using a saturated multi-level structural equation model. The model will be used to compare within and between subject and within and between group means for each variable over time: level one: participant, level two: breathing and stress tasks. The model will then be refined based on any statistically significant relationships. This approach has the added advantage of scalability and can be expanded if the study were repeated at later times. It also has the inherent possibility of treating selected dependent variables as separate observations, artificially increasing the sample size [65].

## 4   Potential Implications

The objective of this study is to determine if undergraduate students can use breath counting and abdominal breathing to regulate physiological responses caused by cognitive load. It examines physiological responses elicited by a computer-based task and if individuals are able to manage these responses through breathing. If evidence emerges that basic breathing exercises can be used by students to manage physiological responses due to cognitive load, these findings would have several implications.

First, it would reinforce what has been long known by members of certain meditative traditions, namely that breathing can be used for self-regulation. What is new, however, is the context in which these breathing protocols are applied and the specific purpose of employing these exercises for self-regulation in learning scenarios. Generally, self-regulation skills are not formally taught beyond elementary school and self-directed learners only gain new self-regulation skills through trial and error. If some undergraduate students are able to use these practices in response to cognitive load, it may support the idea that perhaps these procedures should be formally taught in educational settings. Other questions would then need to be addressed such as which individuals benefit the most from these practices and what factors influence the adoption of these behaviors.

If evidence emerges to the contrary and individuals are unable to effectively use these breathing protocols to manage physiological response, two questions that must be addressed are: (a) if the breathing protocols are appropriate for educational contexts and (b) to what degree is time is a factor in learning how to employ these protocols effectively. Future research could focus exclusively on each protocol to determine if any individual factors influence protocol use and adoption as well as how much time should be invested in practicing these protocols in order to enable one to successfully use the protocol to manage physiological response.

Additionally, there might be implications for human-computer interaction, specifically interface and software design. As affective systems emerge, it will be imperative to consider users' breathing as an indirect measure of cognitive load, especially since it is a physiological factor that can be independently controlled. Computer interfaces and applications that can monitor users' breathing could do two very important things: (a) help users become aware of their breathing so they can adjust it as needed and (b) adapt the systems to users' individual information processing capacities.

# References

1. Lin, I., Peper, E.: Psychophysiological patterns during cell phone text messaging: a preliminary study. Appl. Psychophysiol. Biofeedback **34**, 53–57 (2009)
2. Peper, E., Harvey, R., Tylova, H.: Stress protocol for assessing computer-related disorders. Biofeedback **34**, 57–62 (2006)
3. Peper, E.: The possible uses of biofeedback in education. In: Peper, E., Ancoli, S., Quinn, M. (eds.) Mind/body integration: essential readings in biofeedback. Plenum Press, New York (1979)
4. Grassmann, M., Vlemincx, E., von Leupoldt, A., Mittelstädt, J.M., Van den Bergh, O.: Respiratory changes in response to cognitive load: a systematic review. Neural Plast. **2016**, 16 p. (2016). doi:10.1155/2016/8146809
5. Song, H.-S., Lehrer, P.M.: The effects of specific respiratory rates on heart rate and heart rate variability. Appl. Psychophysiol. Biofeedback **28**, 13–23 (2003)
6. Paul, G., Elam, B., Verhulst, S.: A longitudinal study of students' perceptions of using deep breathing meditation to reduce testing stresses. Teach. Learn. Med. **19**, 287–292 (2007)
7. Sellakumar, G.K.: Effect of slow-deep breathing exercise to reduce anxiety among adolescent school students in a selected higher secondary school in Coimbatore. India. J. Psychol. Educ. Res. **23**, 54 (2015)
8. Tloczynski, J., Tantriella, M.: A comparison of the effects of Zen breath meditation or relaxation on college adjustment. Psychologia **41**, 32–43 (1998)
9. Terai, K., Shimo, T., Umezawa, A.: Slow diaphragmatic breathing as a relaxation skill for elementary school children: a psychophysiological assessment. Int. J. Psychophysiol. **94**, 229 (2014)
10. Fried, R.: The Psychology and Physiology of Breathing: In Behavioral Medicine, Clinical Psychology, and Psychiatry. Springer, New York (1993)
11. Naifeh, K.H.: Basic anatomy and physiology of the respiratory system and the autonomic nervous system. In: Timmons, B.H., Ley, R. (eds.) Behavioral and Psychological Approaches to Breathing Disorders. Plenum Press, New York (1994)
12. Gilbert, C.: Biochemical aspects of breathing. In: Chaitow, L., Gilbert, C., Bradley, D. (eds.) Recognizing and Treating Breathing Disorders: A Multidisciplinary Approach. Churchill Livingstone Elsevier, London (2014)
13. Karlen, W., Gan, H., Chiu, M., Dunsmuir, D., Zhou, G., Dumont, G.A., Ansermino, J.M.: Improving the accuracy and efficiency of respiratory rate measurements in children using mobile devices. PLoS ONE **9**, e99266 (2014)
14. Nakamura, T.: Oriental Breathing Therapy. Japan Publications, New York, Tokyo (1981)
15. Hoshiyama, M., Hoshiyama, A.: Heart rate variability associated with different modes of respiration during Zen meditation. Presented at the Computing in Cardiology Conference (CinC), 22 September 2013
16. Lehmann, D., Faber, P.L., Tei, S., Pascual-Marqui, R.D., Milz, P., Kochi, K.: Reduced functional connectivity between cortical sources in five meditation traditions detected with lagged coherence using EEG tomography. NeuroImage **60**, 1574–1586 (2012)
17. Hooker, K.E., Fodor, I.E.: Teaching mindfulness to children. Gestalt Rev. **12**, 75–91 (2008)
18. Levinson, D.B., Stoll, E.L., Kindy, S.D., Merry, H.L., Davidson, R.J.: A mind you can count on: validating breath counting as a behavioral measure of mindfulness. Conscious. Res. **5**, 1202 (2014)
19. Sessa, S.A.: Meditation, breath work, and focus training for teachers and students - the five minutes a day that can really make a difference. J. Coll. Teach. Learn. TLC. **4**, 57–62 (2007)

20. Kajander, R., Peper, E.: Teaching diaphragmatic breathing to children. Biofeedback **26**, 14–17 (1998)

21. Chaitow, L., Gilbert, C., Bradley, D. (eds.): Recognizing and Treating Breathing Disorders: A Multidisciplinary Approach. Churchill Livingstone Elsevier, London (2014)

22. Biggs, Q., Kelly, K., Toney, J.: The effects of deep diaphragmatic breathing and focused attention on dental anxiety in a private practice setting. J. Dent. Hyg. **77**, 105–113 (2003)

23. Hymes, A., Nuernberger, P.: Breathing patterns found in heart attack patients. J. Int. Assoc. Yoga Ther. **2**, 25 (1991).

24. Busch, V., Magerl, W., Kern, U., Haas, J., Hajak, G., Eichhammer, P.: The effect of deep and slow breathing on pain perception, autonomic activity, and mood processing-an experimental study. Pain Med. **13**, 215–228 (2012)

25. Jerath, R., Edry, J.W., Barnes, V.A., Jerath, V.: Physiology of long pranayamic breathing: neural respiratory elements may provide a mechanism that explains how slow deep breathing shifts the autonomic nervous system. Med. Hypotheses **67**, 566–571 (2006)

26. Bignall, W.J.R., Luberto, C.M., Cornette, A.F., Haj-Hamed, M., Cotton, S.: Breathing retraining for African-American adolescents with asthma: a pilot study of a school-based randomized controlled trial. J. Asthma **52**, 889–896 (2015)

27. Bell, K.M., Meadows, E.A.: Efficacy of a brief relaxation training intervention for pediatric recurrent abdominal pain. Cogn. Behav. Pract. **20**, 81–92 (2013)

28. Moss, D.: The house is crashing down on me: integrating mindfulness, breath training, and heart rate variability biofeedback for an anxiety disorder in a 71-year-old caregiver. Biofeedback **44**, 160–167 (2016)

29. Wang, S.-Z., Li, S., Xu, X.-Y., Lin, G.-P., Shao, L., Zhao, Y., Wang, T.H.: Effect of slow abdominal breathing combined with biofeedback on blood pressure and heart rate variability in prehypertension. J. Altern. Complement. Med. **16**, 1039–1045 (2010)

30. Peper, E., Miceli, B., Harvey, R.: Educational model for self-healing: eliminating a chronic migraine with electromyography, autogenic training, posture, and mindfulness. Biofeedback **44**, 130–137 (2016)

31. Sweller, J.: Cognitive load during problem solving: effects on learning. Cogn. Sci. **12**, 257–285 (1988)

32. Sweller, J.: Cognitive technology: Some procedures for facilitating learning and problem solving in mathematics and science. J. Educ. Psychol. **81**, 457 (1989)

33. Sweller, J.: Cognitive load theory, learning difficulty, and instructional design. Learn. Instr. **4**, 295–312 (1994)

34. Chandler, P., Sweller, J.: Cognitive load theory and the format of instruction. Cogn. Instr. **8**, 293–332 (1991)

35. Quiroga, L.M., Crosby, M.E., Iding, M.K.: Reducing cognitive load. In: Proceedings of the 37th Annual Hawaii International Conference on System Sciences, p. 9 (2004)

36. Ikehara, C.S., Crosby, M.E.: Assessing cognitive load with physiological sensors. In: Proceedings of the 38th Annual Hawaii International Conference on System Sciences, p. 295a (2005)

37. Haapalainen, E., Kim, S., Forlizzi, J.F., Dey, A.K.: Psycho-physiological measures for assessing cognitive load. In: Proceedings of the 12th ACM International Conference on Ubiquitous Computing. pp. 301–310. ACM, New York (2010)

38. Ferreira, E., Ferreira, D., Kim, S., Siirtola, P., Roning, J., Forlizzi, J.F., Dey, A.K.: Assessing real-time cognitive load based on psycho-physiological measures for younger and older adults. In: 2014 IEEE Symposium on Computational Intelligence, Cognitive Algorithms, Mind, and Brain (CCMB), pp. 39–48. IEEE (2014)

39. Wijsman, J., Grundlehner, B., Liu, H., Hermens, H., Penders, J.: Towards mental stress detection using wearable physiological sensors. In: 2011 Annual International Conference of the IEEE Engineering in Medicine and Biology Society, pp. 1798–1801 (2011)

40. Martin, S.: Measuring cognitive load and cognition: metrics for technology-enhanced learning. Educ. Res. Eval. **20**, 592–621 (2014)

41. Paas, F.G.W.C., Merriënboer, J.J.G.V.: Instructional control of cognitive load in the training of complex cognitive tasks. Educ. Psychol. Rev. **6**, 351–371 (1994)

42. Mizuno, K., Tanaka, M., Yamaguti, K., Kajimoto, O., Kuratsune, H., Watanabe, Y.: Mental fatigue caused by prolonged cognitive load associated with sympathetic hyperactivity. Behav. Brain Funct. BBF. **7**, 17 (2011)

43. American College of Health Association: American College Health Association-National College Health Assessment II: Reference Group Executive Summary. American College of Health Association, Hanover (2016)

44. Feldt, R.C.: Development of a brief measure of college stress: the college student stress scale. Psychol. Rep. **102**, 855–860 (2008)

45. Stallman, H.M., Hurst, C.P.: The university stress scale: measuring domains and extent of stress in university students. Aust. Psychol. **51**, 128–134 (2016)

46. Bamber, M.D., Schneider, J.K.: Mindfulness-based meditation to decrease stress and anxiety in college students: a narrative synthesis of the research. Educ. Res. Rev. **18**, 1–32 (2016)

47. Rosen, L., Carrier, L.M., Miller, A., Rokkum, J., Ruiz, A.: Sleeping with technology: cognitive, affective, and technology usage predictors of sleep problems among college students. Sleep Health **2**, 49–56 (2016)

48. Shi, Y., Ruiz, N., Taib, R., Choi, E., Chen, F.: Galvanic skin response (GSR) as an index of cognitive load. In: CHI 2007 Extended Abstracts on Human Factors in Computing Systems, pp. 2651–2656. ACM, New York (2007)

49. Paas, F., Tuovinen, J.E., Tabbers, H., Gerven, P.W.M.V.: Cognitive load measurement as a means to advance cognitive load theory. Educ. Psychol. **38**, 63–71 (2003)

50. Stroop, J.R.: Studies of interference in serial verbal reactions. J. Exp. Psychol. Gen. **121**, 15 (1934)

51. MacLeod, C.M.: Half a century of research on the Stroop effect: an integrative review. Psychol. Bull. **109**, 163 (1991)

52. Karthikeyan, P., Murugappan, M., Yaacob, S.: Descriptive analysis of skin temperature variability of sympathetic nervous system activity in stress. J. Phys. Ther. Sci. **24**, 1341–1344 (2012)

53. Karthikeyan, P., Murugappan, M., Yaacob, S.: Analysis of Stroop color word test-based human stress detection using electrocardiography and heart rate variability signals. Arab. J. Sci. Eng. **39**, 1835–1847 (2014)

54. Wallén, N.H., Held, C., Rehnqvist, N., Hjemdahl, P.: Effects of mental and physical stress on platelet function in patients with stable angina pectoris and healthy controls. Eur. Heart J. **18**, 807–815 (1997)

55. Crabb, E.B., Franco, R.L., Caslin, H.L., Blanks, A.M., Bowen, M.K., Acevedo, E.O.: The effect of acute physical and mental stress on soluble cellular adhesion molecule concentration. Life Sci. **157**, 91–96 (2016)

56. Prinsloo, G.E., Rauch, H.G.L., Lambert, M.I., Muench, F., Noakes, T.D., Derman, W.E.: The effect of short duration heart rate variability (HRV) biofeedback on cognitive performance during laboratory induced cognitive stress. Appl. Cogn. Psychol. **25**, 792–801 (2011)

57. Prinsloo, G.E., Derman, W.E., Lambert, M.I., Rauch, H.G.L.: The effect of a single session of short duration biofeedback-induced deep breathing on measures of heart rate variability during laboratory-induced cognitive stress: a pilot study. Appl. Psychophysiol. Biofeedback **38**, 81–90 (2013)

58. Gwizdka, J.: Using Stroop task to assess cognitive load. In: Proceedings of the 28th Annual European Conference on Cognitive Ergonomics, pp. 219–222. ACM, New York (2010)

59. Renaud, P., Blondin, J.P.: The stress of Stroop performance: physiological and emotional responses to color–word interference, task pacing, and pacing speed. Int. J. Psychophysiol. **27**, 87–97 (1997)

60. Kahneman, D.: Attention to attributes. In: Attention and Effort, pp. 93–111. Prentice-Hall, Englewood Cliffs (1973)

61. Gul, A., Humphreys, G.W.: Practice and colour-word integration in Stroop interference. Psicológica Rev. Metodol. Psicol. Exp. **36**, 37–67 (2015)

62. Yang, E.Z.: Stroop effect - An xhtml 1.0 strict javascript based interactive program. http://ezyang.com/stroop/

63. Feldt, R.C., Koch, C.: Reliability and construct validity of the college student stress scale. Psychol. Rep. **108**, 660–666 (2011)

64. Feldt, R.C., Updegraff, C.: Gender invariance of the college student stress scale. Psychol. Rep. **113**, 486–489 (2013)

65. Huta, V.: When to use hierarchical linear modeling. Tutor. Quant. Methods Psychol. **10**, 13–28 (2014)

# Investigating the Role of Biofeedback and Haptic Stimulation in Mobile Paced Breathing Tools

Antoinette Bumatay[1] and Jinsil Hwaryoung Seo[2(✉)]

[1] Downstream, Portland, OR 97207, USA
aleannab@gmail.com
[2] Texas A&M University, College Station 77843, USA
hwaryoung@tamu.edu

**Abstract.** Previous studies have shown that mindfulness meditation and paced breathing are effective tools for stress management. There are a number of mobile applications currently available that are designed to guide the breath to support these relaxation practices. However, these focus mainly on audio/visual cues and are mostly non-interactive. Our goal is to develop a mobile paced breathing tool focusing on the exploration of haptic cues and biofeedback. We conducted user studies to investigate the effectiveness of the system. This study explores the following questions: Do users prefer control of the breathing rate interval through an on-screen slider (manual mode) or through a physiological sensor (biofeedback mode)? How effective is haptic guidance on its own? And how may the addition of haptic feedback enhance audio-based guidance? Our analysis suggests that while both manual and biofeedback modes are desirable, manual control leads to a greater overall increase in relaxation. Additionally, the findings of this study support the value of haptic guidance in mobile paced breathing tools.

**Keywords:** Haptic guidance · Mobile app · Medication · Paced breathing

## 1 Introduction

Stress is physical response that affects us all in varying degrees throughout our lifetime. Throughout history, people have developed various practices to cope with stress. Many of these focus on bringing awareness to the body and breath. Studies have shown that mindfulness meditation and paced breathing are effective tools for stress management [1, 2]. Within the past year there have been huge strides in development and commercial interest regarding health and fitness portable tools [3]. There are a number of commercial mobile apps currently available designed to guide the breath to support mindfulness meditation and paced breathing practices; however, these focus mainly on audio and visual cues and are non-interactive. And those that are interactive are functional in the sense that they read and display biometric data, but do not use this data to further tailor the experience to the user.

Overall, there has been limited research done towards integrating paced breathing with technology, especially in the realm of haptic use and interactivity in portable

© Springer International Publishing AG 2017
D.D. Schmorrow and C.M. Fidopiastis (Eds.): AC 2017, Part I, LNAI 10284, pp. 287–303, 2017.
DOI: 10.1007/978-3-319-58628-1_23

paced breathing tools. This study focuses on exploring this area by investigating the following questions: What is the role of biofeedback and haptic stimulation in mobile paced breathing tools? Do users prefer control of the breathing rate interval through an on-screen slider (manual mode) or through a physiological sensor (biofeedback mode)? How effective is haptic rhythm guidance on its own? How may the addition of haptic feedback enhance audio-based guidance?

## 2    Background

### 2.1    Living with Stress

Chronic exposure to stress during any stage of life has a negative impact on cognitive and mental health [4]. According to the American Psychology Association, from 2007 to 2012, adults consistently reported their own stress level to be higher than what they believed to be healthy. In 2012, adults rated their own stress level to be 4.9 and a healthy stress level to be 3.6 on a 10-point scale (where 1 is "little to no stress" and 10 is "a great deal of stress"). Approximately 72% of adults surveyed report that their stress level has increased or remained constant in the past five years, and 80% in the past year. 20% report extreme levels of stress. And only 37% feel they are doing an excellent or very good job of stress management. The data reported here support the need for available tools to help control stress.

### 2.2    Traditional Methods of Relaxation

As stress is undeniably universal, there have been many techniques and practices previously developed to assist in stress management and promotion of relaxation.

The use of manipulating and/or bringing awareness to the body to help calm the mind is a common theme in traditional relaxation methods. Through the centuries, physical practices have persevered as a common release of stress. The most well-known of these practices is likely yoga. Although there are many variations, ultimately yoga is considered a moving meditation, focusing on the body and the breath. According to many in the field, yoga is an effective tool in improving stress, anxiety, and mental health, and comparable to other relaxation therapies such as cognitive behavioral therapy [5, 6]. Similarly, the Chinese martial art tai chi is another type of moving meditation, bringing awareness to the breath and movements. Studies have also indicated that tai chi exercise may lead to improvements in stress and overall wellbeing [7, 8].

A common point between the previously mentioned practices is the breath. It appears that this is one of our primary contacts with our parasympathetic nervous system. Often during bouts of stress or panic attacks, our sympathetic nervous system activates "fight or flight" mode. Breathing is the only component of the autonomic nervous system that can be controlled consciously. Practicing yogic paced breathing or mindfulness daily can help form a habit that will be useful during a panic attack, as control of the breath stimulates the vagus nerve which interfaces with the parasympathetic nervous system that is in control of "rest and digest" mode. In other words, this helps trigger a relaxation response [9]. Paced breathing has been shown to be a valid tool in managing stress and anxiety [1].

The relationship of the body to its environment can be obtained through bringing awareness to the senses. Aural and visual stimulation for relaxation have been deeply investigated in research. Although, tactile exploration is underexplored in this particular area, there is evidence of the sense of touch being incorporated in traditional relaxation practices. Touch is an extremely personal and intimate sense. It is used to create a personal space, only experienced to those directly exposed to the action. The use of therapeutic touch is often used to help people relax [10, 11]. Similarly, the tactile sense has also been incorporated in meditation through the physical manipulation of objects with the hands, such as the creation of a zen garden or the handling of baoding/meditation balls and prayer beads [12].

## 2.3    Technology Driven Methods of Relaxation

Recently, there has been a rise in interest in self-monitoring and self-management, as well as non-illness focused methodologies to mental health. In this age of technology and innovation, there exists a lot of opportunity to supplement existing practices. This section first discusses the importance of biofeedback by reviewing previous studies and commercial products. It then reviews current innovative methods for paced breathing applications for mobile devices, and identifies holes in the literature that need investigation.

### Interactive Methods Through Biofeedback

Before delving into the various interactive installations and portable devices, an important distinction must be clarified between adaptive and functional interactivity. This distinction is adapted from Tim Guay's Web Publishing Paradigm. In the case of a functional system, "the user interacts with the system to accomplish a goal or set of goals." The user is provided feedback on their progress towards the goal. In the case of meditation and paced breathing systems, the user is provided a guide, and is made aware of their performance through some form. Although Guay recognizes that "the boundary between functional and adaptive interactivity is blurred," the primary difference between the two is that the adaptive system will modify its own behavior based on some input from the user.

### Functional Interactivity

A few applications are available commercially that offer functional interactivity. The company HeartMath has developed an iPhone application called Inner Balance that uses an ear sensor to capture Heart Rate Variability. The application offers visual guidance for the breath of an expanding and contracting colorful wheel. It also shows real time feedback of the user's heart rate [13]. HeartMath also offers a standalone device line entitled emWave. This device uses heart rate data and provides feedback through graphs and light. It also has an additional software component that allows access to coherence games [14]. RESPeRATE is another commercial paced breathing application. It has a breath sensor and features a simple display with breathe-in/out graphics and audio tones to aide in pacing the breath [15].

**Adaptive Interactivity**

In a study entitled Breathe with the Ocean, three different systems were investigated: a fixed-rate breathing guidance system, an adaptive breathing following system, and an adaptive-rate breathing guidance system. The system featured an environment with audio (ocean wave sounds), haptic (touch blanket), and visual (light) stimuli. It was found that a lack of personalization in a breathing guidance system appeared to be a significant drawback since different users have quite different inhale/exhale patterns and optimal respiration rates. A user can easily become dizzy and uncomfortable if they force their breath to follow a rate or pattern that they cannot adapt to.

Aside from breathing guidance systems, there have been other attempts to help the user bring awareness to their breath through an adaptive system. Sonic Cradle is a large installation designed to cultivate a meditative experience. The user was instructed to wear a breath sensor and was invited to lie in a hammock in a chamber of complete darkness. Users were able to shape peaceful soundscapes using their own respiration [16]. Although there has been limited exploration in the area of adaptive interactivity in portable meditation tools, there is a work-in-progress paper featuring the Heartbeat Sphere [17]. It is spherical object designed to assess and reflect a person's heart rate through soft pulsing vibrations and colorful lights.

**Innovative Methods of Mobile Tools for Paced Breathing**

There has been some effort in consumer companies as well as the academic community to incorporate technology in non-interactive and interactive systems specifically for paced breathing. The primary systems covered in this section focuses on various portable handheld devices that are designed to bring awareness to the user of their own breath.

There are numerous commercial mobile phone applications available in the Google Play Store and the Apple App Store that offer paced breathing guidance. All the mobile phone applications investigated incorporate an option for audio guidance. Audio utilized ranges from guided meditation voice narrative to natural sounds (e.g. water, birds) to percussive sounds (e.g. bell chimes, gongs, meditation bowls). Visual guidance often appears in the form of meters filling and emptying, objects expanding and contracting, or animated graphs. Few offer haptic components, and those that do have abrupt pulses that feel jarring. You Can't Force Calm [18] was an exploratory study that designed and evaluated techniques to support respiratory regulation to reduce stress and increase parasympathetic tone. It incorporated breath sensor input and visual and audio feedback. Evidence from this study supported that auditory guidance was more effective than visual at creating self-reported calm. This was attributed to the users' ability to effectively map sound to respiration, thereby reducing cognitive load and mental exertion. Although visual guidance led to more respiratory change, it resulted in less subjective calm. Thus, motivating users to exert physical or mental efforts may counter the calming effects of slow breathing. It would be interesting to further this exploration of mobile tools into the physical and subjective effects of haptic stimulation. As mentioned previously, personalization of a breathing guidance system is important. Some commercial mobile phone applications offer an option to manually adjust the breathing interval; however, there are currently no mobile tools available that is similar to the adaptive system investigated in the installation Breathe with the Ocean [19]. With the rise in emerging technologies in portable fitness and health, this realm is worth further exploration.

# 3 Case Study

Our goal is to develop a mobile paced breathing tool focusing on the exploration of haptic cues and biofeedback. We conducted user studies to investigate the effectiveness of the system.

## 3.1 System Design

A simple paced breathing application was built in Android Studio to aide in the exploration of these questions. We developed two modes of interaction: manual and biofeedback. The application also has the ability to produce an audio, haptic, or audio-haptic breathing guide. Figure 1 is a diagram of the overall system.

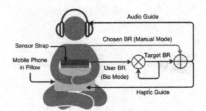

**Fig. 1.** System diagram.

## 3.2 Interaction Type

**Manual Interaction**

In manual interaction mode the user is initially prompted to follow a standard breathing interval of 6 breaths per minute (BPM), an optimal breathing rate for higher HRV values. The user has the ability to manually lengthen or shorten the interval using an unmarked slider. The user may adjust the interval at any time, and the breathing guide is immediately adjusted accordingly.

**Biofeedback Interaction**

Prior to the main session, the user is prompted to breathe regularly for one minute. During this time, the application determines the user's current breathing rate by communicating via Bluetooth with an external physiological sensor, the Zephyr BioHarness. During the main session, the breathing guide is initially set to match the user's breathing rate, slowly increasing the interval to slow down the user's breath. In 30 s intervals throughout the duration of the session, the program monitors the user's ability to match the guide and adjusts the breathing interval accordingly.

### 3.3   Modalities

**Audio**
Sound is utilized in the majority of applications currently on the market. Percussive sounds are a commonly associated with meditation and paced breathing. For this application, the gong chimes used were found on FreeSound.org by D.J. Griffin. We decided on two similar gong sounds in different pitches to help distinguish the inhalation from the exhalation prompt.

**Haptics**
The Immersion Haptic Development Platform for Android was utilized in order to obtain control the vibration of the mobile phone's motor. After testing various haptic patterns, we decided to have the haptic sensations complement the audio. As it has been previously shown that vibration can enhance the experience of audio [19, 20], we decided to have the vibrations mimic the gongs, ringing deeply then fading off. This was made possible by the MagSweepEffect function from the Immersion Haptic SDK.

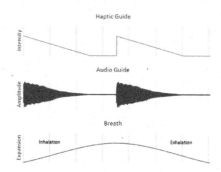

**Fig. 2.**   Audio and haptic patterns for each group.

### 3.4   Creating the Breathing Guide

In order to create the breathing guide, a timer was used in order to trigger the event. The produced event would include audio and/or haptics (Fig. 2). The timer trigger interval was calculated based on the guide's breathing interval (Eq. 1), where the breathing interval is milliseconds per breath and the breathing rate is in breaths per minute. The breathing interval was either chosen by the user via the on-screen slider (manual mode) or dependent on the user's breath via sensor (biofeedback mode) as explained in the biofeedback interaction section.

Equation 1. Conversion of the breathing interval (milliseconds per breath) from the breathing rate (breaths per minute)

$$Breathing\, Interval = \frac{60000}{Breathing\, Rate} \tag{1}$$

## 3.5    Physical Design

After some preliminary user testing with the mobile phone application, we observed some awkwardness in holding a mobile phone for an extended period of time. We decided to create a pillow encasement for the phone in order to allow the user to fully relax with their hands comfortably wrapped around the pillow. This would also soften and amplify the phone's vibrations. A store-bought travel pillow was modified with a pocket along the seam to hold the mobile device in the center of the pillow. Figure 3 displays the final modified pillow in use by the participant.

 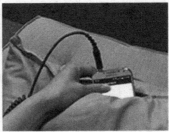

**Fig. 3.** Final modified pillow.

# 4    User Study

## 4.1    Recruitment

For our user study, we recruited 21 university students (14 females and 7 males). Users were separated into three different groups based on a short pre-filter questionnaire. The survey asked the user their self-identified general level of stress (low, medium, high). The participant also noted any previous experience in paced breathing techniques. indicates the division of the participants. Each response was assigned a numerical value between 1 and 5. In the case of deep breathing experience, 1 indicated no experience and 5 indicated a lot of experience. In the case of general level of stress, 1 indicated very low stress level, while 5 indicated a very high stress level. Participants were divided in order to create balance between the three groups. The average deep breathing experience of Group 1, 2, and 3 are all 2.4. The average general level of stress of Group 1, 2, and 3 are 3.3, 3.6, and 3.7 respectively.

## 4.2    Methods

The study concentrated on one dependent variable (stress) and two independent variables (device output and type of interaction). The possible device outputs included the following: haptic, audio, or audio-haptic. The interaction type included manual or biofeedback. Table 1 provides descriptions of each user study case. The study lasted three days for each participant. Table 2 illustrates the division of the cases among each group. Groups contained 3 to 4 participants each.

**Table 1.** Descriptions of user study cases.

| | | Device output | | |
| --- | --- | --- | --- | --- |
| | | A. Haptic | B. Audio | C. Both |
| Interaction type | 1. Manual | Device produces vibration User can manually adjust interval | Device produces sound User can manually adjust interval | Device produces vibration and sound User can manually adjust interval |
| | 2.Biofeedback | Device produces vibration and changes interval based on BR | Device produces sound and changes interval based on BR | Devices produces vibration and sound and changes interval based on BR |

**Table 2.** Group timeline and division of user study cases.

| Groups | Day 1 | Day 2 | Day 3 |
| --- | --- | --- | --- |
| *Group 1.1* | A1 | A2 | Choice of A1 or A2 |
| *Group 1.2* | A2 | A1 | Choice of A1 or A2 |
| *Group 2.1* | B1 | B2 | Choice of B1 or B2 |
| *Group 2.2* | B2 | B1 | Choice of B1 or B2 |
| *Group 3.1* | C1 | C2 | Choice of C1 or C2 |
| *Group 3.2* | C2 | C1 | Choice of C1 or C2 |

Participants were invited to make themselves comfortable in the designated "relaxation station" filled with blankets and a variety of pillows. In order to eliminate environmental noise from the hallways and rooms next door, the user was instructed to utilize noise isolating headphones and a small nearby speaker played various brown and pink ambient noise tracks. The participant was left alone in the area to ensure additional privacy during use of the app. Each participant visited three times and each visit was 1 h.

## 4.3  Data Collection

Both quantitative and qualitative data were used for analysis. Quantitative data collected includes the following: user preference (choice on Day 3), sensor data (heart rate variance, breathing rate, posture), and a short survey (before and after each sit). The short survey consisted of a 5-point Likert scale with a list of adjectives adapted from the Stress Arousal Checklist [21] and an analogue scale for the user to personally rate their relaxation level. Qualitative data was gathered through a series of on-site interviews. A preliminary interview was conducted during the first meeting in order for the user to expand on their experience level in deep breathing and other stress management techniques. A general feedback interview was conducted at the end of each session to discuss the overall experience, what they enjoyed and what they disliked of that particular session. On Day 3 an exit interview was conducted to discuss the overall experience of participation throughout the study. The user elaborated on their last day interaction choice. They also noted what they specifically liked and disliked about both interaction versions of the application. The participant also indicated whether or not they would use this application in their daily lives, and if they would recommend it to their family or friends. The recorded interview data was coded and analyzed focusing on key themes arising from the participants' experiences.

# 5  Results

The results gathered from the conducted user study are divided into four main sections: user group, qualitative data, relaxation response, and physical response.

## 5.1  User Group

Since the user groups were initially chosen to be purely divided based on the user's average stress level and previous experience with paced breathing practices, each group resulted in an unbalanced gender distribution. However, the average emotional and physical results between each gender did not show a significant discrepancy.

## 5.2  Qualitative Data

User interviews were transcribed and coded. Key phrases and themes were extracted from the answer for each open-ended question. All responses were divided into three main sections: interaction mode, breathing guide modality, and overall experience.

### Interaction Modes

*Manual Mode:* Majority of participants had positive feedback about the manual interaction mode. *Only* five participants did not have any positive comments regarding the manual interaction. Twelve users mentioned they liked having the ability to manually control the system, and six of them specifically added that they liked that they could set it at what they personally found comfortable. For instance, some revealed they did not feel comfortable taking long deep breaths at all, noting that they felt more relaxed when taking medium to shallow breaths. Participant R commented, *"I liked how you could control the interval of the breathing, because some people just have massive lungs and other people just shallow breathe all the time... I am a shallow breather, so I just turned it down."*

*Biofeedback Mode:* The majority of participants, fifteen users, had at least one positive comment to provide about the biofeedback interaction. Eleven participants mentioned that they liked the idea of the application easing them into the deep breathing. Participant Q elaborated, *"I felt that it calmed me down more. From going from a normal - what I would usually be breathing at - and then taking me down steadily. I liked that better than me having to think about it."* Six participants reflected that they enjoyed how the system challenged them to help them breathe deeper. Another five users mentioned they liked that there was less to think about. Five participants revealed they felt the biofeedback interaction was more calming. Four participants added that there was a goal or felt they were more focused. A couple users noted that they liked the variation in the pattern, and another couple felt like the rhythm was more natural and less mechanic. Only six users made no comment regarding what they liked about the biofeedback interaction.

### Modality

To iterate, each user only experienced one type of modality for the duration of the study. However, a few users made comments directly addressing the type of feedback they experienced.

*Haptic:* Three users commented that the vibration pulses from the pillow reminded them of a heartbeat or a cat purring. Participant A commented that she liked how subtle the vibrations felt, reflecting *"Normally when I try to meditate on my own I get severely distracted. And I try to set a timer. Do a similar thing... But I liked how the vibrations made you aware that you were doing something. But you weren't really aware of it."* One user initially disliked the vibrations because it reminded him of a phone ringing. He explained, *"The phone vibrating itself is stressful to me. Because when a phone is vibrating it needs immediate attention, so.... I'm not very comfortable with removing my stress with that type of stimulus."* However, the same user said by the end of the session, *"Once I remove it from that association, I was able to relax my body a little more."*

*Audio:* A few people noted specifically that they did like the gong chimes, describing them as *"environmental,"* *"smooth,"* *"relaxing,"* or *"pleasant."* However, some users did not like it at all. They felt it was not very entertaining and a little robotic. Three people said it would be nice if there was more to listen to, like natural sounds or background music. Participant P noted, *"I liked the tones. But I kind of wanted something a little more to listen to... I liked the tones helped me focus. And stay on track. But it wasn't very entertaining to listen to."*

*Audio-Haptic:* Two people commented how they liked how the sounds and the vibrations worked together, helping them feel more immersed. Participant B reflected, *"It was so relaxing. The sounds and the vibrations made it easy to focus on something besides your thoughts. Or anything else. And it was very calming."* Two people specified that the vibrations were actually their favorite part out of the audio-haptic system. They liked that there was an extra something they could feel to complement the sound. Participant H commented, *"I actually found the gong noise a lot more relaxing. I guess maybe that's why I was able to really not think about it. But for some reason I realized this is actually a good noise. I like this. And I felt that had the vibrations not been there I don't know if it would have the same effect."*

### Preferred Interaction Mode

Each participant experienced both types of interactions: manual and biofeedback. On the third day, they chose which interaction to experience they wanted to experience a second time. Out of the 21 participants, 11 chose the manual mode, while 10 chose the biofeedback mode. Two participants clarified that they did not have a preference over either interaction mode. Removing these two users from the preferred interaction count still leaves the count at 10 (48% of participants) for the manual mode and 9 (43% of participants) for the biofeedback mode.

## 5.3   Relaxation Response

The stress survey contained an analog scale that read very tense to very relaxed. Participants marked their current relaxation state on the scale before and after each meditation sit. The participant's mark was converted to a real number on a scale of 1.00 (very tense) to 5.00 (very relaxed). We calculated the user's subjective change in relaxation by the difference of the converted values. Again, this value was again normalized then mapped to a ±10 scale. In general, each group experienced an increase in relaxation state. Overall, users did feel an increased state of relaxation. On average, the three groups were fairly close to each other. The audio group led the greatest average increase in subjective relaxation at 3.8, followed by the haptic group at 3.6 and the audio-haptic group at 3.3. However, if we were to break down these groups further by interaction mode, the haptic group obtained the greatest average change in relaxation at a value of 4.4. This is closely followed by the audio manual group at 4.1. The lowest value was the haptic biofeedback sessions at 2.7. The manual and biofeedback sessions of the audio-haptic group yielded very similar numbers, 3.4 and 3.3 respectively.

## 5.4   Physical Response

*Breathing Rate:* Users did experience a decrease in breathing rate during the session overall. Figure 4 indicates a breakdown of the average breathing rate values observed in each modality and interaction mode.

Difficulty of the session indicates the observed level of difficulty the user had in following the breathing guide. Each session was described using the following adjectives: gradual, flat, and bumpy (Fig. 5). A gradual section is characterized by a steady decrease in average BR. A flat section is characterized by a stable value of average BR. A bumpy section is characterized by an unstable BR.

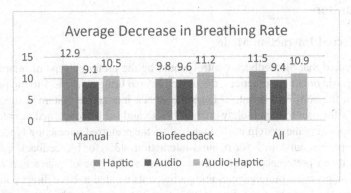

**Fig. 4.** Average highest, lowest, and change in breathing rate (BR) values by group and interaction mode.

**Fig. 5.** Graph descriptions of breathing rate (BR) over the session duration: (a) flat, (b) gradual, and (c) bumpy.

Performance during the manual sessions was divided up into five different categories based on the order observed of the previous characteristics: (1) gradual and flat, (2) flat, (3) bumpy and flat, (4) flat and bumpy, and (5) bumpy. Similarly, biofeedback sessions were divided into the following five categories: (1) gradual and flat, (2) gradual, (3) bumpy and gradual, (4) gradual and bumpy, and (5) bumpy. Gradual and flat patterns are desirable, as it indicates the user was able to follow the guide within reason. They were then reclassified as smooth.

In the majority of sessions, the participant was able to follow the guide. 57% of sessions in the haptic and the audio-haptic guide resulted in smooth breath patterns. This was closely followed by 52% of sessions in the audio group. 33% of users in the audio-haptic group had a breath pattern classified as bumpy then smooth. 24% of sessions in the audio-haptic group the inverse breath pattern, smooth then bumpy. No one in the audio-haptic group experienced a completely bumpy breath pattern. Looking at the audio group, the remaining sessions were evenly split: 17% bumpy then smooth, 19% smooth then bumpy, and 19% bumpy then smooth. In the haptic sessions, 25% of the sessions were classified as bumpy then smooth, and 24% of the sessions were classified as completely bumpy. Only 5% of the haptic sessions were considered smooth then bumpy.

Difficulty following was calculated by determining the fraction of time the user's breath was bumpy throughout the duration of the session. It is on a scale from 0 (completely smooth) to 10 (completely bumpy during the majority of the session).

## 6   Discussion

### 6.1   Preferred Interaction Mode

It was expected that biofeedback control would be the preferred type of interaction. In particular yogic breathing practices, the objective is to bring awareness to the present by focusing on the body and breath. If the biofeedback interactive system is successful, it would allow the user to focus solely on their breath and not be concerned or preoccupied about manipulating the system itself. In actuality, the preferred interaction type was split among the participants: 48% for manual interaction, 43% for biofeedback interaction, and 9% with no preference. It appears that the favored type of interaction is simply dependent on personal preference. Some participants wanted to have direct control over choosing the breathing rate and did not want to release any control to the system. Other participants liked that they could give up some control, and just focus on their breath.

Both types of interaction are still desirable among users. Of the twenty-one participants, sixteen made at least one positive comment regarding the manual interaction, closely followed by fifteen users concerning the biofeedback interaction. One of the participants who had no preference over a group stated, "I like having the option of both. If I really wanted to relax, and I only had nine minutes, then I'd want to do the [manual] one because I would just start right there. But if I maybe had time to do both, then I would start with the [biofeedback] one and slow my breathing down and then do the [manual] one again after it's already there." It appears that the majority of participants liked the option of being able to choose their own breathing rate to follow, but also liked the idea of easing into the deep breathing.

The main complaint regarding the biofeedback system was that it started off too quickly. This perspective could be a result of comparison with prior exposure to the training application used in the informational section of the first day. The breathing guide in the training session was set to 6 BPM. Additionally, when user enters the manual session the breathing rate is initially set to 6 BPM. As a result of having either or both of these experiences before the biofeedback system, the breathing guide would be alarmingly fast. This is interesting, because essentially the system is mirroring back their current breathing rate. Adjustments could be made to the system to make a maximum breathing rate that is still comfortably slow, as to not startle the participant. One participant made an astute observation regarding their breath: *"I felt like yesterday when I was doing [the manual session]. I was relaxed but it was like a little boring. But this gave me something to work towards. Like it showed me how fast my breathing was. And I was like whoa! Okay! I need to slow it down. So yeah, I did like that. I thought it was interesting."* As the system carried on, six users commented that they felt that the system began to prompt them to breathe too slowly. Additionally, four participants explicitly said they felt uncomfortable as a result of the system starting too fast or too slow. This is again the result of system's current limitations. The system would increase the breathing rate if people had a hard time matching it; however, once they were able to reach the target breathing rate, it would challenge the participant to breathe slower once more. A solution could be to stabilize the system once it finds a good match.

## 6.2 Haptic Guidance

As touch is incredibly intimate and important for well-being. By stimulating the tactile sense, the user is provided a personal space where the experience is solely their own. The results of the study support our hypothesis that haptic guidance would be effective on its own. In fact, overall, it appears that the manual haptic guidance was the most effective out of all interaction modality cases.

Users in the haptic group noted they liked the pulses because they were subtle or reminiscent of the cat purring or a heartbeat. There does appear to be a negative initial association with a phone vibrating. Some participants commented that they felt that they were receiving a call. However, by the end of the three sessions, this negative association was faded once the participants became familiar with the vibration pulses as a breathing guide. Another participant mentioned that the fact that the phone was encased in a pillow did help remove this negative association as well.

Out of the three modality groups, the majority of participants in the haptic group were partial to the manual interaction. All seven members of the haptic group had a positive comment regarding the manual interaction mode, compared to only five and four participants in the audio and audio-haptic group respectively. Users in the haptic group also had the least amount of negative comments to give about the manual interaction mode: three users had something negative to say, compared to five and four users in the audio and audio-haptic group respectively. However, the majority of participants in the haptic group did not like the biofeedback interaction at all. Only 23% of the positive comments regarding the biofeedback system were from the haptic group. Additionally, only one haptic user liked that the system eased into the deep breathing, compared to six and four of the audio and audio-haptic group respectively. The haptic group's preference for the manual interaction is also indicative in the emotional responses for both calculated and subjective relaxation.

Out of the three modality groups, the haptic group's manual and biofeedback sessions had the widest discrepancy in relaxation increase. For the average change in calculated relaxation, there was a difference of 1.3 between manual and biofeedback sessions, while the audio and audio-haptic group had gaps of 0.1 and 0.6 respectively. Similarly for the average change in subjective relaxation, the haptic group's manual and biofeedback sessions had the greatest difference of 1.7, while audio and audio-haptic groups had a gap of 0.7 and 0.1 respectively. It is noteworthy that the manual haptic sessions yielded the highest average change in both calculated and subjective relaxation overall.

It is interesting to also note that these differences in the haptic manual and biofeedback sessions are also reflected in the physical responses examined. Overall, participants in the manual haptic session on average achieved the greatest change in decreasing their breathing rate by 12.9 BPM. The haptic group also had the widest discrepancy, 3.1 BPM, between interaction modes for change in breathing rate. The audio and audio-haptic group had a gap of 0.5 BPM and 1.3 BPM respectively.

On average, the haptic group did have the hardest time following the breathing guide. 24% of the session breathing patterns was described as completely bumpy, versus 19 and 0% for audio and audio-haptic groups respectively. However, it is interesting to notice that only 5% of haptic sessions had a breathing pattern of smooth then bumpy, as compared to 19 and 24% of users. This might indicate that if the participant has a good handle on following the guide, they are more focused throughout the duration of the session.

### 6.3   Audio-Haptic Guidance

It was expected that the addition of haptic feedback would enhance the audio based guidance. There have been a few studies that support the effectiveness of vibroacoustic therapy for relaxation [22, 23] and that the simultaneous stimulation of the auditory and tactile senses can be more effective than stimulating one at a time [19, 20]. Additionally, in the particular case of paced breathing, in the previously mentioned study, Breathe with the Ocean [20] that featured a breathing guidance installation, it was noted that most users found the synchronization between the wave-like patterns from the haptic blanket and the audio waves pleasing.

The general feedback interviews from our study supported the comfortable effect from the combined stimulation. A few participants remarked that they liked how the sounds and vibrations worked together, leading to a more immersed feeling. Participant H reflected, *"I actually found the gong noise a lot more relaxing... for some reason I realized this is actually a good noise. I like this... And I felt that... had the vibrations not been there I don't know if it would have the same effect."*

41% of the positive comments for the biofeedback interaction came from the audio-haptic group, compared to 35% and 23% of the audio and the haptic group respectively. They also had the less amount of negative things to say about the biofeedback interaction: 22% versus 44 and 33% for the audio and the haptic group respectively. Only one participant in the audio-haptic group commented that the system started off too fast, compared to four users in the audio and three users in the haptic group.

Interestingly, the audio-haptic group experienced the greatest increase in calculated relaxation for biofeedback sessions, 2.2 versus 1.6 and 1.9 for the haptic and audio group respectively. However, the audio-haptic group also experienced the least amount of calculated relaxation in manual sessions, 1.6 versus 2.9 and 2.0. For subjective relaxation, audio-haptic manual and biofeedback sessions resulted in a similar value, 3.4 and 3.3 respectively. This is interesting to note because the other two groups experienced a 0.7 to 1.7 difference between manual and biofeedback sessions.

Overall, the audio-haptic group did have a significantly easier time following the guide out of the three modalities in both interaction modes with a difficulty value of 0.8 overall versus 2.8 and 2.7. However, it did not necessarily enhance relaxation more over one stimulation alone, and in some cases hindered it. This supports the previous results [18], in which smooth controlled breath does not necessarily lead to a greater sense of relaxation. That being said, participants still expressed pleasure of experiencing both stimulations simultaneously.

# 7   Conclusion

This study investigated the integration of biofeedback and haptic stimulation in mobile paced breathing tools. In order to explore these areas, a mobile phone application was developed. The application was highly received overall among participants. On average, all combinations of interaction and breathing guide modalities resulted in an increase in calculated and subjective relaxation.

Our qualitative analysis suggests that both manual and biofeedback modes are desirable. However, the manual mode resulted in greater average calculated and subjective relaxation. Manual mode was observed to be easier to follow overall. This suggests that biofeedback implementation is not vital in attributing to a greater sense of well-being. This information could potentially aide in therapeutic settings, as it may not be necessary for counselors and the high stress population to invest in expensive biofeedback equipment for stress relief.

The findings of this study also support the effectiveness of haptic guidance on its own. Although, the haptic breathing guide was observed to be the most difficult to follow, manual haptic guidance resulted in the greatest calculated and subjective relaxation. It also led to the greatest decrease in breathing rate. This may be greatly applicable to various situational use. There may be certain conditions where audio guidance is not viable (e.g. too much environmental noise or desire for silence). Many people also have a personal mobile device which contains a motor, and thus, can take advantage of haptic guidance benefits.

Lastly, simultaneous audio-haptic guidance led to a greater decrease in breathing rate over audio guidance, and was the overall easiest to follow. However, it did not necessarily enhance relaxation more over one stimulation alone, and in some cases hindered it. Multimodal audio-haptic stimulation may be beneficial in aiding focus to meet a particular task, but this may impede the user's full potential to relax.

## 8  Limitations and Future Work

There are limitations with the interview and survey data due to self-report error. Participants may also have suffered from the "John Henry" effect, as they entered the study expecting to relax which may have provided a bias. There were also ceiling values in the survey questions, which affected responses of users who came into the session already in a relaxed state. The analog scale design also led some users to fill in the circles rather than mark along the line, resulting in an integer value rather than a real number. In some cases, verbal instruction was necessary to prevent this. It would have also been effective to video record the meditation sit in order to observe how the user interacted with the app. It would also be good as a cross reference to help explain random peaks in the sensor data.

There are also additional limitations with the sensor used. There may be some error with the readings and delay in response of the user's current breathing rate. There is also potentially a timestamp discrepancy between the data from the sensor and from the mobile device. In future work, it would be beneficial to create a file within the application to contain start and end times along with the sensor and guide values. This would also allow us to get a more insight into how close the user was to the guide they were given.

Future work is necessary in order to validate the significance of our findings on a larger sample scale. It would also be beneficial to make improvements to the biofeedback system behavior to eliminate discomfort with the guide moving too slowly or quickly. Future work should also expose participants to experience all three modalities.

## References

1. Grossman, P.: Mindfulness-based stress reduction and health benefits: a meta-analysis. J. Psychosom. Res. **57**(1), 35–43 (2004)
2. Brown, R.P.: Sudarshan kriya yogic breathing in the treatment of stress, anxiety, and depression: part ii-clinical applications and guidelines. J. Altern. Complement. Med. **11**(4), 711–717 (2005)
3. Pitstick, B.: Research Paper: CES 2014 Wearable and Fitness Tech Trends - Going Mainstream —Moor Insights and Strategy (2015). http://www.moorinsightsstrategy.com/research-paper-ces-2014-wearable-fitness-tech-trends-going-mainstream/. Accessed 30 Jan 2015

4. Lupien, S.J., McEwen, B.S., Gunnar, M.R., Heim, C.: Effects of stress throughout the lifespan on the brain, behaviour and cognition. Nat. Rev. Neurosci. **10**(6), 434–445 (2009)
5. Granath, J.: Stress management: a randomized study of cognitive behavioural therapy and yoga. Cogn. Behav. Ther. **35**(1), 3–10 (2006)
6. Smith, C.: A randomised comparative trial of yoga and relaxation to reduce stress and anxiety. Complement. Ther. Med. **15**(2), 77–83 (2007)
7. Jin, P.: Efficacy of Tai Chi, brisk walking, meditation, and reading in reducing mental and emotional stress. J. Psychosom. Res. **36**(4), 361–370 (1992)
8. Sandlund, E.S.: The effects of Tai Chi Chuan relaxation and exercise on stress responses and well-being: an overview of research. Int. J. Stress Manag. **7**(2), 139–149 (2000)
9. Seaward, B.: Managing Stress: Principles and Strategies for Health and Well-Being-BOOK ALONE. Jones & Bartlett Publishers, Burlington (2008)
10. Gagne, D., Toye, R.C.: The effects of therapeutic touch and relaxation therapy in reducing anxiety. Arch. Psychiatr. Nurs. **8**(3), 184–189 (1994)
11. Meek, S.S.: Effects of slow stroke back massage on relaxation in hospice clients. Image. J. Nurs. Scholarsh. **25**(1), 17–22 (1993)
12. Wernik, U.: The use of prayer beads in psychotherapy. Ment. Health Relig. Cult. **12**(4), 359–368 (2009)
13. Inner Balance: Inner Balance: An Innovate Approach to Improving Wellness Through Training, Education and Self Monitoring. HeartMath (2013). http://www.heartmath.com/innerbalance/. Accessed 13 Jan 2015
14. emWave: emWave Technology. HeartMath (2008). http://www.heartmath.com/emwave-technology/. Accessed 13 Jan 2015
15. RESPeRATE: What is RESPeRATE. InterCure, Inc. (2014). http://www.resperate.com/what-is-resperate. Accessed 13 Jan 2015
16. Vidyarthi, J., Riecke, B.E., Gromala, D.: Sonic Cradle: designing for an immersive experience of meditation by connecting respiration to music. In: Proceedings of Designing Interactive Systems Conference, pp. 408–417. ACM, June 2012
17. Thieme, A., Wallace, J., Johnson, P., Lindley, S., McCarthy, J., Olivier, P., Meyer, T.D.: Can we introduce mindfulness practice through digital design. In: Proceedings of BCS HCI (2012)
18. Wongsuphasawat, K., Gamburg, A., Moraveji, N.: You can't force calm: designing and evaluating respiratory regulating interfaces for calming technology. In: Adjunct Proceedings of 25th Annual ACM Symposium on User Interface Software and Technology, pp. 69–70. ACM, October 2012
19. Dijk, E.O., Weffers-Albu, A., De Zeeuw, T.: A tactile actuation blanket to intensify movie experiences with personalised tactile effects. In: Demonstration Papers: Proceedings of 3rd International Conference on Intelligent Technologies for Interactive Entertainment, June 2009
20. Dijk, E.O., Nijholt, A., van Erp, J.B., Kuyper, E., van Wolferen, G.: Audio-tactile stimuli to improve health and well-being (2010)
21. King, M.G., Burrows, G.D., Stanley, G.V.: Measurement of stress and arousal: validation of the stress/arousal adjective checklist. Br. J. Psychol. **74**(4), 473–479 (1983)
22. Wigram, A.L.: The effects of vibroacoustic therapy on clinical and non-clinical populations. Doctoral dissertation, University of London (1996)
23. Patrick, G.: The effects of vibroacoustic music on symptom reduction. IEEE Eng. Med. Biol. Mag. **18**(2), 97–100 (1999)

# Pupil Dilation and Task Adaptation

Cyrus K. Foroughi[1]([⊠]), Joseph T. Coyne[1], Ciara Sibley[1],
Tatana Olson[2], Cory Moclaire[2], and Noelle Brown[3]

[1] U.S. Naval Research Laboratory, Washington, DC, USA
{cyrus.foroughi.ctr, joseph.coyne,
ciara.sibley}@nrl.navy.mil
[2] Naval Aerospace Medical Institute, Pensacola, FL, USA
{tatana.m.olson.mil, cory.m.moclaire.ctr}@mail.mil
[3] U.S. Naval Research Laboratory, Stennis Space Center, MS, USA
noelle.brown@nrlssc.navy.mil

**Abstract.** Individuals adapt to tasks as they repeatedly practice them resulting in increased overall performance. Historically, time and accuracy are two metrics used to measure these adaptations. Here we show preliminary evidence that changes in pupil dilation may be able to capture within-task learning changes. A group of enlisted Sailors and Marines completed forty-eight trials of a cognitive task while their pupils were recorded with a low-cost eye tracking system. As expected, accuracy increased across trials while reaction times significantly decreased. We found a strong, negative correlation of pupil size across the trials. These data suggest that changes in pupil dilation can be used to measure within-task adaptations.

**Keywords:** Pupillometry · Pupil dilation · Task adaptation

## 1 Introduction

When individuals repeatedly complete a task, they improve over time [1]. Understanding how individuals adapt or learn a task has been of long interest to researchers. Traditionally, adapting to a task has been captured by analyzing changes in reaction time and/or accuracy. For example, in neuroscience and psychology, the serial reaction task is used to assess attentional abilities, and researchers often analyze the "learning" of the task by measuring changes in reaction time [2, 3]. Here we propose a different metric that may capture within-task adaptations: changes in pupil dilation.

### 1.1 Cognitive Load

Cognitive load has been defined as "a multidimensional construct representing the load that performing a particular task imposes on the learner's cognitive system [4]". Cognitive load increases as task difficulty increases. Task difficulty can be manipulated in many ways. For example, by increasing the number of objects or elements and individual has to interact with while performing a task.

D.D. Schmorrow and C.M. Fidopiastis (Eds.): AC 2017, Part I, LNAI 10284, pp. 304–311, 2017.
DOI: 10.1007/978-3-319-58628-1_24

In contrast, cognitive load should decrease as an individual repeatedly completes a task over time [5, 6]. Initially, individuals are expected to exert more mental effort as they are adjusting to a new task. As individuals practice, the mental effort required to complete the task should decrease because they will be incorporating new skills and strategies to complete the task. Further, the task should become more automatic over time [6], and reliance on working memory should decrease as they become experts at the task [7].

## 1.2  Pupillometry

Pupillometry, or measuring changes in pupil size, can be used to capture changes in task difficulty and cognitive load. Dating back to the seminal work by Hess and Polt [8], researchers have repeatedly shown that as task difficulty increases, pupils dilate or increase in size. Further, Chen and Epps [9] manipulated cognitive load within a task and showed that as cognitive load (task difficulty) increased, participant's pupil sizes also increased.

Although research has shown that pupils increase in size as task difficulty or cognitive load increases, little research has evaluated how pupils change when individuals are learning a new task. Because a task should become more automatic over time, and cognitive load should decrease, we suspect that pupils will shrink over time.

## 1.3  Goal Summary

To determine whether within-task adaptations can be captured via pupillometry.

## 2  Methods

### 2.1  Participants

Fourty-four ($M_{AGE}$ = 21.2 years, $SD_{AGE}$ = 2.5, 12 females) enlisted Sailors and Marines enrolled in Air Traffic Control school at the Naval Air Training Technical Center in Pensacola, Florida, USA participated in this experiment. The U.S. Naval Research Laboratory Institutional Review Board approved this research.

### 2.2  Direction Orientation Task (DOT)

The Direction Orientation Task (DOT) is a cognitive task that requires participants to orient themselves in space to correctly identify the position of a target relative to an Unmanned Aerial Vehicle's (UAV) heading. This task is currently being used by both the United States Air Force and Navy as part of their selection test batteries for pilots. Participants see two images per trial (see Fig. 1). On the left image, they see a map that shows the heading of the UAV. On the right image, they see a view of four parking lots that are directly ahead of the UAV's position. Participants are asked to correctly choose which lot depicts one of four randomly selected parking lots (viz., North, South, East, or West Parking Lot). For example, if the UAV has a heading of 270° (i.e., heading directly west) and they were asked to choose the west parking lot, the correct answer would be the parking lot at the top of the image (see Fig. 1). If they were asked to choose the west parking lot, the correct answer would be the lot at the top of the camera view. Each trial is randomly generated with heading varying in 30° increments. The DOT has 48 experimental trials. Participants either get the trial correct or not. Completion time for each trial is also recorded. See Ostoin [10] for more information about the DOT.

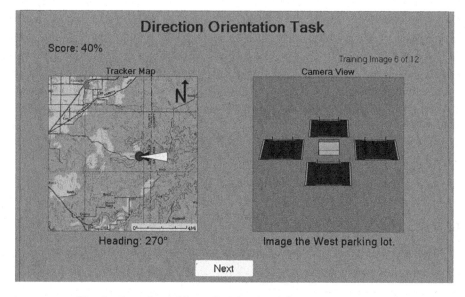

**Fig. 1.** Example trial from the Direction Orientation Task (DOT)

### 2.3 Eye Tracker

Pupil data were collected at 60 Hz using a Gazepoint GP3 Desktop eye tracking system. The eye trackers were calibrated for each participant with the Gazepoint default software before beginning the experiment.

### 2.4 Monitor

Dell 1708FPt monitors were used for this experiment. The DOT was centered at a resolution of 1280 × 1024.

### 2.5 Procedure

All participants read and signed a consent form before beginning the experiment. After becoming comfortable in their seats, the eye trackers were adjusted and calibrated for each participant. Calibration was completed using the Gazepoint's nine point calibration procedure included in their Gazepoint control software. Participants were instructed to minimize their head movements during the experiment. They completed a short tutorial of the DOT, completed a dozen practice trials with feedback, and then completed the 48 experimental trials. See Fig. 2 for an example computer setup.

**Fig. 2.** Example setup using the Gazepoint GP3 Desktop eye tracker

# 3   Results

## 3.1   Pupil Cleaning

Each data type recorded by the Gazepoint system has a corresponding binary quality measure which indicates whether the system considers that data point to be either good or bad. Data that the Gazepoint GP3 system identified as bad were replaced using linear interpolation, and within-subject outliers were corrected using a Hampel filter [11]. Linear interpolation was done using the 'zoo' package [12] in R [13]. Outlier removal (i.e., Hampel filter) was done using the 'pracma' package [14] in R. Data from eleven participants were excluded due to excessive movement during the experiment resulting in more than 90% data loss by the eye-tracker. More information about that data loss (and data loss from other projects) is also being presented at this conference [15]. The final correlation between left and right pupil was high (r = .90) so all analyses were done with the right pupil.

## 3.2   Primary Analyses

Overall, participants answered 61% of the DOT trials correctly with an average response time of 7.95 s. As expected, accuracy on the DOT increased across trials (r = .24, p = .10, see Fig. 3) while reaction time significantly decreased (r = −.58, p < .01, see Fig. 4). Both suggest participants adapted and improved on the DOT across trials. Analysis of the pupil data revealed a strong, negative correlation (r = −.83, p < .01, see Fig. 5) across the trials. That is, participants' pupils shrank as they advanced through the

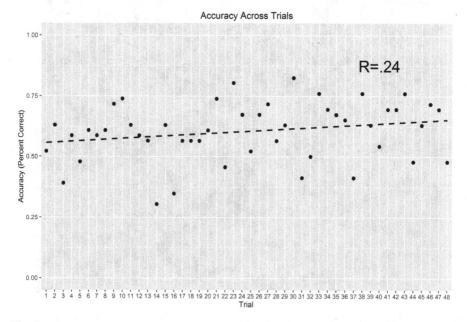

**Fig. 3.** Accuracy (percent correct) for all participants across all trials of the Direction Orientation Task (DOT)

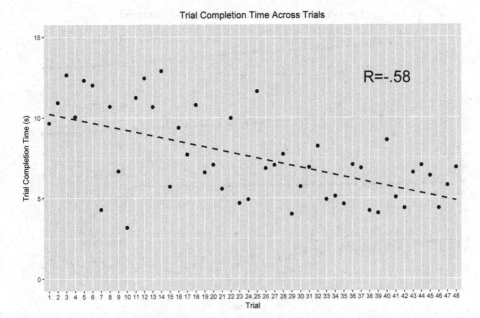

**Fig. 4.** Average trial completion time (seconds) for all participants across all of the trials of the Direction Orientation Task (DOT)

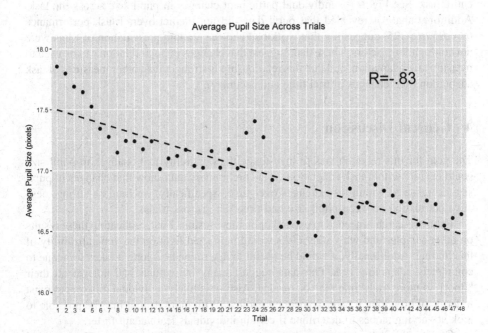

**Fig. 5.** Average pupil size (pixels) for all participants across all of the trials of the Direction Orientation Task (DOT)

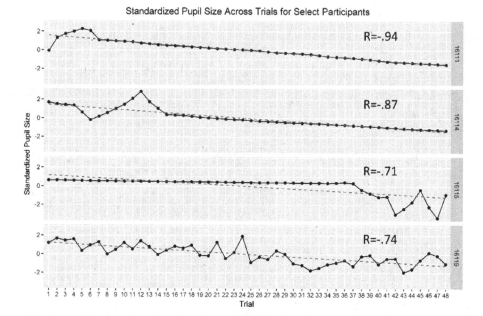

**Fig. 6.** Standardized pupil size for select participants across all of the trials of the Direction Orientation Task (DOT).

entire task. See Fig. 6 for individual participant changes in pupil size across the task. Additional analysis revealed that pupil data did not predict overall task performance ($r = .05$, $p > .25$) suggesting that workload and the random presentation of trials were not confounding factors. These data suggest that changes in pupil dilation can be used to measure task adaptation, and that this relationship is stronger than other measures of task adaptation (i.e., changes in trial time and accuracy).

## 4   General Discussion

The goal for this research was to investigate the possibility that changes in pupil size could capture within-task adaptations. This preliminary data show that changes in pupil size do relate to within-task changes over time. Specifically, we found a strong, negative correlation between pupil size and time (i.e., across trials).

Future research is needed to expand upon these results. First, replicating these results on other samples and with other tasks would help shed light on the generalizability of this finding. Additionally, it would be useful to determine how long it takes someone to completely adapt to a task. Our data suggest many individuals had not yet hit their "floor" so more trials/time may be needed. Also, it is likely individual differences exist in terms of how long it takes someone to adjust. With more data, it may be possible to look at varying slopes to determine if certain individuals learn/adapt faster.

Of note, this data was captured using a low-cost eye-tracking system. Thus, we add to a growing body of literature that shows that low cost eye-tracking systems are capable of collecting meaningful data [16, 17].

# References

1. Newell, A., Rosenbloom, P.S.: Mechanisms of skill acquisition and the law of practice. Cogn. Skills Acquis. **1**, 1–55 (1981)
2. Robertson, E.M.: The serial reaction time task: implicit motor skill learning? J. Neurosci. **27**(38), 10073–10075 (2007). https://doi.org/10.1523/JNEUROSCI.2747-07.2007
3. Unsworth, N., Engle, R.W.: Individual differences in working memory capacity and learning: evidence from the serial reaction time task. Memory Cogn. **33**(2), 213–220 (2005). doi:10.3758/BF03195310
4. Paas, F., Tuovinen, J.E., Tabbers, H., Van Gerven, P.W.: Cognitive load measurement as a means to advance cognitive load theory. Educ. Psychol. **38**(1), 63–71 (2003). http://dx.doi.org/10.1207/S15326985EP3801_8
5. Sibley, C., Coyne, J., Baldwin, C.: Pupil dilation as an index of learning. In: Proceedings of Human Factors and Ergonomics Society Annual Meeting, vol. 55, no. 1, pp. 237–241. SAGE Publications, September 2011. https://doi.org/10.1177/1071181311551049
6. Sweller, J.: Cognitive load theory, learning difficulty, and instructional design. Learn. Instr. **4**(4), 295–312 (1994). http://dx.doi.org/10.1016/0959-4752(94)90003-5
7. Ericsson, K.A., Kintsch, W.: Long-term working memory. Psychol. Rev. **102**(2), 211 (1995). http://dx.doi.org/10.1037/0033-295X.102.2.211
8. Hess, E.H., Polt, J.M.: Pupil size in relation to mental activity during simple problem-solving. Science **143**(3611), 1190–1192 (1964). doi:10.1126/science.143.3611.1190
9. Chen, S., Epps, J.: Using task-induced pupil diameter and blink rate to infer cognitive load. Hum.–Comput. Interact. **29**(4), 390–413 (2014). http://dx.doi.org/10.1080/07370024.2014.892428
10. Ostoin, S.D.: An Assessment of the Performance-Based Measurement Battery (PBMB), the Navy's Psychomotor Supplement to the Aviation Selection Test Battery (ASTB). Naval Postgraduate School, Monterey, CA (2007)
11. Pearson, R.K.: Data cleaning for dynamic modeling and control. In: 1999 European Control Conference (ECC), pp. 2584–2589. IEEE, August 1999
12. Zeileis, A., Grothendieck, G., Ryan, J.A., Andrews, F., Zeileis, M.A.: Package 'zoo'. R package version 1.7-12 (2014). http://CRAN.R-project.org/package=zoo
13. R Development Core Team: R: A Language and Environment for Statistical Computing. R Foundation for Statistical Computing, Vienna (2014)
14. Borchers, H.W.: Package 'pracma'. R package version 1.9.5 (2016). https://cran.r-project.org/web/packages/pracma/pracma.pdf
15. Sibley, C., Coyne, J., Foroughi, C.K., Olson, T., Moclaire C.: Practical considerations for low-cost eye tracking: an analysis of data loss across tasks and time. In: Human-Computer Interaction International 2017 (2017, accepted)
16. Balthasar, S., Martin, M., Camp, F., Hild, J., Beyerer, J.: Combining low-cost eye trackers for dual monitor eye tracking. In: Kurosu, M. (ed.) HCI 2016. LNCS, vol. 9732, pp. 3–12. Springer, Cham (2016). doi:10.1007/978-3-319-39516-6_1
17. Coyne, J., Sibley, C.: Investigating the use of two low cost eye tracking systems for detecting pupillary response to changes in mental workload. In: Proceedings of Human Factors and Ergonomics Society Annual Meeting, vol. 60, no. 1, pp. 37–41. SAGE Publications, September 2016. https://doi.org/10.1177/1541931213601009

# Rim-to-Rim Wearables at the Canyon for Health (R2R WATCH): Correlation of Clinical Markers of Stress with Physiological COTS Data

Lucie Jelinkova, Emily Pearce, Christopher Bossart, Risa Garcia, and Jon Femling[✉]

Department of Emergency Medicine, The University of New Mexico Health Sciences Center, Albuquerque, NM, USA
jfemling@salud.unm.edu

**Abstract.** Commercial off-the-shelf (COTS) wearable devices can provide easily deployable physiologic measurement systems that generate large amounts of crucial health status data. This data, although similar to physiologic data recorded and used routinely in the health care environment, lacks validation in the non-clinical environment. To address this gap in knowledge and to translate clinical expertise to the field we examined healthy volunteers attempting a strenuous task of crossing the Grand Canyon from rim to rim (R2R) in a single day. Subjects completed a pre-crossing questionnaire with baseline biometric measurements and blood collection for analysis of a comprehensive metabolic panel. Enrolled subjects were then asked to wear COTS wearable fitness devices as they attempted the crossing. Subjects were asked to provide a post-crossing questionnaire, repeat biometric measurements and blood collections. We obtained 52 complete sets of pre- and post-hike blood samples. We identified multiple significant changes in metabolic measurements consistent with expected stresses endured. In addition to the subjective fatigue expectedly reported by subjects, subjects had signs of significant muscle breakdown, yet no subject required immediate medical attention upon completing the task. We linked these clinical markers of stress to the physiologic output from COTS wearable devices and are now able to translate the output measures of these devices to meaningful clinical outcomes. In addition, we have begun to establish new expected ranges for physiologic data during extreme stress that does not require immediate medical attention. This data is crucial to defining usage parameters for wearable devices in deployed field settings.

**Keywords:** Health promotion · Medical information system and its application · Quality of life and lifestyle · Real life environments

## 1 Introduction

Hikers in Grand Canyon National Park (GCNP) who choose to hike below the canyon rim face a challenging environment with extreme temperatures, often exceeding 100 °F in the summer shade with heat indices regularly above 120 °F in the baking sun.

© Springer International Publishing AG 2017
D.D. Schmorrow and C.M. Fidopiastis (Eds.): AC 2017, Part I, LNAI 10284, pp. 312–322, 2017.
DOI: 10.1007/978-3-319-58628-1_25

These extreme temperatures, coupled with steep elevation gradients on all hiking trails in the canyon, in addition to limited access to shade and water, can place unprepared hikers into perilous situations in which they encounter significant health risks. GCNP Park Rangers who patrol below the canyon rim are trained emergency medical services (EMS) providers who care for over 300 backcountry patients annually, over 175 of whom require helicopter evacuation from the canyon's depths due to the acuity of their condition [1]. Rangers are highly trained in recognizing and treating common heat illnesses, including dehydration, heat exhaustion, heat stroke, hyponatremia, and rhabdomyolysis. To effectively diagnose and treat patients in the remote backcountry, many rangers carry point-of-care blood chemistry analyzers. These devices are extremely beneficial to the rangers who are tasked with treating ill or injured hikers, however the physiological changes in healthy hikers not presenting with an illness or injury is relatively unknown.

With the advent of a preponderance of wearable devices capable of collecting data on performance metrics and biomarkers [2–5], there is an ability to measure markers of health in the field continuously, which may be a significant benefit in a remote field setting with limited access to equipment or laboratory studies. Studying R2R hikers to determine clinical markers of current health status via blood sampling in conjunction with wearable device metrics provides an opportunity to correlate the two tools, as well as to identify potential markers of extreme physiological stress that exceed traditional physiologically normal parameters but may not require immediate medical attention.

The R2R WATCH study collected data through three methods: (1) wearable devices, (2) survey administration, and (3) blood samples before and after hike. Overall, this data included physiological data, cognitive decision-making abilities, blood chemistries, and a variety of biomarkers including heat shock proteins, arginine vasopressin, and inflammatory markers. By collecting this data, findings may be applied to public health and safety strategy in public lands and backcountry environments. We will describe results from blood sample analysis and correlation with wearable device metric data, and its broader applicability to improving early recognition of physiological stress.

## 2  Study Collaboration

Hiking the Grand Canyon's 24.2 mile R2R hike is an extreme task, requiring hikers to descend 6000 feet from the canyon rim to the canyon bottom, cross the Colorado River via a small footbridge, and then ascend the opposite side of the canyon to the other rim. This hike is only possible in the five months spanning the hot summer season of Arizona, from May to October, as the North Rim of the canyon is closed to the public in the cold, snow-covered winter months. The limited time-frame in which this hike is possible inadvertently pressures hikers to partake in this challenging task in a higher risk environment with heightened temperatures and sun exposure.

The University of New Mexico (UNM) Medical Center's EMS Consortium, a group of EMS physicians, began providing pre-hospital medical direction to the EMS-providing park rangers of GCNP in 2014. As R2R hiking has increased in popularity due to articles in popular hiking, running, and outdoor magazines and newspapers, GCNP rangers began to anecdotally observe an increasing strain on rescue resources in the park. Rangers began to observe the R2R hiking population more closely and counted over 1,000 individuals attempting this strenuous crossing in a single day during the busiest weekends of the year. This massive influx of hikers significantly impacts GCNP in a variety of ways. Increased hiker traffic degrades trail conditions more rapidly, increases the strain on backcountry waste management facilities, and increases the need for urgent/emergent rescue, placing an exhausting tax on the search and rescue (SAR) rangers of GCNP and increasing the risks to rangers as they participate in rescue operations, many of which are inherently high-risk. A former park ranger and a UNM Emergency Medicine physician began collaborating on an interest in understanding in greater detail the nutritional habits and physiological performance of R2R hikers. This was done with the goal in mind of providing more comprehensive information to hikers and increasing their preparedness thereby helping to mitigate the risks they would take.

The R2R study began collecting data on hikers in 2014, and through a partnership with Sandia National Laboratories (SNL), specifically a cognitive psychologist and a geneticist, to examine the efficacy of wearable devices to collect cognitive and physiological data and apply this information to improving warfighter health through early recognition of cognitive of physiological deterioration.

## 3   Empirical Background and Literature Review

### 3.1   Physiological Markers

As the human body experiences physical stressors, many compensatory changes are made in an attempt to maintain a certain level of homeostasis. Many of these changes vary from individual to individual and certain aspects are particularly distinct when comparing fit individuals to their less fit counterparts. Commonly measured physiologic markers include respiratory rate, oxygen saturation, heart rate (HR), temperature, and oxygen delivery/consumption by the body [6].

Respiratory rate is often used as a surrogate for the more clinically important minute ventilation which can increase up to 20-fold from a resting state generally around 5–6 L/min to greater than 100 L/min in a maximal exertional state [6]. This increase in minute ventilation enables the body to maintain oxygen saturations as well get rid of $CO_2$, the byproduct of much of the metabolic activity within the body. Minute ventilation increases as the body's demand for oxygen increases during intense physiologic stress. Interestingly, in a healthy individual, oxygen delivery to tissues is not limited by respiratory rate but rather by the blood's ability to deliver and unload oxygen to tissues at a cellular level [2].

Given the importance of oxygen delivery to tissues via red blood cells (RBCs), it makes intuitive sense that HR would increase during times of stress. This is easily measured non-invasively. However, it is more than simply increasing the rate at which the heart beats which leads to a higher circulating blood volume and cardiac output (CO) [6]. Stroke volume is exceedingly important to maintaining adequate cardiac output and it is here that previous studies have shown that there is a tremendous difference between well trained athletes and those who do not exercise regularly in terms of their body's ability to drastically increase the volume of blood with each coordinated contraction of the heart [6].

The body's blood vessels also help to improve tissue oxygen delivery by vasodilating [6]. As more blood can be delivered to the various tissues in the body, more efficient use of oxygen can be attained. This is measured indirectly by the VO2 max. Many of today's wearable devices can fairly accurately measure VO2 max [6], something that was once only able to be measured in confined labs. In addition to supplying more blood to tissues in need of substrate, vasodilation helps the body cool down. The human body is normally only roughly 25% efficient when it comes to converting nutrients into physical work, thus releasing ample heat as a byproduct. Vasodilation coupled with evaporation are major pathways the body uses to cool down and prevent overheating. Assessing skin temperature as well as electrodermal activity are useful markers of physiologic stress and the body's response and efficiency [6].

All of these physiologic markers likely play a role in how successful an individual is during physical stress and it is our goal to correlate these findings with results in endurance activities such as the R2R in order to better predict who will outperform others and to ascertain a "new normal" when it comes to physiologic stress and performance.

## 3.2  Biomarkers

Along with physiological markers of exertion, several biomarkers can be measured via blood work that reflect the stress of exercise [7]. These biomarkers can be used to monitor fluid status, muscle metabolism, and renal function [7]. Several biomarkers of specific importance to our study include serum creatinine, and creatine kinase.

Serum creatinine is an important marker for kidney function [7]. Clinically it can be used to estimate the glomerular filtration rate (GFR) which is used to monitor kidney function. Creatinine may become elevated in a number of clinical situations, but during exercise it is usually a reflection of dehydration [7]. Acute kidney injury (AKI) is defined as an increase in creatinine and BUN (another marker of renal function). Some criteria for defining AKI describe a sudden twofold increase in creatinine from baseline as injury. It has been suggested that athletes or those conditioned for endurance activities may have higher baseline creatinine and increases may not reflect the same decline in kidney function as the general population [7].

Creatine kinase (CK) can be found in skeletal muscle, the heart, and the brain and is largely measured as a byproduct of muscle use and/or damage [7]. It is commonly elevated in healthy people after exercise and can be used as a qualitative marker for skeletal muscle microtrauma [9, 10]. Correlations have been previously identified between concentrations of CK and intensity as well as duration of exercise [7]. The highest increases generally occurring after intense, endurance activities [7]. A complication of excessive muscle activity, which is reflected by extremely elevated CK, is rhabdomyolysis [9]. This disease process can cause acute renal failure, electrolyte abnormalities, and hypovolemia [9]. Risk factors for developing rhabdomyolysis include heat, stress and dehydration [9]. Interestingly, it has been found that baseline CK may be higher for active people than those who are more sedentary [9]. This has an important implication when monitoring the CK of individuals who have participated in endurance activities. They may remain asymptomatic with levels normally associated with adverse effects. However, persistent elevations in CK may accompany decreased exercise tolerance and decline in performance [7, 8].

It is known that athletes, especially those who participate in endurance activities, may have different reference ranges for common clinical lab values than the general population [10]. In this study, it is the goal to create new reference ranges for active individuals in order to better discern true disease processes from upper limits of normal [7].

## 4    Experimental Design

Data collection occurs over two separate weekends, structured around peak hiker weekends in May and October. Data collection stations are set up at the three main trailheads at the Grand Canyon for hiker enrollment and the collection of start and finish data. A team of researchers also collects data at the bottom of the Grand Canyon, the midpoint of the hike.

Hikers are consented into the study through an institutional review board-approved consent process. They are then enrolled into a three-tier study: (1) survey, (2) blood draw, (3) wearable devices.

### 4.1    Subjects

In October 2016, 288 subjects out of a possible study population of 951 hikers, were enrolled as study subjects. 50 subjects provided wearable device data. In combined efforts between May 2016, one of the original R2R study weekends prior to UNM's collaboration with SNL, and October 2016, 60 subjects provided pre and post blood samples, with 52 complete sets of data.

Data is collected from volunteer hikers, who are not recruited to hike the Rim-to-Rim hike, but instead are enrolled as they approach the trailhead on their already planned hike. This is done to discourage recruiting an unfit subject who may become ill or injured during their hike due to a lack of preparedness.

### 4.2    Survey

Potential subjects are asked to participate in a survey administered at the start, middle, and finish of their hike, assessing nutritional intake, basic biometric data, previous experience, activity times, and self-reports of fatigue and preparedness.

### 4.3   Wearable Devices

Hikers are given wearable devices including fitness wristwatch devices, temperature recording device, an enhanced GPS recording device, environment temperature recording devices, chest straps, smart hats, core temperature devices, and sensor shorts. All wearable devices are non-invasive and COTS products. The goal of this project was to evaluate specifically the efficacy of point estimates of heart rate as measured by a finger oxygen pulse oximeter and the continuous optical heart rate measurements by wearable COTS.

### 4.4   Bloodwork

Subjects are asked to participate in two blood draws (start and finish). Due to logistical limitations, only subjects traveling from the South Kaibab to North Kaibab trail are included in this part of the study. A sample of venous blood is acquired through venipuncture by individuals trained in phlebotomy. One 6 mL tube of blood for serum and an additional 6 mL tube of blood for plasma is drawn from each hiker at the start and finish of the subject's hike. Plasma collection tube contains lithium heparin to prevent clotting. Both collection tubes are centrifuged on site for 15 min at about $1200 \times g$ at ambient temperature, and collected serum and plasma samples are immediately placed on ice. Due to the remote location of the collection site, samples are kept on ice until analysis. A comprehensive metabolic panel and total creatine kinase was obtained from serum samples. Samples were analyzed at the TriCore Reference Laboratory using standard clinical techniques.

## 5   Data Analysis

Peripheral blood samples from subjects before and after the canyon hike were compared for markers of stress and muscle damage. Serum creatine kinase (CK) is a standard clinical marker of muscle damage. Serum CK levels were significantly elevated in subjects after completing the hike ($p < 0.0001$, Fig. 1). In addition, we compared the distribution of serum CK concentrations before and after the task to the distribution of CK concentrations from the large NHANES population database. NHANES is the National Health and Nutrition Survey is a program of studies designed by the Center for Disease Control (CDC) to assess the health and nutritional status of adults and children in the United States [9]. Data from the NHANES project is publically available and data from the 2013–2014 data set was used as a population reference in this study. Figure 2 reveals that our starting concentration distribution closely matches the population data. Conversely, finish CK concentrations had a very different distribution shifted towards higher serum concentrations. These findings are consistent with the canyon hike resulting in a significant physiologic stress causing muscle breakdown. This data also reveals that a CK concentration of 500 IU/L is an important inflection point between starting concentrations and finishing concentrations as well as between normal population values and finish values.

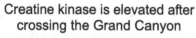

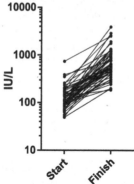

**Fig. 1.** Serum creatine kinase levels in healthy volunteers before and after crossing the Grand Canyon from rim to rim (n = 58 start, 53 finish $p < 0.0001$ for paired T-test).

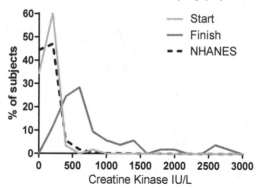

**Fig. 2.** Comparison of creatine kinase distributions. Creatine kinase concentration distributions were binned in 200 IU/L increments. NHANES data represent publicly available population data (n = 6542), Start (n = 58) and Finish (n = 53) data are from healthy volunteers before and after crossing the Grand Canyon.

Using a serum CK concentration of 500 IU/L to stratify our subjects into two groups we evaluated the self-reported fatigue of subjects. All subjects reported high levels of fatigue, but there was no difference between groups defined by CK levels ($p = 0.09$, Fig. 3). Self-reported greatest fatigue was also not significantly different between groups ($p = 0.30$).

We evaluated the ability of heart rate measurements to identify changes in subjects after a canyon crossing. Figure 4 is a comparison of subject heart rate before and after crossing the canyon. Post-crossing heart rates were significantly higher ($p < 0.0001$).

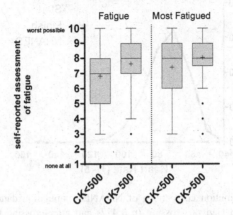

**Fig. 3.** Self-reported assessment of fatigue at the finish of the Grand Canyon crossing. Subjects were asked to rate their fatigue at the completion of the hike and worst fatigue felt during the hike from 1 = none at all to 10 = worst possible (n = 17 for CK < 500, 33 for CK > 500).

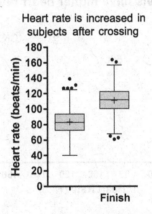

**Fig. 4.** Comparison of starting and finishing heart rates in subjects crossing the Grand Canyon. Box plots with Tukey whiskers from subjects prior to crossing (n = 472) and post crossing (n = 319) $p < 0.0001$ for paired T-test.

We then compared the distribution of start and finish heart rates to NHANES population data (Fig. 5). Both start and finish heart rate distributions were different from resting population norms as well as from each other.

Finally, we examined the continuous heart rate measurements via wearable COTS devices as they related to the clinical measurement of muscle damage via serum CK. Figure 6 reveals that subjects with higher heart rates as measured over the course of their crossing had higher serum CK levels.

**Heart rate distributions vary by population**

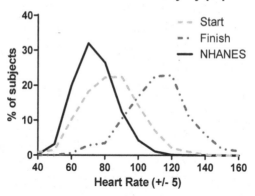

**Fig. 5.** Heart rate distribution comparison of NHANES population data (n = 7549), healthy subjects before a Grand Canyon crossing (n = 472) and after crossing (n = 319). Heart rate values are binned in 10 beat per minute increments and graphed as a percentage of subjects.

**Subjects with higher serum creatine kinase levels have higher heart rates**

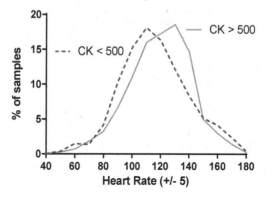

**Fig. 6.** Heart rate distribution of continuous heart rate monitoring in subjects who had both blood work done and wore continuous commercial off the shelf wearable heart rate monitoring devices. N = 11 for CK < 500 and n = 16 for CK > 500.

## 6    Conclusion

We evaluated subjects engaging in a strenuous physical activity as they crossed the Grand Canyon on foot from rim to rim. These subjects endured significant muscle damage as measured by release of intracellular creatine kinase. We then evaluated whether we could ascertain a non-invasive marker that would correlate with the observed muscle damage. Self-reported measures of fatigue were inadequate. This could be because fatigue is the wrong subjective symptom. Future studies could evaluate self-reported measures of muscle soreness as an alternative. In addition, the severity of the task resulted in significant right censoring of subjective data as many of the subjects reported their greatest fatigue as "worse possible". This further emphasized the need for an objective measure of stress.

Heart rate is a relatively easily obtained objective measure of physiologic performance. Many athletes use heart rate responses as an important part of the training, clinicians rely on heart rate measurements for screening, assessing response to therapies, and for continued monitoring of a patient's health. We hypothesized that heart rate measurements in volunteers engaging in a strenuous activity successfully would be very different from established populations norms. We found that Grand Canyon crossers had higher heart rates than NHANES data even before starting their crossing. This was expected as NHANES resting heart rates were taken after sitting still for 4 min. Grand Canyon assessments reported here were while standing immediately before they engaged in the crossing. Many subjects had hiked a small distance or even ran to the trailhead accounting for the shift in heart rates. Importantly, subjects who had successfully completed the Canyon crossing had even higher heart rates. These heart rates if found in a patient in a clinical environment would raise concern for illness, abnormal heart rhythms or other disease processes necessitating intervention. However, in this setting subjects with elevated heart rates were actually successful in completing the task and the only intervention many were looking for was hydration and rest. These data highlight the need for establishing appropriate normal ranges for individuals engaging in strenuous, but not life threatening tasks.

In addition to establishing an expected shift in normal heart rate values in the setting of strenuous activity we were also able to identify an additional rightward shift in subjects who had objective measures of increased muscle damage. In subjects whom we measured both CK levels and had continuous heart rate monitoring we were able to find that higher CK levels were linked with a shift in heart rate values to an even higher level. This has important implications for monitoring subjects during activity. As we continue this study design we hope to refine the signal of increased damage and try to establish the ability to detect this decline in health in real time. This would have the advantage of not only assessing a subject's performance in real time, but offering some prediction into next day performance as the amount of injury an individual sustains will impact their following performance.

COTS device data can be correlated with direct physiologic changes observed in blood work. This holds significant applicability in the austere or remote setting as access to laboratory equipment or point-of-care testing is often limited, inaccessible, and costly. COTS devices, however, are non-invasive, readily available, affordable, and easily analyzed.

# References

1. Grand Canyon National Park Branch of Emergency Services: 2016 Annual Report, Grand Canyon (2017)

2. Li, X., Dunn, J., Salins, D., Zhou, G., Zhou, W., Schüssler-Fiorenza Rose, S.M., Perelman, D., Colbert, E., Runge, R., Rego, S., Sonecha, R., Datta, S., McLaughlin, T., Snyder, M.P.: Digital health: tracking physiomes and activity using wearable biosensors reveals useful health-related information. PLoS Biol. **15**(1), e2001402 (2017). doi:10.1371/journal.pbio. 2001402

3. de Bruin, E.D., Hartmann, A., Uebelhart, D., Murer, K., Zijlstra, W.: Wearable systems for monitoring mobility-related activities in older people: a systematic review. Clin. Rehabil. **22** (10–11), 878–895 (2008). doi:10.1177/0269215508090675

4. Gordon, R., Bloxham, S.: Influence of the Fitbit Charge HR on physical activity, aerobic fitness and disability in non-specific back pain participants. J. Sports Med. Phys. Fit., 8 February 2017. doi:10.23736/S0022-4707.17.06688-9

5. O'Reilly, M., Whelan, D., Ward, T., Delahunt, E., Caulfield, B.: Technology in S&C: tracking lower limb exercises with wearable sensors. J. Strength Cond. Res., 15 February 2017. doi:10.1519/JSC.0000000000001852

6. Burton, D.A., Stokes, K., Hall, G.M.: Physiological effects of exercise. Contin. Educ. Anaesth. Crit. Care Pain. **4**(6), 185–188 (2004). doi:10.1093/bjaceaccp/mkh050

7. Banfi, G., Colombini, A., Lombardi, G., Lubkowska, A.: Metabolic markers in sports medicine. Adv. Clin. Chem. **56**, 1–54 (2012). doi:10.1016/b978-0-12-394317-0.00015-7

8. Banfi, G., Del Fabbro, M., Lippi, G.: Serum creatinine concentration and creatinine-based estimation of glomerular filtration rate in athletes. Sports Med. **39**(4), 331–337 (2009). doi:10.2165/00007256-200939040-00005

9. Warren, J.D., Blumbergs, P.C., Thompson, P.D.: Rhabdomyolysis: a review. Muscle Nerve **25**(3), 332–347 (2002)

10. Clarkson, P.M., Hubal, M.J.: Exercise-induced muscle damage in humans. Am. J. Phys. Med. Rehabil. **81**(Suppl. 11), S52–S69 (2002)

11. National Health and Nutritional Survey. http://cdc.gov/nchs/nhanes/

# Grounded Approach for Understanding Changes in Human Emotional States in Real Time Using Psychophysiological Sensory Apparatuses

Ryan A. Kirk[✉]

Kirk LLC, Seattle, USA
info@ryankirk.info

**Abstract.** This paper discusses the technical and philosophical challenges that researchers and practitioners face when attempting to classify human emotion based upon raw physiological data. It proposes the use of a representational learning approach that adopts techniques from industrial internet of things (IoT) solutions. It applies this approach to the classification of emotional states using functional near infrared spectroscopy (fNIRS) sensor data.

The algorithm used first pre-processes the data using a combination of signal processing and vector quantization techniques. Next, it found the optimal number of natural clusters within human emotional states and used these as the target variables for either shallow or for deep learning classification. The deep learning variant used a Restricted Boltzmann Machine (RBM) to form a compressive representation of the input data prior to classification. A final single layer perception model learned the relationship between the input and output states.

This approach would be useful for detecting real-time changes in human emotional state. It is able automatically create emotional states that are both highly separable and balanced. It is able to distinguish between low v. high emotional states across all tasks (F1-score of 71.4%) and is better at forming this distinction for tasks intended to elicit higher cognitive load such as the Tetris video game (F1-score of 87.1%) or the Multi Attribute Task Battery (F1-score of 77%).

**Keywords:** Affective computing · Cognitive computing · Brain signal processing · Brain computer interfaces · Decision-making · Decision support systems · DSS · Machine learning · Deep learning · Classification

## 1 Background and Problem Definition

### 1.1 Existing Approaches

When it comes to detecting emotional states using sensor data, researchers are often looking for changes in sensory data or for patterns within sensory data. While there are many approaches researchers use to model physiological behaviors, two major approaches are provide useful background upon which to illustrate why it can be a

© Springer International Publishing AG 2017
D.D. Schmorrow and C.M. Fidopiastis (Eds.): AC 2017, Part I, LNAI 10284, pp. 323–341, 2017.
DOI: 10.1007/978-3-319-58628-1_26

challenge to create grounded models. First, many models strives to detect changes in states or it tries to tie recently seen behavioral patterns to known types of patterns [1–4]. Second, many approaches strive to in some way represent the state of a system in order to compare and contrast this representation with historically representations [5–8].

**Signal Detection Models.** These approaches tend to either try to detect changes in physical states by monitoring any of a number of different types of sensors [3, 5, 7]. This relies upon the homeostatic characteristics of physiological systems. When humans engage in activity certain regions become excited relative to their historic baseline. When the activity ceases, these regions return to a state of normalcy. While there is certainly noise in the baseline level of behavior, signal processing approaches can detect the larger changes in state that take place during periods of activity. This approach is highly extensible to a variety of types of sensor modalities.

**Representational Models.** Another approach examines recent patterns in sensory data and compares and contrasts it with previous patterns or with known patterns [4, 9]. This approach can cluster patterns and, in an unsupervised fashion, find the common and less common groupings. Alternatively this approach can try to match a piece of sensory data and see how similar it is to a number of known patterns. This approach is flexible for detecting a number of types of different states.

## 1.2    Existing Challenges

While both the signal detection and representational approaches have advantages, they also can be challenging to use both for researchers and for practitioners. They struggle from a scientific, from a philosophical, and from a technical perspective. Scientifically, it is challenging to generalize the results of one model. Philosophically it is challenging to establish consensus from phenomenological experience. Technically it is challenging to build scalable, real-time models.

**Technical Challenges.** Most models typically strive to either provide state of the art accuracy or state of the art scalability. Both problems are limited by the algorithms and computational power present. From an algorithmic perspective, many models also struggle when the number of features is quite large and when the number of examples is small. This is a common problem encountered by researchers working on creating neural networks for image or for speech recognition [4].

**Scientific Challenges.** The psychophysiological sciences have used quantitative research methods to study and to model psychophysiological data. However, to build an effective model, researchers typically need a large amount of historic data for each participant [1–3]. However, this is not practical in an applied setting since there are often competing demands for researchers to build that work for a variety of individuals with a very short training period. Such difficulties stem from unrealistic requirements for humans to have shared emotion. This means that these models struggle with reproducibility and with generalizability.

**Philosophical Challenges.** Models that strive to represent known emotional states become increasingly fragile for ideas whose properties are challenging to operationalize [10]. If it is hard to capture an idea using language, it can also be hard to measure that idea. Additionally, causality is challenging to establish for complex system whose behavior is non-linear [11, 12].

## 2 Literature Review

### 2.1 Grounding

Grounded models are models that base their representations upon externalized events. In the case of physiological models, external events signify things such as human cognitive or emotional states. However, these states are often subjectively defined either by researchers or by some form of social consensus [11, 13, 14]. The reason for this comes from the question of whether any two humans experience the same emotion and if they do whether their subjective experience is similar. Language is a codified form of social consensus. However, even if researchers have a common language to describe a problem, it does not necessarily mean that they can operationalize this problem. If it is difficult to operationalize, it is difficult to express analytically. Grounded theory is an alternative approach that suggests researchers should first focus upon measuring a system and then find efficient ways to express the system. This approach is analytically useful but critics state it calls to question the classic approach to hypothesis testing.

### 2.2 Cognitive Representation

**Cognitive Spaces.** Humans use perception to form internal representations of stimuli. These representations are influenced by innate perceptual limits and or perceptual biases. For example, humans can only perceive certain colors of light, certain wavelengths of sound, and stimuli that last at least a certain period of time [15, 16]. While these perceptual limits vary slightly from individual to individual but there is enough similarity in these limits across individuals that humans ostensibly have shared perceptual experiences. The geometry of thought is an idea that describes the shape and structure of regions of perceptual sensitivity. These geometries have regions of heightened sensitivity relative to nearby regions. Understanding perceptual biases allows for a grounded understanding of human experience. While it will not predict how an individual will react, it will help predict the degree of sensitive the individual will have to a given perceptual stimuli. Psychometrics uses these cognitive spaces to help design technologies that are more congruent with the human experience.

### 2.3 Limits of Language

While cognitive spaces help researchers build perceptual models, as stimuli become less direct it becomes harder to create grounded models. Language is essential for coordinating cognitive representations. Coordination is necessary to ensure congruency between repeated exposures to similar stimuli. Language is more useful for coordinating when the stimuli represent tangible objects rather than abstract concepts [13, 14]. Material objects allow the individual to tune the way that their internal cognitive representation links to their internal linguistic representation.

**Social Constructivist Narratives.** In addition to communicating shared perceptions of external objects, language can also communicate shared mental states. Such mental states can be emotional or they can be cognitive [13]. Shared cognitive states represent ideas or concepts that language constructs. Social narratives help to construct these ideas. The narratives represent a series of imagined episodic experience. An episodic experience is a type of memory that involves experiences taking place over time that involve one's own sense of self identity. Such narratives are powerful because they are highly relatable. Narratives are relatable because individuals can substitute the experiences in the story with their own.

**Hermeneutical Concerns.** As ideas become more complicated or even abstract, it becomes increasingly difficult to describe an event or object with language. From a learning perspective, we can think of language as a scaffold that shapes and restricts thought. Socially constructed narratives assist in creating consensus amidst ambiguity. However, such narratives are also capable of becoming ungrounded [17]. Whether grounded or not these narratives become ideas that can spread. Such ideas can become pervasive which makes it challenging to separate the grounded from the ungrounded. This affects models since models built on language may not reference a common set of properties and these properties can change over time.

## 2.4 Complexity

Large systems with many variables become technically challenging to analyze. However, complex systems with nonlinear variables become philosophically challenging to analyze. A nonlinear variable is one whose future states are a function of both external influence, such as from neighboring variables, and the previous states of itself [12]. Nonlinearity compounds the challenges that signaling challenges of language. Such systems become ineffable. These variables often have phase transitions that take place. These transitions define the migration of variables between multiple stable states. Multiple states creates non-stationary distributions within these data. Grounded models need a technique to account for the continuously changing nature of these variables.

**Coordination of Action.** Due to the nonlinear properties of complex systems, taking action becomes challenging. Humans tend to interact with such systems in a continuous and dynamic fashion. Action becomes a continuous sequence of making decisions just in time to avoid catastrophe [6, 10]. Previously successful actions will not always guarantee a successful future outcome. Understanding the scope of variables that are currently involved in an undesirable, chaotic state will assist in understanding the scope of action required to control the system.

## 2.5   Internet of Things

The internet of things (IoT) is a recent change in internet technologies has allowed researchers to examine the behavior of many devices simultaneously. This internet of things can be broken up into two kinds: industrial and consumer. The industrial internet refers to the incorporation of telemetry data from computational devices that monitor the behavior of artificial systems. The consumer internet of things is conceptually similar to the industrial internet except that the devices monitor the physiological data of individuals. Beyond their conceptual similarities, these two forms of IoT also have structural similarities.

Industrial scenarios involving sensor apparatuses on interconnected devices lead to data sets that have similar levels of complexity and ambiguity as psychophysiological data. In these scenarios, analytical models also struggle with grounding problems [18]. Such classification models strive to become representational through internalizing certain characteristics of the properties of the external objects or events. They work well in cases where the external object is a physical, external object whose properties are bound by certain constraint. However, these models also become increasingly fragile in cases where objects have as many properties as examples or for ideas whose properties are challenging to operationalize. Rather than using machine learning to perform classification-oriented tasks in these cases, researchers use analytic techniques to first detect aberrant operating conditions. Next they group data based upon similarities. Finally researchers can start to reason about the recurrence of higher order patterns.

Both types of IoT lead to data sets that have similar levels of complexity and ambiguity. Both measure systems capable of forming feedback loops. Finally, both contain a high amount of ambiguity from extensibility, heterogeneity, dynamic scenarios. Because of the conceptual similarity, it seems reasonable that approaches that work well for one form of IoT would work well for another.

## 3   Proposed Solution

Combating these challenges will require an approach that is agnostic to different types of human perception. Drawing from the approaches from the industrial IoT and through employing a combination of supervised and unsupervised learning in efficient, real-time deployments practitioners can overcome some of the challenges mentioned above. This approach involves three stages. First, it creates an efficient lower order representation capable of detecting changes in state in real-time. It does this through efficiently encoding the input variables. Second, it performs a higher order level of inference that allows for cross-modality comparisons to take place. It does this through the use of unsupervised machine learning. Third it connects this representation of the data to external states. It does this using categorical techniques. Finally, by viewing this solution as a generic platform rather than as a single model, this approach can work in conjunction with intelligent systems or with decision-support systems (DSSs) [10, 11].

## 3.1     Lower Order Representation

This approach start by attempting to compress the variable inputs into more efficient representations. It uses the rarity of these representations to detect abnormal events. This process of efficient internal representation combined with change detection is intended to share some of the properties of human cognition. This inductive inference approach allows the model to detect unique states for each individual while also paving the way for more efficient subsequent comparisons.

**Encode.** Representational learning often used as a part of feature engineering. Various techniques can be used to encode the input variables. For example, principal components analysis has become a common way to reduce the dimensionality of input data prior to use within subsequent models [3–5]. Other techniques could include statistical normalization, binning, vector quantization, wavelet transformations, etc. [1, 8].

**Detect.** Once encoded, this approach examines the rarity of this encoded representation. Depending upon the type of encoding this can either be probabilistic or parametric. If the encoding is a quantization or a classification scheme then rarity would be the probability of obtaining this outcome. If the encoding is not discrete then use the distribution of values associated with a variable to assess the probability of obtaining the observed value. If an observation is sufficiently rare, then it indicates a potential change in state. Sufficiency can be explicitly set as in the case of a heuristic threshold. It can also be implicitly set using a kinetic approach that adapts this threshold to ensure that only a certain percentage of observations rise above this limit. Once elevated these observations trigger the next stage of comparison.

## 3.2     Higher Order Inference

The next step of this approach examines starts by grouping input observations based upon similarities. This grouping utilizes unsupervised machine learning techniques to encode the notion of similarity into a new feature. This conceptual grouping of events with similar internal representations is inspired by the way humans conceptually group objects. This higher order feature will allow the last stage of the approach to more efficiently perform compositional learning. Such learning is capable of connecting higher order changes in individual states across participants in reference to objects or events.

**Cluster.** Many types of clustering techniques will allow this technique to detect similarities. For example, centroid-based techniques, higher-dimensional representations, density-based models, etc. In addition this approach can use many different types of metrics to detect similarities for example: co-occurrence, concomitance (rank-order), covariance, correlation, cosine, etc. [8, 11].

**Hierarchical Inference.** Note that so far this technique is a combination of bottom-up detection and top-down cross-correlation. This approach can more accurately bet thought of as an approach that contains potentially many iterations of this process. Each iteration allows this approach to account for an additional layer in the functional hierarchy of the complex system. However, in this case one iteration should be simple enough for the intended use case.

### 3.3 Externalization

Once this approach has efficiently encoded the incoming information and has performed an internal representation of the external states via clustering, it can now connect these representations to external states [10, 13, 14]. Once mapped to external states, this approach can optionally recommend a course of action based upon a relationship between these external states and the relevant action.

**Classification.** This approach performs classification of internal representations by mapping these representations to external states. This will work well in cases where the external object is a physical, external object whose properties are bound by certain constraints. This connection is made possible using examples of known states or through the inference of such states. Known states make use of language and, optionally, domain experts who use such language to label new events. Inferred states from the use of an iterative method where an input stimuli intended to evoke a certain state precedes the analytical representation of the state.

**Action Mapping.** Once labeled, this approach has the option to connect internal representations to potential actions. While this mapping may start out using a set of suggestions, over time it can improve. The success of these actions in turn can influence the future likelihood of taking such actions given the current internal representation. In so doing this is a form of top-down inference influencing bottom-up detection techniques. This form of cross-modality inference allows this technique to yield consistent performance across a variety of use case.

### 3.4 Extensibility and Integration

This approach will offer good scalability as well as high degrees of accuracy. It is flexible in terms of which algorithms constitute the subcomponents of the approach. It will also be extensible to many new types of sensory signals. Its techniques that focus upon change detection and upon creating conceptual groupings are similar to how humans form internal representations of the world. Finally, because it builds in iterative layers that are first based upon efficient representations of the underlying signals, it is also analytically grounded. Because of these properties, this approach should work well in a variety of contexts across deployments that contain a multitude of simultaneous sensory signals so long as such system contain functional hierarchies of complexity.

Viewing this approach as the creation of a platform rather than as the creation of a model focuses upon integration within DSSs and upon the its use within intelligent systems It also helps prevent the over learning that can take place when building models to fit rather than to express a data set.

# 4  Experimental Methods.

To test this approach to creating grounded physiological models of human emotion I applied it to a data set originally used by  _. The inputs for this algorithm are the raw physiological data. The outputs or targets for this algorithm were participants' self-reported emotion data. This algorithm performs several tasks. First it pre-processed the data from the experiment. Next it transformed both the input data and the output data. Finally, it learned the relationship between the target and output data. I build the algorithm using the Python programming language and the Scikit-learn library [19].

## 4.1  Context

The original study had 20 participants who either watched videos intended to elicit specific emotional response or who performed either a multi-attribute task or a Tetris task [1, 2]. Table 1 describes all 11 tasks. Each participant performed each task three times for a total of 33 tasks per participant. While engaging in the task, a sensor apparatus collected raw physiological data using functional near-infrared spectroscopy (fNIRS) brain imaging. This scanner had 52-channels measuring oxy- and 52 measuring deoxy-hemoglobin. The scanner captured data from all 104 of these channels 10 Hz. The data ranged $\{-5,5\}$. The unique combination of participants, tasks, and channel resulted in 68,640 unique streams of data. Tasks lasted for 1 min which resulted in 600 data points per stream and over 41MM observations.

**Table 1.**  Summary of task abbreviation alongside description of that task.

| Task | Description |
| --- | --- |
| vidLVLA | A video with intent to elicit a low valency, low arousal response |
| vidHVLA | A video with intent to elicit a high valency, low arousal response |
| HVHA | A video with intent to elicit a high valency, high arousal response |
| vid-N | A video with intent to elicit a neutral response |
| vid-LVHA | A video with intent to elicit a low valency, high arousal response |
| Matb-L | A multi-attribute task with intent to elicit low mental effort |
| Matb-M | A multi-attribute task with intent to elicit moderate mental effort |
| Matb-H | A multi-attribute task with intent to elicit high mental effort |
| Tet-M | A Tetris task with intent to elicit moderate mental effort |
| Tet-H | A Tetris task with intent to elicit high mental effort |
| Tet-L | A Tetris task with intent to elicit low mental effort |

Following each task, each participant filled out a survey indicating their self-reported emotional response and level of mental effort. This resulted in 660 unique self-evaluations of emotion. The survey was the SAM self-report assessment of arousal, control, and valence all using Likert ratings $\{1,5\}$ [1, 2]. Finally, participants also completed the NASA Task Load Index (TLX) survey following each task [20].

## 4.2 Sampling and Normalization

In order to allow for cross-modality comparisons this data needed to be pre-processed to ensure consistency and to reduce noise. Due to environmental noise some data fell outside of the expected range. This algorithm replaced data below −5 with a floor value of −5. It replaced data above 5 with the ceiling value 5.

**Smoothing.** Cycle noise related to the sampling interval existed within the input data. Because the sampling frequency was 10 Hz, this algorithm replaced each value with the rolling average of the previous 10 data points. This cycle time also agreed with the results of a visual inspection I performed on the raw input data.

**Sampling.** Next the algorithm down sampled the smoothed data from 10 Hz to 1 Hz. Because each point had a 10-point rolling average, it contained some information from these previous time periods. For this reason, a 10-point sampling interval would allow for compression of the input data while still including some of the information from the proceeding time periods. The goal of this procedure is to compress the input data while still representing the longer-term cycles present within the data set.

**Normalization.** Once smoothed and sampled, the data was ready for normalization. While each sensor could theoretically utilize the same range, often times a particular stream of data did not use the full scale. Since the data will eventually undergo a quantization process, each stream will have to use the same scale. Here the algorithm transformed each input vector s.t. the minimum was now 0 and the maximum was now 1.

## 4.3 Vector Quantization

Vector quantization allows algorithms to perform much quicker approximate comparisons. It does this by compressing the size of the input vector. This process approximates a time series vector by breaking this vector into many smaller, optionally overlapping wavelets. It then figures out what the most common wave forms are and expresses these as various exemplars. Finally, it reduces the original input vector into a compressed representation by replacing the wavelets with the id for the most similar exemplar.

At this point sampling and normalization reduced the raw input from length 600 with values spanning all real numbers to a set of data consisting of 60 values spanning 0 to 1. A visual inspection of the sampled, normalized physiological sensor data revealed that a common cycle with a period of approximately 20 points in length. This algorithm used a 20-period rolling window to create the initial set of 2,814,240 possible wavelets.

**Creation.** Many unsupervised clustering techniques are capable of creating the wavelet exemplars [8, 9, 16]. This algorithm used k-means++ to generate centroids that would serve as the exemplars. The minimum tolerance was 0.01 and the maximum number of iterations was 100. Due to memory constraints this algorithm trained on a randomly selected 3% sample. The algorithm tried many different levels of k.

**Evaluation.** The algorithm considered several factors to determine the ideal value for k, the number of centroids. These include tolerance, silhouette score, and the distribution of usage. The tolerance represents the average L2 distance between each data point and the most proximate centroid. As this value gets lower the centroids get closer to the data they represent. The silhouette score attempts to measure the ability of the clusters to differentiate [21]. It is equal to the ratio of the L2 distance to the nearest class compared to the distance to the next nearest class. The distribution of application of centroids refers to the ratio of usage for each centroid. This method combines these usages across class categories by taking their harmonic mean.

For the purposes of sketching vectors the goal was to have a low tolerance while avoiding having a large imbalance in centroid assignment rate. Finally, when considering two alternative values for k with similar results, this algorithm would always choose the smaller.

**Application.** The application of the centroids applies to the sampled wavelets and not to the original input vectors. To further simplify the final set, the algorithm also used a sample interval of 10 points to select wavelets. Each selected wavelet of length 20 had a 50% overlap with both the previous and the subsequent wavelet. This resulted in quantized vectors of length 11 where each point consisted of an integer value ranging from 1 to k where k represents the number of exemplars. Given a set of input wavelets, the application of the centroids simply requires finding the closest centroid. This algorithm used a simple nearest neighbor search with L2 as the distance criteria.

## 4.4    Determining Emotional States

The emotional data went through a very similar treatment as the time series data did during vector quantization. The key difference is that rather than representing a 20-dimensional sequence of events, this data was a 4-dimensional representation of different aspects of emotion.

**Creation.** This algorithm used the same implementation and parameters to generate the emotion centroids. This approach used all of the emotion data as input and tried different values for k.

**Evaluation.** The criteria for evaluation were similar except that the goal of parsimony was more important than tolerance or class balance. This algorithm only considered fairly small values for k and balanced the goal of tolerance with that of centroid use.

**Application.** The application was simpler. Since the data did not represent a sequence of events, all of the data from a given participant for a particular task received a single classification. This classification still used the same nearest-neighbors technique as the vector quantization process.

## 4.5    Predicting Emotional States

Once the algorithm has pre-processed and treated the input data and has also turned the output data into clear targets, it is ready to learn the relationships between the two. I tried two approaches. This algorithm either used a single-stage, "shallow" network or a multi-staged, "deep" network. For both approaches this algorithm first encoded the input data. During the multi-staged approach this the algorithm used a Restricted Boltzmann Machine (RBM) in conjunction with either standard logistic regression or with a single layered perceptron. The single stage model just used a single layered perceptron.

**Encoding Inputs.** Since the processed, treated input data represents discretized states, the algorithm should not treat these labels as continuous features. In order for the algorithm to use probabilistic regression it must encode these inputs using a form of binary representation. This algorithm used one-hot encoding. The 11-point set of 64 centroids then represented as 704 binary digits.

**Restricted Boltzmann Machines.** While the algorithm has already substantially compressed the input data, there is reason to believe that the use of an RBM could increase the representational qualities of the data while serving to further compress the size of the input vector [4]. In practice this technique works well to boost classification on higher dimensional data sets.

To determine the best configuration for an RBM for this problem, I tried many combinations of parameters. This algorithm used a single layered RBM with 704 visible units and 64 hidden units. The algorithm trained the input data using contrastive divergence on a 25% random sample of the encoded input data. Once the algorithm trained the RBM it treated the input data using the RBM and passed this treated data to a second, regression stage.

**Linear Probabilistic Regression Models.** This algorithm used a single-layer logistic neural network model trained using stochastic gradient descent. The regression target was the emotional state classification. This network had as many visible units as were present within the input data 704 binary values associated with the encoded raw data or it was the 64 binary values from the RBM. The single stage algorithm used a multi-batch approach where each partially fit a model using 4,000 training examples and up to 10,000 iterations. The multi-stage approach used the same 25% sample as the RBM.

### 4.6   Combining Evidence

Once trained, the classifier was ready to predict the emotion an individual was experiencing. Since participants wore an apparatus with 104 measurement points, the evidence from these parallel streams could combine to create a richer picture of emotional state. This collective set of sensors represents a mental topology that I expressed as a bipartite graph. Nodes represented measurement streams and edges represented neighboring streams. Since the classifications are discrete, I could not use most graph iteration techniques. Instead, I examined the communities within the graph and used the single largest community as the overall classification outcome for that combination of participant and task.

## 4.7    Evaluating Accuracy

During training this algorithm examined the accuracy of the classifiers on the training data. However, when evaluating the differences between the single-stage or multi-stage approach this algorithm examined the overall accuracy across the entire input set. This gave an indication of overall efficacy of the approach. In order to learn how effective this approach is at generalizing, I facetted accuracy across participants and tasks. I determined overall accuracy for each emotional state and then used this to predict how accurate the classifier should be for each participant and for each task. If the relationship between the predicted and actual accuracy was high, then I would know that the ability to predict task performance related to the ability to predict emotional state.

## 5    Experimental Results

This section will first discuss the results of the creation of the wavelet and emotion centroids. It will then illustrate the accuracy of this algorithm in several different ways. First, it will discuss overall accuracy of the single and multi-stage approaches. Next it will examine the accuracy for each emotional state. Finally, it will further break down this accuracy measurement across participant and task.

### 5.1    Wavelet Centroids Creation Results

Class balance was more important than tolerance for determining centroids that did a good job of reconstructing the initial vectors. Admittedly this was an iterative process where I used both data and my own subjective judgement to gauge reconstructive quality. For regions where the differing values of k did not have as substantial an effect I sampled several reconstructions to see how what type of properties the wavelets were representing. If k was too small the reconstructions tended to under fit some of the important periodic features of the data. Once k was larger than 32 it began including certain periodic properties within the wavelets. If k was much larger than 64 it began to learn certain features as evidenced by increasingly unbalanced usage rates across centroids. Using 64 for k had a good balance between class usages, tolerance, and also appeared to have good reconstructive quality. Figure 1 visually represents the centroids that this approach used.

### 5.2    Emotional State Centroid Creation Results

While the selection of k for wavelet centroids is important for achieving balanced centroid usage, the selection of the proper number of emotional states is critical for the performance of this approach. The tolerance quickly converges if k is 4 or larger. This suggests that the unsupervised learning has the ability to represent all of natural clusters. The silhouette score was much higher for k = 2 and was fairly similar for k = 3 or k = 4. The harmonic mean usage rate was nearly identical to a uniform usage

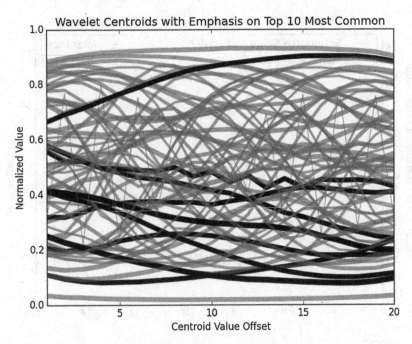

**Fig. 1.** This figure shows all 64 wavelet centroids. Note the normalized value ranging {0,1} and the 20-point width of each. The width of the chart lines is a function of the log frequency of centroid usage. The darker black lines indicate the 10 most highly favored centroids

rate for k = 2 and for k = 3 but precipitously drops if k increases. For these reasons, this approach further cases where k = 2 or where k = 3 (Fig. 2).

## 5.3  Performance Results for Binary Emotional States

The emotional state centroids' values appeared to fall into a low and a high bucket (see Table 2). The use of these buckets was fairly evenly split.

The multi-stage approach was 57.57% accurate. It often tended to classify every instance as the single largest default class. However, the single-stage approach was much better at diffentiating and achieved accuracy of 57.27%. However, the multi-stage approach had much lower precision. Based upon these results the rest of the paper discusses the single-stage approach.

Accuracy on the high state was much higher than the low state. The F1 score for the single-stage approach was 71.46%. Accuracy substantially varied based upon task and participant depending upon the usage level of the high emotional state.

The correlation between the actual and predicted accuracy for these tasks was 0.98. Task accuracy varied from 26.23% to 83.3% (see Table 3). Task performance appears to be a function of how often task elicited heightened emotions. Note the correlation between predicted and actual accuracy and the difference in usage of the *high* class.

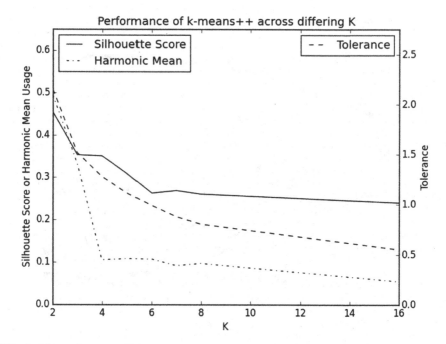

**Fig. 2.** The performance of the unsupervised clustering approach across differs depending upon the initial clusters. Specified by k, the harmonic mean (dash-dotted line) usage of these clusters is balanced for k = 2 and for k = 3. The silhouette score (solid line) is highest for k = 2 and is similar for k = 3 or k = 4. Tolerance (dashed line on secondary axis) converges to a lower bound for k = 4.

**Table 2.** The centroid values and algorithm performance for the high v. low emotional states. Note that the centroid name is linguistic and not statistical; centroid values are not universally higher for the *high* class. The accuracy was much higher for the high emotional state.

| Name | Hits | Total | Accuracy | Arousal | Control | Valence | TLX overall |
|------|------|-------|----------|---------|---------|---------|-------------|
| High | 353 | 370 | 95.40% | 3.47 | 3.19 | 3.13 | 12.68 |
| Low | 25 | 290 | 8.62% | 2.45 | 3.61 | 3.48 | 6.00 |
| Total | 376 | 660 | 57.27% | | | | |

The correlation between actual and predicted accuracy for participants was 0.96. While individual participant scores will be withheld, accuracy ranged from 24.24% to 84.85%. This high correlation between actual and predicted accuracy suggest participant emotional status was a primary contributor to differences in accuracy.

## 5.4    Performance Results for Ternary Emotional States

The emotional state centroids' values did not as succinctly fall into buckets as the binary states. However, their values still support the idea that emotional states fall into various layers. Given their TLX overall values, I will refer to them as low, medium, and high.

**Table 3.** Actual v. predicted classifier performance across task type shows that the accuracy of the classifier for predicting a given task outcome was largely a function of the number of *high* vs. *low* outcomes present within the data. Note performance was substantially higher for the active MATB or Tetris tasks than for the first 5 passive video tasks.

| Task | F1 score | Accuracy | Predicted | High | Low |
|------|----------|----------|-----------|------|-----|
| vidLVLA | 45.95% | 33.33% | 34.66% | 18 | 42 |
| vidHVLA | 50.67% | 38.33% | 39.00% | 21 | 39 |
| HVHA | 74.47% | 60.00% | 65.03% | 39 | 21 |
| vid-N | 34.78% | 26.23% | 28.54% | 14 | 47 |
| vid-LVHA | 50.70% | 41.67% | 34.66% | 18 | 42 |
| Matb-L | 79.41% | 65.85% | 67.89% | 28 | 13 |
| Matb-M | 77.61% | 64.29% | 62.34% | 26 | 16 |
| Matb-H | 73.85% | 59.52% | 58.21% | 24 | 18 |
| Tet-M | 85.29% | 74.36% | 76.49% | 61 | 17 |
| Tet-H | 90.37% | 83.33% | 78.72% | 63 | 15 |
| Tet-L | 83.58% | 71.79% | 73.15% | 58 | 20 |
| All | 71.46% | 57.27% | 57.27% | 370 | 290 |

The single-stage model was 38.94% accurate. It was still had accuracy greater than 90% for classification for the *high* class (see Table 4). The *medium* class was more accurate than the *low* class. Centroid values for TLX performance map to centroid names; however, not all emotional state values agree in direction with TLX performance values.

**Table 4.** The centroid values and algorithm performance for the high, medium, and. low emotional states. Centroid name are linguistic so their values and names do not always agree.

| Name | Hits | Total | Accuracy | Arousal | Control | Valence | TLX overall |
|------|------|-------|----------|---------|---------|---------|-------------|
| High | 218 | 237 | 91.98% | 3.00 | 3.56 | 3.38 | 9.89 |
| Low | 6 | 203 | 2.96% | 2.24 | 3.56 | 3.29 | 4.94 |
| Medium | 33 | 220 | 15.00% | 3.78 | 2.98 | 3.00 | 14.12 |
| Total | 257 | 660 | 38.94% | | | | |

The correlation between the actual and predicted accuracy for these tasks was 0.93. Task accuracy varied from 27.9% to 54.8% (see Table 5). Given the high accuracy of this classifier at detecting high emotional states and the tendency for different tasks to preferentially elicit this state, accuracy.

The correlation between actual and predicted accuracy for participants was 0.9. While individual participant scores will be withheld, accuracy ranged from 18.2% to 75.8%. The high level of correlation between actual and predicted accuracy suggest participant emotional status was a primary contributor to differences in accuracy.

**Table 5.** Actual v. predicted classifier performance across task type shows that the accuracy of the classifier for when k = 3 is lower than for when k = 2. Accuracy still appears to be a function of *high* vs. *low* outcomes present within the data. Accuracy is still poorer for first 5 video tasks.

| Task | Accuracy | Predicted | Low | Medium | High |
|------|----------|-----------|-----|--------|------|
| vidLVLA | 35.00% | 35.72% | 31 | 8 | 21 |
| vidHVLA | 40.00% | 39.49% | 25 | 12 | 23 |
| HVHA | 33.33% | 33.60% | 16 | 27 | 17 |
| vid-N | 27.87% | 24.57% | 41 | 6 | 14 |
| vid-LVHA | 36.67% | 37.20% | 30 | 8 | 22 |
| Matb-L | 48.78% | 52.08% | 8 | 12 | 21 |
| Matb-M | 54.76% | 47.24% | 9 | 14 | 19 |
| Matb-H | 35.71% | 36.65% | 14 | 14 | 14 |
| Tet-M | 47.44% | 48.46% | 7 | 36 | 35 |
| Tet-H | 37.18% | 38.44% | 8 | 45 | 25 |
| Tet-L | 37.18% | 38.50% | 14 | 38 | 26 |
| All | 38.94% | 38.94% | 203 | 220 | 237 |

# 6    Conclusions

The goal of this research was to determine if this approach could yield an algorithm capable of detecting real-time changes in states using a technique that generalizes across participants and across tasks. The approach was straightforward to apply. Once this algorithm creates a model it can detect changes in emotions by applying the existing model. The algorithm can update the model incrementally as new data occurs. The overall accuracy on the Tetris tasks was similar to or even slightly better than previous results. The model performs better at detecting heightened emotional states.

## 6.1    Discussion of Experimental Results

**The Number of States Affect Accuracy.** The classifier tends to favor one outcome over another. This means that the target state with the single highest probability of taking place is a good baseline against which to evaluate the performance of the classifier. The number of states will affect how dominant any state may become. For this reason this approach works better on problems with fewer target states.

**Collective Inference Increases Accuracy.** Combined inference took place in a couple of ways. First, the algorithm combined evidence from 104 sensor channels to create a single prediction for each combination of participant and task. The accuracy for this combined estimate was about 1.5% more accurate than the aggregate estimate of the individual sensors. Because the model combined all sensor readings for the period of the task, it combined evidence across time into one prediction for each sensor channel.

The algorithm also combined both the oxygenated and deoxygenated modalities into a single model. This combined model was more accurate than the combination of two separate models created for each modality. Adding multiple modalities into a single model increased the ability of the algorithm to generalize.

**Heightened Emotion is Easier to Detect.** The highest accuracy took place for tasks and for participants that elicited heightened emotional states. Conversely, the lowest accuracy occurred for tasks designed to elicit neutral emotions. The highest accuracy took place for Tetris tasks designed to elicit mental effort. The second highest accuracy took place on multi-attribute tasks. The video tasks intended to elicit certain emotional responses had the lowest accuracies. This approach may primarily detect changes to a default baseline.

**Emotion Generalizes Despite Individual Differences.** Emotions tend to stratify into discrete states. If using two states, the clusters tended to represent either low or high states. When using three clusters grouped into low, medium, and high. The application of these centroids to participants' emotional data revealed that certain tasks tended to elicit heightened emotional states across participants. It also revealed that there were important individual differences in expression of emotional state. Some individuals rarely exhibited heightened emotional states.

## 6.2  Conclusions About the Approach

This approach is flexible, scalable, and extensible. Once built the approach was fairly easy to implement on different types of input data. Creating states as prediction targets is an approach that will work in a variety of industrial and physiological scenarios. Using an algorithm that incrementally, partially fits data allows this approach to scale well. Furthermore, exerting compression using vector quantization reduces the computational complexity. However, this approach is not without its challenges.

**RBMs Need Enhancements.** RBMs have several advantages including the ability to compress the input representation and the ability to succinctly learn relationships between those same inputs. As noted in the results above, the inclusion of RBMs prior to classification often resulted in a slight increase in overall accuracy. However, this increases seemed due to luck since this approach was strongly favoring the dominant class. Nonetheless, this approach did not make use of the Softmax or of Gaussian visible units. Both of these techniques make RBMs easier to train and to fit the input data [4].

## 7  Next Steps

This research used a fairly straightforward implementation of the approach mentioned within this paper. Now that the approach appears to work on at least one example using a simple implementation, future research can focus upon extending this work further by using different techniques. For example, additional pre-processing techniques such as fast Fourier transformations could assist the model in learning periodic nature of the inputs. Additionally, certain streaming detection techniques could assist in reducing false positive classifications. Moving towards the use of conditional RBMs will increase representational qualities of this algorithm and will hopefully boost the accuracy. Finally, additional forms of graph-based inferencing may help combine evidence across the 104 channels. For example, group sensors together based upon which region of the brain they observe.

**Acknowledgments.** The author thanks Mark Costa, Danushka Bandara, Leanne Hirshfield and Syracuse University for enabling the application of this research to the context of human physiological data. They provided historic data and offered detailed descriptions related to past experiments.

# References

1. Bandara, D., Bratt,S., Hirshfield, L., Velipasalar, S.: Building predictive models of emotion with functional near-infrared spectroscopy. Int. J. Hum.-Comput. Stud. (in press)
2. Bandara, D., Song, S., Hirshfield, L., Velipasalar, S.: A more complete picture of emotion using electrocardiogram and electrodermal activity to complement cognitive data. In: Schmorrow, D.D., Fidopiastis, Cali M.M. (eds.) AC 2016. LNCS (LNAI), vol. 9743, pp. 287–298. Springer, Cham (2016). doi:10.1007/978-3-319-39955-3_27
3. Kalpana, V., Hamde, S.T., Waghmare, L.M.: ECG feature extraction using principal component analysis for studying the effect of diabetes. J. Med. Eng. Technol. **37**(2), 116–126 (2013). doi:10.3109/03091902.2012.753126
4. Taylor, G.W., Hinton, G.E., Roweis, S.: Modeling human motion using binary latent variables. In: 19th Proceedings of 2006 Conference on Advances in Neural Information Processing Systems, vol. 1, pp. 1345–1352. MIT Press (2007)
5. Thompson, D.R., Mandrake, L., Green, O.R., Chen, S.A.: A case study of spectral signature detection in multimodal and outlier-contaminated scenes. IEEE Geosci. Remote Sens. Lett. **10**(5), 1021–1025 (2013)
6. Jaderberg, M., et al.: Reinforcement learning with unsupervised auxiliary tasks. Comput. Res. Repos. 1611 (2016)
7. Chan, M., Lowrance, J., Murdock, J., Ruspini, E.H., Yang, J., Yeh, E.: Human-aided multi-sensor fusion. In: 7th International Conference on Information Fusion, p. 3 (2005). doi:10.1109/ICIF.2005.1591827
8. Pearl, J.: Causality. Cambridge University Press, New York (2000)
9. Michael, J.-B., et al.: Qualitative analysis of culture using millions of digitized books. Science **331**(6014), 176–182 (2011)
10. Veeramachaneni, K., et al.: AI²: training a big data machine to defend. In: 2016 IEEE 2nd International Conference on Big Data Security on Cloud (BigDataSecurity), IEEE International Conference on High Performance and Smart Computing (HPSC), and IEEE International Conference on Intelligent Data and Security (IDS), New York, NY, pp. 49–54 (2016). doi:10.1109/BigDataSecurity-HPSC-IDS.2016.79
11. Kirk, R.A.: Evaluating a cognitive tool built to aid decision making using decision making approach as a theoretical framework and using unobtrusive, behavior-based measures for analysis. Doctoral dissertation (2015). Retrieved from ProQuest (3684297)
12. Kirk, R.A., Kirk, D.A., Pesheck, P.: Decision making for complex ecosystems: a technique for establishing causality in dynamic systems. In: Stephanidis, C. (ed.) HCI 2016. CCIS, vol. 617, pp. 110–115. Springer, Cham (2016). doi:10.1007/978-3-319-40548-3_18

13. Jonassen, D.: Using cognitive tools to represent problems. J. Res. Technol. Educ. **35**, 36–82 (2003)
14. Vygotsky, L.S.: Consciousness as a problem in the psychology of behavior. Russ. Soc. Sci. Rev. **20**(4), 47–79 (2010). [1061–1428] Vygotsky
15. Gardenfors, P.: Conceptual Spaces: The Geometry of Thought. MIT Press, Hong Kong (2000)
16. Russell, J.A.: A circumplex model of affect. J. Pers. Soc. Psychol. **39**(6), 1161–1178 (1980)
17. Moskowitz, G.B.: Social Cognition: Understanding Self and Others. Guilford Publications, New York (2013)
18. Binh, L.N.: Optical Multi-bound Solitons. CRC Press, Boca Raton (2016)
19. Pedregosa, F., et al.: Scikit-learn: machine learning in Python. JMLR **2012**, 2825–2830 (2011)
20. Hart, S.G., Staveland, L.E.: Development of NASA-TLX (task load index): results of empirical and theoretical research. In: Hancock, P.A., Meshkati, N. (eds.) Human Mental Workload. Advances in Psychology, vol. 52, pp. 139–183. North Holland, Amsterdam (1988). doi:10.1016/S0166-4115(08)62386-9
21. Rousseeuw, P.J.: Silhouettes: a graphical aid to the interpretation and validation of cluster analysis. Comput. Appl. Math. **20**, 53–65 (1987). doi:10.1016/0377-0427(87)90125-7

# Augmented Cognition for Continuous Authentication

Nancy Mogire[1]([⊠]), Michael-Brian Ogawa[1], Brent Auernheimer[2],
and Martha E. Crosby[1]

[1] Department of Information and Computer Sciences,
University of Hawaii at Manoa, Honolulu, HI 96822, USA
{nmogire, ogawam, crosby}@hawaii.edu
[2] Computer Science Department,
California State University, Fresno, CA 93740, USA
brent@csufresno.edu

**Abstract.** Authentication serves the gatekeeping function in computing systems. Methods used in authentication fall into three major paradigms: 'what you
know', 'who you are' and 'what you have' of which the first is still the most
commonly applied in the form of passwords authentication. Recall and recognition are the cognitive functions central to the 'what you know' authentication
paradigm. Studies have shown that more secure passwords are harder to recall
and this often leads to habits that facilitate recollection at the expense of
security. Combining the uniqueness of physiological measures, such as brainwave patterns, with memorable augmented passwords shows the promise of
providing a secure and memorable authentication process. In this paper, we
discuss authentication and related problems and considerations in literature. We
then test a password system designed to make use of character property transformations such as color and font to minimize the need for complex passwords
while not compromising security. The findings from this study suggest that
applying transformations to passwords facilitates memorability. We then discuss
a study to combine an augmented password system with physiological measures
that can provide a more secure model for continuous authentication.

**Keywords:** Authentication · Password authentication · Brainwave based
authentication · Recall and recognition · Password memory · Physiological
measures

## 1 Introduction

Authentication is one of the considerations central to system design since it serves the
gate-keeping function in any given system. Authentication can be defined as the process where one entity acquires evidence of the identity claimed by another entity in a
protocol in which both entities are involved. Commonly in consumer computing
systems, this protocol is the login process. Authentication methods fall into three
different paradigms: who you are, what you have and what you know. Various methods
drawn from these different paradigms can be combined to form multi-factor authentication systems. This paper details the weaknesses and trade-offs of each of these

© Springer International Publishing AG 2017
D.D. Schmorrow and C.M. Fidopiastis (Eds.): AC 2017, Part I, LNAI 10284, pp. 342–356, 2017.
DOI: 10.1007/978-3-319-58628-1_27

methods. Password authentication which falls under the 'what you know' paradigm is most commonly used perhaps due to the lower cost and ease of implementation. As it is susceptible to various attacks, we discuss some causes and possible solutions including the use of physiological measurements for authentication. Since we may be able to capture physiological data from the recall and recognition of passwords, we designed a study to test the memorability of augmented passwords with the goal of designing a system aimed at mitigating password problems.

Physiological characteristics are harder to impersonate than any other authentication form because they are pre-cognitively controlled. While a lot of physiological functioning is non-observable in the physical dimension, its measurement can be obtained by measuring performance of an individual on carefully designed and pre-defined tasks that reflect various behavioral and bodily functions. For example, we can detect recognition of a password by observing a P300 brainwave pattern obtained using EEG tools. Our eventual goal is to study how these measures can be reliably combined to distinguish between intended and unintended users.

## 2  Review of the Literature

This review presents the different paradigms of authentication and then focuses on a the 'what you know' model of password-based authentication due to its current dominance in user authentication processes. We review the weaknesses of password authentication and the background problems that lead to these weaknesses. Specifically, we focus on recall and recognition and the attempts that have been made at improving these cognitive processes for the sake of password security. Subsequently we review literature on the workings of the brain as underlies cognition. We then introduce brain computer interaction and review studies that have considered the use of brain data for authentication in the way that passwords are used today. Next, we review security propositions in physiological measurement based authentication and finally we look at some security threats resulting from these physiological measurement methods and the potential effectiveness of attacks to these systems. We close this section by reviewing literature on continuous authentication itself a concept that is still relatively new, and its connection to the brainwave based authentication.

### 2.1  Authentication

Different methods of authentication are susceptible to different attacks. Thorpe et al. [21] summarize the susceptibilities of what-you-know-based authentication such as text and graphical passwords. The threats include shoulder surfing which is made easier by high resolution phone cameras, dictionary attacks which are made easier by poor password choices, acoustic attacks on typing rhythm, and disclosure of password by the user through sharing or writing down to aid in later recall. 'Who you are' authentication traditionally relies on biometric keying such as the use of a fingerprint or iris scanning to authenticate to a system. The problem with this class of authentication methods as Thorpe et al. [21] point out is that they rely on a key whose lifetime is that of the owner. Various authors [4, 14] have discussed several attacks facing physical biometric systems on various levels in the authentication process. If biometric identity is compromised, then the vulnerability of the individual may be permanent due to the lack of a changeability property. As noted by Thorpe et al. [21], physical biometrics are not used for remote authentication.

'What you have' based authentication involves the use of a physical token often in the form of a smart card to authenticate oneself to a system. The problem in this authentication scheme is the fact that authenticating authorities have not found a way of consolidating their functions into a single universal token per single user which means the user must carry a separate token for every system that uses such an authentication scheme. As Thorpe et al. [21] note, this can be inconvenient for the user. The issuance and management of tokens is also an unrealistic cost for many systems, such as social media websites, with high user turnover and often free patronage.

Increasingly, combinations of these factors are used together in what is known as multi-factor authentication. Kiljan et al. [11] conducted a survey on 80 home banking sites, 60 mobile banking applications and 25 mobile banking sites in a study similar to a previous one they conducted in 2013 and compared the results. In their 2015 study they found that most banks in Europe, South America, and Oceania required the use of multiple factors, while most other regions seem to be more divided. However, they found that there was not much change in the overall use of knowledge and possession factors in both mobile applications and sites between 2013 and 2015 except for the introduction of possession-only authentication by a few banks. The authors found that passwords were popular in both multi-factor and single factor usage while PIN numbers were only applied when multi-factor authentication was used, a pattern which can be attributed to the lower complexity of PINs compared to passwords. The authors note that while biometrics based on physical characteristics can be used as an additional or alternative authentication factor for user authentication, the method is faced with disadvantages. These disadvantages include unwillingness of some people to use biometrics due to social stigma, and the limited number of non-replaceable characteristics which can also be absent if the user is disabled. Behavioral characteristics on the other hand are not applicable for initial authentication when based upon anomaly detection since the user has to do some activity first for anomaly to be detected. However, as the authors point out, analysis of usage characteristics such as usual time of login and known location can be used as part of initial authentication.

## 2.2  Password Authentication

Use of passwords is the most common form of authentication perhaps due to its low cost of implementation especially on unmonitored systems. In theory, passwords could offer a high entropy but user choices make it difficult to achieve. As an example, Thorpe et al. [21] discuss in their character based pass-thought system that assuming a textual password scheme where all 95 printable ASCII characters are displayed on a screen and the user must select a sequence of 8 characters, the size of the full pass-thought space is $95^8$, approximately 52 bits could be achieved but the poor choice of passwords by users limits what can be expected.

In a study of web password habits conducted by Florencio and Herley [6] covering half a million accounts over the course of 3 months, users chose passwords with an average bit strength of 40.54 bits. Also, unless forced to do otherwise, the majority chose passwords that contained only lower case letters without any uppercase letters, digits, or special characters. Additionally, the average password was re-used in at least six different sites at times including phishing sites. It is notable similar user habits as related to passwords were found in a smaller study conducted almost two decades earlier [13]. In this experiment, user passwords were easy to crack as lengthy dictionaries could be scanned fast and words could be permuted in different ways. As an example, a dictionary of 250,000 words could be checked in under five minutes. He was also able to crack passwords from languages other than English and even less common words like "fylgjas." His observation was that users typically choose weak passwords, which was confirmed many years later by Florencio and Herley [6]. An explanation for this behavior relates to problems of password recall and recognition. As Forget et al. [7] discuss, more secure passwords are often difficult to remember. In attempting to solve this problem, they conceptualized the *Password Rehearsal Games (PRG)* based on their study of Brain Age games made by Nintendo. They discuss that Nintendo's Brain Age games which involve memory, language, and mathematical exercises, were inspired by neurophysiology and brain mapping research on cognitive functioning. In their work, Forget et al. [7] suggest that password rehearsal games could help users recall their real passwords better. While memory games are not themselves a new idea, their efficacy is not widely agreed upon. Melby-Lervåg and Hulme [17] conducted a meta-analysis of several studies on memory training and arrived at the conclusion that although memory training programs can yield reliable improvements on both verbal and nonverbal working memory tasks, these effects are likely to be short-term. They found that for verbal working memory, near-transfer effects are achieved but are not sustained when reassessed after a delay averaging roughly 9 months. Near-transfer effects are those reflecting in tasks closely related to the ones in the training program. For visuo-spatial memory, the pattern has not been as clear although a few studies suggest that modest training effects can occur and can last up to 5 months after cessation of training.

Another method that has been studied for improving brain function is the stimulation of the dorsolateral prefrontal cortex (DLPFC) using Transcranial Magnetic Stimulation (TMS). Bhattacharyya et al. [2] discuss in their review of neurotechnology that this kind of stimulation has been linked to improvements in basic cognitive functions, including working memory assessed through performance in the N-back task. The N-back task as described by the authors is a continuously performed task in which the subject is given a sequence of images and asked to identify a match within the sequence. For instance, 1-back is a comparison of the current stimulus with the previous one while 2-back is a comparison between the current stimulus and the one 2 steps back, that is the one before the previous one. As they point out, evidence of improvement varies widely across methods and studies. It appears that memory training games could require a lot of conscious effort and motivation while the effects are very moderate, do not last long and may even fail to occur and neurotechnology may be harder to access and require more specialized application with varied usability and results. This reduces the prospects of making password systems more secure through memory and cognition improvement techniques.

## 2.3    Authentication Using Physiological Measurements

In exploring possible alternatives to password authentication, physiological measures have shown the potential to expand the 'who you are' model of authentication which was previously confined to the physical properties of the entity being authenticated. This is due to uniqueness of physiological behavior to an individual, and the measurability of these physiological events. As Ikehara and Crosby [10] discuss, there are many physiological events that can be measured directly using sensors including eye movements, pupil size and skin conductivity. These measures can be used to identify various cognitive states including stress, fatigue, arousal, attention deficit and many others. In their experiments, they used a mobile eye tracking system and a desktop model to obtain gaze position and pupil size. They also used a custom designed electrically isolated physiological sensor system to obtain galvanic skin conductivity (GSR), peripheral temperature, relative blood flow and the pressures applied to a computer mouse. Identification of cognitive states of individuals could be used to authenticate them. The authors suggest that unexpected cognitive measures would lead to a prompt to the user to reauthenticate themselves. Further, the authors propose that if these measures can be obtained continuously, then a continuous authentication model can be created to prevent unauthorized users from slipping into a system and being able to use it. Recognition of various cognitive states has been studied in different contexts and efforts to automate the sensor data collection continue in various contexts.

Picard [19] developed a wristband for measurement of skin conductance, while they worked towards automating the recognition of stress and emotion. Their interest in electrodermal activity (EDA) measurements grew after they found in various tests that skin conductance correlated highly with stress levels. In their experiments focusing on children with autism, a group they selected because of its higher levels of response to stimuli, they saw among other observations that skin conductance measurements grew during tasks that increased cognitive or physical exertion. Conversely, skin conductance decreased during repetitive movements like swinging or rocking, suggesting relaxed feelings. In their work, they continually correlate the EDA data with brain data measurements for reference. As they note, brain studies have shown that a key part of the brain involved in emotion is the amygdala. Taking a closer look at literature in brain studies, many processes happening in the body can be correlated with a visible change in structure or otherwise measurable signal change in the brain. Gonzalez and Berman [8] discuss that brain mapping can be used to associate one physiological process with another or with occurrence of some event. Conversely, brain mapping can also be used to dissociate two or more processes by finding brain regions that respond differently to different experimental manipulations. Brain mapping also helps to draw connections between physiological function and respective anatomical structure in what is known as localization.

The authors suggest that brain imaging is important in research reliant on psychological factors because it enables optimization of techniques towards collection of good data. This is because brain imaging has enabled classification of cognitive actions and led to the understanding of the spatial temporal resolution dynamics. Each of the current brain mapping technologies has either a high temporal resolution or a high spatial resolution but not both. However, some researchers have combined brain mapping methods in order to obtain both optimizations. As Gonzalez and Berman [8] argue, the study of the relevant neuroscience is important when intending to collect and use brain data for various reasons; first it helps in understanding how to set up a good experiment environment that supports collection of good data, it also helps to know how to design questions in a way that can enable one to reach valid conclusions using data from brain mapping as well as how to design the experiment itself, putting in adequate constraints, and being cognizant of various confounding variables.

## 2.4 Neurofeedback of Recall and Recognition Functions

We now highlight recall and recognition which are the cognitive functions central to the 'what you know' authentication paradigm. Cabeza et al. [3], conducted an experiment to compare regions of the brain used for recognition and recall functions. They used positron emission tomography to take measurements while young healthy persons were recognizing or recalling previously studied word pairs. The researchers included some words not previously studied by the participant, to serve as a control to the experiment. Their experiment found that recall tasks caused a higher activation of blood flow in the anterior cingulate, globus pallidus, thalamus, and cerebellum, suggesting a role played by cerebellofrontal pathway in recall but not recognition.

Recognition on the other hand caused a higher activation in right inferior parietal cortex, suggesting a larger perceptual component in recognition than recall. They found that activations of frontal regions were indistinguishable between recognition and recall. As they discuss, this last observation corroborates the notion that frontal activations simply indicate attempts to retrieve some stored information but do not point to the specific mechanism of retrieval. Brain mapping can possibly expand not only the 'who you are' but also the 'what you know' paradigm of authentication because one will recognize or recall what they know.

## 2.5 Brainwave Based Authentication

Brainwave based authentication has been made possible by the progress made in brain computer interaction (BCI) research. BCI research started out with search for solutions for brain control of prosthetics for disabled patients. BCI interfaces link the brain's EEG signals with a computer [1]. The essence of brain computer interaction work is: observe a brain signal evoked by some stimuli, extract its features, translate or classify those features into recognizable command using signal processing and machine learning techniques Thorpe et al. [21]. As Bayliss and Auernheimer [1] found in a study comparing BCI under immersion in a virtual environment versus BCI while simply staring at a computer monitor, there were no significant differences between these two conditions.

A tool commonly used for signal acquisition is the electroencephalogram (EEG). The term electroencephalogram (EEG) is derived from combining 'Electro' meaning electrical activity, 'encephalo' meaning brain, and 'graph' for the picture [14]. As indicated by the name, the EEG measures the brain's electrical activities. It does so using electrodes attached to the scalp. These electrodes are connected to a computer to display and store the measurements. The electrical signal is produced by the combined activity of large number of similarly oriented pyramidal neutrons. In other words the signal is the result of synchronous activity across a large group of cells (Personal Communication: Vibell Lecture Notes 2017). Each person's brain patterns are unique and different from those of other people.

As [14] discuss, brainwave signals are usually decomposed in several frequency bands with each band signaling a particular brain activity. The authors summarize the broad categorizations of the EEG signal bands in their literature review: Gamma - active thought, attention, learning, visual perception, memory; Beta- Alert, Working; Alpha- Relaxed, Reflective; Theta-Drowsy, Meditative; Delta-Sleepy, Dreaming. The authors also summarize the different classes of brain signal: The Slow cortical potentials (SCP) which refers to slow brain signal typically from non-movement tasks from 300 s; The P300 evoked potential generated by auditory, visual & somatosensory stimuli in the parietal cortex region after 300 ms of stimuli exposure; The visual evoked potential (VEP) caused by sail changes in the brain resulting from visual stimulus such as flashing lights; The activity of neural cell which is a measure of firing rate of the neuron in the region of motor; The energy of the brain reflected by the energy of brainwaves at different frequencies; The acknowledge to mental task which is caused by a mental task such as solving an arithmetic expression or imagining a 3D object; The complex neuro-mechanism group is any combination of the other classes.

Feature classification is carried out using different mathematical techniques such as *fourier transformation* which enables signal representation in frequency bands such as delta, theta, alpha, beta, and gamma with each band being classified as a different feature [20], *auto-covariance* which involves finding features which distinguish one EEG signal from others, and other techniques.

The P300 brain signal has proved relevant and useful in cognitive biometrics because it reveals the change in mental state that occurs when a user recognizes some stimuli. Its discreteness property makes it useful for environmental control [1]. Meijer et al. [16] showed that mere recognition was sufficient to elicit a P300 response and that it was not essential that the recognized stimuli be important to the participant. In their experiment, they isolated mere recognition by having participants respond based on an irrelevant dimension of the stimuli such as faces of known public figures with comparison to people important to the participant and people not known by the participant. The authors note that stimuli referring to information relevant to the participant elicits a larger P300 than stimuli referring to incidentally acquired information.

## 2.6 Brainwave Based Authentication System Design and Security Proposition

The availability of low cost EEG sensors has motivated research work in brain computer interactions and brainwave based authentication. Chuang et al. [5] studied the efficacy of single-channel as opposed to multi-channel EEG signals, being that single channel devices are lower end versions of EEG devices. In their experiment, they used a consumer-grade headset that provided a single-channel EEG signal. They designed mental tasks for subjects to perform such as breathing, singing and listening and authenticated subjects based on performance in the specific tasks chosen for them. The authentication involved matching a sample to a pre-recorded identity. They designed a user matching algorithm adapted from the K-Nearest Neighbors (KNN) algorithm for coloring graphs, with their adaptation making the trial signatures the nodes, the subject identities the colors and the cosine similarity being the distance metric. They measured the false acceptance and the false rejection error rates. The findings revealed that single-channel EEG authentication can be just as accurate as multi-channel EEG authentication because single-channel signals do exhibit subject-specific patterns.

Thorpe et al. [21] focused on harnessing the P300 paradigm in their design proposal of a pass-thoughts system that authenticates by applying thoughts in the way that text passwords are traditionally applied to log into a device. Their idea was to use a thought based system as a natural 2-factor system where the changeable thought or measurable response to a stimuli is the first factor and physiological uniqueness of brain signal is the second factor. They proposed a system where the user would select a pass-thought, then to log in they would look at a character set on the screen where the characters would be highlighted one at a time and randomly. When the user sees part of their pass-thought highlighted their P300 would spike. The P300 spikes would be recorded and used to determine whether the user's P300 firing matched the expected template of that user's account's password i.e. after the user completes the pass-thought input, the hash of the pass-thought is compared to the stored pass-thought. They point out that although the size of the pass-thought space for this scheme is dependent on the number of characters on the screen and the number of screens that get presented to the user, in reality the message space is always curbed by user choices.

The security proposition in brainwave based authentication as in other physiological property based authentication is that brainwave patterns are less susceptible to forgery. This is due to various factors including that brain response events are unconsciously controlled, unique for each person and changeable e.g. by changing one's thoughts. As Thorpe et al. [21] argue, a login system such as pass-thoughts would be shoulder-surfing resistant, and also resistant to acoustic attacks and dictionary attacks. The authors are careful to note that although brainwave based authentication could offer better security guarantees than other methods like typing in text passwords, the method is also susceptible to some attacks such as social engineering as well as interception attacks in remote usage. In their coloring-graph-type user matching algorithm Chuang et al. [5] note that user identification proved harder than user authentication. That observation raises the question of whether an attacker could successfully forge identity once they know the custom tasks a system expects from a target. Brainwave based authentication is faced with other limitations as well.

## 2.7 Limitations on Brainwave Based Authentication

As noted earlier, low cost availability of EEG devices has made it easier to explore brainwave based authentication especially being that lower end EEG devices have been shown to reveal subject-specific brain patterns characteristics almost as well as the higher end tools. However, EEG based authentication has been reported to be a slow method of logging in to a system. Thorpe et al. [21] report that the P300 bit rate is 4.8 characters per minute which would make the login process noticeably slower. This could feel like a step in the backward direction for many and is one reason brainwave authentication may not have mass applicability for now. However, it is reasonable to view this as a short-term problem due to the rate of growth of bit processing power. Another problem is that EEG signal collection involves mounting the EEG headset on a user's head to make contact with the scalp. Although this is not considered invasive, it does limit mass applicability. Thorpe et al. [21] mention an interesting direction to explore, that is if the P300 signal could be collected using a touch pin pattern, a technique that could allow the scheme be integrated to a cellphone touchscreen. Another potential problem is that if the tasks are similar then user selection may converge on a similar pool of choices. However, when participants only had to answer a question by thinking of something, a rate of collision of user choices of thoughts was not identified.

## 2.8 Deception Detection in EEG Data

Meijer et al. [16] showed that mere recognition was sufficient to elicit a P300 response and that it was not essential that the recognized stimuli be important to the participant. However, they note that other studies exist which indicate that stimuli referring to information relevant to the subject elicit a larger P300 than stimuli referring to incidentally acquired information. These findings raise the question of whether it is possible to tell between those who honestly acquired or owned some piece of information such as a password and those who had acquired it disingenuously. Some progress has been made towards finding an answer to this question as wavelet analysis of EEG signals has been applied with some success in general deception detection. Merzagora et al. [18] investigated the capacity for EEG measurement to differentiate among the cognitive elements of truth and deception. Neither time-domain nor frequency-domain features revealed any significant difference between channels or responses. However, on analysis of wavelet domain features extracted from the EEG, they found that wavelet coefficients with a joint time-frequency distribution corresponding to the beta rhythm were able to discriminate true and false information in time windows from 300 to 1000 ms. They note however that their work is preliminary and would need larger samples sizes, more diverse protocols, and other considerations in future iterations of the experiment.

Khandelwal et al. [12] in their conceptual study also suggest that EEG could be used to detect basic lying. They reference other methods that already show results. For example, functional magnetic resonance imaging (fMRI) which records brain activity by identifying changes in brain blood flow and the metabolic rate has shown that the conflict between true and false information can be observed when imaging the brain. However, these studies do not reveal if disingenuously obtained information would be detectable. Although acquiring this type of information involves some dishonesty, such information is essentially not a lie.

## 2.9 Attacks on EEG Based Authentication

A study by Martinovic et al. [15] shows the feasibility of side channel attacks on EEG based authentication. In their study of the security implication of consumer grade BCI devices, they found that the signal captured by a consumer-grade EEG device can be used to extract potentially sensitive information from the users. In their experiment, the attack vector was third party developer applications in EEG-based gaming headsets which are low-cost and easily available in the consumer market. The threat model was the fact that the EEG devices developer API provided unrestricted access to the raw EEG signal and allowed applications complete control over the stimuli that could be presented to the users. The attacker in this case could be the ill-meaning third-party developer. The study investigated how third party EEG applications could infer private information about the users, by manipulating the visual stimuli presented on screen and by analyzing the corresponding responses in the EEG signal. They based the success of slipping in irrelevant stimuli to a user on the fact that P300 is elicited during stimuli that are personally meaningful to participants even though not defined by the task. This is consistent with what Meijer et al. [16] found in their literature survey that if the information had some meaning to the participant, P300 could be elicited without any instructions or tasks. In the experiment, the gaming device user who was the target of attack was probed to detect whether certain stimuli such as PIN number, bank name, and month of birth were familiar to or relevant for the user. They found that found that the entropy of the private information is decreased on the average by approximately 15%–40% compared to random guessing attacks. They suggest a remedy where the EEG application API is made more restrictive not giving third party developers access to raw data, a strategy that could limit developers both positively and negatively. Other suggestions include users consciously ignoring non-target stimuli, an expectation that may not be realistic.

## 2.10 Continuous Authentication Using EEG

As discussed, EEG measurement can reliably differentiate between different individuals. However, for the scheme to be applicable towards continuous authentication, there are still questions as to whether a user can be continuously re-identified correctly with changes in the environment over the short term and over an extended timeframe. If the EEG can continue to recognize a user across their changing cognitive states, then it can be applicable for continuous authentication.

Kumari and Vaish [14] in their review of methods in EEG based authentication note among the advantages of using the EEG signal that it can be collected continuously allowing for ascertaining that the subject is alive. They also note that if it is coerced out of subject the EEG signal will be distorted by stress. Additionally, since it is related to genetic information a stable unique pattern for each person can be attained over time. The stability factor is however still being studied. Gupta et al. [9], conducted a study investigating the stability of recognition features noting that the long-term invariance would be necessary for reliable implementation. In their work, they found among other results that the task design can influence stability and they suggested the use of Rapid Serial Visual Paradigm (RSVP) in task design for cognitive biometrics. On task usability, Kumari and Vaish [14] note in their work that this varies based on various factors including boredom level. Overall, the stability of recognition features in brainwave based biometrics has not been extensively studied.

With the eventual goal of developing a secure and memorable password authentication process, we are testing ways to effectively combine the uniqueness of physiological measures, such as brainwave patterns, with memorable augmented passwords. Our initial study was to use augmented passwords to elicit recognition and recall behavior.

## 3   Password Recognition and Recall Study

### 3.1   Setting

This initial study was conducted on a large-enrollment introductory computer science course at a research extensive university. Approximately 200–300 students enroll in this course each semester from over 30 majors. The course includes a lecture meeting and a laboratory component with a teaching assistant. One hundred fifty-seven students participated in the study.

### 3.2   Methods

To determine the recognition and recall accuracy of augmented passwords using font styles, we developed a system parallel to account password generation systems where users enter their passwords twice before using it for account authentication. We created a six-character string password with different font styles for students in the labs. The second character of the password string was modified for the different groups, no font style, bold, italicize, underline, and strikethrough. Students entered the password that was displayed on the projector twice on the first day to assess recognition and mirror password creation. On the second lab day, two days later, students entered their password from memory to assess recall and reflect account authentication. After entering the password on the second day, a survey was administered to determine the methods used to recall the password.

### 3.3   Results

Students had a recognition rate of 70% for no font style (plain text), 76% for bold text, 74% for italicize text, 75% for underline text, and 86% for strikethrough text (see Fig. 1). When asked to recall the password, students responded accurately 64% for no font style, 93% for bold text, 91% for italicize text, 94% for underline text, and 76% for strikethrough text. Performance improved between recognition and recall for bold, italicize, and underline text by 17–19%. Conversely, performance decreased for no font style (−6%) and strikethrough (−9%).

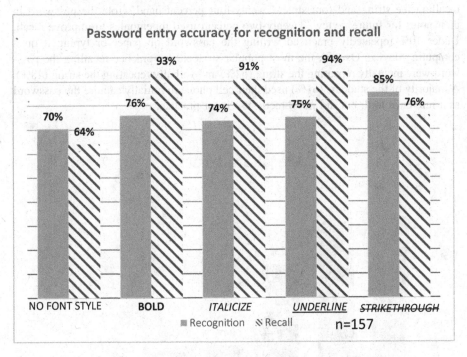

**Fig. 1.** Password accuracy for recognition and recall

Augmented password recall accuracy was higher than the non-augmented passwords with bold, italicize, and underline augmentation having over 90% recall rates and strikethrough having a 76% recall rate. The researchers believe that the augmented characters were distinctive, which made the password string more memorable for participants. The strikethrough augmentation had the lowest recall rate of the augmented passwords which could be attributed to its less use compared to bold, italicize, and underline text. Based on the greater recall rate, the authors believe that augmented passwords could be used in practice. By adding augmented characters to passwords, the total number of possible characters will increase from 95 ASCII characters [21] to 475 characters which enhances password strength.

Recognition accuracy for augmented passwords were also higher than the recognition rate for traditional passwords. Similar to recall, the authors believe that the higher recognition rate is based on one of the characters including augmentation, which helped the participant to focus on the string and accurately replicate it. The increased accuracy for augmented password strings may support its usage in multifactor authentication environments, particularly with a secondary authentication method such as one-time passwords [11].

When asked about recall strategies, 62% of the students took a picture of the password with their phone to review (see Fig. 2). Sixty-one percent mentally repeated the password to visualize the it and improve recall on the second day. Forty-eight percent of the students verbally repeated the password to themselves to practice recalling the string and font style. Twenty-four percent hand wrote the password in their notes for future review. Twenty-two percent used mnemonics to improve recall. Under 10% repeatedly practiced writing the password on paper or typing it on a computing device. Overall, the most popular strategies to practice recalling the password were mentally repeating the string (62%) and verbally repeating the string (48%). A majority of the students (61%) used their cell phone to initially capture the password as a reference tool, but did not directly use it for practice.

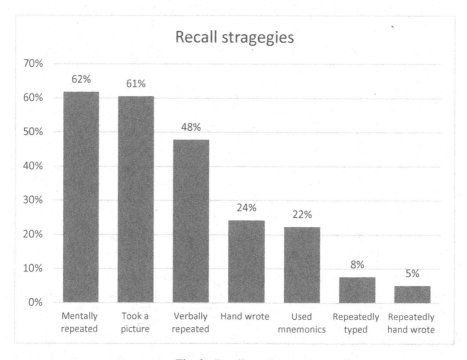

**Fig. 2.** Recall strategies

Given the recall strategies the participants employed, the authors suggest matching rehearsal strategies to the users' practices rather than providing users with practice tools such as rehearsal games [7]. Even though a wide range of rehearsal techniques can improve password recall [17], embedding rehearsal techniques in the users' everyday practices would likely lead greater amounts of practice rather than having to rehearse using a technique that is not a typical practice.

# 4    Password Recall and Recognition Study Using Physiological Measurements

In our proposed next study, whose results are not presented here, we repeat the above study, taking measurement of physiological data elicited by the recall and recognition processes during usage of the system. We can draw physiological patterns but are they accurate enough to be used to authenticate users? The task used in controlling the measurements is their usage of the augmented password system. In essence, the augmented password system provides the first factor while the physiological measures provides the second factor in this study.

## 4.1    Methodology

We are collecting data from 30–50 participants. Three standard-size disposable sensors will be applied to the forearms to measure heart rate. Two standard-sized disposable sensors will be attached to the palm of the subject's non-dominant hand to measure skin conductance. Two sensors will be attached to skin over the orbicularis oculi muscle just below the eye. Two small sensors will also be applied just above the participant's left eyebrow to measure frown muscle activity. Brainwave activity will be recorded over the course of the experimental procedure using an Emotiv EEG data collection headset (http://www.emotiv.com/researchers/). The protocol begins once the physiological data collection, sensors are applied.

The task is to ask individuals to either create and transform a password or to recognize a password transformation previously created by themselves, or to recognize a password, pattern, arithmetic expression previously disclosed to them and modify it in a predefined and pre-discussed way. A session constitutes a combination from the 4 tasks: create, modify, recognize or recall some distinct object such as a character, shape or image. At the end of the tasks, the participant is given a feedback questionnaire. Once the results are analyzed, we will study the stability of these measurements over the short and longer terms and how they could be used in a continuous authentication model.

# References

1. Bayliss, J.D., Auernheimer, B.: Using a brain-computer interface in virtual and real world. Proc. Ninth Int. Conf. Hum.-Comput. Interact. 1, 312–316 (2001)
2. Bhattacharyya, R., Coffman, B.A., Choe, J., Phillips, M.E.: Does neurotechnology produce a better brain? Computer 50(2), 48–58 (2017). doi:10.1109/mc.2017.49
3. Cabeza, R., Kapur, S., Craik, F.I.M., McIntosh, A.R., Houle, S., Tulving, E.: Functional neuroanatomy of recall and recognition: a pet study of episodic memory. J. Cogn. Neurosci. 9(2), 254–265 (1997). doi:10.1162/jocn.1997.9.2.254
4. Chen, L., Pearson, S., Vamvakas, A.: A trusted biometric system - PDF. http://docplayer.net, http://docplayer.net/33351165-A-trusted-biometric-system.html. Accessed 18 Feb 2017

5. Chuang, J., Nguyen, H., Wang, C., Johnson, B.: I think, therefore i am: usability and security of authentication using brainwaves. In: Proceedings of the Workshop on Usable Security, USEC 2013 (2013)

6. Florencio, D., Herley, C.: A large-scale study of web password habits. ACM, New York (2007). doi:10.1145/1242572.1242661. ©2008

7. Forget, A., Chiasson, S., Biddle, R.: Lessons from brain age on password memorability. ACM, New York (2008). doi:10.1145/1496984.1497044. ©2008

8. Gonzalez, R., Berman, M.G.: The value of brain imaging in psychological research. Acta Psychol. Sin. **42**(1), 111–119 (2010). doi:10.3724/SP.J.1041.2010.00111

9. Gupta, C.N., Palaniappan, R., Paramesran, R.: Exploiting the P300 paradigm for cognitive biometrics. Int. J. Cogn. Biometrics **1**(1), 26–28 (2012). doi:10.1504/IJCB.2012.046513

10. Ikehara, C.S., Crosby, M.E.: Physiological measures used for identification of cognitive states and continuous authentication. In: CHI 2010 (2010)

11. Kiljan, S., Simoens, K., Cock, D.D., Eekelen, M.V., Vranken, H.: A survey of authentication and communications security in online banking. ACM Comput. Surv. **49**(4), 1–35 (2016). doi:10.1145/3002170

12. Khandelwal, R.J., Mahajan, J.D., Bombatkar, U.P., Badhe, S.G.: Analysis of EEG signals for deception detection. Int. J. Adv. Res. Elect. Electron. Inst. Eng. **5**(2) (2016). doi:10.15662/IJAREEIE.2016.0502038

13. Klein, D.V.: Foiling the cracker: a survey of, and improvements to, password security. In: Proceedings of the 2nd USENIX Security Workshop (1990)

14. Kumari, P., Vaish, A.: Brainwave based authentication system: research issues and challenges. Int. J. Comput. Eng. Appl. **IV**, I & II (2014). ISSN: 2321 - 3469

15. Martinovic, I., Davies, D., Frank, M., Perito, D., Ros, T., Song, D.: On the feasibility of side-channel attacks with brain-computer interfaces. In: The Proceedings of the 21st USENIX Conference on Security Symposium (2012)

16. Meijer, E.H., Smulders, F.T.Y., Wolf, A.: The contribution of mere recognition to the P300 effect in a concealed information test. Appl. Psychophysiol. Biofeedback (2009). doi:10.1007/s10484-009-9099-9

17. Melby-Lervåg, M., Hulme, C.: Is working memory training effective? A meta-analytic review. Dev. Psychol. **49**(2), 270–291 (2013). doi:10.1037/a0028228

18. Merzagora, A.C., Bunce, S., Izzetoglu, M., Onaral, B.: Wavelet analysis for EEG feature extraction in deception detection. In: 2006 International Conference of the IEEE Engineering in Medicine and Biology Society (2006). doi:10.1109/iembs.2006.260247

19. Picard, R.W.: Automating the recognition of stress and emotion: from lab to real-world impact. IEEE Multimedia **23**(3), 3–7 (2016). doi:10.1109/MMUL.2016.38

20. Safont, G., Salazar, A., Soriano, A., Vergara, L.: Combination of multiple detectors for EEG based biometric identification/authentication. In: 2012 IEEE International Carnahan Conference on Security Technology (ICCST) (2012). doi:10.1109/ccst.2012.6393564

21. Thorpe, J., van Oorschot, P.C., Somayaji, A.: Pass-thoughts: authenticating with our minds. ACM, New York (2005). doi:10.1145/1146269.1146282. ©2005

# Analysis of Social Interaction Narratives in Unaffected Siblings of Children with ASD Through Latent Dirichlet Allocation

Victoria Newton[1,2(✉)], Isabel Solis[1], Glory Emmanuel Aviña[3],
Jonathan T. McClain[2], Cynthia King[4],
and Kristina T. Rewin Ciesielski[1,5]

[1] Pediatric Neuroscience Laboratory, The University of New Mexico,
Albuquerque, NM, USA
vnewton@sandia.gov, ktc@unm.edu
[2] Sandia National Laboratories, Albuquerque, NM, USA
[3] Sandia National Laboratories, Livermore, CA, USA
[4] Department of Psychiatry, School of Medicine,
UNM, Albuquerque, NM, USA
[5] MGH/HMS Athinoula A. Martinos Center for Biomedical Imaging,
Radiology, Massachusetts General Hospital, Harvard Medical School,
Boston, MA 02129, USA

**Abstract.** Children with autism spectrum disorders (ASD) and their unaffected siblings (US) are frequent targets of social bullying, which leads to severe physical, emotional, and social consequences. Understanding the risk factors is essential for developing preventative measures. We suggest that one such risk factor may be a difficulty to discriminate different biological body movements (BBM), a task that requires fast and flexible processing and interpretation of complex visual cues, especially during social interactions. Deficits in cognition of BBM have been reported in ASD. Since US display an autism endophenotype we expect that they will also display deficits in social interpretation of BBM. *Methods.* Participants: 8 US, 8 matched TD children, age 7–14; Tasks/Measurements: Social Blue Man Task: Narrative interpretation with a Latent Dirichlet Allocation [LDA] analysis; Social Experience Questionnaires with children and parents. *Results.* The US displayed as compared to TD: (i) low self-awareness of social bullying in contrast to high parental reports; (ii) reduced speed in identifying social cues; (iii) lower quality and repetitive wording in social interaction narratives (LDA). *Conclusions.* US demonstrate social endophenotype of autism reflected in delayed identification, interpretation and verbalization of social cues; these may constitute a high risk factor for becoming a victim of social bullying.

**Keywords:** Autism spectrum disorder · Unaffected siblings · Biological body movement · Bullying · Social narratives · LDA

---

Sandia National Laboratories is a multi-mission laboratory managed and operated by Sandia Corporation, a wholly owned subsidiary of Lockheed Martin Corporation, for the U.S. Department of Energy's National Nuclear Security Administration under contract DE-AC04-94AL85000. SAND2017-2189C.

© Springer International Publishing AG 2017
D.D. Schmorrow and C.M. Fidopiastis (Eds.): AC 2017, Part I, LNAI 10284, pp. 357–371, 2017.
DOI: 10.1007/978-3-319-58628-1_28

# 1 Introduction

Children with autism spectrum disorders (ASD) and their unaffected siblings (US) are more frequently victims of bullying than typically developing (TD) peers from families not affected by ASD (Sumi et al. 2006). We hypothesize that this greater victimization rate may be related to the primary clinical phenomena in autism: the specific deficit in perceiving, categorizing and understanding social interactions. Prior studies have reported the endophenotype of social deficits in US (Ozonoff et al. 2011). Social interactions are sequences of fast and complex visual experiences that require correct perception of visual-spatial directions of biological body movements (BBM), understanding the social intentions of these movements, and the ability to respond fast to each intention which relies on the correct perception and categorization of the earlier movements in the sequence. We investigate the interpretation of social cues as displayed in BBMs by TD children and US of children with autism. We will examine the level of this complex sequence – perceptual, cognitive, and verbal – on which an abnormality may be manifested in US. The narrative cognitive interpretation of social cues in BBM will be related to personal experiences of bullying. To our knowledge, this relationship has not been studied yet. The long-term goal of this investigation is to better understand in US of children with autism the interplay between difficulties in fast cognitive processing and verbalization of social cues, as displayed in BBM and high risk of these children to bullying victimization.

## 1.1 Social Bullying in ASD and Their Unaffected Siblings

Core clinical symptoms of ASD include anxious insistence on sameness, purposeless ritualistic cognitive and motor acts and severe difficulty to communicate, initiate and maintain social interactions (DSM-V; American Psychiatric Association 2013). Current research shows one in sixty-eight children being diagnosed with ASD (Center for Disease Control 2014). ASD is a heterogeneous and neurodevelopmental disorder with multiple etiological factors including: hereditary (Kabot et al. 2003), metabolic and neurological (Kennedy and Courchesne 2008; Manzi et al. 2008; Minshew and Keller 2010) and neurodevelopmental (Durkin et al. 2008; Nelson et al. 2001; Varcin and Nelson 2016). Currently, special education, behavior modification and an array of pharmacological therapies are used to enhance the individual's overall functioning, but a targeted treatment or preventive approach has not been developed yet.

Evidence is accumulating about genetic and hereditary risks for developing ASD. Siblings of children with ASD are 5–10 times more likely to experience a pervasive developmental disorder than a child from the general population (Sumi et al. 2006). Siblings not diagnosed clinically with the disorder are also more likely to have an ASD trait endophenotype, that is expressing characteristics in cognition (attention, learning) and brain function similar to ASD to a much higher degree than in typically developing (TD) children in the population at large (Ozonoff et al. 2011). Consistent with the apparent differences between children with ASD and TD in social interaction and communication, children with ASD are reported to experience more peer victimization. Bullying experiences of clinically unaffected siblings have not attracted yet attention of researchers.

Olweus (1993) defines bullying as aggressive, intentional, and repeated behaviors that involve a power imbalance and inflict mental and physical harm. Bullying can occur in physical, verbal, social, or cyber forms (Cappadocia et al. 2012). In the traditional view, the behavior of a child who bullies others have been correlated with drugs and alcohol abuse, school dropout, earlier sexual activity, criminal convictions, and abusiveness (Olweus 1993). The current view of "bully" has been broadened with sophisticated relational manipulations and cyber abuse. Negative consequences for victims of bullying could be severe, and include depression, anxiety, physical and psychological health concerns, decreased academic performance, reduced social involvement, suicidal ideations and in extreme cases the school shootings (Sterzing et al. 2012). Bullying of a child may have a devastating impact on families, and thus becomes a major social problem to be solved. We are focusing here exclusively on perceptual and cognitive characteristics of a child who experiences social victimization or bullying.

Recent research has shown an increase in prevalence of school bullying. For TD school children, the prevalence of peer victimization averages at 30% (Molcho et al. 2009). However, in children with ASD reports show peer victimization between 34–94% (Cappadocia et al. 2012; Carter 2009; Little 2002; Van Roekel et al. 2010). The large range in victimization of children with ASD is in part due to the difference in report styles (i.e. who reports the bullying, length of time considered). The accuracy of self-reports by individuals with ASD has also been questioned due to the perception of social knowledge and interpretation of bullying involvement.

One theoretical framework about communication and social deficits in children with ASD that may be related to their susceptibility to bullying is their deficits in the Theory of Mind (ToM). ToM is the mental ability to attribute beliefs and attitudes to others and has been used to describe social behavior in autism (Baron-Cohen et al. 1985). Van Roekel et al. (2010) conducted a study that considered the ToM and perception of bullying in adolescents with ASD and found a relationship between weaker ToM and greater exposure to victimization. In a comprehensive literature review of the ToM and ASD, Baron-Cohen (2000) suggested that ToM deficits are universal in individuals with ASD therefore those with ASD are more likely to experience peer victimization. Our study will permit characterization of these risk factors and their interplay in bullying, as we will be asking US children to assign intentions and social behavioral aims to stimuli expressing BBM.

Another study examined if certain characteristics might lead to greater victimization in ASD (Sterzing et al. 2012). The results showed that: (1) Individuals with ASD who had less deficits in social skills were less likely to be bullied due to their more socially appropriate responses; (2) Those engaging in conversational interactions, however, were more likely to be bullied, because they exposed the poverty and inappropriateness of verbal expressions to be negatively seen by their peers; (3) Children in general education classrooms were more likely to be bullied because of the unprotected environment; (4) Children who had at least one peer whom they considered a friend were less likely to be victimized, and (5) Children who had comorbid conditions (e.g. attention-deficit/hyperactivity disorder) were more likely to be bullied. The findings were consistent with other studies showing that children attending a public school and diagnosed with Asperger syndrome are at the greatest risk of being a victim of social bullying in the forms of rumor spreading or exclusion (Zablotsky et al. 2014; Cappadocia et al. 2012). The more friends a child has, the less likely they are to experience victimization, which highlights the impact of the social component as a factor for resilience to victimization (Cappadocia et al. 2012). The above evidence suggests that a relationship exists between bullying and social interactions, interpretations, and communication as an explanation for higher victimization rates. These finding form a foundation for our study.

As far as we know, no research has been reported on peer victimization of clinically unaffected siblings. Most investigators consider these US individuals as a typically developing group (Nowell et al. 2014). Nowell et al. (2014) however, made an important observation that children with an ASD diagnosis are more frequently bullied than their siblings without a diagnosis. This study is inspiring in directing our attention to the cognitive risk factors of social bullying in unaffected siblings of children with ASD in comparison to their TD peers. Due to the role of genetics in ASD, we predict that clinically unaffected siblings are more likely to experience the trait endophenotype of difficulties in social communication or interaction that we see in ASD, and, thus, will be more susceptible to social bullying than their TD peers.

## 1.2 Visual Processing of Biological Body Movements (BBM)

BBM paradigms have been successfully used to test the perception of biological body movement in humans. Studies have shown that the perceptual system is able to accurately and quickly identify the biological body motion and distinguish it from other types of motion patterns (Hubert et al. 2007). Researchers have found that typically developing persons can accurately determine social meanings associated with bodily movements such as the gender of an individual walking or emotions/attitudes (Hubert et al. 2007). However, individuals with ASD have been found to have difficulties when perceiving actions of others', their subjective states, and emotions as compared to TD (Koldewyn et al. 2001; Lainé et al. 2011; Swettenham et al. 2013). Specifically, children with ASD were impaired when distinguishing expressive/emotional states (e.g. bored, tired, hurt) when compared with TD and peers with other developmental disorders who have intact the interpretation of object motions (Moore et al. 1997). Thus, BBM tasks can be useful when testing perception of social intentions expressed in body motion.

Little research has been conducted on social perception in unaffected siblings. Those reported relate mostly to perception of faces. Dalton et al. (2007) reported that the gaze fixations and brain activation patterns of US during face-processing is similar to children with ASD and largely different than their typically developing group indicating differences in social processing as well as underlying neural circuitry. Further, Kaiser et al. (2010) using fMRI found distinctly different pattern of brain activation to body motion when compared to typically developing children, even though their behavioral responses were similar. These studies showed that US display neural signatures of increased compensatory activity in regions implicated in social perception and cognition, significantly different than those in the TD and ASD subjects. This could indicate protective genetic factors that are vital for understanding treatment and intervention in those with ASD.

## 1.3 Rationale

Social interactions belong to very complex and multi-stage visual events that require a fast and accurate perception and interpretation of another's actions. In addition, one must then be able to quickly and adequately evaluate the event and respond in a socially appropriate manner so not to be rejected or penalized. Examining one's interpretation of social interactions as displayed by BBM could provide an important insight into the risk factors that contribute to the vulnerability of becoming a victim of bullying.

We examine the interpretation of social content of BBM and compare it to both parental reports about the child's experience with bullying and to the child's self-reported social interactions questionnaire. The ultimate goal of this study is to contribute to developing a new line of research on prevention of social bullying among healthy children and children with psychopathological disorders. We predict that: (i) In clinically unaffected siblings (US) the self-reports and parental reports will reveal significantly more prevalent social bullying events than in their TD peers; (ii) US Children, compared to their TD peers, will require a significantly longer time for perception and interpretation of social interactions as expressed in BBM, and (iii) In US the quality and quantity of narratives about the social meaning of BBM will be lower than in TD.

## 2 Methods

### 2.1 Participants

Sixteen children participated in this study: eight unaffected siblings of children with ASD (US; 5 males, mean age = 11y6m, SD = 2y5m) and eight typically developing controls (TD; mean age = 11y0m, SD = 2y8m) ranging from 7 to 14 years for both groups. TD children were matched to US for age, sex, SES, and the developmental markers of speaking and walking onset (p > .05 for all demographics).

The inclusion criteria for TD involved: age 6–16, both genders and normal academic achievements at school. The exclusion criteria involved: no current Central Nervous System medication, no history of premature birth or TBI, and no history or current DSM diagnosis including substance abuse or ADHD; no first- or second-degree family members diagnosed with ASD, psychotic and bipolar disorders; no neuropsychological scores consistently −2SD below age norms. TD children were recruited by flyers on the UNM Campus and by personal contacts. The inclusion and exclusion criteria for US were identical except that US must have had a first- or second-degree family member diagnosed with ASD: six had a sibling diagnosed, one had a cousin with ASD and another had a second degree cousin with Asperger's Syndrome and a parent with OCD. All family members who had an ASD diagnosis were males. The US children were recruited from Clinical Centers for Children with ASD, by contact to Pediatric Psychiatrists and by personal contacts.

All participants underwent a telephone or in-person screening interview ensuring they met all inclusion/exclusion requirements before being invited to participate in our study. However, in one US subject we found out only after the data was processed that the child was taking a low dose of cognition enhancing medication (open on shelf) and was diagnosed with ADD. One US participant was removed from our analysis due to the consistently −2SD scores below her age normative scores and more than two standard deviations below normalized scores of other US participants. This child was undergoing a clinical diagnostic process that was revealed to us only after we completed testing.

## 2.2    Procedures and Measurements

All participants were tested in the Pediatric Neuroscience Laboratory, Psychology Clinical Neuroscience Center, The University of New Mexico. Child participants and their parent were briefed on the components of our study prior to signing the IRB approved consent/assent forms. The assent forms and the parental consent forms were signed before the testing began. The University of New Mexico (UNM) Institutional Review Board Committee for the School of Medicine (North Campus) approved this study. All participants were compensated $30 for their time and travel expenses.

The study constituted of two parts. Part I included two related tasks: first, visual-spatial perception task of the blue cartoon characters (Blue Man Test, BMT, Ciesielski 2003, 2007; based on The Blue Man Group, www.blueman.com/boston) while recording the performance accuracy, time of processing and the brain Event-Related Potentials (ERPs). After completing this task and a short resting break, the second task was administered. This involved table-paper presentation of two different characters from the BMT arranged into a socially meaningful interactions and we record the child's narrative description of the social interaction between two blue characters expressed by their biological body movements (BBM). Part II of the study involved also the neuropsychological battery of tests for assessing child's cognitive functions and clinical interviews. For details of the visual-spatial perception task and ERPs methods, see Bouchard et al. (2016; under review) and Newton et al. (2016).

### 2.2.1    Social Blue Man Task (SBMT): Interpretation of Social Cues in BBM

To investigate how US interpret social interactions as expressed by BBM of two interacting individuals, we present our figures in pairs. We will use the Social Blue Man Test (SBMT; Ciesielski et al. 2015) which is derived from the Blue Man Task (BMT; Ciesielski 2007). The SBMT involves static little blue characters that depict posture of a biological body motion and may be interpreted as expressing different intentions towards the second character in the image (Fig. 1). They are faceless to remain as simple as possible and thus do not require participants to observe both body motions and facial expressions. SBMT provides an opportunity to assess social interactions without an overload on sensory levels in children with ASD - which is a common occurrence in autism. The blue characters can be arranged into social interactions and can represent humans interacting with each other as a snapshot of human BBM.

Participants were shown 10 images consisting of 2 blue characters depicting a social interaction. First, the participant had to decide if the blue men's' interactions

**Fig. 1.** Example of social scenario represented by a snapshot of BBM in social blue man test (SBMT, Ciesielski et al. 2015). (Color figure online)

were either good (happy and nice) or bad (mean and angry) and press the button immediately: green if good and black if bad. The stress on the speed of the response was emphasized. Response "I don't know" was permitted only if encouragements failed. The main task was to "imagine what the blue men are doing and create a story about it, including information such as who they are, where they are right now, and why they are doing all of this." Responses were recorded with a digital voice recorder and were later transcribed. There was no time limitation but the response time on completion of the task was recorded.

### 2.2.2 Self- and Parent-Reports on Bullying Experiences

To gain an understanding of each participant's daily social interactions, we created a questionnaire in the Pediatric Neuroscience Laboratory called the "Social Interactions Questionnaire". Some questions asked were, "Do you know what bullying is?" "How many friends do you have?", "Are children nice to you at school or during after-school programs?", "Have you ever seen someone who was bullied?", and "Have you experienced any bullying?" The answers to these questions provide information on the participants' awareness of being a target of bullying and the child's resilience to bullying, as well as their social adjustment.

Finally, a confidential clinical interview with each participant's parents were conducted. Detailed information was collected about the child's prenatal and early postnatal life history, family history of DSM-V disorders, current status of family health, constitution and social-economic status. Additionally, a Traumatic Experiences Questionnaire (Ciesielski et al. 2015, Manual, PNL) was used to obtain parental knowledge about their child's exposure to peer victimization. Among several other questions the following were posed to the parent: (1) "Has your child experienced any rejection, teasing and/or aggressive behaviors from his/her peers in school or other places? – please describe." and (2) "Has your child experienced any psychological or physical punishment, aggression by other or isolation from others?"

## 2.3    Statistical Data Analysis

The data analysis was conducted using three approaches: t-tests for independent samples, Pearson correlations and a Latent Dirichlet Allocation analysis. The independent samples t-test was used to analyze: between-group contrasts in performance accuracy and reaction time during the SBMT and all neuropsychological tests scores. Pearson correlation coefficients were used to find within-group correlations on neuropsychological tests and the results on severity of bullying questionnaires. Latent Dirichlet Allocation (LDA) as a method of text analytics via topic modeling was used to analyze the transcribed stories from the SBMT in an unbiased manner (Blei et al. 2003). Each word in the collection of documents is treated as a finite mixture of an unobservable set of topics so that the LDA provides topic representation in each document. The t-tests and correlations were conducted on SPSS 23 and the LDA was completed with software developed by researchers at Sandia National Laboratories.

# 3    Results

We examined the association between the quality and quantity of verbal narratives regarding social interactions of BBM with the parent- and self-reports of exposure to bullying (Newton et al. 2016). Details of the ERP data were processed separately (Bouchard et al. 2016). TD children showed no significant neuropsychological deviations, except for significantly prolonged time of recognition of complex visual figures with ambiguous meaning ($p > 0.05$). There were also no differences found in US in visual-spatial perception of BBM.

While initiating this study, we predicted significantly more frequent social bullying events to be reported by the US children and their parents than in their TD peers. As shown in Fig. 2, parental- and self-reports regarding bullying experiences significantly differed. Parents-reported five times more bullying incidents in US (M = 1.38, SD = .74) than in TD (M = .25, SD = .46; p = .003, d = −1.8) and more bullying than was reported by self-reports by US children (M = 2.21, SD = .32). Self-reports show no significant differences in number of bullying events from those reported by TD children (M = 2.34, SD = .30, p = .42, d = .44). This result may need to be discussed in context of considerable frequency of bullying reported by TD children, but also as a result of poor insight of US children into being a target of bullying.

US children's parents reported that 88% of children experienced some form of consistent peer victimization while only 38% of self-reporting US children admitted being bullied. A reverse statistic is observed in TD children: TD parents reported that 25% of their children experienced being bullied while 43% of TD children admitted victimization. Our data provide support to and extend our earlier prediction: US are more frequently bullied when we carefully consider parental reports. This observation of discrepancy between US parental reports and US children's reports is important as it may suggest low awareness of social victimization in US. Additionally, we found that TD children also report a considerable exposure to bullying.

Our second prediction was also supported. Unaffected siblings needed significantly more time to decide if the BBM represent a "good" or "bad" social interaction. The

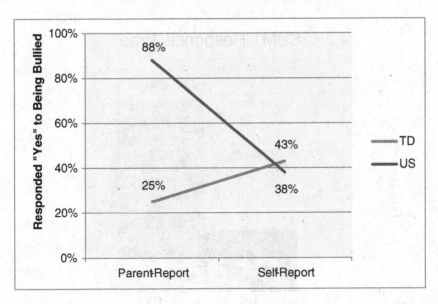

**Fig. 2.** Percentage of parent- and self- reports that responded "yes" to experiencing peer victimization in both unaffected siblings and typically developing.

Social Blue Man Task provided participants with images of social interactions and were told to decide as quickly as they could if the image displayed good or bad situations. They were informed that there were no incorrect answers but to respond with how they perceived the image. The response time was measured from the first view of the image and the response of "good" or "bad". We found that there is a significant delay in response time in US (M = 6.86, SD = 4.26) as compared to TD (M = 2.22, SD = 0.74, p = .01 d = −1.52). Figure 3 shows the relationship of the RT for both tasks in each group. Furthermore, a significant negative correlation of r = − 0.92, p < .001 was found between time delay in decision making about the good/bad social content of the BBM displayed in SBMT stimuli and the lower report rate of bullying by US. This suggests that the slower the US are in their social judgment the less insight they have and therefore report less bullying incidents.

Finally, we predicted that the quality and quantity of narratives about the social meaning of BBM would be lower in US than in TD and negatively correlated with high frequency of social bullying in US. We conducted the LDA analysis by combining all TD and all US responses into their two separate groups. As seen in Fig. 4, our TD participants weighed heavily on Topic 1 while our unaffected siblings weighed heavily on Topic 0. This unbiased model therefore distinguished differences between our two populations in SBMT responses.

The greatest differences between Topic 0 and Topic 1 are the amount of words and the diversity of words chosen, not on their content. By examining word clouds of the transcriptions, we can determine frequency of root words used in each topic. The larger the word in the cloud, the more frequently it is used. Topic 0 has many words that are used frequently and almost all of the words are fairly large in size. This indicates

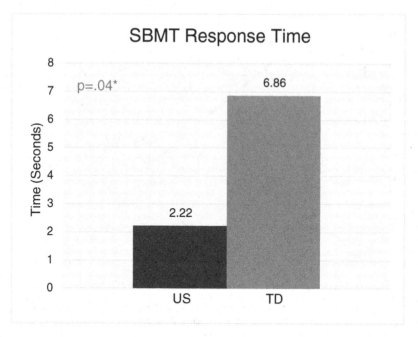

**Fig. 3.** Delayed response time during the SBMT in US.

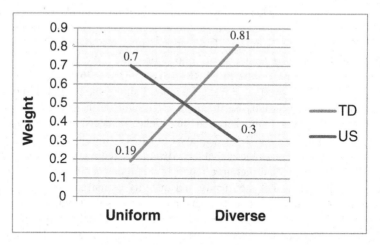

**Fig. 4.** The relationship between weight of each topic and subject group from LDA analysis of transcribed responses to the social blue man task. An inverse relationship exists between each group and the topic they are categorized into according to the unbiased LDA.

several words were used often by many of our unaffected siblings and that most words were used more than once. However, in Topic 1, only a few words had great frequency while majority of the words were unique. Therefore, Topic 0 is labeled "Uniform" and

Topic 1 is labeled "Diverse." This tells us that our US group provided narratives that were repetitive and lacked quality and flexibility in word choices (Fig. 5).

Unaffected Siblings            Typically Developing

**Fig. 5.** The word clouds indicate that there was a lack of variation in words used by all unaffected siblings when describing social narratives of the SBMT images.

## 4  Discussion

We examined the effects of bullying, as measured by both a parent-and self-report, in unaffected siblings of children with ASD. We collected unique information regarding the specific mechanism of underreporting of bullying by US children. We also analyzed the quality of narratives used by US and TD children to describe socially meaningful BBM snapshots to determine if any differences existed between US and TD in perception, interpretation, and reporting of social cues. US displayed significantly delayed interpretations and poorer social narratives. This may be indicative that US struggle to adequately process and interpret social interactions and then report and interpret them, but also that they may be unaware of their difficulties. This is an important insight into creating preventative measures for the US population. Programs that will be able to effectively help US children to increase the processing speed and improve the interpretation and communication of bullying experiences, would likely see more successful outcomes.

Delays in processing visual complex information may vastly interfere with identifying, interpreting, and responding to the fast, continuously changing, and often ambiguous social cues. As a result, unaffected siblings participating in our study might have had difficulty recognizing they were in fact a target of social bullying at school, hence they did not report about it during our testing. Their parental reports unravel a high frequency of victimizing events towards US children, which is consistent with the most recent literature (Nowell et al. 2014). While the parent-reports reveal significantly higher frequency of bullying experiences, the latent Dirichlet allocation showed in US poor verbal flexibility when describing social interactions. This difficulty might have reduced the ability of US to inform accurately, but also could be a foundation of their poor verbalization and poor awareness of bullying incidents. These findings are consistent with the Van Roekel et al. (2010) study, which showed a correlation between weaker ToM in ASD and greater exposure to victimization. To form a ToM with the interacting person one needs time to process the social messages and also verbal tools for understanding them and translating them into a socially-acceptable response. Baron-Cohen (2000) suggested that ToM deficits make individuals more likely to experience peer victimization. ToM may be one of the contributing factors responsible for the slow and partial only interpretation of social meaning of BBM by US children in our study.

The SBMT responses were recorded in relation to social interactions. The children who are typically developing are better able to describe their social surroundings than our US group. US of those with ASD showed a tendency to repeat words and did not use alternative words to describe the various social situations depicted. Since there were no statistically significant group differences on the neuropsychological tasks, with many of our US children outperforming our TD children, we cannot conclude that the results of LDA analysis is due to a lack of verbal abilities as such in the US. Considering the prolonged response times, we conclude that unaffected siblings of children with ASD perform equally well as TD on perception of visual-spatial characteristics of the BBM of the little blue man characters, but show significant deficiencies when they are required to describe the social meaning of the BBM of blue man interactions.

While this study improves our understanding of the mechanism underlying the social bullying in children displaying the endophenotype of ASD, there were some limitations that need to be addressed in future studies. First, our population consists of unaffected siblings of children with ASD- it will be important to examine children diagnosed with ASD with different levels of severity, and how this impacts the perception and interpretation of BBM. In addition, we aim to develop methods of nonverbal measurement of interpretation of BBM that should allow subjects with ASD to participate despite their verbal deficits. Further, our study does not consider causation between interpretation of BBMs and bullying. Thus, future research should attempt to determine causal relationships. In the future, we would like to obtain a more rigorous and holistic perspective of the child's bullying exposure and impacts to the child's mental and physical health. Finally, we intend to continue testing children in larger samples.

There is some debate as to whether parent- or self-reports reveal more accurate bullying experiences. The most accepted conclusion is that parents tend to over report their child's bullying experiences while individuals tend to under report their own bullying experiences. Regardless, that is the case whether children have a disorder or are typically developing. Therefore, to monitor the group differences in parent reports and children self-reports still provide an important insight into the status of bullying experienced in our schools. On the other hand, parents of a child with an ASD may be overly sensitive or even more involved with their children's social interactions than parents of typically developing children, so they may have better insight to their child's social interactions than a parent of a child who is TD.

This research provides some insight into the mechanism of bullying experienced by unaffected siblings of children with ASD. Although the cognitive abilities are similar in our TD and US subjects with no evident neuropsychological test deficits, a distinct and specific difference has been identified in the increased parent-report of peer victimization, delayed perception and interpretations on social interactions, and poorer quality of social narratives. The delay in interpretation and low quality of narratives may be characteristics of risk factors for the high exposure to bullying in unaffected siblings. Our findings might give rise to studies on improving the US child's ability to perceive and absorb complex social cues.

# References

American Psychiatric Association: Diagnostic and Statistical Manual of Mental Disorders, 5th edn. Washington, DC (2013)

Baron-Cohen, S.: Theory of mind and autism: a fifteen year review. In: Baron-Cohen, S., Tager-Flusberg, H., Cohen, D.J. (eds.) Understanding Other Minds: Perspectives From Developmental Cognitive Neuroscience, pp. 3–20. Oxford University Press, New York (2000)

Baron-Cohen, S., Leslie, A.M., Frith, U.: Does the autistic child have a 'theory of mind'? Cognition 21, 37–46 (1985)

Blei, D.M., Ng, A.Y., Jordan, M.I.: Latent Dirichlet allocation. J. Mach. Learn. Res. 3(1), 993–1022 (2003)

Bouchard, C., Solis, I., Seaman, B., Pesko, J.C., Ciesielski, K.R.: Developmental and familial characteristics of top-down inhibitory control networks and performance strategies: ERPs to the blue man stop-response task. Program No. 90.12. 2016 Neuroscience Meeting Planner. Society for Neuroscience, San Diego (2016)

Cappadocia, M.C., Weiss, J.A., Pepler, D.: Bullying experiences among children and youth with autism spectrum disorders. J. Autism Dev. Disord. 42(2), 266–277 (2012). doi:10.1007/s10803-011-1241-x

Carter, S.: Bullying of students with Asperger syndrome. Issues Compr. Pediatr. Nurs. 32, 145–154 (2009). doi:10.1080/01460860903062782

Centers for Disease Control: Autism Spectrum Disorder (ASD) (2014). http://www.cdc.gov/ncbddd/autism/facts.html#ref

Ciesielski, K.T.R.: Blue Man N-Back Test: Visual-Spatial Working Memory Paradigm (MGH/MIT AA Martinos Center for Biomedical Imaging, Radiology, Massachusetts General Hospital). (RN 0008929/2003, 2007) (2007)

Ciesielski, K.T.R., Newton E.V., Solis, I.: Social Blue Man Test. Manual. Pediatric Neuroscience Laboratory, PCNC, Psychology, University of New Mexico, Albuquerque, NM 87131 (2015)

Dalton, K.M., Nacewicz, B.M., Alexander, A.L., Davidson, R.J.: Gaze fixation, brain activation, and amygdala volume in unaffected siblings of individuals with autism. Soc. Biol. Psychiatry 61, 512–520 (2007)

Durkin, M., Maenner, M., Newschaffer, C., Lee, L., Cunniff, C., Daniels, J.L., Schieve, L.A.: Advanced parental age and the risk of autism spectrum disorder. Am. J. Epidemiol. 168(11), 1268–1276 (2008)

Hubert, B., Wicker, B., Moore, D.G., Monfardini, E., Duverger, H., Da Fonséca, D., Deruelle, C.: Brief report: recognition of emotional and non-emotional biological motion in individuals with autistic spectrum disorders. J. Autism Dev. Disord. 37(7), 1386–1392 (2007). doi:10.1007/s10803-006-0275-y

Kabot, S., Masi, W., Segal, M.: Advances in the diagnosis and treatment of autism spectrum disorders. Prof. Psychol. Res. Pract. **34**, 26–33 (2003)

Kaiser, M.N., Hudac, C.M., Schultz, S., Lee, S.M., Cheung, C., Berken, A.M., Pelphry, K.A.: Neural signatures of autism. Proc. Nat. Acad. Sci. USA **107**(49), 21223–21228 (2010)

Kennedy, D.P., Courchesne, E.: The intrinsic functional organization of the brain is altered in autism. Neuroimage **39**(4), 1877–1885 (2008)

Koldewyn, K., Whitney, D., Rivera, S.M.: Neural correlates of coherent and biological motion perception in autism. Dev. Sci. **14**(5), 1075–1088 (2001). doi:10.1111/j.1467-7687.2011. 01058.x

Lainé, F., Rauzy, S., Tardif, C., Gepner, B.: Slowing down the presentation of facial and body movements enhances imitation performance in children with severe autism. J. Autism Dev. Disord. **41**(8), 983–996 (2011). doi:10.1007/s10803-010-1123-7

Little, L.: Middle-class mothers' perceptions of peer and sibling victimization among children with Asperger's syndrome and nonverbal learning disorders. Issues Compr. Pediatr. Nurs. **25**, 43–57 (2002)

Manzi, B., Loizzo, A., Giana, G., Curatolo, P.: Autism and metabolic diseases. J. Child Neurol. **23**(3), 307–314 (2008)

Minshew, N.J., Keller, T.A.: The nature of brain dysfunction in autism: functional brain imaging studies. Cur. Opin. Neurol. **23**(2), 124–130 (2010)

Molcho, M., Craig, W., Due, P., Pickett, W., Harel-Fisch, Y., Overpeck, M.: Cross-national time trends in bullying behaviour 1994–2006: findings from Europe and North America. Int. J. Public Health **54**, 225–234 (2009)

Moore, D.G., Hobson, R.P., Lee, A.: Components of person perception: an investigation with autistic, nonautistic retarded and typically developing children and adolescents. Br. J. Dev. Psychol. **15**, 401–423 (1997)

Nelson, K.B., Greather, J.K., Croen, L.A., Dambrosia, J.M., Dickens, B.F., Jeliffe, L.L.: Neuropeptides and neurotrophins in neonatal blood of children with autism or mental retardation. Ann. Neurol. **49**, 597–606 (2001)

Newton, V., Solis, I., Avina, G.E., McClain, J.T., King, C., Bouchard, C., Ciesielski, K.R.: Cognition of biological body movement as a risk factor for social bullying in unaffected siblings of children with autism spectrum disorders. Presentation at Neuroscience 2016, San Diego, California (2016)

Nowell, K.P., Brewton, C.M., Goin-Kochel, R.P.: A multi-rater study on being teased among children/adolescents with autism spectrum disorder (ASD) and their typically developing siblings: associations with ASD symptoms. Focus Autism Other Dev. Disabil. **29**(4), 195–205 (2014)

Olweus, D.: Bullying at School: What We Know and What We Can Do. Blackwell, Oxford (1993)

Ozonoff, S., Young, G.S., Carter, A., Messinger, D., Yirmiya, N., Zwaigenbaum, L., Stone, W. L.: Recurrence risk for autism spectrum disorders: a baby siblings research consortium study. Pediatrics **128**, e488–e495 (2011)

Sterzing, P.R., Shattuck, P.T., Narendorf, S.C., Wagner, M., Cooper, B.P.: Bullying involvement in autism spectrum disorders: prevalence and correlates of bullying involvement among adolescents with an autism spectrum disorder. Arch. Pediatr. Adolesc. Med. **166**(11), 1058–1064 (2012). doi:10.1001/archpediatrics.2012.790

Sumi, S., Taniai, H., Miyachi, T., Tanemura, M.: Sibling risk of pervasive developmental disorder estimated by means of an epidemiologic survey in Nagoya, Japan. J. Hum. Genet. **51**, 518–522 (2006)

Swettenham, J., Remington, A., Laing, K., Fletcher, R., Coleman, M., Gomez, J.C.: Perception of pointing from biological motion point-light displays in typically developing children and children with autism spectrum disorder. J. Autism Dev. Disord. **43**(6), 1437–1446 (2013). doi:10.1007/s10803-012-1699-1

Varcin, K.J., Nelson, C.A.: A developmental neuroscience approach to the search for biomarkers in autism spectrum disorder. Curr. Opin. Neurol. Apr. **29**, 123–129 (2016). doi:10.1097/WCO.0000000000000298

Van Roekel, E., Scholte, H.J., Didden, R.: Bullying among adolescents with autism spectrum disorders: prevalence and perception. J. Autism Dev. Disord. **40**, 63–73 (2010). doi:10.1007/s10803-009-0832-2

Zablotsky, B., Bradshaw, C.P., Anderson, C.M., Law, P.: Risk factors for bullying among children with autism spectrum disorders. Autism **18**(4), 419–427 (2014). doi:10.1177/1362361313477920

# Smart Watch Potential to Support Augmented Cognition for Health-Related Decision Making

Blaine Reeder[✉], Paul F. Cook, Paula M. Meek,
and Mustafa Ozkaynak

University of Colorado College of Nursing, Aurora, CO, USA
{blaine.reeder,paul.cook,paula.meek,
mustafa.ozkaynak}@ucdenver.edu

**Abstract.** In this paper, we review current smart watch research in the health domain to inform an Augmented Cognition (AugCog) research agenda for health-related decision making and patient self-management. We connect this AugCog research agenda to prior Clinical Decision Support (CDS), workflow, and informatics research efforts using Persons Living With HIV (PLWH) and Chronic Obstructive Pulmonary Disorder (COPD) patients as examples to illustrate potential research directions.

**Keywords:** Smart watch · Smartwatch · Consumer health · Health behavior · Usability

## 1 Introduction

Smart watches have seen rapid and widespread adoption by consumers in the past few years, with an expected market demand for these devices reaching up to 214 million units in 2018 [1]. These network-enabled, wrist-worn devices represent an unprecedented opportunity to support improved patient self-management and health monitoring in everyday life through an array of on-board sensors, computing capability, and communication features. Indeed, two recent systematic reviews found smart watch studies targeting numerous health-related applications have appeared at an increasing rate in the scientific literature in a few short years [2, 3].

The objective of this paper is to illustrate potential uses and challenges of smart watches for health-related decision making by describing these devices in relation to an Augmented Cognition (AugCog) research approach. We first conduct a brief review of AugCog research, relate AugCog research to that of Clinical Decision Support (CDS) research in the health domain, and discuss smart watch applications based on prior research with these devices. We then outline potential augmented cognition research directions in the health domain using smart watches by describing sensing modalities and potential mitigation strategies in relation to Persons Living With HIV (PLWH) [4–7], Chronic Obstructive Pulmonary Disorder patients [8–12], and emerging patient-centered workflow paradigms [13–18].

© Springer International Publishing AG 2017
D.D. Schmorrow and C.M. Fidopiastis (Eds.): AC 2017, Part I, LNAI 10284, pp. 372–382, 2017.
DOI: 10.1007/978-3-319-58628-1_29

## 1.1 Augmented Cognition

The goal of AugCog is to enhance end user cognitive capacity and capability in support of human task performance via automated adaption of technical system function and information presentation in a closed loop system [19, 20]. Three principal AugCog research areas are: Cognitive State Assessment (CSA) enabled by sensor-based capture of cognitive or functional state; Mitigation Strategies (MS) that respond to cognitive state through closed-loop system adjustments; and Robust Controllers (RC) that allow systems to function with resilience under diverse operating conditions [20, 21].

## 1.2 Clinical Decision Support

A clinical decision support (CDS) system is "designed to be a direct aid to clinical decision making, in which the characteristics of an individual patient are matched to a computerized clinical knowledge base and patient-specific assessments or recommendations are then presented to the clinician or the patient for a decision" [22]. Prior CDS research has identified a rank-ordered list of ten grand challenges to improve the design of CDS systems [23]. Four of these ten grand challenges have been designated as necessary to improve the effectiveness of CDS interventions; the remaining six pertain to creation of new CDS interventions and dissemination of existing CDS knowledge.

The four grand challenges for improved effectiveness of CDS interventions are ranked as follows: *Improve the human–computer interface* (first out ten); *Summarize patient-level information* (third out of ten); *Prioritize and filter recommendations* (fourth out of ten) and; *Synthesize recommendations for comorbidities* (sixth out of ten) [23]. These four grand challenges are relevant to two cognitive bottlenecks identified from AugCog research [24]. Table 1 displays these four CDS grand challenges [23] with the associated cognitive bottleneck and the AugCog approach to overcome the bottleneck [24]. *Narrow user input capabilities* refer to limitations of system designs that present barriers to information entry. *Information overload* refers to the inability of users to process vast amounts of system output. A *cognitive state sensor* "acquires physiological and behavioral parameter(s) that can be reliably associated with specific cognitive states, which can be measured in real time while an individual or team of individuals is engaged with a system" [21].

**Table 1.** CDS grand challenges and AugCog approaches to overcome cognitive bottlenecks

| CDS grand challenge | Cognitive bottleneck | AugCog approach |
| --- | --- | --- |
| Improve the human–computer interface | Narrow user input capabilities | Cognitive state sensor |
| Summarize patient-level information Prioritize and filter recommendations Synthesize recommendations for comorbidities | Information overload | Adaptive filtering Data aggregation Clustering Advanced visualization |

### 1.3    Linking Augmented Cognition and Clinical Decision Support

Notably, the top-ranked CDS grand challenge of *Improve the human–computer interface* [23] represents the greatest opportunity for AugCog integration with CDS systems. Figure 1 illustrates how the concept of a CDS system aligns with the Fundamental Theorem of Biomedical Informatics, which states: "A person working in partnership with an information resource is 'better' than that same person unassisted" [25].

**Fig. 1.**  Graphic demonstrating the fundamental theorem of biomedical informatics [25]

In describing seminal AugCog efforts, Schmorrow and Kruse state:

AugCog will enable computational systems to adapt to the user, rather than forcing the user to adapt to the computational systems. In this way the AugCog program moves beyond the traditional approach to redesigning human-computer interfaces - which often fail to take the state of the user into account [19].

Taken together, these statements illustrate that the AugCog approach of cognitive state assessment using a cognitive state sensor is complementary to the notion of a CDS system that aligns with the Fundamental Theorem of Biomedical Informatics. However, the health domain represents a context with stakeholders who may have conflicting goals (e.g.: patients, family members, and health care providers with different roles). As a result, there may be fewer parallels between the health domain of patients in everyday life, the military domain where AugCog research originated [19, 21], and nuclear power plant control rooms where AugCog approaches have translated [20]. In particular, "operators" in military and control room environments possess specialized training, skills, and protocols designed to facilitate achievement of organizational objectives whereas patients in everyday life may not. Still, there have been recent AugCog forays into the health research domain [26–28]. In addition, while there is a large body of clinical decision support research, much of it is focused on health care provider decision making in clinical contexts using data from electronic health records [22, 23, 29]. Therefore, advances in smart watch technology represent new opportunities to support health-related decision making for patients in everyday life using AugCog and CDS approaches. Our proposed health research agenda will expand the types of sensors and sensor data for AugCog purposes, beyond those of physiological data, in a similar way that others have already begun [28].

## 2  Sensors in Health Research

Sensors have long been posited as a means to support health-related activities outside clinical care settings through incorporation of sensor data in health applications. Some common sensor types in health studies include smart home sensor technologies installed in the residential environment that enable passive monitoring of health [30–33] and wearable technologies [34, 35]. Each has its own trade-offs in terms of technology function and acceptance. For instance, smart homes require no user interaction beyond initial agreement to install the technology yet only collect data when a person is home and have difficulty distinguishing between multiple residents [31]. Wearable technologies can enable activity data collection anywhere, matched to an individual, but can present adherence issues if technologies are not worn properly [34].

### 2.1  Smart Watches in Health Research

Smart watches are a relatively new innovation in wearable technology. That being said, numerous smart watch health studies have been conducted since 2014 [2, 3]. While research with these wearable devices is still at a nascent stage, the purposes for which they have been put to use vary widely by sensing modality and study focus. Smart watches have been used for detection of activity levels, emotional state, seizures, tremor, posture, heart rate, temperature, speech therapy progress, and eating, medication-taking, and scratching behaviors [2]. These studies have employed a variety of onboard sensing modalities including accelerometers, gyroscopes, microphones, optical sensors, contact sensors, ambient light sensors, and received signal strength indication (RSSI) localization. Smart watch applications have been primarily used during proof-of concept studies to determine if smart watches are feasible for research. Studies that enrolled persons living with targeted conditions were few and focused on Parkinson's disease, epilepsy, and diabetes management.

### 2.2  Rapid Technology Change as a Challenge

In a previous AugCog paper focused on technology-supported health measures for congestive heart failure (CHF) patients [36], we described the Lab of Things platform [37, 38] and Pebble smart watches (http://www.getpebble.com) as promising technologies for integration in the home. However, rapid changes due to market forces and business initiatives can cause technologies to become unavailable or unsupported. As of 2016, the Pebble smart watch company went out of business and the Lab of Things [37, 38] Internet of Things platform is no longer supported by Microsoft Research.

## 3  Future Research

### 3.1  Patient Cases

#### 3.1.1  Smart Watch Potential to Support AugCog

Prior smart watch research shows promise to support specific needs for PLWH and COPD patients. Table 2 illustrates smart watch sensor types for cognitive state

**Table 2.** Technologies and recommendations for AugCog health research using smart watches

|  | PLWH[1] | COPD[2] |
|---|---|---|
| Cognitive State Assessment (CSA) | Sensor types<br>• Daily activity monitoring [39]<br>• Activity-based detection of eating behavior [40]<br>• Activity-based detection of medication-taking behavior [41]<br>• Detection of emotional state [42]<br>• Chronic disease self-management [43] | Sensor types<br>• Daily activity monitoring [39]<br>• Activity, heart rate, and temperature monitoring [44]<br>• Activity-based detection of medication-taking behavior [41]<br>• Detection of emotional state [42]<br>• Chronic disease self-management [43]<br>• COPD activity monitoring [45] |
| Mitigation Strategies (MS) | • Tailored messages delivered in everyday contexts<br>• Tailored messages delivered in high-risk geo-locations<br>• Tailored messages based on participant's emotional state<br>• Visual, text, or haptic cues for healthy behavior<br>• Alarms or notifying a collateral if behaviors (e.g. medication) are *not* done | • Tailored environmental messages<br>• Tailored activity messages based on current physical sensations and environmental conditions<br>• Visual, text or haptic cues for delivery of MDI medications<br>• Tailored messages based on participants anxiety or mood |
| Robust Controllers (RC) | Studies need:<br>Integration with Internet of Things platforms [46]<br>Workflow research [13, 15–17]<br>Analytics software to manage deluge of data [47] | |

[1]PLWH: Persons Living with HIV;
[2]COPD: Chronic Obstructive Pulmonary Disorder

assessment, mitigation strategies these sensors may support, and the types of studies needed to develop robust controllers for health-related AugCog.

### 3.1.2    Persons Living with HIV (PLWH)

PLWH must manage everyday behaviors related to antiretroviral medication use, which requires a higher level of adherence than most drugs, and prevention behaviors, which protect them from other STDs and reduce the chances that they will spread HIV to others. These behaviors can be hard to maintain, even with the best of intentions. Mobile technology has proven effective in improving antiretroviral therapy (ART) adherence through daily tailored messages [4–7]. Future research could extend these findings to more immediate messaging delivered via smart watches, use of haptic cues as reminders to take medication, or geolocation to deliver specific messages at specific times when PLWH are in higher-risk environments. Mobile cues to engage in other healthy behaviors are also particularly relevant to PLWH, who have higher rates of smoking, alcohol, and drug use than the general population, and must manage nutrition and exercise to counteract medication-related increases in cardiovascular risk. Table 2 shows smart watch potential to support PLWH.

### 3.1.3   Chronic Obstructive Pulmonary Disorder (COPD)

COPD is a chronic progressive disease that requires the individual to monitor their breathing, daily activity patterns, and self-manage medications such as metered dose inhalers (MDIs) [8]. There are multiple steps to effective deliver of MDI medications with individuals with COPD, only successful about half of the time. The interplay of these behaviors requires significant cognitive skills such as sensation, temperature, humidity, and air quality monitoring and appraisal within the overlay of daily activity expectations and successful medication deliver. Individuals with COPD do have some cognitive challenges in managing their health and well-being and the stress and anxiety of being short of breath while processing multiple sources of information to determine whether to take action or simply rest and continue monitoring would totally benefit from AugCog [8–12]. Providing summary information, monitoring physical cues such as heart rate or respiratory rate as well as mobile cues as to environmental concerns would move COPD self-management forward and is the next frontier for health care-focused mobile technology research. Table 2 shows smart watch potential to support COPD.

## 3.2   Types of Studies Needed

### 3.2.1   Workflow

Workflow research, which traditionally focuses on activities and temporal relationships between them, can contribute to understanding of the relationship between AugCog and health-related decision making, and also inform the design, implementation and evaluation of technology-based interventions that support decision making [14, 16]. Workflow research typically yields three types of deliverables: Rich workflow descriptions (narratives); quantitative representations (e.g. Petri Nets or Markov Chains); and visual depictions (e.g. workflow diagrams) [14]. These three deliverables are beneficial in the examination of the relationships between AugCog and decision making at a high-level as described in Table 1. Workflow research can be particularly helpful in highlighting temporal relationships that translate correlations into causal relationships about how AugCog approaches can improve decision making. The informatics literature shows that if workflows that represent current practice are not accounted for in the design and implementation of new systems, technology changes can disrupt workflow in intended and unintended ways and leads to poor performance and outcomes [48]. Thus, the effect of AugCog research on decision making must take workflow into account to realize the full potential of AugCog interventions. One gap in current workflow research is that field studies typically focus on behavioral indicators without regard to cognitive activities. Cognitive activities are either ignored or they are assumed. The ability to understand the role of cognitive activities as an underlying feature of behavioral indicators can allow researchers to examine workflow and cognition in the temporal context of health-related activities as whole. Smart watches can play a critical role in narrowing this gap by providing by providing real-time, in situ assessment of cognitive state through onboard sensors and communication features.

### 3.2.2   Technology Function and Acceptability

Studies must be conducted to validate and understand behaviors from data collected by smart watches. Smart watch technical function must be validated through comparison studies using known research-grade devices as the gold standard. This research should also explore strategies to overcome the challenge of device and platform obsolescence due to rapid change in the technology landscape [49]. Studies that develop new methods to estimate behavior from activity data, and other types of data, will be required on a continuous basis as more and different types of sensor-based measurements become available [50–53]. Important to understand are the factors related to why a given individual will use or abandon a wearable device like a smart watch [54]. Not surprisingly, smart watch acceptance research is at an early stage due to recent availability of smart watches as a consumer-grade device [55–59].

### 3.2.3   Informatics Study Types and Task Complexity

Friedman et al. define a set of informatics study classifications that describe the range of what can be studied based on type of research question [60]. Studies are classified as: needs assessment ("what is the problem?"); design validation ("is the development method appropriate?"); structure validation ("does the system function as intended?"); usability test ("can targeted stakeholders use it as intended?"); laboratory function ("does it have potential for benefit?"); field function ("does it have the potential for benefit in the real world?"); laboratory user effect ("is it likely to change behavior?"); field user effect ("does it change behavior in the real world?"); problem impact ("does it have a positive impact on the defined problem?") [60]. These informatics study types are non-exclusive and should be conducted iteratively using smart watches to support health-related decision making for PLWH and COPD.

  These studies should be designed with the aim of providing task advantages that deliver real-time resources to meet the personal goals of PLWH and COPD patients [36]. Prior research on task complexity [61] can inform the design and conduct of these studies using smart watches as an integral data collection and communication device. For example, the first Apple Watch applications for COPD currently do not gather or summarize the appropriate information and coordinate this with reminders or alarms that allow the patient to fully self-manage their condition. Patients must manually self-monitor but these data should be seamlessly integrated with environmental conditions, current emotional state, and complexity of medication regimes. At present, these smart watch applications have heavy input requirements with little synthesis or summary of material in ways that patients could use to modify activities, take preventive actions or address a current physical sensation.

## 4   Conclusion

In this paper, we have reviewed current health-related research using smart watches in terms of an Augmented Cognition research agenda. In doing so, we have connected this AugCog research agenda with prior Clinical Decision Support, workflow, and health informatics research using Persons Living With HIV (PLWH) and Chronic Obstructive

Pulmonary Disorder (COPD) as examples of future AugCog research directions for health-related decision making.

Chronic disease management and health care domain areas differ greatly from the original AugCog military research domain. However, AugCog research approaches have great potential to facilitate improved decision making, self-management and health outcomes for PLWH, COPD, and others, by using information collected over the long-term. One potential way to improve patient self-management and health outcomes is through automated and passive collection of information about activity levels, emotions, risky situations, or other health behaviors from smart watches to support augmented cognition for the wearer. However, before that happens, interdisciplinary researchers must understand where AugCog meshes with these domains and identify potential advantages of smart watch information for patients, family members, and health care providers. Ultimately, the goal is to enable community-based field studies that enroll persons living with the conditions targeted by smart watch interventions.

# References

1. Rawassizadeh, R., Price, B.A., Petre, M.: Wearables: has the age of smartwatches finally arrived? Commun. ACM **58**, 45–47 (2015)
2. Reeder, B., David, A.: Health at hand: a systematic review of smart watch uses for health and wellness. J. Biomed. Inform. **63**, 269–276 (2016)
3. Lu, T.-C., Fu, C.-M., Ma, M.-M., Fang, C.-C., Turner, A.M.: Healthcare applications of smart watches. Appl. Clin. Inform. **7**, 850–869 (2016)
4. Cook, P.F., Hartson, K.R., Schmiege, S.J., Jankowski, C., Starr, W., Meek, P.: Bidirectional relationships between fatigue and everyday experiences in persons living with HIV. Res. Nurs. Health **39**, 154–163 (2016)
5. Langness, J., Cook, P.F., Gill, J., Boggs, R., Netsanet, N.: Comparison of adherence rates for antiretroviral, blood pressure, or mental health medications for HIV-positive patients at an academic medical center outpatient pharmacy. J. Managed Care Pharm. **20**, 809–814 (2014)
6. Cook, P.F., Carrington, J.M., Schmiege, S.J., Starr, W., Reeder, B.: A counselor in your pocket: feasibility of mobile health tailored messages to support HIV medication adherence. Patient Prefer. Adherence **9**, 1353 (2015)
7. Cook, P.F., McElwain, C.J., Bradley-Springer, L.A.: Brief report on ecological momentary assessment: everyday states predict HIV prevention behaviors. BMC Res. Notes **9**, 9 (2016)
8. Mason, L.M., Meek, P.M.: Cognitive function patterns In: COPD C107. New Interventions and Outcomes in Pulmonary Rehabilitation, p. A5290. American Thoracic Society (2015)
9. Effing, T.W., Vercoulen, J.H., Bourbeau, J., Trappenburg, J., Lenferink, A., Cafarella, P., Coultas, D., Meek, P., van der Valk, P., Bischoff, E.W.: Definition of a COPD self-management intervention. In: International Expert Group consensus. European Respiratory Journal ERJ-00025-02016 (2016)
10. Sood, A., Petersen, H., Qualls, C., Meek, P.M., Vasquez-Guillamet, R., Celli, B.R., Tesfaigzi, Y.: Analysis of severity staging of chronic bronchitis reveals frequent instability of diagnosis. B43. COPD: Phenotypes and Clinical Outcomes, p. A3524. American Thoracic Society (2016)

11. Meek, P.M., Petersen, H., Washko, G.R., Diaz, A.A., Kim, V., Sood, A., Tesfaigzi, Y.: Chronic bronchitis is associated with worse symptoms and quality of life than chronic airflow obstruction. CHEST J. **148**, 408–416 (2015)

12. Fan, V.S., Meek, P.M.: Anxiety, depression, and cognitive impairment in patients with chronic respiratory disease. Clin. Chest Med. **35**, 399–409 (2014)

13. Ozkaynak, M., Brennan, P.F., Hanauer, D.A., Johnson, S., Aarts, J., Zheng, K., Haque, S.N.: Patient-centered care requires a patient-oriented workflow model. J. Am. Med. Inform. Assoc. **20**, e14–e16 (2013)

14. Ozkaynak, M., Unertl, K.M., Johnson, S.A., Brixey, J.J., Haque, S.N.: Clinical workflow analysis, process redesign, and quality improvement. In: Finnell, J.T., Dixon, B.E. (eds.) Clinical Informatics Study Guide, pp. 135–161. Springer, Cham (2016). doi:10.1007/978-3-319-22753-5_7

15. Ozkaynak, M., Johnson, S.A., Tulu, B., Donovan, J.L., Kanaan, A.O., Rose, A.: Exploring the effect of complex patients on care delivery tasks. Int. J. Health Care Qual. Assur. **28**, 494–509 (2015)

16. Ozkaynak, M., Johnson, S., Shimada, S., Petrakis, B.A., Tulu, B., Archambeault, C., Fix, G., Schwartz, E., Woods, S.: Examining the multi-level fit between work and technology in a secure messaging implementation. In: AMIA Annual Symposium Proceedings, vol. 2014, p. 954. American Medical Informatics Association (2014)

17. Ozkaynak, M., Jones, J., Weiss, J., Klem, P., Reeder, B.: A workflow framework for health management in daily living settings. Stud. Health Technol. Inform. **225**, 392–396 (2016)

18. Ozkaynak, M.: Capturing self management of chronic disease in daily life. In: 48th Annual Communicating Nursing Research Conference (22–25 April 2015) (2015)

19. Schmorrow, D., Kruse, A.A.: DARPA's augmented cognition program-tomorrow's human computer interaction from vision to reality: building cognitively aware computational systems. In: Proceedings of the 2002 IEEE 7th Conference on Human Factors and Power Plants, p. 7. IEEE (2002)

20. Fuchs, S., Hale, K.S., Axelsson, P.: Augmented cognition can increase human performance in the control room. In: 2007 IEEE 8th Human Factors and Power Plants and HPRCT 13th Annual Meeting, pp. 128–132. IEEE (2007)

21. Reeves, L.M., Schmorrow, D.D., Stanney, K.M.: Augmented cognition and cognitive state assessment technology – near-term, mid-term, and long-term research objectives. In: Schmorrow, D.D., Reeves, L.M. (eds.) FAC 2007. LNCS, vol. 4565, pp. 220–228. Springer, Heidelberg (2007). doi:10.1007/978-3-540-73216-7_25

22. Sim, I., Gorman, P., Greenes, R.A., Haynes, R.B., Kaplan, B., Lehmann, H., Tang, P.C.: Clinical decision support systems for the practice of evidence-based medicine. J. Am. Med. Inform. Assoc. **8**, 527–534 (2001)

23. Sittig, D.F., Wright, A., Osheroff, J.A., Middleton, B., Teich, J.M., Ash, J.S., Campbell, E., Bates, D.W.: Grand challenges in clinical decision support. J. Biomed. Inform. **41**, 387–392 (2008)

24. Dorneich, M.C., Whitlow, S.D., Ververs, P.M., Rogers, W.H.: Mitigating cognitive bottlenecks via an augmented cognition adaptive system. In: IEEE International Conference on Systems, Man and Cybernetics, vol. 1, pp. 937–944. IEEE (2003)

25. Friedman, C.P.: A "Fundamental Theorem" of Biomedical Informatics. J. Am. Med. Inform. Assoc. **16**, 169 (2009)

26. Navarro, R.F., Rodriguez, M.D., Favela, J.: Intervention tailoring in augmented cognition systems for elders with dementia. IEEE J. Biomed. Health Inform. **18**, 361–367 (2014)

27. Glenn, L.M., Boyce, J.A.S.: At the nexus: augmented cognition, health care, and the law. J. Cogn. Eng. Decis. Making **1**, 363–373 (2007)

28. Alam, M.A.U., Roy, N., Holmes, S., Gangopadhyay, A., Galik, E.: Automated functional and behavioral health assessment of older adults with dementia. In: 2016 IEEE First International Conference on Connected Health: Applications, Systems and Engineering Technologies (CHASE), pp. 140–149. IEEE (2016)

29. Karsh, B.-T.: Clinical practice improvement and redesign: how change in workflow can be supported by clinical decision support. US Department of Health and Human Services. Publication, Agency for Healthcare Research and Quality (2009)

30. Chan, M., Campo, E., Estève, D., Fourniols, J.Y.: Smart homes - current features and future perspectives. Maturitas **64**, 90–97 (2009)

31. Reeder, B., Meyer, E., Lazar, A., Chaudhuri, S., Thompson, H.J., Demiris, G.: Framing the evidence for health smart homes and home-based consumer health technologies as a public health intervention for independent aging: a systematic review. Int. J. Med. Inform. **82**, 565–579 (2013)

32. Liu, L., Stroulia, E., Nikolaidis, I., Miguel-Cruz, A., Rincon, R.A.: Smart homes and home health monitoring technologies for older adults: a systematic review. Int. J. Med. Inform. **91**, 44–59 (2016)

33. Rantz, M.J., Skubic, M., Popescu, M., Galambos, C., Koopman, R.J., Alexander, G.L., Phillips, L.J., Musterman, K., Back, J., Miller, S.J.: A new paradigm of technology-enabled 'vital signs' for early detection of health change for older adults. Gerontology **61**, 281–290 (2014)

34. Allet, L., Knols, R.H., Shirato, K., de Bruin, E.D.: Wearable systems for monitoring mobility-related activities in chronic disease: a systematic review. Sens. (Basel, Switzerland) **10**, 9026–9052 (2010)

35. Evenson, K.R., Goto, M.M., Furberg, R.D.: Systematic review of the validity and reliability of consumer-wearable activity trackers. Int. J. Behav. Nutr. Phys. Act. **12**, 159 (2015)

36. Reeder, B., Richard, A., Crosby, M.E.: Technology-supported health measures and goal-tracking for older adults in everyday living. In: Schmorrow, D.D., Fidopiastis, C.M. (eds.) AC 2015. LNCS, vol. 9183, pp. 796–806. Springer, Cham (2015). doi:10.1007/978-3-319-20816-9_76

37. Samuel, A., Brush, A., Mahajan, R.: Lab of things: building a research platform for connected devices in the home and beyond. ACM SIGMOBILE Mob. Comput. Commun. Rev. **18**, 37–40 (2015)

38. Brush, A.B., Mahajan, R., Samuel, A.: Lab of things: simplifying and scaling deployments of experimental technology in homes. In: van Hoof, J., Demiris, G., Wouters, E.J.M. (eds.) Handbook of Smart Homes, Health Care and Well-Being, pp. 1–9. Springer, Cham (2014)

39. Ahanathapillai, V., Amor, J.D., Goodwin, Z., James, C.J.: Preliminary study on activity monitoring using an android smart-watch. Healthcare Technol. Lett. **2**, 34–39 (2015)

40. Thomaz, E., Essa, I., Abowd, G.D.: A practical approach for recognizing eating moments with wrist-mounted inertial sensing. In: Proceedings of the 2015 ACM International Joint Conference on Pervasive and Ubiquitous Computing, pp. 1029–1040. ACM, Osaka (2015)

41. Kalantarian, H., Alshurafa, N., Sarrafzadeh, M.: Detection of gestures associated with medication adherence using smartwatch-based inertial sensors. IEEE Sens. J. **16**, 1054–1061 (2016)

42. Kamdar, M.R., Wu, M.J.: PRISM: a data-driven platform for monitoring mental health. In: Pacific Symposium on Biocomputing. Pacific Symposium on Biocomputing, vol. 21, pp. 333–344 (2016)

43. Arsand, E., Muzny, M., Bradway, M., Muzik, J., Hartvigsen, G.: Performance of the first combined smartwatch and smartphone diabetes diary application study. J. Diab. Sci. Technol. **9**, 556–563 (2015)

44. Jovanov, E.: Preliminary analysis of the use of smartwatches for longitudinal health monitoring. In: 2015 Annual International Conference of the IEEE Engineering in Medicine and Biology Society. IEEE Engineering in Medicine and Biology Society, pp. 865–868 (2015)

45. Hataji, O., Kobayashi, T., Gabazza, E.C.: Smart watch for monitoring physical activity in patients with chronic obstructive pulmonary disease. Respir. Invest. **54**, 294–295 (2016)

46. Feminella, J., Pisharoty, D., Whitehouse, K.: Piloteur: a lightweight platform for pilot studies of smart homes. In: Proceedings of the 1st ACM Conference on Embedded Systems for Energy-Efficient Buildings, pp. 110–119. ACM, Memphis (2014)

47. Demiris, G., Thompson, H.: Smart homes and ambient assisted living applications: from data to knowledge - empowering or overwhelming older adults? Contribution of the IMIA smart homes and Ambiant assisted living working group. IMIA Yearb. 2011: Towards Health Inform. 3.0 **6**, 51–57 (2011)

48. Ratwani, R.M., Fairbanks, R.J., Hettinger, A.Z., Benda, N.C.: Electronic health record usability: analysis of the user-centered design processes of eleven electronic health record vendors. J. Am. Med. Inform. Assoc. **22**, 1179–1182 (2015)

49. Huh, J., Nam, K., Sharma, N.: Finding the lost treasure: understanding reuse of used computing devices. In: Proceedings of the SIGCHI Conference on Human Factors in Computing Systems, pp. 1875–1878. ACM (2010)

50. Freedson, P.S., Melanson, E., Sirard, J.: Calibration of the computer science and applications, inc. accelerometer. Med. Sci. Sports Exerc. **30**, 777–781 (1998)

51. Lyden, K., Keadle, S.K., Staudenmayer, J., Freedson, P.S.: A method to estimate free-living active and sedentary behavior from an accelerometer. Med. Sci. Sports Exerc. **46**, 386–397 (2014)

52. Ellingson, L.D., Schwabacher, I.J., Kim, Y., Welk, G.J., Cook, D.B.: Validity of an integrative method for processing physical activity data. Med. Sci. Sports Exerc. **48**, 1629–1638 (2016)

53. Lyden, K., Kozey-Keadle, S.L., Staudenmayer, J.W., Freedson, P.S.: Validity of two wearable monitors to estimate breaks from sedentary time. Med. Sci. Sports Exerc. **44**, 2243 (2012)

54. Lazar, A., Koehler, C., Tanenbaum, J., Nguyen, D.H.: Why we use and abandon smart devices. In: Proceedings of the 2015 ACM International Joint Conference on Pervasive and Ubiquitous Computing, pp. 635–646. ACM (2015)

55. Wu, L.-H., Wu, L.-C., Chang, S.-C.: Exploring consumers' intention to accept smartwatch. Comput. Hum. Behav. **64**, 383–392 (2016)

56. Choi, J., Kim, S.: Is the smartwatch an IT product or a fashion product? A study on factors affecting the intention to use smartwatches. Comput. Hum. Behav. **63**, 777–786 (2016)

57. Kim, K.J., Shin, D.-H.: An acceptance model for smart watches: implications for the adoption of future wearable technology. Internet Res. **25**, 527–541 (2015)

58. Chuah, S.H.-W., Rauschnabel, P.A., Krey, N., Nguyen, B., Ramayah, T., Lade, S.: Wearable technologies: the role of usefulness and visibility in smartwatch adoption. Comput. Hum. Behav. **65**, 276–284 (2016)

59. Jung, Y., Kim, S., Choi, B.: Consumer valuation of the wearables: the case of smartwatches. Comput. Hum. Behav. **63**, 899–905 (2016)

60. Friedman, C.P., Wyatt, J.C., Owens, D.K.: Evaluation and technology assessment. In: Shortliffe, E.H., Cimino, J.J. (eds.) Biomedical Informatics: Computer Applications in Health Care and Biomedicine, pp. 403–443. Springer, Heidelberg (2006)

61. Crosby, M.E., Iding, M.K., Chin, D.N.: Research on task complexity as a foundation for augmented cognition. In: 2003. Proceedings of the 36th Annual Hawaii International Conference on System Sciences, 9 p. IEEE (2003)

# Multidimensional Real-Time Assessment of User State and Performance to Trigger Dynamic System Adaptation

Jessica Schwarz$^{(\boxtimes)}$ and Sven Fuchs

Fraunhofer Institute for Communication,
Information Processing and Ergonomics,
Department of Human-Systems Engineering,
Fraunhoferstr. 20, 53343 Wachtberg, Germany
{jessica.schwarz,sven.fuchs}@fkie.fraunhofer.de

**Abstract.** In adaptive human-machine interaction, technical systems adapt their behavior to the current state of the human operator to mitigate critical user states and performance decrements. While many researchers use measures of workload as triggers for adjusting levels of automation, we have proposed a more holistic approach to adaptive system design that includes a multidimensional assessment of user state. This paper outlines the design requirements, conceptual framework, and proof-of-concept implementation of a Real-time Assessment of Multidimensional User State (RASMUS). RASMUS diagnostics provide information on user performance, potentially critical user states, and their related impact factors on a second-by-second-basis in real-time. Based on these diagnoses adaptive systems are enabled to infer when the user needs support and to dynamically select and apply an appropriate adaptation strategy for a given situation. While the conceptual framework is generic, the implementation has been applied to an air surveillance task, providing real-time diagnoses for high workload, passive task-related fatigue and incorrect attentional focus.

**Keywords:** Multidimensional user state · Physiological measures · Workload · Attention · Fatigue · Performance · Real-time assessment · Adaptation · Augmented Cognition

## 1 Introduction

Automation of technical systems has greatly increased, but it is usually still the human operator who is responsible for the safety and effectiveness of the human-machine-system. Hence, adverse user states that impair the operator's effectiveness can have severe consequences, especially in safety-critical task environments. A notable example was the crash of Air France flight AF447 in 2009. According to the flight accident report [1] technical failure followed by an autopilot disconnection provoked multiple adverse mental states of the pilots (e.g. confusion, overload, inadequate situation awareness). As a consequence pilots were not able to regain control over the aircraft and it crashed (cf. [2] for a more detailed discussion).

© Springer International Publishing AG 2017
D.D. Schmorrow and C.M. Fidopiastis (Eds.): AC 2017, Part I, LNAI 10284, pp. 383–398, 2017.
DOI: 10.1007/978-3-319-58628-1_30

To prevent such critical user states in highly automated systems, approaches of adaptive system design have been developed, e.g. Adaptive Aiding [3], Adaptive Automation [4], and Augmented Cognition [5]. In adaptive human-machine systems, technology adapts its behavior to the current state of the human operator to mitigate critical user states and performance decrements. However, researchers have faced a number of challenges transferring those approaches from the laboratory to the real world. One major challenge is that human-machine systems are impacted by a wide range of influencing factors in the real world that are often not accounted for in laboratory settings. Researchers have therefore concluded that context, environmental parameters, system state and goals must be considered in order to successfully apply adaptation strategies (e.g., [6–8]).

Additionally, as illustrated in the crash of flight AF447, human error and performance decrements can be the result of multiple critical user states that are both intertwined and interrelated. Hence, a one-dimensional consideration of user state (e.g., by focusing on high workload) may not be sufficient to successfully select and apply appropriate adaptation strategies in real-world settings. We have therefore proposed to also account for the multidimensional nature of user state in adaptive system design [2]. Our approach of a multidimensional user state assessment focuses on six dimensions of user state that we have found to be able to substantially impact human performance, namely workload, fatigue, attention, situation awareness, motivational aspects of engagement, and emotional states characterized by negative valence and high arousal. Evidence of their effect on performance is summarized in Table 1.

This paper introduces our diagnostic engine. "RASMUS" (Real-time Assessment of Multidimensional User State) enables the technical system to detect performance declines of the user and to infer potential causes of performance declines based on diagnosed critical user states and related environmental and individual impact factors. The next section outlines the main findings of our analysis phase and summarizes

**Table 1.** User states considered in RASMUS and their effect on user performance

| User state | Effect on user performance |
|---|---|
| Workload | Performance is likely to decrease if mental workload is either too high or too low [9, 10] |
| Fatigue | Fatigue impairs information processing and decreases attention, vigilance and situation awareness. It is estimated that fatigue contributes to 20 to 30% of transport accidents [11] |
| Motivational aspects of engagement | High engagement can improve task performance even during sleep deprivation [12] |
| Attention | Lack of attentional resources and inadequate focus of attention (e.g. attentional tunneling) can decrease performance [13] |
| Situation Awareness (SA) | 69.1% of the operational errors in air traffic control and 88% of aviation accidents involving human error could be attributed to SA problems [14] |
| Emotional states | Emotions that are characterized by negative valence and high arousal (such as anxiety) can narrow attention and impair information processing [15] |

corresponding design requirements, used for the conceptual design of RASMUS. The generic conceptual framework is detailed in Sect. 3. Subsequently, we present a proof-of-concept implementation of RASMUS that provides real-time diagnoses for high workload, passive task-related fatigue and incorrect attentional focus in an air surveillance task. We also present some preliminary results of a recent validation study (Sect. 4). The article concludes with a discussion and an outlook on future work (Sect. 5).

## 2 Design Requirements

Analysis of related work revealed that previous studies have mainly focused on just one dimension of user state. For example, workload is often used as a trigger for Adaptive Automation [16–18]. Many studies also focus on a specific field of application, e.g. command and control, aviation, driving. In contrast, our multidimensional approach is more holistic and not domain-specific. During the review phase of our work we therefore analyzed studies across different domains focusing on different types of user states. Literature reviews lead to the identification of five aspects that appeared particularly relevant to our approach. The following subsections deal with each of the five aspects and describe which design requirements were derived for the conceptual development of RASMUS. These findings and design requirements are summarized in Sect. 2.6.

### 2.1 Indicators of User State

The six user states considered for multidimensional user state assessment are hypothetical constructs that cannot be measured directly. But various assessment methods have been established to provide indicators of those states: subjective measures, performance-based measures, physiological and behavioral metrics, as well as model-based assessment. Considering their properties, psychophysiological and behavioral metrics appear to be particularly well-suited for user state assessment in adaptive systems, as they provide continuous indicators of user state in real time. Moreover, many of those metrics can be measured by sensors that are rather unobtrusive (e.g. remote eye trackers). However, previous research has also revealed some shortcomings:

- Physiological measures are influenced not only by user state but also by other factors not related to user state which may cause misleading results [5, 19], e.g. pupil dilation is also influenced by lighting conditions.
- Physiological measures are not indicative of a single user state, e.g. heart rate can increase due to high workload but it can also increase as a result of emotional states with high arousal e.g. anxiety or anger [20].
- Adaptive systems should address the causes rather than the symptoms of critical user states and performance decrements [7]. Even if physiological and behavioral measures did reflect changes in user state, they would not provide any information about what provoked those state changes.

In order to compensate for these shortcomings, our approach of multidimensional user state assessment combines physiological and behavioral measures (e.g. pupil dilation, heart rate, breathing rate, mouse click frequency) with environmental and individual impact factors on user state. Environmental factors involve all factors that externally impact user state and performance including task properties, context factors, conditions of the surrounding, objectives and events. Individual factors refer to long-term and short-term properties of the human that impact his/her state and performance internally (e.g. level of experience, capabilities, skills, constitution, mood, or well-being). These indicators were identified in previous analyses and integrated into a self-developed generic model of user state (cf. [2]).

## 2.2    Self-Regulation of the Human Operator

When designing an adaptive technical system it must be considered that humans are adaptive systems themselves. By applying self-regulation strategies, e.g. investing more effort if task demands increase or drinking coffee to combat fatigue, the human operator is also able to mitigate critical user states. For Adaptive Automation, researchers strongly recommend consideration of the human's effort-regulation processes [9, 21]. Veltman and Jansen [21] point out that increases in workload can be a sign of a successful adaptation of the operator to changing task demands as he or she is investing more effort to meet the demands. Thus, if these changes in workload were used by the technical system to reduce the task load, it might result in counterproductive interaction between the two adaptive systems. However, as accidents caused by critical user states indicate, there are also situations (e.g. extreme underload or overload) when the operator's state regulation processes fail to successfully maintain the operator's effectiveness. Veltman and Jansen [21] therefore propose that adaptive technical systems are more likely to work successfully if adaptation is triggered only in those situations when the operator's effort regulation mechanisms are unable to adequately react to changing task demands. As our approach does not only focus on workload as a trigger and is not limited to adjusting the level of automation, we extend this recommendation and suggest to not counteract any productive self-regulation strategies of the operator by technical adaptation strategies. Consequently, we decided to use performance measures as a trigger for adaptation because a decline in performance is a clear indication that self-regulation has failed and the operator needs support.

## 2.3    Individual Differences

User state is often examined at a group level, trying to demonstrate significant effects of assessment methods between task conditions (e.g. [19, 22]). However, individuals differ in their physiological reactions. Accordingly, physiological measures that are sensitive at the group level have been shown to lack sensitivity in single-trial analysis needed for real-time adaptation (e.g. [23]). We were able to replicate these findings in previous experimental studies [24, 25]. Results supported the sensitivity of most physiological measures to indicate changes in user state and performance at a group level. At an individual level, however, we found outcomes to vary strongly between individuals even when using normalized data. This finding may indicate that the sensitivity of a physiological metric is user-specific which means that certain measures are sensitive indicators for some subjects but not for others. Veltman and Jansen [23] make two suggestions how to deal with individual differences in Adaptive Automation: (1) Increase the sensitivity at an individual level by combining different physiological measures, and (2) use individual sets of baseline data from different sensors to select those measures that are most sensitive for the given individual. Additionally, it might be useful to weigh indicators in the assessment according to their user-specific sensitivity. However, individual weighting of indicators would only be appropriate if the indicators' sensitivity was temporally stable.

## 2.4 Temporal Stability

For assessing the temporal stability of our findings, we conducted a retest experiment one year after the initial experiment involving the same task conditions and participants (cf. [25]). Related work testing the temporal stability of physiological measures is rather sparse and findings are reported predominantly at a group level (e.g. [26]). These studies indicate moderate levels of temporal stability for different kinds of physiological measures. Likewise, our retest experiment confirmed the temporal stability of three out of four tested physiological metrics at the group level. However, analysis at an individual level revealed that outcomes differ strongly not only between but also within individuals from test to retest. Some indicators that showed high sensitivity for one participant in the first test showed rather weak sensitivity for the same participant in the retest and vice versa.

We assume these variations in time were a result of environmental and individual impact factors that we could not control for in test and retest, e.g. learning effects, different degrees of initial fatigue or motivation, differences in mood or different fitting and tracking quality of sensors. Considering real-world settings, there are even more uncontrollable impact factors causing some indicators to be more and some less sensitive for variations in user state in a specific situation. Consequently, we propose to refrain from user-specific selection and weighting of user state indicators. Instead the results highlight the importance of combining different kinds of measures to compensate for potentially biased or invalid measurements.

## 2.5 Oscillation

Researchers have pointed out that adaptation triggered by a threshold algorithm may evoke undesirable oscillation or "yo-yoing" [5, 27, 28]. Particularly physiological gauges have been observed to frequently pass a predetermined threshold resulting in adaptations being switched on and off in short time intervals. This oscillation of adaptation has been shown to produce detrimental effects on operator performance as it can confuse the user and increase workload [5]. To prevent oscillation effects it has been suggested to smooth physiological measures e.g. by filters or moving-mean estimation and to define a minimum time interval between switches in adaptation (coined as "refractory period" [27] or "deadband" [28]). As our approach uses performance decrements to trigger adaptation, these effects are avoided. Nevertheless, we consider these suggestions when using physiological measures for user state assessment.

## 2.6 Summary

Table 2 provides a summary of the main findings of our analysis phase and lists the corresponding design requirements we formulated for the conceptual development of RASMUS. Findings and design requirements refer to each of the five aspects detailed in Sects. 2.1–2.5 (indicated in the left column of Table 2).

**Table 2.** Summary of literature findings and corresponding design requirements

| Section | Finding | Design requirement |
|---------|---------|--------------------|
| 2.1 | Symptom-based adaptation is not sufficient [7] Physiological measures are affected by multiple factors [5, 19, 20] | Combine physiological and behavioral measures with other factors that impact user state Combine different kinds of measures |
| 2.2 | Self-regulation strategies have to be considered [21] | Only adapt, when the human's self-regulation failed → Use performance measures to trigger adaptation |
| 2.3 | Individual differences in physiological reactions have to be considered [23] | Perform analyses at an individual level Compare to an individual baseline |
| 2.4 | Physiological measures differ both between and within individuals [25] | Refrain from person-specific selection and weighting of user state indicators Combine different kinds of measures |
| 2.5 | Adaptation triggered by gauges passing a threshold may evoke oscillation [5, 27, 28] | Define a minimum time interval between adaptation changes Apply methods to smoothen physiological measures |

# 3 Real-Time Assessment of Multidimensional User State (RASMUS)

The "Real-Time Assessment of Multidimensional User State" (RASMUS) is part of a larger dynamic adaptation framework. A simplified model is depicted in Fig. 1. The "information processing" component represents the basic functionality of traditional technical systems in human-machine-interaction. It analyses and displays data from the environment and processes operator inputs. To enable adaptive behavior of the technical system we added a state regulation component that is modeled after the four-stage model of human information processing and the corresponding classes of system functions proposed in [29]. It includes four stages of state regulation: data acquisition,

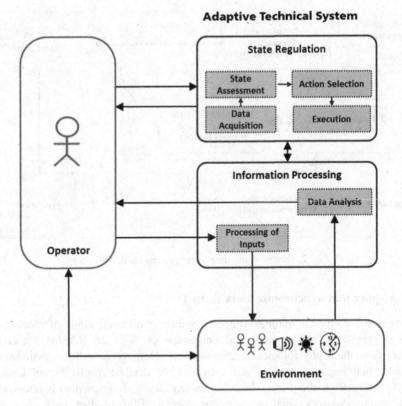

**Fig. 1.** Simplified model of our dynamic adaptation framework

user state assessment, action selection and execution (action implementation). RASMUS diagnostics introduced in this paper address the first two stages of state regulation: the acquisition of data from the operator and the environment and the subsequent assessment of the user state. The stages of action selection and action implementation refer to the selection and application of appropriate adaptation strategies, accomplished through an Advanced Dynamic Adaptation Management (ADAM) detailed in another paper within this volume [30].

The diagnostic process of RASMUS is broken down into four consecutive steps depicted in Fig. 2: "Acquire and synchronize data", "Evaluate need for support", "Analyze critical user states and impact factors" and "Display and forward diagnostic results". The black arrows in Fig. 2 indicate the sequence of the diagnosis and stage regulation process. Information gathered on one step is required not only for the immediate next step but also to accomplish subsequent steps. These dependences are indicated by the grey arrows in Fig. 2. The four steps are explained in more detail below.

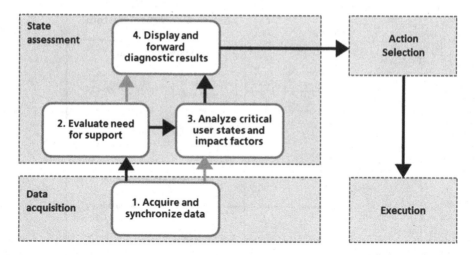

**Fig. 2.** Steps of the diagnostic process in RASMUS

### 3.1 Acquire and Synchronize Data (Step 1)

Literature and empirical findings suggest combining different kinds of measures in order to gain more robust and valid diagnoses (cf. Sect. 2). RASMUS therefore acquires data about physiological and behavioral reactions as well as environmental and individual impact factors. These measures are derived from different kinds of sources. Information about individual factors (e.g. level of experience) is obtained by questionnaires. Sensors, such as an eye tracker, an EEG headset, or a chest strap provide physiological metrics. Additionally, the experimental system logs data on environmental parameters and user activity (e.g. number of current tasks, number of mouse clicks). These data streams are merged and synchronized in real-time, using the iMotions biometric research platform (iMotions, Inc., MA, USA). To normalize physiological measures RASMUS records a baseline at the beginning of each session to compare subsequent data to individual baseline states (cf. Sect. 2.3).

### 3.2 Evaluate Need for Support (Step 2)

This step determines when to trigger adaptation. In RASMUS, this decision is based on an evaluation of the operator's performance. Using performance declines to detect a need for support further ensures that the adaptive system does not counteract productive self-regulation mechanisms of the human (cf. Sect. 2.2). Declines in performance clearly indicate that self-regulation has failed and the operator needs support. Diagnosis of performance decrements is based on rules stored and processed in a rule engine. The researcher can define and edit these rules in a self-developed software tool. As an example, the researcher may define that a performance decrement should be detected when a certain task is not completed within a specified time frame (e.g. 60 s).

It must be noted that not every detected decrement in performance triggers adaptation. As stated in Sect. 2.5, unfavorable oscillation effects can occur that may produce rapid adaptation changes in short time intervals. To prevent rapid oscillation, we use a deadband to suppress new adaptation if further performance decrements occur within a given time interval after the previous adaptation.

### 3.3 Analyze Critical User States and Impact Factors (Step 3)

As noted in Sect. 2.1 adaptive systems should address the causes rather than the symptoms of performance decrements and critical user states. When a performance decrement, and thus a need for support, is detected, RASMUS determines potential causes for the performance decrement by evaluating user states and associated contextual indicators. This information can later be used to select an appropriate adaptation strategy (cf. [30]).

The assessment of indicators used for the evaluation of critical user states is accomplished in a similar way as the detection of performance decrements. The researcher defines rules for each indicator to detect potentially adverse outcomes. Likewise, rules are defined to link indicators (or combinations of indicators) with potentially critical user states. Both high and low thresholds may be selected to indicate a critical state. For example, a low heart rate (compared to that individual's baseline state) may indicate fatigue while a large positive deviation from baseline can indicate high workload.

As stated in Sect. 2.4 the sensitivity of indicators can unpredictably vary over time. Hence, whenever possible, the detection of critical user states is not based on a single indicator but on a combination of different indicators. A critical state is detected only in those cases when the majority of its indicators support the diagnosis.

### 3.4 Display and Forward Diagnostic Results (Step 4)

RASMUS forwards all diagnostic results to the adaptation management component where they are processed to select, configure, and execute appropriate adaptation strategies. Diagnostic results are also saved for later offline analyses. Additionally, RASMUS diagnostics are visualized in real-time in a "Performance and User State Monitor" application. This software allows researchers or other observers to monitor diagnoses of performance decrements, critical user states, and all indicators used for user state assessment. This is helpful to observe and demonstrate the mechanisms of RASMUS.

## 4 Proof-of-Concept Implementation

In a first proof-of-concept implementation the generic diagnostic framework detailed in Sect. 3 was applied and tailored to the specific requirements of a naval Anti-Air-Warfare (AAW) task paradigm. For this purpose it was necessary to determine appropriate indicators for performance and user state assessments and to specify the rule base for critical outcomes.

### 4.1    Task Environment

RASMUS diagnostics were implemented as a Java-based research testbed and connected to an existing AAW simulation. Figure 3 shows the research testbed with the sensors currently utilized for user state assessment: an SMI REDn eye tracker underneath the monitor, the Zephyr' BioHarness3 multisensor chest strap on the left, and a webcam positioned on top of the monitor. The monitor shows the user interface of the AAW simulation. The Tactical Display Area (TDA) located in the center displays virtual contacts in the surroundings of the ownship.

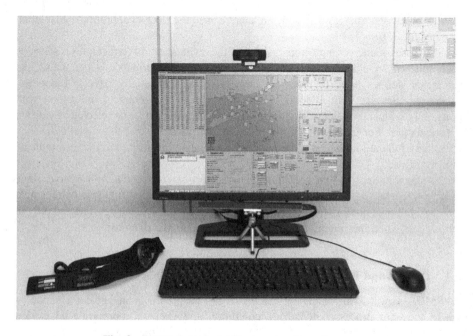

**Fig. 3.**   Research testbed with user monitor and sensors

The simulation includes four simplified AAW-tasks (cf. Table 3 for task descriptions). These tasks occur at scripted times throughout the scenario and may also occur simultaneously. In this case the task with the highest priority must be performed first. Each task is associated with a time limit for task completion. Time limits were assigned based on outcomes of an earlier study that employed the same tasks and simulation software [31]. If a task is not completed within the time limit or if task completion is incorrect, RASMUS detects a performance decrement. Table 3 provides the priorities (with 500 being highest and 100 being lowest) and the respective time limits of each task.

**Table 3.** Task descriptions and task properties

| Task | Description | Priority | Time limit |
|------|-------------|----------|------------|
| Identify | Any unidentified contacts must be identified as friendly, neutral, or hostile based on predefined criteria. Identified contacts may change their behavior in a way that requires reassigning their identity | 100 (outside ISR), 300 (within ISR) | 60 s |
| Create NRTT | When a message appears in the message panel a contact (NRTT) must be added manually to the TDA. Information required to create the NRTT is displayed in the message | 200 | 90 s |
| Warn | Contacts identified as hostile must be warned as soon as they enter the Identification Safety Range (ISR; indicated on the TDA by a blue circle around the own ship) | 400 | 30 s |
| Engage | Contacts identified as hostile that have been warned must be engaged as soon as they enter the Weapon Range (WR; indicated on the TDA by a red circle around the own ship) | 500 | 10 s |

Abbreviations: ISR – Identification Safety Range; TDA – Tactical Display Area; NRTT – Non-real-time track; WR – Weapon Range

## 4.2 User States and Assessment Criteria

The proof of concept implementation focused on three out of the six user state dimensions introduced in Sect. 1. These three dimensions, namely workload, attention, and fatigue, were regarded as particularly relevant for air surveillance tasks by domain experts. RASMUS was implemented to provide diagnoses for the potentially adverse states of high workload, passive task related fatigue, and incorrect attentional focus, all detailed below.

**High Workload.** The state of high workload can arise if task processing is highly demanding. According to Neerincx [32], task demand or task load can be modulated in experimental conditions by changing the task complexity, task volume, and number of task-set switches. We therefore designed a scenario in which high workload states are provoked by increasing the number of different tasks that have to be performed simultaneously. High workload is assessed through a combination of different indicators: heart rate variability, respiration rate, pupil dilation as physiological measures, the number of mouse clicks as a behavioral measure, and the number of tasks as an environmental factor. These indicators were chosen as they had proven sensitive for the assessment of high workload in previous studies. High workload is detected if at least three of these five indicators show critical outcomes.

**Passive Task Related Fatigue.** Following May and Baldwin [33], we distinguish between sleep-related (SR) and task-related (TR) fatigue. SR fatigue is influenced by sleep deprivation and the circadian rhythm (time of day) while task-related fatigue is induced by task properties and time-on-task. TR fatigue can be further subdivided into a passive and active form (cf. [33]). We focus on the passive form that is induced by monotonous tasks with a low level of cognitive demand. Passive TR fatigue is associated with a low level of arousal resembling the contrary problem state to high workload. Thus, we used the same indicators for assessment of passive TR fatigue as for high workload but with opposite criteria (cf. Table 4).

**Table 4.** Indicators and rule base for problem states

| High workload | Passive TR fatigue | Incorrect attentional focus |
|---|---|---|
| • number of tasks > 2 | • number of tasks < 2 | • number of tasks > 1 and |
| • click frequency > 10 | • click frequency < 3 | no processing of highest priority task |
| • HRV low | • HRV high | • number of tasks = 1 and |
| (>1 SD neg. dev.) | (>1 SD pos. dev.) | no processing of task |
| • pupil dilation high | • pupil dilation low | |
| (>1 SD pos. dev.) | (>1 SD neg. dev.) | |
| • respiration rate high | • respiration rate low | |
| (>1 SD pos. dev.) | (>1 SD neg. dev.) | |

**Incorrect Attentional Focus.** This state is closely related to Wickens' concept of "attentional tunneling" which is defined as "allocation of attention to a particular channel of information, diagnostic hypothesis or task goal, for a duration that is longer than optimal, given the expected cost of neglecting events on other channels, failing to consider other hypotheses, or failing to perform other tasks" ([13], p. 1). Our focus is on correctly prioritized task processing. Hence, RASMUS detects incorrect attentional focus if a higher priority task is neglected because the user is processing a lower priority task or if he/she missed a task in the absence of an alternative task. We included the latter rule as we observed that monitoring contacts on the TDA also requires attention even though it is not associated with processing a specific task.

### 4.3    Rule Base

To account for individual differences in physiological reactions (cf. Sect. 3.1), critical outcomes of physiological measures are detected by analyzing the deviation of current recordings from a baseline. We use the standard deviation (SD) as criterion for a critical deviation. As physiological measures fluctuate in short time intervals (cf. Sect. 2.5), RASMUS calculates moving averages over a time window of 30 s to smoothen the data. The physiological indicator is labeled as critically high or low if the current mean deviates by more than 1 SD from the baseline mean.

For indicators "number of tasks" and "frequency of mouse clicks", outcomes are labeled as critically high or low if the number of tasks/click frequency during the current time interval falls above or below a threshold value that has been derived from previous observations. Incorrect attentional focus is detected if the task that is currently being processed is not the highest priority task. Indicators and corresponding rules for critical outcomes are summarized in Table 4.

## 4.4   Validation

We recently conducted a validation experiment with 12 participants to examine the validity of RASMUS diagnostics for the detection of high workload, passive TR fatigue, and incorrect attentional focus. Participants performed the AAW tasks described in Sect. 4.1 in a scenario-based simulation. The scenario was designed to provoke states of high workload, passive TR fatigue, and incorrect attentional focus. Whenever RASMUS detected a performance decrement the scenario was paused and the participant was asked to rate his or her current user state with respect to the six state dimensions introduced in Sect. 1. We then compared RASMUS' user state diagnostics at the time of performance decrements with outcomes of the user rating. First of all, analyses revealed that most performance decrements were associated with at least one user state evaluated as potentially critical. For those states with critical outcomes corresponding user ratings mostly showed consistent deviations from the baseline. Hence, these preliminary results indicate that the validity of RASMUS diagnostics can be confirmed. More detailed results from this experiment will be reported in a future publication.

## 5   Conclusions and Future Work

With our concept of a real-time assessment of multidimensional user state (RASMUS) we address some major challenges that have been identified for real-world applications of adaptive system design. For example, RASMUS considers self-adaptation of the human as it detects a need for support when performance is declined, and thus self-adaptation has failed to successfully maintain the operator's effectiveness. Also, user state assessment in RASMUS is based on the combination of different kinds of measures to provide more robust and valid diagnoses. With the assessment of several potentially problematic user states and associated contextual indicators RASMUS enables dynamic adaptive systems to not only determine when the user needs support but to infer what kind of support is most appropriate to restore the user's effectiveness. To that end, RASMUS diagnostics have already been combined with a dynamic adaptation management component to accomplish near real-time selection and configuration of adaptation strategies (cf. [30]).

With our proof-of-concept implementation of RASMUS we also demonstrated the feasibility of applying our generic concept to the domain of naval Anti-Air Warfare. Initial results of a validation experiment support the validity of RASMUS diagnostics in the event of a performance decrement within this task environment. As indicators and rule base are variable entities in our framework, they may be modified to further improve the diagnostic capabilities or tailor our dynamic adaptation framework to various application areas in which human-machine systems act in safety-critical task environments. Visualization of real-time diagnostics on our "Performance and User State Monitor" may also be beneficial for adaptive training, e.g. to verify and monitor the deliberate induction of adverse user states to develop coping strategies.

The current implementation is limited in that it only provides diagnoses for three specifically relevant problem states out of the six dimensions covered by our generic concept of multidimensional user state assessment. We plan to expand the rule base to cover additional user states in the near future. Also, it is important to note that the purpose of RASMUS' user state assessment is to identify factors that likely contributed to an observed decline in performance. A critical state diagnosis therefore indicates that the respective state deviates considerably from the optimal condition which, by itself, does not necessarily imply that the user is on the edge of a breakdown and requires assistance. Therefore, RASMUS user state assessment cannot be used for proactive prevention of critical user states and performance decrements. However, while proactive adaptation may appear superior to our post-hoc approach, intervening too early may provoke conflicts with the user's self-adaptation mechanisms and favor complacency [34]. We therefore believe that combining reasonable performance thresholds as a trigger for adaptation with user state assessment for root-cause analysis is still an effective way to enable dynamic, context-sensitive adaptation.

# References

1. BEA (2012) Final Report on the accident on 1st June 2009 to the Airbus A330-203 registered F-GZCP operated by Air France flight AF447 Rio de Janeiro – Paris. https://www.bea.aero/docspa/2009/f-cp090601.en/pdf/f-cp090601.en.pdf. Accessed 10 Feb 2017
2. Schwarz, J., Fuchs, S., Flemisch, F.: Towards a more holistic view on user state assessment in adaptive human-computer interaction. In: Proceedings of the IEEE International Conference on Systems, Man, and Cybernetics, San Diego CA USA, pp. 1247–1253 (2014). doi:10.1109/SMC.2014.6974082
3. Rouse, W.B.: Adaptive aiding for human/computer control. Hum. Factors **30**(4), 431–443 (1988)
4. Scerbo, M.W.: Theoretical perspectives on adaptive automation. In: Parasuraman, R., Mouloua, M. (eds.) Automation and Human Performance: Theory and Applications, pp. 37–63. Erlbaum, Mahwah (1996)
5. Stanney, K.M., Schmorrow, D.D., Johnston, M., Fuchs, S., Jones, D., Hale, K.S., Ahmad, A., Young, P.: Augmented cognition: an overview. In: Durso, F.T. (ed.) Reviews of Human Factors and Ergonomics, HFES, Santa Monica, vol 5, pp. 195–224 (2009). doi:10.1518/155723409X448062
6. Fuchs, S., Hale, K.S., Stanney, K.M., Berka, C., Levendowski, D., Juhnke, J.: Physiological sensors cannot effectively drive system mitigation alone. In: Schmorrow, D.D., Stanney, K.M., Reeves, L.M. (eds.) Foundations of Augmented Cognition, 2nd edn, pp. 193–200. Strategic Analysis Inc., Arlington (2006)
7. Steinhauser, N.B., Pavlas, D., Hancock, P.A.: Design principles for adaptive automation and aiding. Ergon. Des. **17**(2), 6–10 (2009)
8. Dorneich, M.C., Verver,. P.M., Mathan, S., Whitlow, S., Hayes, C.C.: Considering etiquette in the design of an adaptive system. J. Cogn. Eng. Decis. Making **6**(2), 243–265 (2012). doi:10.1.1.981.8586
9. Hancock, P.A., Chignell, M.H.: Input information requirements for an adaptive human-machine system. In: Proceedings of the Tenth Department of Defense of Conference Psychology, vol 10, pp. 493–498 (1986)
10. Veltman, J.A., Jansen, C.: The role of operator state assessment in adaptive automation. TNO Report, TNO-DV3 2005 A245, Soesterberg (2006)

11. Akerstedt, T., Mollard, R., Samel, A., Simons, M., Spencer, M.: The role of EU FTL legislation in reducing cumulative fatigue in civil aviation (2003). Paper prepared for ETSC

12. Wilkinson, R.T., Edwards, R.S., Haines, E.: Performance following a night of reduced sleep. Psychon. Sci. **5**, 471–472 (1966). doi:10.3758/BF03328474

13. Wickens, C.D.: Attentional tunneling and task management. Technical report, AHFD-05-01/NASA-05-10, NASA Ames Reseach Center, Moffett Field CA (2005)

14. Endsley, M.R.R.: Situation awareness and human error: designing to support human performance. In: Proceedings of the High Consequence Systems Surety Conference, Albuquerque NM (1999)

15. Staal, M.A.: Stress, Cognition, and Human Performance: A Literature Review and Conceptual Framework. National Aeronautics & Space Administration, Hanover (2004)

16. Hilburn, B., Jorna, P.G., Byrne, E.A., Parasuraman, R.: The effect of adaptive air traffic control (ATC) decision aiding on controller mental workload. In: Mouloua, M., Koonce, J. (eds.) Human Automation Interaction: Research and Practice, Erlbaum, Mahwah NJ, pp. 84–91 (1997). doi:10.1518/155534310X522851

17. Kaber, D.B., Prinzel, L.J. III, Wright, M.C., Clamann, M.P.: Workload-matched adaptive automation support of air traffic controller information processing stages. Technical report NASA/TP-2002-211932, NASA, Hampton VA (2002)

18. Parasuraman, R.: Adaptive automation matched to human mental workload. In: Hockey, G.R.J., Gaillard, A.W.K., Burov, O. (eds.) Operator Functional State Assessment: The Assessment and Prediction of Human Performance Degradation in Complex Tasks, pp. 177–193. IOS Press, Amsterdam (2003). doi:10.1518/001872007X249875

19. Greef, T., Lafeber, H., Oostendorp, H., Lindenberg, J.: Eye movement as indicators of mental workload to trigger adaptive automation. In: Schmorrow, D.D., Estabrooke, Ivy V., Grootjen, M. (eds.) FAC 2009. LNCS (LNAI), vol. 5638, pp. 219–228. Springer, Heidelberg (2009). doi:10.1007/978-3-642-02812-0_26

20. Jorna, P.G.A.M.: Heart-rate and workload variations in actual and simulated flight. Ergonomics **36**(9), 1043–1054 (1993). doi:10.1080/00140139308967976

21. Veltman, H.J.A., Jansen, C.: The adaptive operator. In: Vincenzi, D.A., Mouloua, M., Hancock, P.A. (eds.) Human Performance, Situation Awareness, and Automation: Current Research and Trends, vol. 2, pp. 7–10. Erlbaum, Mahwah (2004)

22. Berka, C., Levendowski, D., Lumicao, M., Yau, A., Davis, G., Zivkovic, V., Craven, P.L.: EEG correlates of task engagement and mental workload in vigilance, learning and memory tasks. Aviat. Space Environ. Med. **78**(5, Section II, Suppl.), B231–B244 (2007). http://www.ncbi.nlm.nih.gov/pubmed/17547324

23. Veltman, J.A., Jansen, C.: Differentiation of mental effort measures: consequences for adaptive automation. In: Hockey, G.R.J., Gaillard, A.W.K., Burov, O. (eds.) Operator Functional State, pp. 249–259. IOS Press, Amsterdam (2003)

24. Schwarz, J., Fuchs, S.: Efficacy of metrics from a low-cost EEG sensor for multi-dimensional user state assessment. In: Presentation held at 11. Berliner Werkstatt Mensch-Maschine-Systeme, Berlin, 07–09 October 2015 (2015)

25. Schwarz, J., Fuchs, S.: Test-retest stability of eeg and eye tracking metrics as indicators of variations in user state - an analysis at a group and an individual level. In: Hale, K.S., Stanney, K.M. (eds.) Advances in Neuroergonomics and Cognitive Engineering, pp. 145–156. Springer International Publishing, Cham (2016). doi:10.1007/978-3-319-41691-5_13

26. Tomarken, A.J.: A psychometric perspective on psychophysiological measures. Psychol. Assess. **7**(3), 387–395 (1995)

27. Diethe, T.: The future of augmentation managers. In: Schmorrow, D.D. (ed.) Foundations of augmented cognition, pp. 631–640. Erlbaum, Mahwah NJ (2005)

28. Barker, R.A., Edwards, R.E., O'Neill, K.R., Tollar, J.R.: DARPA improving warfighter information intake under stress - augmented cognition Concept Validation Experiment (CVE). Analysis Report for the Boeing Team, pp. 1–112 (2004)

29. Parasuraman, R., Sheridan, T.B., Wickens, C.D.: A model of types and levels of human interaction with automation. IEEE Trans. Syst. Man Cybern. Part A Syst. Hum. 30, 286–297 (2000). doi:10.1109/3468.844354

30. Fuchs, S., Schwarz, J.: Towards a dynamic selection and configuration of adaptation strategies in augmented cognition. In: Schmorrow, D.D., Fidopiastis, C.M. (eds.) AC 2017. LNCS (LNAI), vol. 10285, pp. 101–115. Springer, Cham (2017)

31. Schwarz, J.: Benutzerzustandserfassung zur Regelung Kognitiver Assistenz an Bord von Marineschiffen. In: Söffker, D. (ed.) 2. Interdisziplinärer Workshop Kognitive Systeme: Mensch, Teams, Systeme und Automaten, DuEPublico, Duisburg-Essen (2013). doi:10. 17185/duepublico/31351

32. Neerincx, M.A.: Cognitive task load design: model, methods and examples. In: Hollnagel, E. (ed.) Handbook of Cognitive Task Design, pp. 283–305. Lawrence Erlbaum Associates, Mahwah NJ (2003)

33. May, J.F., Baldwin, C.L.: Driver fatigue: the importance of identifying causal factors of fatigue when considering detection and countermeasure technologies. Transp. Res. Part F: Psychol. Behav. 12(3), 218–224 (2009)

34. Billings, C.E., Lauber, J.K., Funkhouser, H., Lyman, G., Huff, E.M.: NASA aviation safety reporting system. Technical Report TM-X-3445, NASA Ames Research Center, CA (1976)

# An Affordable Bio-Sensing and Activity Tagging Platform for HCI Research

Siddharth[1,2(✉)], Aashish Patel[1], Tzyy-Ping Jung[2], and Terrence J. Sejnowski[2,3]

[1] Department of Electrical and Computer Engineering, University of California, San Diego, USA
{ssiddhar,anp054}@eng.ucsd.edu

[2] Institute for Neural Computation, University of California, San Diego, USA
jung@sccn.ucsd.edu, terry@salk.edu

[3] The Computational Neurobiology Laboratory, Salk Institute, La Jolla, USA

**Abstract.** We present a novel multi-modal bio-sensing platform capable of integrating multiple data streams for use in real-time applications. The system is composed of a central compute module and a companion headset. The compute node collects, time-stamps and transmits the data while also providing an interface for a wide range of sensors including electroencephalogram, photo-plethysmogram, electrocardiogram, and eye gaze among others. The companion headset contains the gaze tracking cameras. By integrating many of the measurements systems into an accessible package, we are able to explore previously unanswerable questions ranging from open-environment interactions to emotional-response studies. Though some of the integrated sensors are designed from the ground-up to fit into a compact form factor, we validate the accuracy of the sensors and find that they perform similarly to, and in some cases better than, alternatives.

**Keywords:** Bio-sensing · Multi-modal bio-sensing · Emotion studies · Brain-computer interfaces

## 1 Introduction

Electroencephalogram (EEG) systems have experienced a renewed interest by the research community for use in non-clinical studies. Though being deployed in large-scale studies, many of the advances have not been translated to substantial real-world applications. A major challenge is that the hardware and software typically used to make measurements limit their use to controlled environments. Additionally, the low spatial resolution of EEG itself limits the amount of usable information that can be extracted from noise in dynamic recording environments. Lastly, the absence of a method to automatically extract user-environment interactions for tagging with EEG data introduces an immense overhead to researchers - having to manually tag events or limit experimental design by requiring the subjects to provide information during the experiments.

© Springer International Publishing AG 2017
D.D. Schmorrow and C.M. Fidopiastis (Eds.): AC 2017, Part I, LNAI 10284, pp. 399–409, 2017.
DOI: 10.1007/978-3-319-58628-1_31

Most of the EEG research from the past decades has been conducted under laboratory based controlled environments as opposed to practical daily-use applications. On the other hand, there are many fitness trackers available today capable of providing accurate heart-rate, blood pressure, galvanic skin response (GSR), steps taken etc. Under controlled laboratory conditions, EEG researchers have been able to control a quadcopter [1], control robots [2], control wheelchair to move around [3] etc. Unfortunately, research labs have been unable to show applications of EEG "into the wild" due to constraints imposed by the existing EEG decoders [17].

EEG research often studies event-related brain responses evoked or elicited by a visual or auditory stimulus. But, for real-world experiments with EEG, the stimulus onset is not measured or is ill-defined. A solution is to use saccadic eye movements and fixations as the time-locking mechanism for analyzing naturalistic visual stimuli [26–28]. Hence, we need to simultaneously record and synchronize EEG and eye-gaze data in real-world neuroimaging studies. For real-world experiments with EEG there is also a need to pinpoint the stimulus that is causing the changes in EEG. Hence, user's visual perspective is necessary to be recorded for EEG recordings in real-world experiments.

For the analysis of emotional responses, recent research [8, 10] (in NeuroCardiology) has shown that the heart also has a role to play in generation of emotions. This falsifies the wide ranging decades old belief that the brain is solely responsible for the generation and subsequent emotional feelings. But, there is no currently available system which can reliably sense and record EEG and electrocardiogram (ECG) together in a mobile environment. Furthermore, ECG complicates the experimental setup since subjects have to wear a belt or place several sensors on their chest. A workaround is to use photoplethsmogram (PPG) from commercially available devices that derive PPG from the wrist. But, such devices usually use low sampling rates to save battery power and hence can only measure heart rates, but not heart-rate variability (HRV) that is typically only estimated by commercial devices.

Addressing the above key limitations of existing systems, we present an affordable, wearable multi-modal bio-sensing platform that is capable of monitoring EEG, PPG, eye-gaze, and limb dynamics (Fig. 1). The platform also supports the addition of other biosensors including galvanic skin response (GSR) and lactate levels. Leveraging the capabilities of this system, a new breadth of applications can be explored that allow for better translations to impactful solutions.

## 2  System Overview

We use modular design to increase the flexibility and efficiency of multiple measurements of the multi-modal bio-sensing platform. Selecting a control board that is well supported by the open-source community and had capable expansion was a priority. To this end, this study has explored different solutions including the Arduino, Raspberry Pi, LeMaker Guitar, and other ARM-based embedded controllers. The hardware evaluation metric that determined viability was the ability for the systems to hit lower-bound frame-rates and collect data from multiple sensors in real-time using the Lab-Streaming Layer (LSL [23]). The last but one of the most important evaluation metrics was the expandability via general input/output or communication protocols.

**Fig. 1.** Portable multi-modal bio-sensing platform paired with an Emotiv Epoc for EEG, PPG behind ear and eye-gaze collection.

After evaluation of the different platforms, the Raspberry Pi 3 (RPi3) was identified as being the system that best balances cost, support, and capabilities. The sensors that were selected for preliminary use are explored in detail below.

## 2.1 Electroencephalogram (EEG)

Non-invasive EEG is used to collect neural signals from individuals. Any EEG system that is supported by LSL can be used in the proposed multi-modal bio-sensing framework. The Emotiv Epoc+ system is shown in Fig. 1 as it has a suitable tradeoff between ease-of-use and performance. The Epoc allows for wireless collection of data that can be time-stamped and synchronized in real-time by RPi 3. The sampling frequency of the system is on the lower end of new commercial systems at 128 Hz, but has 14 channels (saline activated) and a gyroscope allowing for collection of cleaner signals. Independent Component Analysis (ICA) [5, 6, 21] is used in real time using ORICA [20, 24] toolbox in Matlab to separate the sources of EEG recordings in real-time and plot them. For each of the independent components, the scalp map is plotted in real-time to better depict the source localization. ICA is also used to remove EEG artifacts due to eye blinks, muscles and other movements.

## 2.2 Photoplethsmogram (PPG)

Due to the uncomfortable nature of existing heart-rate and heart-rate variability sensors, a new miniaturized PPG sensor (Fig. 2) was developed that magnetically clipped to the ear. The miniaturization was achieved by integrating a high-precision and high-sampling rate ADC to the sensor. Additionally, to eliminate noise, a third-order filter (bandpass 0.8–4 Hz) was also integrated on the board such that only the digitized and filtered signals are transmitted to the control board. To also account for motion artifacts in the heart-rate signals, a 3-axis accelerometer was integrated into the board. The two data streams, once collected by the core controller, are integrated using an adaptive noise cancellation algorithm (ANC) [7, 18] (Fig. 3). Addressing the discomfort and bulk associated with existing systems, the device was developed to be mountable to the ear-lobe using magnets [7]. Because the system is low-profile and capable of resting behind the ear [9, 16], more mobile studies can be conducted without the constrained natures of existing systems.

**Fig. 2.** Miniaturized PPG sensor with scale reference. (A) 3-axis accelerometer, (B) 100 Hz 12-bit ADC, (C) IR emitter and receiver, (D) third-order filter bank.

## 2.3   Eye Gaze

The next sensor of the multi-modal system is a pair of cameras. One camera, an IR emitting device, is capable of accurately capturing the pupil location. A pupil-centering algorithm is also integrated into the platform and is capable of maintaining the exact location even under perturbation. An algorithm developed by Pupil Labs [4] for pupil detection and eye-gaze calibration is utilized. Refer to the results section for quantification of tracking accuracy.

The second integrated camera in the system is a world-view camera. The camera provides a wide-angle view of what the wearer is seeing. While being small and integrated into the headset, the camera itself is a standard easily-accessible module. With the information that is retrievable from both the pupil and the world cameras, it is possible to retrospectively reconstruct the full-view that the user was observing. The primary problem that stems from this type of mass video collection is that the amount of data that must be manually labelled is enormous. There are machine-learning tools that are capable of labelling video post-hoc, but limit the types of experiments that can be performed. To create a truly portable system, the system's video can be streamed to a computer and processed using deep-learning libraries such as You Only Look Once (YOLO) [19] that are capable of labelling 20 objects in real-time (trained on Pascal VOC [20] dataset). By labelling exactly what the user is looking at and allowing labelled data to be accessible during the experiment, the experimental rigidity can be

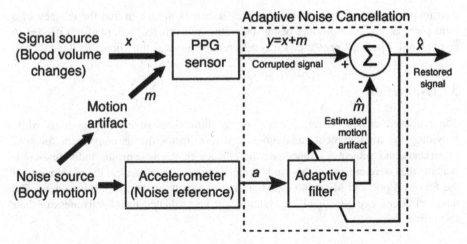

**Fig. 3.** Schematic overview of adaptive noise cancellation integration with PPG.

relaxed allowing for more natural free-flowing behavior to be measured with minimally intrusive cues (Fig. 4).

## 2.4    Galvanic Skin Response (GSR)

The final sensor considered for addition to our multi-modal setup is a galvanic skin response sensor. GSR specifically allows for the measurement of arousal through the

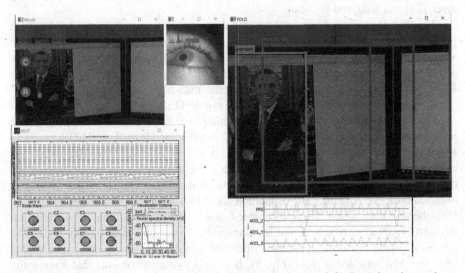

**Fig. 4.** Pupil and world views from companion headset device (top-left). Deep-learning package used to classify objects in real-time (top-right). EEG with real-time ICA and PPG signals capture (bottom panels).

measurement of the skin's impedance. This sensor is unique in that the efficacy of a third party commercial product being integrated into this research platform needed to be explored. The GSR sensor that was selected for use was the Microsoft Band 2 [14].

# 3 Evaluation

The proposed device addresses many of the limitations of existing systems while providing the measurement capabilities in a form-factor that is convenient for both researchers and subjects. To evaluate the efficacy of the system, the individual components that were created in this study were evaluated. In particular, the evaluations of the Emotiv Epoc and Microsoft Band are not explicitly evaluated in this review. The novel PPG and eye-gaze tracking systems will be evaluated for effectiveness in their respective areas.

## 3.1 PPG Evaluation

To quantify the performance of the miniaturized PPG sensor, different scenarios are considered that are representative of real-world uses. The baseline system for comparison is an EEG/ECG collection system from the Institute of Neural Engineering of Tsinghua University, Beijing, China. It is capable of measuring EEG/ECG at 1,000 Hz. Because the reference system takes measurements from electrodes placed near the heart, the artifacts introduced from movements or other physiological responses are minimized. Simultaneously while taking measurements from the reference system, the PPG is collecting the ECG signal from the user's ear at a rate of 100 Hz. As both systems can be connected in parallel, they are synchronized using the lab-streaming layer [23] and analyzed post-hoc.

The first experiment was a resting scenario - the user remained seated for a fixed period of two minutes. For the PPG sensor, the data were compared to the reference with and without the adaptive noise cancellation filter. The second experiment was an active scenario where the user was instructed to walk in-place at a normal pace to simulate an active walking scenario. Again the data after using adaptive noise cancellation was compared against the standard raw PPG signal.

A peak detection algorithm [25] using minimum distance to next peak as one of the parameters to eliminate false peaks was used to calculate Heart Rate (HR) from ECG and PPG Data. Fifteen-second trails were used to calculate the HR using the peak-detection algorithm. Figures 5 and 6 show the normalized errors, the ratio of the difference in HR between PPG and ECG-based methods divided by the mean HR obtained by PPG. A perfect HR estimation should result in 0%. Examining the results from the reference signal, the ANC enabled, and ANC disabled signals, it is clear that the ANC enabled signals have the least amount of noise and most closely match the reference signal. For resting, the ANC-disabled signals were nearly undistinguishable from the ANC-enabled signals (Fig. 5). It is in active environments that having the ANC filtering provide a marked improvement in noise rejection (Fig. 6).

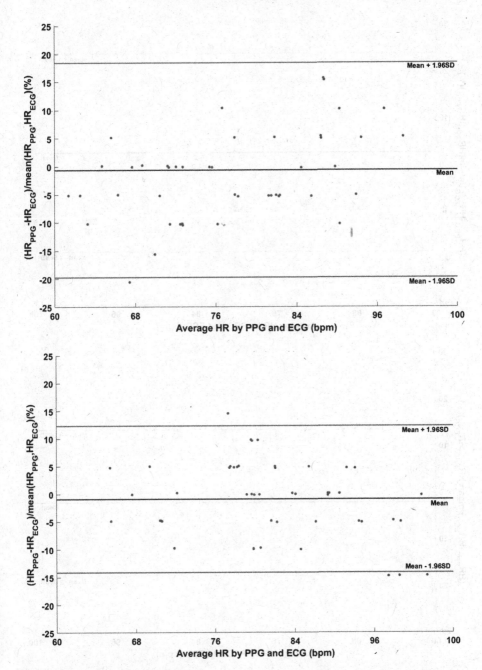

**Fig. 5.** Bland-Altman plot comparing the measured PPG signal to a reference while at rest (top). Similarly comparing the measured PPG signal using an adaptive noise cancellation filter to reference while at rest (bottom).

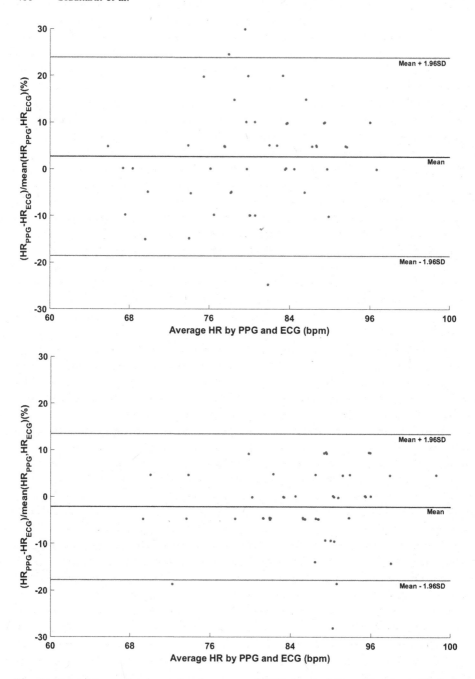

**Fig. 6.** Bland-Altman plot comparing the measured PPG signal while walking (top). Similarly comparing the measured PPG signal using an adaptive noise cancellation filter while walking (bottom).

## 3.2  Eye Gaze Evaluation

The performance of the paired pupil- and world- view cameras was evaluated using a structured visual task to measure precision and accuracy during use. The user sat 2–2.5 ft away from a computer monitor such that the world camera was >90% of the camera view was composed of the task screen. Both cameras were streamed at 30 fps. For the first task, the participant was instructed to fix their head movement and only move their eyes to gaze at static targets that appeared on the screen. A calibration step where 9 targets appeared in a regular fashion on the screen calibrated the user's gaze marker. Immediately following the calibration process, a series of 20 unique targets are collected in distributed manner across the full screen accounting for the majority of the field of view. This process was followed by a period of 30 s of rest where the user was asked to move their head around without removing the headset. This action was designed to simulate the active movement scenarios when wearing the headset. Next, the participant is instructed to return to a preferred position and maintain head position. Twenty new unique points are shown on the screen to measure the precision and accuracy of the eye-tracking system after active use. This process was repeated for a total of three trials per subject.

Examining the results for the patients, we are able to observe that the accuracy and precision of the eye gaze setup does not drift significantly from the expected output. The accuracy is measured as the average angular offset (distance in degrees of the visual angle) between fixation locations and the corresponding fixation targets (Fig. 7). The precision is measured as the root-mean-square of the angular distance (degree of visual angle) between successive samples during a fixation (Fig. 8). Compared to literature, the gaze accuracy drift of 0.42 degrees is significantly less than the 1–2 degree drift found in commercial systems [11, 12]. The precision, on the other hand, experiences only a 0.2 degree shift post movement, indicating a minimal angular distance shift.

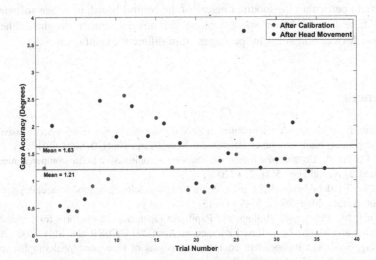

**Fig. 7.** Gaze accuracy analysis comparing the mean after calibration (red) and after 30 s of dynamic head movement to simulate active conditions (blue). (Color figure online)

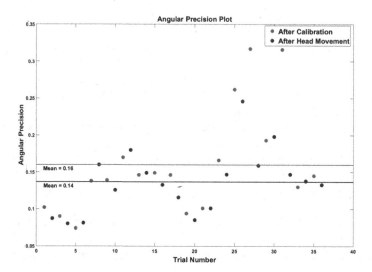

**Fig. 8.** Angular precision analysis comparing the mean after calibration (red) and after 30 s of dynamic head movement to simulate active conditions (blue). (Color figure online)

## 4  Conclusion

There are numerous sensors capable of measuring useful metrics for human behavior and interactions, however, limitations in the collection hardware and software hinder their use in experiments spanning multiple modalities. By developing a low-cost, portable, multi-modal bio-sensing platform that is capable of interfacing with numerous different sensors, we are able to explore richer experimental questions that have previously been unable to be accessed due to the constrained nature of the measurement hardware. In particular, the modular nature of the control board, interface software, and headset, time can be better spent looking for novel research insights rather than wrangling devices and software packages from different manufacturers.

## References

1. LaFleur, K., et al.: Quadcopter control in three-dimensional space using a noninvasive motor imagery-based brain–computer interface. J. Neural Eng. **10**(4), 046003 (2013)
2. Bell, C.J., et al.: Control of a humanoid robot by a noninvasive brain–computer interface in humans. J. Neural Eng. **5**(2), 214 (2008)
3. Carlson, T., del Millan, R.J.: Brain-controlled wheelchairs: a robotic architecture. IEEE Robot. Autom. Mag. **20**(1), 65–73 (2013)
4. Kassner, M., Patera, W., Bulling, A.: Pupil: An Open Source Platform for Pervasive Eye Tracking and Mobile Gaze-Based Interaction, April 2014. CoRR abs 1405.0006 (2014)
5. Makeig, S., et al.: Independent component analysis of electroencephalographic data. In: Advances in Neural Information Processing Systems, pp. 145–151 (1996)

6. Makeig, S., et al.: Blind separation of auditory event-related brain responses into independent components. Proc. Natl. Acad. Sci. **94**(20), 10979–10984 (1997)
7. Poh, M.-Z., Swenson, N.C., Picard, R.W.: Motion-tolerant magnetic earring sensor and wireless earpiece for wearable photoplethysmography. IEEE Trans. Inf. Technol. Biomed. **14**(3), 786–794 (2010)
8. Van der Wall, E.E., Van Gilst, W.H.: Neurocardiology: close interaction between heart and brain. Neth. Heart J. **21**(2), 51–52 (2013)
9. Patterson, J.A.C., McIlwraith, D.C., Yang, G.-Z.: A flexible, low noise reflective PPG sensor platform for ear-worn heart rate monitoring. In: Sixth International Workshop on Wearable and Implantable Body Sensor Networks, BSN 2009. IEEE (2009)
10. Samuels, M.A.: The brain–heart connection. Circulation **116**(1), 77–84 (2007)
11. Morgante, J.D., Zolfaghari, R., Johnson, S.P.: A critical test of temporal and spatial accuracy of the Tobii T60XL eye tracker. Infancy **17**(1), 9–32 (2012)
12. Hansen, D.W., Ji, Q.: In the eye of the beholder: a survey of models for eyes and gaze. IEEE Trans. Pattern Anal. Mach. Intell. **32**(3), 478–500 (2010)
13. Notch Motion Tracking System. https://wearnotch.com/
14. Microsoft Band. https://www.microsoft.com/microsoft-band/
15. Da He, D., Winokur, E.S., Sodini, C.G.: A continuous, wearable, and wireless heart monitor using head ballistocardiogram (BCG) and head electrocardiogram (ECG). In: 2011 Annual International Conference of the IEEE Engineering in Medicine and Biology Society, EMBC (2011)
16. He, D.D.: A wearable heart monitor at the ear using ballistocardiogram (BCG) and electrocardiogram (ECG) with a nanowatt ECG heartbeat detection circuit. Dissertation Massachusetts Institute of Technology (2013)
17. Vaughan, T.M., Wolpaw, J.R., Donchin, E.: EEG-based communication: prospects and problems. IEEE Trans. Rehabil. Eng. **4**(4), 425–430 (1996)
18. Widrow, B., et al.: Adaptive noise cancelling: principles and applications. Proc. IEEE **63**(12), 1692–1716 (1975)
19. Redmon, J., et al.: You only look once: unified, real-time object detection. In: Proceedings of the IEEE Conference on Computer Vision and Pattern Recognition (2016)
20. Everingham, M., et al.: The Pascal visual object classes (voc) challenge. Int. J. Comput. Vis. **88**(2), 303–338 (2010)
21. Bell, A.J., Sejnowski, T.J.: An information-maximization approach to blind separation and blind deconvolution. Neural Comput. **7**(6), 1129–1159 (1995)
22. Kothe, C.A., Makeig, S.: BCILAB: a platform for brain–computer interface development. J. Neural Eng. **10**(5), 056014 (2013)
23. Kothe, C.: Lab streaming layer (LSL). https://github.com/sccn/labstreaminglayer. Accessed 2015
24. Hsu, S.-H., et al.: Online recursive independent component analysis for real-time source separation of high-density EEG. In: 2014 36th Annual International Conference of the IEEE Engineering in Medicine and Biology Society (EMBC). IEEE (2014)
25. Matlab Signal Processing Toolbox. www.mathworks.com/help/signal/
26. Devillez, H., Nathalie, G., Guérin-Dugué, A.: An eye fixation–related potentials analysis of the P300 potential for fixations onto a target object when exploring natural scenes. J. Vis. **15**(13), 20 (2015)
27. Kamienkowski, J.E., et al.: Fixation-related potentials in visual search: a combined EEG and eye tracking study fixation-related potentials in visual search. J. Vis. **12**(7), 4 (2012)
28. Acqualagna, L., Blankertz, B.: Gaze-independent BCI-spelling using rapid serial visual presentation (RSVP). Clin. Neurophysiol. **124**(5), 901–908 (2013)

# Machine Learning in Augmented Cognition

# Facial Expression Recognition from Still Images

Bilge Süheyla Akkoca Gazioğlu[1]([⊠]) and Muhittin Gökmen[2]

[1] Istanbul Technical University, Istanbul, Turkey
bakkoca@itu.edu.tr
[2] MEF University, Istanbul, Turkey
muhittin.gokmen@itu.edu.tr
http://www.itu.edu.tr/,
http://www.mef.edu.tr//

**Abstract.** With the development of technology, Facial Expression Recognition (FER) become one of the important research areas in Human Computer Interaction. Changes in the movement of some muscles in face create the facial expressions. By defining these changes, facial expressions can be recognized. In this study, a cascaded structure consists of Local Zernike Moments (LZM), Local XOR Patterns (LXP) and Global Zernike Moments (GZM) methods is proposed for the FER problem. The generally used database is the Extended Chon - Kanade (CK +) in FER problems. The database consists of image sequences of 327 expressions of 118 people. Most FER system includes recognition of 7 classes of emotions happiness, sadness, surprise, anger, disgust, fear and contempt, and we use Library of Support Vector Machines (LIBSVM) classifier for multi class classification with the leave one out cross-validation method. Our overall system performance is measured as 90.34% for FER.

**Keywords:** Facial Expression Recognition · Local Zernike Moments · Local XOR Patterns · Global Zernike Moments

## 1 Introduction

Speaking is very important in human-human interaction from previous ages till today. Besides talking, facial expressions is also important in communication because how a person is affected by conversation can be understandable from his gestures and expressions. With the development of technology, Facial Expression Recognition (FER) become one of the important research areas in Human Computer Interaction. Facial expressions can be recognized by computers hardly. Also, it becomes harder with the differences in facial images like skin color, hair type, age, gender and each person's response to the same feeling. Furthermore, illumination changes, image resolution and acquisition difficulties do not facilitate the solution of problem.

Changes in the movement of some muscles in face create the facial expressions. By defining these changes, facial expressions can be recognized. Most FER system includes recognition of 7 classes of emotions happiness, sadness, surprise, anger, disgust, fear and contempt.

© Springer International Publishing AG 2017
D.D. Schmorrow and C.M. Fidopiastis (Eds.): AC 2017, Part I, LNAI 10284, pp. 413–428, 2017.
DOI: 10.1007/978-3-319-58628-1_32

## 1.1 Related Work

Recognition of facial expressions is one of the important research areas in human - computer interaction. There are many studies in the literature on automatic recognition of facial expressions by using different methods. In previous studies, many feature extraction and machine learning methods have been tested for the FER problem.

Deng et al. is intended to recognize facial expressions with a system based on Gabor features using the New Local Gabor Filter Bank [1]. When extracting Gabor attributes, a Global Gabor Filter Bank with 5 frequency and 8 orientation information is used. During the computation of the performance of the Local Gabor Filter Bank method, they use Principal Component Analysis (PCA) and Linear Discriminant Analysis (LDA) methods, which are two-stage compression methods, to compress and select Gabor features. Then the minimum distance classifier is included in the system to calculate the facial expression recognition performance of the system.

Local Binary Pattern (LBP) method can be used to recognize facial expressions. The operator used in the LBP method takes the center pixel value of a $3 \times 3$ window as the threshold value and performs a labeling process (assigning 1 or 0) by comparing all the neighboring pixels with this value [2]. This process is repeated for all pixel values in the image, so a new binary image is obtained. The 8-bit two-base number is converted to the decimal number and it is assigned as new value of the center pixel. After that, histograms are generated from new image and the recognition process is performed by using these histograms as descriptors. The LBP method can be used effectively in recognizing personally independent facial expressions. Thus, in the literature, we can find many studies such as Boosted-LBP method, which is a slightly improved version of the original LBP method [3]. This study also used LBP method as a representation based on statistical local properties for facial expressions. In order to reveal the most distinctive LBP features in the mentioned study, the Boosted LBP method has been formulated. With this new method, recognition of facial expressions has been classified with Support Vector Classifiers(SVC) and the performance of the system is improved. In the other study, the Compound Local Binary Patterns (CLBP) method was applied to the FER problem [4]. In the Local Binary Patterns (LBP) method, the LBP operator encodes the sign of the difference between the gray values of the center pixel and the neighboring pixel P with the P bit, however in the proposed CLBP method, encoding is performed by using 2P bits. The other P bits are used to code the amplitude information of the difference between the gray values of the center and given number of neighborhood pixels with a threshold value. This method discards some neighborhood information to reduce the length of the feature vector. In order to include the locational information into the histogram up to a certain point, they used the developed CLBP histogram in the method. In this study, the recognition process was implemented with Support Vector Machines (SVM) as the classification algorithm.

There is a study worked on Local Directional Pattern (LDP), which is a property descriptor for FER problem [5]. The LDP features are obtained by calculating the edge response values of each pixel position and the eight directions of this pixel, and then a new code based on the power of the relative amplitude is obtained. Therefore, each expression is expressed as a distribution of LDP codes. Template Matching and Support Vector Machines have been used to measure the success of the method. With LDP histograms, detailed information such as edges, corners and local texture properties can be obtained. However, since histograms are calculated on all image, position information for micro-samples can not be kept in histograms. In order to possess this information, the images are generally divided into sub-regions and the position information can be included in the general histogram by calculating the histograms over those regions.

Sariyanidi et al. used Quantified Local Zernike Moments (QLZM) and Local Zernike Moments (LZM) methods in their FER study [6]. Various numbers of images were generated for each image by using Localized Zernike moments by being calculated Zernike moments around each pixel in the image. When these images are generated, the expression image is divided into $N \times N$ subregions and LZM method is applied to each of the subregions. Then, the real and imaginary parts of each generated ZM coefficient are converted into binary values by using the signum function. With this conversion quantification process is carried out. With this approach, low-level features are determined by using LZM calculations, realized non-linear coding by using quantization, and combined features encoded on local histograms. The mentioned work has the very high success on the database used for face expressions recognition.

Another study on recognition of facial expressions is based on using the Local Directional Number Patterns method [7]. In this study, directional information of the tissues on the face is coded. The structure of each micro pattern is calculated with a mask and this information is coded with using significant direction indices (directional numbers) and pointers. The face is divided into many sub-regions and the distribution of the Local Directional Number Pattern features is obtained from these sub-regions. Then all features are concatenated to create an feature vector and it is used as a face descriptor.

A slackness is suggested to parallel hyperplane constraints; thus, a method called as modified correlation filters (MCF) has been proposed [8]. This method is inspired by Support Vector Machines and correlation filters and described as supervised binary classification algorithm. The MCF method provides energy minimization by using linear constraints. The usage of this method reduces the effect of outliers and noises in the training set. This study is applied for the recognition of facial expressions.

## 2    Feature Extraction Methods

In this section, the methods used in this study are mentioned. These methods are Global Zernike Moments(GZM), Local Zernike Moments(LZM) and Local XOR Patterns (LXP).

## 2.1   Global Zernike Moments

Moment based approaches are frequently used in pattern recognition processes and in image processing studies. The location, size, position and orientation information of the object are very important in pattern recognition studies. However, such these problems can be handled easily by using moment based approaches [9].

Zernike moments (ZM) are one of the methods used in image processing and computer vision problems. ZMs can produce successful results in some research areas such as Character recognition [10], fingerprint recognition [11] and pattern analysis [12] etc. ZMs are invariant to rotation. Also, it can be used as successful feature extraction method [13] (Fig. 1).

**Calculation of Global Zernike Moments.** Zernike moments can be defined as projections on complex Zernike polynomials. Zernike polynomials are expressed as an orthogonal polynomial set to the unit disk. Zernike Moments −f$(\rho,\theta)$ of a Gray level image is defined as [14]

$$Z_{nm} = \frac{n+1}{\pi} \int_{\theta=0}^{2\pi} \int_{\rho=0}^{1} V_{nm}^*(\rho,\theta)f(\rho,\theta)\rho d\rho d\theta, \quad |\rho| \le 1. \tag{1}$$

where $V_{nm}(\rho,\theta)$ is Zernike polynomials, $n$ is the moment degree and $m$ is number of iterations. $V_{nm}(\rho,\theta)$ polynomials are calculated as

$$V_{nm}(\rho,\theta) = R_{nm}(\rho)e^{-jm\theta} \tag{2}$$

where $R_{nm}(\rho)$ is radial polynomials and calculated as s

$$R_{nm}(\rho) = \sum_{k=0}^{\frac{n-|m|}{2}} (-1)^k \frac{(n-k)!}{k!(\frac{n+|m|}{2}-k)!(\frac{(n-|m|)}{2}-k!)} r^{n-2k} \tag{3}$$

In these equations, $n$ and $m$ values are selected according to the $n \ge 0$, $0 \le |m| \le n$, $n - |m|$ is even rules.

Calculated Zernike Moments in Eq. (1) cannot be used in images. It should be converted to the discrete form. New equation can be shown as

$$Z_{nm} = \lambda(n,N) \sum_{i=0}^{N-1} \sum_{j=0}^{N-1} R_{nm}(\rho_{ij})e^{-jm\theta_{ij}}f(i,j), \quad 0 \le \rho_{ij} \le 1 \tag{4}$$

$$\rho = \sqrt{(c_1 i + c_2)^2 + (c_1 j + c_2)^2} \tag{5}$$

$$\theta = tan^{-1}(\frac{c_1 j + c_2}{c_1 i + c_2}) \tag{6}$$

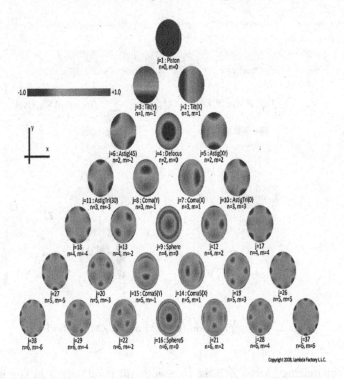

**Fig. 1.** Images of Zernike Polynomials that corresponding to $n = 0, 1, 2, 3, 4$ values. [15].

## 2.2 Local Zernike Moments

When image moments are applied globally, they give successful results when used in classification or recognition processes where the shapes in the images are obvious [9]. One of these moments, Zernike moments, is based on the calculation of complex moment coefficients from the whole image; but this method is successful when working on such studies like character recognition.

Zernike moments make a unique definition on the whole image. These definitions are due to the use of radial polynomials at different degrees. Thanks to each of the variables used, different characteristic features of images are emerging [16]. It is seen that these holistic moment components are inadequate in face images and that the local features of images are more important. Thus, by localizing the Zernike moments method, that is, by calculating a new moment value around each pixel, Local Zernike moments (LZM) representations have been proposed, and successful results have been obtained in the face recognition by using this method [9]. The results which are obtained by applying Global Zernike moments and the application of Local Zernike Moments are shown in Fig. 2.

In facial expression recognition, the local changes in the face image play very important role. LZM method was applied twice successively in this study because it provides that local features which are independent of illumination changes are obtained with the first application and shape statistics are determined with the second one.

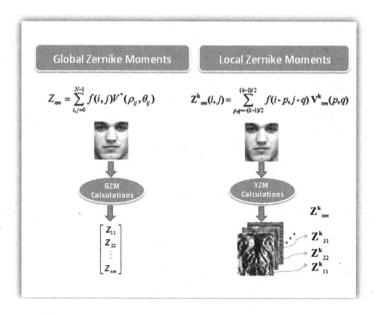

**Fig. 2.** The application of GZM and YZM methods.

While calculating global Zernike moments, all pixel values in the image are used; in Local Zernike Moments method, localization is performed by making these calculations for each pixel in the image. This localization process is used to extract the shape information in the image pattern.

**Calculation of Local Zernike Moments.** In LZM formula, moment-based operators, $V_{mn}^k$ is calculated as

$$V_{nm}^k(i,j) = V_{nm}(\rho_{ij}, \theta_{ij}) \tag{7}$$

$k \times k$ kernels can be considered as 2D convolution filters used in image filtering. According to these kernels, LZM transformation can be defined as

$$Z_{nm}^k(i,j) = \sum_{p,q=-\frac{k-1}{2}}^{\frac{k-1}{2}} f(i-p,j-q)V_{nm}^k(p,q) \tag{8}$$

There are many different parameters in the LZM method. One of the most important of these parameters is $n$, which is expressed as moment degree. Different numbers of real and imaginary $V_{mn}^k$ kernels are obtained depending on this moment degree. The real and imaginary components of the first 8 kernels obtained for $k = 9$ are shown in Fig. 3.

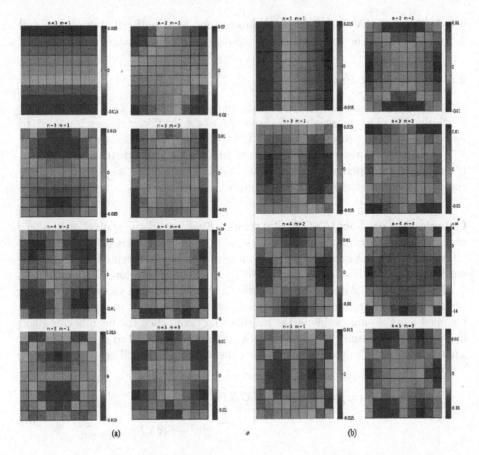

**Fig. 3.** (a) The real components of the first 8 kernels obtained for $k = 9$ (b) the imaginary components of the first 8 kernels obtained for $k = 9$ [17].

Real and imaginary images are produced corresponding to the number of real and imaginary $V_{mn}^k$ kernels used, as seen from the Eq. 8. In this study, we discarded the images that produced by $m = 0$ valued filters from $V_{mn}^k$ kernels since the imaginary parts of the images produced with these filters are 0.

The number of complex valued images obtained by the LZM transformation can be calculated as:

$$K(n) = \begin{cases} \dfrac{n(n+2)}{4} & \text{n is even,} \\ \dfrac{(n+1)^2}{4} & \text{n is odd.} \end{cases} \tag{9}$$

In most face recognition applications, the advantages of dividing the images into subregions are discussed. Therefore, the LZM images are divided into sub-regions and this process is performed in two stages. At first stage, the images are divided into sub-regions of equal size $N \times N$. In the second step, the images are divided into $(N-1) \times (N-1)$ sub-regions by a half-cell shifted grid and $N^2 \times (N-1)^2$ is the total number of subregions for each image.

## 2.3   Local XOR Patterns

Original study about Local XOR Patterns are defined as Local Gabor XOR Patterns [18]. The sensitivity of Gabor phases to different poses is aimed to be reduced in the proposed method. If two phases are in the same range (ex. $[0°, 90°]$, it is expressed that they have similar local characteristics. Also, it is explained that phase values that do not fall within the same range reflect completely different characteristics from each other.

**Calculation of Local XOR Patterns.** First of all, new pixel values are obtained by quantizing the phase values in $[0°, 360°]$ range according to different intervals, in this LXP method. If the interval number is specified as 4, the values between $[0°, 90°])$ are 0; $90^{circ}, 180°])$: 1; $[180^{circ} mathrm, 270° mathrm])$: 2; $[270°, 360°])$: 3. After the quantization is performed, the value of the center pixel value and neighboring pixels are subjected to the XOR process. If the center pixel has the same value as the neighboring pixel, then the neighboring pixel has 0; if not the same, the pixel is written as 1. It is resulted a binary image. This binary form is then converted to the decimal form. The corresponding formula is

$$LGXP\,\mu, v(z_c) = [LGXP^P_{\mu,v}, LGXP^{P-1}_{\mu,v}, \ldots, LGXP^1_{\mu,v}]_{binary}$$
$$= [\sum_{i=1}^{P} 2^{i-1} * LGXP^i_{\mu,v}]_{decimal}. \tag{10}$$

The processing steps of the LXP method are shown in Fig. 4.

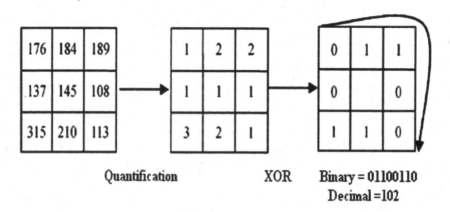

Fig. 4. Example of quantizing LXP method with 4 phase range and obtaining binary and decimal numbers [18].

where $z_c$ is center pixel position in phase map, $\mu$ is orientation, $v$ is scale. $LGXP(\mu, v)^i (i = 1, 2, \ldots, P)$ is the calculated example between $z_c$ and its neighbor $z_i$. It is calculated as

$$\boldsymbol{LGXP}^i_{(\mu,v)} = q(\phi_{(\mu,v)}(z_c)) \bigotimes q(\phi_{(\mu,v)}(z_i)), i = 1, 2, \ldots, P. \tag{11}$$

Where $\phi_{(\mu,v)} \odot$ is the phase, $\bigotimes$ defines XOR process, $q \odot$ specifies the quantization process. They can be defined as

$$c \bigotimes d = \begin{cases} 0, & c = d, \\ 1, & c \neq d. \end{cases} \tag{12}$$

$$q(\phi_{(\mu,v)} \odot) = i; \frac{360 * i}{b} \leqslant (\phi_{(\mu,v)} < \frac{360 * (i+1)}{b}, i = 0, 1, \ldots, b-1 \tag{13}$$

where b is th number of phase ranges.

# 3   Experimental Studies

## 3.1   Database

The Cohn-Kanade(CK) database is one of the most used databases in automatic facial expression recognition studies [19]. In this study we use uses the latest version of CK database, the CK + database (Extended CK database) [20]. In this database, there are 327 facial expression image of 118 different persons. The database contains image sequence of a facial expression of one person. These images starts from the natural expressions to the real expressions. In the database, there are a total of 7 expression classes including anger, disgust, fear, happiness, surprise, upset and contempt. The images of these classes are shown in Fig. 5. The distribution of expressions according to classes is given in Table 1.

## 3.2   Preprocessing on Images

Facial expression images must be processed before classification process. In this study, we used the peak image of expressions as a result of the tests carried out. We performed our recognition system for only one still image. As a pre-process step, we choose some regions, such as the eyes and the mouths are very important in recognition, on the face while the expression occurs. In this study, 9 patches were specified on each face image and all patches are aligned. Specified patches on an image are shown in Fig. 6. The extracted patches according to the active appearance model points are shown in Fig. 7.

## 3.3   Generating Feature Vectors

There are 3 steps for generating the feature vectors.

- New images are generated with the application of LZM.
- The binary images are obtained by applying LXP Method to the real and imaginary parts of the images, that are generated by LZM.
- GZM approach is applied to these final images and features are obtained.

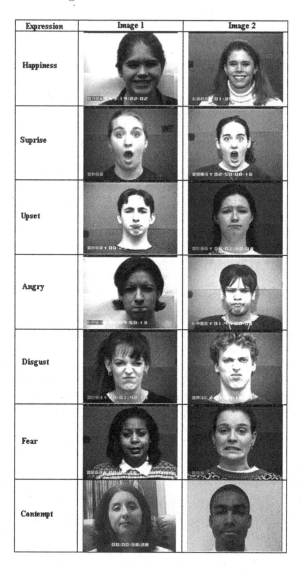

**Fig. 5.** Expression images in dataset.

**Application of Local Zernike Moments.** LZM has previously been applied to the FER problem [21]. In the mentioned work, very high system performance can not be achieved by applying the LZM directly on the whole image, but the results are promising. Therefore, in this study, Local Zernike Moments is applied on each patch. With LZM, a new moment image with the same size as the original image is obtained by taking into account the values of the adjacent pixels to that pixel. This process is repeated for each moment degree to obtain a set of images. The real and imaginary parts of the images obtained as a result of applying LZM once can be seen in Fig. 8.

**Table 1.** Distribution of the expressions according to the classes.

| Expression | Number of samples |
|------------|-------------------|
| Angry      | 45                |
| Contempt   | 18                |
| Disgust    | 59                |
| Fear       | 25                |
| Happiness  | 69                |
| Upset      | 28                |
| Surprised  | 83                |

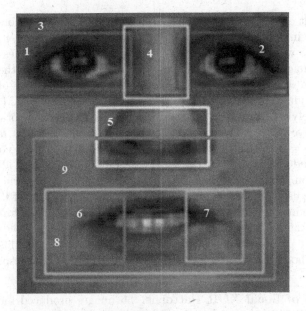

**Fig. 6.** Specified patches on a face image.

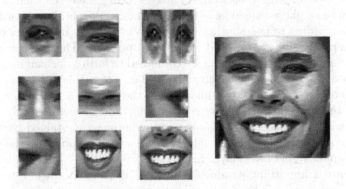

**Fig. 7.** The extracted patches from the image.

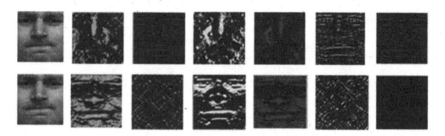

**Fig. 8.** The real and imaginary parts of the images obtained as a result of applying LZM once. Real images are shown in first line, Imaginary images are shown in second line. [21].

As a result of all the tests performed, it is seen that application of the LZM method twice improves the performance of the system. Therefore, $n = 3$, $m = 3$, $k_1 = 5$, $k_2 = 5$ were selected as the most suitable parameter values in this case. 36 moment images are obtained from a patch image according to the given parameters. When $n = 3$, $m = 3$, 4 real and 4 imaginary images are obtained as a result of applying the first layer LZM. With the second layer LZM, we have 32 image by applying LZM to 4 images from first layer and the total number of images we have is 36 as the second layer result. In the case of a facial expression, $36 \times 10 = 360$ images are obtained. In facial expression recognition, the phase amplitude histograms of the LZM images were calculated [21]. However, the recognition of facial expressions has not been able to perform successfully with only the use of LZM, due to the fact that the calculation of histograms in facial expressions does not produce very successful results. Therefore, the loss of position information with histograms can be considered as a disadvantage. For this reason, we proposed a cascaded method for FER problem in this study. This cascaded method consists of 3 methods, LZM, LXP and GZM respectively.

**Application of Local XOR Patterns.** 36 images produced for each patch with LZM contain images with real and imaginary components. The Local XOR Pattern method obtains phase-valued images using these real and imaginary images. On these phase-valued images, binary images are obtained by using XOR operation according to neighborhood values. When binary images are obtained, the central pixel value is processed with XOR operation. Then, in the clockwise direction, obtained binary numbers are combined to form a decimal number, and this number is assigned to the center pixel value. Then, this process is repeated for the each pixels in the whole image with the help of $3 \times 3$ or $5 \times 5$ filters according to the neighboring degree as in the sliding window method. Thus, an image with new pixel values is obtained. The images obtained by the LXP method are shown in Fig. 9. In the figure, LZP method is applied to the resulting images of application of first layer LZM.

There are 2 important parameters in LXP method. According to the test results for determining phase angle value and neighborhood value, both parameters are assigned as.

**Fig. 9.** Face images after LXP method applied.

**Application of Global Zernike Moments.** GZM is a method based on the calculation of complex moment coefficients from the whole image. This method is successful in images that contain significant shape information, such as characters. Thus, instead of applying this method directly to the entire face image, it is understood that the use of patches will produce more successful results.

The most important parameter used in GZM method is the parameter which determines the moment degree. As this parameter is changed, the generated number of moments changes, so the calculated moments depend on this number of moments. That is, the dimension of the generated feature vector changes. In this study, we specified the moment degree parameter as 11.

Furthermore, we analyzed the performance of each patch. Each patch performance can be seen in the graphic in Fig. 10.

## 3.4 Classification Results

In this system, LZM, LXP and GZM approaches are applied to each patch. After GZM Method applied, the moment values of each patch are concatenated.

After the feature vectors are generated, the performance of the system can be tested by classification methods. For this reason, we applied LibSVM classification algorithm.

**LibSVM.** LibSVM, Support Vector Machine Library, method is frequently used in the multi-classification problem. In this study, LibSVM approach was applied to the vectors because we have 7 classes to classify. There are 4 core types used in this method, and one of these cores must be selected. For this reason, system performance has been tested with the use of all cores. The highest performance

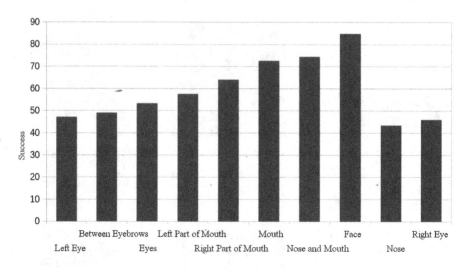

**Fig. 10.** The graphical representation of each patch success.

is achieved with the use of a linear kernel, as shown in the Table 2. So, we use LibSVM with Linear Kernel.

**Table 2.** Test results of LibSVM kernels.

| Kernel type | Success rate % |
| --- | --- |
| **Linear kernel** | **90.2** |
| Polynomial kernel | 83.8 |
| Radial basis function kernel | 75.5 |
| Sigmoid kernel | 66.1 |

We test the all 3 methods independently and we get the best results with the cascaded structure includes all of 3 methods. The confusion matrix containing the recognition rate for each expression is given in Table 3.

Our study is compared the other studies uses the same dataset. This is shown in Table 4.

## 3.5  Conclusion and Future Works

In this study, we proposed a new cascaded method which consists of Local Zernike Moments (LZM), Local XOR Patterns (LXP) and Global Zernike Moments (GZM) methods Facial Expression Recognition problem. Most common dataset, CK+ dataset, is used. The database possess image sequences of 327 expressions of 118 people. These expressions are happiness, sadness, surprise, anger, disgust, fear and contempt. We select the most emoted image and

**Table 3.** Confusion matrix.

|  | Angry | Contempt | Disgust | Fear | Happiness | Upset | Surprised |
|---|---|---|---|---|---|---|---|
| Angry | **35** | 1 | 3 | 0 | 1 | 4 | 1 |
| Contempt | 1 | **17** | 0 | 0 | 0 | 0 | 0 |
| Disgust | 2 | 0 | **57** | 0 | 0 | 0 | 0 |
| Fear | 0 | 0 | 0 | **20** | 0 | 3 | 2 |
| Happiness | 0 | 0 | 0 | 1 | **68** | 0 | 0 |
| Upset | 5 | 1 | 0 | 1 | 1 | **20** | 0 |
| Surprised | 2 | 1 | 1 | 1 | 0 | 0 | **78** |

**Table 4.** The comparison of the results in other studies.

| Method | Classifier | Success rate % |
|---|---|---|
| CAPP | SVM(Linear) | 70.1 |
|  | SVM(Linear) | 89.3 |
| LDNP | SVM(RBF) | 89.3 |
|  | SVM(Polynomial) | 81.7 |
| Gabor | SVM(Linear) | 91.8 |
| LBP | SVM(Polynomial) | 82.4 |
| BOW | SVM(Linear) | 95.9 |
| QLZM | SVM(RBF) | 96.2 |
| **LZM + LXP + GZM** | **SVM(Linear)** | **90.2** |

we applied the methods and obtained the feature vector. As a final step, Lib-SVM classifier with linear kernel is used as a classification algorithm. Calculated feature vectors are classified with LibSVM according to the leave one out cross-validation method. Facial expression recognition rate is measured as 90.34% for overall system.

We are planning to use the more than one image in the image sequence and add some features about the difference between those images to our feature vector. We can also try a cascaded structure with different classification algorithms in the classification step. As another future work, it is planned that histograms of the images after LZM and LXP applied can be calculated and used for feature vector.

# References

1. Deng, H., Jin, L., Zhen, L., Huang, J.: A New Facial Expression Recognition Method Based on Local Gabor Filter Bank and PCA plus LDA (2007)
2. Shan, C., Gong, S., McOwan, P.W.: Robust facial expression recognition using local binary patterns. IEEE Int. Conf. Image Process. ICIP **2**, 370 (2005)

3. Shan, C., Gong, S., McOwan, P.W.: Facial expression recognition based on local binary patterns: a comprehensive study. Image Vis. Comput. **27**, 803–816 (2009)
4. Ahmed, F., Hossain, E., Bari, A., Shihavuddin, A.: Compound local binary pattern (CLBP) for robust facial expression recognition. In: Computational Intelligence and Informatics (CINTI), pp. 391–395 (2011)
5. Jabid, T., Kabir, M.H., Chae, O.: Facial expression recognition using local directional pattern (LDP). In: 17th IEEE International Conference on Image Processing, pp. 1605–1608 (2010)
6. Sariyanidi, E., Gunes, H., Gokmen, M., Cavallaro, A.: Local Zernike moment representation for facial affect recognition. In: BMVC (2013)
7. Rivera, A.R., Castillo, J.R., Chae, O.O.: Local directional number pattern for face analysis: face and expression recognition. IEEE Trans. Image Process. **22**, 1740–1752 (2013)
8. Chew, S.W., Lucey, S., Lucey, P., Sridharan, S., Conn, J.F.: Improved facial expression recognition via uni-hyperplane classification. In: Computer Vision and Pattern Recognition (CVPR), pp. 2554–2561 (2012)
9. Sariyanidi, E., Dagli, V., Tek, S.C., Tunc, B., Gokmen, M.: Local Zernike moments: a new representation for face recognition. In: 2012 19th IEEE International Conference on Image Processing (ICIP), pp. 585–588 (2012)
10. Kan, C., Srinath, M.D.: Invariant character recognition with Zernike and orthogonal Fourier-Mellin moments. Pattern Recognit. **35**, 143–154 (2002)
11. Zhai, H.L., Hu, F.D., Huang, X.Y., Chen, J.H.: The application of digital image recognition to the analysis of two-dimensional fingerprints. Anal. Chim. Acta **657**, 131–135 (2010)
12. Sim, D.G., Kim, H.K., Park, R.H.: Invariant texture retrieval using modified Zernike moments. Image Vis. Comput. **22**, 331–342 (2004)
13. Khotanzad, A., Hong, Y.H.: Invariant image recognition by Zernike moments. Pattern Anal. Mach. Intell. **12**, 489–497 (1990)
14. Mukundan R., Ramakrishnan K.R.: Moment Functions in Image Analysis: Theory and Applications (1998)
15. http://www.lambda-factory.co.jp/Free/zer_wp
16. Chong, C.W., Raveendran, P., Mukundan, R.: A comparative analysis of algorithms for fast computation of Zernike moments. Pattern Recognit. **36**, 731–742 (2003)
17. Basaran, E.: Traffic sign classification with quantized local Zernike moments. Istanbul technical University (2013)
18. Xie, S., Shan, S., Chen, X., Chen, J.: Fusing local patterns of Gabor magnitude and phase for face recognition. Trans. Image Process. **19**, 1349–1391 (2010)
19. Kanade, T., Cohn, J.F., Tian, Y.: Comprehensive database for facial expression analysis. In: Fourth IEEE International Conference on Automatic Face and Gesture Recognition, pp. 46–53 (2000)
20. Lucey, P., Cohn, J.F., Kanade, T., Saragih, J., Ambadar, Z., Matthews, I.: The extended Cohn-Kanade Dataset (CK+): a complete dataset for action unit and emotion-specified expression. In: Computer Vision and Pattern Recognition Workshops (CVPRW), pp. 94–101 (2010)
21. Akkoca, B.S., Gokmen, M.: Facial expression recognition using local Zernike moments signal processing and applications (2013)

# CHISSL: A Human-Machine Collaboration Space for Unsupervised Learning

Dustin Arendt[1]([✉]), Caner Komurlu[2], and Leslie M. Blaha[1]

[1] Pacific Northwest National Laboratory, Richland, WA, USA
{dustin.arendt,leslie.blaha}@pnnl.gov
[2] Illinois Institute of Technology, Chicago, IL, USA
ckomurlu@hawk.iit.edu

**Abstract.** We developed CHISSL, a human-machine interface that utilizes interactive supervision to help the user group unlabeled instances by her own mental model. The user primarily interacts via correction (moving a misplaced instance into its correct group) or confirmation (accepting that an instance is placed in its correct group). Concurrent with the user's interactions, CHISSL trains a classification model guided by the user's grouping of the data. It then predicts the group of unlabeled instances and arranges some of these alongside the instances manually organized by the user. We hypothesize that this mode of human and machine collaboration is more effective than Active Learning, wherein the machine decides for itself which instances should be labeled by the user. We found supporting evidence for this hypothesis in a pilot study where we applied CHISSL to organize a collection of handwritten digits.

**Keywords:** Human-machine interface · Interactive clustering · Active learning · Semi-supervised learning · Direct manipulation

## 1 Introduction

A typical assumption for machine learning is that training instances are abundant and fully observed (i.e., each instance is correctly labeled by a human expert and all features are measured). Unfortunately, this assumption does not hold in many real-world problems. Often, there are plenty of instances, but labels are not available. To make matters worse, acquiring a set of labels can be very expensive when it requires the judgment of an expert user. In such cases, we need to be selective when determining which instances we ask a user to label, as all instances will not be equally helpful for training the model.

Active learning is a maturing sub-field of machine learning that approaches this missing label problem by optimizing the order in which experts are asked to provide labels. However, the missing label problem is not completely solved with a pure machine solution. As Kulesza et al. discuss, human labelers (even experts) may not label instances consistently [17]. Some instances may have multiple candidate labels of which each labeler's choice is subjective and somewhat

© Springer International Publishing AG 2017
D.D. Schmorrow and C.M. Fidopiastis (Eds.): AC 2017, Part I, LNAI 10284, pp. 429–448, 2017.
DOI: 10.1007/978-3-319-58628-1_33

arbitrary. Choice of label is often context dependent; for example, a bird may simply be labeled "bird" if the image occurs amongst many animals, but may be labeled "sparrow" if presented amongst only images of other birds.

Users' conceptions of a class can evolve, possibly becoming better defined over time as they label more instances. Furthermore, the most uncertain instance to the machine learner may not be the most important or relevant for the labeler. Some errors (i.e., misclassifications) are more tolerable than others, and the user should have some control over which to address first. Finally, in some cases the human labelers may have no conception *a priori* of the type or number of classes that should exist in the data, and they may want to explore the data to construct a better mental model for the data space.

We address these issues with CHISSL,[1] a user interface and framework for semi-supervised clustering. With CHISSL, the user is presented instances spatially arranged into separate groups. Each group consists of instances the user has labeled as well as instances the machine has predicted to belong within that group. The user's task is to improve the meaningfulness of the groups by reorganizing the instances to reflect better membership consistency or accuracy. We do not query the user directly for explicit labels of any particular instances. We only require the user to move instances between groups or into new groups as she sees fit. The user can determine both the number of groups and the group assignments she deems appropriate for the data at hand. While the user is interacting, a machine learning classifier is continuously re-trained and is predicting the group membership of unlabeled instances. When the user re-assigns an instance between groups, the machine will re-assign additional instances. Over a series of user interactions, the machine clustering is guided toward reflecting the user's mental representation of the groupings within the data. As the machine becomes more predictive of the user's mental model, it becomes increasingly effective in the organization of the instances, accelerating the user at her task.

Starting with a set of instances with any amount of labeling (partial or even completely unlabeled data), the human and the machine cooperating through CHISSL produce the following outcomes:

- *Label induction*—group assignments for the unlabeled instances are predicted. The user can continue to refine the model until she is confident in the quality of the predicted group assignments.
- *User-assigned training set*—the small set of instances assigned to clusters by the user form a training set that can be exported to bootstrap the training of other classifiers.
- *Predictive model*—a lightweight classifier is available to predict the cluster assignments for yet-to-be-seen instances, which can be applied to an expanding data set or in a streaming context. The classifier does not rely on a database of previously labeled instances for prediction.

---

[1] CHISSL stems from a concatenation of the acronyms for computer-human interaction (CHI) and semi-supervised learning (SSL).

## 2    Related Work

Related work spans three broad research domains: machine learning, visual analytics, and human-computer interaction (HCI). In the machine learning field, the areas of semi-supervised learning and active learning are most relevant. These approaches are both concerned with classification involving a combination of labeled and unlabeled data. Broadly, semi-supervised learning focuses on how to propagate labels from a small training set to a larger unlabeled set, and how to leverage the distribution of the unlabeled set to improve classification accuracy [29]. Active learning, on the other hand, is concerned with techniques for selecting unlabeled instances for an expert to label [22]. It is assumed that the user has a fixed budget (e.g., time, mental resources, money) to spend on labeling, so the crucial problem in active learning is determining the ideal instances to label that improve the classification accuracy with the fewest iterations. Some common techniques in active learning are uncertainty sampling [18] wherein the user is asked to provide a label for the least certain predicted instance, query-by-committee [23] wherein instances on which an ensemble of models disagree most are selected for labeling, and expected error reduction [21] wherein instances that promise highest reduction in prediction error when labeled by a human expert are selected for labeling.

A useful distinction exists between transductive and inductive learning [29]. Inductive classifiers build models that can predict labels for unseen data not originally part of the original data set. This concept was first introduced by Vapnik and Vapnik [27]. Transductive learning techniques only seek to assign labels to the unlabeled data in the original data set. Inductive learning is valuable, for example, when we wish to train a classifier to act autonomously. We can apply this categorization to understand related works in visual analytics, most of which we discuss are transductive. CHISSL is an inductive learning system.

### 2.1    Spatializations

Visual analytics systems have been recently developed to help the user arrange large amounts of unlabeled data according to her own mental model. Several of these systems center around a 2-D distance-preserving projection of the data, sometimes referred to as a spatialization, to help the user organize or cluster data. Choo et al. developed iVisClassifier [8], an interactive visualization using linear discriminant analysis and labels supplied by the user. ForceSPIRE [12] and Dis-function [6] infer the user's intent through direct manipulation of the projected instances, resulting in a change to the underlying model. Spatializations capitalize on the fact that allowing a user to spatially arrange a set of objects is an efficient and natural approach to eliciting insight into her mental organization of those objects [14].

Spatialization techniques are transductive; they primarily help organize a given dataset. It is not immediately clear how new data points should be handled without simply incorporating those data points into the original dataset and re-running the analysis. For example, Dis-function "exports" the user's mental model as a parameterized distance metric, but this alone is not sufficient to reproduce the spatial arrangement the user sees with new data. This requires the original data, which should be considered part of the model in some sense. Frequently, the goal of the user when interacting with projected data is to discover meaningful groupings of instances. This can be hindered by the projection algorithm which may sometimes place distant points close together in the projected space, which can be detrimental to the user's trust in the system [9] and has the potential to result in visual inference errors.

### 2.2 Interactive Clustering

Supporting formation or discovery of groups may be more helpful to the user than spatializations for some tasks. However, fully automated clustering algorithms are frequently not satisfying, often producing arbitrary or uninteresting clusters. "Interactive clustering" allows the user to help guide the clustering algorithm to find meaningful groups. A recent example by Srivastava et al. allows the users to reject uninteresting clusters until they are satisfied [25]. Their work builds on the interactive clustering techniques by Bilenko et al. [4] and Cohn and Caruana [10]. These approaches take feedback from the user in terms of linkage constraints (e.g., "these two instances do or do not belong together"), criticism (e.g., "this cluster is not what I'm looking for"), or a small amount of labeled data (e.g., "this instance belongs in this cluster"). A shortcoming of these approaches is that they do not often consider the user interface that would be used to elicit user feedback in a continuous loop, rather they assume this user feedback as input to their algorithm. Also, because the algorithm is transductive, it not clear how to add new instances to existing clusters without re-running the original clustering or resorting to a $k$ nearest neighbor classifier.

CHISSL is similar to Basu et al.'s "assisted clustering" [2] and Kulesza et al.'s "structured labeling" [17]. Assisted clustering is a hybrid metric learning/classification approach for document clustering [2]. Part of Basu et al.'s system uses a logistic regression classifier that is trained to predict which instances belong to which user-created groups. While not the main contribution of their paper, they created a user interface that could recommend clusters for unclustered documents by drawing a line between the document and the cluster. However, this was disabled during the user study, so the advantage of the classifier feedback for the user was not evaluated. Similar to this is Kulesza et al.'s structured labeling [17], which is an interface that is intended to address the problem of concept evolution when humans are providing labels in an active learning context. They also propose how a nearest-neighbor approach can be used to recommend labels for instances. We leverage the user-defined groups and similarity-based recommendations in CHISSL.

Our approach is also similar to Amershi et al.'s ReGroup [1], which was designed to help users build a classifier to act as a group filter for a social network. ReGroup trains a binary Naïve Bayes classifier from a user-defined grouping. ReGroup shows suggested instances (i.e., Facebook users) to help the user add examples to the training set. The user is presented with suggestions drawn from the classifier's most certain predicted instances. In contrast with ReGroup, CHISSL presents the user with a mixture of training data and the classifier's most *uncertain* predicted instances. Additionally, CHISSL is designed to support multi-class classification/clustering, whereas ReGroup trains a binary classifier designed to act as a filter allowing instances to be labeled as either in or out of the class. ReGroup requires both positive and negative training examples, whereas CHISSL, which uses a multi-class classifier, only requires positive examples. A positive example for one group is a negative example for all other groups in our interface. ReGroup may also be misleading when it hand picks the most likely predicted instances to show the user. CHISSL shows the user the most challenging instances to classify as candidate group members. Finally, ReGroup's evaluation focused on the usability of the overall system whereas our evaluation is a more direct comparison to active learning to understand the advantage of user- versus machine-selected instances.

## 3 Approach

We designed CHISSL to help the user organize unlabeled instances according the user's own mental model. CHISSL allows the user to flexibly create and modify groups of instances. While the user is interacting with CHISSL, the system is training a supervised classification model to predict group membership of a data set. CHISSL, depicted in Fig. 1, represents groups to the user as a collection of instances containing both training (user-grouped) and machine-predicted instances. We refer to the visible training instances as exemplars and the visible predicted instances as delegates. Delegates are presented to the user so she has the opportunity to correct any mistakes made by the machine.

We designed CHISSL to trade-off between *overwhelming* the user and making the user *overconfident* in the model. If too many instances are shown to the user, then the UI becomes taxing to use—if there is no bound on the number of instances shown, the UI is not scalable. Alternatively, if too few predicted instances are shown, the UI can misrepresent the model by giving an inflated impression of accuracy. We accomplish this balance by ensuring the user sees at least a fixed amount of the most uncertain predicted instances in each group. We prevent the user from being overwhelmed by showing no more than a fixed amount of the labeled data in each group. We help preserve the user's mental map by ensuring that, as much as possible, the same instances (assigned and unassigned) are shown to the user before and after interactions. This should prevent a radical shift of the organization captured in the UI that may cause frustration for the user. Below we describe in detail how CHISSL accomplishes this.

CHISSL allows a user to group instances according to her own mental model, showing this grouping in a grid (see Fig. 1). Within each group, training (i.e., labeled) instances and predicted instances are shown together. Human-assigned instances have a solid outline, initial machine-assignment predictions have a dashed outline, and un-assigned delegates have no outline but are placed into

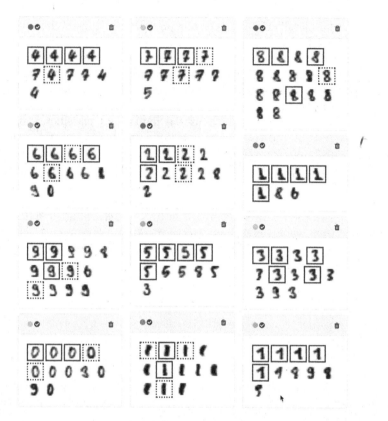

**Fig. 1.** The CHISSL grid arranges instances by predicted group assignment. The user drags instance between groups, and the model is re-trained, learning to predict the user-desired groupings. The UI also contains controls to delete groups (trash icon in upper right), or accept all predicted instances in the group (check mark in upper left).

machine-predicted group positions for user consideration. The user communicates her mental model to the machine by dragging instances between existing groups or into a newly created group, merging groups, or deleting groups. The user never directly provides labels for instances or for groups; instead, the machine learns to predict the user's grouping, and is re-trained after each interaction. The assigned or predicted group of an instance determines the visual cluster in which that instance appears in the UI. Whenever user interactions result in delegates being re-assigned to new groups by the machine learner, their corresponding images move to the new groups in the UI as necessary.

We conceptualize CHISSL's behavior in terms of changes to the set membership of instances (see Fig. 2). We define CHISSL as having sets $I$, $H$, $M$, and $D$, which are the set of all instances, human-assigned instances, initial machine-assigned instances, and machine-predicted delegates, respectively. $M$ are selected as instances with high probability of membership in the initial clusters from

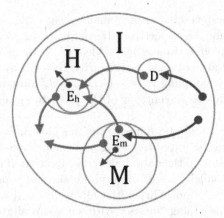

**Fig. 2.** CHISSL can be understood as instances changing set membership as a result of actions taken by the human or the machine. Red arrows indicate set membership changes caused by the machine, whereas blue lines indicate set transitions caused directly by the user through the interface. $I$ is the set of instances, $H$ and $M$ are instances assigned by the human and machine, respectively. $E_h$, $E_m$, and $D$ are the exemplars and delegates, which are the only instances visible to the user in the interface. (Color figure online)

the initial machine learner training, prior to human interaction. Instances in $H \cup M$ have been assigned to groups, and form the training set for the classifier. $E_m \subseteq M$ (dashed outlines in Fig. 1) and $E_h \subseteq H$ (solid outlines in Fig. 1) are the "exemplars" of each group, which are subsets of the human- and machine-assigned instances that are visible to the user in the interface. Instances in $D$, which we refer to as "delegates," are also visible in the UI without any boxes or borders, but their group assignments have been predicted by CHISSL, rather than assigned directly by the user. Next, we discuss the responsibilities of the human and the machine as they use CHISSL, and how their actions affect these sets.

### 3.1  CHISSL UI Design

We assume that for scalability and tractability reasons, the human is not usually able to view all of the instances at once. So, except for smaller data sets, a key role of the machine, beyond training the model on user-provided groupings, is to decide which instances the user will see in the UI. Because the user is usually interacting with tentatively assigned delegates, the number of delegates in the visualization decreases, and the number of human-assigned instances increases. Without intervention, the interface would quickly comprise of assigned instances only.

This problem is addressed by two parameters, a bound $b$ on the number of total exemplars $E_h + E_m$ and a quota $q$ on the number of delegates that are shown to the user at a given iteration. Per group, only the $b$ most recent human- or machine-assigned instances remain in the exemplar sets $E_h$ and $E_m$; the rest return to $H$ and $M$ respectively. If group $g$ has $d_g$ delegates, and $q > d_g$, then $q - d_g$ un-assigned instances are added to $D$ to maintain the delegate quota. New delegates are not chosen arbitrarily. Instead, we rely on a technique similar to uncertainty sampling to select the $q - d_g$ most uncertain instances. We measure uncertainty as the entropy of the predicted probability distribution of the instance.

Given a new, fully unlabeled dataset, the machine finds an initial exemplar set, $E_m$. CHISSL could be initialized using any unsupervised learning technique of preference appropriate to the data under consideration. If the data set contain partial or incomplete labels, a semi-supervised learning approach could also be used to initialize the system. This initial clustering is done to bootstrap the learning process, by providing the user with some initial groups to start from. Otherwise, the interface could be initialized with a random selection of instances, which runs the risk of all instances in the UI belonging to the same group. We believe some degree of initial organization is helpful when the user has no knowledge of the underlying structure or classes in the data.

In the present work, we selected the initial machine exemplars with DBSCAN [11], an unsupervised clustering technique. We set the parameters of DBSCAN to produce a few dense clusters surrounded by a majority of outliers, which we ignore, treating them as un-assigned delegates. Note that in this example on handwritten digit image data [16], we ignored the available digit labels and completed the DBSCAN initialization as an unsupervised process. After the determination of an initial unsupervised clustering, and subset of machine-predicted instances are selected as the $E_m$ to be displayed in the initial UI. All initial $E_m$ are shown with the dashed box, as seen in Fig. 3a. The clusters provided by DBSCAN are then further partitioned using $k$-means where we let $k = b$. The centroids of these sub-clusters constitute $E_m$, providing us with a diverse set of exemplars for each cluster found by DBSCAN.

## 3.2    Human Responsibility

The user is responsible for imposing her mental model on the data by organizing the visible instances into groups that are consistent with her model. As a shorthand notation below, we define $A[, B] \rightarrow C$ to mean that an instance belonging to $A$ or $B$ has changed its set membership to $C$. The user can perform the following actions when interacting with exemplars or delegates (represented by blue arrows in Fig. 2):

- **Change the group of an instance** by dragging it from one group area to another, $E_h, E_m \rightarrow E_h$. In the newly assigned group the instance is now outlined in a solid box, because the user assigned it to the group, and the instance has joined $E_h$.
- **Create a new group** by dragging an instance to the new group drop area, $E_h, E_m \rightarrow E_h$. This creates a new group within the CHISSL grid. The instance used to start the group is included, becomes an exemplar $E_h$, and has a solid outline. This is illustrated in Fig. 3.

- **Accept the assignment of an instance** by double clicking the instance $D \rightarrow E_h$. The delegate then gains a solid black line and stays in the group in the UI.
- **Accept the assignments of all instances in a group** by clicking the check icon for the group, $D \rightarrow E_h$. All these instances gain solid borders, and remain in the current group in the UI.
- **Merge two or more groups** by dragging the groups to the merge area and clicking merge. The assignments of the human- and machine-assigned instances in the $2^{nd}$ through $n^{th}$ group are changed to the group assignment of the $1^{st}$ group, causing the now-redundant groups to disappear. Exemplars remain so, and no delegates become exemplars. All delegates not originally from the $1^{st}$ group now appear in this group.
- **Delete a group** by clicking the delete icon for the group, $H, M \rightarrow I$. All machine- and human-assigned instances leave these sets and become unassigned delegates. The deleted group disappears from the user interface.

An example of how CHISSL's groups change over time as a result of its human-in-the-loop approach is shown in Fig. 3. This graphic illustrates the splitting of the group in (a) to the two groups in (c) by moving a delegate. (a) contains a set of machine-assigned exemplars in dashed boxes, and a set of uncertain delegates without boxes. The delegate has selected a delegate and moved it (b) to a new group; this delegate then gains a solid outline in (c), indicating it was user-assigned to the new group. This move causes the classifier to assign the other digits (1s) from (a) to the new group in (c) based on their similarity to the user-assigned instance. The machine also supplies additional delegates from $I$ to both groups through uncertainty sampling, shown as the images without boxes. Additional reassignments of the erroneous elements in subsequent steps results in the more consistent groups in (d).

### 3.3 Machine Responsibility

The machine is responsible for understanding the user's mental model by learning a function that predicts the group assignment of an instance according to the user's organization of the data. The machine trains a classification model from $\{(x_i, y_i) : i \in H \cup M\}$ where $x_i$ is an instance from the given dataset $I$, and $y_i$ is the group assigned to that instance by the user. Once the classification model has been trained, the model predicts group assignments for the remaining data $\{x_i : i \in I - (H \cup M)\}$, and uses the predicted probabilities (across all group assignments) to help determine which new instances (e.g., delegates) to show.

It is important to recall that labels are not explicitly assigned by the user; group assignments are inferred by the groupings in the visualization. Within the algorithm, an internal label or tagging scheme is used to track the groups, but the labels have arbitrary meaning, more or less. In other words, the user may group together all handwritten digits that resemble "four." But this may be assigned an internal arbitrary tag of $y_i = 2$. Internal group references are hidden from the user's perspective, and will work within the algorithm as long as the

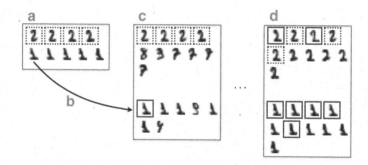

**Fig. 3.** An example to illustrate the UI responding to user interaction. (a) The user identifies an inconsistent group. (b) The user moves one of the 1s out of this group into another group. (c) The other 1s from the original group follow and additional delegates are suggested for both groups. But the classifier is not perfect. (d) After repeating this process a few more items, both classes appear more consistent or correct.

machine can effectively predict the user's grouping given the available features and training data.

The machine can take the following actions (represented by red arrows in Fig. 2):

- **Provide an initial assignment for the instances** by selecting a few representative instances with unsupervised clustering, $I \rightarrow E_m$. These are shown in the interface with a dashed outline to indicate they were assigned to a group, but not by the user.
- **Identify un-assigned instances as delegates** by selecting instances the machine is uncertain about, $I \rightarrow D$. Delegates are shown in the interface without an outline.
- **Stop showing some exemplars** by removing old exemplars from the display, $E_m \rightarrow M$ and $E_h \rightarrow H$.

## 4    Evaluation

Our hypothesis is that the human and machine together produce a more accurate classifier with a smaller training set compared to more automated approaches like Active Learning. Active Learning techniques decide the instance for which the user will provide a label. In contrast, our technique gives the user control over which instances enter the training set. If CHISSL learns more quickly than Active Learning, then the flexibility provided by CHISSL is a plausible explanation for the improvement. We conducted a carefully designed pilot experiment to compare CHISSL to test this hypothesis. We designed an Active Learning baseline algorithm so that the same instance selection, assignment, and scoring algorithms were used for both CHISSL and the baseline. The active learning algorithm selects one instance about which to query an oracle for a label at each iteration.

For the evaluation we refer to our two conditions as "human + machine" and "machine + oracle." The "human + machine" condition was users (members of the project team) following a self-selected strategy. The "machine + oracle" condition was active learning querying an oracle model for the ground truth labels in the dataset. For both conditions, we used a dataset of 1797 instance of $8 \times 8$ grayscale images of handwritten digits [16].[2] We split this dataset into training and testing sets across 3 different random cross-validation folds. For both conditions, we used the same preprocessing pipeline and model, a multi-class logistic regression classifier [28], using defaults without hyper-parameter optimization.

We ran a {3 fold} × {2 user} × {2 human sub-strategy} experimental matrix to further understand differences between human and machine strategies. The users were two of the authors of this paper. Below we discuss details relevant to the "machine + oracle" and "human + machine" strategies, and compare the learning curves for these strategies across the folds.

### 4.1   Machine + Oracle Strategy

Our instance selection approach for Active Learning is the same uncertainty sampling technique used by CHISSL discussed previously. The machine finds the 5 instances with the most uncertainty (i.e., largest entropy) and randomly selects one of these to be labeled by the oracle. Without this randomization, the active learning algorithm would be deterministic, and would produce the same learning curve each time. The randomization allows us to find the average learning curve across multiple runs within the same fold. Given a selected instance, the machine then queries the oracle for its ground truth and assigns the instance to the group with the most labeled instances having the same ground truth labels as the unlabeled instance. This is our adaptation of the oracle model commonly used to evaluate Active Learning with ground truth labels. This process was repeated for 500 steps per fold.

### 4.2   Human + Machine Strategies

The humans used CHISSL combined with a simple strategy during the evaluation. For fairness, the users were restricted to only assigning instances to groups one at a time to prevent them from using features in CHISSL that were not available for the machine + oracle (e.g., merging groups). The pilot users' strategies were simply to prioritize correcting wrongly predicted instances over confirming correct predictions. In other words, when a delegate (or machine exemplar) appeared in the wrong group, the users moved this instance to the correct group. When all groups appear internally consistent, the users could select a single correctly predicted delegate to confirm, adding that delegate to the training set. This process was undertaken for 15 min per fold, long enough to produce a training set of at least 300 instances for each fold.

---

[2] Data available from the UCI Machine Learning Repository [19], as "Optical Recognition of Handwritten Digits Data Set".

Each user ran through with two slightly different sub-strategies. With sub-strategy 1 (s1) the user creates exactly 10 groups, one for each digit. Whereas, with sub-strategy 2 (s2) the user creates more than 10 groups, in order to capture the different visual instantiations of the digits (e.g., fours closed on top, or not, sevens with a hatch, or not, etc.).

## 4.3 Evaluation Metrics

Evaluating our system is not as straightforward as a traditional classification model evaluation, where standard metrics such as the F1 score can be applied. Instead of measuring the accuracy of the classifier against some ground truth, we are actually interested in measuring how well our system supports eliciting the user's mental model. There are different ways to think about this, which is complicated by the fact that the labels the user provides may not match the labels in any ground truth validation set (at best they could be a permutation of the ground truth labels). Therefore, we implemented several metrics that we use to understand the progress of CHISSL over time in different ways as the user interacts with the system. The metrics, which can also be applied to our active learning baseline are

- Adjusted rand index ($ARI$) – consistency with ground truth,
- Maximum entropy ($max(H)$) – confidence of least confident instance,
- Average delta ($avg(\Delta)$) – stability of predictions, and
- Average entropy ($avg(H)$) – average confidence.

Our only metric to understand the accuracy of CHISSL (i.e., with respect to ground truth) is indirectly via the adjusted rand index (ARI) [15]. A direct measurement of accuracy would not be appropriate because CHISSL is not predicting the ground truth labels. Rather, it is predicting the user-defined group to which each instance belongs. The group assignments may be (but are not necessarily) a permutation of the ground truth label, and ARI will be maximum in this case. ARI will be minimum when the user's group assignment provides no information about the ground truth labels.

The remaining thee metrics do not evaluate CHISSL against ground truth, because such information is not assumed to be available during real-world scenarios. So, these metrics instead measure properties related to the internal state of the model, and are designed to provide information about how quickly the machine learning model is converging to the user's mental model. Entropy is calculated over the predicted probability distribution over labels for a given sample. Maximum entropy is the largest entropy in the validation set, whereas average entropy is averaged across the validation set. Average delta is the number of instances in the validation set whose predicted label is different in the current time step compared to the previous.

## 4.4 Result–Learning Curves

In Fig. 4, we show how the metrics for the human + machine system compare to the machine + oracle system across our experimental matrix. Results for

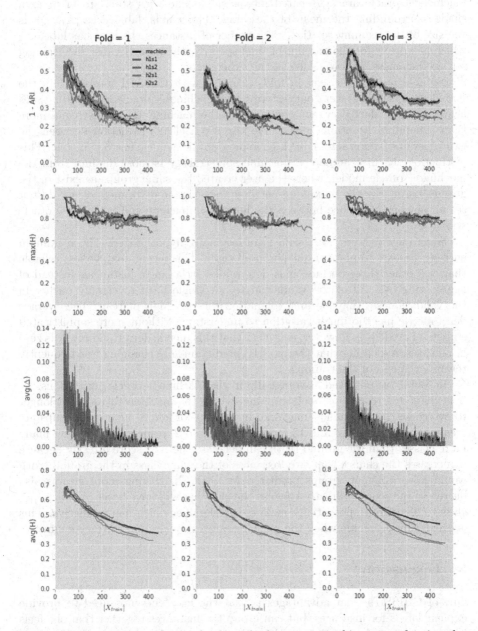

**Fig. 4.** Results from our pilot study show the human + machine outperforming the machine + oracle in several cases. Notably, this occurs with the ARI metric in folds 2 and 3, which indicate the human + machine system achieves the same level of accuracy as the machine + oracle many iterations ahead.

machine + oracle are aggregated into a single line with standard error area shaded surrounding the mean of the series. The $x$-axis, labeled as $|X_{train}|$, is the size of the training set (i.e., the number of instances the user has labeled), which is a proxy for the amount of time spent by the user, because the training set size increases monotonically in the experiment.

Notable results are seen in folds 2 and 3 with the ARI metric. Here the human + machine system outperforms the machine + oracle system, at times achieving equivalent accuracy compared to the machine + oracle system, more than a hundred iterations ahead. We also see a clear distinction between the two types of systems across all three folds with the average entropy metric. This distinction the first human + machine sub-strategy is most distinct from the machine + oracle model, where the user created the same groups as exist in the ground truth. For the maximum entropy and average delta metrics, we do not see an obvious difference between the human + machine and machine + oracle strategies.

Some metrics were less useful than originally hypothesized. The maximum entropy appears to plateau quickly in all cases. This metric may be less reliable than the other three because it is determined by a single instances, instead of aggregating over all of the validation set. A single hard to classify outlier in the validation set may be an explanation for this high plateau. The average delta metric has too much variation to understand without more sophisticated statistical modeling. However, it is clear that this metric does trend towards zero in all cases, indicating that the models' predictions are changing less frequently towards the end of the training.

In fold 3, we observed a strange dip in the machine + oracle curve. This, we believe, is due to a poor bootstrapping, which the machine takes much longer to overcome than human + machine. In the case of fold 3, 17 initial groups are created compared to 14 and 13 for fold 1 and fold 2, respectively. Having many more classes than the ground truth can decrease the ARI score directly because it increases the chance that two instances of the same class in the ground truth would have different groups predicted by CHISSL. Having more groups also decreases the score indirectly because the classifier will have fewer instances per class to learn from, potentially making the classifier much less predictive. This is eventually overcome when the machine strategy picks an arbitrary winner.

## 5    Discussion

One of CHISSL's clear advantages is that the user does not need to provide explicit labels for instances, but can group the instances together that she feels belong together. An example of where this is beneficial is shown in Fig. 5, where the user could have easily supplied an explicit class for groups (a) and (c), such as "one" and "seven", respectively. But the user may have labeled instances in the group (b) inconsistently as "one" or "seven". This is a case where the same semantic label would be applied to objects with different visual features. Instead, CHISSL allows the user to easily create a separate group to account for ambiguity a                    b                    c

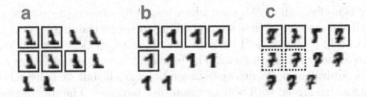

**Fig. 5.** CHISSL allows the user to create arbitrary groups to handle ambiguous classes. In this case, the user has created (a) one class that is clearly for 1's, (c) one class that is clearly for 7's, and a third class (b) that contains digist that could be labeled as 1 or 7. Regardless of the intended labels (or lack thereof), it is clear that the perceptually distinguishing characteristic is the presence/absence and placement of the horizontal stroke.

or variability within semantic categories like in (b), which is distinguished from the others by the lack of a horizontal stroke. So although handwritten digits are a data set that has an obvious choice of labels with strong semantic meaning, the user can create groups based on the pure perceptual properties (the perceived similarity or group-ness) of the instances.

Research in human categorization has repeatedly demonstrated that people are capable of learning both explicit and implicit category structures, which may be supported by different functional neural areas and cognitive mechanisms [24]. An explicit category structure is one in which the classification rules are easily verbalized (e.g., green objects in one category, red in another). Implicit categories have classification rules that are not as easily articulated and entail the integration of information across multiple dimensions. Because it does not prescribe the use of a label set, CHISSL enables users to leverage whichever organization system seems the most logical scheme to them, regardless of the verbaliz-ability of the organization schema. By studying the variability among category schemes created by different CHISSL users on the same set of instances, we may better understand the natural mental models for organizing various sets of data, or even explore how the choice of graphical or glyph representation of abstract data shapes the user's structuring of those data.

## 5.1 Scalability and Computational Complexity

CHISSL is designed to be scalable by constraining the number of instances that appears in the user interface. The bounds and quotas we place on exemplars and delegates ensure that $O(q + b)$ instances are shown at any given time, per user-defined group. Determining which instances to show is also computationally efficient. Given $n$ $d$-dimensional instances, calculating the uncertainty given predicted probabilities from the model is $O(n \cdot d)$. Finding additional delegates to meet the quota per group is $O(n \cdot \log n)$, as this only requires sorting the instances and picking (at most) the top $q$ per group.

The responsiveness of CHISSL depends largely on the complexity of the classifier's training and prediction routines. Some classifiers are faster than others, but there is no free lunch. We must often trade-off between the accuracy of the model and the amount of time we are willing to spend training it. Our philosophy was to rely on faster, and perhaps less accurate, models to provide a more interactive experience for the user. The user may have to supply more labels to achieve an equivalent performance between two models, but we believed the user would be less frustrated with a more responsive interface. The cost of training is also kept low because the model is only trained on instances belonging to $H \cup M$, which is potentially much smaller than the set of available instances $I$. Thus, we can avoid some of the cost of training by building a training set incrementally until the classifier's performance is acceptable to the user.

## 5.2  Limitations

A limitation of CHISSL is that, for simplicity, we currently re-train the classifier from scratch each iteration. This obviously becomes intractable when the training set becomes large, but solutions like incremental learning exist for support vector machines [20] and other classifiers. An additional problem may occur when using CHISSL with classifiers that rely on random number generation during training (e.g., random forests). Training from scratch each iteration may cause delegates to be less stable in the user interface compared to deterministic models (e.g., support vector machines).

CHISSL can be applied, in theory, to any data representable as real-valued feature vectors. However, because it relies on human visual perceptual groupings, CHISSL requires the instance's features to be meaningful when shown as a small image or icon, and that the similarities between instances are easily discernible in this representation. While this will be possible for handwriting and some image datasets, other domains will require different representations. For data with few features, a star glyph [5] might be effective [3]. However, for unstructured data like text, where the number of dimensions is very high, it is unlikely that we can capture enough detail in such a small space. In these cases, a larger view of the data could become available when the user interacts with the icon, allowing the icon to serve to trigger the user's memory when they were not viewing the full data. Alternatively, the icon could be replaced with keywords or a very short summary of the document.

Identification of delegates needing reassignment relies on a combination of visual search and "odd man out" identification. Change blindness becomes a more prevalent problem in cases where the differences between instances are not rapidly discerned, that is, when the user cannot rapidly scan a group and spot the "odd man out." As the groups become well-learned in CHISSL, there are fewer uncertain delegates in the display. Depending on the locus of attention when a new delegate is selected and displayed, the user may not immediately notice its presence. Similarly, the similarity of an odd-man-out delegate may be very high to the other delegates, as in the Fig. 5(c), requiring attention-intensive serial visual search.

The interface can assist the user with this challenge by using pre-attentive cues (e.g., color, motion) to indicate which delegates have recently changed groups, or which groups have recently lost or gained delegates. Techniques such as storyline visualization [22, 30], which show how entities interact over time, could help the user track changes to delegates' predicted assignments. Delegates would be represented as storylines, and two delegates would be "interacting" if they have the same predicted assignment at the same time, providing a history of the model in terms of predicted groupings. This could help the user spot trends or anomalies and catch when an instance unexpectedly changes groups. Evaluation of these additional interface features is left for a full user-in-the-loop study.

# 6   Conclusions and Future Work

The principles behind CHISSL could be integrated into other systems that offer interactive visual analytics features for the evaluation of more complicated data types. In the case of document exploration and analytics, a system that is constructed for coordinated views of document content and linking document themes might leverage the CHISSL human-in-the-loop approach to shape and correct the theme identification and linking. The CHISSL approach could also be used to link social media threads between users and across social media formats. Basically, in any place where associations between instances are of interest, the CHISSL approach can be leveraged to steer the analytical models.

The category structures and associated labels that a human observer will bring to a set of instances is a function of his/her expertise, as experts will have more labels available to them than novices [13, 26]. Extensive perceptual training on a set of objects hones the visual system in order to know which details are important and which are uninformative in the classification process. Experts are more attuned to fine details that may not be obvious or readily available to the novice observer. Because they can classify instances into both high level and subordinate level categories, experts may naturally produce more categories than novices, or their categories will follow a different semantic interpretation scheme. We can consider, then, using the collaborative nature of CHISSL as a vehicle not only for translating human expertise into the machine learning process but also to train other human observers. This could be done by simply providing a semi-trained model (trained by a combination of machine and human expert) to the novice to work with. Or this could be a collaborative process wherein the novice and expert work together on coordinated CHISSL systems, so the expert can guide and correct the novice's group assignments.

Perceptual expertise is hard to document as experts cannot often articulate their expert skills [7]. Session histories provided by CHISSL offer a novel means of documenting expert behavior while simultaneously leveraging that expertise to inform the machine learning. It remains to be seen if these session histories might facilitate the articulation of expert strategies for other humans. But, like implicit category structures, even if we cannot verbalize well an expert strategy for associating data instances with each other, CHISSL will learn and utilize the same categorization structure as the expert by interactively learning how the expert is assigning delegates to groups.

CHISSL offers a novel technique to use machine learning to track the development of expertise, offering a means to support future modeling of how experience and expertise development shapes the process by which users select which objects to reassign, which clusters to merge, etc. Our pilot study provided evidence that supports our hypothesis–that it is beneficial to allow the user some flexibility in determining what instances are labeled. CHISSL appears to provide more advantage over active learning earlier in the training process, because users are able to detect and correct misclassifications early on that have a large impact on the classifier performance. We found least two additional metrics that, in the absence of ground truth, could provide a helpful signal to the user about the stability of the model. These signals could help the user determine when she should stop adding labels to the training set.

For future work, we plan on providing these signals to the user in real-time via the CHISSL interface. Because CHISSL appears to be an effective tool for rapidly training models to explore unlabeled data, we also plan to allow the user to create, manage, and visually interpret multiple classification models simultaneously as different lenses on the data. Our broader goal is to develop a visual analytics system for exploring massive datasets by enabling the user to interact with a representative "tip of the iceberg", build classifiers representative of her mental models, and then summarize the remaining unlabeled data using these classifiers.

**Acknowledgments.** The research described in this document was sponsored the U.S. Department of Energy (DOE) through the Analysis in Motion Initiative at Pacific Northwest National Laboratory. The views and conclusions contained in this document are those of the authors and should not be interpreted as representing the official policies, either expressed or implied, of the U.S. Government.

# References

1. Amershi, S., Fogarty, J., Weld, D.: Regroup. In: Proceedings of the 2012 ACM Annual Conference on Human Factors in Computing Systems - CHI 2012, p. 21. ACM, New York (2012)
2. Basu, S., Drucker, S.M., Lu, H.: Assisting users with clustering tasks by combining metric learning and classification. In: AAAI, pp. 394–400 (2010)
3. Fuchs, J., et al.: The influence of contour on similarity perception of star glyphs. IEEE Trans. Vis. Comput. Graph. **20**(12), 2251–2260 (2014)
4. Bilenko, M., Basu, S., Mooney, R.J.: Integrating constraints and metric learning in semi-supervised clustering. In: Twenty-First International Conference on Machine Learning - ICML 2004, p. 11 (2004)
5. Borgo, R., Kehrer, J., Chung, D.H.S., Maguire, E., Laramee, R.S., Hauser, H., Ward, M., Chen, M.: Glyph-based visualization: foundations, design guidelines, techniques and applications. In: Eurographics State of the Art Reports, pp. 39–63 (2013)
6. Brown, E.T., Liu, J., Brodley, C.E., Chang, R.: Dis-function: learning distance functions interactively. In: 2012 IEEE Conference on Visual Analytics Science and Technology (VAST), pp. 83–92. IEEE (2012)

7. Chi, M.T., Glaser, R., Farr, M.J.: The Nature of Expertise. Psychology Press, Hove (2014)
8. Choo, J., Lee, H., Kihm, J., Park, H.: iVisClassifier: an interactive visual analytics system for classification based on supervised dimension reduction. In: 2010 IEEE Symposium on Visual Analytics Science and Technology, pp. 27–34. IEEE (2010)
9. Chuang, J., Ramage, D., Manning, C.D., Heer, J.: Interpretation and trust: designing model-driven visualizations for text analysis. In: Proceedings of the SIGCHI Conference on Human Factors in Computing Systems, pp. 443–452 (2005)
10. Cohn, D., Caruana, R.: Semi-supervised clustering: incorporating user feedback to improve cluster utility. In: Proceedings of the Conference on Artificial Intelligence (2000)
11. Daszykowski, M., Walczak, B.: Density-based clustering methods. In: Comprehensive Chemometrics, vol. 96, pp. 635–654. Elsevier (2009)
12. Endert, A., Fiaux, P., North, C.: Semantic interaction for sensemaking: inferring analytical reasoning for model steering. IEEE Trans. Vis. Comput. Graph. 18(12), 2879–2888 (2012)
13. Gauthier, I., Skudlarski, P., Gore, J.C., Anderson, A.W.: Expertise for cars and birds recruits brain areas involved in face recognition. Nat. Neurosci. 3(2), 191–197 (2000)
14. Goldstone, R.: An efficient method for obtaining similarity data. Behav. Res. Methods, Instrum. Comput. 26(4), 381–386 (1994)
15. Hubert, L., Arabie, P.: Comparing partitions. J. Classif. 2(1), 193–218 (1985)
16. Kaynak, C.: Methods of combining multiple classifiers and their applications to handwritten digit recognition. Master's thesis, Institute of Graduate Studies in Science and Engineering, Bogazici University (1995)
17. Kulesza, T., Amershi, S., Caruana, R., Fisher, D., Charles, D.: Structured labeling for facilitating concept evolution in machine learning. In: Proceedings of the 32nd Annual ACM Conference on Human Factors in Computing Systems - CHI 2014, pp. 3075–3084. ACM, New York (2014)
18. Lewis, D.D., Gale, W.A.: A sequential algorithm for training text classifiers. In: Proceedings of the 17th Annual International ACM SIGIR Conference on Research and Development in Information Retrieval, pp. 3–12. Springer, New York (1994)
19. Lichman, M.: UCI machine learning repository (2013). http://archive.ics.uci.edu/ml
20. Poggio, T., Cauwenberghs, G.: Incremental and decremental support vector machine learning. Adv. Neural Inf. Process. Syst. 13, 409 (2001)
21. Roy, N., McCallum, A.: Toward optimal active learning through sampling estimation of error reduction. In: ICML, pp. 441–448 (2001)
22. Tanahashi, Y., Hsueh, C.-H., Ma, K.-L.: An efficient framework for generating storyline visualizations from streaming data. IEEE Trans. Vis. Comput. Graph. 21(6), 730–742 (2015)
23. Seung, H.S., Opper, M., Sompolinsky, H.: Query by committee. In: Proceedings of the Fifth Annual Workshop on Computational Learning Theory, pp. 287–294. ACM (1992)
24. Smith, J.D., Berg, M.E., Cook, R.G., Murphy, M.S., Crossley, M.J., Boomer, J., Spiering, B., Beran, M.J., Church, B.A., Ashby, F.G., et al.: Implicit and explicit categorization: a tale of four species. Neurosci. Biobehav. Rev. 36(10), 2355–2369 (2012)
25. Srivastava, A., Zou, J., Sutton, C.: Clustering with a Reject Option: Interactive Clustering as Bayesian Prior Elicitation, pp. 120–126, February 2016

26. Tanaka, J.W., Curran, T., Sheinberg, D.L.: The training and transfer of real-world perceptual expertise. Psychol. Sci. **16**(2), 145–151 (2005)
27. Vapnik, V.N., Vapnik, V.: Statistical Learning Theory, vol. 1. Wiley, New York (1998)
28. Yu, H.F., Huang, F.L., Lin, C.J.: Dual coordinate descent methods for logistic regression and maximum entropy models. Mach. Learn. **85**(1–2), 41–75 (2011)
29. Zhu, X.: Semi-supervised learning literature survey. Technical report 1530, Computer Sciences, University of Wisconsin-Madison (2005)
30. Liu, S., et al.: Storyflow: tracking the evolution of stories. IEEE Trans. Vis. Comput. Graph. **19**(12), 2436–2445 (2013)

# Toward an Open Data Repository and Meta-Analysis of Cognitive Data Using fNIRS Studies of Emotion

Sarah Bratt[✉]

M.I.N.D. Lab S.I. Newhouse School of Public Communications,
Syracuse University School of Information Studies, Syracuse, NY, USA
sebratt@syr.edu

**Abstract.** HCI research has increasingly incorporated the use of neurophysiological sensors to identify users' cognitive and affective states. However, a persistent problem in machine learning on cognitive data is generalizability across participants. A proposed solution has been aggregating cognitive and survey data across studies to generate higher sample populations for machine learning and statistical analyses to converge in stable, generalizable results. In this paper, I argue that large data-sharing projects can facilitate the aggregation of results of brain imaging studies to address these issues, by smoothing noise in high-dimensional datasets. This paper contributes a small step towards large cognitive data sharing systems-design by proposing methods that facilitate the merging of currently incompatible fNIRS and FMRI datasets through term-based metadata analysis. To that end, I analyze 20 fNIRS studies of emotion using content analysis for: (1) synonym terms and definitions for 'emotion,' (2) the experimental stimuli, and (3) the use or non-use of self-report surveys. Results suggest that fNIRS studies of emotion have stable synonymy, using technical and folk conceptualizations of affective terms within and between publications to refer to emotion. The studies use different stimuli to elicit emotion but also show commonalities between shared use of standardized stimuli materials and self-report surveys. These similarities in conceptual synonymy and standardized experiment materials indicate promise for neuroimaging communities to establish open-data repositories based on metadata term-based analyses. This work contributes to efforts toward merging datasets across studies and between labs, unifying new modalities in neuroimaging such as fNIRS with fMRI datasets, increasing generalizability of machine learning models, and promoting the acceleration of science through open data-sharing infrastructure.

**Keywords:** Data repository · Cognitive data · fNIRS · Emotion · Metadata · Machine learning · HCI

## 1 Introduction

Human Computer Interaction (HCI) research has increasingly incorporated the use of neurophysiological sensors to identify users' cognitive and affective states. From the development of brain computer interfaces (BCI) (Hennrich et al. 2015) to the

© Springer International Publishing AG 2017
D.D. Schmorrow and C.M. Fidopiastis (Eds.): AC 2017, Part I, LNAI 10284, pp. 449–467, 2017.
DOI: 10.1007/978-3-319-58628-1_34

evaluation of affective responses to social media, devices such as functional near-infrared spectroscopy (fNIRS) are making significant headway in the refinement of experimental design and machine learning (ML) algorithms to make sense of mental and emotional states.

However, a persistent problem in machine learning on cognitive data is the generalizability across participants given the 'curse of dimensionality.' To complicate this problem, under experimental conditions researchers often use self-report surveys to train machine learning algorithms or to inform statistical analyses of cognitive data. Further exacerbating the 'curse of dimensionality,' subjective surveys can prove inaccurate and affect classification accuracy (Hirshfield et al. 2014).

In this paper, it is argued that an automated meta-analysis of current methods in cognitive data processing and experiment design specific to emotion will help move toward the merging of currently incompatible datasets (fNIRS and fMRI) to build more accurate models and higher sample populations that converge in stable, generalizable results. Large data-sharing projects facilitate the aggregation of results of brain imaging for smoothing of noise in high-dimensional datasets. For example, to improve classification accuracy, the fMRI community has begun unifying datasets in the open data movement as exemplified by Neurosynth, a "platform for automatically synthesizing the results of many different neuroimaging studies" (Neurosynth 2016).

Drawing from a previous provisional framework which classifies the challenges of employing machine learning on cognitive data (Costa and Bratt 2016), this paper addresses the problem of establishing a gold standard with fallible, subjective surveys. Collective results afford the exploration of opportunities to improve machine learning classification labels vulnerable to being false positive or negatives. Through this meta-analysis of data scraped from SCOPUS and Web of Science I report of extant approaches in neurophysiological data analysis with a focus on fNIRS studies involving emotion. This overview is a first step at mapping the stimuli and survey techniques to create metadata for unifying cognitive data.

In the first section, I provide literature and background on the devices used for neuroimaging and detecting BOLD signal data, including the motivation of their use and previous studies in merging data between fMRI and fNIRS with each other and between homogenous data sets, and briefly discuss the domain of interest: neuroimaging studies of emotion. The *Methodology* section details the data collection and analysis procedures. The next section presents *Results* by describing and synthesizing the data, providing an overall summary of findings of 20 studies of emotion definitions (naming conventions and synonyms), stimuli used to 'induce emotion,' and survey forms used to ground the cognitive state in self-report class labels for machine learning and statistical analysis. This section has detailed description, comparison, and metadata recommendation analysis of the studies' use of naming conventions, stimuli, and class-labeling approaches. The final section, *Discussion* presents opportunities for merging data based with policy and scholarly digital infrastructure precedents in cyber-enabled data repositories and incorporation of demographic data, and concludes with a summary and vision of future work.

## 2 Literature Review

### 2.1 Background

**Neuroimaging Technology.** Functional imaging technology has many advantages as an approach for eliciting human subject data. While self-report surveys are widely used, they are vulnerable to well-known drawbacks to self-assessment measures. For example, participant self-report surveys often inaccurately report cognitive load, misrepresent responses due to social desirability (Edwards 1953), and distort data due to the participants' difficulty remembering behavior and emotional experiences when surveys are administered after the task is finished (postdictively). Other studies show that subjective, self-report responses correlate only moderately with others' reports of their actions or observed behavior (Sackett and Larson 1990). For these reasons, these measures can be limited in accurately collecting real-time information in experimental and research settings.

In compensation for these limitations, cognitive data measurement techniques have come to the fore in research and commercial spheres. Popular technologies such as functional magnetic resonance imaging (fMRI) and electroencephalography (EEG) have been used to quantify workload and emotional states in human and animal subjects (Grimes et al. 2008; Nicholson et al. 2017; Soleymani et al. 2016). While fMRI provides valuable neurophysiological information, it is prone to disadvantages for emotion research because it confines the subjects to a supine position, requiring them to lie immobile in a chamber with a large magnet. The noise of the machine also makes fMRI data collection limited in its ability to experimentally simulate realistic settings (Bunce et al. 2006). Although fMRI studies suggest that we can objectively measure affective states (Phan et al. 2002; Wiebking et al. 2011), it cannot be used outside of a lab for operational situations such as sitting at a computer, conversation, and other medical and social situations where quantifying affective state would be extremely valuable, especially in naturalistic settings conducive to emotionally challenging tasks.

Functional near-infrared spectroscopy (fNIRS) has appeared as a relatively new research modality that is non-invasive, silent, allows for participant movement, and has been validated as a device for capturing the BOLD signal at the cortical level (Yuan and Ye 2013) (Fig. 1). fNIRS monitors brain function through measuring changes in the concentrations of oxygenated and deoxygenated hemoglobin based on the technique developed by Chance and Leigh who found that hemoglobin changes its color when the oxygen content of blood changes (Sevick et al. 1991).

Due to the frequently-cited advantages for naturalistic, more ecologically-valid experimentation, fNIRS has been used in affective computing to investigate emotional brain states for HCI and BCI applications from authentication systems and entertainment to suspicion and marketing (Abdul Serwadda 2015; Bigliassi et al. 2015; Glotzbach et al. 2011; Noah et al. 2015). In medical contexts, fNIRS are used to develop emotion recognition models for diagnosing and evaluating autism spectrum disorders therapy (Kaliouby et al. 2006).

**Fig. 1.** The Hitachi 52-channel fNIRS device recording cognitive data while a participant completes a task.

## 2.2   Research Setting

**Functional Neuroimaging Studies of Emotion.** Cognitive-affective approaches for eliciting, measuring, and validating techniques for measuring emotion have varied widely. Research communities outside of HCI and bioengineering have debated the conceptual definition and physiological correlates of affect, and engaged in the ongoing research challenge quantifying emotions. Scholars in organizational psychology, feminist socio-technical systems theory, neuroscience, and philosophy have proposed conceptual frameworks for exploring emotion, such as from theoretical paradigms of performativity in emotion (Ekman and Friesen 1971), cultural and gender contingencies (Codispoti et al. 2008), and language taxonomies to describe distinctions among, for example, "affect, emotion, mood, sentiment, and feeling-states" (Hengehold 2003; Scherer 2005).

While there is a great deal of debate about the conceptual definitions of emotion as well as methodological approaches for its quantification, I define emotion provisionally in concert with widely-accepted definition by prominent scholars in neurophysiological research. That is, emotion is defined as intense, short-lived affective responses to stimuli or events with three components: (1) behavioral (e.g. facial movement), (2) autonomic (neurophysiological activity) and (3) subjective (the reported experience of a feeling-state) (Phan et al. 2002). Because behavioral and subjective components are not always reliable predictors of emotion and do not consistently encompass 'full emotional experiences,' neurophysiological activation is a promising approach for studying emotion. Brain-based emotion has been reported across studies to occur in centers such as the prefrontal cortex, the cingulate cortex, and the amygdala. These functional regions have been connected with affect and autonomic control (Thayer et al. 2012); (Thayer and Lane 2009).

**Obstacles in Neuro-Physiological Analyses of Emotion.** Though fNIRS and fMRI studies have successfully analyzed emotional responses in many settings, these technologies face generalizability and validity challenges. Previous research that investigated employing machine learning on cognitive data articulated these issues, namely, that machine learning models overfit and are prone to errors due to the limitations of subjective, self-report surveys and the "curse of dimensionality." That is, cognitive-function data has a large number of features and a relatively small number of participants who may misreport their cognitive state, making primary component analysis difficult (Costa and Bratt 2016).

A further complication for generalizability and cognitive data analysis is demographic differences in between individuals' brain function. While researchers may assume that the same experimental conditions and stimulus material will elicit comparable cognitive responses, there are two distinct scenarios that put pressure on the reliability these assumptions, especially in the context of emotion.

First, different affective responses can result from identical experimental stimuli. For example, what is perceived as 'sad' for one might be 'intensely nostalgic' for another. Listening to classical music might be pleasant and calming for Participant A, while Participant B experiences unease, boredom, and distraction. One might attempt to address this worry by requiring self-report surveys to report emotion; yet, it is simple to imagine a scenario in which Participant B inaccurately reports her affective state, failing to report boredom or distraction in the post-task survey because she has a desire to perform well for the research lab technicians. Demographic differences such as culture, age, ethnicity, and participant gender have well-documented influences on affective perception and experience of emotion. For example, fNIRS studies have suggested that prefrontal cortex (PFC) activity may be associated with individuals' trait-based responses. In one such study, emotional stimuli elicited brain activity that were colored by gender differences (Whittle et al. 2011). Further, another fNIRS study in gender differences recognized that the region of the brain involved in emotion processing "exhibits valence-dependent sex differences in activation to emotional stimuli" (Stevens and Hamann 2012).

Second, studies have found that the same affective response can activate a different cognitive functional region. Differences in functionality between individuals' brain activity in response to experimental manipulations can be seen in analyses of cognitive language processing and emotional regulation. For example, being right or left handed affects the part of the brain which language processing dominantly occurs (Shimoda et al. 2008). In participants with brain damage, neuro-plasticity allows brain functions to "relocate" brain processes sing when a part of the tissue is damaged, such as in the development of cognitive compensatory mechanisms in people with aphasia (Thomas et al. 1997).

Because the underlying mechanisms of demographic and cultural differences remains an unsolved challenge in neuroimaging studies, there is a crucial need to incorporate demographic data and personalized elicitation method for investigating the effects of emotional stimuli in human subjects. Thus, to progress toward the frequently quoted goals of developing generalizable, adaptive HCI technologies, we must develop strategies for addressing these problems not least of which are merging cognitive data.

**Merging Data: fMRI and fNIRS and Science of Science Initiatives.** To address these challenges, I argue that there is a need to aggregate and combine data for meaningful macro-analyses of affective state research across scientific disciplines. High-level synthesis of research data sets has the potential to accelerate facilitate cross-communication between research labs that use different measurement techniques, and combined data could help to improve classification and experiment-design accuracy.

There are precedents for developing systems for standardized sharing of data to increase the number of participants' data, cross-check cognitive data results, and make explicitly the phenomenon of study by identifying metadata that can link studies.

Previous studies which triangulate numerous sensors have shown that combining studies to better understand affective states improves classification accuracy and provides another level of validity in ascertaining the intended emotional state was successfully induced. For example, a study was conducted with fMRI and EEG to understand vascular responses in the brain (Yuan and Ye 2013) that manually compared the results of the two modalities to identify the relationship between neuronal activity and the blood oxygenation level-dependent (BOLD) signal. They identified multiple functional processes such as "neuronal activity, synaptic activity, vascular dilation, blood volume and oxygenation changes" which were common to both EEG and fMRI signals, the electrophysiological and vascular response, respectively.

Neuroscience data repositories such as Open fMRI and the Collaborative Informatics and Neuroimaging Suite (COINS) have sprung up to facilitate the storage, sharing, and communication of researchers and affiliate institutions. Other systems like Neurosynth (Neurosynth 2017) act as wrappers around cognitive data through term-based meta-analysis of studies to map active brain regions by identifying, retrieving, and aggregating data. Such aggregators address the curse of dimensionality and subjective surveys errors to be addressed with a higher number of participants to cancel noisy data.

However, these aggregators and repositories do not include fNIRS data. They only include fMRI, MRI, ERP, EEG, and MEG ("Neuroimaging databases" 2014) as of the writing of this paper. Yet there is promise for uniting these different neuroimaging modalities because of shared technological characteristics. Underlying both fNIRS and FMRI modalities are MNI coordinates, which delineate the precise location of the BOLD signal activity. Given the probe configuration of the device and cranial circumference of the individual participant, MNI coordinates serve as a universal language, so to speak, for combining datasets between different devices and devices of the same type, such as the fNIRS technologies Hitachi ETG 4000 and NIRSOptix. Therefore, fMRI and fNIRS data can be merged or compared through the conversion of fNIRS data to MNI coordinates suggesting that these sensors can "communicate" to inform analyses.

Dataset storage, retrieval, and aggregation is only possible for datasets with standardized metadata or computational techniques that identify naming conventions between datasets. Combining data and processed results to develop an open data repository for fNIRS requires standardization practices, as evidenced in fMRI-community database precedents. Such common aggregation techniques in open neuroscience data repositories include natural language processing analyses and the creation of metadata associated with neuroimaging datasets such as demographic, neurophysiological activity, or task-type metadata. For example, a researcher interested in gender and working memory can retrieve datasets by querying metadata identifying gender, age, and task-type to acquire neuroimaging datasets of n-back test performance of females aged 25–40 years.

Thus, a first step in the effort to standardize descriptions by evaluating fNIRS studies and describing commonalities and differences in terminology used in a subset of fNIRS literature. To effectively identify similar studies and merge fNIRS datasets with other neuroimaging studies, I conduct a provisionary meta-analysis of fNIRS studies on emotion to begin the descriptive standardization process, as detailed in the methodology, results, and discussion sections below.

## 2.3  Methodology

**Data.** The data is composed of publications in fNIRS research studies of emotion. I collected the data per these parameters and used simple search terms to simulate a computational approach to scraping metadata, cognizant of the goal for future development of an automated term-based system. I conducted a SCOPUS and Web of Science search on keywords "fNIRS" and "emotion." Other terms synonymous to emotion were attempted as search terms, but the results were sparse (i.e., 11 total results when including "affect" as a query-term). The SCOPUS search algorithm scrapes data from the text of the publication metadata, including abstract, title, keywords, among other fields. A total of 62 studies were scraped with 50 published between 2013 and 2017, with the majority belonging to the subject areas of neuroscience, medicine, psychology, computer science, and engineering. While the bulk are articles or conference proceedings on human subjects, several results included reviews and animal studies. I excluded reviews and animal results because of the focus for this paper is scoped to publications on cognitive affective activity in humans using fNIRS measurements.

Twenty of these results were selected for analysis based on their citation counts (by highest citation count, descending) and relevance. Citation count and topical relevance were the criterion for data selection because metadata development using term-based search will use these citation metrics to indicate impact and relevance to studies of emotion.

**Analysis.** I downloaded the SCOPUS metadata and annotated the full text articles through searching online for available articles and proceedings. Using deductive content analysis (Elo and Kyngäs 2008), I constructed a coding-framework developed through previous experience reading and conducting fNIRS studies, iteratively annotating the documents for three thematic components: (1) definition of emotion (or lack thereof), (2) stimuli or experimental manipulation and (3) surveys employed (or lack thereof). Throughout analysis, contextual codes were generated as per the framework but also included emergent themes such as "combination of emotion and cognitive processes" in a study on Theory of Mind and empathy as they surfaced. Additional contextual codes were generated, such as the following meta-analytic categories: Number of study Participants, Stimulus/Task Type(s), Stimulus/Task/Treatment Type (s), Device(s) Used, Regions of Interest (ROI), Labeling Technique, Analysis technique (ML, or Statistical Significance, Ensemble, etc.), Statistical Significance Analysis, and ML algorithm employed (e.g., SvM, Naive Bayes, decision tree), among others. Codes were merged, and I converged similar categories across the descriptive aspects of each study. Discussions with collaborators and mind-mapping were used to augment this process, and during my analysis and synthesis of results.

# 3  Results

## 3.1  Defining Emotion: Conceptualizations and Synonymous Terms Used

A working definition or provisional conceptual model of emotion, whether implied or explicitly defined, undergirds every research study of emotion. Emotion is a complex concept that has been the subject of debate in many research disciplines, from organization psychology to affective computing. Although there is a lack of convergence among scholars in these and other HCI and social sciences, numerous neurophysiological studies are focused on measuring emotion. For the purposes of this paper, it is less crucial to define emotion precisely or mark the boundaries of the field than to identify terms and descriptions common to fNIRS efforts that affiliate with the project of quantifying emotion in the brain. One such definition offered by a meta-review of functional neuroanatomy of emotion by prominent scholars in the field is that emotions are intense, transitory affective responses to stimuli or events composed of a combination of behavioral, autonomic (neurophysiological) and subjective components (Adolphs et al. 1996; Blair 1999; Phan et al. 2002).

**Defining Emotions Indirectly: Technical and Folk Synonyms.** In this study, the data showed that no universally-defined or commonly cited theoretical framework was used when describing emotion. Across the 20 papers, authors used a wide variety of terms to refer to 'emotion,' and provided details ranging from (a) the absence of definition to (b) a brief discussion in the final paragraphs of the paper to (c) a highly-detailed description with citations of foundational literature. In all studies, 'emotion' and a mix of other terms were used and often implied as linguistic synonyms. For example, eleven of the studies did not include an explicit definition of emotion, but described emotional phenomenon richly, using terms linguistically-related to emotion throughout the text. In one such study, the authors incorporated no less than eight synonyms, including "temperament" "emotion" "empathy" "feelings" and "affect" (see Table 1). The studies that incorporated many emotion terms were frequently developing or testing fNIRS technological methods or elicitation paradigms, which thus required a range of emotions to analyze multiple, contrasting, emotional situations.

Of the studies that used multiple technical or common terms, most used the terms interchangeably. That is, "disposition" was used as a synonym for "mood," and "affective style" interchanged with "negative and positive emotions" (Balconi et al. 2015). In contrast to the use of many synonymous terms, four studies used a single, specific term throughout the analysis (i.e., "empathy" and "frustration") to refer to the emotional state of interest (Brink et al. 2011; Gygax et al. 2013; Perlman et al. 2014; Rutkowski et al. 2011). These studies appear to be a distinct sub-genre within the fNIRS emotional literature, one characterized by an exclusive focus on a specific affective response, where the authors use specific emotion phrases that correspond with the specific affective experience.

**Defining Emotions Indirectly: Using Neurophysiological and Co-constituent Cognitive Processes Terms.** First, a common approach to defining emotion was to reference neurophysiological language. For example, a study that did not provide an explicit definition of emotion (Tupak et al. 2013) conceptualized emotion by describing

**Table 1.** A sample of five fNIRS publications involving neurophysiological measurement of emotion. The title and citation of the study are provided with the verbatim terms used within the paper that describe emotion or otherwise synonymously reference affective states.

| Study | Emotion terms |
|---|---|
| Activation of the rostromedial PFC during the experience of positive emotion in the context of esthetic experience: an fNIRS study (Kreplin and Fairclough 2013) | *Pleasantness, affect, emotion, positive evaluation, attraction, internal processes of positive and negative feelings* |
| Prefrontal activation patterns of automatic and regulated approach-avoidance reactions - a functional near-infrared spectroscopy (fNIRS) study (Ernst et al. 2013) | *Approach/avoidance, emotional regulation, volitional control, cognitive-emotional, negative emotions, fear, disgust, positive emotions, excitement, amusement, awe, contentment* |
| fNIRS evidence of prefrontal regulation of frustration in early childhood (Perlman et al. 2014) | *Frustration, temperament, emotion regulation, mood* |
| Resting lateralized activity predicts the cortical response and appraisal of emotions (Balconi et al. 2015) | *Valence, positive emotion, negative emotion, appetitive (approach-related), aversive (withdrawal-related), motivation, dispositional mood, affective style, emotional expressions, anger, sadness, subjective response, affective behavior, subjective appraisal, emotional stress* |
| Interactive component extraction from fEEG, fNIRS, and peripheral biosignals for affective brain-machine interfacing paradigms (Rutkowski et al. 2011) | *Emotional synchrony, emotional empathy signatures, feelings, emotional arousal, emotional processes, affective human/brain–computer interfacing paradigm, human factors and human behavioral aspects of emotion* |

brain region activation as constitutive of emotion. Emotion, thus, was considered equivalent and reflexively defined by neurophysiological activation as opposed to the previously mentioned definition of emotion as constituted of three components (i.e. behavior, subjective perception, autonomic experience). Nine studies similarly drew from physiological language to describe and define emotion. In (Hosseini et al. 2011), emotion was defined as a decoding process of human affective states manifesting through "various biosignals." The authors referred to emotions as originating in brain-anatomy, such as subcortical areas, the limbic system, and the "prefrontal cortex (PFC) in emotion induction and regulation." Similarly, another study grounded emotion in internal brain activity, external physical reactions, and related these signals with human perception of emotion:

> *Electric field activity and oxygenation changes localized in cortical areas of the brain and additional peripheral body measurements such as skin conductance, heart-rate, breath and pulse variability, as well facial muscle and eye-movement characteristics also correlate to emotional arousal...These physically based measures provide an objective way to explore the realm of perception, experience, mind, and emotional processes...*(Rutkowski et al. 2011).

The authors implicitly define emotion in this description of affective responses. They allude to three aspects of human experience of emotion: autonomic, behavioral, and perceptive, a description consistent with the three-component conceptual model of emotion presented earlier in this section by (Phan et al. 2002).

Second, a predominant sub-theme related to neurophysiological synonyms was that emotion and functional processing states are defined as co-constituent processes. Roughly one-third of the papers (seven) suggested this result or argued that emotion was conceptually misunderstood as a single, monolithic brain event or personality trait. For example, the emotional experiences involved in flow were associated with subjective experiences and behavioral actions indicating emotions as well as PFC activity, leading the authors to conclude that emotional aspects of flow are associated with functions such as "maintenance of internal goals, and reward processing" (Yoshida et al. 2014). Another study of a complex emotion suggested a multi-faceted definition of frustration. The authors defined frustration as "the obstruction to a desired goal," and suggested the affective experience is a combination of emotion and cognitive load (Perlman et al. 2014). Studies of emotional responses to music, experiences of empathy, and altruism included emotional and other cognitive processes. For example, (Brink et al. 2011) reported:

*Empathy, defined as the ability to understand and share another person's inner life, consists of two components: affective (emotion-sharing) and cognitive empathy (Theory of Mind).*

The affective experience of empathy is suggested to be defined as involving two process: social cognition as well as other aspects of emotional processing in the brain. An fNIRS study of affective responses to music enlisted multiple aspects of human behavior, perception, physiology to describe emotional response, where the reaction to the music "involves personality traits as well as the unconscious," arguing:

*Given that the brain is the center of sensory reception, interpretation, integration, and responses, music likely affects specific areas related to these functions* (Bigliassi et al. 2015).

These studies illuminate opportunities for text mining for meta-data generation and systems development. Such automated processes can leverage these patterns in identifying studies of emotion. For example, patterns of synonymy and the use of indirect referents for concepts such as emotion can inform NLP algorithm-design specific to the fNIRS emotion cognitive data to develop repositories or aggregators. Thus, metadata of affective studies should not preclude the cognitive processes that are not ostensibly associated with emotional brain states, but rather merge data that refers to emotion indirectly as well as peripheral or co-constituent processes, such as reward-processing and emotion regulation. In this preliminary results paper, it is not my intention to make prescriptive judgements of best practices but to point out that no clear definition within fNIRS emotion studies is adhered to. Rather, synonymy often is assumed between varied emotional phrases and terms, underscoring a challenge in requirements gathering when developing metadata and naming conventions in fNIRS the development of cognitive database systems.

## 3.2    Eliciting Affective States: Experiment Manipulation and Stimuli Selection

Neurophysiological experiments operate on the premise that emotion can be elicited and measured in a lab setting. Researchers use manipulations to induce empathy, sadness, happiness, anger, and other feeling-states among diverse participants. These manipulations, or "stimulus materials" are available as standardized images and audio samples. The fNIRS studies of emotion fall broadly into three categories: standardized image and in-house methods of passive multimedia, interactive games, and performative or immersive techniques. For example, previous studies in studies with fMRI, EEG, and fNIRS have used self-selected music, citing the need for personalized emotional experienced given the "subjectivity of emotion" (Bigliassi et al. 2015). Other studies use visual media such as music videos, movie clips, and animation-audio pairings to engage participants' emotional processing centers. For example, León-Carrión et al. used "distressing, disgusting, and amusing" movie clips to show that the prefrontal cortex (PFC) can be activated by overriding emotional circuits (Banks et al. 2007; Leon-Carrion et al. 2006). In concert with this effort to create more realistic emotional experiences, other research approaches enlist behavioral and immersive techniques like virtual reality (VR) environments and theatrical performance (Diemer et al. 2015; Gorini et al. 2009; Iacucci and Kuutti 2002). For example, an fMRI study of emotion led by a research group at CMU used a theatrical method, hiring student actors and instructing them to read words like 'happiness,' 'anger,' 'lust,' 'shame,' 'pride,' and 'sadness' and performatively "bring themselves to experience" each term-correspondent emotional state (Kassam et al. 2013).

In the data collected for this study, the most commonly used stimuli for emotion elicitation were standardized and included the International Affective Picture System (IAPS) (Blood et al. 1999) and International Affective Digital Sounds (IADS) (Breiter et al. 1996). A total of ten studies used the International Affective Digitized Sound System (IADS), two used IAPS, and one the Berlin Affective Word List (Võ et al. 2009) (Table 2).

**Table 2.** The three categories of valanced words (negative, positive, and neutral) in English and German, used as the stimulus materials for a German study of emotional regulation (Kopf et al. 2013).

| Negative words | Positive words | Neutral words |
| --- | --- | --- |
| TYPHUS (typhus) | RETTER (savior) | ABLAUF (sequence) |
| BEFEHL (order) | WISSEN (knowledge) | AFFEKT (affect) |
| ARREST (warrant) | MUTTER (mother) | BANNER (banner) |

## Berlin Affective Word List

The remainder of the fNIRS studies used variants of these standardized stimuli or developed in-house manipulations. The visual and audio stimuli developed by researchers were predominantly multi-media. For example, seven studies selected film clips, such as (León-Carrión et al. 2007) in their study of emotion:

*Two scenes from Salo o le 120 giornate di Sodoma were selected as unpleasant emotional stimuli one reflecting explicit physical pain...and another showing a revolting act. The scenes selected as pleasant stimuli were a fade out of an aerial view of an island from The Beach and a cartoon scene of Roadrunner and the Coyote.*

Another study presented participants with images from a database of visual art and directed participants to engage in emotional introspection during image-viewing (Kreplin and Fairclough 2013). Similarly, the paper reporting NIRS measurement of emotion elicited by motivational music used a series of audio clips from calm and motivational songs (Bigliassi et al. 2015). A novel method was proposed that addressed the issue of interacting effects of facial expressions and gender (Breiter et al. 1996; Codispoti et al. 2008) in affective response by developing a stimulus based on walking patterns. This manipulation developed a video showing emotions embodied in gait pattern by instructing the actors to imagine "sentimental past life events" to authentically simulate emotions for the video stimulus. These videos were then developed into the stimulus material of "faceless avatars expressing fearful, angry, sad, happy or neutral gait patterns" (Schneider et al. 2014). In three of studies, the research team developed a game to elicit emotion. For example, the "Frustrative Emotion Task for Children (FETCH)" was an in-house game developed by (Perlman et al. 2014) played by children. In the game, a "desired and expected prize was 'stolen' by an animated dog" to elicit frustration in 4-year-old to 6-year-old children.

Tetris, fictional stories, and other stimuli were developed to induce affective experiences in classifiable categories that suggest standardization across studies is feasible. Such classification can inform metadata development and computational models for data aggregation. The manipulations and stimulus materials can also be abstracted into categories for classification of different types of stimuli. As of now, keywords are not standardized or structured in a way that would facilitate extraction of metadata for data sharing systems. However, classification categories such as those mentioned above contribute to the identification of the manipulation type-similarity across studies. With standard terms for stimulus material, similar studies can be merged and contrasting can be compared for more effective analysis of different conditions.

### 3.3    Measuring Affective States: Use of Self-report Surveys

Self-report surveys are frequently administered to assign a "class label" to a segment of recorded cognitive data for subsequent machine learning and analysis. While other methods for class-label assignment are often used such as the stimulus-type (e.g. arithmetic, image-matching), surveys lend additional validity by allowing participant feedback to be incorporated during subjective mental and emotional state experiments. The latter class-labeling technique segments the data based on the experimental manipulation type rather than the participant-reported state. For example, in the latter labeling technique, a video clip from a violent part of a horror movie would be labeled as "unpleasant/negative" (Brink et al. 2011). Further, pre-experiment surveys can be used to collect demographic information such as IQ, education, and mental or physical health conditions.

Participants report their affective state during each manipulation period by entering a description of their experience or by completing a scalar-survey question. Widely used, standardized surveys include Ekman's basic emotions (Ekman 1993) for quantitatively identifying discrete types of emotions and Russell's Pleasure-Arousal-Dominance scale (Russell and Mehrabian 1977) to classify emotions along dimensional models using the Self Assessment Manikins (Bracley and Lang 1994) (see Fig. 2).

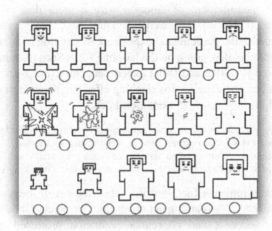

**Fig. 2.** The Self Assessment Mannequin. A rating scale used to quantitatively describe emotion along the dimensions Pleasure, Arousal, and Dominance (Bracley and Lang 1994).

Five of the twenty studies did not use post-task surveys and all studies included demographic surveys. The majority of the studies that administered post-task surveys used the standardized surveys of the Self-assessment mannequins (SAM) and Positive Affect Negative Affect Schedule (thirteen of twenty) (Bradley and Lang 1994; Watson et al. 1988). In language-other-than-English studies, appropriate version of the standardized surveys were used, e.g., the German version of the PANAS (Ernst et al. 2013). Others developed their own self-report measures, though two of these in-house surveys were used as augmentations of standardized measures (SAM or PANAS). Two studies used verified but less-common (within emotion studies) scales. The first evaluated the "current mood states" with scales called the Hamilton Depression Rating Scale (HDRS) (Williams 1988) and the Young Mania Rating Scale (YMRS) (Young et al. 1978), and the second used *Child Behavior Questionnaire (CBQ)-Long Form* (Rothbart et al. 2001).

Of those who developed their own surveys, the measures were specific to a novel stimulus or specific to the emotional state elicited, such as in the novel methodological evaluation of emotion using gait, the study using motivational music, and another using an approach-avoidance task which employed the use of a joy stick to assess attraction/aversion in opinion polls (Ernst et al. 2013). In-house surveys were developed when novel methods were developed, such as in the gait experiment survey where participants were instructed to evaluate the emotion they perceived the walking avatar to portray (Schneider et al. 2014). Eight studies used textual, open-ended survey questions to verify participants' emotional experiences, prompted by questions such as:

*What emotions does [the artwork] trigger in you? Does it make you feel sad/happy/angry etc.? Does it remind you of an emotional event you have experienced in the past?*

As seen in this sample of fNIRS studies of emotion, surveys are often used to quantitatively identify emotions. Post-experiment surveys have been a central topic in neurophysiological measurement of emotion with a great deal of methodological research advancements. For one, researchers acknowledge that current baseline mood or affect could influence the participants' experience of emotion insofar that the level of intensity may be different depending on the baseline state. Second, resting states, which are traditionally used in fNIRS and fMRI experiments to "come back to baseline," are not emotion-bereft because there are overlapping effects in the default network regions. As one fMRI study in rest states and emotion finds:

*Our demonstration of a relationship between induced activity during rest within regions of the DMN and emotions, which was reduced here to identification of emotions, are in line with previous findings that show that emotions, as induced by the presentation of emotional stimuli, impact upon neural response changes in subsequent rest periods* (Wiebking et al. 2011).

Further, the measurement effect, that is, "when the act of measuring changes the properties of the observed" has an impact on emotion research. One fMRI study found that participants' awareness and conscious evaluation prompted by self-reporting emotional states can alter emotional processes (Kassam and Mendes 2013).

Thus, the description of surveys used in fNIRS studies of emotion would provide valuable metadata to aggregate studies and identify patterns in cognitive data per the various input factors, such as survey response or a generated feature such as the use or non-use of a post-task survey. Addressing the overarching goal of identifying metadata for eventual merging of fNIRS and other compatible cognitive data, I found that both pre-experiment (demographic, or "trait data") and post-task (self-report survey, or "state data") data in these studies might be recorded and stored in standardized format, creating an opportunity for metadata scraping for merging between and across studies.

## 4  Discussion

**Metadata Development for fNIRS Cognitive Data.** The limitations of current fNIRS studies' metadata development standards and collection are manifold: a lack of synonyms for emotion, no control of the classification criterion for the study, bereft weighting fields that indicate a higher relevance to the query for the term-based search, and failure to include demographic metadata. Metadata development not only promises to improve statistical models of factor analysis and identify false positives in machine learning on cognitive data and to smooth noise in self-report surveys, but also for filtering and sub-setting datasets, mining for patterns across types of participants. Furthermore, as referred to in the *Literature* section above, trait-based differences such as cultural background and gender-identity can influence affective processing. For example, the experimental manipulation of a "Slow zoom in and out of the Virgin Mary's face" in the (León-Carrión et al. 2007) is likely to elicit a culturally-contingent emotional experience. Given that emotion is performative and gendered, demographic data of gender is crucial in analysis of cognitive and affective studies of emotion (Codispoti et al. 2008; Goffman et al. 1978; Hudson et al. 2015).

**Systems and Protocol Precedents in Big Science Repositories.** While the fNIRS studies of emotion face many limitations, merging fNIRS datasets has precedence in other data sharing and scholarly digital infrastructure collaborations. As fNIRS research develops, institutional trends in cyber-enabled science and open repositories will propel these relatively niche disciplines and research modalities toward data sharing procedures. Large scholarly data repositories such as GenBank, Long Term Ecological Research Network (LTER), and the Laser Interferometer Gravitational-Wave Observatory (LIGO) have established institutional data sharing and metadata creation protocols to facilitate the storage, sharing, and merging of data, testifying to this accelerating paradigm. More recently, projects proposing to merge datasets of electronic trace data from online communities by creating an "Open Collaboration Data Factory" (OCDF) have been proposed by social and information scientists. Such infrastructure for merging datasets can serve a parallel or collaborative purpose to such repositories, acting as a "boundary negotiating artifact for developing modes of cross-disciplinary collaboration," across neurophysiological sensors to "address differences in research aims, data, and methods, and enable a new, interdisciplinary synthesis of knowledge" (Link et al. 2016).

# 5   Conclusion

In summary, large-scale, aggregating repositories for data merging in neuroimaging studies such as fNIRS and fMRI will require metadata governed by naming conventions. Previous established precedents in cyber-enabled repositories such as Open fMRI already provide a path forward for meta-analyses of cognitive data, such as memory and workload tasks {Citation}. The ambitious promises of accurate BCI and personalized authentication will require the generalized descriptions of data, and sharing of data.

Future work will involve collaborators with fNIRS labs on the national and international levels on the technical feasibility of converting MNI coordinates for the BOLD signal matching and prototyping metadata techniques and conducting requirements gathering. Protocols similar to Open fMRI and similar repositories in SDRs such as policies for sharing data, anonymity, and others will be researched to incorporate research protocols such as the currently instated Declaration of Helsinki (Association et al. 2002). Overall, this paper contributes steps toward developing metadata for informing generalizability of fNIRS machine learning on cognitive data models, accelerating scientific data sharing initiatives, and promoting scientific and public communication across current disciplines in neuroscience, psychology, and information and computer science.

**Acknowledgements.** The author thanks the Syracuse University Media Interface Network Design (M.I.N.D.) Lab at S.I. Newhouse School of Public Communications and colleagues for support.

# References

Abdul Serwadda, V.P.: fNIRS: A New Modality for Brain Activity-Based Biometric Authentication (2015)

Adolphs, R., Damasio, H., Tranel, D., Damasio, A.R.: Cortical systems for the recognition of emotion in facial expressions. J. Neurosci. **16**(23), 7678–7687 (1996)

Association, W.M., et al.: World medical association declaration of Helsinki. Ethical principles for medical research involving human subjects. Nurs. Ethics **9**(1), 105 (2002)

Balconi, M., Grippa, E., Vanutelli, M.E.: Resting lateralized activity predicts the cortical response and appraisal of emotions: an fNIRS study. Soc. Cogn. Affect. Neurosci. **10**(12), 1607–1614 (2015). doi:https://doi.org/10.1093/scan/nsv041

Banks, S.J., Eddy, K.T., Angstadt, M., Nathan, P.J., Phan, K.L.: Amygdala-frontal connectivity during emotion regulation. Soc. Cogn. Affect. Neurosci. **2**(4), 303–312 (2007). doi:https://doi.org/10.1093/scan/nsm029

Bigliassi, M., Barreto-Silva, V., Altimari, L.R., Vandoni, M., Codrons, E., Buzzachera, C.F.: How motivational and calm music may affect the prefrontal cortex area and emotional responses: a functional near-infrared spectroscopy (fNIRS) study. Percept. Mot. Skills **120**(1), 202–218 (2015). doi:https://doi.org/10.2466/27.24.PMS.120v12x5

Blair, R.J.R., Morris, J.S., Frith, C.D., Perrett, D.I., Dolan, R.J.: Dissociable neural responses to facial expressions of sadness and anger. Brain **122**(5), 883–893 (1999)

Blood, A.J., Zatorre, R.J., Bermudez, P., Evans, A.C.: Emotional responses to pleasant and unpleasant music correlate with activity in paralimbic brain regions. Nat. Neurosci. **2**(4), 382–387 (1999). doi:https://doi.org/10.1038/7299

Bradley, M., Lang, P.J.: Measuring emotion: the self-assessment manikin and the semantic differential. J. Behav. Ther. Exp. Psychiatry **25**(1), 49–59 (1994)

Breiter, H.C., Etcoff, N.L., Whalen, P.J., Kennedy, W.A., Rauch, S.L., Buckner, R.L., Rosen, B.R.: Response and habituation of the human amygdala during visual processing of facial expression. Neuron **17**(5), 875–887 (1996)

Brink, T.T., Urton, K., Held, D., Kirilina, E., Hofmann, M.J., Klann-Delius, G., Kuchinke, L.: The role of orbitofrontal cortex in processing empathy stories in 4- to 8-year-old children. Front. Psychol. **2**, (2011). doi:https://doi.org/10.3389/fpsyg.2011.00080

Bunce, S., Izzetoglu, M., Izzetoglu, K., Onaral, B., Pourrezaei, K.: Functional near infrared spectroscopy: an emerging neuroimaging modality. IEEE Eng. Med. Biol. Mag. Special Issue Clin. Neuroeng. **25**(4), 54–62 (2006)

Codispoti, M., Surcinelli, P., Baldaro, B.: Watching emotional movies: affective reactions and gender differences. Int. J. Psychophysiol.: Official J. Int. Organ. Psychophysiol. **69**(2), 90–95 (2008). doi:https://doi.org/10.1016/j.ijpsycho.2008.03.004

Costa, M., Bratt, S.: Truthiness: challenges associated with employing machine learning on neurophysiological sensor data. In: Schmorrow, D.D., Fidopiastis, C.M. (eds.) AC 2016. LNCS (LNAI), vol. 9743, pp. 159–164. Springer, Cham (2016). doi:10.1007/978-3-319-39955-3_15

Diemer, J., Alpers, G.W., Peperkorn, H.M., Shiban, Y., Mühlberger, A.: The impact of perception and presence on emotional reactions: a review of research in virtual reality. Frontiers Psychol. **6** (2015). doi:https://doi.org/10.3389/fpsyg.2015.00026

Edwards, A.: The relationship between the judged desirability of a trait and the probability that the trait will be endorsed. J. Appl. Psychol. **37**, 90–93 (1953)

Ekman, P.: Facial expression and emotion. Am. Psychol. **48**(4), 384 (1993)

Ekman, P., Friesen, W.V.: Constants across cultures in the face and emotion. J. Pers. Soc. Psychol. **17**(2), 124–129 (1971). doi:https://doi.org/10.1037/h0030377

Elo, S., Kyngäs, H.: The qualitative content analysis process. J. Adv. Nurs. **62**(1), 107–115 (2008)

Ernst, L.H., Plichta, M.M., Lutz, E., Zesewitz, A.K., Tupak, S.V., Dresler, T., Fallgatter, A.J.: Prefrontal activation patterns of automatic and regulated approach-avoidance reactions - a functional near-infrared spectroscopy (fNIRS) study. Cortex; J. Devoted Study Nerv. Syst. Behav. **49**(1), 131–142 (2013). doi:https://doi.org/10.1016/j.cortex.2011.09.013

Glotzbach, E., Mühlberger, A., Gschwendtner, K., Fallgatter, A.J., Pauli, P., Herrmann, M.J.: Prefrontal brain activation during emotional processing: a functional near infrared spectroscopy study (fNIRS). Open Neuroimaging J. **5**, 33–39 (2011). doi:https://doi.org/10.2174/1874440001105010033

Goffman, E., et al.: The presentation of self in everyday life. Harmondsworth (1978). https://books.google.com/books?hl=en&lr=&id=TllAzT5uT-IC&oi=fnd&pg=PA120&dq=presentation+of+self+goffman+&ots=IsLafkHokc&sig=A4r-dgPr27CTiUgisyfD_3QH6n4

Gorini, A., Mosso, J.L., Mosso, D., Pineda, E., Ruíz, N.L., Ramíez, M., Riva, G.: Emotional response to virtual reality exposure across different cultures: the role of the attribution process. Cyberpsychol. Behav.: Impact Internet, Multimedia Virtual Real. Behav. Soc. **12**(6), 699–705 (2009). doi:https://doi.org/10.1089/cpb.2009.0192

Grimes, D., Tan, D.S., Hudson, S.E., Shenoy, P., Rao, R.P.N.: Feasibility and pragmatics of classifying working memory load with an electroencephalograph. In: Proceedings of the SIGCHI Conference on Human Factors in Computing Systems, pp. 835–844. ACM, New York (2008). doi:https://doi.org/10.1145/1357054.1357187

Gygax, L., Reefmann, N., Wolf, M., Langbein, J.: Prefrontal cortex activity, sympatho-vagal reaction and behaviour distinguish between situations of feed reward and frustration in dwarf goats. Behav. Brain Res. **239**, 104–114 (2013). doi:https://doi.org/10.1016/j.bbr.2012.10.052

Hengehold, L.: "My body, this paper, this fire": the fate of emotion in Foucault's Kantian legacy. Philos. Today **47**, 45–55 (2003)

Hosseini, S.M., Mano, H., Rostami, Y., Takahashi, M., Sugiura, M., Kawashima, R.: Decoding what one likes or dislikes from single-trial fNIRS measurements. Neuroreport, **22**(6), 269–273 (2011). doi:https://doi.org/10.1097/WNR.0b013e3283451f8f

Hudson, M.B., Nicolas, S.C., Howser, M.E., Lipsett, K.E., Robinson, I.W., Pope, L.J., Friedman, D.R.: Examining how gender and emoticons influence facebook jealousy. Cyberpsychol. Behav. Soc. Network. **18**(2), 87–92 (2015). doi:https://doi.org/10.1089/cyber.2014.0129

Iacucci, G., Kuutti, K.: Everyday life as a stage in creating and performing scenarios for wireless devices. Pers. Ubiquitous Comput. **6**(4), 299–306 (2002). doi:https://doi.org/10.1007/s007790200031

El Kaliouby, R., Picard, R., Baron-Cohen, S.: Affective computing and autism. Ann. New York Acad. Sci. **1093**(1), 228–248 (2006). doi:https://doi.org/10.1196/annals.1382.016

Kassam, K.S., Markey, A.R., Cherkassky, V.L., Loewenstein, G., Just, M.A.: Identifying emotions on the basis of neural activation. PLoS ONE **8**(6), e66032 (2013)

Kassam, K.S., Mendes, W.B.: The effects of measuring emotion: physiological reactions to emotional situations depend on whether someone is asking. PLOS ONE, **8**(6), e64959 (2013). doi:https://doi.org/10.1371/journal.pone.0064959

Kopf, J., Dresler, T., Reicherts, P., Herrmann, M.J., Reif, A.: The effect of emotional content on brain activation and the late positive potential in a word n-back task. PLOS ONE, **8**(9), e75598 (2013). doi:https://doi.org/10.1371/journal.pone.0075598

Kreplin, U., Fairclough, S.H.: Activation of the rostromedial prefrontal cortex during the experience of positive emotion in the context of esthetic experience. an fNIRS study. Front. Hum. Neurosci. 7 (2013). doi:https://doi.org/10.3389/fnhum.2013.00879

Leon-Carrion, J., Damas, J., Izzetoglu, K., Pourrezai, K., Martín-Rodríguez, J.F., Barroso y Martin, J.M., Dominguez-Morales, M.R.: Differential time course and intensity of PFC activation for men and women in response to emotional stimuli: a functional near-infrared spectroscopy (fNIRS) study. Neurosci. Lett. **403**(1–2), 90–95 (2006). doi:https://doi.org/10.1016/j.neulet.2006.04.050

León-Carrión, J., Martín-Rodríguez, J.F., Damas-López, J., Pourrezai, K., Izzetoglu, K., y Martin, J.M.B., Domínguez-Morales, M.R.: A lasting post-stimulus activation on dorsolateral prefrontal cortex is produced when processing valence and arousal in visual affective stimuli. Neurosci. Lett. **422**(3), 147–152 (2007). doi:https://doi.org/10.1016/j.neulet.2007.04.087

Link, G.J., Germonprez, M., Goggins, S., Hemsley, J., Rand, B., Squire, M.: The open community data exchange: advancing data sharing and discovery in open online community science. In: Proceedings of the 12th International Symposium on Open Collaboration Companion, p. 7. ACM (2016). http://dl.acm.org/citation.cfm?id=2962142

Neuroimaging databases, 15 July 2014. https://www.openeuroscience.com/data-collaboration-projects/neuroimaging-databases/

Neurosynth (n.d.). Accessed 20 Oct 2016. http://neurosynth.org/

Nicholson, A.A., Rabellino, D., Densmore, M., Frewen, P.A., Paret, C., Kluetsch, R., et al.: The neurobiology of emotion regulation in posttraumatic stress disorder: amygdala downregulation via real-time fMRI neurofeedback. Hum. Brain Mapp. **38**(1), 541–560 (2017)

Noah, J.A., Ono, Y., Nomoto, Y., Shimada, S., Tachibana, A., Zhang, X., Hirsch, J.: fMRI validation of fNIRS measurements during a naturalistic task. J. Vis. Exp. (100) (2015). doi: https://doi.org/10.3791/52116

Perlman, S.B., Luna, B., Hein, T.C., Huppert, T.J.: fNIRS evidence of prefrontal regulation of frustration in early childhood. NeuroImage, **85** Pt 1, 326–334 (2014). doi:https://doi.org/10.1016/j.neuroimage.2013.04.057

Phan, K.L., Wager, T., Taylor, S.F., Liberzon, I.: Functional neuroanatomy of emotion: a meta-analysis of emotion activation studies in PET and fMRI. Neuroimage **16**(2), 331–348 (2002)

Rothbart, M.K., Ahadi, S.A., Hershey, K.L., Fisher, P.: Investigations of temperament at three to seven years: the children's behavior questionnaire. Child Dev. **72**(5), 1394–1408 (2001)

Russell, J.A., Mehrabian, A.: Evidence for a three-factor theory of emotions. J. Res. Pers. **11**(3), 273–294 (1977)

Rutkowski, T.M., Tanaka, T., Cichocki, A., Erickson, D., Cao, J., Mandic, D.P.: Interactive component extraction from fEEG, fNIRS and peripheral biosignals for affective brain–machine interfacing paradigms. Comput. Hum. Behav. **27**(5), 1512–1518 (2011)

Scherer, K.R.: What are emotions? And how can they be measured? Soc. Sci. Inf. **44**(4), 695–729 (2005). doi:https://doi.org/10.1177/0539018405058216

Schneider, S., Christensen, A., Häußinger, F.B., Fallgatter, A.J., Giese, M.A., Ehlis, A.-C.: Show me how you walk and i tell you how you feel — a functional near-infrared spectroscopy study on emotion perception based on human gait. NeuroImage, **85**, Part 1, 380–390 (2014). doi: https://doi.org/10.1016/j.neuroimage.2013.07.078

Sevick, E.M., Chance, B., Leigh, J., Nioka, S., Maris, M.: Quantitation of time-and frequency-resolved optical spectra for the determination of tissue oxygenation. Anal. Biochem. **195**(2), 330–351 (1991)

Shimoda, N., Takeda, K., Imai, I., Kaneko, J., Kato, H.: Cerebral laterality differences in handedness: a mental rotation study with NIRS. Neurosci. Lett. **430**(1), 43–47 (2008). doi: https://doi.org/10.1016/j.neulet.2007.10.016

Soleymani, M., Asghari-Esfeden, S., Fu, Y., Pantic, M.: Analysis of EEG signals and facial expressions for continuous emotion detection. IEEE Trans. Affect. Comput. **7**(1), 17–28 (2016)

Stevens, J.S., Hamann, S.: Sex differences in brain activation to emotional stimuli: a meta-analysis of neuroimaging studies. Neuropsychologia **50**(7), 1578–1593 (2012). doi: https://doi.org/10.1016/j.neuropsychologia.2012.03.011

Thayer, J.F., Åhs, F., Fredrikson, M., Sollers, J.J., Wager, T.D.: A meta-analysis of heart rate variability and neuroimaging studies: implications for heart rate variability as a marker of stress and health. Neurosci. Biobehav. Rev. **36**(2), 747–756 (2012). doi:https://doi.org/10.1016/j.neubiorev.2011.11.009

Thayer, J.F., Lane, R.D.: Claude Bernard and the heart–brain connection: further elaboration of a model of neurovisceral integration. Neurosci. Biobehav. Rev. **33**(2), 81–88 (2009)

Thomas, C., Altenmüller, E., Marckmann, G., Kahrs, J., Dichgans, J.: Language processing in aphasia: changes in lateralization patterns during recovery reflect cerebral plasticity in adults. Electroencephalogr. Clin. Neurophysiol. **102**(2), 86–97 (1997). doi:https://doi.org/10.1016/S0921-884X(96)95653-2

Tupak, S.V., Dresler, T., Badewien, M., Hahn, T., Ernst, L.H., Herrmann, M.J., Fallgatter, A.J.: Inhibitory transcranial magnetic theta burst stimulation attenuates prefrontal cortex oxygenation. Hum. Brain Mapp. **34**(1), 150–157 (2013). doi:https://doi.org/10.1002/hbm.21421

Võ, M.L., Conrad, M., Kuchinke, L., Urton, K., Hofmann, M.J., Jacobs, A.M.: The Berlin affective word list reloaded (BAWL-R). Behav. Res. Methods **41**(2), 534–538 (2009)

Watson, D., Clark, L.A., Tellegen, A.: Development and validation of brief measures of positive and negative affect: the PANAS scales. J. Pers. Soc. Psychol. **54**(6), 1063–1070 (1988)

Whittle, S., Yücel, M., Yap, M.B.H., Allen, N.B.: Sex differences in the neural correlates of emotion: evidence from neuroimaging. Biol. Psychol. **87**(3), 319–333 (2011). doi:https://doi.org/10.1016/j.biopsycho.2011.05.003

Wiebking, C., de Greck, M., Duncan, N.W., Heinzel, A., Tempelmann, C., Northoff, G.: Are emotions associated with activity during rest or interoception? An exploratory fMRI study in healthy subjects. Neurosci. Lett. **491**(1), 87–92 (2011)

Williams, J.B.: A structured interview guide for the Hamilton depression rating scale. Arch. Gen. Psychiatry **45**(8), 742–747 (1988)

Yoshida, K., Sawamura, D., Inagaki, Y., Ogawa, K., Ikoma, K., Sakai, S.: Brain activity during the flow experience: a functional near-infrared spectroscopy study. Neurosci. Lett. **573**, 30–34 (2014). doi:https://doi.org/10.1016/j.neulet.2014.05.011

Young, R.C., Biggs, J.T., Ziegler, V.E., Meyer, D.A.: A rating scale for mania: reliability, validity and sensitivity. Br. J. Psychiatry **133**(5), 429–435 (1978)

Yuan, Z., Ye, J.: Fusion of fNIRS and fMRI data: identifying when and where hemodynamic signals are changing in human brains. Front. Hum. Neurosci. **7** (2013). doi:https://doi.org/10.3389/fnhum.2013.00676

# Establishing Ground Truth
# on Pyschophysiological Models for Training
# Machine Learning Algorithms: Options
# for Ground Truth Proxies

Keith Brawner[(⊠)] and Michael W. Boyce

Army Research Laboratory, Orlando, FL, USA
{keith.w.brawner.civ,michael.w.boycell.civ}@mail.mil

## 1 Introduction

One of the core aspects of human-human interaction is the ability to recognize and respond to the emotional and cognitive states of the other person, leaving human-computer interaction systems, at their core, to perform many of the same tasks. This can take the form of robotic interaction systems that respond to 'anger' [33], instructional systems that take different actions according to 'confusion' [27], and intelligent aiding systems which dynamically adjust levels of autonomy (i.e. task allocation to the human or the system) depending on continuously changing levels of 'workload' [9]. A well-designed system responds to information about the user, tailoring the experience for the purposes of enjoyment, effectiveness, or both. The emphasis of this paper focuses on understanding that emotional state to maximize human performance.

While there are many reasons why one might want to recognize emotional states within a population of individuals for the purpose of designing systems, the model creation process is fundamentally the same across much of the research. Briefly, this process can be described as the below:

1. Data about 'state' is collected, features of this data.
2. The features are distilled into markers for easier machine learning classification.
3. These markers are fed into one or more model creation algorithms.
4. Affective classification models are created.
5. Affective models are used.

While models can be built from numerous and disparate data sources, the underlying affective data is frequently suspect. Let us consider a labeled datapoint in a set which indicates 'frustration'. Is the user frustrated because they said so right now? Because they said that they were frustrated with the overall experience? Because models calibrated on another frustration event said they were? How do you know that the user is truly frustrated? Is either cognitive underload/overload [12] causing the frustration? During analysis, how can you be assured of the quality of the label in the spreadsheet?

The common aphorism is that "all models are wrong, but some are useful." The quality of labels is frequently dubious, due to the way that the labels are collected (subject to experimenter or experiment design bias), but that does not mean that it

© Springer International Publishing AG 2017
D.D. Schmorrow and C.M. Fidopiastis (Eds.): AC 2017, Part I, LNAI 10284, pp. 468–477, 2017.
DOI: 10.1007/978-3-319-58628-1_35

cannot be applied to useful applications. Further, the quality can be improved through the combination of more than one labeling technique. Researchers have begun to develop adaptive multimodal recognition systems which focus on good quality samples to form training data and thus assisting to reject bad samples. The multimodal adaptive system has the added advantage of achieving better performance and a lower failure rate [11]. There are many options for collecting labeled data, each with its own advantages, disadvantages, limitations for collections, and workarounds for attempting to assure that the label is of high quality. Two significant research design problems exist, both in matching the collection technique to its intended use and the combination of labels from multiple schemes.

While a singular strong state (e.g. rage, surprise, exhaustion) is relatively easy to label, the majority of the states useful for Human Computer Interaction (HCI) research are nuanced (e.g. annoyance, confusion, underload). Distinguishing nuanced states, such as 'underload' from 'boredom', into a labeled category can be difficult. The careful selection of the method chosen for labeled data collection can help to mitigate the problem with wrong model for a specific application or use case.

Research efforts are beginning to apply hybrid techniques of multiple methods for dealing with data to improve quality [24]. Specifically, it is possible to take a qualitative analysis technique such as Grounded Theory, and apply it iteratively when performing sampling to support a machine learning algorithm. Both approaches are derived from the data, with the machine learning looking for features and the Grounded Theory looking for theories or themes that describe those features. In terms of the ability to detect affect from this data, researchers have generally tried to pull together a series of measurements via different types of physiological sensors, such as research that shows the ability to properly classify Valence and Arousal with over a 90% success rate [25], using a combination of Skin Conductance, Heart Rate, and Electromyography. Using a combination of techniques can assist in beginning to target more complex responses. As a part of their research, Noguiera et al. [25] built a regression model which runs through several iterations to assist with data scaling. Then they perform a second pass with several machine learning algorithms to merge the outputs of the regression model into an aggregated score. They use objective player modeling techniques (OPEM), which have been shown to be very consistent between administrations. Even with all these methods to collect data, a key challenge in establishing ground truth is understanding proportionally how to adjust the importance (i.e. weights) of the various data collection measures.

This paper reviews different options for obtaining "ground truth" labeled data from users. The methods examined include:

1. Using pre-existing and validated models created from a standard dataset
2. Using pre-existing and validated models created from multiple contexts of experience
3. Using manually labeled datasets
4. Through self-reported labeled ask soon after or during after the experience
5. Through self-report labeled feedback asked after a number of experiences
6. Creating sensor-based models from theory directly.

Each of these options has advantages, disadvantages, limits or restrictions, and mitigations or workarounds. This paper lightly reviews the literature for groups which have used various techniques in an effort to inform future research on the selection of the experimental labeling design best suited for the end application or use case. The expertise of the authors lies in training system applications, so the labeling techniques discussed within this paper are an extension of that lense through pragmatic application. It is an expansion on some of last years' points from the "truthiness" paper by Mark Costa and Sarah Bratt for the HCII community [8].

## 2   Calibrate from a Standard Dataset

One of the most attractive methods for creating emotional recognition work is to calibrate from an existing dataset. Examples of baseline datasets are the Pose Illumination and Expression (PIE) database [30], or the SEMAINE affective dataset [23]. The advantage of such a dataset is that either paid actors or in-the-wild observations of ground truth that can be used to baseline. The significant disadvantage of the approach is that the models made from such a dataset, while useful for facial detection, haven't made much, if any, progress into realtime applications. The models have been useful in the methods to develop generalized facial detection models, but have not demonstrated use in in-the-wild affect detection problems. Part of the reason for this is that the mapping between the observed face, the Facial Action Coding System (FACS) of Action Unit (AU) identification, and the actual emotion is tenuous [28].

Other work includes Conati's probabilistic assessment models and Pantic and Rothkrantz's audio/video combination methods [26]. In Conati's model, user emotions are defined through several different dimensions: student goals, variables describing student personality traits, actions to be taken by the agent, and variables describing the user's emotional state [7]. They expressed the importance of using the ability of recognizing affective state to make interactions more affective. They argue that communicative cues such as facial expressions and body movements are affected by individual's arousal. Likewise, when humans are interacting with each other humans can interpret these cues while machines have a much more difficult time. They explained that to analyze human affective feedback there needs to be an architecture which supports information coming from the visual system, information coming from the processing of audio, and information coming from touch or tactile sensors. This data in turn would undergo both feature level fusion across information types and data information interpretation to help make decisions on the appropriate feedback. Pantic and Rothkrantz classify it as data level fusion, feature level fusion, and decision level fusion [26].

While fewer emotional datasets exist for physiological signals, the reader should note the lessons from the above, such as establishing similar items from a commonly available physiological model, can be expected to encounter similar difficulties. When discussing classification for the purposes of building affective models from physiology, the authors are only generally aware of two common-access databases for the purpose: the Deap database for emotion analysis using physiological signals [21], and a dataset made available by the authors [5].

## 3    Calibrate from an Existing Validated Model

The general scope of this paper is to discuss evidence that all measures are a proxy of the true ground truth. While the real truth certainly exists in the brain as measured by electroencephalogram (EEG) signals, there is always the concern of the accuracy of measurement. The true brain signal is spread across the skull, subject to noise in measurement, to significant individual differences in brain topology, and varies by day and sensor placement. However, EEG signals are reliable for certain tasks and some systems have been extensively evaluated. As an example, the Advanced Brain Monitoring system can generate real-time indices of alertness, cognition, and memory [2], or measures of drowsiness/alertness [16]. There have been many (20+) studies where the patented detection algorithms have been validated over relatively stable timeframes (minutes). The studies which use functional magnetic resonance imaging (fMRI) have similarly levels of validation, with early research indicating success at tracking moment-to-moment changes in affect [20]. Each of these systems can be relied upon to give fairly accurate information in regards to labeling.

The purpose of a system may to be analyze affect during task performance, with findings useful to the system creators. An example of such a finding would be an interface which causes high levels of workload and dissatisfaction among its users. The finding can be used to redesign the system in such a way to reduce cognitive load. More frequently, however, the purpose of the system is to respond to the users' needs as they need them. An example would be an interface that re-configures based on the high workload, or a teaching system that uses knowledge of the user frustration to make changes in courseware/courseflow. The use one EEG or fMRI system for each user is fundamentally impractical.

An alternative to the use of such systems is to use the high-accuracy systems as the 'ground truth' for a series of, presumably, lower accuracy systems. In the same manner that video systems can use lipreading to distinguish words without audio, systems can be designed to use low-cost wearables and stand-off sensors in order to capture the emotion [22]. The authors have publicly shared such a dataset in the past [5]. The advantage of such an approach is that the ground truth can be considered reasonably reliable, but the disadvantage is the compounding of errors. A classifier which predicts with 80% accuracy on a signal with 80% accuracy in a system which may be barely usable with 64% accuracy. Experimenters should consider this potential compounding of inaccuracies when designing systems, but low levels of accuracy may be acceptable for systems which make slow and reliable decisions.

## 4    Manual Expert Label

One method of addressing the flaws of inability to attain ground truth information is to begin relying on post-hoc added labels to existing recorded data. The process of doing this relies on capturing the nuanced emotions experienced during the desired event using the classifiers in an operational setting. This is the basis for many qualitative research methods that categorize participant actions in a hope to provide more general, overarching themes. Such qualitative approaches include thematic analysis [4] and Interpretative Phenomenological Analysis [3, 31]. On the other end of the spectrum is labeling based on physiological data such as eye fixations and saccades, as was done with an intelligent tutoring system called Metatutor [15]. As an example, consider the tasks of the classification of a fatigued driver. An experimental setup would allow for the driver to perform their normal function while being observed via a combination of bodily (e.g. EEG) and standoff sensors (e.g. webcam). The video data can then be carefully combed by expert labellers at the second-by-second resolution. These "ground truth" labels can then be used to train automatic classifiers for the bodily sensors (EEG), the standoff sensors (webcam), or use a combination of data fusion to attempt to train both.

The advantage of this approach is that, through the use of expert labellers and time-delayed recording, the ground truth information can be captured at relatively fine resolution. As an example, the first moments of affective information can be traced to their earliest FACS movements. A further advantage is that the classifiers trained are applicable in the desired application.

The first disadvantage of the approach is that the methods of classifications are not particularly guaranteed to transition beyond their initial domain. The second disadvantage is that the classifiers in this instance have the tendency to be 'jittery', rapidly classifying emotions at their earliest onset. Jittery classification can be overcome at the labeling instance, by labeling an emotion only when it is fully manifested in the desired application, or at the runtime instance, where simple rules can dampen system actions (e.g. "only act when the emotion has been present for greater than 80% of a 3 min window").

## 5 Self Report

All self-report data, arguably, has the same advantage that it is the ground truth, as the participant has reported it. In some manner, it is very difficult to contradict a participant which responded that they were 'bored' and 'unchallenged' (low workload) by a series of educational content presentations. Hoskin details the typical problems with self-reported data [14]. In brief, these include:

- Individual differences in introspective ability
- Individual variations in interpretation of a question
- Individual variations in rating scales, especially with large variations, such as [0–100]
- Response bias, especially in yes/no questions

Simply using a survey measure such as the NASA-Task Load Index (TLX) [13] to label a 30-second window of time can be subject to all of the above flaws. These flaws may even out over a large amount of samples, on the whole, but using them to label 1000s of datapoints from raw sensors is a gross measure, at best. This limitation is overcome if the experimenter desires a gross measure of the particular affect (e.g. 'confused' at 30 s resolution is sufficient in production).

The accuracy concerns can be mitigated through the use of the more validated instruments, such as the TLX. However, the experimenter should be aware how the frequency of polling can affect the data overall. Additionally, the experimenter should be aware that asking about an experience can change the perception of the experience. An example study where this effect is observed is in an educational study, where significant difficulties were encountered during the learning environment, but reported as interest and enjoyment after the fact [19]. It is worth noting that early results to try to build a system at the same time that it is being used have had sufficient predictive accuracies to be useful in both simulation [6] and practice [10].

## 5.1 Post-hoc Self-report

The general advantages and disadvantages of self-report are discussed above, being that subjects' estimate of their own emotions is arguably better than expert annotation. The notable disadvantage of post-hoc self-report is typical of most video game and learning experiences: the experience itself is somewhat challenging. When asked after an experience about the emotions experienced during the situation, the experience tends to be cast through the lens of the final moment (e.g. winning, losing, learning, etc.). The most useful workaround for this problem is to use a group-based model to create distinctive groups, each of which can be targeted for action [32].

## 5.2 In-Situ Self-report

The general advantages and disadvantages of self-report are discussed above. The alternative method of gathering self-report data is to ask the participant in situ to report their emotions or experience. The "think aloud protocol" allows for the experimenter to obtain a continuous feed of user affective states, resulting in a higher granularity of samples for model creation. The largest disadvantage of this approach is that the experience of "think aloud" can have a modest effect on workload and task performance [29]. This effect can be mitigated by having the "think aloud" be related to the task.

# 6  Physiological Sensors

The advantage of using physiological sensors, as opposed to any of the other above methods, is that the "ground truth" is objective. The raise in Galvanic Skin Response (GSR) or increase of blood flow to an area of the brain, or the frequency of brain operation, are resistant to subject recall, self-report, rater bias, or the error rate of a previously established model. These advantages are significant, but do not come without costs. The costs are that the measurement is usually not suited for the intended environment, individual responses vary significantly and change daily, and that the measurements are usually gross proxies for the things that they are measuring.

The measurement via sensors is usually not appropriate for the intended environment. As an example, much of the emotion-based research in the educational domain is eventually intended to influence the decisions of systems or teachers about the content presented to the student within the classroom. With the average classroom size in the United States around 25 students per teacher, and the cost of an fNIRS system in the range of $50,000, the educational benefits of emotional detection are simply not justified in the cost. Furthermore, many sensor-based systems require extensive set-up, which consumes time that could have been spent on the performance task.

Another downside lies simply in the quality of the data collected versus any interference that is potentially associated with it. Depending on the sensor used, what might be considered a response from a classification algorithm can be noise associated with the electronics, noise associated with the participant, or noise associated with the environment. As a very simple example, consider electrodermal activity being collected to measure arousal. Using many of the electrodermal sensors currently on the market, factors such as the ambient room temperature, skin temperature due to clothing, contact with the skin, and charge of the battery on the sensor can all lead to artifact. This does not even include gross motor movements, which can drastically impact results and the connectivity of the sensors.

Next, sensors frequently measure only a proxy of what they intend to measure. Taking the example of electrodermal activity sensor which measures the changes in skin conductance. These changes proxy are measurements for the autonomic nervous system ("fight/flight") activity, which is linked to emotional and cognitive states. A raise in GSR response can indicate stress, fear, anxiety, excitement, interest, or the anticipation of any of these things. The sensors can be calibrated over time to compensate for this weakness, but the measurement of a sensor is rarely conclusive evidence of an emotional state. Researchers, such as Picard's group, maintain a successful line of research in artifact detection and have developed screening tools to help identify responses, clear noise, and process signals against a predefined set of transformations, with tools released for others [19].

# 7  Conclusions

It is worth noting that early results to try to build a system at the same time that it is being used have had sufficient predictive accuracies to be useful in both simulation [6] and practice [10], which neatly avoids much of the problems of labeling.

With the development of technologies such as crowdsourcing, researchers have begun to address labeling of content in new innovative ways. Katsimerou et al. used a database of over 180 long videos which contained three different visual cues involving face and body, as well as a physical depth-based data stream from the Microsoft Kinect [18]. They used crowdsourcing to be able to make large numbers of annotations related to mood and emotion by non-expert coders. They also compared this against laboratory trained annotations to validate the non-expert inputs. As more and more information becomes available via cloud services, it is likely that labeling accomplished by larger groups of people may become the norm.

Automated detection algorithms are becoming a popular source for labeling data as well. Other researchers have used a multimodal approach (appearances collected from a camera vs context specific behaviors captured by the application) to train different classifiers to interpret affective state [1]. Kapoor and Picard used a multimodal approach in where they combined posture based data with camera based data to achieve an 86% accuracy rating of affective state, the approach was a unified Bayesian approach using Gaussian process classifiers that used expectation propagation (EP) [17].

The intended takeaway from this paper is that no *one* technique is probably sufficient for the accurate representation for the ground truth classification of affective state. However, a number of hybrid techniques can be investigated to mitigate the difficulties in any individual approach. Many experiments under various contexts using semi-reliable self-report information can be combined into reasonably reliable labels. Hybrid approaches may use active machine learning to intelligently select datapoints for labeling, with crowdsourced labeling experts providing annotations, making use of both machine learning techniques and within-task self report information [6]. Another hybrid approach may have an individual baselining period which bootstraps the machine learning classifier in batched training, updating it based on after-task self report information [10]. The authors believe that these multi-point labeling approaches tend to produce higher-quality labels overall, which result in models which are less brittle.

# References

1. Alyuz, N., Okur, E., Oktay, E., Genc, U., Aslan, S., Mete, S.E., Stanhill, D., Arnrich, B., Esme, A.A.: Towards an emotional engagement model: can affective states of a learner be automatically detected in a 1:1 learning scenario. In: Proceedings of the 6th Workshop on Personalization Approaches in Learning Environments (PALE 2016), 24th Conference on User Modeling, Adaptation, and Personalization (UMAP 2016), CEUR Workshop Proceedings, this volume (2016)
2. Berka, C., Levendowski, D., Cvetinović, M., Petrović, M., Davis, G., Lumicao, M.P., Živković, V., Olmstead, R.: Real-time analysis of EEG indices of alertness, cognition and memory acquired with a wireless EEG headset. Int. J. Hum.-Comput. Interact. 17(2), 151–170 (2004)
3. Boyce, M.W., Cruz, D., Sottilare, R.: Interpretative phenomenological analysis for military tactics instruction. In: Kantola, J.I., Barath, T., Nazir, S., Andre, T. (eds.) Advances in Human Factors, Business Management, Training and Education. AISC, vol. 498, pp. 623–634. Springer, Cham (2017). doi:10.1007/978-3-319-42070-7_58
4. Braun, V., Clarke, V.: Using thematic analysis in psychology. Qual. Res. Psychol. 3(2), 77–101 (2006)
5. Brawner, K.: Data sharing: low-cost sensors for affect and cognition. In: Proceedings of the Educational Data Mining, London, UK (2014)
6. Brawner, K.W.: Modeling learner mood in realtime through biosensors for intelligent tutoring improvements. Department of Electrical Engineering and Computer Science University of Central Florida, p. 500 (2013)

7. Conati, C.: Probabilistic assessment of user's emotions in educational games. Appl. Artif. Intell. **16**(7–8), 555–575 (2002)
8. Costa, M., Bratt, S.: Truthiness: challenges associated with employing machine learning on neurophysiological sensor data. In: Schmorrow, D.D.D., Fidopiastis, C.M.M. (eds.) AC 2016. LNCS, vol. 9743, pp. 159–164. Springer, Cham (2016). doi:10.1007/978-3-319-39955-3_15
9. de Winter, J.C., Happee, R., Martens, M.H., Stanton, N.A.: Effects of adaptive cruise control and highly automated driving on workload and situation awareness: a review of the empirical evidence. Transp. Res. Part F Traffic Psychol. Behav. **27**, 196–217 (2014)
10. Fairclough, S.H., Karran, A.J., Gilleade, K.: Classification accuracy from the perspective of the user: real-time interaction with physiological computing. In: Proceedings of the 33rd Annual ACM Conference on Human Factors in Computing Systems, pp. 3029–3038. ACM (2015)
11. Gupta, R., Khomami Abadi, M., Cárdenes Cabré, J.A., Morreale, F., Falk, T.H., Sebs, N.: A quality adaptive multimodal affect recognition system for user-centric multimedia indexing. In: Proceedings of the 2016 ACM on International Conference on Multimedia Retrieval, pp. 317–320. ACM (2016)
12. Hancock, P.A., Chignell, M.H.: Mental workload dynamics in adaptive interface design. IEEE Trans. Syst. Man Cybern. **18**(4), 647–658 (1988)
13. Hart, S.G., Staveland, L.E.: Development of NASA-TLX (Task Load Index): results of empirical and theoretical research. Adv. Psychol. **52**, 139–183 (1988)
14. Hoskin, R.: The dangers of self-report. In: Science Brainwaves (2012). http://www.sciencebrainwaves.com/the-dangers-of-self-report/
15. Jaques, N., Conati, C., Harley, J.M., Azevedo, R.: Predicting affect from gaze data during interaction with an intelligent tutoring system. In: Trausan-Matu, S., Boyer, K.E., Crosby, M., Panourgia, K. (eds.) ITS 2014. LNCS, vol. 8474, pp. 29–38. Springer, Cham (2014). doi:10.1007/978-3-319-07221-0_4
16. Johnson, R.R., Popovic, D.P., Olmstead, R.E., Stikic, M., Levendowski, D.J., Berka, C.: Drowsiness/alertness algorithm development and validation using synchronized EEG and cognitive performance to individualize a generalized model. Biol. Psychol. **87**(2), 241–250 (2011)
17. Kapoor, A., Picard, R.W.: Multimodal affect recognition in learning environments. In: ACM Multimedia 2005, pp. 677–682 (2005)
18. Katsimerou, C., Albeda, J., Huldtgren, A., Heynderickx, I., Redi, J.A.: Crowdsourcing empathetic intelligence: the case of the annotation of EMMA database for emotion and mood recognition. ACM Trans. Intell. Syst. Technol. (TIST) **7**(4), 51 (2016)
19. Kennedy, G., Lodge, J.M.: All roads lead to Rome: tracking students' affect as they overcome misconceptions (2016)
20. Knutson, B., Katovich, K., Suri, G.: Inferring affect from fMRI data. Trends Cogn. Sci. **18**(8), 422–428 (2014)
21. Koelstra, S., Muhl, C., Soleymani, M., Lee, J.-S., Yazdani, A., Ebrahimi, T., Pun, T., Nijholt, A., Patras, I.: Deap: a database for emotion analysis; using physiological signals. IEEE Trans. Affect. Comput. **3**(1), 18–31 (2012)
22. Kokini, C., Carroll, M., Ramirez-Padron, R., Hale, K., Sottilare, R., Goldberg, B.: Quantification of trainee affective and cognitive state in real-time. In: The Interservice/Industry Training, Simulation & Education Conference (I/ITSEC) NTSA, pp. 2155–2166 (2012)
23. McKeown, G., Valstar, M., Cowie, R., Pantic, M., Schroder, M.: The semaine database: annotated multimodal records of emotionally colored conversations between a person and a limited agent. IEEE Trans. Affect. Comput. **3**(1), 5–17 (2012)

24. Muller, M., Guha, S., Baumer, E.P., Mimno, D., Shami, N.S.: Machine learning and grounded theory method: convergence, divergence, and combination. In: Proceedings of the 19th International Conference on Supporting Group Work, pp. 3–8. ACM (2016)
25. Nogueira, P.A., Rodrigues, R., Oliveira, E., Nacke, L.E.: A hybrid approach at emotional state detection: merging theoretical models of emotion with data-driven statistical classifiers. In: Proceedings of the 2013 IEEE/WIC/ACM International Joint Conferences on Web Intelligence (WI) and Intelligent Agent Technologies (IAT)-vol. 02, pp. 253–260. IEEE Computer Society (2013)
26. Pantic, M., Rothkrantz, L.J.: Toward an affect-sensitive multimodal human-computer interaction. Proc. IEEE $91(9)$, 1370–1390 (2003)
27. Pedro, M.O., Baker, R., Bowers, A., Heffernan, N.: Predicting college enrollment from student interaction with an intelligent tutoring system in middle school. In: Educational Data Mining 2013 (2013)
28. Picard, R.W., Vyzas, E., Healey, J.: Toward machine emotional intelligence: analysis of affective physiological state. IEEE Trans. Pattern Anal. Mach. Intell. $23(10)$, 1175–1191 (2001)
29. Pike, M.F., Maior, H.A., Porcheron, M., Sharples, S.C., Wilson, M.L.: Measuring the effect of think aloud protocols on workload using fNIRS. In: Proceedings of the 32nd Annual ACM Conference on Human Factors in Computing Systems, pp. 3807–3816. ACM (2014)
30. Sim, T., Baker, S., Bsat, M.: The CMU pose, illumination, and expression (PIE) database. In: Proceedings of the Fifth IEEE International Conference on IEEE Automatic Face and Gesture Recognition, pp. 46–51 (2002)
31. Smith, J.A.: Reflecting on the development of interpretative phenomenological analysis and its contribution to qualitative research in psychology. Qual. Res. Psychol. $1(1)$, 39–54 (2004)
32. Valle, A., Núñez, J.C., Cabanach, R.G., González-Pienda, J.A., Rodríguez, S., Rosário, P., Cerezo, R., Muñoz-Cadavid, M.A.: Self-regulated profiles and academic achievement. Psicothema $20(4)$, 724–731 (2008)
33. Zhang, L., Jiang, M., Farid, D., Hossain, M.A.: Intelligent facial emotion recognition and semantic-based topic detection for a humanoid robot. Expert Syst. Appl. $40(13)$, 5160–5168 (2013)

# The Impact of Streaming Data on Sensemaking with Mixed-Initiative Visual Analytics

Nick Cramer[1], Grant Nakamura[1], and Alex Endert[2(✉)]

[1] Pacific Northwest National Laboratories, Richland, WA, USA
[2] School of Interactive Computing, Georgia Institute of Technology, 85 5th Street NW, Atlanta, GA, USA
endert@gatech.edu

**Abstract.** Visual data analysis helps people gain insights into data via interactive visualizations. People generate and test hypotheses and questions about data in context of the domain. This process can generally be referred to as sensemaking. Much of the work on studying sensemaking (and creating visual analytic techniques in support of it) has been focused on static datasets. However, how do the cognitive processes of sensemaking change when data are changing? Further, what implication for design does this create for mixed-initiative visual analytics systems? This paper presents the results of a user study analyzing the impact of streaming data on sensemaking. To perform this study, we developed a mixed-initiative visual analytic prototype, the Streaming Canvas, that affords the analysis of streaming text data. We compare the sensemaking process of people using this tool for a static and streaming dataset. We present the results of this study and discuss the implications on future visual analytic systems that combine machine learning and interactive visualization to help people make sense of streaming data.

**Keywords:** Sensemaking · Streaming data · Visual analytics

## 1 Introduction

The creation and storage of data from increasing sources creates important challenges for not only the design of technology, but may change the cognitive processes that humans exhibit when analyzing data. Streaming data is becoming more commonly available, as data is more continuously created, sensed, and stored. The speed (or velocity) of how often streaming data updates varies greatly. For example, news updates may happen daily, new email may arrive every few minutes, while packets of network activity or Twitter feeds may occur with sub-second intervals. Nonetheless, streaming data signifies a shift in the persistence of datasets to a model where the data is no longer complete or static throughout the analysis. In turn, this impacts what we know about data analysis – both from a technical system requirements standpoint of how to design and build visual analytic systems, and also from a cognitive, analytical reasoning perspective of what we know about how people reason about data and perform sensemaking.

© Springer International Publishing AG 2017
D.D. Schmorrow and C.M. Fidopiastis (Eds.): AC 2017, Part I, LNAI 10284, pp. 478–498, 2017.
DOI: 10.1007/978-3-319-58628-1_36

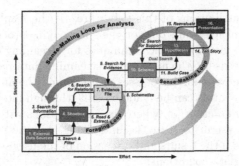

**Fig. 1.** The sensemaking loop, depicting a notional model for the cognitive stages involved in analyzing and understanding data.

Visual analytic techniques are one way to gain insight into data. These techniques foster sensemaking and discovery through visual data exploration [16, 33]. They combine the computational power of analytics with the advantages of interactive visualization to produce insights into data. Incorporating the user into the analysis process creates an analytic discourse between the analyst and the data [10]. Such processes are often described as sensemaking [24]. The "sensemaking loop" (shown in Fig. 1), presented by Pirolli and Card [24], depicts a notional model of cognitive stages that users progress through during a typical exploratory data analysis task. The model was created based on a series of interviews and observations of intelligence analysts performing their professional jobs. This model has been widely adopted by the visual analytics and information visualization community given its applicability to many of the tasks these technologies support.

However, the studies which created this model used static data. Thus, there is an inherent assumption that the data is constant during the immediate analysis session. Further, the design of many visual analytic techniques assert that the dataset remains unchanged throughout the analysis. This raises the important questions of: how do the cognitive reasoning processes of analysts change when data is changing or streaming? what design principles become critical to the success of visual analytic techniques intended to function on non-static data?

In this paper we present the results of a user study examining the impact of streaming data on sensemaking and visual data exploration. We are primarily interested in understanding how introducing new data impacts an ongoing sensemaking task. Our study observed two conditions of the same dataset (static and streaming conditions). For both conditions, the study consisted of 5 one-hour sessions spread over 5 days. The static condition was given the entire dataset at the beginning, while the streaming condition had new data introduced at each session. Finally, we present a set of design guidelines for future visual analytic tools for streaming data.

The primary contributions of this paper are: (i) the results of a user study showing the impact of streaming data on the sensemaking process, and (ii) design guidelines for future visual analytic techniques for streaming data.

Our findings give rise to the notion that streaming data requires tighter coupling between the sensemaking processes of users, and the analytic processes of systems. We show how this can be made possible through interaction techniques such as *semantic interaction* [5], where user interactions with the interface are interpreted by the system to steer the underlying analytic models. We illuminate this need through the results and discussion of the user studying comparing static to streaming data conditions.

## 2    Related Work

The research presented in this paper is grounded in prior work discussed below.

### 2.1    Sensemaking and Analytical Reasoning

Analyzing data for the purpose of gaining insight is largely a cognitive process. This process of increasing one's knowledge or understanding about a domain or phenomena through analyzing data has been widely studied. One commonly used concept to describe this process is sensemaking, a cognitive activity of gaining understanding about the world, through the analysis of data [28]. For example, Pirolli and Card depict the cognitive stages of sensemaking in a notional model called the "sensemaking loop" [24]. This model emphasizes the importance of foraging and extracting content from data, as well as synthesizing these pieces of data inter higher-level insights. This complex, iterative process entails generation and testing hypotheses, as well as more low-level data filtering and retrieval tasks. Sensemaking involves internalizing and understanding the information in the context of the person's experiences and prior knowledge. For instance Klein et al. describe the process as refining one's "data-frames" [18], where the refining and augmenting of one's understanding about a phenomena is explained through framing and re-framing. The fluidity of these tasks was more recently emphasized by Kang and Stasko [15], who comment that stages and tasks of sensemaking to not necessarily follow a given order, and people may switch between them at any given time. Zhang and Soergel [37] proposed an iterative sensemaking model to more fully describe the iterative nature of this synthesis process. This process is at times also called "signature discovery" [13].

### 2.2    Visual Text Analytics

Visual analytic systems have been developed in support of sensemaking for text corpora. These systems tactfully combine statistical and data analytic models with interactive visual interfaces to enable people to reason about their data [33]. Specific to text analytics, several prior examples exist. For instance, Jigsaw [31] provides people with multiple views generated from extracted terms and frequencies.

One common visual metaphor to support sensemaking is a spatial layout, or canvas. The fundamental grounding of this metaphor is the geospatial understanding people have of objects with relative geographic locations between each other (i.e., objects closer together are more similar) [30]. Andrews et al. found that providing analysts with the ability to manually organize information in a spatial workspace enabled them to extend their working memory for a sensemaking task [2]. They found that analysts created spatial constructs that represented knowledge artifacts corresponding to intermediate findings throughout the process (e.g., timelines, lists, piles, etc.). Shipman et al. coined this process of refining intermediate spatial structures over time as "incremental formalism" [29]. They discuss how people were better able to express their knowledge structures spatially because freely organizing information in space does not require people to explicitly specify what the construct means. For example, analysts can create piles or lists without specifying the parameters used to create them. For text analysis in particular, these spatial constructs have been shown to encode significant amounts of semantic information about an analyst's process and insights [9]. Examples of visual analytic applications built to enable users to manually create spatial data layouts that aid their analytical reasoning include Analyst's Workspace [3], the nSpace Sandbox [36], and others.

## 2.3   Streaming Data Visual Analytics

Streaming data is a growing challenge in the way of data complexity for visual analytics [11,25]. There are areas of related work for streaming data analytics, ranging from algorithmic advances to handle the technical challenges of incorporating additional data during runtime (e.g., [22]), to visualization techniques for showing data changes over time. Mansmann et al. describe the concept of "dynamic visual analytics" and point out that streaming data presents additional challenges over temporal data due to caching and other data storage challenges [19]. A key difference comes through the realization that streaming data (ranging for various speeds of data arrival or updates) has impacts on the human reasoning process, and thus the design of visualizations. Specific to streams of textual data, Rohrdantz et al. have enumerated and discussed several of the challenges [26].

For example, STREAMIT shows users a spatial clustering of text documents, where similarity functions are used to place similar documents near each other [1]. While this is a familiar technique for showing text visually (i.e., [35], this work showed how as new data is imported, it can be added to the existing clusters so that users can observe how the new information maps to existing user-defined clusters. Further, Fisher et al. demonstrate how both interaction and visualization designs specific for streaming data must be carefully considered [12].

Similarly, Stolper et al. have presented the concept of "progressive visual analytics" [32] to describe a visual analytic technique for giving users incremental results for queries of large, complex data. While not specific to streaming data, the key challenge approached by this work is to understand how to show users incomplete results of queries. With streaming data, the assumption that the data is "not yet compete" (and may never be) may hold true. Thus, some of their findings may be valuable to consider for the design of streaming data visual analytic systems.

# 3    Streaming Canvas Description

To study the impact of streaming data on sensemaking, we first created a visual analytic prototype that enables the analysis of streaming and static text datasets. The Streaming Canvas is a visual analytics tool for spatially organizing and analyzing textual datasets (see Figs. 2 and 3). The user interface consists mainly of a spatial workspace, or canvas, that enables people to create and organize groups of documents. Specifically, this visual analytic prototype supports streaming, or updating, datasets (i.e., datasets where incremental updates are periodically received).

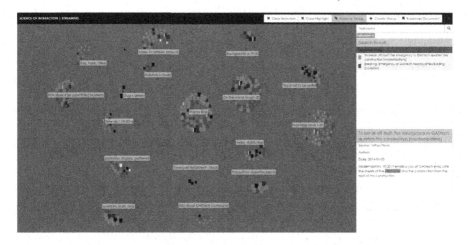

**Fig. 2.** The Streaming Canvas lets users group documents into user-defined clusters. The system adds new documents to these clusters based on similarity to existing documents.

## 3.1    Data Model and Import

The Streaming Canvas models documents using a vector space model similar to the data models used in many other visual analytic tools. We have adopted a model familiar to us from previous work. We provide a brief description here as background. The details of our model are more fully described in [27,35].

Each document is treated as a "bag of words" in that the model considers the presence of words, but not their sequence. The words are extracted and counted for each document, and the resulting counts are used to create a vector space.

Each document is assigned a numeric vector that can be interpreted as a set of coordinates specifying a position in the vector space. Such a vector can also be used as the basis for additional computation; for the Streaming Canvas, this is the key characteristic required of the vector space model.

In our particular model, the features in our vector consist of the top-scored 200 terms in the dataset, which we call topics (extracted and weighted using the entity extraction technique from Rose et al. [27]). These topics form the basis for the vector space, with each dimension corresponding to a topic term.

For the user study, the application augments the vector space model with an additional set of relevance weights for tracking user interest in topics. The application interprets some user interactions as indicators of interest in a document or documents, triggering a boost in the relevance weights for the dimensions most important for the document(s). The application immediately updates document badge sizes based on the modified weights. Subsequent vector space computations such as group assignment of new documents also account for the updated weights.

The application displays documents in groups that are statistical clusters within our vector space model. Our data model makes the group assignments for the initial set of documents on the basis of X-Means clustering [23]. Each group has a centroid vector that is the mean of the vectors for its documents. The application uses multidimensional scaling to convert these n-dimensional centroid vectors to the 2D coordinates in the display space.

The Streaming Canvas is intended to import, process, and display an initial set of documents, to be followed by zero or more increments of additional documents. The description of how streaming data is handled by the system is described in a later section.

## 3.2   User Interface

The Streaming Canvas is presented as a single-page Web application. The user interface consists of a canvas pane, a reading pane, and a menu bar (shown in Fig. 2). The primary visualization component of this interface is the canvas. The canvas represents documents as small rectangles, grouped based on similarity. The reading pane presents details about selections, including the text of the current document (if any). The menu bar contains additional operations and the application title.

The canvas shows documents appear as rectangular icons against a gray background (we refer to these as "badges"). Documents are clustered into roughly circular groups. The application assigns each document one of four badge sizes, where the size represents content magnitude as measured using the vector space model (normalized for document length). Each such group is labeled with gray text on a white central badge. Each label consists of a small number of prominent features computed based on the text content of the group's documents (shown in Fig. 3).

The application also positions the group badges relative to each other such that proximity correlates to content similarity. The application positions document badges using a force-directed layout, so document badge proximity does not imply content similarity [14].

## 3.3  User Interactions

The Streaming Canvas supports a number of user interaction in the canvas, and other user interface components. Specifically, the canvas supports:

**Selecting a group** - The user clicks on a group badge to select a group and all documents belonging to that group. The document badges become highlighted in orange. The document titles are listed in the reading pane.

**Selecting a document** - The user clicks on a document to select an individual document. That document's title is listed in the reading pane's document list, and selected, causing the document text to be displayed in the lower part of the pane. The document is colored blue in both the canvas and list.

**Moving a group** - The user can drag a group to any empty space on the Canvas, to move the group (and its documents) there.

**Moving a document** - The user can drag a document badge from one group and drop it on another group's badge, changing the group assignment of the document.

**Panning, Zooming** - The user can pan and zoom on the canvas.

The reading pane supports the following user interactions:

**Selecting a document** - The user clicks on a title in the Document List. The application displays the text for that document in the lower part of the pane.

**Highlighting** - The user drag-selects a passage in the document text, causing the passage to be highlighted. The application also bookmarks the document.

**Searching** - The user searches by typing a search query into the search box. The application highlights the resulting documents' badges in orange and lists their titles in the Document List.

The menu bar provides for the following user interactions:

**Renaming a group** - The user replaces the label via a dialog.

**Creating a new group** - A new group badge will appear in the canvas. The new group will initially contain no documents.

**Bookmarking the current document** - The application decorates the document's badge with a green vertical stripe, both in the document list and the canvas.

The user interaction design for the Streaming Canvas follows previously-established *semantic interaction* principles. Semantic interaction is an approach to interaction design for visual analytic tools that tightly couples exploratory user interaction with analytic model steering [8]. In prior work, examples of this coupling include using interactions such as highlighting phrases of text and grouping documents as a means to steer underlying dimension reduction, entity extraction [8], and information retrieval models [4]. User studies of semantic interaction show that this coupling of user interaction with model steering provides a good match between the insights users have during analysis and the parameterization of the model over time [6]. In general, the design decision to use semantic interaction stems from the intended functionality of the system being grouping and spatial organization of documents. For these tasks, specifically, semantic interaction has been shown to be effective [7]. Finally, the document and feature vectors systematically generated help in the data analysis stages of the study.

The Streaming Canvas implements semantic interactions as follows. Some of the user interactions afforded in the user interface directly correspond to data model updates. Of the user interactions listed above, the two that are coupled to model steering operations are: moving a document from one cluster to another, and bookmarking a document. The resulting model steering impacts document and feature weight vectors to update. These vectors are integrated into the clustering and entity extraction models described in Sect. 3.1, and therefore make them helpful for the spatial organization and grouping functions supported by the system.

In the case of moving a document from one group to another, the vectors involved are those of the document being moved, and the vectors for any documents already in the new group. The highest-magnitude features are selected for each such vector, using a threshold of 1.5 standard deviations above the mean. The weighting coefficient for each of those features is increased by 0.05. No features are down weighted. In the bookmarking case, the only vector involved is that of the bookmarked document. Otherwise the steering computation is exactly the same.

Additionally, as user interacts with the application, the appearance of documents evolves in subtle but noticeable ways. As a document is accessed more, its color may change. Darker shades indicate a greater amount of handling, following a smudge metaphor where more handling of a document makes it less pristine over time. Prior work has shown how this technique can be applied to graphical user interface widgets to indicate more commonly used functions [21].

Document sizes also evolve depending on use. The application interprets some user interactions as indicators of interest in some features in preference to others. It therefore tries to upweight content associated with the preferred features.

## 3.4   Incorporating Streaming Data

When a new set of documents arrives, the application assigns each new document to an existing user-generated or system-generated group. The application computes a term vector for the new document by extracting terms from new documents using the same method as the initial document import. Weights of these terms are assigned based on the term weights for the current dataset and state of the system. That is, if the user has steered the system to assign certain terms significantly more weight than others, those weights will carry over to the new documents. Then, the document is assigned to the nearest group in the vector space model, where distance is the Euclidean distance from the group centroid to the document term vector. The goal is to assign newly arriving documents to the user- or system-generated groups which most relate.

# 4    Study Description

The purpose of the study was to explore differences in sensemaking behaviors between user groups faced with an analysis task over a static document collection versus a streaming document collection. We did this via a between-subjects design, testing a streaming versus a static dataset using the Streaming Canvas prototype. Thus, the primary research question this study seeks to understand is *how does streaming data impact the cognitive process of sensemaking in a visual data analysis scenario?*

## 4.1    Task and Dataset

Each participant was given the same task, stated as "identify suspicious behavior of individuals or organizations contained in this dataset." This task embodies the canonical structure of a sensemaking task, emphasizing open-ended exploration and discovery.

The dataset used for this study consists of 378 short documents modeled after intelligence reports. These documents are a subset of the data from the VAST Challenge 2014 [34]. Documents are typically one or two paragraphs in length, and contain details of some event or action that a person saw that may be of interest to a larger group of analysts. This fictitious dataset describes the events of an island of Kronos where events have unfolded surrounding the kidnapping of 10 GASTech company employees. Two organizations, GASTech and Protectors of Kronos (POK), and their members are of primary interest. The data for analysis is a set of historic news articles spanning from 1982 to 2013 and news articles and blogs covering current events January 19, 20 and 21 of 2014. The dataset has a known ground truth used to evaluate the accuracy of findings by our participants. Also, the dataset includes several "dead ends", consisting of lines of investigation that seem relevant, but ultimately do not result in the correct answer to the task.

## 4.2    Procedure

Participants were asked to analyze the dataset (either streaming or static) over 5 days. In total, each participant analyzed a collection of 378 text documents with an available time of 4 h 15 min for analysis. The participation time was 1 h per day over a 5 day period with 30 min the first day for tool training and 15 min the last day for post-analysis interview. For analysis time, participants had 30 min on day 1, 1 h on days 2–4, and 45 min on day 5.

Users in both streaming and static conditions analyzed the exact same collection of documents but each group received subsets differently. All users received the same documents in the same sequence. The static group received an initial set of 95 historic documents which spanned approximately 20 years. On day 2, an additional 283 documents were added to the visual analytics tool. On subsequent days, the dataset remained static and no new documents were introduced.

For the streaming condition, users received the same initial set of 95 historic documents on day 1. On day 2, they received an increment of 18 new documents. On days 3, 4, and 5, they received an increments of 83, 139, and 43 documents respectively. The binning of these documents was based on the clean monthly breaks in the temporality of the dataset. Each participant was given a 10 min tutorial on day 1 demonstrating the functionality of the Streaming Canvas software. A one page "cheat sheet" was provided to act as an aid to remind users of the meaning the visual encodings and query syntax options.

On day 1, both static and streaming user groups are asked to "Organize and understand this document set to become familiar with the history of the POK, GASTech, and of the region overall." For subsequent days, streaming users are to "Monitor and explain the activity and events unfolding over the next 3 days" while static users are to "Explain the activity and events which have unfolded over the past 3 days."

### 4.3   Participant Demographics

We recruited and randomly assigned participants into one of two groups: static or streaming. We recruited 9 volunteers (6 male), aged 21 to 36, with a range of modest data analysis and analysis tool experience. Volunteers had degrees in criminal justice, mathematics, operations research, computer science, civil engineering. We had 3 PhD students, 1 Master's student, 1 Bachelor's student, and 4 post-Bachelors.

A total of 11 people were recruited to participate in the study of which 9 were able to fully participate (5 performing the streaming condition, 4 the static). Partial data from 2 participants was excluded from any analysis because they were unable to participate for the full period of time. Participants with odd numbered identifiers are members of the static data condition while participants with even numbered identifiers are members of the streaming data condition. User01 and User05 (both in the static data condition) did not complete the study and were excluded from the analysis and results.

### 4.4   Data Capture and Analysis

We collected a variety of data to support the analysis of this study. For each trial, we recorded the audio and video of the participant for the entire duration. We also used screen recording to capture all the user interactions and visualization states of the system throughout the study. Further, the server uses a custom logging facility to capture every call made to server. Some state information from the data model is also logged for events, in order to provide additional context for analysis. Specifically we logged the term weight vectors for the cluster centroids so that we can analyze the content in the cluster compared to the cluster centroid. Throughout the study, one investigator was present to administer the think-aloud approach, taking notes and observing the participants. Finally, at the conclusion of the study, we administered a verbal questionnaire to ask about their findings and process. We analyzed all of this data to more fully understand the sensemaking process of each participant and condition, as described in the results section below.

## 5   Results

We present the results of the user study as follows. We describe how the system was used by each condition (streaming compared to static). This includes a description of the user' interactions and functionality of the system. Second, we describe how users in the two conditions leveraged spatial constructs, groups, and other affordances to organize and analyze their information in the workspace.

### 5.1   User Interactions Performed

The participants were tasked with using the Streaming Canvas visual analytics tool to build an understanding of the history and current unfolding events in the dataset. The Streaming Canvas supports a collection of user interaction which allow the user to accomplish this task. Interactions include selecting document full text to read, executing a keyword search, labeling a group of documents, and several more. As the user performs interactions during the course of analysis, these are logged (see Table 1).

**Table 1.** Overview of interactions performed. Total indicates the number of times each interaction was performed by all users over the duration of the study. Averages indicate how many times, on average, a user in each condition performed the interactions.

| Interaction type | Total | Avg. streaming | Avg. static |
|---|---|---|---|
| Get document | 8964 | 1065 | 910 |
| Search | 889 | 116 | 78 |
| Move Doc to group | 875 | 146 | 36 |
| Re-position group | 860 | 114 | 72 |
| Label group | 123 | 19 | 7 |
| Bookmark document | 118 | 10 | 17 |
| Create group | 90 | 14 | 5 |
| Annotate document | 55 | 4 | 8 |

On average, users working in the streaming data scenario performed more interactions of most types compared to users working with static data. Static data users only performed more bookmarking and annotating interactions (see Table 1). These are raw totals and averages. Given the small population size, no statistical significance is computed.

## 5.2    Spatial Constructs Created

The Streaming Canvas visualization allowed users to create named groups of documents as a mechanism to externalize and aid in their sensemaking. Based on prior work on "incremental formalism", the Streaming Canvas does not require users to explicitly specify the label or analytic reasoning associated with a group [29]. Instead, users can create and modify group labels, and group membership, through a more informal process. Across all users, groupings of documents were created for a variety of reasons but some commonalities emerged. Groups were formed around metadata such as document publication date and news source. Groups were also formed around an entity or topic. Groups for low value documents was created by 4 of the 9 users with labels like "junk", "trash", "less informative", and "too small". Lastly, one user created groups labeled explicitly for evidence to be gathered related to hypotheses.

We analyzed the labels of these user-created groups into concepts. These concepts (shown below) were created based on the meaning that our participants applied to these groups during their investigation. We derived these based on the data collected during the think-aloud protocol, and show examples of labels applied by participants.

User-generated group labels observed during this study include:

*Entity-centric:* "Karel", "Background on POK"
*Topic-centric:* "Pollution in Elodis", "Plane that left"

**Fig. 3.** Study participant User10 made extensive use of document groups representing time periods. Space was used to arrange these groups temporally with recent events at the top ranging to historic groups at the bottom.

*Date-centric:* "Jan 19 Details", "Late 1/20"
*Source-centric:* "Breaking", "Voices"
*Low Value:* "Junk", "Trash", "Less Informative"
*Evidence:* "H1 Evidence"

In the Streaming Canvas, users could re-position groups anywhere in the two dimensional space as they saw fit. While many users had document groups representing important dates, these groups were often not organized in temporal order within the space. However, a strong use of space to represent time emerged with two users, User2 and User10. In both cases, time was encoded vertically. User10 created a 2 column layout with groups for recent events at the top and groups for older dates descended down (see Fig. 3). User2 organized groups temporally using the vertical space as well but with older groups at the top and recent events at the bottom.

## 5.3 Grouping Documents

The Streaming Canvas provides several interactions in support of manipulating groupings of documents. Users can create a group, label a group, re-position a group, and move a document into a group. This subset of interactions lets the user organize the documents to fit their mental model and externalize their thinking as a cognitive aid.

The streaming data users performed notably more group-related interactions than the static data users. Looking at document moves into groups day-by-day shows that streaming users performed this interaction more on days where larger numbers of documents are streamed into the visualization (see Fig. 4).

**Document Move Count per Day by User**

|  | Day1 | Day2 | Day3 | Day4 | Day5 | Grand Total |
|---|---|---|---|---|---|---|
| ⊟ Streaming | 36 | 102 | 240 | 287 | 65 | 730 |
| User02 | 8 | 19 | 96 | 124 | 46 | 293 |
| User04 | 4 | 52 | 84 | 45 | 2 | 187 |
| User06 |  | 3 | 36 | 105 | 12 | 156 |
| User10 | 3 | 28 | 24 | 13 | 5 | 73 |
| User08 | 21 |  |  |  |  | 21 |
| ⊟ Static | 7 | 29 | 36 | 23 | 50 | 145 |
| User03 | 6 | 5 | 23 | 13 | 1 | 48 |
| User05 | 1 |  | 8 |  | 49 | 58 |
| User11 |  | 24 |  |  |  | 24 |
| User09 |  |  | 5 | 10 |  | 15 |

**Fig. 4.** Document move interactions per day by user shows notably more for users in the streaming data scenario.

## 5.4 Interaction Sequences

Exploring the interaction sequences provided an interesting view into user sensemaking patterns. Sequence diagrams were generated for all interactions on all days grouped by user and data scenario. Figure 5 gives an example which includes a legend for interaction type encoded in each data point. Each column represents

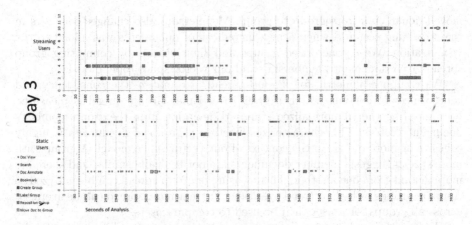

**Fig. 5.** An interaction sequence diagrams displaying when users performed interactions. User IDs are on the y-axis, with interactions (encoded by color and size) shown across the time of day 3 of the study. (Color figure online)

a study participant with each data point representing an interaction performed at a point in time during the user's analysis session. Time is represented vertically in seconds from start of the analysis session.

We posit that interaction types relate to the two major loops within Pirolli and Card's model of sensemaking [24] (foraging and synthesis) shown in Fig. 1. Triaging interactions such as Search, Read, Bookmark, and Annotate relate to foraging. While grouping interactions such as create, label, re-position, and move document relate to synthesis.

This mapping to the foraging and synthesis loops was included in the interaction sequence diagrams using smaller icons for foraging and larger for synthesis (Fig. 1). Visual patterns in the sequence diagrams show periods of foraging where users focus primarily on searching and reading. While other time periods show intense synthesis behavior with sequences of group manipulation interactions occurring. This is consistent with the sensemaking literature that indicates users performing foraging and synthesis in iteration. However, we found that users performing sensemaking on streaming data perform far more interactions to perform their task.

During user study observation on day 3, User2 expressed as the end of the allotted time approached that they were going to "get things organized for tomorrow". This was a notable statement from a user doing analysis on streaming data. The interaction sequence diagrams show that several of the streaming users performed more grouping-related interactions in the latter portion of their analysis time (see Fig. 5).

## 5.5 Group Spread

During the course of their analysis, users would group documents together as they saw fit. Document membership to groups would fluctuate over time as users moved documents from group to group. Membership also changed for users in the streaming scenario when a new increment of documents was added to the visualization. We characterized groups and their change by computing group spread given document membership and our vector space topic model.

We compute a metric for "group spread" to analyze the consistency and cohesiveness of content within a group over time. Group spread is measured by computing the L1 normalized standard deviation from the group member's document vectors. This characterizes whether a group of documents is highly cohesive or more diffuse in the context of our vector space model. A group with more spread suggests member documents are not topically similar and therefore more distant from one another. This measure of group spread can be analyzed to compare groups or look at trend over time. Furthermore, spread can be averaged across all groups for a user then be used to compare users.

We hypothesized that low value groups with labels such as "Junk" or "Trash" would exhibit higher relative measures of spread. For User06, a plot of group spread over time showed that the group labeled "Junk" was created about midway through analysis. Spread for the "Junk" group increased over the remainder of the analysis time to eventually become the most diffuse group which supports our hypothesis (see Fig. 6).

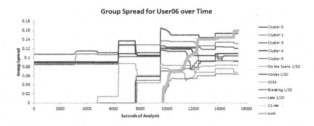

**Fig. 6.** Group spread for User06's groups over the course of their analysis shows the "Junk" group becoming increasingly diffuse.

An interesting pattern across users is observed when mean group spread is plotted over time for the streaming users. Not surprisingly, when an increment of new documents is introduced there is a jump in mean group spread. Then generally as the user manages group document membership in support of their analysis, mean group spread decreases. Groups become on average more cohesive as analysis progresses (see Fig. 7). This may indicate that the organization of information became more consistent and structured over time. In context of sensemaking, this echoes the iterative progression of internalizing and understanding information. As we found, streaming data has a way of disrupting that process, yet users adjusted over time to compensate for this.

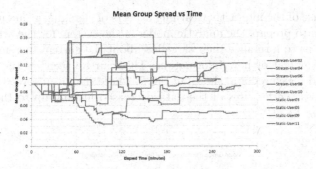

**Fig. 7.** Mean document group spread over time for users in the streaming versus static data condition. New data was introduced at roughly times: 50, 110, 170, 220.

# 6   Implications for Design

Users repeated several activities while performing analysis under steaming data conditions. While the Streaming Canvas successfully supported some of these analysis activities, there is certainly room for improvement in both the visualization and interaction design to fully support sensemaking for streaming data. We observed users progressively iterating through three phases. These include (1) thinking about current data, (2) organizing information in anticipation of more data, and (3) integrating new data into their thinking. These observed analysis activities have implication for design of future streaming visual analytics tools.

When users were given a collection of documents, they would spend time consuming the information to make sense of it. Users performed a variety of interactions to explore documents and externalize their thinking. Reading and searching were the most common interactions. Users would take notes in an accompanying Word document as they discovered key information sometimes copying and pasting snippets of text. Users would also bookmark important documents or annotate specific words, phrases or paragraphs. While these features were used as thinking aides, additions should be considered. Users requested the ability to resize the icon representing a document to convey importance, add notes directly to the Canvas, and draw connecting lines between documents. These suggest the need for features which allow a users to further integrate their knowledge into the visual metaphor, beyond the forming of groups and editing of group membership spatially.

As the analytic processes of the users progressed, they started organizing documents by forming groups and appling meaningful labels to create some higher-level structure. Users formed groups which ranged greatly in precision of definition. Some groups had precise definition such as all documents from a news source, a date range, or contained a specific keyword or name. Other groups were more informal where they revolved around a theme such as "POK violence" or "environmental effects". In anticipation of receiving new documents, users refined document membership within groups and spatially arranged groups.

They made use of the interactive learning aspects of changing group membership of documents to prepare the analytic model in the system for the arrival of new data, as well as to formalize their thoughts about the current increment of data prior to the arrival of new information. This can be seen by the amount of cluster spread measured and shown in Fig. 7, where the mean spread of a cluster centroid across the features of the data decreased leading up to the arrival of new data (Fig. 8).

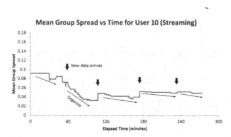

**Fig. 8.** The behavior of User 10 (from the streaming condition) shows interactions which decreased mean group spread over time before new documents arrive.

With the arrival of new documents, the Streaming Canvas mapped these documents into the user's existing groups which represent an externalization of their mental models. Our technical approach used a nearest neighbor measure to decide group assignments for new documents. While this worked in some cases such a topic-centric groups, document assignment did not always match the user's expectations. For more precisely defined groups such as source or date-centric groups, new documents would "contaminate" these groups as they did not match a user's specific and under-specified meaning for the cluster. The user would then spend time cleaning up these groups and moving documents elsewhere. The system and user would have benefited from support for optionally defining groups with precise queries when the users reached a state of formalism about the meaning of a cluster where they could directly specify it.

## 7   Discussion

The ways by which people use space as a means for organizing information has been widely studied for situations where the data (or physical objects) do not change [2,9,17,20,29]. From these studies, we learn that people create spatial constructs and fluid spatial arrangements as an inherent part of their process. For example, some of the groupings reflect process-specific artifacts, such as "todo lists", incremental knowledge structures such as groups of important documents, and in the physical example the methods by which a mechanic organizes the parts on the shop floor gives him or her spatial cues to remember how to re-assemble the components. For each of these, the persistence of the information (both in the spatial location, and as the complete set of the items) provided people the cues to recall aspects of their process or knowledge associated with that information.

However, in this study we observed how data that is changing over time impacts this ability for people to offload parts of their process and working memory into spatial constructs. Our results indicate important distinctions in terms of the canvas usage. Primarily, one of the differences was found in the activities that people perform to "prepare" for the new data. For example, we found users spending more time and effort to organize and label groups so that they would be better able to recall their current state of the investigation when returning the next day to their spatial workspace with additional information.

Our current design decision in the Streaming Canvas was to place the new documents in the labeled group that is most related (based on the term weighting). However, other design alternatives exist. For example, one might choose to create an "inbox-like" view that shows new data, and has the user decide where to place the information. This could be potentially overwhelming when too much new data arrives at any given time increment.

We contend that designers and developers of visual analytic systems for streaming data should take into consideration additional affordances for people to do this "preparation" for new data. The Streaming Canvas allowed for user-defined spatial locations of groups and group labels. This allows people an implicit way to blend the new data with the current investigation state. However, in future iterations of such tools, visual analytic researchers may want to consider other, more explicit techniques for people to inform the system of where they want the new data to visually appear, which data to ignore, and how to prioritize which sub-sets of the new data he or she should read first.

## 8   Conclusion

Visual data analysis is an effective approach for giving people a greater understanding of their data through techniques such as data visualization and visual analytics. By offloading complex cognitive tasks in part to peoples' perceptual systems, visualizations enable people to think (and interact with) their data. This process is often referred to as sensemaking.

However, much of the work on understanding this cognitive task, and the development of visual analytic systems, has been focused on static datasets. While iteration is assumed and depicted in many popular sensemaking models, the fundamental assumption and study design of much prior research is that all the data to analyze is present at the beginning of a study, and that this set of data does now change. The study presented in this paper seeks to understand how incorporating the assumption that data will update over time impacts sensemaking.

We built a prototype streaming text visual analytics tool, called Streaming Canvas, to test this effect. We compared streaming and static conditions of people analyzing a dataset intended to simulate a sensemaking task. Our results indicate that people in the streaming data condition are more explicit about tracking their analytic process than people analyzing static data. Streaming data analysts "prepared" their workspace for the arrival of new data, which required them to be more explicit about the status of their investigation. We believe that this, along with other findings, reveals important design guidelines for future streaming data visual analytic tools.

**Acknowledgments.** The research described in this paper is part of the Analysis In Motion Initiative and the Signature Discovery Initiative at Pacific Northwest National Laboratory. It was conducted under the Laboratory Directed Research and Development Program at PNNL, a multiprogram national laboratory operated by Battelle for the U.S. Department of Energy.

# References

1. Alsakran, J., Chen, Y., Zhao, Y., Yang, J., Luo, D.: STREAMIT: dynamic visualization and interactive exploration of text streams (2011)
2. Andrews, C., Endert, A., North, C.: Space to think: large high-resolution displays for sensemaking. In: Proceedings of the SIGCHI Conference on Human Factors in Computing Systems (CHI 2010), pp. 55–64 (2010)
3. Andrews, C., North, C.: Analyst's workspace: an embodied sensemaking environment for large, high-resolution displays. In: 2012 IEEE Conference on Visual Analytics Science and Technology (VAST), pp. 123–131 (2012)
4. Bradel, L., North, C., House, L.: Multi-model semantic interaction for text analytics. In: Proceedings of IEEE Conference on Visual Analytics Science and Technology (VAST 2014), pp. 163–172 (2014)
5. Endert, A.: Semantic interaction for visual analytics: inferring analytical reasoning for model steering. Synth. Lect. Vis. 4(2), 1–99 (2016)
6. Endert, A., Chang, R., North, C., Zhou, M.: Semantic interaction: coupling cognition and computation through usable interactive analytics. IEEE Comput. Graph. Appl. 35(4), 94–99 (2015)
7. Endert, A., Fiaux, P., North, C.: Semantic interaction for sensemaking: inferring analytical reasoning for model steering. In: IEEE Conference on Visual Analytics Science and Technology (2012)
8. Endert, A., Fiaux, P., North, C.: Semantic interaction for visual text analytics. In: Proceedings of the SIGCHI Conference on Human Factors in Computing Systems (CHI 2012), pp. 473–482 (2012)
9. Endert, A., Fox, S., Maiti, D., Leman, S.C., North, C.: The Semantics of Clustering: Analysis of User-Generated Spatializations of Text Documents (2012)
10. Endert, A., Hossain, M.S., Ramakrishnan, N., North, C., Fiaux, P., Andrews, C.: The human is the loop: new directions for visual analytics. J. Intell. Inf. Syst. 1–25 (2014)
11. Endert, A., Pike, W.A., Cook, K.: From streaming data to streaming insights: the impact of data velocities on mental models (2012)
12. Fischer, F., Mansmann, F., Keim, D.A.: Real-time visual analytics for event data streams. In: Proceedings of the 27th Annual ACM Symposium on Applied Computing, SAC 2012, pp. 801–806. ACM, New York (2012)
13. Jolaoso, S., Burtner, R., Endert, A.: Toward a deeper understanding of data analysis, sensemaking, and signature discovery. In: Abascal, J., Barbosa, S., Fetter, M., Gross, T., Palanque, P., Winckler, M. (eds.) INTERACT 2015. LNCS, vol. 9297, pp. 463–478. Springer, Cham (2015). doi:10.1007/978-3-319-22668-2_36

14. Kamada, T., Kawai, S.: An algorithm for drawing general undirected graphs. Inf. Process. Lett. **31**(1), 7–15 (1989)
15. Kang, Y.-A., Stasko, J.: Characterizing the intelligence analysis process: informing visual analytics design through a longitudinal field study (2011)
16. Keim, D., Andrienko, G., Fekete, J.-D., Görg, C., Kohlhammer, J., Melançon, G.: Visual analytics: definition, process, and challenges. In: Kerren, A., Stasko, J.T., Fekete, J.-D., North, C. (eds.) Information Visualization. LNCS, vol. 4950, pp. 154–175. Springer, Heidelberg (2008). doi:10.1007/978-3-540-70956-5_7
17. Kirsh, D.: The intelligent use of space. Artif. Intell. **73**(1–2), 31–68 (1995)
18. Klein, G., Moon, B., Hoffman, R.: Making sense of sensemaking 2: a macrocognitive model. IEEE Intell. Syst. **21**(5), 88–92 (2006)
19. Mansmann, F., Fischer, F., Keim, D.A.: Dynamic visual analytics–facing the real-time challenge. In: Dill, J., Earnshaw, R., asik, D., Vince, J., Wong, P.C. (eds.) Expanding the Frontiers of Visual Analytics and Visualization, pp. 69–80. Springer, Heidelberg (2012)
20. Marshall, C.C.: Spatial hypertext: designing for change. **38**, 88–97
21. Matejka, J., Grossman, T., Fitzmaurice, G.: Patina: dynamic heatmaps for visualizing application usage. In: Proceedings of the SIGCHI Conference on Human Factors in Computing Systems, CHI 2013, pp. 3227–3236. ACM, New York (2013)
22. O'callaghan, L., Meyerson, A., Motwani, R., Mishra, N., Guha, S.: Streaming-data algorithms for high-quality clustering. In: ICDE, p. 0685. IEEE (2002)
23. Pelleg, D., Moore, A.W.: X-means: extending k-means with efficient estimation of the number of clusters. In: Proceedings of the Seventeenth International Conference on Machine Learning, ICML 2000, pp. 727–734. Morgan Kaufmann Publishers Inc., San Francisco, CA, USA (2000)
24. Pirolli, P., Card, S.: The sensemaking process and leverage points for analyst technology as identified through cognitive task analysis. Proc. Int. Conf. Intell. Anal. **5**, 2–4 (2005)
25. Robertson, G., Ebert, D., Eick, S., Keim, D., Joy, K.: Scale and complexity in visual analytics. Inf. Vis. **8**(4), 247–253 (2009)
26. Rohrdantz, C., Oelke, D., Krstajic, M., Fischer, F.: Real-time visualization of streaming text data: tasks and challenges (2011)
27. Rose, S., Engel, D., Cramer, N., Cowley, W.: Automatic Keyword Extraction from Individual Documents. Wiley, Hoboken (2010). pp. 1–20
28. Russell, D.M., Slaney, M., Qu, Y., Houston, M.: Being literate with large document collections: observational studies and cost structure tradeoffs, p. 55. IEEE Computer Society (2006). 1109739
29. Shipman, F.M., Marshall, C.C.: Formality considered harmful: experiences, emerging themes, and directions on the use of formal representations in interactive systems. Comput. Support. Coop. Work (CSCW) **8**(4), 333–352 (1999)
30. Skupin, A.: A cartographic approach to visualizing conference abstracts. IEEE Comput. Graph. Appl. **22**, 50–58 (2002)
31. Stasko, J., Goerg, C., Liu, Z.: Jigsaw: supporting investigative analysis through interactive visualization. Inf. Vis. **7**(118–132), 2 (2008)
32. Stolper, C.D., Perer, A., Gotz, D.: Progressive visual analytics: user-driven visual exploration of in-progress analytics. IEEE Trans. Vis. Comput. Graph. **20**(12), 1653–1662 (2014)
33. Thomas, J.J., Cook, K.A.: Illuminating the path: the research and development agenda for visual analytics. IEEE Computer Society Press (2005)

34. Whiting, M., Cook, K., Grinstein, G., Liggett, K., Cooper, M., Fallon, J., Morin, M.: Vast challenge 2014: the kronos incident. In: 2014 IEEE Conference on Visual Analytics Science and Technology (VAST), pp. 295–300, October 2014

35. Wise, J.A., Thomas, J.J., Pennock, K., Lantrip, D., Pottier, M., Schur, A., Crow, V.: Visualizing the non-visual: spatial analysis and interaction with information for text documents. pp. 442–450. Morgan Kaufmann Publishers Inc, Burlington (1999). 300791

36. Wright, W., Schroh, D., Proulx, P., Skaburskis, A., Cort, B.: The sandbox for analysis: concepts and methods, pp. 801–810. ACM (2006)

37. Zhang, P., Soergel, D., Klavans, J.L., Oard, D.W.: Extending sense-making models with ideas from cognition and learning theories. Proc. Am. Soc. Inf. Sci. Technol. **45**(1), 23 (2008)

# Some Syntax-Only Text Feature Extraction and Analysis Methods for Social Media Data

Monte Hancock[1], Charles Li[2], Shakeel Rajwani[3(✉)], Payton Brown[3],
Olivia Hancock[3], Corinne Lee[3], Yaniv Savir[3], Nicolas Nuon[3],
and Francesca Michaels[3]

[1] 4Digital Inc., Webster University, Melbourne, FL, USA
[2] Mercy College, Dobbs Ferry, NY, USA
[3] Sirius 17B Team, Melbourne, FL, USA
Shakeel.Rajwani@gmail.com

**Abstract.** Automated characterization of online social behavior is becoming increasingly important as day-to-day human interaction migrates from expensive "real world" encounters to less expensive virtual interactions over computing networks. The effective automated characterization of human interaction in social media has important political, economic, social applications.

New analytic concepts are presented for the extraction and enhancement of salient numeric features from unstructured text. These concepts employ relatively simple syntactic metrics for characterizing and distinguishing human and automated social media posting behaviors. The concepts are domain agnostic, and are empirically demonstrated using posted text from a particular social medium (Twitter).

An innovation uses a feature-imputation regression method to perform feature sensitivity analysis.

**Keywords:** Twitter · Text processing · Social media · Feature selection

## 1 Background

The characterization of text threads in social media can be done using either or both of syntactic methods (e.g., "bag-of-words"), and semantic methods (e.g., Latent Semantic Indexing). Syntactic methods are much more mature and usually much less complex than semantic methods. For the purposes of this work, syntactic methods will refer to fundamentally distributional techniques that do not rely on semantic mapping. Syntactic methods will be those that do not require parsing, resolution of pronominal reference, geotagging, dictionary lookups, etc., but derive their results from term statistics.

Note: A "social medium" is defined here as any venue supporting public-access pseudo-anonymous self-initiated asynchronous data sharing.

© Springer International Publishing AG 2017
D.D. Schmorrow and C.M. Fidopiastis (Eds.): AC 2017, Part I, LNAI 10284, pp. 499–509, 2017.
DOI: 10.1007/978-3-319-58628-1_37

## 2  The Venue: Twitter

The empirical demonstrations done during this research focuses on the characterization of user-generated content on Twitter, one of the simpler social media domains.

Twitter users submit ("post") time-ordered sequences of text (called "tweets", maximum of 140 text characters) through a simple text-window interface. These are made available to other Twitter users in several ways (e.g., "friending", "following").

The term thread refers to a time-ordered sequence of tweets posted by a particular user. Aggregation is facilitated by each user's unique User Id number (a 1 to 17 digit positive integer) and a tweet time-stamp (epoch time). Tweets are not point-to-point communications; they generally function as personal status updates, but also frequently contain opinions about social issues, and items of general cultural interest (movies, sports, politics, world events, etc.) Twitter does not filter tweets for content (e.g., vulgarisms, hate speech).

The simplicity and lack of content constraints also makes Twitter an attractive venue for advertising, subscription services (e.g., weather/traffic reports, alerts), and other automated content. Tweets can contain any combination of free text, emoticons, chat-speak, hash tags, and URL's. Because Tweets can contain URL's, they can be malware vectors.

## 3  Types of Natural Language Text

Depending upon the type and amount of embedded structure used to present text, it is said to fall into two broad categories:

Structured text is text data that is organized into labeled units. The units are often referred to as "fields". The labels are referred to as "metadata", and give contextual information about the field (e.g., what data the field contains, its metric units and ranges, what the data "mean", etc.)

Unstructured text is text data that is not organized into labeled units. In particular, unstructured text has relatively little embedded metadata. The content must provide its own context.

## 4  The Data Source

Twitter maintains a website for servicing data requests posted by those holding Twitter Developer credentials. Developers obtain these credentials through an online application process.

Credentialed developers may request information for Twitter user accounts by posting requests to the Twitter API (application program interface) at a URL (uniform resource locator) provided by Twitter. Requests can be made for specific accounts based upon their User Identification Numbers. Requests can also be made for random samples of accounts selected by Twitter. Requested data are returned as a hierarchical data structure called JSON (JavaScript Object Notation).

## 5 Data Form

Data for this work consist of the threads for 8,845 users, each having at least one tweet, and no more than 200 tweets. The users were randomly selected by Twitter from its international user base. Most, but not all, tweets used are in English.

## 6 Text Data Ground Truth Tagging

Tweet text for 101 user threads was evaluated manually by a team of English-speaking readers, all experienced users of social media. Because the intention is to model the perceptions of human content consumers, readers were instructed not to collaborate, and to use their personal intuition to decide which of the threads they reviewed were likely the result of human posting behaviors, and which were likely the result of automated posting (BOT's). Ten readers participated, with each of the threads evaluated by at least 2 readers.

Sixty-five of the 101 threads were tagged as either "human generated" or "BOT generated" by majority vote of the readers of that thread. That experienced readers could not agree on the tagging of 36 out of 101 threads illustrates the difficulty of ground-truth assignment in this domain.

## 7 Extrapolation of Ground Truth Tags

The BOT-NotBOT tags from the 65 manually tagged threads were extrapolated to the larger corpus of 8,845 threads using a population-weighted N-Nearest Neighbor Classifier having the 65-thread set as the standard. N was allowed to vary from 1 to 20; the tagging for N = 5 was chosen for the extrapolation, because it best matched the class proportions of the 65-thread standard.

Following Hancock et al. [4], several angles-only metrics were used to project each feature vector into a low (nominally 4–8) dimensional Euclidean space for visualization and analysis.

## 8 The Content Data Elements and Their Encoding

The text constituting each of the 8,845 user threads was rolled up into a normalized 23-dimensional numeric feature vector quantifying certain low-level syntactic user posting behaviors the user (more complete description below).

Below are linguistic attributes that our team felt would be useful for discriminating automated posting behaviors from human posting behaviors. These attributes provide the rationale for the features that were encoded from the twitter text. The resulting features were used to generate mathematical "signatures" for online behaviors. In this way, they augment account-level demographic features (e.g., user time-zone, user language) to create a rich, high-fidelity information space for behavior mining and modeling.

1. The relative size and diversity of the account vocabulary
   Content generated by automated means tends to reuse complex terms, while naturally generated content has a more varied vocabulary, and terms reused are generally simpler.
2. The word length mean and variance
   Naturally generated content tends to use shorter but more varied language than automatically generated content.
3. The presence/percentage of chatspeak
   Casual, social users often employ simple, easy to generate graphical icons, called emoticons. Sophisticated non-social users tend to avoid these unsophisticated graphical icons.
4. The presence and frequency of hashtags
   Hash tags are essentially topic words. Several hash tags taken together amount to a tweet "gist". A table of these could be used for automated topic/content identification and categorization.
5. The number of misspelled words
   It is assumed that sophisticated content generators, such as major retailers, will have a very low incidence of misspellings relative to casual users who are typing on a small device like a phone or tablet.
6. The presence of vulgarity
   Major retailers are assumed to be unlikely to embed vulgarity in their content.
7. The use of hot-button words and phrases ("act now", "enter to win", etc.)
   Marketing "code words" are regularly used to communicate complex ideas to potential customers in just a few words. Such phrases are useful precisely because they are hackneyed.
8. The use of words rarely used by other accounts (e.g., Tf.Idf scores) [1]
   Marketing campaigns often create words around their products. These created words occur nowhere else, and so will have high Tf.Idf scores.
9. The presence of URLs
   To make a direct sale through a tweet, the customer must be engaged and directed to a location where a sale can be made. This is most easily accomplished by supplying a URL. URL's, even tiny URL's, can be automatically followed to facilitate screen scraping for identification/characterization.
10. The generation of redundant content (same tweets repeated multiple times)
    It is costly and difficult to generate unique content for each of thousands of online recipients. Therefore, automated content (e.g., advertising) tends to have a relatively small number of stylized units of content that they use over and over.

A vector of text features is derived for each user. This is accomplished by deriving text features for each of the user's tweets, then rolling them up. Therefore, one content feature vector is derived for each user from all of that user's tweets, as follows:

1. Collect the user's most recent (up to 200) tweet strings into a single set (a thread).
2. Convert the thread text to upper case for term matching.
3. Scan the thread for the presence of emoticons, chat-speak, hash tags, URL's, and vulgarisms, setting bits to indicate the presence/absence of each.

4. Remove special characters from the thread to facilitate term matching
   (a) Create a frequency histograms for the thread. Vocabulary word from a twitter word list. The bins represent the 5,000 most frequently used Twitter words, arranged in order of decreasing Twitter frequency.

5. Create a Redundancy Score for the Thread. This is done by computing and rolling up (sum and normalize) the pairwise similarities of the tweet strings within the thread using six metrics: Euclidean Distance, RMS-Distance, L1 Distance, L-Infinity Distance, Cosine Distance, and the norm-weighted average of the five distances.

6. The thread text feature vector then contains as vector components the emoticon flag, the chat-speak flag, the hash tag flag, he URL flag, the vulgarity flag, the Redundancy score, and the selected term histogram (Fig. 1).

| UID | Thread | PostInThread | Tweet |
|---|---|---|---|
| ANON_A | 1 | 1 | Up Next: Johnson & Johnson $JNJ #Baby #Powder #Talc #Ovarian #Cancer #Lawsuits https://t.co/KO9iV5YAlt |
| ANON_A | 1 | 2 | New United States Food and Drug Commissioner .@US_FDA Dr. Robert Califf Responsible for #KILLER $JNJ #Xarelto https://t.co/BNYVroR4Rb |
| ANON_A | 1 | 3 | Death by Johnson and Johnson $JNJ #Levaquin (levofloxacin) Anti-Biotic https://t.co/QDOqGkfoAs |
| ANON_A | 1 | 4 | United States Senate HELPless Committee https://t.co/bYEh42aE0P |
| ANON_A | 1 | 5 | Johnson and Johnson $JNJ #Risperdal US Black Box DEATH Warning for Elderly Dementia NOT Applied in Australia https://t.co/h064XWKM5q |
| ANON_A | 1 | 6 | Michelle Obama and the Johnson and Johnson $JNJ CEO Gorsky $5 Billion #Risperdal, Omnicare, #Medicaid #Scandal https://t.co/PjU27zTu1B |
| ANON_A | 1 | 7 | $70 Million Punitive Judgment Against Johnson & Johnson $JNJ Subsidiary #Ethicon https://t.co/CBcVdCirMh |
| ANON_A | 1 | 8 | Asthma Rates Reduce After Toxic Chems Removed from Johnson & Johnson $JNJ Baby Products https://t.co/98hS13BkNp |
| ANON_A | 1 | 9 | Why US Senate HELP Committee MUST SHUT DOWN Johnson and Johnson $JNJ https://t.co/7OqCuiiqX6 |
| ANON_A | 1 | 10 | Up Next: Johnson & Johnson $JNJ Baby Powder Talc Ovarian Cancer Lawsuits https://t.co/kZzZTRygh5 |
| ANON_B | 2 | 1 | #TheHuntsmanWintersWar is about as generic as it.s title #moviereview https://t.co/YNOMjL2Wn1 |
| ANON_B | 2 | 2 | Who wins the fight? #BatmanvSuperman #MovieReview https://t.co/l2Lw2BI3hg |
| ANON_B | 2 | 3 | #AWalkintheWoods was a pleasant movie that worked really well because of the great chemistry and banter between Redford and Nolte. |
| ANON_B | 2 | 4 | Despite the shitty reviews. I.ve got my ticket for tomorrow night. Still pumped to see it. #BatmanvSuperman |
| ANON_B | 2 | 5 | Finally rewatched #ManofSteel. Liked it even better this 2nd time around. I.m ready for some #BatmanvSuperman! |
| ANON_B | 2 | 6 | Why do I want to follow this douche w/a camera. Was just waiting for him to finally kick it. Go hangman! #TheGallows |
| ANON_B | 2 | 7 | #InfinitelyPolarBear is an interesting look at bipolar/manic depressive parenting. Really good performance by Ruffalo. |
| ANON_B | 2 | 8 | #Minions need to stick to comic relief. An entire movie of them is TOO MUCH! Boy, they started to get on my nerves. |
| ANON_B | 2 | 9 | Watching #HeNamedMeMalala made me feel like I.ve accomplished nothing. but the movie was so good. What an amazing, inspirational kid! |
| ANON_B | 2 | 10 | Better late than never. right? #Top10 of 2015: https://t.co/DKeHV8hPZT |
| ANON_B | 2 | 11 | Watched Ant-Man again. Luis is one of my favorite characters in the MCU. Hope we get more @realmichaelpena |
| ANON_B | 2 | 12 | #PaperTowns So. a bunch of HS kids can take a road trip from Orlando to NY w/o telling parents and no repercussions? #NotWhenIWasAKid |
| ANON_B | 2 | 13 | My kids eat a lot of nuggets....maybe I shouldn.t have watched #Cooties. |
| ANON_B | 2 | 14 | #TheRevenant is a beautiful and brutal film: https://t.co/2UI4Pi69xd |
| ANON_B | 2 | 15 | A different kind of top 10 for 2015 https://t.co/cgaXXavDkR |
| ANON_B | 2 | 16 | #TheSecondBestExoticMarigoldHotel lived up to it.s name by being second best |

**Fig. 1.** For the sake of definiteness and intuition building, the figure above shows actual tweet threads for two Twitter users.

# 9    Experiment 1: Feature Selection by Brute Force

Direct blind-evaluation of all $2^{23} = 8,388,608$ possible feature sets was performed to provide definitive feature evaluation.

When many columns of data are available, choosing the "right" ones to use is hard, for a number of reasons:

1. Having many columns means many "dimensions" when viewed geometrically
2. The data consist of columns that can interact in complicated ways. For example, two "weak" pieces of evidence together sometimes provide more information than one "strong" piece of evidence alone.
3. There are a huge number of possible combinations in which columns could be chosen/rejected as features for a data mining project, so it is time-consuming to check them all. For example, if there are 20 columns, there are $2^{20} - 1 > 1,000,000$ ways to choose which subset of features to use.

The information assessment begins by reading in the data to be analyzed, and computing the means and standard deviations for each of the ground truth classes. That is, the means and standard deviations are computed for each column for all the rows that are in ground truth class 1, giving the "center" and "variability" of the class 1 data; then, for class 2 rows, and so on.

To determine which columns contain information useful for classification of the data into its ground truth classes, all possible subsets of the available columns are tested; the subsets giving the best results with a weighted nearest-neighbor classifier are cataloged. The process proceeds as follows:

Step 1: Read in the data file containing the numericized feature data
Step 2: Segment the data file in calibration, training and validation files
Step 3: Compute the centroids, feature standard deviations calibration data
Step 4: Select a subset of the columns to test (a "clique")
Step 5: Use the centers and standard deviations computed in Phase A for the clique to assign each data point in the training segment to a class as depicted in Fig. 2.

Repeat steps 4 and 5 for all possible feature cliques. With 23 features, this is $2^{23} = 8,388,608$ unique feature representations of the data. The features in the "best" clique (had the highest accuracy score on the test set) are the ones that, as a group, have the most useful information for classification of those tested. This "winning team" comprises our selected feature set.

To create a numeric measure of the classification power of a subset of the available features, this very fast weighted nearest-neighbor classifier is run repeatedly on a calibration set with various sets of features, and the best collection is remembered. Also, if the same feature appears in many high-performing feature sets, it is reasonable to conclude that it is probably "good". In this way, the clustering algorithm described here is used to "game" feature sets in a "Monte Carlo" fashion.

The spreadsheet below shows the classification power of various feature sets. In the table below, "1" means that columns feature was present in that set, while "0" means it was not. In this experiment, only the 2,500 highest blind-accuracy feature sets were cataloged. This output gives the performance measures for all of them so the user can see the value of including/excluding the various feature combinations (Fig. 3).

Each feature clique is a row; a "0" means that feature was not used in that clique, excluded, and a "1" means that feature was used in that clique. Performance for each clique is in columns 2 and 3. The bottom row shows the proportion of the top 2,500 cliques that used the feature in the corresponding column. For example, the feature indicating the use of adjectives was used in 72.7% of the 2,500 best feature sets. This provides a relative ranking of features with respect to how they contribute in context.

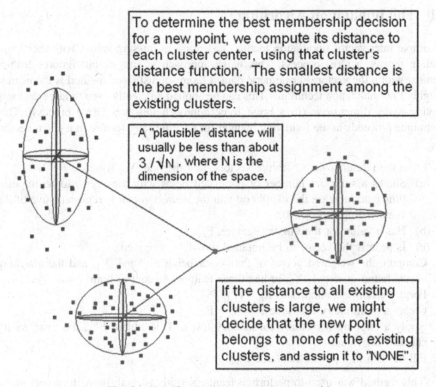

**Fig. 2.** Classification by nearest class centroid

| Fea COUNT | fmeasure | %Acc | tweets | adj | adv | art | comm | conj | interj | prep | pron | Propn | verb | stopword | vulgar | hash | urls | case | punc | emo_chat | good_len | good_cnt | bad_len | bad_cnt | redund |
|---|---|---|---|---|---|---|---|---|---|---|---|---|---|---|---|---|---|---|---|---|---|---|---|---|---|
| 16 | 91.740143 | 95.2381 | 0 | 1 | 1 | 1 | 1 | 1 | 1 | 1 | 1 | 1 | 0 | 1 | 0 | 1 | 1 | 0 | 1 | 1 | 0 | 0 | 0 | 1 | 1 |
| 16 | 91.740143 | 95.2381 | 0 | 1 | 1 | 1 | 1 | 1 | 1 | 1 | 1 | 1 | 0 | 1 | 1 | 0 | 1 | 0 | 1 | 1 | 0 | 0 | 0 | 1 | 1 |
| 16 | 91.740143 | 95.2381 | 0 | 1 | 1 | 1 | 1 | 1 | 1 | 1 | 1 | 1 | 0 | 1 | 1 | 1 | 0 | 0 | 1 | 1 | 0 | 0 | 0 | 1 | 1 |
| 16 | 91.740143 | 95.2381 | 0 | 1 | 1 | 1 | 1 | 1 | 1 | 1 | 1 | 1 | 0 | 1 | 1 | 1 | 0 | 0 | 1 | 0 | 0 | 0 | 0 | 1 | 1 |
| 16 | 91.740143 | 95.2381 | 0 | 1 | 1 | 1 | 1 | 1 | 1 | 1 | 1 | 1 | 0 | 1 | 1 | 1 | 0 | 0 | 1 | 1 | 0 | 0 | 0 | 1 | 0 |
| 17 | 91.740143 | 95.2381 | 0 | 1 | 1 | 1 | 1 | 1 | 1 | 1 | 1 | 1 | 0 | 1 | 1 | 1 | 1 | 0 | 1 | 1 | 0 | 0 | 0 | 1 | 1 |
| | | FREQ: | 0 | 0.727 | 0.626 | 0.678 | 0.727 | 0.56 | 0.499 | 0.591 | 0.514 | 0.955 | 0 | 0.455911 | 0.5 | 0.38 | 0.73 | 0.104 | 0.499 | 0.667308 | 0 | 0 | 0 | 0.65422 | 0.5429 |

**Fig. 3.** Feature sets and their effectiveness

## 10 Experiment 2: Sensitivity Testing by Feature Imputation

An "intra/inter-vector" feature imputation scheme is now described that uses a reference data set to determine the most likely fill values for the features of a feature vector (this is called "feature imputation"). For example, if a vector has all features present except one, the existing features and the reference set are used to make a best estimate of the missing feature. This is equivalent to asking, "What feature value should be placed here, given the values of the other features in the vector?"

The imputation software ingests a feature vector file, and infers, in this way, a new value for *every* feature of *every* vector in the whole file, using patterns from a reference feature vector file as the standard.

## 11   The Imputation Algorithm

A simple inter-vector imputation method just replaces missing values with their population means, a $O(n)$ process. This naïve approach is simple, but ignores feature context within the vector. For numeric data, a more sophisticated method is the nearest neighbor normalization technique. This can be applied efficiently even to large data sets having many dimensions (in a brute force approach this is a $O(n^2)$ process). This technique proceeds in the following manner for each missing feature in a given vector, $V_1$:

1. From the reference set of feature vectors, find the one, $V_2$, which:
    (a) Shares a sufficient number of populated fields with the vector to be imputed (this is to increase the likelihood that the nearest vector is representative of the vector being processed).
    (b) Has a value for the missing feature, $F_m$.
    (c) Is nearest the vector to be imputed (possibly weighted).
2. Compute the weighted norms of the vector being imputed, $V_1$, and the matching vector found in step 1, $V_2$, in just those features present in both.
3. Form the normalization ratio $R_n = |V_1|/|V_2|$.
4. Create a preliminary fill value $P = R_n * F_m$.
5. Apply a clipping (or other) consistency test to $P$ to obtain $F'_m$, the final, sanity checked fill value.
6. Fill the gap in $V_1$ with the value $F'_m$.

This method was used to perform a feature sensitivity analysis with respect to the ground truth in the following way:

The 8,845 thread set described above was divided into two sets by inferred ground truth: Those tagged as BOT were placed in one file, and those tagged as non_BOTS in another.

The 8,845 thread set was divided into two sets by inferred ground truth: Those tagged as BOT were placed in one file, and those tagged as non_BOTS in another.

The imputation scheme was then used to impute the non-BOT feature vectors using the BOT file as the reference set. Comparing the before and after imputation versions of the non-BOT file addresses Question A:

"Which features must be altered, in what ways, by how much, to make a non-BOT resemble a BOT?"

This process was repeated, this time using the Intra/Inter-Vector Regression scheme to impute the BOT feature vectors using the non-BOT file as the reference set. Comparing the before and after imputation versions of the BOT file addresses Question B:

"Which features must be altered, in what ways, and by how much, to make a BOT resemble a non-BOT?"

These are important and interesting questions that, among other things, provide objective insight into how BOT-characterization is seen in each feature. They also provide insight into how to disguise a BOT as a non-BOT. It is interesting to note that the changes required to make a BOT look like a non-BOT are the reverse of the changes required to make a non-BOT look like a BOT (Figs. 4 and 5).

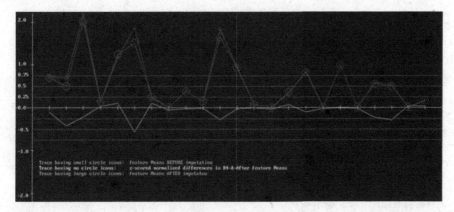

**Fig. 4.** The figure immediately above shows the "before" and "after" feature means for BOT data imputed from Non-BOT data. The light colored line is the z-weighted delta between the "before" and "after" representations.

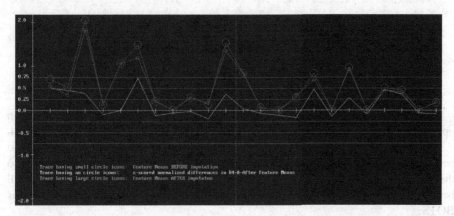

**Fig. 5.** The "before" and "after" feature means for the non-BOT data imputed from the BOT data. The light colored line is the z-weighted delta between "before" and "after" featuress.

The following is a tabulation of some "before imputation" and "after imputation" statistics for each of the 23 features. The first two columns give the feature number and name, respectively. Columns 3 and 4 are the feature means of the BOT data before and after imputation from the non-BOT data. Column 5 is column 4 minus column 3 (the change in the means due to imputation). Columns 6 and 7 are the feature standard deviations of the BOT data before and after imputation from the non-BOT data. Column 8 is column 7 minus column 6 (the change in the standard deviations due to imputation) (Fig. 6).

Columns 9 and 10 are the feature means of the non-BOT data before and after imputation from the BOT data. Column 11 is column 10 minus column 9 (the change in the means due to imputation). Columns 12 and 13 are the feature standard deviations of the non-BOT data before and after imputation from the BOT data. Column 14 is column 13 minus column 12 (the change in the standard deviations due to imputation).

| Imputation Experiment | | Bots imputed from Non-Bots (before & After) | | | | | | Non-Bots imputed from Bots (before & After) | | | | | |
|---|---|---|---|---|---|---|---|---|---|---|---|---|---|
| Fea # | FeaName | μ_B4 | μ_AFT | μ_Delta | σ_B4 | σ_Aft | σ_Delta | μ_B4 | μ_Aft | μ_Delta | σ_B4 | σ_Aft | σ_Delta |
| 1 | #tweets/200 | 0.73 | 0.699 | -0.03 | 0.28 | 0.24 | -0.041 | 0.56 | 0.704 | 0.147 | 0.3 | 0.26 | -0.03 |
| 2 | redundancy | 0.7 | 0.51 | -0.192 | 0.45 | 0.34 | -0.118 | 0.34 | 0.524 | 0.179 | 0.39 | 0.29 | -0.102 |
| 3 | adjectives | 2.18 | 2.01 | -0.166 | 0.79 | 0.64 | -0.151 | 1.84 | 2.048 | 0.21 | 0.54 | 0.49 | -0.052 |
| 4 | adverbs | 0.15 | 0.149 | 0.004 | 0.12 | 0.1 | -0.023 | 0.15 | 0.14 | -0.009 | 0.1 | 0.09 | -0.013 |
| 5 | articles | 1.18 | 1.253 | 0.069 | 0.66 | 0.58 | -0.08 | 1.07 | 1.071 | -0.001 | 0.49 | 0.52 | 0.03 |
| 6 | comm noun | 1.86 | 1.51 | -0.351 | 0.62 | 0.38 | -0.246 | 1.19 | 1.489 | 0.295 | 0.4 | 0.45 | 0.043 |
| 7 | conjunctions | 0.23 | 0.248 | 0.019 | 0.19 | 0.16 | -0.03 | 0.22 | 0.203 | -0.017 | 0.14 | 0.13 | -0.015 |
| 8 | interjections | 0.01 | 0.009 | -0.002 | 0.04 | 0.03 | -0.004 | 0.01 | 0.007 | -0.001 | 0.02 | 0.02 | -0.002 |
| 9 | prepositions | 0.38 | 0.377 | -0.005 | 0.26 | 0.2 | -0.062 | 0.3 | 0.294 | -0.004 | 0.18 | 0.18 | -0.008 |
| 10 | pronouns | 0.16 | 0.153 | -0.002 | 0.17 | 0.14 | -0.039 | 0.16 | 0.137 | -0.025 | 0.14 | 0.12 | -0.013 |
| 11 | Proper nouns | 1.83 | 1.653 | -0.181 | 0.65 | 0.51 | -0.135 | 1.36 | 1.538 | 0.182 | 0.5 | 0.5 | 0.003 |
| 12 | verbs | 0.95 | 0.933 | -0.013 | 0.51 | 0.42 | -0.087 | 0.83 | 0.85 | 0.016 | 0.39 | 0.39 | -0.001 |
| 13 | stopwords | 0.08 | 0.075 | 0 | 0.09 | 0.07 | -0.02 | 0.07 | 0.063 | -0.004 | 0.07 | 0.06 | -0.011 |
| 14 | vulgarisms | 0 | 0.001 | 0 | 0 | 0 | 0 | 0 | 0.001 | -0.001 | 0.01 | 0.01 | -0.004 |
| 15 | hashtags | 0.34 | 0.367 | 0.025 | 0.33 | 0.29 | -0.039 | 0.34 | 0.292 | -0.044 | 0.28 | 0.27 | -0.012 |
| 16 | urls | 0.84 | 0.816 | -0.024 | 0.24 | 0.24 | -0.004 | 0.69 | 0.834 | 0.144 | 0.3 | 0.22 | -0.08 |
| 17 | Upp/Low case | 0.01 | 0.009 | -0.002 | 0.09 | 0.07 | -0.02 | 0.02 | 0.009 | -0.013 | 0.1 | 0.06 | -0.04 |
| 18 | punctuation | 0.98 | 0.98 | 0 | 0.06 | 0.06 | -0.005 | 0.94 | 0.972 | 0.034 | 0.12 | 0.07 | -0.048 |
| 19 | emojis/chat | 0.01 | 0.009 | -0.001 | 0.05 | 0.04 | -0.008 | 0.01 | 0.007 | -0.003 | 0.03 | 0.03 | -0.004 |
| 20 | good_chrs/140 | 0.58 | 0.557 | -0.023 | 0.1 | 0.09 | -0.006 | 0.45 | 0.51 | 0.059 | 0.13 | 0.11 | -0.019 |
| 21 | good_wrds/28 | 0.53 | 0.499 | -0.028 | 0.1 | 0.09 | -0.01 | 0.42 | 0.455 | 0.038 | 0.11 | 0.1 | -0.002 |
| 22 | bad_chrs/140 | 0.01 | 0.009 | 0 | 0.01 | 0.01 | -0.001 | 0.01 | 0.01 | -0.001 | 0.01 | 0.01 | -0.002 |
| 23 | bad_wrds/28 | 0.17 | 0.17 | 0.005 | 0.14 | 0.12 | -0.025 | 0.19 | 0.178 | -0.009 | 0.12 | 0.11 | -0.013 |

**Fig. 6.** Before and after imputation statistics

Notice that imputation from non-BOTs to BOTS moves the means in the direction opposite the direction of imputation from BOTs to non-BOTs, as would be expected.

To verify the effectiveness of imputation in "nudging" vectors from one class to another, a classifier that discriminates between BOT and non-BOT data is applied to the imputed data. If the imputation has been effective, the post-imputation BOTS will be classified as non-BOTs, and the post imputation non-BOTs will be classified as BOTS.

In fact, when the imputed data is classified by the original data using a nearest neighbor classifier, the ground truth tags are reversed for 100% of the vectors, as expected.

## 12   Future Work

This work describes a characterization method for content data. Future work will leverage the factor analysis it provides, which previous work has shown [1] can be used to determine which members of a forum are least committed to their clique, and exactly what would be required to move them out of their current clique. This is a type of "cultural terrain-forming".

These observations suggest that opportunities for objective, quantitative proactive social media psy-ops planning could use the imputation sensitivities to estimate the following:

1. How each feature's effect on BOT-non-BOT assignment is quantified
2. How to optimally impersonate a member
3. How to identify imposters/impersonators (psycho-anomaly detection)
4. Deriving posts that would tend to foment or mitigate conflict among cliques.

# References

1. Hancock, M., et al.: Modeling of social media behaviors using only account metadata. In: 8th International Conference on Applied Human Factors and Ergonomics, Orlando, Florida, July 2016
2. Hancock, M., et al: Multi-cultural empirical study of password strength vs. ergonomic utility. In: 18th International Conference on Human Computer Interaction, Toronto, Canada, July 2016
3. Hancock, M., et al.: Field-theoretic modeling method for emotional context in social media: theory and case study. In: Schmorrow, D.D., Fidopiastis, C.M. (eds.) AC 2015. LNCS (LNAI), vol. 9183, pp. 418–425. Springer, Cham (2015). doi:10.1007/978-3-319-20816-9_40
4. Hancock, M., Sessions, C., Lo, C., Rajwani, S., Kresses, E., Bleasdale, C., Strohschein, D.: Stability of a type of cross-cultural emotion modeling in social media. In: Schmorrow, D.D., Fidopiastis, C.M. (eds.) AC 2015. LNCS (LNAI), vol. 9183, pp. 410–417. Springer, Cham (2015). doi:10.1007/978-3-319-20816-9_39
5. Hancock, M.: Novel methods for adjudicating multiple cognitive decision models. In: 2nd International Augmented Cognition Conference, San Francisco, CA, October 2006
6. Hancock, M., Day, J.: Exploring human cognition by spectral decomposition of a Markov random field. In: 1st International Augmented Cognition Conference, Las Vegas, NV, July 2005
7. Hancock, M.: A cognitive engineering methodology for building multi-level fusion applications. In: Northrop Grumman Data Fusion Conference, Aurora, CO, November 2007
8. Hancock, M.: Automating the characterization of social media culture, social context, and mood. In: Science of Multi-Intelligence Conference (SOMI), Chantilly, VA (2014)
9. Hancock, M.: Data mining: technology and practice in the real world. In: Tutorial Notes of the SIAM International Data Mining Conference (SDM 2003) (2003)

# Using the Hash Tag Histogram and Social Kinematics for Semantic Clustering in Social Media

Monte Hancock[1], Chloe Lo[4], Shakeel Rajwani[4(✉)], Shai Neumann[2],
Dale Franklin[3], Esnet Gros Negre[3], Tracy Hollis[3], Steven Knight[3],
Vikram Tutupalli[3], Vineet Chintamaneni[3], Sheila Daniels[3],
Brian Gabak[3], Venkata Undavalli[3], Payton Brown[4],
and Olivia Hancock[4]

[1] 4Digital Inc., Webster University, Melbourne, FL, USA
[2] Eastern Florida State College, Melbourne, FL, USA
[3] Webster University, Melbourne, FL, USA
[4] Sirius 17 Team, Melbourne, FL, USA
Shakeel.Rajwani@gmail.com

**Abstract.** This work addresses automated semantic clustering of twitter users by analysis of their aggregated text posts (tweets). This semantic clustering of text is an application of a theory we refer to as Social Kinematics. Social Kinematics is a term coined by our team to refer to the field-theoretic approach we develop and describe in [1–3, 5]. It is used here to model human interaction in social media. This social modeling technique regards social media users as field sources, and uses the Laplacian to model their interaction. This yields a natural analogy with physical kinematics. Automation is described that allows social media text posts (organized by author into "threads") to self-organize as a precursor to analysis and characterization. The goal of this work is to automate the characterization of user-generated text content in terms of its semantics (meaning). Characterization here means the determination of intuitive "categories" for content, and the automatic assignment of user-generated content to these categories. Categories might include: Advertising, Subscribed feeds (news, weather, traffic, etc.), Discussion of current events (politics, sports, popular culture, etc.), and Casual conversation (filial, friend-to-friend, etc.) Characterization is performed by retrieving text posts by Twitter users; numericizing these using a field model; and clustering them by their semantics. An innovation is the application of the field model to semantic characterization of text. This is based upon the observation that user hash tags are a priori semantic tags, making expensive and brittle semantic mapping of the tweet text unnecessary.

## 1 Background

Text data is a finite set of characters. It might, or might not, show structure or meaning.

Unstructured text is text data that is not organized into labeled units. In particular, unstructured text does not usually have much associated metadata. It must provide its own context.

© Springer International Publishing AG 2017
D.D. Schmorrow and C.M. Fidopiastis (Eds.): AC 2017, Part I, LNAI 10284, pp. 510–520, 2017.
DOI: 10.1007/978-3-319-58628-1_38

The processing of natural language text has been an area of research for many years. The hierarchy of complexity depicted below shows some of the many problems into which automated text processing can be partitioned. The complexity increases from the top of the list to the bottom:

Integration of semi-structured text
    Automatically generate prose reports from data
Term-space disambiguation
    Use NLP to disambiguate names/addresses/identities
    derive networks of suspicious money transfers, using Belief Net
Concept extraction from structured text
Use NLP, and Belief Net to infer adversary "intent" from Reuters news reports
Understanding of unstructured text snippets
Semantic mapping using a comprehensive ontology
Mode analysis from unstructured text
    Characterize user behaviors/processes from unstructured text (no ontology)
Semantic mapping of semi-structured text
    Document reduction for searching and sorting
Semantic mapping of unstructured text ß the work in this paper
    XML tagging of transcribed spoken prose using a comprehensive ontology
Semi-structured text understanding
    Normalize, interpret, understand, and repair a knowledge repository
Understanding of unstructured text

For completeness, a tabulation of major semantic text processing methods is below [4] (Table 1):

**Table 1.** The characteristics and limitations of four text mining methods

| Models | Characteristics/limitations |
|---|---|
| Latent Semantic Analysis (LSA) | Characteristics<br>• Reduces dimensionality of tf-idf using Singular Value Decomposition<br>• Captures synonyms of words<br>• Not robust statistical background<br>Limitations<br>• Difficult to determine the number of topics<br>• Difficult to interpret loading values with probability meaning<br>• Difficult to label a topic in some cases using words in the topic |
| Probabilistic Latent Semantic Analysis (PLSA) | Characteristics<br>• Mixture components are multinomial random variables that can be viewed as representations of "topics"<br>• Each word is generated from a single topic; different words in a document may be generated from different topics<br>• PLSA partially handles polysemy<br>Limitations<br>• No probabilistic model at the level of documents |

(continued)

**Table 1.** (*continued*)

| Models | Characteristics/limitations |
|--------|------------------------------|
| Latent Dirichelet Allocation (LDA) | Characteristics<br>• Provides full generative model with multinomial distribution for words in topics and Dirichlet distribution over topics<br>• Handles long-length documents<br>• Shows adjectives and nouns in topics<br>Limitations<br>• Incapable to model relations among topics |
| Correlated Topic Model (CTM) | Characteristics<br>• Considers relations among topics using logistic normal distribution<br>• Allows the occurrences of words in other topics<br>• Allows topic graphs<br>Limitations<br>• Requires complex computations<br>• Contains too general words in topics |

Data clustering ([6]) is a valuable non-parametric technique for detecting and exploiting patterns of interaction in abstract data sets. If detected clusters can be assigned empirical significance, clustering can be used as a classification method [6] (Fig. 1):

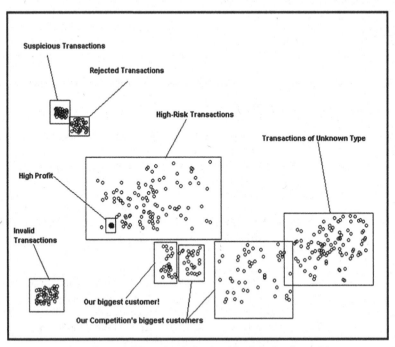

When "meaning" can be determined for "clusters", useful
patterns and discriminators can sometimes be revealed.

**Fig. 1.** Notional clustering of demographic data

## 2  Social Media Psychology is Virtual Action-at-a-Distance

Just as masses and charges give rise to gravitational and electric fields, the online behaviors of individuals engaged in social discourse give rise to an "ambient culture" that conditions, and is conditioned by, these behaviors.

Apply classical methods from:

Information Theory
Information Geometry
Differential Geometry
Machine Learning

A mathematical field theory of online discourse is described [3]. This has been implemented in software as an application that characterizes and visualizes a multi-dimensional vector field ("social context") arising from this discourse:

The general mathematical model for the social context of a social media venue as a set of field equations in [3] is used to extract the features from the hash tag histogram.

Using the Field-Theoretic Approach to the Electrostatic and Gravitational Problems, physicists found that, instead of the impossibly complicated problem of modeling many dynamically interacting things (e.g., free electrical charges moving in space-time), they could characterize systems by modeling one thing: the field they generate.

In the same way, the Field-Theoretic Approach to the Social Media Culture Mining Problem proceeds, not by considering the impossibly complicated problem of modeling many dynamically interacting things (e.g., asynchronously-posting persons moving in virtual space-time), it is necessary to model one thing: the field they generate.

The following is a summary excerpt from [3] describing the field arising from posting behavior in a social medium:

Let $\mathcal{F}$ be a collection of finite length character strings ("threads"):

$$\mathcal{F} = \{A_j\} = \{A_1, A_2, \cdots, A_M\}$$

Let $d_{ij}(A_i, A_j) = d_{ij}$ be a metric on $\mathcal{F}$. Form the distance matrix:

$$D(A_i, A_j) = [d_{ij}], \quad i, j = 1, 2, \ldots M$$

This matrix will be symmetric, zero diagonal, and non − negative.
Let:

$$S = \{\vec{a_j}\} = \{\vec{a_1}, \vec{a_2}, \cdots \vec{a_M}\} \in \mathbb{R}^N$$

be a (hypothetical) set of vectors having distance matrix D Regarding the $\vec{a_j}$ as <u>field sources</u>, we define a discrete scalar potential $\wp$ on $S$ by:

$$\wp(\overrightarrow{a_i}) = \mathscr{g} \sum_{j=1}^{M} \left( \|\overrightarrow{a_i} - \vec{a}_j\| - d_{ij} \right)^2 \quad (*)$$

It will be seen that analysis of this vector field provides information sufficient to identify semantically meaningful cliques of users among the posters.

## 3 Advantages of the Field-Theoretic Approach to Document Clustering

The field-theoretic approach offers important advantages over current linguistic approaches:

1. Language independence: no initial requirement for linguistic support, lexicon's, parsers, stemmers, etc.
2. Computational tractability: will not scale unless the computational complexity is low in the size of the term space, post space, and membership space.
3. More mature foundation: Classical Analysis vs. Discrete Mathematics. Repurposing an existing body of technical methods reduces risk and cost, and presents many opportunities for extension by others.

## 4 The Software Prototype

A software prototype has been built to infer and characterize cliques of users in social media. No a priori assumptions are made, so the software processing is "domain agnostic". The prototype can infer and numerically characterize co-posting cliques, as well as topically homogeneous cliques.

The prototype produces a characterization of the "social context" that the user can both survey as a set of tables, and interrogate visually.

The application can incrementally superpose new data as it arrives, and remove old data for aging (e.g., no "priors" to update, or graph structures to retool) (Fig. 2).

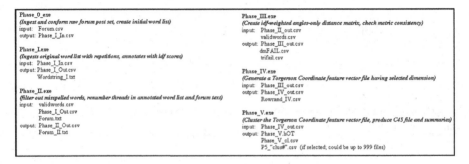

**Fig. 2.** The field-theoretic clustering process

## 5   Applications of the Method

The field-equations can be used to impose an inherent, a priori clustering of entities in the space. Clustering determines, and is determined by, the terrain geometry. These are in dynamic tension. Clusters correspond to topically homogeneous discussions.

The techniques are able to identify cliques of "like-minded" posters. More importantly, the "social distance" between cliques can be quantified, supporting assessment of the "ideological separation" of cliques, and individuals within cliques. Further, the level of commitment to a stated position can be estimated.

## 6   Inputs and Outputs

Twitter maintains a website for servicing data requests posted by those holding Twitter Developer credentials. Developers obtain these credentials through an online application process.

Credentialed developers may request information for Twitter user accounts by posting requests to the Twitter API (application program interface) at a URL (uniform resource locator) provided by Twitter. Requests can be made for specific accounts based upon their User Identification Numbers. Requests can also be made for random samples of accounts selected by Twitter.

Requested data are returned as a hierarchical data structure called JSON (JavaScript Object Notation). There are hard limits on the amount and type of information that can be requested. If these limits are exceeded, the requestor's credentials are revoked by Twitter.

## 7   The Content Data Elements and Their Encoding

Content data (tweets) are returned (in the JSON structure) as character strings of length 1 to 140 characters. They may be in any language, or no language at all. Tweets can contain any combination of free text, emoticons, chat-speak, hash tags, and URL's. Twitter does not filter tweets for content (e.g., vulgarisms, hate speech). Below is a segment showing tweets from two users, here called "1" and "2" (Fig. 3):

| Thread | Tweet | Tweet_Text |
|---|---|---|
| 1 | 1 | Up Next: Johnson & Johnson $JNJ #Baby #Powder #Talc #Ovarian #Cancer #Lawsuits https://t.co/KO9IV5YAlt |
| 1 | 2 | New United States Food and Drug Commissioner .@US_FDA Dr. Robert Califf Responsible for #KILLER $JNJ #Xarelto https://t.co/BNYVroR4Rb |
| 1 | 3 | Death by Johnson and Johnson $JNJ #Levaquin (levofloxacin) Anti-Biotic https://t.co/QDQqGkfoAs |
| 1 | 4 | United States Senate HELPless Committee https://t.co/bYEh42aE0P |
| 1 | 5 | Johnson and Johnson $JNJ #Risperdal US Black Box DEATH Warning for Elderly Dementia NOT Applied in Australia https://t.co/h064XWKMSq |
| 1 | 6 | Michelle Obama and the Johnson and Johnson $JNJ CEO Gorsky $5 Billion #Risperdal. Omnicare. #Medicaid #Scandal https://t.co/PJU27zTu1B |
| 1 | 7 | $70 Million Punitive Judgment Against Johnson & Johnson $JNJ Subsidiary #Ethicon https://t.co/C8cVdCirMh |
| 1 | 8 | Asthma Rates Reduce After Toxic Chems Removed from Johnson & Johnson $JNJ Baby Products https://t.co/98hS13BkNp |
| 1 | 9 | Why US Senate HELP Committee MUST SHUT DOWN Johnson and Johnson $JNJ https://t.co/7OqCuilqX6 |
| 1 | 10 | Up Next: Johnson & Johnson $JNJ Baby Powder Talc Ovarian Cancer Lawsuits https://t.co/kZzZTRyghS |
| 2 | 1 | #TheHuntsmanWintersWar is about as generic as it.s title #moviereview https://t.co/YNOMjL2Wn1 |
| 2 | 2 | Who wins the fight? #BatmanvSuperman #MovieReview https://t.co/J2Lw2Bi3hg |
| 2 | 3 | #AWalkintheWoods was a pleasant movie that worked really well because of the great chemistry and banter between Redford and Nolte. |
| 2 | 4 | Despite the shitty reviews. I.ve got my ticket for tomorrow night. Still pumped to see it. #BatmanvSuperman |
| 2 | 5 | Finally rewatched #ManofSteel. Liked it even better this 2nd time around. I.m ready for some #BatmanvSuperman! |
| 2 | 6 | Why do I want to follow this douche w/a camera. Was just waiting for him to finally kick it. Go hangman! #TheGallows |
| 2 | 7 | #InfinitelyPolarBear is an interesting look at bipolar/manic depressive parenting. Really good performance by Ruffalo. |

**Fig. 3.**   Two tweet text threads

A vector of text features is derived for each user. This is accomplished by deriving text features for each of the user's tweets, then rolling them up. Therefore, one content feature vector is derived for each user from all of that user's tweets.

The extraction of numeric features from text is a multi-step process:

a. Collect the User's most recent (up to 200) tweet strings into a single set (a Thread).
b. Convert the thread text to upper case for term matching.
c. Scan each tweet for the presence of hash tags, creating a Hash Tag Histogram (described below) for each thread.

A Hash Tag Dictionary was created from a collection of 180,000 tweets.

The bins represent the 2,500 most frequently used Twitter hash tags, arranged in order of decreasing frequency (Fig. 4):

| TermRank | HashTag | Frequency | WEIGHT | | TermRank | HashTag | Frequency | WEIGHT |
|---|---|---|---|---|---|---|---|---|
| 1 | #quote | 1007 | 0.00099305 | | Continued... | | | |
| 2 | #Marketing | 691 | 0.00144718 | | 2716 | #voicesavekorin | 7 | 0.14286 |
| 3 | #Periscope: | 550 | 0.00181818 | | 2717 | #Volkswagen | 7 | 0.14286 |
| 4 | #retail | 480 | 0.00208333 | | 2718 | #walkingholiday | 7 | 0.14286 |
| 5 | #Job | 464 | 0.00215517 | | 2719 | #webhosting | 7 | 0.14286 |
| 6 | #FF | 415 | 0.00240964 | | 2720 | #webinars | 7 | 0.14286 |
| 7 | #osrs | 399 | 0.00250627 | | 2721 | #weddings | 7 | 0.14286 |
| 8 | #socialmedia | 393 | 0.00254453 | | 2722 | #wednesdaymotivation | 7 | 0.14286 |
| 9 | #health | 390 | 0.0025641 | | 2723 | #WeHelpYouSellMore | 7 | 0.14286 |
| 10 | #giveaway | 362 | 0.00276243 | | 2724 | #WeHonorVeterans | 7 | 0.14286 |
| 11 | #Travel | 355 | 0.0028169 | | 2725 | #what | 7 | 0.14286 |
| 12 | #ad | 349 | 0.00286533 | | 2726 | #WomensHistoryMonth | 7 | 0.14286 |
| 13 | #photography | 346 | 0.00289017 | | 2727 | #WoO | 7 | 0.14286 |
| 14 | #love | 336 | 0.00297619 | | 2728 | #words | 7 | 0.14286 |
| 15 | #FREE | 328 | 0.00304878 | | 2729 | #working | 7 | 0.14286 |
| 16 | #sponsored | 316 | 0.00316456 | | 2730 | #writetip | 7 | 0.14286 |
| 17 | #music | 293 | 0.00341297 | | 2731 | #wsnc | 7 | 0.14286 |
| 18 | #Leadership | 258 | 0.00387597 | | 2732 | #ww | 7 | 0.14286 |
| 19 | #gameinsight | 256 | 0.00390625 | | 2733 | #WWENetwork | 7 | 0.14286 |
| 20 | #arts | 255 | 0.00392157 | | 2734 | #yesrealestate | 7 | 0.14286 |
| 21 | #tech | 238 | 0.00420168 | | 2735 | #youdonthavealife | 7 | 0.14286 |
| 22 | #innovation | 233 | 0.00429185 | | 2736 | #yyc | 7 | 0.14286 |
| 23 | #Business | 230 | 0.00434783 | | 2737 | #3: | 6 | 0.16667 |
| 24 | #SEO | 222 | 0.0045045 | | 2738 | #312 | 6 | 0.16667 |
| 25 | #Celiac | 216 | 0.00462963 | | 2739 | #5167BoulDocario | 6 | 0.16667 |

**Fig. 4.** Hash tag frequencies from a large tweet corpus

- The inverse hash tag frequencies are used to weight the histogram bins. In this way, common hash tags have less impact on the hash tag histogram than rarer hash tags. Because the Twitter term space follows a Zipf Distribution, the hash tag histograms tend to be relatively "level" in amplitude: less frequent terms are given a higher per occurrence weight (Fig. 5).

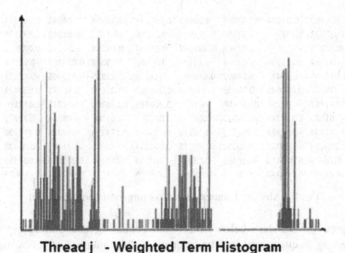

**Thread j - Weighted Term Histogram**

**Fig. 5.** A hash tag histogram for a single thread

## 8 Feature Encoding by the Field-Theoretic Model

Each weighted hashtag histogram consists of 2,500 bins containing real numbers. These hashtag histograms can be processed to provide the geometric features that serve as the basis for the inter-vector distance matrix which in turn is inputted into the field model (Fig. 6).

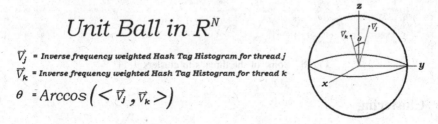

*Unit Ball in $R^N$*

$\vec{V}_j$ = *Inverse frequency weighted Hash Tag Histogram for thread j*

$\vec{V}_k$ = *Inverse frequency weighted Hash Tag Histogram for thread k*

$\theta$ = $Arccos\left(<\vec{V}_j, \vec{V}_k>\right)$

**Fig. 6.** Notional depiction of the 2,500-dimensional hash tag hypersphere

The hashtag histograms were normalized to become points on the surface of a 2,500-dimensional unit ball. The Cosine Distance was computed between each pair of points on the ball to create a pairwise distance matrix for the hashtag histograms.

The field model was then used to generate an 8-dimensional representation of the distribution of hashtag histograms, and so, of the user thread text.

The table below is a snippet of the file containing the 8-dimensional vectors developed for each hashtag histogram using the field model (Fig. 7):

Feature conditioning may be applied as part of pre-processing, such as z-scoring by vector components, pre-analysis missing-value imputation, etc.

| 1 | 0.025169 | -0.01201 | 0.047568 | -0.04669 | 0.014571 | 0.016004 | -0.06642 | 0.003044 | 1 |
|---|---|---|---|---|---|---|---|---|---|
| 2 | 0.017522 | 0.107598 | 0.07996 | 0.281586 | 0.02658 | -0.1727 | -0.01848 | 0.095179 | 1 |
| 3 | -0.18135 | -0.18526 | -0.03966 | 0.232847 | -0.01334 | -0.04288 | -0.09912 | 0.077531 | 1 |
| 4 | -0.01534 | -0.19964 | -0.02284 | 0.12466 | -0.20199 | 0.15248 | 0.029929 | -0.14193 | 1 |
| 5 | 0.090745 | -0.19437 | -0.06603 | 0.014603 | -0.23673 | -0.15835 | 0.079368 | -0.02575 | 1 |
| 6 | 0.075262 | 0.053645 | -0.20159 | 0.098872 | 0.045082 | 0.02697 | 0.10321 | 0.227433 | 1 |
| 7 | 0.141487 | -0.04998 | 0.388106 | -0.5013 | 0.204486 | 0.134308 | -0.37212 | 0.112196 | 1 |
| 8 | -0.01628 | 0.100243 | -0.24517 | 0.064772 | 0.066054 | -0.03307 | -0.09965 | -0.21775 | 1 |
| 9 | 0.141494 | -0.04998 | 0.388113 | -0.50128 | 0.204494 | 0.134298 | -0.37213 | 0.112206 | 1 |
| 10 | 0.215054 | -0.16724 | -0.05899 | 0.240515 | 0.054287 | -0.035 | 0.031461 | -0.01402 | 1 |
| 11 | -0.16474 | 0.068415 | -0.16626 | -0.08697 | -0.0389 | 0.056693 | 0.208658 | 0.013495 | 1 |
| 12 | -0.04236 | 0.009244 | -0.09684 | 0.029325 | -0.0189 | -0.33958 | 0.002511 | -0.0629 | 1 |

**Fig. 7.** Abstract features derived as torgersen coordinates [1]

The figure immediately below shows the beginning and ending entries in the Twitter hashtag frequency table. The frequency is the number of times that hashtag occurs in the tweet reference sample. The weight is just the reciprocal of the frequency (as suggested by the Zipf distribution) (Fig. 8).

| User# | Cluster# | HashTag | Freq | Freq_Weighted | HashTag | Freq | Freq_Weighted | HashTag | Freq | Freq_Weighted | HashTag | Freq | Freq_Weighted | H |
|---|---|---|---|---|---|---|---|---|---|---|---|---|---|---|
| 1228 | 9 | #FF | 2 | 0.011797314 | #SOCIALMEDIA | 1 | 0.005585957 | #TRAVEL | 5 | 0.025229195 | #MUSIC | 2 | 0.008329188 | #O |
| 1286 | 9 | #TRAVEL | 4 | 0.020183356 | #FOLLOWFRIDAY | 3 | 0.006993106 | #1 | 1 | 0.002245754 | #DEALS | 1 | 0.001364509 | #M |
| 1295 | 9 | #MARKETING | 1 | 0.009821619 | #FF | 5 | 0.029493284 | #SOCIALMEDIA | 1 | 0.005585957 | #HEALTH | 2 | 0.011086632 | #T |
| 1362 | 9 | #TRAVEL | 4 | 0.020183356 | #PHOTOGRAPHY | 1 | 0.004917916 | #FUN | 2 | 0.001989908 | #FUNNY | 1 | 0.000895459 | #A |
| 1423 | 9 | #QUOTE | 1 | 0.014313126 | #HEALTH | 1 | 0.005543316 | #TRAVEL | 23 | 0.116054296 | #INNOVATIC | 1 | 0.003311776 | #O |
| 1465 | 9 | #TRAVEL | 1 | 0.005045839 | #YELP | 1 | 0.001392936 | #CRUISE | 1 | 0.000213204 | | | | |
| 25 | 10 | #JOB | 2 | 0.013190249 | #JOBS | 1 | 0.002288395 | #CONSTANTCONT | 1 | 0.001208159 | #RESTAURA | 4 | 0.001193945 | #H |
| 169 | 10 | #JOB | 190 | 1.253073698 | | | | | | | | | | |
| 455 | 10 | #JOB | 14 | 0.092331746 | #BUSINESS | 2 | 0.00653827 | #MOBILE | 2 | 0.00363869 | #MONDAYM | 4 | 0.004946344 | #E |
| 586 | 10 | #JOB | 1 | 0.006595125 | #FINTECH | 1 | 0.000568545 | #GAMEOFTHRON | 1 | 0.000426409 | #INVESTME | 1 | 0.000213204 | #H |
| 664 | 10 | #INFOGRAPH | 6 | 0.004349371 | | | | | | | | | | |
| 770 | 10 | #JOB | 57 | 0.375922109 | #GOOGLE | 1 | 0.001364509 | #FAIL | 1 | 0.000611186 | | | | |
| 1329 | 10 | #JOB | 3 | 0.019785374 | #UK | 1 | 0.00285694 | #WEATHER | 1 | 0.002800085 | #BLOG | 1 | 0.000994954 | #S |
| 1406 | 10 | #JOB | 182 | 1.2003127 | #INTERVIEW | 1 | 0.0003127 | #JOBSEARCH | 1 | 0.000255845 | | | | |
| 59 | 11 | #TECH | 1 | 0.003382844 | #CONTENTMARKE | 1 | 0.002999076 | #MOBILE | 15 | 0.027290171 | #DIGITAL | 2 | 0.002757444 | #T |
| 515 | 11 | #TECH | 3 | 0.010148532 | #JOBS | 6 | 0.013730367 | #ECOMMERCE | 15 | 0.034112714 | #MOBILE | 2 | 0.00363869 | #E |
| 517 | 11 | #TECH | 1 | 0.006595125 | #TECH | 2 | 0.006765688 | #IOT | 2 | 0.003723971 | #MOBILE | 2 | 0.00363869 | #A |
| 553 | 11 | #SOCIALMED | 1 | 0.005585957 | #HEALTH | 1 | 0.005543316 | #TRAVEL | 1 | 0.005045839 | #MUSIC | 3 | 0.012493782 | #H |
| 638 | 11 | #MOBILE | 1 | 0.001818245 | | | | | | | | | | |

**Fig. 8.** Some of the threads in clusters 9–11

# 9  Clustering

Coherent clustering was visually apparent in the output of the field model. K-Means clustering was used to assign the abstract 8-dimensional spatial feature vectors to 150 disjoint clusters.

The figure below is a perspective projection of a 4-dimensional field-theoretic representation of the hashtag data. It has been colorized using a K-Means algorithm. The light-colored "halo" of points at the upper left (and scattered to the lower right) were found by manual review of the corresponding text tweets to be BOTs. The dark sphere was found to be typical social exchanges between persons; and, the single point at the lower right was found to consist of approximately 200 accounts generated by BOTs. The most significant observation to make here is that these subpopulations show significant coherence: they are not just random scatterings of points (Fig. 9).

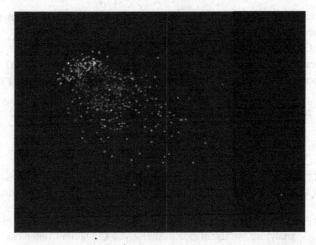

**Fig. 9.** Hashtag histogram data clustered using the field model

A number of animations of the formation of these clusterings have been prepared, in which one can see the process by which the data self-organize.

## 10  A Classification Experiment

Ground truth was assigned manually to whole clusters by readers independently reviewing the original tweet.

A classifier was trained on part of the manually tagged data, and applied in a blind test to the other part. Accuracy in detecting "advertising" in the blind set was 97%. This is not surprising, given that advertisers can be expected to use hashtags in a way that is somewhat different from their use by social posters.

## 11  Future Work

This work describes a characterization method for content data. Future work will leverage the factor analysis it provides, which we have shown can be used to determine which members of a forum are least committed to their clique, and exactly what would be required to move them out of their current clique. This is a type of "cultural terrain-forming" (this application is not discussed here).

The field equations impose a set of non-isotropic pseudo-metrics on the attribute space that define its geometry, which in turn conditions the kinematics of the space. The resulting dynamics has only approximate conservation laws and fundamental constants, most of which await formulation. These observations suggest that opportunities for objective, quantitative proactive social media psy-ops planning could use the field equation to determine the following:

1. How each member's effect on all other members is quantified, so numeric measures of "influence" could be derived
2. How to optimally impersonate a member
3. How to identify imposters/impersonators (psycho-anomaly detection)
4. Deriving posts that would tend to foment or mitigate conflict among cliques

# References

1. Hancock, M., et al.: Modeling of social media behaviors using only account metadata. In: 8th International Conference on Applied Human Factors and Ergonomics, Orlando, Florida, July 2016
2. Hancock, M., et al.: Field theoretic modeling method for emotional context in social media: theory and case study. In: 9th International Augmented Cognition Conference, Los Angeles, CA (2015)
3. Hancock, M., Lo, C., et al.: Stability of a type of cross-cultural emotion modeling in social media. In: 9th International Augmented Cognition Conference, Los Angeles, CA (2015)
4. Lee, S., Song, j., Kim, Y.: An empirical comparison of four text mining methods (2010)
5. Hancock, M.: Automating the characterization of social media culture, social context, and mood. In: 2014 Science of Multi-Intelligence Conference (SOMI), Chantilly, VA (2014)
6. Hancock, M.: Practical Data Mining. CRC Press, Boca Raton (2011)
7. Delmater, R., Hancock, M.: Data Mining Explained: A Manager's Guide to Customer-centric Business Intelligence. Digital Press, Boston (2001)

# Interface Metaphors for Interactive Machine Learning

Robert J. Jasper[✉] and Leslie M. Blaha

Pacific Northwest National Laboratory, Richland, WA, USA
{robert.jasper,leslie.blaha}@pnnl.gov

**Abstract.** To promote more interactive and dynamic machine learning, we revisit the notion of user-interface metaphors. User-interface metaphors provide intuitive constructs for supporting user needs through interface design elements. A user-interface metaphor provides a visual or action pattern that leverages a user's knowledge of another domain. Metaphors suggest both the visual representations that should be used in a display as well as the interactions that should be afforded to the user. We argue that user-interface metaphors can also offer a method of extracting interaction-based user feedback for use in machine learning. Metaphors offer indirect, context-based information that can be used in addition to explicit user inputs, such as user-provided labels. Implicit information from user interactions with metaphors can augment explicit user input for active learning paradigms. Or it might be leveraged in systems where explicit user inputs are more challenging to obtain. Each interaction with the metaphor provides an opportunity to gather data and learn. We argue this approach is especially important in streaming applications, where we desire machine learning systems that can adapt to dynamic, changing data.

**Keywords:** Interactive machine learning · User interface · Interface metaphor

## 1 Introduction

Following the introduction of the desktop as a user interface for personal computers, together with the mouse as an extension of the user's hand for interacting with the desktop, metaphors have dominated the design of user interfaces. Indeed, the use of metaphors is highlighted in early interface guidelines for the Macintosh: "You can take advantage of people's knowledge of the world around them by using metaphors to convey concepts and features of your application" [2]. This increased the accessibility of computational systems for everyone by rendering the systems intuitive and familiar.

A user-interface metaphor provides a visual or action pattern that leverages a user's knowledge of another domain. Metaphors provide the user a quick understanding of context and meaning of interface contents based on familiarity with another, typically physical, domain. For example, files, folders, tabs,

© Springer International Publishing AG 2017
D.D. Schmorrow and C.M. Fidopiastis (Eds.): AC 2017, Part I, LNAI 10284, pp. 521–534, 2017.
DOI: 10.1007/978-3-319-58628-1_39

stick-on notes are common user-interface metaphors based on a user's knowledge of office environments. Roots, trunks, branches, and leaves are metaphors for structural or hierarchical organization based on a user's knowledge of trees. These metaphors not only provide the user an understanding of concepts and structural relationships, but also permissible actions and potential consequences of actions. In the office environment, files, folders and tabs have implications for intuitive means of organizing information in a nested fashion, while stick-on notes carry implications about methods for annotating information.

Metaphors derive their power from the user's experiences with the real world prior to encountering them in the computational setting. This experience can be gained by direct experience in the world (e.g., working in an office) or by indirect observation of other people's interactions (e.g., watching a master chef in a kitchen setting). People learning through observations of others' interactions with the world gives inspiration to how machines could learn by observing user interactions through user-interface metaphors.

Despite the ubiquity of user-interface metaphors in practical applications, much of their use has been ad-hoc, based on intuition rather than formalism. We leverage an existing user-interface metaphor taxonomy [4,5] to help formalize the notion of metaphor and its role in user interfaces. We extend the use of this interface metaphor taxonomy for interactive machine learning. Such formalisms provide us with a more nuanced view of the role of these metaphors and how machines might learn from our interactions with them.

The crux of our argument is that, if it is "things" that make people smart about how to interact with the world [18], and metaphors about those things have made complex computational machines intuitively accessible to users [3,10], then those same metaphors can be leveraged by machine learning to render the computational systems smarter about the meanings of the interactions from the people who use them.

We believe that computers can learn by observing user interactions with user-interface metaphors. Our goal in the present paper, however, is not to simply reiterate the body of literature on how to select a good metaphor. Rather, our goal is to explore how machine learning might exploit good metaphors selected for (graphical) user interfaces to advance the capabilities of the machine learning-based system. We do not wish to be prescriptive about which metaphors should be used. We hope to identify synergies between user-interface metaphors, particularly those already familiar to users, and the goals and needs of machine learning to suggest fruitful next steps for using metaphors to support interactive machine learning.

## 2    The User-Interface Metaphor Taxonomy

We adopt the metaphor taxonomy of Barr et al. [4] which presents an extension to the seminal work of Lakoff and Johnson [16]. This framework provides a taxonomy of metaphors and introduces several important concepts. Figure 1 depicts their taxonomy (the subset of the image with squared corners); we note that the elements of this taxonomy are not mutually exclusive. We provide a short summary of these elements for completeness.

**Orientational** metaphors organize a set of concepts in terms of a space. For example, GOOD IS UP, and BAD IS DOWN. They provide at least one dimension (e.g., goodness, time) along which we can relate concepts to one another. The fast-forward (right-pointing arrow) and rewind (left-pointing arrow) buttons on a media player are simple examples of orientational user-interface metaphors.

**Ontological** metaphors support understanding of system concept based on understanding of objects or entities in the physical world. A common ontological metaphor is TIME AS AN OBJECT with quantity (e.g., having enough time). In a computational system, DATA AS A FILE is a common ontological metaphor, where the file can be quantified and manipulated.

**Structural** metaphors characterize the structure of one concept through another concept. Where ontological metaphors state that X is an object, structural metaphors state the object that X is, which implies its structure. For example, the FOLDER AS AN OBJECT in the user interface is an ontological metaphor, and the FOLDER AS A CONTAINER for holding documents is a structural metaphor for the object [7]. Structural metaphors speak to how the user experiences the concept.

**Process** and **element** metaphors are types of structural metaphors introduced by Barr and colleagues [4], inspired by the work of Nielsen and Molich [17]. Process metaphors explain how something works, indicating functionality. For example, tools are process metaphors that use icons or words to indicate functionality within graphics software, such as SCISSORS to CUT CONTENT. Element metaphors are part of the user interface that indicate which process metaphors are applicable. Toolboxes containing collections of tools with common functionality are familiar element metaphors. Because of their common functionality for adding visual content, BRUSH, PENCIL, and PAINT BUCKET AS DRAWING IMPLEMENTS are collected into a PAINTING TOOLBOX.

**Metonymy** metaphors substitute the name or adjunct of an object for the object itself. For example, PEN FOR WORDS, as in "the pen is mightier than the sword." Within computational systems, examples of metonymy include the MAGNIFYING GLASS FOR SEARCH and ZOOM, and a QUESTION MARK FOR HELP MENU.

Not included in the taxonomy diagram, but referred to in practice, there is also a concept of a conventional metaphor [6]. A conventional metaphor is one with which users are already familiar, and so it continues to be used. Common examples include BUSY PROCESSOR AS SPINNING ICON (replacing the cursor) and DATA AS DOCUMENT.

Metaphors connote meanings and potential affordances to the users through a concept of metaphoric entailment. A metaphoric entailment describes what one thing (the signifier) implies about another (the signified). This concept is both fundamental to Lakoff and Johnson's work in language, and it is fundamental

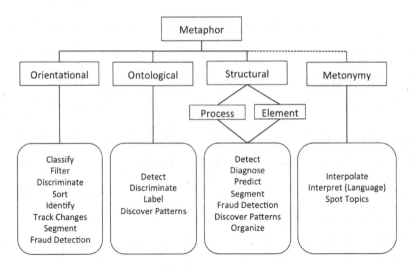

**Fig. 1.** User-interface metaphor taxonomy from [4] augmented with the types of machine learning activities that might benefit from leveraging each type of metaphor.

to user interface design. An example provided by [6] is USING THE DATA-STORAGE SYSTEM IS FILING. Entailments for this user-interface metaphor include:

a. There are files in the data-storage system.
b. There are folders in the data-storage system.
c. Files can be placed (recursively) in folders in the data-storage system.

Entailments provide a way of transferring the user's knowledge about the signifier onto the signified. These can be used to construct deductive arguments, hence the use of the verb entails. For example:

```
A FOLDER IS A FILE.
FILES CAN BE DUPLICATED.
--------------------------------------
Therefore: A FOLDER CAN BE DUPLICATED.
```

## 2.1 Why Are User-Interface Metaphors Important for Humans?

Interface metaphors allow users to more quickly learn and adapt to new user interfaces through reasoning by analogy. Analogical reasoning is central to cognition [12–14]. Analogies operate as a mapping between domains, providing context for finding patterns and relationships between patterns. Analogies provide a way of recreating complex patterns from personal feeling and experience. They form the foundation of mental models to support mental simulation and prediction for novel situations. In the context of data analytics, analogical reasoning is a foundation for contextualizing cues and using them for appropriate recall and inferences over the course of the analytics process [19]. By tapping into analogical reasoning, user-interface metaphors take advantage of the extensive cognitive capabilities supported by analogy. When user-interface metaphors are successful, they seem invisible to the users, providing an intuitive and seamless user experience [10].

Interfaces that do not rely on user-interface metaphors (or worse yet, break them) make learning a new interface or system more difficult. Many user-interface metaphors have become ubiquitous because interfaces that break with them frustrate users, which limits adoption. One of the most familiar cases is the aforementioned personal computer OPERATING SYSTEM AS DESKTOP interface metaphor. Most non-specialist users (non-computer-scientist or engineer) are comfortable navigating the desktop environment, but they are not comfortable working within the command line interface. The ubiquity of the desktop and the familiarity of the metaphor have established user expectations for system interactions. The additional time and effort needed to work from the command line to accomplish the same goals are costs that many users do not want to pay. In fact, one can argue that the use of the metaphor itself becomes a kind of metaphor for other applications. Because of the desktop work environment, nearly every operating system using a graphic interface employs the TRASH CAN AS CONTAINER metaphor for unwanted files. Emptying the trash can becomes the metaphor for permanently removing files. Not using this metaphor or adopting a new metaphor would have to provide significant benefits over the existing metaphor for people to want to make the change.

## 2.2   Why Are User-Interface Metaphors Important for Machines?

In addition to supporting intuitive user interface design, we can conceive of metaphors as an additional rich source of data for machine learning systems. Many traditional machine learning approaches rely on pre-labeled training data with minimal direct user input into the training process. The resulting trained algorithms are non-adaptive during application; even if the user's understanding of the data has changed, the machine algorithm remains fixed. Active learning approaches have resulted in more adaptive machine learning systems that are responsive to explicit user feedback [1]. Such systems require humans to engage in the training process by providing explicit inputs, such as labels for images, to create a training data set for semi-supervised machine learning. But human-interface interactions can provide additional implicit data to the system. For the image labeling situation, for example, the speed at which labels are input, the similarity in labels between images, and the number of other activities with which the user engages concurrent to the labeling task could all provide information to the machine.

Metaphors have the potential to provide critical contextual information and constraints on user interactions that can be leveraged to guide machine learning. Paralleling the human use of interface metaphors, they might provide a mechanism for a process akin to analogical reasoning for the machine learner. Past interaction with data via metaphors, for example, offers a template for how to handle new data [20]. Consider a case where a user places all email from advertisers into the trash can, using the TRASH CAN AS CONTAINER metaphor. Explicitly, the user has input to the system a specific set of data that need to go into a cluster with all other objects in that container. Implicitly, the user is indicating a set of data that s/he wishes to eliminate or not even receive in the inbox. Knowledge of this intention can be derived from the DELETE FILES AS EMPTY TRASH CAN metaphor. If the machine learner could access this metaphor, it could derive implicitly the user's intention from the explicit actions. From this, perhaps the system could learn to predictively place new messages from advertisers into the trash can as well. Thus, the user input provides direct feedback to the machine learner, and the metaphor provides the context critical for interpreting and generalizing the user's actions. This approach has obvious benefits (off-loading the effort from the user) as well as risks (the machine places something important in the trash). We anticipate that transparency into how the system is handling new data will be important for avoiding overgeneralizations from user interaction with metaphors. User feedback or guidance to the system to correct machine errors can aid in avoiding the overgeneralization as well.

As described above, user-interface metaphors provide both context for interpretation as well as constraints on the possible user interactions afforded by the metaphor. Continuing our trash can metaphor, one would naturally fill and empty the trash, but one does not usually organize the trash, as one might with a file system metaphor. Machines capable of learning metaphors could leverage the affordance constraints to make predictions about future interactions, with the interpretation grounded in the metaphor-provided context. Metaphor entailments would further augment the machine's ability to interpret and generalize user behaviors. The user-interface taxonomy in Fig. 1 offers a way to consider the classes of possible metaphors in a way that describes the context and constraints within each class, as we have defined above. Certain contexts and their associated interactions have variable amounts of usefulness for different machine learning tasks. We augment the user-interface taxonomy with sets of machine learning tasks for which each class should have a high degree of usefulness. Our hypothesized associations are shown in the rounded-corner boxes in the lower tier of Fig. 1. Specific choices of user-interface metaphors, however, should be made in the context of the desired system. We do recommend leveraging common user-interface metaphors as much as possible from existing systems. To aid a system designer in thinking through metaphor selection for interactive machine learning systems, we next discuss a set of questions that define ways in which metaphors could shape system development.

## 3   Metaphor Considerations

As in user interface design, choice of metaphor is critical to promoting effective user engagement and understanding of an IML system. It is also a design decision made at the discretion of the designer, though often shaped and honed by user evaluations. Erickson [10] posed five critical questions that should be asked in the process of user-interface metaphor generation to evaluate candidate choices. These questions are also applicable to selection of metaphors for use in machine learning:

1. *How much structure does the metaphor provide?* This speaks to the usefulness of the metaphor for aiding the user in analogical reasoning and scaffolding knowledge.
2. *How much of the metaphor is actually relevant to the problem [for which the interface is designed to solve]?* The inclusion of too much irrelevant detail could be misleading or result in misuse or overgeneralization of the metaphor.
3. *Is the interface metaphor easy to represent?* Simplicity is key to adoption because the analogical reasoning will not place heavy cognitive demands on the user.
4. *Will your audience understand the metaphor?* Metaphors cannot help users if the users cannot understand the metaphor.
5. *What else do the proposed metaphors buy you?* Metaphors can be selected that provide useful structure that can be built upon later with additional metaphors or additional functionality.

IML from metaphors is one way that good choice of metaphors can be built upon for additional system functionality, going more deeply than just user interaction functionality implied by the last question. But this suggests that we should start the process of developing IML systems on the metaphors that have already proven successful in interface design, such as the desktop and toolboxes. Moving toward IML with metaphors wherein the user interactions and the content of the metaphor become additional inputs to the machine learner (in addition to the data of interest), we should pose some additional questions to inform good choices of metaphors.

6. *How consistent is the structure of the user interactions with the metaphor?* Metaphors that encourage consistent interaction patterns within and across users will provide consistent structure to the interaction-based inputs to the machine learner. This includes both the volume (number of types of interactions, frequency of interaction) and the variability of the interactions. Of particular concern in the process of learning is how many interpretations could be attributed to the same user input. For example, double clicking a mouse can mean open a file, launch an application, highlight a word, or zoom in/out, depending on the context. Context learned from the metaphor and metonymy (icons) become critical for disambiguating user behavior for machine interpretability.
7. *How many machine learning tasks can be supported with a selected metaphor or method of representation?* This speaks to an IML-specific dimension of usefulness for the metaphor. If a metaphor supports a basic machine learning task (cluster, rank) in a manner that is not strictly tied to a data type or domain, then that metaphor may be re-usable across systems that all need the same basic task. VOTING AS AGREEMENT is an example of a simple

metaphor (up/down orientational metaphor) that can be represented with straightforward interactions (select up/down button, which may be depicted as arrows, ✓ and × marks, or thumbs up and thumbs down). Depending on the context, voting can signify agreement between users or between user and machine, individual user preferences, rankings, correctness, or popularity. As we will discuss later, metaphors may be scaffolded upon each other to develop more complex systems, so the development of metaphor-based IML approaches may benefit from starting with combinations erring on the side of simplicity over complexity.

8. *Does the metaphor seamlessly integrate the machine learning into the user's natural activities on the system?* Even if a selected metaphor is intuitive and easy for the user to grasp and use, if it does not integrate naturally into their activities or workflow then it will may be deemed a burden or distraction by the user, who will avoid it altogether. Active learning suffers a pitfall of placing a cognitive burden on the user of providing explicit labels or supervision to the machine learner, which can detract from a user's primary goals or needs for using the computational system and machine learner in the first place. A promise of IML systems is the ability to extract supervision for the machine learner from natural interactions by the user within their normal workflow. Choice of metaphor may be crucial to this smooth integration.

9. *What can the machine learner learn from the metaphor?* We address this at length in the next section.

## 4   Learning from Metaphors

Metaphors make complex computational machines intuitively accessible to users. By analogy, those same metaphors can be leveraged by machine learning to render the computational systems smarter about the meanings of the interactions from the people who use them. We argue that metaphors provide a natural focal point for learning from the user. This learning may occur at two levels. When the metaphor is fixed and well known (e.g., trash can), we can learn about the user's goals, preferences, and needs through their interaction with the metaphor. When the metaphor is not obvious (e.g., organizing objects on a canvas), machines can learn the metaphor by looking at how the user interacts with user interface elements. For example, if user is organizing objects horizontally based on chronology, the machine might infer the user is applying a TIME AS LINE metaphor. Machines can learn these metaphors much in the same way we learn these metaphors, by observing the actions of others.

Each interaction with the metaphor provides an opportunity to gather data and learn. Placing a file in the trash suggests the file has little future utility for the user. Organization of elements on a canvas may suggest how those objects relate to one another. These insights come from how the user interacts with the particular metaphor. The trash can provides a structural metaphor; spacial grouping on a canvas suggests an orientational metaphor. We focus herein on learning from interactions, specifically interaction with metaphors. Interactions provide the clearest insight into user intentions, preferences, goals, and needs. Metaphors provide structure that may be absent from non-metaphorical user interface elements.

User-interface metaphors are typically more constrained due to inherent limitations of the physical objects and processes they represent. This provides a level of consistency and regularity that makes learning from them easier than from a metaphor-free user interfaces, which is unconstrained. Furthermore, the metaphorical entailments by definition follow a particular form and can be reasoned about.

Organization of objects into folders and subfolders or grouping objects on a desktop provides clues to the relationship between those objects. If like items are clustered, the machine can learn to leverage the SIMILARITY AS PROXIMITY metaphor. Changing the sort order of a list or reordering individual list items provides clues to our preferences. The machine can learn the VALUE AS POSITION metaphor. Each user interaction with a metaphor is a potential clue and opportunity for machine learning to better support the user. When the metaphor is unknown, we want to learn these metaphors from user interaction. This approach provides the opportunity to learn new metaphors that maybe unknown to the designer of the system.

Fails and Olsen [11] presented an approach to constructing a perceptual user interface (PUI) using an IML model. IML departs from the standard machine learning (SML) model in which models are built offline then used interactively. IML creates a loop in which the user supports training of the classifier, which is built incrementally and interactively. Done properly, user interactions in IML provide both benefit to the user and feedback to the underlying machine learning system. Crayons is a system described in [11] that uses IML to create image classifiers. Crayons leverages the ITEM TAGGING AS PAINTING and USER FEEDBACK AS TUTOR metaphors. Crayons users can refine the image classifiers by iteratively adding more tags until satisfied with the machine learning performance.

Machine learning can be used to learn metaphors and leverage those metaphors to better support users. Orientational and structural metaphors provide the greatest opportunity to leverage machine learning. The following two sections provide more detail into how we can learn from interaction with these classes of metaphors.

## 4.1   Learning from Orientational Metaphors

Orientational metaphors provide meaning to objects in terms of a space. Examples include, GOOD IS UP, BAD IS DOWN, PAST TIME IS LEFT, FUTURE TIME IS RIGHT, HOT IS ABOVE COLD. Orientational metaphors extend to and are embedded in everyday objects, symbols and speech. Examples from speech include "she was at the top of her class" or "left of boom" referring to time prior a horrible event. Most typically, organizational metaphors provide meaning to a collection of objects and therefore describe how they relate to one another along an important dimension. For example, using the common orientational metaphor TIME AS LINE, users can depict the temporal ordering of events by organizing them along a horizontal line from left (earliest) to right (latest). We can depict that "$A$ occurred before $B$" and "$B$ occurred before $C$" by placing these symbols horizontally organized from left to right. This metaphor implies a number of entailments such as: $A$, $B$, and $C$ are different events; $A$, $B$, and $C$ didn't occur at the same time; and $A$ occurred before $C$.

When the metaphor is unknown, we would like the machine to learn from user interaction with orientational interface metaphors while avoiding the hardcoding or pre-programming of specifics into a system (e.g., good := up, bad := down).

As previously discussed, learning can occur at two levels. First, we discuss how we could learn the metaphor itself from user interaction.

While we could pre-program a particular orientational metaphor into a system, such a system would always be brittle. Suppose the user is given a 2-d canvas in which to organize objects needed to perform a task, and s/he is employing an organizational metaphor. Given sufficient access to the underlying structure and attributes of objects, a system could learn the metaphor being employed by the user. For example, one user might be organizing hotter objects on the right and colder objects on the left. A second user could similarly be organizing hotter objects on the top and the colder objects on the bottom of the canvas. The machine should learn the metaphor TEMPERATURE AS LINE regardless of the orientation on the screen.

Given sufficient examples, the system could review the attributes of each object and determine the attribute that provides an ordering consistent with the user's layout. This could be employed in both dimensions across all the attributes. Of course, it is possible that there are multiple (or no attributes) that result in a consistent ordering. Multiple attributes providing a consistent ordering suggests some level of ambiguity on the part of the learner. Finding no consistent order may suggest that the user is not using an orientational metaphor, or they are organizing by an attribute not available to the learner.

Regardless, there exists opportunities for the machine learning to make plausible inferences regarding the use of orientational metaphors by the user. Similar techniques could be used to derive metaphorical entailments the user has made based on the organization of objects.

The second level entails learning the user's preferences, goals, and concepts. Given the system understands the metaphor, the system could learn the user's preferences based on interactions with those metaphors. User interaction with objects organized in a space provides clues into how the objects are related based on the metaphor. For example, the user places important items above less important items in a list. Second level learning would have to determine what makes items important, which could be obtained by examining the items. Having learned which items are important and not important, the system could recommend where to place incoming items based on their importance.

Such an intelligent system could warn the user when they are using the metaphor inconsistently. Widely used metaphors across users could be suggested to new users of the system. Entailments that have found to be useful could be leveraged with new users.

## 4.2  Learning from Structural Metaphors

Structural metaphors reveal the structure of one object (signified) through reference of another object (signifier). They are more powerful than orientational or ontological metaphors as they often leverage more of our personal experiences. ARGUMENT IS WAR is a classic example, where ARGUMENT is the signified and WAR is the signifier. People "attack" and "defend" themselves in argument. There are "winners" and "losers" or someone might "come to my defense". Such metaphors are powerful in that they can aid the user in more quickly discovering how a system works though the analogy.

iTunes uses many orientational and structural metaphors, including the album/song metaphor and stop, reverse, forward, and play button metaphors. In fact, these metaphors arise from multiple sources. The album/song metaphor comes from vinyl records. The control button metaphors come from the cassette recorder. These metaphors instantly clue the user into what operations are valid and what consequences the associate actions have on the iTunes system. They bring forth a number of entailments.

- You can organize songs into albums.
- You can play, reverse, or forward a song.
- You can play an album.
- Playing an album starts with the first song.

They also indicate which actions you cannot perform.

- You can not put in album in an album.
- You can play an album, but not reverse an album.

Because the metaphors are, by design, abstracted away from the unchangeable properties of the physical objects, the computational system can combine multiple metaphors to introduce new functionality. For example, iTunes songs are not hardcoded on media in a fixed order. The system can take advantage of the LIST AS DECK OF CARDS metaphor, providing a new shuffle entailment, which randomly reorders the song list.

Similarly, learning from structural metaphors can occur at two levels. When the metaphor is fixed and well known, we're interested in learning the user's needs through their use of the metaphor. When the metaphor is not known, the system must first learn the structure being implied by the metaphor. A learning system could learn the types of relationship and hierarchies that are possible based on user interaction. Again, we would like to avoid hard coding learning systems.

An IML system, having learned the iTUNES AS ALBUM PLAYER metaphor, could further leverage the metaphor and related user interactions to support a system for DATA STREAM AS MEDIA PLAYER metaphor. Samples of data could be treated as songs. Activation icons can be re-used for the interface. The IML system takes advantage of the metaphor entailments:

- User can organize samples into into data stream albums (related groupings).
- You can play, reverse, or forward a data stream sample.
- You can play an album of data streams.
- Playing a data stream album starts with the first sample.

The efforts of the analyst, then, can be re-focused on more challenging problems of stream fusion or out-of-order samples. Further, because of the ability of the IML approach to learn metaphors, ongoing interactions by the user on the streaming player system could evolve additional metaphors. The IML system can also learn which metaphor elements are not useful in the new setting (e.g., track shuffle would render the stream out of temporal order and may not be useful for stream interpretation). The adoption of existing metaphors serves to facilitate the learning and system development process.

## 5   Limitations and Implications

We believe the most promising applications for learning from metaphors will be through interactive machine learning (IML). General purpose learning-based agent support faces a number of challenges identified by Horvitz [15]. Such a learning system may make poor guesses about the user's goals and intents, or the costs and benefits of taking action to support the user. These limitations stem from a number of underlying root causes.

- Data is limited.
- The number of user interactions may not be sufficient for the system to generalize about the user's goals and intent.
- The user's goals may not be static but may change over time.
- The underlying data may also be shifting over time.
- The underlying object may not reveal enough information for a learning system.
- The user may be making decisions based on background knowledge or insights unavailable to the machine learner.

While Horvitz [15] proposed mixed-initiative systems to address these limitations, our goals are more modest. IML systems focus on solving a more limited set of problems that center-around machine learning. These systems, by definition, focus on learning from user interaction on a continuous basis. This seems like the natural place to leverage metaphors for the purpose of learning.

We share a vision for machine learning, packaging algorithms into small, discrete components. Designers and developers will then build systems using pre-built learning components. This is a departure from traditional systems which rely on a centralized learning component. Ideally, we would like to support specific tasks (e.g., filter, sort, organize) through a collection of suitable component-level interface metaphors. Each metaphor would have its own learning algorithm, learning from interactions with that component. Machine learning will need to understand context (e.g., user, time, environment) to be effective.

Learning could occur at multiple levels in a hierarchical fashion. General purpose learning could be used to identify orientational or structural metaphors. Higher level learning could be used to determine orientational axis or structure of a metaphor. Other learning algorithms could focus on individual preferences, goals, and priorities of the user through interaction. Such an approach would be much more flexible than hard-coded single learner systems.

Interactive machine learning from user-interface metaphors is especially appealing in streaming data environments. Relative to static or batch analytics environments, streaming data is characterized by increased velocity and volatility. That is, data captured from an inherently dynamic and streaming world can result in a user environment that is shifting, with changing context and constraints. Leveraging user interfaces for analytics that learn through metaphors supports adaptation of the machine learner to the changing context and constraints without the need for explicit user input. This enables an analyst to be continually supported by the machine analytics and focus mental efforts on the data interpretations, rather than supervising the machine learning. Recent work in visual analytics has demonstrated the utility of leveraging interface interactions to learn functions of the data and make visualization recommendations [8,9,20]. User-interface metaphors smoothly integrated into interactive machine learning could be the key to extending such learning to streaming analytics environments.

**Acknowledgments.** The research described in this document was sponsored the U.S. Department of Energy (DOE) through the Analysis in Motion Initiative at Pacific Northwest National Laboratory. The views and conclusions contained in this document are those of the author and should not be interpreted as representing the official policies, either expressed or implied, of the U.S. Government.

# References

1. Amershi, S., Cakmak, M., Knox, W.B., Kulesza, T.: Power to the people: the role of humans in interactive machine learning. AI Mag. **35**(4), 105–120 (2014)
2. Apple Computer Inc: Macintosh Human Interface Guidelines. Addison-Wesley, Boston (1992)
3. Barr, P.: User-interface metaphors in theory and practice. Master's thesis, University of Wellington, Victoria (2003)
4. Barr, P., Biddle, R., Noble, J.: A taxonomy of user-interface metaphors. In: Proceedings of the SIGCHI-NZ Symposium on Computer-Human Interaction, pp. 25–30. ACM (2002)
5. Barr, P., Biddle, R., Noble, J.: A semiotic model of user-interface metaphor. In: Liu, K. (ed.) Virtual, Distributed and Flexible Organisations, pp. 189–215. Springer, Dordrecht (2004)

6. Barr, P., Khaled, R., Noble, J., Biddle, R.: A taxonomic analysis of user-interface metaphors in the microsoft office project gallery. In: Proceedings of the Sixth Australasian Conference on User interface, vol. 40, pp. 109–117. Australian Computer Society, Inc. (2005)
7. Brockerhoff, R.: User interface metaphors. In: MacHack Conference proceeding (2000)
8. Brown, E.T.: Learning from users' interactions with visual analytics systems. Ph.D. thesis, Tufts University (2015)
9. Brown, E.T., Ottley, A., Zhao, H., Lin, Q., Souvenir, R., Endert, A., Chang, R.: Finding waldo: learning about users from their interactions. IEEE Trans. Vis. Comput. Graph. **20**(12), 1663–1672 (2014)
10. Erickson, T.D.: Working with interface metaphors. In: Baecker, R.M. (ed.) Readings in Human-Computer Interaction: Toward the Year 2000, vol. 11, pp. 147–151 (1995)
11. Fails, J.A., Olsen, D.R.: Interactive machine learning. In: Proceedings of the 8th International Conference on Intelligent User Interfaces, pp. 39–45. ACM (2003)
12. Gentner, D.: Structure-mapping: a theoretical framework for analogy. Cogn. Sci. **7**(2), 155–170 (1983)
13. Gentner, D., Holyoak, K.J.: Reasoning and learning by analogy: introduction. Am. Psychol. **52**(1), 32–34 (1997)
14. Gentner, D., Holyoak, K.J., Kokinov, B.N.: The Analogical Mind: Perspectives from Cognitive Science. MIT Press, Cambridge (2001)
15. Horvitz, E.: Principles of mixed-initiative user interfaces. In: CHI (1999)
16. Lakoff, G., Johnson, M.: Metaphors We Live By. University of Chicago Press, Chicago (1980)
17. Nielsen, J., Molich, R.: Heuristic evaluation of user interfaces. In: Proceedings of the SIGCHI Conference on Human Factors in Computing Systems (1990)
18. Norman, D.A.: Things that Make us Smart: Defending Human Attributes in the Age of the Machine. Basic Books, New York (1993)
19. Patterson, R.E., Blaha, L.M., Grinstein, G.G., Liggett, K.K., Kaveney, D.E., Sheldon, K.C., Havig, P.R., Moore, J.A.: A human cognition framework for information visualization. Comput. Graph. **42**, 42–58 (2014)
20. Saket, B., Kim, H., Brown, E.T., Endert, A.: Visualization by demonstration: an interaction paradigm for visual data exploration. IEEE Trans. Visual Comput. Graph. **23**(1), 331–340 (2017)

# Classifying Tweets Using User Account Information

John Khoury[1], Charles Li[2], Chloe Lo[3], Corinne Lee[3],
Shakeel Rajwani[3(✉)], David Woolfolk[3], Alexis-Walid Ahmed[3],
Loredana Crusov[3], Arnold Pérez-Goicochea[3], Christopher Romero[3],
Rob French[3], and Vasco Ribeiro[3]

[1] Eastern Florida State College, Melbourne, FL, USA
neumanns@easternflorida.edu
[2] Mercy College, Dobbs Ferry, NY, USA
[3] Sirius17, Melbourne, FL, USA
shakeel.rajwani@gmail.com

**Abstract.** Twitter is a short-text message system developed 6 years ago. It now has more than 100 million users generating over 300 million tweets every day. Twitter accounts are used for diverse purposes, such as social, advertising, political, religious, benevolent or vicious ideologies, among other activities. These activities can be communicated by humans, a machine or a robot. The purpose of this paper is to build predictive models, such as Logistic Regression, K Nearest Neighbors and Neural Network in order to identify the best variables that help predict, based on the contents, whether the tweets are coming from a human or a machine with the least possible error.

**Keywords:** Twitter · Social media · Predictive models

## 1 Background

Social media activity data, in the case of this paper Twitter account activity, can be understood as consisting of two primary components, metadata or demographics, and content data. Metadata involves external characteristics such as time of activity, time of account creation, location, type of platform used for activity, number of friends, followers, and more. Content data involves syntactic and semantic characteristics. The focus of this paper is on content data, in particular, content feature extraction that can be implemented on a large set of text data in order to enable categorization of types of activities and classification of activities as automated versus non-automated.

This paper is an attempt to build a model to make prediction based only on content data. Among various available modeling tools, Linear Regression Model, K-Nearest Neighbor Model and a Neural Nets Model, abbreviated as LR Model, KNN Model and NN Model respectively, were of the highest interest.

© Springer International Publishing AG 2017
D.D. Schmorrow and C.M. Fidopiastis (Eds.): AC 2017, Part I, LNAI 10284, pp. 535–542, 2017.
DOI: 10.1007/978-3-319-58628-1_40

## 2  Method

### 2.1  Data

Twitter account activity data is available through the Twitter API (application program interface) which returns requests for random samples of data in JSON (JavaScript Object Notation) data structure containing both demographics and content.

Content data (tweets) are returned (in the JSON structure) as character strings of length 1 to 140 characters. They may be in any language or no language at all. Tweets can contain any combination of free text, emotions, chat-speak, hash tags, and URL's. Twitter does not filter tweets for content (e.g., vulgarisms, hate speech).

A vector of text features is derived for each user. This is accomplished by deriving text features for each of the user's tweets, then rolling them up. Therefore, one content feature vector is derived for each user from all of that user's tweets.

The extraction of numeric features from text is a multi-step process:

1. Collect the User's most recent (up to 200) tweet strings into a single set (a Thread).
2. Convert the thread text to upper case for term matching.
3. Scan the thread for the presence of emoticons, chat-speak, hash tags, URL's, and vulgarisms, setting bits to indicate the presence/absence of each of these text artifacts.
4. Remove special characters from the thread to facilitate term matching.
5. Create a Redundancy Score for the Thread. This is done by computing and rolling up (sum and normalize) the pairwise similarities of the tweet strings within the thread using six metrics: Euclidean Distance, RMS-Distance, L1 Distance, L-Infinity Distance, Cosine Distance, and the norm-weighted average of the five distances.

The thread text feature vector contains vector component user scores based on features such as the emoticon flag, chat-speak flag, hash tag flag, URL flag, vulgarity flag, and the Redundancy score.

For this study, a sample of the activity of 8845 Twitter accounts containing 1,048,395 tweets was collected for content analysis.

A list of 23 potential content related features was created and calculated for each of the 8845 Twitter accounts in the sample. These features were used for modeling in this paper (Table 1).

**Table 1.** The list of 23 features for analysis

| Feature | | Description |
|---|---|---|
| 1 | tweets | Number of tweets up to 200 |
| 2 | adj | Number of adjectives per tweet |
| 3 | adv | Number of adverbs per tweet |
| 4 | art | Number of articles per tweet |
| 5 | commnoun | Number of common nouns per tweet |
| 6 | conj | Number of conjunctions per tweet |

(*continued*)

**Table 1.** (*continued*)

| Feature | | Description |
|---|---|---|
| 7 | interj | Number of interjections per tweet |
| 8 | prep | Number of prepositions per tweet |
| 9 | pron | Number of pronouns per tweet |
| 10 | propnoun | Number of proper nouns per tweet |
| 11 | verb | Number of verbs per tweet |
| 12 | stopword | Number of stop words matching a list - per tweet |
| 13 | vulgar | Number of vulgar words matching a list - per tweet |
| 14 | hash | Number of hash tags per tweet |
| 15 | urls | Number of urls per tweet |
| 16 | case | Relative frequency of usage of both lower and upper case |
| 17 | punc | Relative frequency of usage of punctuation |
| 18 | emo_chat | Number of emoticons per tweet |
| 19 | good_len | Number of *characters* in correctly spelled words per tweet |
| 20 | good_cnt | Number of *words* of correctly spelled words per tweet |
| 21 | bad_len | Number of *characters* of incorrectly spelled words per tweet |
| 22 | bad_cnt | Number of *words* of incorrectly spelled words per tweet |
| 23 | redund | Redundancy Score for the Thread |

## 2.2 Software

XLMiner is used to sort out the most important features for model building and model assessment/validation.

## 2.3 Procedures

For the purpose of predicting whether a tweet was automated or not, a manual rating process of a sample tweet content coming from 101 active accounts was carried out. Of the 101 accounts, 65 were jointly classified as 35 bot accounts and 30 non-bot accounts with a high level of confidence. Those 65 accounts were then assigned a dependent variable value of 1 if identified as a bot, and 0 otherwise.

An analysis on the correlation of each of the 23 features to the dependent variable (bot or not) was carried out to identify the 10 most important predictive features (with the highest correlation scores) from this set of data with 65 accounts.

The BOT-NotBOT tags from the 65 manually tagged threads were extrapolated to the larger corpus of 8,845 threads using a population-weighted N-Nearest Neighbor Classifier having the 65-thread set as the standard. N was allowed to vary from 1 to 20; the tagging for N = 5 was chosen for the extrapolation, because it best matched the class proportions of the 65-thread standard.

XLminer's Feature Selection tool was then used to identify the best subset of features to be used as input to a classification or prediction method from the extrapolated dataset. After the 10 most important features were selected, they were considered in conjunction with the set of important features obtained from the correlation analysis using the set of 65 manually tagged tweet accounts. A preliminary analysis using LR Model was performed to figure out the best subset of features for modeling by trial and error, where the process was aided by, but not limited to, the union of the two sets of best features obtained from the two preliminary analyses.

The resultant subset of best features was then used in building a LR Model, KNN Model and a NN Model. The set of 8845 data was split into two portions, where 60% became the training set and the remaining 40% became the validation set. The training set was used to build the model, and the validation set was used to evaluate the accuracy of each aforementioned model. Each model would try to predict whether a tweet account in the set was a bot or not, and then the result would be compared with the BOT-notBOT tag either flagged manually by readers or determined by the afore-mentioned extrapolation.

Cumulative gains charts for all models were plotted to evaluate the predictive power of each model.

## 3    Result

### 3.1    Feature Selection

The following predictors were returned as the 10 most important features, sorted in descending order of importance (Table 2):

**Table 2.** The list of most important features (common features highlighted)

|  | Correlation Analysis | Feature Selection by XLminer |
|---|---|---|
| 1 | redund | good_len |
| 2 | urls | commnoun |
| 3 | good_len | good_cnt |
| 4 | adj | redund |
| 5 | tweets | propnoun |
| 6 | vulgar | tweets |
| 7 | good_cnt | urls |
| 8 | commnoun | punc |
| 9 | emo_chat | adj |
| 10 | art | prep |

The feature "good_cnt" was dropped as it correlates highly with "good_len", due to the fact that more correctly spelled words implies more characters of correctly spelled words. The grammatical features "art", "punc", "adj" and "prep" were considered to be of little importance, and therefore were dropped. The feature "hash", which did not appear in the top 10 features from both analysis, were included as it was deemed important by observing the tweet data. The following 9 features were singled out as the best features for model building:

1. tweets
2. redund
3. commnoun
4. propnoun
5. vulgar
6. hash
7. urls
8. emo_chat
9. good_len

## 3.2  Modeling

After training the models with the training set, the results given by the validation set were as follows (Tables 3, 4 and 5; Figs. 1, 2 and 3):

**Table 3.**  a, b The results of LR model

(a)

| Actual Class | | Predicted Class | |
|---|---|---|---|
| | | Bot | Not Bot |
| | Bot | 646 | 75 |
| | Not Bot | 237 | 2579 |

(b)

| Class | Cases | Error | % Error |
|---|---|---|---|
| Bot | 721 | 75 | 10.40% |
| Not Bot | 2816 | 237 | 8.42% |
| Overall | 3537 | 312 | 8.82% |

**Table 4.**  a, b The results of KNN model

(a)

| Actual Class | | Predicted Class | |
|---|---|---|---|
| | | Bot | Not Bot |
| | Bot | 513 | 208 |
| | Not Bot | 86 | 2730 |

(b)

| Class | Cases | Error | % Error |
|---|---|---|---|
| Bot | 721 | 208 | 28.85% |
| Not Bot | 2816 | 86 | 3.05% |
| Overall | 3537 | 294 | 8.31% |

**Table 5.** a, b The results of NN model

**(a)**

|              |         | Predicted Class | |
|--------------|---------|------|---------|
|              |         | Bot | Not Bot |
| **Actual**   | **Bot** | 588 | 133 |
| **Class**    | **Not Bot** | 120 | 2696 |

**(b)**

| Class | Cases | Error | % Error |
|-------|-------|-------|---------|
| **Bot** | 721 | 133 | 18.45% |
| **Not Bot** | 2816 | 120 | 4.26% |
| **Overall** | 3537 | 253 | 7.15% |

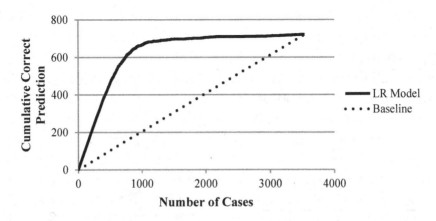

**Fig. 1.** The cumulative gains chart of LR model

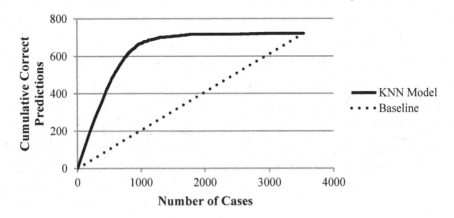

**Fig. 2.** The cumulative gains chart of KNN model

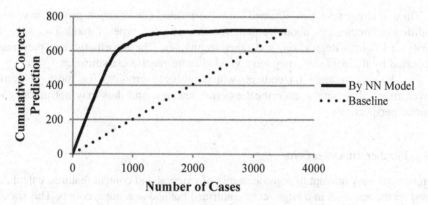

**Fig. 3.** The cumulative gains chart of NN model

# 4 Discussion

## 4.1 Findings

We can see that overall percentage error for NN model lowest among the models built. Therefore we conclude that NN model is best for classifying the new tweet as BOT or NOTBOT. It has the lowest classification error rate (Table 6).

**Table 6.** The summary of results of all models

| Model | Overall percentage error | Percentage error predicting bots | Percentage error predicting non-bots |
|-------|--------------------------|----------------------------------|--------------------------------------|
| LR    | 8.82%                    | 10.40%                           | 8.42%                                |
| KNN   | 8.31%                    | 28.85%                           | 3.05%                                |
| NN    | 7.15%                    | 18.45%                           | 4.26%                                |

As observed from the results, there is more error related to classifying the designation BOT. If we want to correctly classify more BOTs we may need to lower the cut-off value than 0.5 which is default in XLMiner.

By observing the curvature of the cumulative gain charts of all models, it was evident that the predictive power of all models were better than a random guess without a model, as all curves lay above the baseline. This confirmed that all models had significant predictive power in determining whether a tweet account is automated or not.

## 4.2 Limitations

A number of significant limitations must be noted.

First, the data set may not be a representative sample of the current state of affairs when it comes to bot versus non-bot activity in the Twitter medium.

Second, the process of manually classifying a small set of accounts and reaching a consensus in roughly two-thirds of the cases may not be without errors.

Third, a larger set when obtained from the manual classification process may lead to different conclusions about content features and the type of modeling, such as penalized Logistic Regression, and other techniques. These methods, had they been supported by the data size, may have yielded more precise classification.

Fourth, concentrating on content, which probably provides the most predictive power, may still ignore some critical external features, and thus may not produce an optimal perspective.

### 4.3   Further Investigations

Future work may attempt to consider a mix of external and content features, calculated based on the activities in a large set of confirmed bot and non-bot accounts. This should enable a much more reliable subset of predictive or discriminating features, which in turn may lead to more reliable descriptive and predictive models.

## 5   Conclusion

This paper demonstrates one way by which content of social media activities may be processed in terms of mathematical "signatures" of different types of online behaviors that may be used for descriptive and predictive modeling of automated versus non-automated activities.

## References

1. Alarifi, A., Alsaleh, M., Al-Salman, A.: Twitter turing test: identifying social machines. Inf. Sci. **372**, 332–346 (2016). doi:10.1016/j.ins.2016.08.036
2. Azaria, A., Durst, S., Ferrara, E., Flammini, A., Galstyan, A., Kagan, V., Lerman, K., Menczer, F., Subrahmanian, V.S., Zhu, L.: The DARPA Twitter bot challenge. IEEE Comput. **49**, 38–46 (2016)
3. Benton, M.C., Radziwill, N.M.: Bot or Not? Deciphering Time Maps for Tweet Interarrivals. CoRR, abs/1605.06555 (2016)
4. Carapinha, F., et al.: Modeling of social media behaviors using only account metadata. In: Schmorrow, D., Fidopiastis, M. (eds.) AC 2016. LNCS, vol. 9744, pp. 393–401. Springer, Cham (2016). doi:10.1007/978-3-319-39952-2_38
5. Gilani, Z., Wang, L., Crowcroft, J., Almeida, M., Farahbakhsh, R.: Stweeler: a framework for Twitter bot analysis. In: Proceedings of the 25th International Conference Companion on World Wide Web - WWW 2016 Companion (2016). doi:10.1145/2872518.2889360
6. Kolesnikov, D.A., Ovchinnikov, G.V., Oseledets, I.V.: Algebraic reputation model RepRank and its application to spambot detection. CoRR, abs/1411.5995 (2014)
7. Hancock, M.: Automating the characterization of social media culture, social context, and mood. In: 2014 Science of Multi-Intelligence Conference (SOMI), Chantilly, VA (2014)
8. Hancock, M., Sessions, C., Lo, C., Rajwani, S., Kresses, E., Bleasdale, C., Strohschein, D.: Stability of a type of cross-cultural emotion modeling in social media. In: Schmorrow, D., Fidopiastis, C. (eds.) AC 2015. LNCS, vol. 9183, pp. 410–417. Springer, Cham (2015). doi:10.1007/978-3-319-20816-9_39

# Machine Learning-Based Prediction of Changes in Behavioral Outcomes Using Functional Connectivity and Clinical Measures in Brain-Computer Interface Stroke Rehabilitation

Rosaleena Mohanty[1], Anita Sinha[2], Alexander Remsik[3],
Janerra Allen[4], Veena Nair[5], Kristin Caldera[6], Justin Sattin[7],
Dorothy Edwards[3,7], Justin C. Williams[2],
and Vivek Prabhakaran[2,5,7(✉)]

[1] Department of Electrical Engineering,
University of Wisconsin-Madison, Madison, USA
rmohanty@wisc.edu
[2] Department of Biomedical Engineering,
University of Wisconsin-Madison, Madison, USA
amsinha@wisc.edu, jwilliams@engr.wisc.edu,
VPrabhakaran@uwhealth.org
[3] Department of Kinesiology, University of Wisconsin-Madison, Madison, USA
{aremsik, dfedwards}@wisc.edu
[4] Department of Material Science and Engineering,
University of Wisconsin-Madison, Madison, USA
jdallen4@wisc.edu
[5] Department of Radiology, University of Wisconsin-Madison, Madison, USA
VNair@uwhealth.org
[6] Department of Rehabilitation, University of Wisconsin School of Medicine
and Public Health, Madison, USA
kcaldera@wisc.edu
[7] Department of Neurology, University of Wisconsin School of Medicine
and Public Health, Madison, USA
sattin@neurology.wisc.edu

**Abstract.** The goal of this work is to evaluate if changes in brain connectivity can predict behavioral changes among subjects who have suffered stroke and have completed brain-computer interface (BCI) interventional therapy. A total of 23 stroke subjects, with persistent upper-extremity motor deficits, received the stroke rehabilitation therapy using a closed-loop neurofeedback BCI device. Over the course of the entire interventional therapy, resting-state fMRI were collected at two time points: prior to start and immediately upon completion of therapy. Behavioral assessments were administered at each time point via neuropsychological testing to collect measures on Action Research Arm Test, Nine-Hole Peg Test, Barthel Index and Stroke Impact Scale. Resting-state functional connectivity changes in the motor network were computed from pre- to post-interventional therapy and were combined with clinical data corresponding to each subject to

© Springer International Publishing AG 2017
D.D. Schmorrow and C.M. Fidopiastis (Eds.): AC 2017, Part I, LNAI 10284, pp. 543–557, 2017.
DOI: 10.1007/978-3-319-58628-1_41

estimate the change in behavioral performance between the two time-points using a machine learning based predictive model. Inter-hemispheric correlations emerged as stronger predictors of changes across multiple behavioral measures in comparison to intra-hemispheric links. Additionally, age predicted behavioral changes better than other clinical variables such as gender, pre-stroke handedness, etc. Machine learning model serves as a valuable tool in predicting BCI therapy-induced behavioral changes on the basis of functional connectivity and clinical data.

**Keywords:** Brain-computer interface · Stroke rehabilitation · BCI therapy · Upper extremity motor recovery · Resting-state fMRI · Machine learning · Predictive model

# 1  Introduction

Approximately 800,000 individuals in the U.S. experience a new or recurrent stroke (ischemic or hemorrhagic) each year [7]. In recent years, there has been a significant decrease in stroke mortality, indicating that most stroke subjects survive their initial stroke event; however, survivors are often left with life-long impairments involving one or more of their motor, speech, visual etc., abilities. Specifically, upper extremity motor deficits are frequently observed in 30–66% of stroke survivors after six months of the stroke [6]. The majority of subjects have some spontaneous functional recovery after a stroke event. However, rehabilitative therapies can further improve motor recovery several months after stroke to enhance quality of life for survivors [13].

An emerging technology for stroke rehabilitation that has been shown to stimulate additional recovery is brain-computer interface (BCI). Electroencephalogram (EEG)-based BCI detects neural signals and uses them as inputs to provide real-time feedback, enabling users to modulate their own brain activity. This is a promising therapy for those with motor disabilities by allowing self-modulation of neural signals to control assistive devices such as computers during rehabilitative tasks without relying on residual muscle control [3]. Previous studies have shown potential functional benefits associated with the use of BCI technology in stroke rehabilitation including neural reorganization and improved behavioral and motor function [8, 10, 11, 13]. Real-time feedback in the form of reward for the production of certain brain activity patterns relative to others while performing a task raises the possibility that there are changes in brain activation patterns produced during tasks similar to those involved in BCI therapy; an important implication could be that BCI therapy can induce detectable changes in brain activation patterns in stroke subjects.

Studies have suggested that an association exists between resting-state networks and the reorganization of neural processes in post-stroke motor recovery [2, 11]. Resting-state functional magnetic resonance imaging (rs-fMRI) is a powerful tool to measure the temporal correlation of the spontaneous, low-frequency (<0.1 Hz) blood oxygenation level dependent (BOLD) signals across regions in the resting brain. Oscillations in the BOLD fMRI signals are indicative of self-organizing dynamic behavior of the brain, and these fluctuations are suggested to be associated with the flexibility and variability in motor function and cognition [1, 5]. Recent neuroimaging studies have demonstrated that there are overlapping networks involved during resting-state fMRI as well as motor imagery and motor execution fMRI tasks [4, 8]. The motor network commonly includes cortical areas such as the primary motor area (M1), pre-motor cortex (PMC) and supplementary motor area (SMA) as it is widely accepted that activity in these cortical regions maintains a dynamic equilibrium at resting-state and is modulated during task performance. Prior work indicates that resting-state brain connectivity can be potentially used to track brain changes following brain-computer interface (BCI) therapy [8], which serves as the motivation for this present study.

EEG-based BCI intervention is a promising rehabilitation therapy for improving motor function after stroke; however, the changes in functional connectivity in the brain following this therapy are not fully understood. Changes in resting-state functional connectivity (rs-FC) were examined in eight seed regions of interest within the motor network that play a dominant role in motor development, specification and execution. Specifically intra-hemispheric and inter-hemispheric connectivity measures were compared within this network. The aim of this present study was to investigate the effect of BCI interventional therapy using a closed-loop neurofeedback device intended to improve motor function in stroke subjects on behavioral performance metrics using changes in rs-FC in the motor network by analyzing data of 23 stroke subjects. To study the change in FC and behavior over time, we chose to utilize rs-fMRI data from two different time points, namely before starting and immediately upon completion of the interventional therapy. Additionally, clinical variables associated with the subjects were factored in. A number of behavioral measures were collected during neuropsychological assessments that served as the behavioral outcome variables. With the help a non-linear machine learning regression model, we analyzed the correlation between change in FC and clinical variables to change in behavioral outcomes.

## 2 Materials and Methods

### 2.1 Study Design

A permuted-block design that included subject characteristics such as gender, stroke chronicity and severity of motor impairment was employed to randomly assign subjects to either the Crossover Control group or BCI therapy group (Experimental Only). Subjects in the BCI therapy group received interventional rehabilitation therapy with functional assessment and MRI scans at four time points: (1) pre-therapy, (2) mid-therapy, (3) post-therapy and (4) 1 month after completing the last BCI therapy. Subjects in the Crossover Control group first received three functional assessments and MRI scans during the control phase in which no BCI therapy was administered, and their assessments were spaced at intervals similar to those given during the BCI therapy phase. After completing the control phase of the study, the Crossover Control group moved to the BCI therapy phase of the study. This study paradigm, as illustrated in Fig. 1, was chosen to determine if any outcome effects were attributable to BCI training vs. practice effects. All subjects completed at least 9 and up to 15 two-hour sessions of interventional BCI therapy. For the purposes of this study, we chose to analyze the change in rs-FC and change in behavior between time points (1) and (3) i.e. pre-therapy

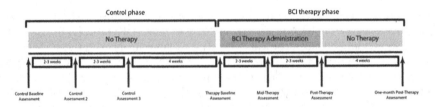

**Fig. 1.** Study paradigm of BCI-EEG interventional therapy [13]

to post-therapy. Furthermore, we combined the subjects from the Crossover Control group and the BCI therapy into a single sample group to provide more power to the analysis.

## 2.2    Sample Characteristics

Subjects were recruited as part of an ongoing stroke rehabilitation study to evaluate interventional therapy using a BCI device targeting upper extremity motor function. Inclusion criteria were as follows: (1) at least 18 years or older; (2) persistent upper extremity motor impairment resulting from ischemic or hemorrhagic stroke; (3) ability to provide written informed consent. Exclusion criteria included: (1) concurrent neurodegenerative or other neurological disorders; (2) psychiatric disorders or cognitive deficits that would preclude a subject's ability to provide informed consent; (3) pregnant or likely to become pregnant during the study; (4) allergies to electrode gel, metal and/or surgical tape, contraindications to MRI; (5) concurrent treatment for infectious disease. All participants provided written informed consent. The Health Sciences Institutional Review Board of the University of Wisconsin-Madison approved the study, including all of the measures assessed and therapies administered to subjects. The mean age of the sample was 63 years. The sample included 10 female and 13 male subjects; 20 right-handed subjects, 2 left-handed subjects and 1 ambidextrous subject; 13 subjects with a right-hemispheric lesion and 10 subjects with a left-hemispheric lesion. Individual study subject characteristics are summarized in Table 1 below.

**Table 1.**  Subject demographics and characteristics

| Subject ID | Age (years) | Gender | Affected arm | NIH stroke scale | Time since stroke (months) | Pre-stroke handedness | Lesion hemisphere |
|---|---|---|---|---|---|---|---|
| 1 | 52 | Male | Right | 8 | 15 | Right | Left |
| 2 | 61 | Female | Right | 8 | 16 | Right | Left |
| 3 | 68 | Male | Right | 0 | 3 | Right | Left |
| 4 | 66 | Male | Right | 6 | 23 | Right | Left |
| 5 | 73 | Female | Right | 0 | 2 | Ambi | Left |
| 6 | 59 | Male | Right | 2 | 28 | Right | Left |

(*continued*)

**Table 1.** (*continued*)

| Subject ID | Age (years) | Gender | Affected arm | NIH stroke scale | Time since stroke (months) | Pre-stroke handedness | Lesion hemisphere |
|---|---|---|---|---|---|---|---|
| 7 | 45 | Female | Left | 6 | 99 | Right | Right |
| 8 | 71 | Female | Left | 6 | 26 | Right | Right |
| 9 | 80 | Male | Left | 2 | 20 | Right | Right |
| 10 | 76 | Male | Left | 3 | 132 | Right | Right |
| 11 | 43 | Male | Right | 2 | 12 | Right | Left |
| 12 | 75 | Female | Left | 7 | 23 | Right | Right |
| 13 | 61 | Male | Right | 0 | 17 | Right | Left |
| 14 | 48 | Male | Left | 3 | 6 | Left | Right |
| 15 | 56 | Male | Right | 2 | 17 | Right | Left |
| 16 | 50 | Male | Left | 4 | 16 | Right | Right |
| 17 | 77 | Male | Left | 1 | 22 | Left | Right |
| 18 | 69 | Male | Left | 1 | 90 | Right | Right |
| 19 | 82 | Female | Right | 0 | 19 | Right | Left |
| 20 | 74 | Female | Left | 8 | 6 | Right | Right |
| 21 | 64 | Female | Left | 1 | 6 | Right | Right |
| 22 | 42 | Female | Left | 3 | 87 | Right | Right |
| 23 | 57 | Female | Left | 7 | 12 | Right | Right |

## 2.3   BCI Intervention Procedure

The BCI-EEG setup is presented in Fig. 2. The closed-loop neurofeedback device used in therapy incorporates feedback from EEG from visual display, tongue stimulation and functional electrical stimulation. Subjects received no more than three sessions of interventional therapy per week, and the total BCI therapy lasted up to six weeks. The BCI therapy ran on the BCI2000 software 9 version 2 with modifications for administering tongue stimulation (TDU 01.30, Wicab Inc.), along with functional electrical stimulation (FES) (LG-7500, LGMedSupply; Arduino 1.0.4). EEG signals were detected and recorded from a 16-channel EEG cap and amplifier (Guger Technologies) during the BCI therapy.

Each session started with an open-loop screening task to optimize the control signals. During this screening task, each subject was asked to move either their left or right hand with resting periods in between; this was conducted using words on a screen as cues, "right", "left" or "rest", in blocks of 4 s. The specific movements, that subjects chose, ranged from opening or closing one's hand, squeezing hand and wrist flexion; these movements served as baseline abilities for each individual. During the screening session, the subjects were not given any feedback. Attempted movement was used for the initial screening and closed-loop feedback conditions to structure the neurofeedback training conditions similar to the mental processes used when performing real-world movement. For this reason, control signals were based on neural activity patterns of subjects performing movement to aid in strengthening the persistence of movement-related brain

**Fig. 2.** BCI-EEG interventional therapy setup [8]

activity patterns. Following the initial screening, subjects performed a closed-loop task, where they received real-time visual feedback in the context of a game to gain training on how to modulate brain activity while moving each hand. In the game, subjects were prompted to move a cursor (ball) onto a target area, and target areas were positioned on the left or right side of the computer screen. Subjects were told to move his/her left or right hand to control the movement of the ball towards the direction of the target presented on the screen. Real-time EEG signals were used to calculate lateral cursor movement. During each BCI therapy session, all subjects completed 10 runs of the game, each run including 8–12 trials, with visual feedback.

Once subjects successfully completed 10 runs of the game with visual feedback and achieved consistent accuracy ( $\geq 70\%$ ), both tongue stimulation and functional electrical stimulation (FES) were incorporated into the session. Tongue stimulation, continuous electro-tactile stimulation of the tongue on an electrode grid, was administered in each following trial. FES was administered to muscles of the impaired arm when neural activity signals corresponding to impaired arm movement were detected on EEG during a trial in which subjects had to move the cursor to a target on the screen that matched the side of the impaired arm. In order to keep subjects engaged in the tasks, the size of the target on the screen could be changed to increase the difficulty of the task if they showed normal cursor control and accuracy. Additionally, if subjects were unable to perform the task with proper cursor control, the task difficulty could be reduced.

## 2.4   Data Acquisition

Neuroimaging scans were acquired at all the four time points mentioned previously. However, we chose to use the imaging data from two of those four time points, namely: time point (1) i.e. prior to starting the intervention and time point (3) i.e. immediately upon completion of intervention. Rs-fMRI scans were acquired on GE 750 3T MRI scanners (GE Healthcare, Waukesha, WI) using an 8-channel head coil. 10-minute resting state scans were acquired while subjects' eyes were closed using single-shot echo-planar T2*-weighted imaging: TR = 2.6 s, 231 time-points, TE = 22 ms, FOV = 22.4 cm, flip angle = 60°, voxel dimensions of $3.5 \times 3.5 \times 3.5$ mm$^3$, 40 slices. T1-weighted axial images were obtained at the start of each scan using FSPGR BRAVO sequence (TR = 8.132 ms, TE = 3.18 ms, TI = 450 ms) over a $256 \times 256$ matrix with 156 slices (flip angle = 12°, FOV = 25.6 cm and slice thickness = 1 mm).

## 2.5  Neuropsychological Assessment

In order to assess the behavioral impact of the BCI therapy, neuropsychological assessments were administered at the four previously specified time points. Corresponding to the imaging data, we were interested in behavioral changes between pre-therapy to post-therapy. The following standard behavioral measures were evaluated each time: Action Research Arm Test (ARAT) [9, 14], the 9-Hole Peg Test (9-HPT) [15], Barthel Index [18], and Stroke Impact Scale (SIS) [16, 17]. Scores for the 9-HPT were calculated using the mean of two attempts with the impaired hand. ARAT scores reflect a total score assigned for the subject's impaired hand. The SIS scores encompass multiple aspects of which we take into account the following standard domains: Activities of Daily Living, Hand Function, Mobility and Strength. In accordance with standard SIS scoring practice, SIS domain scores were transformed to yield a percentage of possible points obtained that have been used for the analysis here.

## 2.6  Data Preprocessing

Rs-fMRI data were preprocessed using Analysis of Functional NeuroImages [20] and FMRIB Software Library [21]. The preprocessing steps included: removing the first three volumes of each scan, images despiking, slice time correction, alignment with anatomical scan, spatial smoothing with a 4-mm FWHM (full width at half maximum) Gaussian kernel, transformation into TLRC space (3.5 mm isotropic), motion censoring (per TR motion > 1 mm or 1°), nuisance regression, bandpass filtering (0.009–0.08 Hz). We did not perform global signal regression. Additionally, motion within each volume was computed, and volumes with motion > 1 mm were censored.

## 2.7  Functional Connectivity in the Regions of Interest

Seed regions within the motor network were based on prior findings that have looked at resting-state connectivity in stroke population [4, 8]. The areas identified were based on a network of cortical and subcortical areas activated during visually paced hand movements. The regions of interest (ROIs) of this network include the primary motor cortex (M1), supplementary motor area (SMA), thalamus and lateral premotor cortex (PMC) in the right and left hemispheres visualized in Fig. 3, [12] and are abbreviated as per Table 2. The MNI coordinates for the 8 ROIs were used to create 8-mm spherical seed ROIs for this study. For each subject, time series from the 8 ROIs were extracted from the spatially standardized residuals for the resting EPI data. The motor mask constituting the 8 ROIS was then used to extract the time series for each region, and an $8 \times 8$ ROI correlation matrix was computed for each subject. The computed correlation coefficients were standardized to their z-scores. The change in FC from time-point before BCI therapy to time-point after BCI therapy were used as input features for the machine learning regression model.

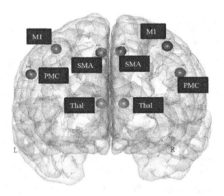

**Fig. 3.** Motor network with seed regions used in analysis [8]

**Table 2.** Shorthand representation of the eight ROIs used for the analysis

| ROI | Shorthand |
| --- | --- |
| Left primary motor cortex | L.M1 |
| Right primary motor cortex | R.M1 |
| Left premotor cortex | L.PMC |
| Right premotor cortex | R.PMC |
| Left supplementary motor area | L.SMA |
| Right supplementary motor area | R.SMA |
| Left thalamus | L.Thal |
| Right thalamus | R.Thal |

## 2.8   Clinical Data

Often times, factors such as age and gender can impact the changes in behavior over time and need to be taken into account. Thus, in the regression model for this work, we consider the following clinical variables: age, gender, side of affected arm, NIH Stroke Scale (NIHSS), time since last stroke (TSS) and pre-stroke handedness score (pre-hand). These clinical factors were evaluated separately, as well as combined with FC features, in order to predict change in behavioral measures.

## 2.9 Data Analysis

We model this data by fitting a machine learning based regression model to FC and clinical data in order to predict behavioral measures. In particular, supervised learning support vector machines (SVM) [19] are employed. Typically used as a classifier, SVM can also be used for regression analysis [22] and is known as Support Vector Regression (SVR). SVR forms a non-parametric method by implementing the kernel trick. The principle behind the using SVR analysis is described below:

Consider pair of multiple data points, $\{(x_1, y_1), \ldots (x_l, y_l)\} \subset X \times \mathbb{R}$, X being the input space. While the $x_i$s represent the input features, the $y_i$s represent the outcome variable. Here, the $x_i$s are the FC values or the clinical data corresponding to each subject and $y_i$s stand for the behavioral outcomes such as 9-HPT, ARAT, BI, SIS measures. The goal, then, is to find a non-linear function that fits the $x_i$s such that the estimated value of $y_i$s within a specified small margin of error from the true $y_i$s. If $f$ is the estimated function, we have:

$$f(x) = <w, x> + b$$

where, $w \in X$, and $b \in \mathbb{R}$, $<, >$ denotes the dot product in X.

Ensuring that $w$ turns out to be small ensures that the estimated $y_i$s will deviate from true $y_i$s within a small margin. This problem can be rewritten in the form of a convex optimization as follows:

$$minimize \frac{1}{2}||w||^2$$

$$subject\ to \begin{cases} y_i - <w, x_i> - b \leq \varepsilon \\ <w, x_i> + b - y_i \leq \varepsilon \end{cases}$$

where, $\varepsilon$ is the small allowable margin of error between true $y_i$ and estimated $y_i$.

The above can be reformulated again to cope with possible infeasible constraints that may arise in the optimization problem by incorporating slack variables. This is analogous to the concept of "soft margin" in SVM classifiers that allow for marginally higher error to get a more superior performance overall. The reformulation, then, becomes:

$$minimize \frac{1}{2}||w||^2 + C \sum_{i=1}^{l}(\zeta_i + \zeta_i^*)$$

$$subject\ to \begin{cases} y_i - <w, x_i> - b \leq \varepsilon + \zeta_i \\ <w, x_i> + b - y_i \leq \varepsilon + \zeta_i^* \\ \zeta_i, \zeta_i^* \geq 0 \end{cases}$$

where, $C > 0$ is a constant that determines the extent to which error more than $\varepsilon$ are allowed. The given method for regression can be applied to the linear case where a linear estimate between input and output values is predicted. With the use of SVM, a kernel method [23] can be applied which can predict non-linear relationships between the input and the output variables, thus, giving a better fit to the data. We implemented the SVR using a Gaussian radial basis function for a kernel given by:

$$k\left(x_i, x_j\right) = \exp\left(-\frac{||x_i - x_j||^2}{2\sigma^2}\right)$$

where, $||x_i - x_j||^2$ is the squared Euclidean distance between two input feature points and $\sigma$ is a free parameter. The kernel transforms the input feature dataset into a higher dimensional feature space where a linear separation may exist.

A leave-one-out-cross-validation (LOOCV) was used to predict the outcome variable since it is a method that gives the most unbiased estimate of test error [25]. In a LOOCV approach, the same dataset can be used for both the training and testing phases. During each fold of LOOCV, a data point is left out and training is performed on the remaining data points. The left out data point is used as a testing point to predict the outcome corresponding to it and evaluate the error measure of prediction. Each data point is left out only once, and so, the number of folds is equal to the number of data points in the sample. We assessed the performance of the SVR using the root mean squared error given by the following equation:

$$RMSE = \sqrt[2]{\frac{1}{l}\sum_{i=1}^{l}(y_{est_i} - y_i)^2}$$

where, $y_{est_i} - y_i$ term is the measure of error between the estimated outcome and the true outcome. A good SVR should have low values of RMSE.

Three cases of SVR were implemented, namely: (a) change in FC from pre-intervention to post-intervention as the input features to predict behavioral outcomes, (b) clinical variables as input variables to predict behavioral outcomes, (c) change in FC and clinical variables together as input variables to predict behavioral outcomes. The SVR generates a weighting system to rank the various input features in the order of their importance in predicting the outcome variables. We implemented SVR on MATLAB (R2015b; MathWorks, Natick, MA, USA) with the help of The Spider Machine Learning Toolbox library for SVR [24].

## 3    Results

We present the results of using a non-linear SVR with a Gaussian kernel by the following cases: The prediction of changes in behavioral outcomes from pre-intervention to post-intervention was performed using (a) changes in FC only (b) clinical variables only and (c) changes in FC and clinical variables combined. Among the top 10 ranked predictors, a greater number of inter-hemispheric FC changes were observed compared to intra-hemispheric FC changes for almost all the behavioral measures in cases (a) and (c). Also in both these instances, while intra-hemispheric FC change between left M1 and left PMC was ranked within top 10 predictors, inter-hemispheric FC change between left M1 and right M1 was ranked within top 5 predictors corresponding to changes across all behavioral measures. Age emerged as the top ranked clinical variable associated with changes in all the behavioral outcomes in (b) as expected. In (c), however, age predicted changes particularly in ARAT for affected side, BI, SIS for strength of affected side and SIS for mobility. Although the difference is small, reduced RMSE values were observed in case (c), thus, suggesting that combining FC changes with clinical variables might form a better predictive model as compared to cases (a) and (b) with a larger sample size. Detailed list of top 10 ranked predictors by the SVR weights can be found in Tables 3, 4 and 5 below. The behavioral outcomes are listed by the following shorthand: 9HPT (A) for 9-HPT of affected side, 9HPT (U) for 9-HPT of unaffected side, ARAT (A) for ARAT of affected side, ARAT(U) for ARAT of unaffected side, SIS (Str) for Strength, SIS (ADL) for Activities of Daily Living, SIS (Mob) for Mobility and SIS (Hand) for Hand Function.

Each SVR is evaluated using RMSE for assessment of quality of prediction. Lower RMSE values represent better performance. The RMSE for the three SVRs are presented by case in Table 6 below. RMSE_FC, RMSE_Clinical, RMSE_FC+Clinical are used as shorthand to denote the three cases of SVR respectively.

**Table 3.** The top 10 ranked predictors of change in behavioral measures using change in FC as input features from pre-intervention to post-intervention

| ID | 9HPT (A) | 9HPT (U) | ARAT (A) | ARAT (U) | Barthel Index | SIS (Str) | SIS (ADL) | SIS (Mob) | SIS (Hand) |
|---|---|---|---|---|---|---|---|---|---|
| 1 | L.Thal-R.Thal | L.M1-R.M1 | L.SMA-L.Thal | L.Thal-R.PMC | L.Thal-R.SMA | R.PMC-R.SMA | R.M1-R.Thal | L.Thal-R.Thal | L.SMA-R.SMA |
| 2 | L.M1-R.M1 | L.Thal-R.M1 | L.Thal-R.PMC | L.PMC-R.SMA | L.PMC-L.Thal | L.PMC-R.SMA | L.M1-R.M1 | L.PMC-R.SMA | L.PMC-L.SMA |
| 3 | L.M1-L.PMC | L.PMC-R.SMA | L.M1-R.M1 | R.PMC-R.Thal | L.PMC-R.SMA | R.PMC-R.Thal | L.Thal-R.M1 | L.M1-R.M1 | L.M1-R.M1 |
| 4 | L.SMA-R.SMA | L.M1-L.PMC | L.Thal-R.SMA | L.M1-R.M1 | L.M1-R.M1 | L.Thal-R.PMC | L.M1-L.PMC | L.M1-L.PMC | L.SMA-R.Thal |
| 5 | L.PMC-L.SMA | L.SMA-R.PMC | L.Thal-R.M1 | L.SMA-L.Thal | L.SMA-R.Thal | L.M1-R.M1 | L.Thal-R.PMC | R.PMC-R.SMA | L.M1-L.PMC |
| 6 | L.PMC-R.PMC | L.M1-R.PMC | L.PMC-L.M1 | L.M1-L.PMC | L.SMA-R.SMA | L.SMA-R.PMC | L.Thal-R.SMA | L.SMA-R.PMC | L.SMA-R.PMC |
| 7 | L.PMC-R.SMA | L.M1-L.SMA | R.Thal-R.SMA | L.M1-R.PMC | R.M1-R.Thal | L.M1-L.PMC | L.M1-R.PMC | L.SMA-R.Thal | L.M1-R.PMC |
| 8 | L.SMA-R.PMC | L.SMA-L.Thal | L.Thal-L.PMC | L.M1-L.SMA | L.Thal-R.Thal | L.M1-R.PMC | L.SMA-R.Thal | L.Thal-R.M1 | R.SMA-R.Thal |
| 9 | R.PMC-R.Thal | L.M1-R.SMA | L.SMA-R.Thal | R.SMA-R.Thal | L.M1-L.PMC | L.Thal-R.SMA | R.SMA-R.Thal | L.Thal-R.SMA | L.Thal-R.Thal |
| 10 | L.M1-R.PMC | L.M1-L.Thal | L.M1-R.PMC | L.PMC-L.Thal | L.M1-R.PMC | L.PMC-R.Thal | L.M1-L.SMA | R.SMA-R.Thal | L.M1-L.SMA |

**Table 4.** Ranked predictors of change in behavioral measures from pre-intervention to post-intervention using clinical data as input features

| ID | 9HPT (A) | 9HPT (U) | ARAT (A) | ARAT (U) | Barthel Index | SIS (Str) | SIS (ADL) | SIS (Mob) | SIS (Hand) |
|---|---|---|---|---|---|---|---|---|---|
| 1 | Age | Age | Age | Age | Age | Age | Age | Age | Age |
| 2 | NIHSS | TSS | TSS | Affected arm | Affected arm | NIHSS | TSS | Pre-hand | Affected arm |
| 3 | Pre-hand | Pre-hand | NIHSS | Pre-hand | Pre-hand | Affected arm | Pre-hand | TSS | Pre-hand |
| 4 | Affected arm | Gender | Affected arm | Gender | TSS | Pre-hand | Gender | Gender | TSS |
| 5 | Gender | Affected arm | Gender | TSS | Gender | Gender | Affected arm | Affected arm | Gender |
| 6 | TSS | NIHSS | Pre-hand | NIHSS | NIHSS | TSS | NIHSS | NIHSS | NIHSS |

**Table 5.** The top 10 ranked predictors of change in behavioral measures using change FC from pre-intervention to post-intervention and clinical data as input features

| ID | 9HPT (A) | 9HPT (U) | ARAT (A) | ARAT (U) | Barthel Index | SIS (Str) | SIS (ADL) | SIS (Mob) | SIS (Hand) |
|---|---|---|---|---|---|---|---|---|---|
| 1 | L.M1-R.M1 | L.Thal-R.SMA | Age | L.Thal-R.SMA | Age | Gender | L.M1-R.M1 | L.PMC-R.SMA | L.PMC-L.Thal |
| 2 | L.M1-L.PMC | R.PMC-R.Thal | L.SMA-R.Thal | L.SMA-R.Thal | L.SMA-L.Thal | L.PMC-L.Thal | L.M1-L.PMC | L.PMC-R.Thal | L.Thal-R.SMA |
| 3 | L.PMC-L.Thal | L.PMC-R.Thal | L.PMC-R.Thal | L.SMA-R.PMC | L.PMC-R.Thal | L.PMC-R.Thal | L.M1-R.PMC | L.M1-R.M1 | L.M1-R.M1 |
| 4 | Gender | L.M1-R.M1 | R.SMA-R.Thal | L.M1-R.M1 | L.M1-R.M1 | Affected Arm | L.M1-L.SMA | L.M1-L.PMC | L.M1-L.PMC |
| 5 | L.PMC-R.Thal | L.Thal-R.PMC | L.M1-R.M1 | L.M1-L.PMC | R.SMA-R.Thal | L.M1-R.M1 | L.M1-R.SMA | Gender | L.M1-R.PMC |
| 6 | L.M1-R.PMC | L.M1-L.PMC | L.PMC-R.SMA | L.M1-R.PMC | L.M1-L.PMC | R.SMA-R.Thal | L.Thal-R.Thal | L.SMA-R.Thal | L.SMA-R.Thal |
| 7 | L.M1-L.SMA | L.M1-R.PMC | L.SMA-L.Thal | L.M1-L.SMA | NIHSS | Age | L.M1-L.Thal | R.SMA-R.Thal | Time since stroke |
| 8 | L.M1-R.SMA | L.M1-L.SMA | L.SMA-R.SMA | L.M1-R.SMA | L.Thal-R.Thal | L.SMA-R.Thal | L.M1-R.Thal | Age | L.M1-L.SMA |
| 9 | L.Thal-R.SMA | Affected Arm | L.M1-L.PMC | Affected Arm | L.M1-R.PMC | L.M1-L.PMC | NIHSS | L.M1-R.PMC | L.SMA-L.Thal |
| 10 | L.M1-L.Thal | L.M1-R.SMA | L.M1-R.PMC | NIHSS | L.M1-L.SMA | L.SMA-L.Thal | L.PMC-R.M1 | L.M1-L.SMA | L.M1-R.SMA |

# 4    Conclusion

## 4.1    Summary

Changes in functional connectivity and clinical measures, together, can predict behavioral changes in subjects undergoing BCI-aided rehabilitation for stroke recovery and

**Table 6.** Root meant squared errors by outcome for the three SVRs implemented

| Behavioral outcome | RMSE_FC | RMSE_Clinical | RMSE_FC+Clinical |
|---|---|---|---|
| 9HPT (A) | 1.0231 | 1.5527 | 1.023 |
| 9HPT (U) | 1.0208 | 1.3261 | 1.021 |
| ARAT (A) | 1.0261 | 1.1257 | 1.0252 |
| ARAT (U) | 1.0409 | 1.0969 | 1.0371 |
| Barthel Index | 1.0215 | 1.0984 | 1.0216 |
| SIS (Str) | 1.0264 | 1.5703 | 1.0261 |
| SIS (ADL) | 1.0241 | 1.0566 | 1.0238 |
| SIS (Mob) | 1.0282 | 1.5258 | 1.0274 |
| SIS (Hand) | 1.0238 | 1.272 | 1.0237 |
| **Mean SVR RMSE** | 1.0261 | 1.2916 | 1.0254 |

machine learning can help rank the predictors of change in behavior. Notably, it was demonstrated that inter-hemispheric changes in FC in the motor network are more significant than intra-hemispheric changes in driving the prediction for most of the behavioral scales included in the neuropsychological battery. Among the clinical variables, age appeared to be a significant factor in assessing changes in behavioral outcomes.

## 4.2 Discussion and Future Scope

This study highlights that machine learning based statistical tools such as the SVR can provide information correlating neuroimaging changes to behavioral changes, although it can be limited by the sample size used in the analysis. Additionally, the heterogeneity of the cohort in terms of their lesion location, lesion volume and affected side due to stroke may influence the result of the predictive model. A left hemispheric dominance was observed among the top weighted features predicting behavioral measures. This could potentially arise due to most subjects being right-handed prior to occurrence of the stroke and would require inclusion of comparable number of left-handed subjects in the sample in order to further analyze the effect of handedness. Furthermore, we have not taken into consideration, the relationship between the multiple behavioral outcomes in this work. Also, the direction of change in behavioral measurements has not been considered. In particular, future work could assess the relationship between behavioral gains and functional connectivity changes. The complete BCI-aided intervention involved collection of imaging as well as behavioral data at four different time points, of which the pre- and post-intervention data have been used in the current analysis. The analysis, here, uses only two of the four time-points and could be expanded further by considering the changes in FC over all the four time points and correlating it to behavioral changes. This current approach, however, provides a basic framework for future work to build a larger predictive model that incorporates data from additional predictors in the form of other imaging modalities such as diffusion tensor imaging (DTI), task-based fMRI, lesion maps, implements a multiple-output SVR to control for possible correlations between outcome variables and utilizes a larger sample size.

**Acknowledgments.** The authors would like to thank all the subjects and their families for their participation in the stroke rehabilitation program. Thanks to the study coordinator Theresa Jungae Kang and the MRI technicians Sara John and Jenelle Fuller at the Wisconsin Institutes for Medical Research. This study was supported by NIH grants RC1MH090912-01, K23NS086852, T32GM008692, UL1TR000427, T32EB011434 and TL1TR000429. Additional funding was also provided through a Coulter Translational Research Award, an American Heart Association Postdoctoral Fellow Research Award, AHA Midwest Grant-in-Aid Award, AHA National Innovation Award, UW Milwaukee-Madison Intercampus Grants, UW Graduate School, Grants from Shapiro Foundation and Foundation of ASNR award.

# References

1. Bajaj, S., Butler, A.J., Drake, D., Dhamala, M.: Functional organization and restoration of the brain motor-execution network after stroke and rehabilitation. Front. Hum. Neurosci. **9**(173), 1–14 (2015)

2. Carter, A.R., Astafiev, S.V., Lang, C.E., Connor, L.T., Rengachary, J., Strube, M.J., Pope, D.L.W., Shulman, G.L., Corbetta, M.: Resting inter-hemispheric fMRI connectivity predicts performance after stroke. Ann. Neurol. **67**(3), 365–375 (2010)

3. Felton, E.A., Radwin, R.G., Wilson, J.A., Williams, J.C.: Evaluation of a modified Fitts law brain-computer interface. J. Neural Eng. **6**, 1–7 (2009)

4. Grefkes, C., Eickhoff, S.B., Nowak, D.A., Dafotakis, M., Fink, G.R.: Dynamic intra- and interhemispheric interactions during unilateral and bilateral hand movements assessed with fMRI and DCM. NeuroImage **41**(4), 1382–1394 (2008)

5. Lee, M.H., Smyser, C.D., Shimony, J.S.: Resting state fMRI: a review of methods and clinical applications. AJNR Am. J. Neuroradiol. **34**(10), 1866–1872 (2013)

6. Kwakkel, G., Kollen, B.J., van der Grond, J., Prevo, A.J.H.: Probability of regaining dexterity in the flaccid upper limb: impact of severity of paresis and time since onset in acute stroke. Stroke **34**(9), 2181–2186 (2003)

7. Mozaffarian, D., Benjamin, E.J., Go, A.S., Arnett, D.K., Blaha, M.J., Cushman, M., et al.: Execute summary: heart disease and stroke statistics – 2016 update: a report from the American heart association. Circulation **133**(4), 447–454 (2016)

8. Nair, V.A., Young, B.M., Nigogosyan, Z., Remsick, A., Weber, S., Diffee, K., Walton, L., Tyler, M., Sattin, J., Edwards, D.F., Williams, J., Prabhakaran, V.: Abstract 6: resting-state functional connectivity changes after stroke rehabilitation using closed loop neurofeedback. Stroke **4**, A6 (2015)

9. Carroll, D.: A quantitative test of upper extremity function. J. Chronic Dis. **18**, 479–491 (1965). doi:10.1016/0021-9681(65)90030-5

10. Soekadar, S.R., Birbaumer, N., Slutzky, M.W., Cohen, L.G.: Brain-machine interfaces in neurorehabilitation of stroke. Neurobiol. Dis. **83**, 172–179 (2015)

11. Varkuti, B., Guan, C., Pan, Y., Phua, K.S., Ang, K.K., Kuah, C.W.K., Chua, K., Ang, B.T., Birbaumer, N., Sitaram, R.: Resting state changes in functional connectivity correlate with movement recovery for BCI and robot-assisted upper-extremity training after stroke. Neurorehabil. Neural Repair **27**(1), 53–62 (2013)

12. Xia, M., Wang, J., He, Y.: BrainNet Viewer: a network visualization tool for human brain connectomics. PLoS ONE **8**(7), e68910 (2013)

13. Young, B.M., Nigogosyan, Z., Walton, L.M., Song, J., Nair, V.A., Grogan, S.W., Tyler, M.E., Edwards, D.F., Caldera, K., Sattin, J.A., Williams, J.C., Prabhakaran, V.: Changes in functional brain organization and behavioral correlates after rehabilitative therapy using a brain-computer interface. Front. Neuroeng. **7**(26), 1–15 (2014)

14. Lang, C.E., Wagner, J.M., Dromerick, A.W., Edwards, D.F.: Measurement of upper-extremity function early after stroke: properties of the action research arm test. Arch. Phys. Med. Rehabil. **87**, 1605–1610 (2006). doi:10.1016/j.apmr.2006.09.003

15. Beebe, J.A., Lang, C.E.: Relationships and responsiveness of six upper extremity function tests during the first six months of recovery after stroke. J. Neurol. Phys. Ther. **33**, 96–103 (2009). doi:10.1097/NPT.0b013e3181a33638

16. Duncan, P.W., Wallace, D., Lai, S.M., Johnson, D., Embretson, S., Laster, L.J.: The stroke impact scale version 2.0. Evaluation of reliability, validity and sensitivity to change. Stroke **30**, 2131–2140 (1999). doi:10.1161/01.str.30.10.2131

17. Carod-Artal, F.J., Coral, L.F., Trizotto, D.S., Moreira, C.M.: The stroke impact scale 3.0: evaluation of acceptability, reliability and validity of the Brazilian version. Stroke **39**, 2477–2484 (2008). doi:10.1161/STROKEAHA.107.513671

18. Mahoney, F.I., Barthel, D.: Functional evaluation: the Barthel Index. Maryland State Med J. **14**, 56–61 (1965)

19. Scholkopf, B., Smola, A.J.: Learning with Kernels: Support Vector Machines, Regularization, Optimization, and Beyond. MIT Press, Cambridge, (2001)

20. http://afni.nimh.nih.gov/afni

21. www.fmrib.ox.ac.uk/fsl

22. Vapnik, V.: The Nature of Statistical Learning Theory. Springer, New York (1995)

23. Schölkopf, B., Smola, A.J.: Learning with Kernels: Support Vector Machines, Regularization, Optimization and Beyond, p. 633. MIT Press, Cambridge (2002)

24. Weston J., Elisseeff A., Bakir G., Sinz F.: The Spider Machine Learning Toolbox. Resource object oriented environment. http://people.kyb.tuebingen.mpg.de/spider/main.html

25. Hastie, T., Tibshirani, R., Friedman, J.H.: The Elements of Statistical Learning: Data Mining, Inference, and Prediction. Springer Publishing Company Inc., New York (2001). pp. 193–224

# Content Feature Extraction in the Context of Social Media Behavior

Shai Neumann[1], Charles Li[2], Chloe Lo[3], Corinne Lee[3],
Shakeel Rajwani[3(✉)], Suraj Sood[3], Buttons A. Foster[3], Toni Hadgis[3],
Yaniv Savir[3], Frankie Michaels[3], Alexis-Walid Ahmed[3],
Nikki Bernobic[3], and Markus Hollander[3]

[1] Eastern Florida State College, Melbourne, FL, USA
neumanns@easternflorida.edu
[2] Mercy College, Dobbs Ferry, NY, USA
[3] Sirius17, Melbourne, FL, USA
shakeel.rajwani@gmail.com

**Abstract.** Twitter accounts are used for a multitude of reasons, including social, commercial, political, religious, and ideological purposes. The wide variety of activities on Twitter may be automated or non-automated. Any serious attempt to explore the nature of the vast amount of information being broadcast over such a medium may depend on identifying a potentially useful set of content features hidden within the data. This paper proposes a set of content features that may be promising in efforts to categorize social media activities, with the goal of creating predictive models that will classify or estimate the probabilities of automated behavior given certain account content history. Suggestions for future work are offered.

**Keywords:** Twitter · Social media · Content feature extraction

## 1 Background

### 1.1 Introduction

Social media activity data, in the case of this paper Twitter account activity, can be understood as consisting of two primary components, metadata or demographics, and content data. Metadata involves external characteristics such as time of activity, time of account creation, location, type of platform used for activity, number of friends, followers, and more. Content data involves syntactic and semantic characteristics. The focus of this paper is on content data, in particular, content feature extraction that can be implemented on a large set of text data in order to enable categorization of types of activities and classification of activities as automated versus non-automated.

### 1.2 The Content Data Elements and Their Encoding

Below are some linguistic features that can be extracted from the text content generated by Twitter users. These features can be used to generate mathematical "signatures" for

© Springer International Publishing AG 2017
D.D. Schmorrow and C.M. Fidopiastis (Eds.): AC 2017, Part I, LNAI 10284, pp. 558–570, 2017.
DOI: 10.1007/978-3-319-58628-1_42

different types of online behaviors. In this way, they augment account demographic features to create a rich, high-fidelity information space for behavior mining and modeling.

1. *The relative size and diversity of the account vocabulary*
   Content generated by automated means tends to reuse complex terms, while naturally generated content has a more varied vocabulary, and terms reused are generally simpler.
2. *The word length mean and variance*
   Naturally generated content tends to use shorter but more varied language than automatically generated content.
3. *The presence/percentage of chat-speak*
   Casual, social users often employ simple, easy to generate graphical icons, called emoticons. Sophisticated, non-social users tend to avoid these unsophisticated graphical icons.
4. *The presence and frequency of hashtags*
   Hashtags are essentially topic words. Several hashtags taken together amount to a tweet "gist". A table of these could be used for automated topic/content identification and categorization.
5. *The number of misspelled words*
   It is assumed that sophisticated content generators, such as major retailers, will have a very low incidence of misspellings relative to casual users who are typing on a small device like a phone or tablet.
6. *The presence of vulgarity*
   Major retailers are assumed to be unlikely to embed vulgarity in their content.
7. *The use of hot-button words and phrases ("act now", "enter to win", etc.)*
   Marketing "code words" are regularly used to communicate complex ideas to potential customers in just a few words. Such phrases are useful precisely because they are hackneyed.
8. *The use of words rarely used by other accounts (e.g., tf-idf scores)*
   Marketing campaigns often create words around their products. These created words occur nowhere else, and so will have high tf-idf scores, which is the term frequency–inverse document frequency score.
9. *The presence of URL's*
   To make a direct sale through a tweet, the customer must be engaged and directed to a location where a sale can be made. This is most easily accomplished by supplying a URL. URL's, even tiny URL's, can be automatically followed to facilitate screen scraping for identification/characterization.
10. *The generation of redundant content (same tweets repeated multiple times)*
    It is costly and difficult to generate unique content for each of thousands of online recipients. Therefore, automated content (e.g., advertising) tends to have a relatively small number of stylized units of content that they use over and over. The result is an account with "redundant" content.

## 2  Method

### 2.1  Data

Twitter account activity data is available through the Twitter API (application program interface) which returns requests for random samples of data in the JSON (JavaScript Object Notation) data structure containing both demographics and content.

Content data (tweets) are returned (in the JSON structure) as character strings of length 1 to 140 characters. They may be in any language or no language at all. Tweets can contain any combination of free text, emoticons, chat-speak, hashtags, and URL's. Twitter does not filter tweets for content (e.g., vulgarisms, hate speech).

For this study a sample of the activities of 8845 Twitter accounts containing the content of 1,048,395 tweets was collected for content analysis.

### 2.2  Procedures

A vector of text features is derived for each user. This is accomplished by deriving text features for each of the user's tweets and then rolling them up, i.e. summing and normalizing the data. Therefore, one content feature vector is derived for each user from all of that user's tweets.

The extraction of numeric features from text is a multi-step process:

1. Collect the user's most recent (up to 200) tweet strings into a single set (a Thread).
2. Convert the thread text to upper case for term matching.
3. Scan the thread for the presence of emoticons, chat-speak, hashtags, URL's, and vulgarisms, setting bits to indicate the presence/absence of each of these text artifacts.
4. Remove special characters from the thread to facilitate term matching.
5. Create a Redundancy Score for the Thread. This is done by computing and rolling up (sum and normalize) the pairwise similarities of the tweet strings within the thread using six metrics: Euclidean Distance, RMS-Distance, L1 Distance, L-Infinity Distance, Cosine Distance, and the norm-weighted average of the five distances.
6. The thread text feature vector then contains as vector components user scores based on features such as the emoticon flag, the chat-speak flag, the hashtag flag, the URL flag, the vulgarity flag, and the Redundancy score.

A list of 23 potential content related features was created and calculated for each of the 8845 Twitter accounts in the sample (Tables 1 and 2).

For the purpose of classifying accounts as automated (bots) versus non-automated, a manual rating process of a sample of tweet content coming from 101 active accounts was executed. The sample was divided into 5 subsets with each set being rated by multiple volunteers who read the content of approximately 20 accounts in each subset,

**Table 1.** Sample of raw data

| Feature | | Set 1 | Set 2 | Set 3 |
|---|---|---|---|---|
| UserID | | 22821737 | 22822092 | 22823578 |
| 1 | tweets | 10 | 190 | 133 |
| 2 | adj | 1.7 | 2.247368 | 1.774436 |
| 3 | adv | 0 | 0.2684211 | 0.09774436 |
| 4 | art | 0.1 | 1.994737 | 1.338346 |
| 5 | commnoun | 4.2 | 1.215789 | 1.736842 |
| 6 | conj | 0.6 | 0.6947368 | 0.3458647 |
| 7 | interj | 0 | 0.005263158 | 0.007518797 |
| 8 | prep | 0.6 | 0.3736842 | 0.3383459 |
| 9 | pron | 0 | 0.368421 | 0.03759398 |
| 10 | Propnoun | 1.4 | 1.931579 | 1.699248 |
| 11 | verb | 0.4 | 1.215789 | 0.6315789 |
| 12 | stopword | 0 | 0.06842105 | 0.04511278 |
| 13 | vulgar | 0 | 0.01578947 | 0 |
| 14 | hash | 0.6 | 0.4894737 | 0.1052632 |
| 15 | urls | 1 | 0.1473684 | 0.9774436 |
| 16 | case | 0 | 0 | 0 |
| 17 | punc | 1 | 0.9842106 | 1 |
| 18 | emo_chat | 0 | 0 | 0 |
| 19 | good_len | 82.2 | 74.14211 | 70.9624 |
| 20 | good_cnt | 13.3 | 16.08947 | 12.59398 |
| 21 | bad_len | 0.7 | 1.394737 | 1.233083 |
| 22 | bad_cnt | 0.1 | 0.2 | 0.1954887 |
| 23 | redund | 0.7686407 | 0.7453661 | 0.740773 |

**Table 2.** The list of 23 features for analysis

| Feature | | Description |
|---|---|---|
| 1 | tweets | Number of tweets up to 200 |
| 2 | adj | Number of adjectives per tweet |
| 3 | adv | Number of adverbs per tweet |
| 4 | art | Number of articles per tweet |
| 5 | commnoun | Number of common nouns per tweet |
| 6 | conj | Number of conjunctions per tweet |
| 7 | interj | Number of interjections per tweet |
| 8 | prep | Number of prepositions per tweet |
| 9 | pron | Number of pronouns per tweet |
| 10 | Propnoun | Number of proper nouns per tweet |

(*continued*)

**Table 2.** (*continued*)

| Feature | | Description |
|---|---|---|
| 11 | verb | Number of verbs per tweet |
| 12 | stopword | Number of stop words matching a list- per tweet |
| 13 | vulgar | Number of vulgar words matching a list- per tweet |
| 14 | hash | Number of hashtags per tweet |
| 15 | urls | Number of urls per tweet |
| 16 | case | Relative frequency of usage of both lower and upper case |
| 17 | punc | Relative frequency of usage of punctuation |
| 18 | emo_chat | Number of emoticons per tweet |
| 19 | good_len | Number of *characters* in correctly spelled words per tweet |
| 20 | good_cnt | Number of *words* of correctly spelled words per tweet |
| 21 | bad_len | Number of *characters* of incorrectly spelled words per tweet |
| 22 | bad_cnt | Number of *words* of incorrectly spelled words per tweet |
| 23 | redund | Redundancy Score for the Thread |

each subset containing a few thousand tweets. The rating of each account involved classification as a bot or not and also the assignment of a level of confidence associated with such classification, then a brief explanation of the main reasons was given for the relevant decisions. Of the 101 accounts, 65 were classified as 35 bot accounts and 30 non-bot accounts with a high level of confidence. Those 65 accounts were then assigned a dependent variable value of 1 if identified as a bot, and 0 otherwise.

## 3  Results

Excel was used to generate a correlation matrix for the 23 content features for the large sample of 8845 feature vectors (Table 3).

Similarly, correlations between the 23 content features and the dependent variable for the small set of 65 accounts were calculated and sorted based on absolute value (Table 5).

Absolute values of the correlations between features and the dependent variable ranged from 0.003 to 0.603. Ranking such absolute values of correlations resulted in the following list of top predictors of bot-like behavior: "redund", "urls", "good_len", "adj", "tweets", "vulgar", "good_cnt", "commnoun", "emo_chat" and "art".

Charts were created to examine the distributions of features that were deemed to be significant in terms of their correlation with the dependent variable in the small sample. Charts were created to examine joint distributions. Following some interpretation of the nature of distributions, some hypotheses were made as to potential statistical learning tools that may be useful in modeling based on such content features (Figs. 1, 2, 3, 4, 5, 6, 7, 8, 9, 10 and 11).

**Table 3.** Correlation among the 23 features of tweet data (correlation scores above 0.6 are bolded)

| | 1 | 2 | 3 | 4 | 5 | 6 | 7 | 8 | 9 | 10 | 11 |
|---|---|---|---|---|---|---|---|---|---|---|---|
| 1 | 1.000 | | | | | | | | | | |
| 2 | 0.029 | 1.000 | | | | | | | | | |
| 3 | -0.019 | 0.044 | 1.000 | | | | | | | | |
| 4 | 0.032 | 0.110 | 0.436 | 1.000 | | | | | | | |
| 5 | 0.094 | 0.086 | 0.135 | 0.292 | 1.000 | | | | | | |
| 6 | 0.019 | 0.076 | 0.407 | **0.630** | 0.214 | 1.000 | | | | | |
| 7 | -0.041 | -0.066 | 0.031 | -0.104 | 0.104 | -0.079 | 1.000 | | | | |
| 8 | 0.040 | 0.088 | 0.144 | 0.417 | 0.267 | 0.321 | -0.113 | 1.000 | | | |
| 9 | -0.078 | 0.070 | 0.400 | 0.339 | 0.090 | 0.387 | 0.043 | 0.128 | 1.000 | | |
| 10 | 0.039 | 0.054 | 0.302 | 0.545 | 0.533 | 0.431 | 0.078 | 0.322 | 0.245 | 1.000 | |
| 11 | 0.006 | 0.115 | 0.424 | **0.701** | 0.279 | 0.544 | -0.134 | 0.381 | 0.360 | 0.448 | 1.000 |
| 12 | -0.007 | 0.069 | 0.216 | 0.263 | 0.076 | 0.262 | -0.063 | 0.179 | 0.285 | 0.152 | 0.277 |
| 13 | -0.052 | -0.014 | 0.072 | 0.038 | -0.031 | 0.038 | 0.037 | -0.059 | 0.120 | -0.020 | 0.059 |
| 14 | -0.010 | -0.021 | -0.028 | 0.021 | 0.119 | -0.054 | -0.013 | 0.077 | -0.072 | 0.061 | 0.068 |
| 15 | 0.299 | -0.066 | -0.254 | -0.216 | 0.028 | -0.257 | -0.106 | 0.059 | -0.296 | -0.147 | -0.199 |
| 16 | -0.149 | 0.190 | -0.022 | -0.093 | -0.134 | -0.026 | -0.001 | -0.091 | 0.010 | -0.144 | -0.070 |
| 17 | 0.207 | -0.009 | -0.034 | 0.123 | 0.156 | 0.053 | -0.068 | 0.146 | -0.100 | 0.148 | 0.069 |
| 18 | -0.044 | 0.127 | 0.011 | 0.096 | -0.006 | -0.014 | 0.014 | 0.048 | 0.053 | -0.002 | 0.123 |
| 19 | 0.160 | 0.101 | 0.216 | 0.490 | 0.590 | 0.326 | -0.026 | 0.470 | 0.088 | 0.580 | 0.473 |
| 20 | 0.081 | 0.298 | 0.390 | **0.702** | **0.650** | 0.538 | 0.023 | 0.502 | 0.309 | **0.752** | **0.665** |
| 21 | -0.047 | -0.177 | -0.131 | -0.280 | -0.170 | -0.183 | 0.054 | -0.134 | -0.110 | -0.220 | -0.254 |
| 22 | -0.035 | -0.172 | -0.068 | -0.255 | -0.105 | -0.136 | 0.079 | -0.101 | -0.091 | -0.166 | -0.237 |
| 23 | 0.352 | 0.178 | -0.015 | -0.001 | 0.073 | 0.011 | 0.018 | 0.021 | 0.001 | 0.061 | -0.027 |

## 4 Discussion

### 4.1 Findings

Approximately 10% of the 8845 accounts had the maximum level of activity measured (200 tweets). This may provide some lower bound estimate of the rate of accounts exhibiting bot-like behavior.

Examination of the content features correlation matrix reveals that correlations are generally low with some explainable exceptions. Features such as good_len and good_cnt refer to the number of characters that are part of correctly spelled words and the number of correctly spelled words, respectively. The high correlation of 0.86 is to be expected, and such is the case for bad_len and bad_cnt with a correlation of 0.841

**Table 4.** Correlation among the 23 features of tweet data

| | 12 | 13 | 14 | 15 | 16 | 17 | 18 | 19 | 20 | 21 | 22 | 23 |
|---|---|---|---|---|---|---|---|---|---|---|---|---|
| 12 | 1.000 | | | | | | | | | | | |
| 13 | 0.009 | 1.000 | | | | | | | | | | |
| 14 | -0.014 | -0.054 | 1.000 | | | | | | | | | |
| 15 | -0.048 | -0.225 | 0.088 | 1.000 | | | | | | | | |
| 16 | -0.018 | 0.038 | -0.136 | -0.264 | 1.000 | | | | | | | |
| 17 | 0.018 | 0.158 | 0.118 | 0.567 | -0.350 | 1.000 | | | | | | |
| 18 | 0.004 | 0.025 | 0.019 | -0.037 | -0.010 | -0.021 | 1.000 | | | | | |
| 19 | 0.189 | -0.131 | 0.380 | 0.313 | 0.277 | 0.433 | 0.042 | 1.000 | | | | |
| 20 | 0.266 | -0.038 | 0.208 | -0.045 | -0.159 | 0.271 | 0.078 | 0.861 | 1.000 | | | |
| 21 | -0.117 | -0.029 | 0.086 | 0.104 | -0.017 | 0.055 | -0.008 | -0.102 | 0.211 | 1.000 | | |
| 22 | -0.087 | -0.030 | 0.109 | 0.064 | -0.008 | 0.057 | -0.020 | -0.009 | -0.112 | 0.841 | 1.000 | |
| 23 | 0.027 | -0.052 | 0.007 | 0.159 | -0.187 | 0.145 | 0.007 | 0.103 | 0.098 | -0.007 | -0.039 | 1.000 |

(both highlighted in Table 4). In both situations, consideration may be given to selecting only one of each pair for the purpose of predictive modeling.

The top ten content features appear to contain discriminating information that may be relevant in an attempt to classify Twitter accounts as bot or non-bot accounts. Separation issues and the skewed nature of the majority of the distributions of content features may justify an expectation that a nonparametric approach may perform better than a parametric one.

The distribution of the redundancy scores appears to be approximately normal, while all other distributions examined are skewed. As in the case of an earlier study of external features, most relevant distributions that quantify social media behaviors do not appear to be normal, a fact that may later support preference for nonparametric modeling techniques or the application of some feature transformations.

Examination of the scatter plots of joint distributions seems to support the selection of the top content features listed above. One can note that in the case of vulgarity score

**Table 5.** Correlation of the 23 features to the dependent variable (bot or not Boolean value)

| | Feature | r score |
|---|---|---|
| 23 | redund | 0.602903665143099 |
| 15 | urls | 0.552239841627008 |
| 19 | good_len | 0.499866059699615 |
| 2 | adj | 0.439996556749289 |
| 1 | tweets | 0.405312199707016 |
| 13 | vulgar | -0.386187081404597 |
| 20 | good_cnt | 0.361167846205383 |
| 5 | commnoun | 0.336302040152226 |
| 18 | emo_chat | -0.322361395640107 |
| 4 | art | -0.306464242615507 |
| 6 | conj | -0.266514973936451 |
| 12 | stopword | -0.256512790006307 |
| 9 | pron | -0.23235623235559 |
| 17 | punc | 0.22984473910942 |
| 8 | prep | 0.217071031951804 |
| 10 | Propnoun | 0.215136062319311 |
| 7 | interj | -0.202111817921263 |
| 14 | hash | 0.125290858127832 |
| 3 | adv | -0.0933858445685339 |
| 16 | case | -0.0477397194562674 |
| 21 | bad_len | 0.0373329649121563 |
| 22 | bad_cnt | 0.0035443689757518 |
| 11 | verb | 0.0027851841588802 |

there is no presence of vulgarity among the bot accounts, while non-bot accounts may or may not include vulgar language.

Taking all this into account, a starting set of content features that may be selected for modeling may involve the following nine features: redund, urls, good_len, adj, tweets, vulgar, commnoun, art, emo_chat.

## 4.2  Limitations

A number of significant limitations must be noted.

First, the data set may not be a representative sample of the current state of affairs when it comes to bot versus non-bot activity in the Twitter medium.

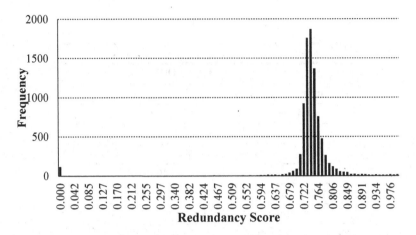

**Fig. 1.** Histogram of the distribution of redundancy score

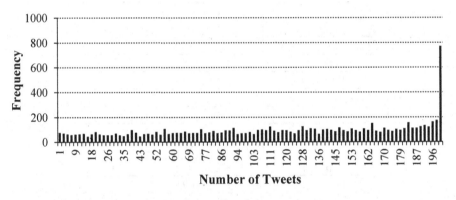

**Fig. 2.** Histogram of the distribution of number of tweets

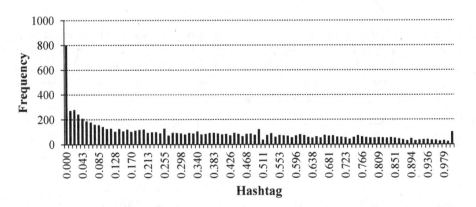

**Fig. 3.** Histogram of the distribution of hashtag

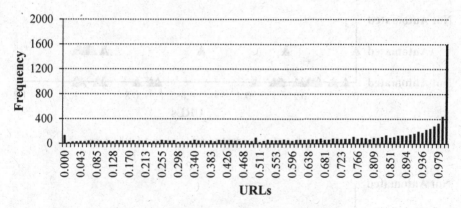

**Fig. 4.** Histogram of the distribution of URLs

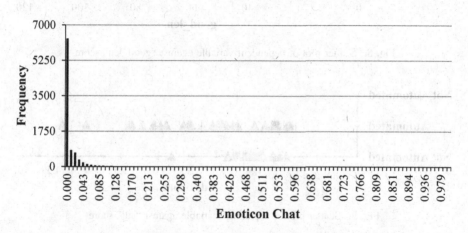

**Fig. 5.** Histogram of the distribution of emoticon_chat

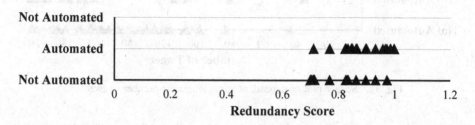

**Fig. 6.** Scatter plot of dependent variable against redundancy score

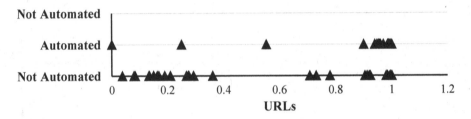

**Fig. 7.** Scatter plot of dependent variable against URLs score

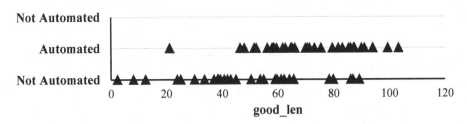

**Fig. 8.** Scatter plot of dependent variable against "good_len" score

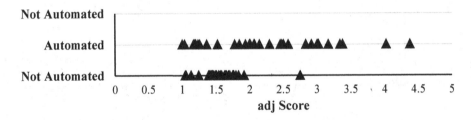

**Fig. 9.** Scatter plot of dependent variable against "adj" score

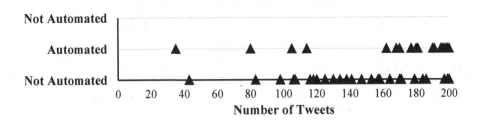

**Fig. 10.** Scatter plot of dependent variable against number of tweets

Second, the process of manually classifying a small set of accounts and reaching a consensus in roughly two-thirds of the cases may not be without errors.

Third, a larger sample set from the manual classification process may lead to different conclusions about content features and the type of modeling that may be expected to perform best.

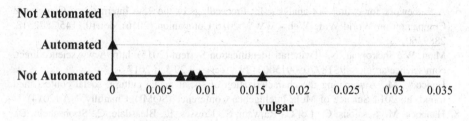

**Fig. 11.** Scatter plot of dependent variable against vulgarism score

Fourth, concentrating on content, which probably provides the most predictive power, may still ignore some critical external features, and thus may not produce an optimal perspective.

### 4.3 Further Investigations

Future work may attempt to consider a mix of external features and content features, calculated on a large set of known bot and non-bot accounts for better feature selection, description, and classification. This should enable a much more reliable subset of predictive or discriminating features, which in turn may lead to more reliable descriptive and predictive models.

## 5 Conclusion

This paper demonstrates one way by which content of social media activities may be processed in terms of mathematical "signatures" of different types of online behaviors that may be used for descriptive and predictive modeling of automated versus non-automated activities.

## References

1. Alarifi, A., Alsaleh, M., Al-Salman, A.: Twitter turing test: identifying social machines. Inf. Sci. **372**, 332–346 (2016). doi:10.1016/j.ins.2016.08.036
2. Carapinha, F., et al.: Modeling of social media behaviors using only account metadata. In: Schmorrow, D.D., Fidopiastis, C.M. (eds.) AC 2016. LNCS (LNAI), vol. 9744, pp. 393–401. Springer, Cham (2016). doi:10.1007/978-3-319-39952-2_38
3. Chu, Z., Gianvecchio, S., Jajodia, S., Wang, H.: Detecting automation of Twitter accounts: are you a human, bot, or cyborg? IEEE Trans. Dependable Sec. Comput. **9**, 811–824 (2012)
4. Dickerson, J.P., Kagan, V., Subrahmanian, V.: Using sentiment to detect bots on Twitter: are humans more opinionated than bots? In: 2014 IEEE/ACM International Conference on Advances in Social Networks Analysis and Mining (ASONAM 2014) (2014). doi:10.1109/asonam.2014.6921650

5. A framework for twitter bot analysis. In: Proceedings of the 25th International Conference Companion on World Wide Web - WWW 2016 Companion (2016). doi:10.1145/2872518.2889360

6. Main, W., Shekokhar, N.: Twitterati Identification System (2015). http://www.sciencedirect.com/science/article/pii/S1877050915003129. Accessed 29 Jan 2017

7. Hancock, M.: Automating the characterization of social media culture, social context, and mood. In: 2014 Science of Multi-Intelligence Conference (SOMI), Chantilly, VA (2014)

8. Hancock, M., Sessions, C., Lo, C., Rajwani, S., Kresses, E., Bleasdale, C., Strohschein, D.: Stability of a type of cross-cultural emotion modeling in social media. In: Schmorrow, D.D., Fidopiastis, C.M. (eds.) AC 2015. LNCS (LNAI), vol. 9183, pp. 410–417. Springer, Cham (2015). doi:10.1007/978-3-319-20816-9_39

# Detecting Mislabeled Data Using Supervised Machine Learning Techniques

Mannes Poel[✉]

Human Media Interaction, University of Twente, Enschede, The Netherlands
m.poel@utwente.nl

**Abstract.** A lot of data sets, gathered for instance during user experiments, are contaminated with noise. Some noise in the measured features is not much of a problem, it even increases the performance of
many Machine Learning (ML) techniques. But for noise in the labels
(mislabeled data) the situation is quite different, label noise deteriorates
the performance of all ML techniques. The research question addressed
in this paper is to what extent can one detect mislabeled data using a
committee of supervised Machine Learning models. The committee under
consideration consists of a Bayesian model, Random Forest, Logistic classifier, a Neural Network and a Support Vector Machine. This committee
is applied to a given data set in several iterations of 5-fold Cross validation. If a data sample is misclassified by all committee members in
all iterations (consensus) then it is tagged as mislabeled. This approach
was tested on the Iris plant data set, which is artificially contaminated
with mislabeled data. For this data set the precision of detecting mislabeled samples is 100% and the recall is approximately 5%. The approach
was also tested on the Touch data set, a data set of naturalistic social
touch gestures. It is known that this data set contains mislabeled data,
but the amount is unknown. For this data set the proposed method
achieved a precision of 70% and for almost all other tagged samples the
corresponding touch gesture deviated a lot from the prototypical touch
gesture. Overall the proposed method shows high potential for detecting mislabeled samples, but the precision on other data sets needs to be
investigated.

**Keywords:** Mislabeled data · Supervised Machine Learning

## 1 Introduction

A lot of data sets, gathered for instance during user experiments, are contaminated with noise. Some noise in the measured features is not much of a problem,
it even increases the performance of many Machine Learning (ML) techniques
Quinlan (1986). But for noise in the labels the situation is quite different, label
noise deteriorates the performance of all ML techniques (Brodley and Friedl
1999). Hence the detection of mislabeled data is of utmost importance in many
ML applications. The research question we address in this paper is "To what

© Springer International Publishing AG 2017
D.D. Schmorrow and C.M. Fidopiastis (Eds.): AC 2017, Part I, LNAI 10284, pp. 571–581, 2017.
DOI: 10.1007/978-3-319-58628-1_43

extent can one detect mislabeled data using a committee of supervised Machine Learning models?"

The outline of the paper is as follows, in Sect. 2 we give an overview on the related work concerning detecting mislabeled data. In Sect. 3 we introduce the methodology for applying supervised Machine Learning techniques in order to detect mislabeled data. The results of this methodology on two cases is presented in Sect. 4. These results are discussed in Sect. 5 and we round off with conclusions and future work in Sect. 6.

## 2    Related Work

### 2.1    Statistical Outlier Methods

One of the traditional approaches to outlier detection is to model a mislabeled sample as an outlier and apply standard statistical outlier detection methods Barnett and Lewis (1994). In such an approach the subset of samples with the same label is modelled as a probabilistic (mixture) model $p(x)$ or a kernel based nearest neighbor estimator (Parzen windows) and a threshold $\theta$ is determined such that if the likelihood of a sample $s$ is less than the threshold, i.e. $p(s) < \theta$, then the sample $s$ is tagged as a mislabeled sample. Hence the approach is similar to outlier detection in, for instance, medicaid fraud van Capelleveen et al. (2016).

### 2.2    Local Based Methods

Another local based model compares the label of a sample with the labels of the $k$-nearest neighbors. Based on the labels of these $k$-nearest neighbors the label of the sample under consideration can be classified as mislabeled. For instance, if all the $k$-nearest neighbors have the same label and this label is different from the label of the sample then the label could be considered noise. See for instance the work of Wilson (1972).

### 2.3    Single Model Based Methods

Two typical examples of the use of single classification models for detecting mislabeled data are Support Vector Machines (SVMs) and Adaboost

**Support Vector Machines.** The classification by a SVM is determined by an optimal hyperplane in feature space and this hyperplane is completely determined by the so-called support vectors. Moreover these support vectors are a subset of the training set (Bishop 2007). The intuition behind these support vectors (data points) is that they are close to the boundary between the different classes and are hard to classify. Hence these support vectors could be an indication of mislabeled data points. This is the approach explored by Ekambaram et al. (2016). They showed that the support vectors can reduce the search space for mislabeled data. These support vectors are deleted from the training set and after retraining the generalization performance on the test set is evaluated. The main goal was to investigate the performance but not the detection of mislabeled data. But one can deduce in advance that the precision for detecting mislabeled data is low due to the fact that a SVM always has support vectors and thus also in cases where all data is correctly labeled.

**Adaboost.** Adaboost (Freund et al. 1996) is an iterative algorithm which constructs a strong committee classifier based on weak classifiers. It is an iterative procedure in which hard to classify examples get more weight than easy to classify examples. In each iteration a new weak classifier is trained based on the weights of each data sample. The weight of the data sample denotes the relative contribution of this data sample to the error function. After training, the data samples with the highest weights are those data samples which are hard to classify by the committee. The approach discussed in (Cao et al. 2012) is that mislabeled data are in general hard to classify and thus get high weights when applying Adaboost. These examples are deleted from the training set and after retraining the performance increase on the test set is evaluated. The main goal of this study is to evaluate the performance after deleting data samples with high weights (potentially mislabeled data) and does not focus on precision or recall. Once again this reduces the search space for mislabeled data but the precision is low.

## 2.4   Ensemble Based Methods

The use of ensemble based methods for detecting mislabeled data is already discussed in the paper by Brodley and Friedl (Brodley and Friedl 1999), which is one of the first papers on using Supervised Machine Learning for the detection of mislabeled data. The ensemble they used consisted of Decision Trees, k-Nearest Neighbor and Linear Discriminant. Moreover the difference between majority voting and consensus to tag an instance as mislabeled was investigated. The approach was empirically validated on 5 data sets. The overall conclusion was that detecting and filtering out the data tagged as mislabeled improves the generalization performance, but if the mislabel rate is too high then, as expected, the method breaks down. The main focus was to investigate the generalization performance but they also looked into the precision of their method, by introducing artificial noisy labels. As expected the consensus approach has higher precision than majority voting, but the precision was not optimal. This means that sometimes samples with correct labels (probably the hard to classify samples) were discarded from the training set. A more extensive overview of classification in the presence of mislabeled data can be found in Frénay and Verleysen (2014).

The focus of the research described in this paper is different: the main focus here is on precision and recall of mislabeled data using an ensemble based method. The overall aim is to detect mislabeled samples with high precision and in a second step, not covered in this paper, to remove the samples from the training set or relabel these samples, for instance by manual inspection, in order to improve classification performance.

# 3   Methodology

Recall that we want to investigate in how far one can detect mislabeled data using supervised ML techniques. Normally mislabeled data is detected by humans (visually) analyzing the data and checking wether for a given data sample the corresponding label is correct. This analysis can be supported by automatic clustering techniques (an unsupervised technique) to detect suspicious (data sample, label) pairs. In this paper we follow a different approach. The idea is to replace the human inspectors by a committee of trained supervised Machine Learning models, such as Bayesian Classifiers, Random Forest and Logistic regression. If a data sample is misclassified by all models then this sample is tagged as suspicious. These models are trained in the given data set, which in theory contains mislabeled data, so they are not optimal. To compensate for this non optimality we train and apply the models several times using k-fold Cross Validation (k-CV). Since we want to detect mislabeled data, high performance of a model is not required, but of course it is an advantage. Moreover investigating data samples can be very time consuming, for instance if one has to check the video or sound recordings, so we strive for a high precision as opposed to high recall with many false positives. The overall method is as follows. Select a diverse set of supervised ML models, the more diverse the more independent the models are. In our case we selected a Bayesian model, Random Forest, Logistic classifier, a Neural Network and a Support Vector Machine. Next train and apply the models to the given data set using k-CV, and determine how many times a data sample is misclassified. For one run of k-CV and five models the maximum number of misclassifications is also five. This result could depend on the partition of the k-folds and moreover the training of the ML models is non-optimal due to the presence of mislabeled data. Hence we repeat this k-CV approach several times, say 10 times, and data samples which are misclassified all the time (in this case $5 \times 10 = 50$ times) are flagged as suspicious and are candidates for future investigation by for instance human experts. We investigated the precision and recall of the above approach on the well-known Iris Plants data set Fisher (1936) by introducing mislabeled data by randomly switching the label of randomly selected data samples. Afterwards we tested our approach on the touch data set Jung et al. (2016), a data set more prone to mislabels. For this touch data set the mislabels are unknown and hence we only focus on precision.

## 3.1   Iris Data Set

The Iris Plant data set is a well known (toy) data set for validating Machine Learning methods, see Fisher (1936). The data set consists of 150 samples of three different Iris species and each sample coded by four numerical features; sepal width, sepal length, petal width and petal length. First we test our approach on the original data set and afterwards introduce artificial mislabeled data in order the analyse the precision and recall of our methodology. Randomly 1 up to 30 data samples were selected for which the label was randomly switched to another class. Since we randomly select mislabeled data we repeated each experiment of introducing mislabels twenty times.

## 3.2 Touch Data Set

The touch data set, introduced in Jung et al. (2016), is a corpus consisting of social touch gestures. The main goal of this data set (corpus) is to work towards a data driven approach for touch recognition and benchmarking. The corpus was constructed by a user experiment in which 32 subjects had to perform 14 different social touch gestures in three different variations (gentle, normal and rough) on a sensor grid wrapped around an artificial mannequin arm, see Fig. 1 for how the user experiment was conducted. The participants first saw a movie in which

**Fig. 1.** Setup of the touch experiment.

the 14 different touch gestures on the mannequin arm where demonstrated. In order to practice participants were instructed to repeat every gesture. After this demonstration and practice each subject had to perform 252 gestures in random order. The reason to show the instruction at the start of and not during the experiment was to allow for individual freedom in performing the requested touch gestures. But this also led to forgetting the instruction, being uncertain about the gesture to be performed or recalling the wrong instruction, and therefore not performing the right touch gesture, leading to a corpus containing mislabeled data.

The experiment was video recorded and this gives an opportunity to inspect the label of a given recorded touch gesture. But this is a very time consuming procedure. For this research we focus only on the rough touch gestures in this data set, in total 2602.

For our analyses we first normalized the features between $-1$ and $1$ and afterwards projected the normalized features on the first 12 principal components. We ran the experiments for 1000 iterations and each iteration applied a 5-fold CV for all the 5 members of the committee of classifiers. This gives the opportunity to investigate the effect of the number of iterations on the number of tagged samples. Afterwards a random subset of 20 samples is used to investigate the precision of our approach. Observe that we cannot assess the recall of our approach on this data set because the subset of mislabeled samples is unknown.

## 4   Results

We tested our approach on the Iris Plant and Touch data sets. The results are reported below.

### 4.1   Iris Plant Data Set

If we apply our methodology with 10 iterations of 5-CV no data samples were flagged as misclassified.

The maximum number misclassifications was 8 and in order to be flagged a data sample must be misclassified 10 times. This makes the Iris Plant data set a good candidate for a supervised approach by introducing mislabeled data. We randomly selected between 1 and 30 data samples for which we randomly switched the label to another class. Since we randomly introduce mislabeled data we repeated each experiment of introducing mislabels twenty times. The results for precision and recall can be found in Fig. 2.

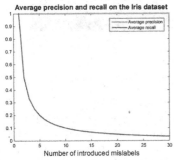
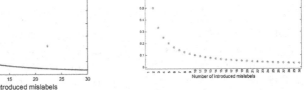

(a) The average precision and recall over 20 runs.

(b) Box plot for the recall.

**Fig. 2.** The average precision and recall over 20 runs, including a boxplot for the recall.

Observe that the average recall is dropping but stays above zero, but the precision is always one. This means that the data samples flagged by our method are in the set of mislabeled data samples. It also follows that by an iterative approach all the mislabeled data can be detected. Since the precision is one we can remove or relabel the flagged data points. For this new data set the number mislabeled is less and it follows from Fig. 2(a) that the precision is still 1. Hence we can apply the method over and over again, removing or relabel the flagged data samples. We will end up with a data set with no mislabeled data. Wether this also holds for other data sets needs be investigated.

## 4.2   Touch Data Set

On the Touch data set we applied 1000 iterations of 5-CV. In each iteration the performance of the classifiers was between 55 and 60% and on average 550.7 samples were tagged in each iteration with a standard deviation of 11.2. The development of the number of samples which were always misclassified is depicted in Fig. 3.

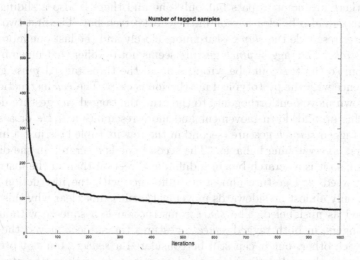

**Fig. 3.** Number of tagged samples plotted against the number of iterations.

Observe that the curve flattens after approximately 200 iterations and after 1000 iterations 70 samples are tagged as mislabeled. Some statistics on the tagged samples, the number of tags per gesture are: *grab* 3, *hit* 10, *massage* 3, *pat* 10, *pinch* 5, *poke* 2, *press* 9, *rub* 6, *scratch* 3, *slap* 4, *squeeze* 4, *tap* 5 and *tickle* 0. Meaning that only three gestures – *hit*, *pat* and *press* – are responsible for 29 out of 70 (41%) tagged samples. With respect to the subjects, subject 23 was responsible for 7 of the tagged examples, subject 27 for 6 and subject 9, 21 and 30 for 5. Meaning that only 5 out of 32 subjects are responsible for 40% of all tagged samples. A factor analysis reveals that for subject 9 the gesture *pat* was tagged 3 times and for subject 23 the gesture *grab* was tagged 3 times, so all tagged *grab* gestures are from this subject.

From these 70 tagged samples we randomly took 20 samples for further inspection, meaning watching the video in order to detect what actually happened, see Table 1. For each tagged gesture we have depicted the instruction as the first picture in the row followed by pictures showing the most characteristic (distinctive) property of the tagged gesture.It is clear from these screenshots that for the *grab* gesture the tagged sample is substantially different from the instruction touch, it is in principle a *tickle* gesture. For the *hit* gesture the first two are substantially different from the instruction (the prototypical gesture), not using a fist but the flat hand, but the last one seems to resemble the instructions a lot. Looking at the *massage* gesture one can clearly see that the participant is not focusing purely on performing the gesture but is also reading from a piece of paper. Moreover the performed gesture resembles a stroke. For the *pat* gesture it is hard to see from the screenshots if there is a substantial difference between the instruction and the performed gesture. The instruction is two times a vertical pat on the sensor grid, inspection of the videos reveals that in the tagged samples there are not two pats but only one and there is also a sliding movement. This can also be clearly seen in the third screenshot. The first two tagged *pat* gestures resemble the *slap* gesture more closely and the last one more (three times) a *stroke*. The tagged *pinch* gesture seems not to differ that much from the instruction, so the tag could be wrong. For all the three tagged *press* gestures the difference with the prototypical instruction is clear. The *rub* instruction is an up and down movement orthogonal to the arm, the tagged *rub* gesture does not contain this up and down movement and more resembles a *tickle* or a *scratch*. The first tagged *scratch* gesture (second in the row in Table 1) is just a hit using the fingers, no scratching behavior. The second one is a scratch in the direction of the arm, so it is a scratch but in a different direction than in the instruction. For the tagged *slap* gesture almost no difference with the instruction can be detected, only almost no sidewards movement, so it is not clear why this sample was tagged as mislabeled. The *squeeze* instruction is a squeeze without moving the fingers, in both tagged *squeeze* gestures the subject moved the fingers towards each other, but it can still be considered a *squeeze* but not prototypical (similar to the instruction). For the last gesture to analyse, the *stroke*, it is already clear from the screenshot that the first one is mislabeled, it is a *grab*. The second gesture is depicted by two screenshots, the first part is a *stroke* but only using two fingers and the last part is a stroke using the fist. So it is more a sequence of different types of *strokes*, first two fingers and afterwards the fist.

Summarizing, for the sample of 20 tagged samples 14 tagged samples were clearly mislabeled, a precision of 70%. For most of the other tagged samples the touch gesture differs a lot from the prototypical instruction but still could be considered as labeled correctly.

## 5    Discussion

The goal of the study was to construct a method based on a committee of different supervised ML models to detect mislabeled samples in corpus. The

**Table 1.** Screenshots per touch class. Touch instruction (first in the row) and then the tagged samples. The last two screenshots in the last row (*stroke* gesture) are from the same gesture.

| Gesture label | Screenshots |
|---|---|
| *grab* | |
| *hit* | |
| *massage* | |
| *pat* | |
| *pinch* | |
| *press* | |
| *rub* | |
| *scratch* | |
| *slap* | |
| *squeeze* | |
| *stroke* | |

committee used consists of five different types of models, a Bayesian model, Random Forest, Logistic classifier, a Neural Network and a Support Vector Machine. The reason for selecting different types of models was to assure that the models are independent. But it is not clear in how far the models are really independent because they are trained on the same data set and how far the results depend on the chosen models. First we tested the approach on the Iris data set. Initially no mislabeled samples were detected, but this was not validated by experts or visual inspection of the data set. The next step was to contaminate this data set with artificially mislabeled data. These artificially mislabeled samples were detected with high precision and low but sufficient recall, see Fig. 2(a). This makes it possible to remove all mislabeled samples from the data set.

But for the Touch data set the situation is quite different. There are mislabeled samples in the data set, as can be seen in the results described in Sect. 4, but the exact set of mislabeled samples is unknown and also depends on personal interpretation. In the construction of the Touch data set the participants were given instructions on how to perform the touch gesture at the start of the experiment, on the one hand to give the participant a clue about the gestures to perform and on the other hand to allow for personal interpretation and freedom. This is for instance clear from one of the tagged *scratch* gestures, which is definitely a scratch but differs in the direction from the instruction. If in all other trials for the *scratch* gesture the participants followed the instruction then this tagged *scratch* gesture is quite different from the prototypical *scratch* gesture and hence always misclassified. But this instruction at the start can also cause the participants to make a mistake in the recall of the instruction and perform a different touch gesture, as can be seen in one of the tagged *grab* gestures which is a *tickle*. One can conclude that in a naturalistic setting such as the investigated Touch corpus the correctness of the labeling depends on the personal interpretation of the touch label by the participant (personal freedom of interpretation) and the goal for and methodology by which the corpus is constructed.

In the related work described by Brodley and Friedl (1999), Ekambaram et al. (2016), Frénay and Verleysen (2014), Guan and Yuan (2013) the main focus is classification performance on the test set by removing tagged mislabeled samples from the training set. Hence it is hard to compare our findings with their results.

## 6   Conclusions

It is known that mislabeled data can adversely affect the performance of supervised ML methods. In order to detect such mislabeled data samples we proposed a detection method based on a committee of five different supervised ML models; a Bayesian model, Random Forest, Logistic classifier, a Neural Network and a Support Vector Machine. The precision of this committee was evaluated on the Iris and Touch data sets. The results show that on the contaminated Iris data set the committee had always a precision of one and the recall was low, around 10%, but sufficient.

On the Touch data set the situation is quite different due to the nature of the data set. The generation of the data set allows for personal freedom and interpretation of touch gestures. In total 70 samples were tagged as potentially mislabeled. A random sample of 20 tagged instances was selected and evaluated by inspecting the corresponding videos. The result was a precision of 70%. For most of the other tagged samples the touch gesture differs a lot from the prototypical instruction but still could be considered as labeled correctly.

Overall the proposed method shows high potential for detecting mislabeled samples, but the precision on other data sets needs to be investigated.

**Acknowledgments.** This work was partially supported by the Dutch national program COMMIT.

# References

Barnett, V., Lewis, T.: Outliers in Statistical Data. Wiley, Chichester (1994)

Bishop, C.: Pattern Recognition and Machine Learning, 2nd edn. Springer, New York (2007)

Brodley, C.E., Friedl, M.A.: Identifying mislabeled training data. J. Artif. Intell. Res. **11**, 131–167 (1999)

Cao, J., Kwong, S., Wang, R.: A noise-detection based AdaBoost algorithm for mislabeled data. Pattern Recognit. **45**(12), 4451–4465 (2012)

van Capelleveen, G., Poel, M., Mueller, R.M., Thornton, D., van Hillegersberg, J.: Outlier detection in healthcare fraud: a case study in the medicaid dental domain. Int. J. Account. Inf. Syst. **21**, 18–31 (2016)

Ekambaram, R., Fefilatyev, S., Shreve, M., Kramer, K., Hall, L.O., Goldgof, D.B., Kasturi, R.: Active cleaning of label noise. Pattern Recognit. **51**, 463–480 (2016). http://www.sciencedirect.com/science/article/pii/S0031320315003519

Fisher, R.A.: The use of multiple measurements in taxonomic problems. Ann. Eugen. **7**(2), 179–188 (1936)

Frénay, B., Verleysen, M.: Classification in the presence of label noise: a survey. IEEE Trans. Neural Netw. Learn. Syst. **25**(5), 845–869 (2014)

Freund, Y., Schapire, R.E., et al.: Experiments with a new boosting algorithm. ICML **96**, 148–156 (1996)

Guan, D., Yuan, W.: A survey of mislabeled training data detection techniques for pattern classification. IETE Tech. Rev. **30**(6), 524–530 (2013)

Jung, M.M., Poel, M., Poppe, R., Heylen, D.K.J.: Automatic recognition of touch gestures in the corpus of social touch. J. Multimodal User Interfaces **11**, 1–16 (2016). http://dx.doi.org/10.1007/s12193-016-0232-9

Quinlan, J.R.: Induction of decision trees. Induction Decis. Trees Mach. Learn. **1**(1), 81–106 (1986)

Wilson, D.L.: Asymptotic properties of nearest neighbor rules using edited data. IEEE Trans. Syst. Man Cybern. **3**, 408–421 (1972)

# Author Index

Printed in the United States
By Bookmasters